Introduct

Conflict of Laws is to legal studies what number theory is to mathematics–a subject "so attractive that only extravagant incompetence could make it dull."[1] Whether I have met that exacting standard in this Concise Hornbook is for readers to determine. Either way, I am firm in my conviction that Conflicts is not only a topic of great (and increasing) practical importance both in domestic American law and in the international sphere, but also a subject of intrinsic beauty and even wonder.

My approach in this book has been to focus on the *concepts* underlying the law of Conflicts, which can be bewildering for experts on the subject, let alone students encountering it for the first time. Therefore, this is less a treatise or reference work that discusses every nook and cranny of conflicts law, or that summarizes hundreds of cases, than a discursive essay treating what I take to be the most salient aspects of Conflicts doctrine in the United States. In organizing the chapters that follow, I've been guided and motivated by the kinds of questions that have been raised by my students in the basic Conflicts course I have taught for a decade and a half. I'm hopeful that the approach I've taken here will also make this book useful for lawyers and law professors who know little about Conflicts but seek a basic introduction to the subject.

The fact that I've focused on general concepts doesn't mean that there aren't discussions of cases, and even footnotes, in what follows; there are. To a large extent, this Concise Hornbook follows the basic organization of most Conflicts casebooks. I illustrate many of the basic concepts with discussions of the famous (sometimes rather old) cases that conventionally appear in those casebooks. In other instances, I've not hesitated to discuss other (frequently more recent) cases when they better illustrate the point at hand. In fact, this book should serve well as a companion to the main casebooks in the field.

A word on this book's structure and organization:

Traditionally, the field of Conflicts in American law has been thought to include the topics of Choice of Law; Recognition of Judgments; and Personal Jurisdiction. In this Concise Hornbook, I take up only the first two of these. Nowadays most first-year classes in Civil Procedure cover personal jurisdiction, and few Conflicts classes bother with it, so there's no need to include it here. Excellent discussions of

---

1. G.H. Hardy & E.M. Wright, An Introduction to the Theory of Numbers ix (6th ed. 2008).

personal jurisdiction can be found in Professor Kevin Clermont's Concise Hornbook on Civil Procedure and in many other sources.

The first four chapters concern choice of law. Chapter 1 treats the traditional or "territorial" approach to choice of law, which still informs much of modern conflicts law and which is the best vehicle for surfacing the basic conceptual problems raised by choice of law. Chapter 2 proceeds, in fairly conventional fashion, to consider more "modern" choice-of-law methodologies–those that have emerged in part as a reaction against the traditional approach. In Chapter 3, I focus briefly on a few topics of particular interest in present-day conflicts law. Since Chapters 1 and 2 tend to focus the reader's attention on more general conceptual issues, Chapter 3 is designed to apprise the reader of some specific conflicts issues that arise with some frequency today, and that raise some particularly difficult problems. Chapter 4 concerns constitutional limits on choice of law–that is, limits on the power of the forum to apply forum law (and not some other state's law) to a dispute.

Chapter 5 treats the general area of Recognition of Judgments, which, after Choice of Law, is the most important component of American conflicts law. The question of judgments and *res judicata* is not confined, of course, to multistate problems (those in which the "recognition court" is in a different state from that in which the "rendering court" sits). Since an understanding of interjurisdictional recognition (which is a conflicts problem) relies heavily on an understanding of *res judicata* in the purely domestic context (which is not), I have devoted considerably more attention in Chapter 5 to a detailed review of the basics of *res judicata* than do the authors of most conflicts books. After that review, I proceed to a discussion of interjurisdictional preclusion, focusing on the constitutional principle of full faith and credit.

The remainder of the book deals with more specific topics; I think that some exposure to each of these topics is important for conflicts students. Chapter 6 deals with the distinctive role of conflicts law, in particular interjurisdictional recognition, in the area of family law. The advent of same-sex marriage and the problems of interstate recognition that it raises makes this subject obviously quite topical, but interjurisdictional problems relating to child custody and support orders are equally pressing and have been for generations. Chapter 7 treats what is known as the "*Erie* problem." Traditionally, *Erie* has been the curricular possession of courses in Civil Procedure and Federal Courts and is not customarily treated as a "conflicts" issue, but I've discovered that my students no longer are exposed to *Erie* in those other courses with regularity. So I usually cover the subject in my conflicts course, and I've included a chapter on it in this book as well. After discussing *Erie* and its "progeny," I briefly take up the issue of post-*Erie* federal common law, although I do so in much less detail than would an analogous treatment in a book on federal courts.

West's Law School Advisory Board

PRINCIPLES
OF
CONFLICT OF LAWS

By

Clyde Spillenger
UCLA School of Law

CONCISE HORNBOOK SERIES®

A Thomson Reuters business

Mat #40730076

© 2010 Thomson Reuters

    610 Opperman Drive
    St. Paul, MN 55123
    1–800–313–9378

Printed in the United States of America

ISBN: 978–0–314–19102–1

To my father

Finally, in Chapter 8, we turn to Conflict of Laws in the international context. Just as the origins of modern conflicts law is to be found in the law of nations and other "transnational" sources, it's clear that the stage upon which the most important conflicts questions will appear in the next generation is the international sphere. Postponement of these issues to this book's final chapter is, therefore, no comment on the importance of the topic. In keeping with the general focus of this book, most of Chapter 8 considers the question of international conflicts from the perspective of American courts. Examples include the extraterritorial application (by American courts) of U.S. law, the Act-of-State Doctrine, and recognition (by American courts) of foreign-country judgments. Most scholars and teachers of the subject agree that, over the next generation, a variety of international issues–for example, arbitration in international transactions, civil and criminal procedure in international dispute resolution, and conflict-of-laws provisions in various international treaties and conventions, to name a few–will continue to move to the forefront of American conflicts law.

Conflicts scholars are not always in perfect agreement with one another concerning proper "arrangement" of the subject and, indeed, what the subject is fundamentally about. There is even less consensus on what the basic rules and assumptions of conflicts law should be. Although I've attempted to give a fair and objective view of the field in this book, undoubtedly my own views on some of the contested questions have influenced my presentation. Readers should therefore consider themselves invited to think for themselves concerning the interpretations presented here. And I apologize in advance to any of the numerous scholarly giants in this field if I have given their views short shrift, or simply don't see things quite the way that they do.

* * *

For his consistent support in the preparation of this Concise Hornbook, I would like to thank Ryan Pfeiffer of West. Catherine Fisk provided a helpful dissection, complete with formaldehyde, of the first chapter; thanks, Catherine. I'd also like to thank Antonia E. Stamenova–Dancheva, Class of 2009 at UCLA School of Law, for the use of her helpful research on the problem of "libel tourism." To all my students at UCLA, particularly those who have taken my Conflicts class over the years, I would like to express my appreciation for all they have taught me, much of which is reflected in the text of this book. And my profoundest debt is to my wife, Andrea Bell, for reasons too humorous to mention.

Summary of Contents

Table of Contents

PRINCIPLES
OF
CONFLICT OF LAWS

Chapter 1

THE TERRITORIAL APPROACH TO CHOICE OF LAW: CONCEPTS AND LIMITATIONS

"Choice of law" is the centerpiece of the study of conflicts, at least in the domestic sphere. Even the other topics that have traditionally formed part of the field of conflict of laws, such as jurisdiction and recognition of judgments, have close conceptual relationships with the problem of choice of law.

The general problem of choice of law is easily stated: When a dispute has meaningful connections with more than one state, and the respective laws of those states differ with respect to some relevant issue, which state's law should apply? Consider a few examples of the choice-of-law problem:

Example 1. Alan and Barbara, airline passengers, are killed when the plane they are on crashes in Iowa. The airplane, owned and operated by Jetstream Airlines, took off from an airport in Illinois (where Alan and Barbara boarded the plane) and was bound for Denver, Colorado. Alan is a domiciliary of New Mexico; Barbara, a domiciliary of New Jersey. Jetstream Airlines is incorporated in Delaware and has its principal place of business in Illinois. The plane's manufacturer, Fuchs Aircraft, is incorporated under the laws of Washington State and has its principal place of business there. Alan, from his home in New Mexico, had purchased his ticket online from a ticket dealer whose online server is located in California. Barbara, from her home in New Jersey, purchased her ticket directly from Jetstream Airlines by phone, speaking with a ticket agent physically located in India. With respect to a number of important issues, the laws of the various states with a connection to the episode are likely to differ. For example, they may differ concerning the measure of damages a tort plaintiff can recover in such cases. Some of the states strictly limit the amount that may be recovered for "noneconomic" damages (principally pain and suffering), while others do not. Some may place a ceiling on the amount of punitive damages that are available, while others do not. Suppose the survivors of Alan and Barbara bring a lawsuit against Jetstream and Fuchs. Somehow we have to determine which state's

1

law will apply to the various issues, and the answers will have enormous consequences for the parties.

Example 2. Lucy, a systems engineer, signs an employment contract with Widgets, Inc., which is incorporated and has its principal place of business in Texas. The contract provides that, once Lucy leaves the employment of Widgets, Inc., she will not accept a position with any other widgets manufacturer for a period of five years. Lucy quits her job with Widgets, Inc., and within a year she moves to Florida, where she takes a similar engineering position with Seminole Products, Inc., a widgets manufacturer which is incorporated and has its principal place of business in Florida. The law of Texas regards so-called "covenants not to compete" as void and unenforceable; the law of Florida regards them as fully enforceable. Widgets, Inc. sues Lucy for breach of contract. Should Florida law apply, rendering the noncompete covenant enforceable, or should Texas law apply, in which case Lucy would not be held liable for breach? Should the answer depend on whether Widgets, Inc. sues in Texas or in Florida court?

Example 3. Edward and Philip are married in a ceremony in the state of Massachusetts, whose law recognizes same-sex marriage. Massachusetts law provides a cause of action for wrongful death, which may be brought by the surviving spouse of a person wrongfully killed through the negligence of another. While Edward and Philip are vacationing in Alabama, Edward is killed in an auto accident caused by the negligence of Patricia, an Alabama domiciliary who was driving carelessly. The law of Alabama gives a remedy for wrongful death, permitting surviving spouses to bring such an action, but under the law of Alabama, the term "surviving spouse" does not include persons who are the same sex as the decedent. Thus, if Alabama wrongful death law applies, it seems likely that Philip will not recover if he sues Patricia, while the opposite result will obtain if Massachusetts law applies. Which state's law should govern if Philip brings a wrongful death action against Patricia? Again, should the answer be the same regardless of whether the case is brought in Massachusetts or in Alabama?

In each of these scenarios, a choice-of-law problem is likely to arise if a lawsuit is brought. In Example #1, determining which state's law on the availability of damages for noneconomic harm is likely to be very complex. The conflicts law of many states places some emphasis on the domicile of the decedent in such cases. Would it be acceptable to apply the law of different states, and thus reach different results, for the claims brought on behalf of the estates of the two decedents, each of whom was domiciled in a different state? In Example #2, should the noncompete covenant be enforced? Should the answer to that question depend on the court (California or Texas) in which the action is brought? Note that in all three

examples, the choice-of-law question may be the single most important legal issue in the case. For instance, in Example #3, if there is
no dispute concerning the defendant's negligence or other facts in
the case, everything will come down to whether Massachusetts or
Alabama law applies to the question of whether Philip should be
considered a "surviving spouse."

One of the beguiling aspects of Conflicts is that readers coming
to these questions for the first time often have strong intuitions as
to how questions like these should be resolved. For example, many
people think it obvious that the law of the place where an accident
occurs should govern any ensuing dispute. As we will see, however,
even if it seems clear which law should apply in a particular case, it
is harder to devise a *general* choice-of-law theory or methodology
that will produce results that accord with our intuitions in most or
all cases that might arise. It is the search for such a methodology
that has occupied jurists in the area of conflicts for hundreds of
years.

**Some Preliminary Observations on Choice of Law in the
United States.** The purpose of this chapter and the next one is to
introduce you to the basic principles of choice of law, and to the
primary conflicts methodologies used by courts in the United
States. Before we work our way through the different choice-of-law
methodologies, using the three foregoing examples as guides, let us
set out a few general points.

First: The choice-of-law rules and principles applied by a court
themselves constitute a body of law. In short, *every state has a "law
of choice of law,"* consisting of rules or principles for resolving
particular kinds of conflicts problems. Just as there is a law of torts
or a law of contracts, there is a law of choice of law. As with the law
of jurisdiction, which concerns when a court may validly hear and
reach a judgment in a particular case, the law of choice of law is
ancillary to the substantive law that may be involved in a particular
case; choice of law and substantive law are analytically distinct
from one another.

Second: The law of choice of law is invariably *forum* law; a
court applies its own law (or, more precisely, its own *state's* law) of
choice of law. (Sometimes you will see the phrase *"lex fori"*—Latin
for "the law of the forum"—to refer to the application of forum
law.)[1] One immediate consequence of this fact is that, if the
plaintiff is able to sue the defendant in two different states, each of
whose choice-of-law principles differ from one another, a forum-
shopping opportunity may arise for the plaintiff if the case features
a conflicts problem: If each state's court would resolve that conflicts

---

1. In conflicts law, the word "forum" refers both to the court hearing a
case and to the state in which that court
sits, as in "the law of the forum."

problem differently, by "choosing" a different state's substantive law from what the other state would, one of those outcomes may be more favorable for the plaintiff and will likely influence her choice of forum.

Third: Remember that, even if it appears that a dispute has plausible connections with more than one state, a conflicts problem only arises if the rules of decision[2] supplied by each of those states differ from one another, and then only if those differences would affect the outcome of the case. If, in a tort case, one state with a plausible connection to the case would apply a strict liability test, while another would apply a negligence test, we are likely to have a conflicts problem to resolve. If, to take a counterexample, the statutory limitations period in one state is two years, and in the other is one year, the difference in rules will not produce a conflict of laws if the plaintiff has brought her claim six months after the events in question.

A. *Lex Loci*: The Traditional Approach to Choice of Law

Until well into the twentieth century, most American choice-of-law rules directed a court to apply the substantive law of a particular, predefined *place* that, for various reasons, was regarded as the proper reference for a particular type of legal issue. The traditional phrase for this concept, going back hundreds of years, was *lex loci*—Latin for "the law of the place." And when we say "the law of the place," we mean "the law of the place where some event that is characteristically an important part of this kind of cause of action took place." Examples of such *lex loci* rules are *lex loci contracti* (the law of the place of the contract) or *lex loci delicti* (the law of the place of wrong). American jurists refer variously to this *lex loci* approach as the "territorial" approach, or the "traditional" approach, or the "First Restatement" approach (since most of the provisions of the (First) Restatement of Conflict of Laws, promulgated in 1934, reflect the *lex loci* concept), or even on occasion the "Bealean" approach, after its most erudite American expositor, Professor Joseph Beale (1861–1943) of Harvard Law School. For the most part, these terms will be used interchangeably in the remainder of the book.[3]

---

2. I use the phrase "rule of decision" from time to time in this book. The phrase is essentially synonymous with "the legal rule that governs the disputed issue."

3. To use all these terms synonymously does risk conflating variations among those who advocated the territorial approach. The First Restatement

was not adopted until 1934, but the "territorial" conception of choice of law goes back centuries; several cases discussed in this chapter predate 1934. Not all adherents of the territorial approach would necessarily have agreed with each of the specific *lex loci* rules set forth in the First Restatement. Moreover, Beale, who was the official Reporter for the

The notion that choice of law should be about "place" seems intuitively obvious. Plainly, no matter what choice-of-law methodology is used, the law of some *place* is going to end up being applied. The distinguishing characteristic of the *lex loci* rules, however, is that they specify this place in advance of, and independently of, the details of any particular case. The *lex loci* rules are thus examples of what are called "jurisdiction-selecting" rules of choice of law. By design, they are (at least in theory) blind to the specifics of any particular case. Thus, for example, the choice-of-law rule *lex loci delicti* for torts—the law of the place of wrong—specifies that, in Example 3 above, the law of Alabama should apply, meaning that Philip will be unable to recover on his wrongful-death claim. In theory, the jurisdiction-selecting *lex loci* rule reaches this result with no further consideration of the facts of the case or other nuances that might militate in favor of another state's law being applied—for example, the fact that Edward and Philip had been married in Massachusetts, and made their home there.

Whether or not they like the particular result in Example 3 that it generates, many—perhaps most—people find the *lex loci* approach in general to be intuitively attractive and sensible. The rather remorseless or "mandatory" quality of the territorial rules is, in the eyes of some, an advantage. "Justice is blind" is an oft-cited ideal of the law, and consistent recourse to a predetermined choice-of-law reference means that all cases of a similar type are treated equally, avoiding subjective, case-by-case judicial determinations of the proper choice-of-law reference. Moreover, many of the specific territorial rules, such as *lex loci delicti* for tort cases, accord reasonably well with people's intuitions about which state's laws should govern their behavior. One frequently hears the view, for example, that if a person drives into a state, she naturally expects (or should expect) to be governed by that state's laws, such as the posted speed limits. It might seem to follow from this view that the place where an accident (or perhaps the negligent behavior causing the accident)[4] occurred should supply the governing law in the case of a conflict. Here's another example of a *lex loci* rule: The traditional choice-of-law principle of *lex loci rei sitae* for real property cases similarly dictates that disputes concerning land (whose location is rarely if ever ambiguous) should be governed by the law

---

First Restatement, attempted in his scholarly work to establish an all-encompassing theoretical foundation for choice of law that should be distinguished from the concept of territoriality itself. Nevertheless, for our purposes it is appropriate to use the various terms interchangeably.

    4. Under the *lex loci delicti* rule, it is sometimes ambiguous whether it is the place of injury, or the place of wrongful behavior, that is the appropriate reference, since these sometimes can be different places. For purposes of exposition, we can ignore the problem of distinguishing between the place of injury and the place of wrongful act, since in the cases we discuss this will usually be the same.

of the place where the real property is situated. These intuitions about whose law should govern a dispute are linked to traditional, if slowly fading, conceptions of sovereignty; to many people, a state *should* have final if not exclusive authority to regulate the behavior of people driving within their states, or to have its law govern the disposition of property situated there.

Even if particular *lex loci* rules don't strike everyone as intuitively providing the "right" answer in all conceivable situations, as a *general* approach it seems to offer a certain stability and predictability. At least in situations where people realistically can plan in advance for the possibility of a dispute—such as when people form a contract, dispose of property, or execute a will—jurisdiction-selecting rules such as those specified by the *lex loci* approach seem to promise more predictability than *ad hoc*, subjective choice-of-law determinations by courts that evaluate all the circumstances in each case. That *ad hoc* approach, as we'll see, might avoid the irrational results in particular cases to which remorseless application of *lex loci* rules can occasionally lead; but if *all* conflicts problems were decided in such an *ad hoc* way, the ability to predict in advance what law would apply to a dispute would be seriously compromised. Moreover, another advantage of the jurisdiction-selecting approach is that, if all courts apply the same *lex loci* rules honestly and fairly, then litigants supposedly cannot seek better choice-of-law results by "forum shopping"; presumably *any* court applying the principle of *lex loci delicti* would find, for example, that the accident in Example 3 took place in Alabama, and thus would reach the same result, reducing the utility of forum shopping to the parties. By contrast, no one can be certain how factually identical cases would come out under an *ad hoc* conflicts approach in which the court "balances all the interests" of the relevant states—even if all courts professed to apply that approach in good faith. Later in this chapter we will further scrutinize the claims sometimes made on behalf of certain choice-of-law methodologies concerning the certainty, consistency, and predictability that they promote; but in principle it is certainly true that jurisdiction-selecting rules, such as the territorial approach, offer more hope for certainty and predictability than do approaches that are more *ad hoc* in nature.

1.   The Lex Loci *Approach in Tort Cases: The* Carroll *Case*

The *lex loci* approach prevailed in the United States without major protest for a very long time; it is still in use in a number of states for particular kinds of cases; and it undoubtedly leads to acceptable, if not necessarily perfect, results in the great majority of cases to which it is applied. Nevertheless, as a choice-of-law methodology in this country it came under withering attack beginning in the 1920s, and remained a veritable punching bag for many conflicts scholars until the 1990s if not beyond. The case of *Alabama Great Southern R. Co. v. Carroll* (Ala. 1892),[5] which you may have read since it is a leading case in almost every Conflict of Laws casebook, illustrates many of the reasons why this criticism emerged—although the case is far from demonstrating that the territorial approach is somehow "wrong."

Carroll, a domiciliary[6] and citizen of Alabama, was a brakeman for the Alabama Great Southern Railroad Co., which was incorporated in Alabama. Their employment contract had been made in Alabama. The route of the freight train on which Carroll worked originated in Chattanooga, Tennessee, passed through Tennessee and Alabama, and terminated in Meridian, Mississippi. On the day in question, Carroll was injured when, while the train was in Mississippi, a link between two of the cars broke. It appears that the link broke because it was defective and, while the train was stopped in Alabama, a fellow employee of the railroad had failed properly to inspect it while attaching one car to another. The law of Mississippi retained the American common-law rule (which, in reality, was itself but a few decades old at the time) barring an employee from recovering from the employer for injuries caused by the negligence of a fellow employee. In Alabama, however, the law was different. The Alabama legislature, by contrast, had some years previously enacted an Employers' Liability Act, one provision of which abrogated the common-law "fellow servant rule" and allowed an injured employee to recover under the circumstances presented by the *Carroll* case. Carroll brought an action against the railroad in Alabama court. The Alabama Supreme Court, applying the *lex loci delicti* rule, ruled that Mississippi law, including its common-law fellow-servant rule, must apply to the case, and that therefore Carroll could not recover against the railroad.

Carroll is an ideal case for latter-day authors of Conflicts casebooks because it illustrates many of the potential vulnerabilities of the *lex loci* approach, and it does so in a case whose result will strike most people as unfortunate. Today there are few defenders of the outcome in *Carroll*. One reason, of course, is that most people probably find the "fellow servant rule" to be both unfair and

---

5. 97 Ala. 126, 11 So. 803 (1892).

6. The term "domiciliary" is a term of art in Conflicts law; many legal problems that traditionally have fallen within the domain of Conflicts require consideration of the "domicile" of one or both of the parties or of some other person who is relevant to the case. Because "domicile" is a criterion in resolving so many problems traditionally regarded as lying within Conflict of Laws, older treatments of conflicts actually devoted a great deal of attention to the problem of defining domicile in particular situations. For purposes of our consideration of the *Carroll* case, it is sufficient to think of Mr. Carroll as a "resident" of Alabama—someone whose permanent and habitual home was in Alabama.

bad policy. That distaste has nothing to do with conflicts law as such. But, from a conflicts perspective, the principal reason that many people condemn the court's ruling is that the employee was deprived of a remedy provided by Alabama law, despite the fact that both the employee and the employer were domiciliaries of that state. (It is conventional to regard a corporation as domiciled in its state of incorporation.) The court's opinion in *Carroll*, however, was in keeping with then-prevailing legal ideas. The general concept of *lex loci* had been around for centuries and was well known to all educated jurists. *Conceptually*, then, the decision in *Carroll* was not out of the ordinary for its time.

What *had* begun to change not long before *Carroll* was decided, however, was the nature of many of the conflicts questions that confronted courts. *Carroll* featured a "conflict" between a rule of the common law (the fellow-servant rule) and an Alabama statute that, in order to further the state's policy with respect to industrial accidents and to facilitate compensation of injured workers, abrogated that rule. The post-Civil War proliferation of protective state legislation that abrogated traditional common-law rules, such as Alabama's Employers' Liability Act, was jarring to some jurists. Nineteenth-century jurists adhered to a conceptual distinction between statutes and common-law rules that is no longer observed today. In particular, courts expressed great concern about giving state statutes "extraterritorial" effect; to give the forum's statute extraterritorial effect violated the limits of the forum's political authority. In fact, if you read the *Carroll* decision closely, you will see that the language in that case differs somewhat from the modern choice-of-law opinion. The Court in *Carroll* does not speak of resolving a conflict of laws nor of "choosing" one of two rules of law, each with some rational claim to application, as would be the case today. Rather, it speaks of the sheer unthinkability of applying the Alabama Employers' Liability Act to events (namely, the injury) occurring outside of Alabama. Today, no one speaks of such rigid intrinsic limitations on the extraterritorial application of state statutes; that is a meaningless concept in a nation where overlap among the regulatory authority of the contiguous states is a reality, if not a practical necessity. In this respect, the *Carroll* decision bears the jurisprudential marks of its time, and would not have been regarded in precisely the same way by contemporaries as we are apt to do today. One should keep this in mind before coming down too hard on the Alabama Supreme Court in the *Carroll* case.

Nevertheless, let us examine *Carroll* as a way of exploring some implications of the territorial approach to choice of law. The *lex loci* approach results in the application of Mississippi law, since that is where the accident occurred and the injury inflicted. But notice how modest and fortuitous are the dispute's connections with Mississippi, and how much more substantial are the connections with Alabama.

Alabama	Mississippi	Tennessee
Π's domicile	injury (link breaks)	origin of train
Δ's domicile	terminus	
"seat" of relationship[7]		
negligent act		
train passes through		
court		
law: recovery	law: no recovery	law: ??

The fact that the railroad line terminated in Mississippi would appear to be of negligible significance at best—certainly of no greater relevance than the fact that the train's route originated in Tennessee—leaving the place of injury as the single meaningful event that took place in Mississippi. Even that detail may appear to be of debatable significance. The link could have failed, and the injury suffered, at any time once the train left its stop in Alabama; the fact that it did so in Mississippi is at least somewhat fortuitous. By contrast, the allegedly negligent behavior, an event that is to a far greater extent under human control (*i.e.* not "fortuitous"), took place in Alabama when the link was not properly inspected.[8] Moreover, one might well argue that Alabama's statute should govern in cases where both the injured party and the allegedly responsible party are Alabama domiciliaries.

The *Lex Loci* Reference Sometimes Appears Arbitrary. What is it, precisely, that seems troubling about application of the *lex loci delicti* rule in this case? First, despite what we said above about the intuitive attractiveness of the *lex loci* approach, *Carroll* reveals that the particular reference made by a *lex loci* rule can seem far from intuitive and even downright perverse. A personal injury claim, for example, requires (among other things) both (1) negligence on the part of the defendant and (2) a resulting injury to the plaintiff. Sometimes, as in *Carroll*, the location of (1) and of (2) can be in different states. The traditional *lex loci* rule as applied in

---

7. Courts and scholars today sometimes treat the place where a relationship between plaintiff and defendant was formed—the "seat" of the relationship—as a relevant consideration in assessing the relative interests of a state in a particular transaction or dispute. It may appear that this factor is already addressed by taking account of the domicile of the plaintiff and the defendant, but sometimes the parties may have formed their relationship in a state different from that of their respective domiciles. *See Tooker v. Lopez*, 24 N.Y.2d 569, 301 N.Y.S.2d 519, 249 N.E.2d 394 (1969), discussed in Chapter 2. In the *Carroll* case, of course, the employer and employee formed their relationship in Alabama.

8. To be completely accurate, there was more than one place along the route where the link could have been inspected, meaning negligence conceivably could have occurred outside Alabama as well.

Carroll, however—*lex loci delicti*—tended to place all of the emphasis on (2) and none on (1). Why should the location of the injury be more significant than the place of the wrongful act? Defenders of the *lex loci delicti* rule replied that, *temporally*, the fact of plaintiff's injury was always the "last event" necessary to "make the cause of action complete"; therefore it was the proper reference for purposes of *lex loci*. Let's concede that this chronological, indeed metaphysical, distinction may have been, in the minds of pre-twentieth-century lawyers, a significant one. Today it isn't. The fact that negligent behavior necessarily precedes the injuries it causes is not by itself a good enough reason for selecting the "place of injury" as a universal choice-of-law reference—not, at least, if that rule will lead often enough to results that don't sit well with us. Of course, this observation alone doesn't undermine the principle of *lex loci*; perhaps we've just selected the wrong "locus" to refer to in negligence cases. But it's not clear that simply replacing the "place of injury" with the "place of negligence" would necessarily be more defensible—although the fact that negligence, while not itself intentional, usually results from purposeful human behavior may make the state where it occurs a more sensible general reference than the place of injury.

The Characterization Problem. Second, the territorial approach provides one *lex loci* rule for tort cases, another *lex loci* rule for contract cases, and so on. But first we must be able to determine whether we have a tort case or a contract case or something else.[9] The *lex loci* or territorial approach relies on the ability of courts to "characterize" the legal issue as to which there is a conflict, so that the proper *lex loci* rule can be identified and applied. Unlike some modern choice-of-law methodologies, which engage in an assessment of a variety of factors regardless of the type of conflict involved, categorization or "characterization" of a dispute is essential to the territorial approach. That fact alone is not troubling, of course—most of the time the proper characterization of the relevant issue isn't especially controversial—but *Carroll* illustrates some of the problems it can present. Faced with the *lex loci delicti* rule and its reference to Mississippi law, Mr. Carroll's attorney also argued that what was really involved in the case was the enforcement of his client's *contractual* rights. He arrived at this conclusion by noting that Carroll and the railroad had formed their employment contract in Alabama, at a time when the Alabama Employers' Liability Act was in force. That law, he argued, must be

---

9. The editors of one conflicts casebook analogize this problem to "Kipling's Painted Jaguar, who complained that his mother had told him that if he found a tortoise he should scoop it out of its shell and that if he found a hedgehog he should hold it under water, but that she had not told him how to tell which was a hedgehog and which a tortoise." Currie, Kay, Kramer & Roosevelt, *Conflict of Laws: Cases—Comments—Questions* (7th ed. 2006), 46 n.2.

considered to have been "incorporated" in the contract, essentially giving Carroll a right to recover from the railroad compensation for injuries (wherever suffered) caused by the negligence of other employees. Since the traditional choice-of-law reference for contract enforcement actions is *lex loci contracti*—the state where the contract was made—Alabama law, argued Carroll's attorney, should apply to the dispute, regardless of where the injury was ultimate suffered.

Is this wrong? Many people seem to think so, believing instinctively that *Carroll* is "really" a tort case, yet it is difficult to state in more analytical terms what, precisely, is wrong with the attorney's argument. The argument for regarding the matter as a contract dispute is not frivolous. The Alabama legislature enacted its employers' liability act for the benefit of those employed by railroads doing business within the state. Employees who theretofore would have been unable to recover from their injuries were now able to recover; the statute thus altered, in an important way, the legal *relationship* between railroads and their employees. Henceforth their contracts for employment necessarily were made against the background of the statute's terms. Should the railroad be able to evade the duties placed on it by the Alabama legislature simply by sending its employees out of the state to do their work? These arguments don't conclusively demonstrate that the case should be regarded as a contract rather than a tort case. But even if we were to conclude that *Carroll* is in fact better seen as a tort case, the case does demonstrate that proper characterization of a dispute for purposes of identifying the appropriate *lex loci* rule is not simply a given, but rather is frequently contestable. That fact alone does not undermine the territorial approach, but it introduces a note of uncertainty and subjectivity into a choice-of-law methodology whose hallmark supposedly is certainty and objectivity.

Don't Both Laws "Apply"? Finally, application of the rigid *lex loci delicti* rule in *Carroll* simply evades the fact that more than one state has supplied a rule of decision that, on its face, seems to cover the situation. Neither the Alabama statute nor the Mississippi common-law rule explicitly provides that its application is limited to events occurring within the state; by their terms, both would seem to apply.[10] If we are nevertheless to decide that only one of them will actually govern the case, we need a more discriminating

---

10. In fact, one could argue that *any* rule of law governing injuries caused to a railroad worker by the negligence of a fellow employee, promulgated by *any* sovereign in the world, would *prima facie* apply, assuming that the law did not specify any geographical limitations. This fact should get you thinking about what criteria we should use to limit the list of contenders for possible application in a particular case. Whatever its other merits or demerits, the *lex loci* approach has the advantage of avoiding this problem, since its rules simply designate a single place as the appropriate choice-of-law reference.

examination of the scope and significance of each of the laws competing for recognition. That would seem to call for an exercise in statutory interpretation.[11] At one point in its opinion in *Carroll*, the Alabama Supreme Court actually attempts to address this question, stating that "universally recognized principles" require that the Alabama Employers' Liability Act "is to be interpreted . . . as if its operation had been expressly limited to this state, and as if its first line read as follows: 'When a personal injury is received in Alabama by a servant or employe,' etc." This is statutory interpretation, of a sort. But what compels this conclusion? If the Alabama legislature *didn't* actually include these words in its statute, why should the statute be interpreted as if it did?

If we are to engage in statutory interpretation, based on the intent of the legislature or on something else, we might note that neither the *lex loci delicti* rule, nor the Alabama Supreme Court in *Carroll*, gives any consideration whatever to the *domicile* of the parties. That is, in assessing the applicability of a state law to a particular multistate situation, one might rationally consider the domicile of one or both parties to be relevant. One reason that *Carroll* strikes many modern readers as troubling is that, whatever the outcome of the case were to be, its most immediate impact would be on an Alabama plaintiff (not to mention his immediate family, who presumably relied on his earnings) and an Alabama defendant, in a case decided by an Alabama court—yet Mississippi law ended up being applied, and the very notion that Alabama law might apply was rudely dismissed by the Alabama Supreme Court. Some of the traditional *lex loci* rules took domicile into account,[12] but many of the most important, such as the rules for torts, contracts, and property did not. This may strike us as odd. Today,

---

11. Territorial rules like those specified by the First Restatement are an example of what is called a "multilateral" approach to choice of law. The aim of such a multilateral approach is to arrive at a choice-of-law reference in particular kinds of cases that is *exclusive*: To say that a state's law to a case applies is also to say that no other state's law can apply. All courts, wherever situated, applying such a multilateral approach would in theory reach the same result. By contrast, "unilateral" approaches to choice of law are concerned first and foremost with whether forum law applies to the case; if it does, it should apply. The unilateral approach, unlike the multilateral approach, does not deny that more than one state's law can "apply" to the case, but regards forum law, if applicable, as the presump-

tive choice among those that might apply. Brainerd Currie's "interest analysis," discussed at length in Chapter 2, is a good example of a unilateral approach to choice of law. The terms "unilateral" and "multilateral," while very important in the history of continental theories of choice of law, seldom play a major role in discussions of domestic American conflicts law, so they will not be further considered in this book. For an excellent general discussion, see William S. Dodge, *Extraterritoriality and Conflict-of-Laws Theory: An Argument for Judicial Unilateralism*, 39 HARVARD INTERNATIONAL LAW JOURNAL 101, 106–21 (1998).

12. For example, most of the territorial choice-of-law rules pertaining to domestic relations referred to the law of the jurisdiction of the marital domicile or the domicile of one of the parties.

when a state enacts a law (such as Alabama's employer liability statute), we understand it to be an expression of the state's policy, and state policy often concerns itself with the protection or regulation of the state's residents. Such statutes usually do not *expressly* limit their effect to state domiciliaries—it is doubtful that they could do so without raising some serious constitutional issues—but we sense that those laws have at least *something* to do with the state's own residents. When a decision like *Carroll* seems to disregard entirely the domiciliary relationship between the legislature that enacted the law and the parties in the case, we sense that something may be awry.

That sense, though, is based on a conception of law and governance that is widely held today, but that was not yet ascendant in 1892, the year *Carroll* was decided. Until the twentieth century, most of the law that was likely to govern civil litigation in traditional private-law areas like contract, tort, and property was common law. There were statutes aplenty prior to 1900, but, until the last quarter of the nineteenth century, statutes that created causes of action, or that altered the rules governing claims and defenses in traditional common-law actions, were the exception. Although the common law of one state might differ in specifics from the common law of another state, "the common law" was still regarded as the core body of law throughout the United States, not the sovereign possession or the expression of the governmental "policy" of a particular state. For the most part, the common law retained, in the minds of most jurists, its character as the product of reason applied to human experience, an adjudicative process that was universal rather than the command of a particular state. Therefore, the *lex loci* rules that applied in the relatively infrequent instances where the common law of one state differed from that of another in the areas of tort or contract law did not emphasize the domiciles of the parties; whatever differences that might exist in the governing law reflected, not the different "policies" of states acting politically on behalf of their residents, but the specific conditions within the territory of a state that perhaps differed from those in another state.

Things were somewhat different, however, where a state *statute* was involved. Today we view the statutes of a state and the common law of that state simply as being two styles of what is essentially the same thing: the law of that state. Thus, choice-of-law problems today are treated the same way whether the competing laws are based on statute or on common law. Late-nineteenth-century jurists were more apt to see statutes and common law as significantly different in many ways, including this one: The enactment of a statute, unlike the application by a court of a common-law rule, was an exercise of the state's *political* jurisdiction. For that reason, as mentioned earlier, courts were concerned about the *extraterritorial* effect of a statute—its application to events taking place outside the state of enactment—in a way that did not concern them where application of the common law was involved. The Alabama Supreme Court in *Carroll*, for example, would probably not have disputed the fact that Alabama's Employers Liability Act had been enacted as "protective" legislation for the benefit of Alabama railroad workers. But that did not mean that the parties' domicile should be a factor in determining whether the law applied in *Carroll*, because it simply was not permissible to give the Alabama statute extraterritorial effect (*i.e.* to the accident/injury in Mississippi). So far as the exercise of Alabama's "political" jurisdiction—the permissible scope of its statutes—was concerned, what mattered was the extent of the state's territory, not the domicile of those affected by the state's laws.

The traditional theory's general indifference to party domicile—an indifference no longer characteristic of modern conflicts law in the United States—underscores a more general way in which that theory differs from choice-of-law methodologies that have come to center stage in the last 40 years. Today, we see law as an expression of state *policy*. Beginning almost a century ago, American legal reformers argued that governmental power should be exercised *purposefully* to promote beneficent social and economic policies. This view called on judges, when interpreting and applying statutes or assessing their constitutionality, to consider their *purposes* and to construe them in a way that would best promote those purposes. "Modern" choice-of-law theories extend this idea to the realm of conflict of laws; in resolving a conflict, a court should consider (to the extent this is possible) the purposes lying behind the respective state laws. Sometimes this can simplify the analysis, by revealing that the purposes lying behind the laws of one of the states would not be advanced by applying its law in the dispute. The traditional theory did not concern itself with the "policies" or "purposes" behind the law of a state in a choice-of-law situation, much less a state's desire to protect its beneficiaries.

The First Restatement. This discussion has been by way of noting how we can justly criticize the result and reasoning in *Carroll*, while recognizing that the result was unremarkable when measured against the legal conceptions of its own time. By the early-to-mid-twentieth century, important changes in the nature and substance of American law had begun to make the territorial approach in *Carroll* appear quaint. Those developments are discussed in Chapter 2. For now, let us note that the First Restatement's rules for tort cases embodied most of the conceptual premises underlying the decision in *Carroll*. For example, § 384 of the First Restatement set forth the basic "place of wrong" rule for torts. Other sections (§§ 377ff.) supply rules for particular issues, such as standard of care, vicarious liability, wrongful death claims, and so on; most of them refer to the "place of wrong."

Beale and "Vested Rights." The Principal Reporter for the First Restatement, Joseph Beale, had in his scholarly work supplied a comprehensive theoretical rationale for the *lex loci* system. Prior to Beale, the most influential treatment of conflict of laws by an American had been Joseph Story's 1834 treatise on the subject. Story, while fully embracing the *lex loci* approach to choice-of-law rules, believed that the phenomenon of a court's applying foreign law in appropriate cases was founded on *comity*—not a strict legal obligation to apply foreign law where a relevant *lex loci* rule might call for it, nor an untrammeled discretion, but a general disposition (based on considerations of justice and reciprocity) on the part of tribunals in all civilized countries to acknowledge the rightful scope of foreign law. The particular choice-of-law references he favored were by and large the same as those specified by the First Restatement, but in Story's view the foundation for the whole approach was the principle of comity. Beale, however, insisted that the duty to apply foreign law as per the *lex loci* rules was more obligatory than implied by Story's approach. He set forth a theory of "vested rights," according to which courts everywhere are obliged to enforce the rights (as well as duties) acquired by persons by virtue of their having acted in a particular way in a particular place (as determined by the applicable *lex loci* rule). The whole "vested rights" idea was expressed economically and memorably by Justice Holmes: "The theory of the foreign suit is that, although the act complained of was subject to no law having force in the forum, it gave rise to an obligation, an *obligatio*, which, like other obligations, follows the person, and may be enforced wherever the person may be found."[13]

Beale's "vested rights" theory was to some extent a generalization of an idea that had existed for a century or more in English and American jurisprudence: the "transitory" cause of action. The idea of the transitory cause of action was that certain legal rights, such as compensation for an injury wrongly inflicted in the locus, could and should be enforced anywhere. Beale thus was building on some familiar ideas in proposing his system. Before very long, though, the "vested rights" idea was subjected to devastating criticism. Without going into the details here (more are provided in Chapter 2), the most obvious problem with the "vested rights" idea is that the legal source of the universal "obligation" it imposes on courts everywhere to apply the law of the locus is mysterious. In an age when most believe that all judicially enforceable law is positive

13. *Slater v. Mexican National R.R.*, 194 U.S. 120, 126 (1904).

law, that is a serious problem. In retrospect, Story's "comity" approach is a more convincing, and certain more accurate, explanation of why courts do and should sometimes apply foreign law.

2. The Lex Loci Approach in Contract Cases: Milliken v. Pratt

We've used *Carroll*, a tort case, to explore the basic features of the territorial approach to choice of law. We can take a look at how that approach treated conflicts in other kinds of cases, albeit in somewhat less detail. *Milliken v. Pratt* (Mass. 1878)[14] is as historically venerable an example of the territorial approach to conflicts in contract cases as *Carroll* is in the area of torts. In *Milliken*, Mr. Pratt, a resident of Massachusetts, applied to the Deering, Milliken company for credit; the company was located in Maine. At the company's request, Mrs. Pratt agree to be her husband's guarantor up to the amount of $500. The company drew up the guaranty papers in Maine; Mrs. Pratt signed them in Massachusetts; Mr. Pratt mailed them back to the company in Maine. Over time, Mr. Pratt purchased goods from the company, but eventually he failed to pay his bills and Mrs. Pratt did not make good on the guaranty. The company sued Mrs. Pratt in Massachusetts court for breach of contract to recover the amount due under the guaranty. One final piece of information: At the time the contract was made, Massachusetts law regarded contracts to which a married woman was party as unenforceable; Maine had altered that rule, to make such agreements enforceable. You might consider making a diagram of what seem to you to be the relevant connections of the case with the states of Maine and Massachusetts, respectively, as we did in our discussion of the *Carroll* case.

You can probably see where this is heading. The territorial approach to choice of law held that the validity of a contract is governed by *lex loci contracti*—the law of the place where the contract had been made.[15] Mainstream contract law doctrine at the time considered that the contract in *Milliken* had been "completed" in Maine, when the company received the signed guaranty. The conflicts question concerned the contract's validity: Massachusetts law regarded such contracts as unenforceable and Maine regarded them as enforceable. After a rather hesitant discussion, the Massachusetts Supreme Court concluded in *Milliken* that the contract was governed by Maine law, and that therefore the company's

---

14. 125 Mass. 374 (1878).

15. In reality, courts were never wholly consistent concerning whether *lex loci contracti* referred to the place where the contract was to be *made*, or to the place where the contract was to be *performed*. In general, questions concerning contract validity were governed by the law of the place where the contract had been made, and questions concerning contract interpretation were governed by the law of the place where the contract was to be performed.

action for breach was enforceable in the Massachusetts courts. It's a more or less conventional result under the territorial approach.

The result in *Milliken v. Pratt* does not on the surface seem wrong in the way that the result in *Carroll* does, partly because the legal disability imposed by Massachusetts law on married women repels us today, but it is nevertheless a revealing example of traditional conflicts reasoning. Here, unlike in *Carroll*, we have parties from different states. The Deering, Milliken company might reasonably have expected its home state's general rule—that contracts, whether or not made by a married woman, are enforceable—to apply; Mrs. Pratt might reasonably have expected her home state's rule, making contracts unenforceable against the married women who sign them, to apply (although it's hard to sympathize with someone who relies on her home state's law to invalidate the very agreement she is signing). We sense, then, that it would not be outrageous for either state's law to be applied. But, as in *Carroll*, we can ask whether the applicable *lex loci* rule hits the mark when it peremptorily designates the "place of the contract" as the place of crucial significance. Is the automatic selection of that "place" any more logical than the automatic selection of the "place of harm" for tort cases?

The basic assumption underlying the *lex loci contracti* rule is far from irrational. In the classic statement of the rule, Lord Mansfield, Chief Justice of England, wrote, "[T]he general rule . . . is, that the place where the contract is made, and not where the action is brought, is to be considered in expounding and enforcing the contract. But this rule admits of an exception, where the parties (at the time of making the contract) had a view to a different kingdom."[16] *The lex loci contracti* rule, then, had its origin in the notion that the parties' wishes as to the law governing the contract should be, to the extent possible, respected; and it is *presumed* (unless otherwise shown) that the parties want their contract to be governed by the law of the place where they make it. Certainly this presumption made sense at a time when most contracts were signed and sealed in person, and the time and location of the making of the contract could hardly be in doubt.

What makes the *lex loci contracti* rule seem more doubtful in *Milliken v. Pratt*, however, is that determining where a contract has been completed when it has been made at a distance (for example, by mail) is fundamentally an arbitrary exercise, not necessarily according with human intuition. The law of contract provides rules, such as the "mailbox rule," for determining for various kinds of contracts *when* an offer has been accepted and a contract has been made, and we may as well draw on those rules for determining

---

16. *Robinson v. Bland*, 2 Burr. 1077 (K.B. 1760).

where the contract has been made. But those rules are based more on the need for a rule, any rule, than on any congruence with basic human intuitions. Whereas it might be acceptable to presume that parties sitting down together to sign a contract intend the law of the place where they are sitting to govern the contract, it's doubtful that parties to a contract made by mail have the intention that their contract should be governed by the law of the place that the "mailbox rule" or some other arbitrary (if necessary) rule dictates is the place where the contract has been "completed."

In fact, once we consider that states might differ with respect to their legal rules for determining when and where a contract has been made, the *lex loci contracti* rule can lead to an exercise in question-begging, especially if the legal issue being disputed is whether in fact a contract was ever in fact made. If we're trying to figure out if there even *is* a contract, how can we use the choice-of-law rule "the law of the place where the contract was made" to choose between the law of two relevant states whose rules differ on the matter? The term "contract" is a legal construction, not a definitive description of a real-world event. The First Restatement recognized the problem, albeit in terms that seem today amusing:

> Under its Conflict of Laws rules, in determining the place of contracting, the forum ascertains the place in which, *under the general law of Contracts*, the principal event necessary to make a contract occurs. The forum at this stage of the investigation does not seek to ascertain whether there is a contract. It examines the facts of the transaction in question only so far as is necessary to determine the place of the principal event, if any, which, under the general law of Contracts, would result in a contract. Then, and not until then, does the forum refer to the law of such state to ascertain if, under that law, there is a contract, although of course there normally will be a contract unless the local law of Contracts of the state to which reference is thus made differs from the general law of Contracts as understood at the forum.[17]

Today we do not recognize the existence of something called "the general law of Contracts"; all law enforceable in American courts is the positive law of some state or nation. The First Restatement's effort to deal with the problem is therefore unpersuasive to a present-day reader. In fact, a purely logical approach would require us first to perform a choice-of-law analysis on the question of whether "there is a contract," and only then (if necessary), proceed to the matter of which law should govern the question of the

17. Restatement of Conflict of Laws, § 311 (Comment d) (emphasis added).

contract's validity. We may be embarking on an endless voyage as we seek to chase down a stable starting point from which to begin the analysis. Let's not, however, get too carried away with this point. Relatively few contract disputes are about whether a contract even exists; most are about some question of contract *interpretation*. On most questions of contract formation, the law does not differ very much from state to state, meaning that conflicts of laws on such matters are rare. And the fact that, in theory, some *lex loci* rules can devolve into second- or third-order questions that logically would require additional *lex loci* rules to solve *those* questions doesn't mean that *lex loci contracti* can't be an acceptable approach to conflicts in contract cases. It simply illustrates that when *lex loci* rules identify a "principal event" to determine the proper choice-of-law reference, that principal event (such as the place where a contract has been made) isn't always a simple "fact"; sometimes it's a legal conclusion as to which the laws of different states may differ.

The more important point is that, however one determines where a contract has been made, that particular detail can often seem like a rather irrelevant factor in resolving a conflicts problem. Professor Brainerd Currie developed an elaborate series of hypotheticals based on the *Milliken v. Pratt* case to dramatize the problem. In one permutation, he observed that had Mrs. Pratt and the Deering, Milliken company both been domiciliaries of Massachusetts, but made their contract in Maine, it would have been "incredibly perverse" for a Massachusetts court to apply Maine law to uphold the contract, contrary to Massachusetts's policy of "protection" for its married women. Yet this is what the *lex loci contracti* rule, remorselessly applied, would have required.[18] Currie had an excellent eye for the dramatic illustration, and there are features of this hypothetical that make it perhaps too facile a target. Nevertheless, the point is a valid one: *Lex loci* rules can, in practice, overemphasize seemingly irrelevant factors at the expense of relevant ones. We will consider Currie's analysis at greater length in Chapter 2.

The First Restatement took the usual *lex loci* approach to conflicts in contract disputes, although it did distinguish (§ 332) between disputes involving contract validity (in which the law of the place of contract should apply) and disputes involving performance (in which the law of the place of performance should apply). Again, a series of provisions concerning more specific contract issues were set forth. Discussing comprehensively the numerous kinds of knotty problems to which the Restatement's conflict rules for contract disputes—not to mention its rather formalistic concep-

---

18. Brainerd Currie, *Married Women's Contracts: A Study in Conflict-of-* *Laws Method,* 25 University of Chicago Law Review 227, 240 (1958).

tion of the law of Contracts itself—led, in theory if not practice, would be more tiresome than illuminating. Several provisions, such as that governing conflicts concerning whether there had been an actual acceptance of a contract offer where the acceptance was sent from one state to another, made reference to the "general law of Contracts" as discussed above. In truth, though, the First Restatement's treatment of conflicts in the area of contracts was not a major spur to criticism of the territorial approach. Throughout the twentieth century, conflicts in the area of torts, particularly with respect to the law governing personal injuries, have played a much greater role in highlighting the shortcomings of the traditional approach.

3. The Lex Loci *Approach in Property Cases*

Real Property. Property is the third in the common-law trilogy of tort, contract, and property. For real property, traditional learning posited that *lex loci rei sitae*—the law of the place where the real property is situated—is the proper choice-of-law reference, and, even today, it is harder to quarrel with this one.[19] Of course, sometimes one state can claim a plausible interest in a dispute pertaining to real property situated in another. Occasionally we might even conclude that that interest is the more compelling one. But, in contrast with the *lex loci contracti* rule, rarely if ever would we say that the location of real property is an *arbitrary* or *irrelevant* consideration in determining whose law should govern a dispute concerning it. Partly this is attributable to the time-honored view (relevant to a variety of legal questions, not just conflict of laws) that the state in which real property sits has exclusive sovereign authority over it. This view, which originally reflected the reality in medieval England that ownership of land was the key to political power, may have lost a bit of its force, but it still exerts a strong grip on conflict-of-laws thinking. Conflicts cases involving real property, especially questions pertaining to title, do not play as large a role in the parade of horribles cited by critics of the territorial approach as do tort (and, occasionally, contract) cases.

At the same time, it's not hard to see how arguments could be made in particular cases for the application of some law besides that of the state where real property is situated. Many of these situations constitute examples of the "characterization" problem that we have already mentioned and that will be discussed at greater length below. For example, nuisances emanating from real property in one state can cause injury to person or property in another state; whether the resulting cause of action "sounds" in tort or property for purposes of determining the proper *lex loci* rule

---

19. The basic *"situs"* rule was spelled out in §§ 214–254 of the First Restatement.

seems unanswerable in principle. But if it is regarded as a "nuisance" case, and hence a question of "property," and the laws of the two states differ on the matter, perhaps the law of the state of the party whose person or property is injured would have a plausible claim to application. Similarly, a contract for the purchase or sale of real property can lead to disputes that bear elements of both contract and property. The admission of estates to probate regularly features the disposition of real property located in a state other than that in which that property is located. Obviously, in these cases a state other than that in which the real property sits might have a good claim to have its law apply. The fact of the matter, though, is that some form of *lex loci rei sitae* is still the dominant choice-of-law principle in real property cases, and, as the cases featuring the application of that principle don't seem too controversial, conflicts casebooks tend to focus more on tort and contract cases to illustrate the pros and cons of different choice-of-law methodologies.

Personal Property. The territorial approach to conflicts involving personal property presents a somewhat more complicated story.[20] In fact, the traditional view of choice of law tended to favor a *situs* rule for personal property just as it did for real property.[21] A number of factors, however, generate more difficulties in this area than in the area of real property. First, unlike land, personal items do not necessarily "stay at home." In fact, one might say that most litigation with respect to items regarded as "personal property" arise out of events that take place while goods are in transit. This does not call into question the basic concept underlying the *lex loci sitae* rule for personal property, but it does suggest that the actual location of the personal property in question at the relevant moment (the time of destruction, spoliation, etc.) can be a knotty problem, making a simple *lex loci* rule difficult to apply. Second, an important species of personal property is *intangible*—shares of stock, bank accounts, indebtedness. The place that the law regards as the *"situs"* of such property, for purposes of the *lex loci sitae* choice-of-law rule as well as other legal questions, does not necessarily accord with human intuition. In fact, it's a little bit like the question of where a contract has been made, discussed above: We need a rule establishing *situs*, and the choice the law makes is motivated more by the need for certainty than by the logical merits

---

20. Actually, the conventional approach in the law of property is to distinguish between "movables" and "immovables" rather than between "personal" and "real" property. The principal significance of this terminology is that leaseholds, which technically constitute "personal" rather than "real" property, are regarded as falling within the category "immovables." I use the terminology of "personal" and "real" property because it will likely be more familiar to most readers.

21. See §§ 255–310 of the First Restatement.

of the choice itself. One example, made famous by the U.S. Supreme Court's decision in *Shaffer v. Heitner* (1977),[22] is a Delaware statute declaring that the "situs" of all shares of stock in a corporation organized under the laws of Delaware is—Delaware.

Finally, many legal questions concerning personal property can equally appropriately be categorized as falling within another area of law. For example, many problems concerning the destruction or spoliation of goods in a commercial context are likely to be regarded as "contract" questions (if not commercial law questions governed by the Uniform Commercial Code), so conflicts regarding them would be governed by the appropriate *lex loci* rule for contracts. Similarly, disputes concerning wills and probate obviously involve property, both real and personal. The First Restatement offered some specific rules for conflicts pertaining to succession to personal property, usually pointing to the law of the decedent's domicile, which obviously might be a different state from that of the relevant personal property. A *lex loci domicilii* rule for such situations certainly makes sense, so that one law can govern succession to a variety of personal property that might be far-flung. Unfortunately, the First Restatement did not adopt the same solution for succession to real property. Evidently the principle that the state where real property is situated has exclusive sovereign authority over the disposition of such property was too deeply ingrained and too fundamental to give way to the interests of simplicity and uniformity in having questions of succession governed by a single law.

4. Other Areas

The territorial approach to choice of law, and in particular the First Restatement which attempted to codify its principles, provided *lex loci* rules for a large variety of legal problems. It's unnecessary here to itemize these rules further; the interested reader can consult the First Restatement to learn more about them. For at least a century now, the conflicts problems that have proved most significant in the development of conflicts law and theory have fallen into the categories of tort and contract law. Criticism of the results generated by the territorial approach in these areas of law has, by extension, become criticism of the territorial approach in its entirety.

B. "Escape Devices"

One reason the First Restatement approach could never attain the overall certainty and predictability claimed for it by its proponents is that there were numerous ways by which courts could avoid the results that strict adherence to the *lex loci* rules would

---

22.   433 U.S. 186 (1977).

have dictated, while still appearing to be working within the *lex loci* system. How often this happened, and what were the precise motivations of the individual judge when it did, are matters of conjecture. But it happened often enough to suggest to critics of the First Restatement approach that no system of purely "jurisdiction-selecting" rules was going to achieve uniform or even truly consistent results. After all, judges simply are not oblivious to the results that application of a particular choice-of-law rule will produce in the manner that the "jurisdiction-selecting" concept envisions. If uniformity and predictability are the major advantages of the territorial approach—and that is a big "if," since there are other features of that approach that some cite in its favor—then this criticism is a major indictment of that approach.

1. *Characterization*

The Basic Problem. We have already mentioned, in our discussion of the *Carroll* case, the vagaries of "characterization" and its importance to the *lex loci* approach. That is, if the rules (say) of *lex loci delicti* and *lex loci contracti* would refer in a particular case to different states, then characterization of the dispute as either a tort or a contract question will be crucial. Many texts (like this one) label characterization as an "escape device," implying that it is a means by which a court applying the First Restatement approach can reach a choice-of-law result, and thus a substantive outcome, that is different from (and, from the court's point of view, more desirable than) what the "correct" *lex loci* rule would have dictated. Unquestionably some courts have done this, characterizing legal issues in unconvincing ways to reach results the courts thought desirable.

But before we write off "characterization" as nothing more than an "escape device," let's remember two things: (1) In any jurisdiction-selecting conflicts approach, characterization is a necessary step in the analysis, and in fact it occurs at least tacitly in the resolution of *every* choice-of-law problem. In many cases it may seem so obvious that a particular issue is "a tort issue" or "a contract issue" that explicit characterization is unnecessary, but that does not mean that there has been no characterization of the dispute. (2) Not infrequently, the proper characterization of an issue is legitimately debatable; a court could reasonably characterize the issue in more than one way, each of which would lead to invocation of a *lex loci* rule that points to a different source for the substantive rule of decision. There are many situations in which a legal question embraces aspects of both property and contract, or contract and tort, or tort and family law, to give only a few examples. Sometimes there is judicial precedent in a state as to how particular issues should be characterized, but in general there is no pre-existing set of rules prescribing the proper characterization for particular situations.[23] In cases where reasonable people could differ concerning proper characterization of the dispute, we should be cautious about describing a characterization with which we disagree as an exercise in "escape."

A famous illustration of the characterization problem is the case of *Haumschild v. Continental Casualty Co.* (Wis. 1959).[24] The Haumschilds, Wisconsin domiciliaries, were involved in an auto accident while driving in California. Ms. Haumschild sued her husband, the driver, in Wisconsin court for the injuries she had suffered. California law at the time recognized the doctrine of "interspousal immunity," barring spouses from suing one another in tort; Wisconsin law did not recognize the doctrine and would have permitted the suit. The territorial approach held that the law of the place of injury should govern conflicts in "tort" cases, whereas the law of the place of (marital) domicile should govern conflicts with respect to the issue of "legal capacity to be sued." Since, in the *Haumschild* case, one of these "places" was in California and the other in Wisconsin, each of whose rules on interspousal immunity differed, much depended on how the disputed issue should be characterized. That proper characterization of the disputed issue was not entirely self-evident is indicated by the fact that Wisconsin precedent had held that such a dispute concerned a "tort" matter and should be governed by *lex loci delicti*, whereas California precedent had held that such a dispute concerned a matter of "legal capacity" arising from a family relationship, traditionally regarded as governed by the law of the domicile.

The Wisconsin Supreme Court in *Haumschild* overruled its own precedent and held that the law of the domicile—Wisconsin— should govern. (Interestingly, in so doing, it cited the earlier California decision as persuasive—though obviously not binding— authority.) The court examined rather carefully both decisions in

23. Actually, if one wanted to try to resolve characterization problems, while being faithful to the self-consistent, "territorial" system that Beale and the First Restatement envisioned, one would logically have to posit a "law of characterization" in each state, and a choice-of-law rule for choosing among them. This can be illustrated by the *Haumschild* case, discussed in the next paragraph of the text. Prior to the decision in *Haumschild*, Wisconsin law characterized the disputed issue as a "tort" issue, while California law characterized it as a "legal capacity" issue. After all, the principles governing correct characterization have to come from somewhere. And wouldn't there have to be a choice-of-law rule to govern ques-

tions of characterization? (One might imagine that *lex fori* should govern such a problem—the court should apply the law of the forum with respect to characterization questions—but neither Beale nor the First Restatement discussed the matter in much detail.) Fortunately for all of us, courts applying First Restatement principles (including the *Haumschild* court) never took conflicts questions to quite this level of meta-exploration. But the problem dramatizes the fact that the effort to attain a self-consistent and internally closed choice-of-law system, like the effort to provide such a foundation for the principles of basic arithmetic, is futile.

24. 7 Wis.2d 130, 95 N.W.2d 814 (1959).

other jurisdictions and the writings of scholars in coming to its conclusion that the interspousal immunity issue should be governed by the law of the marital (or family) domicile. It is possible, of course, that the court was motivated by considerations going beyond the dry academic analysis of the relative merits of the *lex loci delicti* and *lex loci domicilii* rules for resolving "interspousal immunity" conflicts. After all, a court usually has some strong motivation when it overrules its own precedent. The Wisconsin Supreme Court was obviously not blind to the facts of the case, or to its sense of the justice of the matter. The court may have wished to provide a remedy for its own domiciliary, Ms. Haumschild (or, conversely, to impose an enforceable duty on Mr. Haumschild); it may have regarded the doctrine of interspousal immunity as unjust and outdated, and thus wished to avoid its application where possible without explicitly disavowing it; it may even have come to doubt the wisdom of the entire *lex loci* regime as a way of resolving ticklish conflicts problems. Or, perhaps, it simply believed that it is more rational to characterize questions of "interspousal immunity" as a "legal capacity" issue.

The question is whether the fact that courts do this from time to time is, by itself, an indictment of the entire *lex loci* approach. After all, there is probably no area of law in which courts do not occasionally find ways of evading the impact of a legal rule through indirect means. *Haumschild* demonstrates that, in resolving such authentically debatable questions of characterization, courts will be aware of how their characterization of the issue, in determining the proper *lex loci* rule, will influence the resolution of the particular issue and perhaps even of the entire case. That observation may serve to undermine the claims of some who have defended the territorial approach as being a neutral, wholly self-consistent system, or as capable of producing uniform results. But that only undercuts the most extravagant pretensions of the territorial approach; it doesn't demonstrate that approach's lack of utility as a conflicts methodology altogether.

Tort or Contract? The Impact of Third Parties. There are thus many situations in which a disputed legal issue might reasonably be characterized in more than one way. Consider the problem of whether an issue should be characterized as one of tort or as one of contract. You'll recall that this was one of the subsidiary issues in the *Carroll* case. Among other things, Mr. Carroll argued that he should receive the benefit of Alabama's plaintiff-protective employer's liability law; that law, he claimed, should be regarded as a background principle incorporated into all employment contracts entered into in Alabama, and his employment agreement with the railroad had been made in Alabama. The matter, so he argued, concerned the enforcement of a contractual provision, and so *lex* *loci contracti* should apply. As we noted, this argument doesn't seem altogether unreasonable, even if the claim in *Carroll* may "sound" more like a tort claim; since Alabama's employer's liability act was by definition addressed to employers and employees engaged in a contractual relationship, it seems a bit odd to say that the duties imposed by that law (including vicarious liability imposed upon an employer for injuries caused to one employee by the negligence of another employee)—that is, the legal nature of the employer-employee relationship—should be changed when the train leaves the state of Alabama.

The difficulties with any rigid characterization of a situation as a tort problem rather than a contract problem are especially vivid in situations where three rather than two actors are involved. Take, for example, the general principle of vicarious or imputed liability, which often involves the relationship among employer, employee, and an unrelated third-party victim of the employee's negligence. In *Venuto v. Robinson* (3d Cir. 1941),[25] a North Carolina trucker agreed to lease his truck to a North Carolina company and transport a load of the company's goods to New England. During the trip, the trucker was involved in a collision in New Jersey in which several people were killed. A diversity action based on wrongful death was brought against the North Carolina company in federal district court in New Jersey. The key issue was whether the trucker's negligence should be imputed to the company. Both North Carolina and New Jersey recognized the general principle of an employer's vicarious liability for the torts of its employees. The difference, though, was that while New Jersey law regarded this particular relationship between the North Carolina company and the trucker as one of employer and employee, North Carolina law regarded the trucker as an independent contractor (in which case vicarious liability would not attach). The First Restatement flatly characterized the question of vicarious liability as one of tort law, saying it should be governed by *lex loci delicti*, and the Third Circuit in *Venuto* accordingly applied New Jersey law, resulting in a finding of vicarious liability.

Whatever conflicts methodology we may favor, the situation in *Venuto*, which really involves three actors, confounds any attempt to claim that *either* North Carolina or New Jersey is a superior choice for the governing law. From the perspective of the decedents' survivors (who we'll assume were New Jersey domiciliaries), there is *no* reason why North Carolina should apply; nothing alerted them or their decedents to the relevance of that state in framing their behavior. Why should their ability to recover hinge on where the trucker and the company for which he was working made their

---

25. 118 F.2d 679 (3d Cir. 1941).

agreement? On the other hand, the trucker and the company did make their agreement in the shadow of North Carolina law; the company could, perhaps, have guessed at the possibility that the trucker would at some point drive through New Jersey on his way north, but why should the consequences for the company of an agreement made in North Carolina depend on the fortuity of the trucker's driving negligently (or having his negligence cause an accident) in one rather than another state? On this reasoning, perhaps the heart of the dispute is the contractual relationship between the trucker and the North Carolina company, and should be governed by *lex loci contracti* (North Carolina).

Any general solution to this problem would thus be subject to legitimate objections, but the First Restatement's categorical pronouncement that questions of vicarious liability are governed by *lex loci delicti* seems particularly poorly adapted to the *Venuto* situation. The duties of care imposed on a person by tort law, such as the negligence principle, tend to be owed to a large universe of people (say, all drivers on the road); but the question of vicarious liability pertains to particular *relationships*, including contractual relationships. At a formal level, the doctrine of vicarious liability allocates liability between employer and employee, not between wrongdoer and victim (although, of course, the doctrine also usually serves to make it more likely that the victim will receive an actual recovery). In *Venuto*, the truckers' negligence was not the issue; the question was whether that negligence should be imputed to the North Carolina company. That question does seem to be more related to the trucker-contractual relationship than it does to the circumstances of the actual collision. The point here is that *no* inflexible, *ex ante lex loci* rule can be wholly satisfactory in a case like *Venuto*, which concerns the implications for an unrelated third party of a contractual relationship between two others.

An interesting comparison with *Venuto* is *Levy v. Daniels' U–Drive* (Conn. 1928),[26] a case that appears in many conflicts casebooks. A Connecticut statute imposed liability on anyone renting or leasing a car to another for damages to person or property caused by "the operation of" the care while it was being rented or leased.[27] A Connecticut man rented a car from Daniels' U–Drive in Connecticut; he drove the car with a Connecticut passenger into Massachusetts, where his negligent driving caused injuries to the passenger. The passenger sued Daniels' U–Drive, citing the Connecticut statute. Predictably, Daniels' U–Drive argued that the cause of action

---

26. 108 Conn. 333, 143 A. 163 (1928).

27. Although the statute did not explicitly require the vehicle operation to have been "negligent" in order for the renter/lessor to be liable for damages, the Connecticut Supreme Court held in *Levy* that such negligence was in fact a predicate for liability.

was a tort claim, and that liability must be governed by the law of Massachusetts, which had no statute or principle of liability analogous to the one imposed by the Connecticut statute. The Connecticut Supreme Court held that the liability asserted by the plaintiff was "in its nature contractual," and that the Connecticut statute must govern.

The court in *Daniels' U–Drive* went to some length to characterize the issue as one, not of "vicarious liability," but of a direct liability imposed by statute on rental car companies. The Connecticut statute did not, in so many words, *impute* driver-renter's negligence to the rental car company, but rather created an incentive for the company to rent its cars only to "competent and careful operators," essentially by imposing on the company an independent liability for its own failures to identify such drivers, with damages to be measured by the harm caused by the driver's negligent driving. That observation alone, of course, by itself doesn't make *Daniels' U–Drive* a "contract case" instead of a "tort case." The court, though, went on to observe that the liability created by the statute must be regarded as implicitly incorporated into rental agreements made by the rental company (similar to the argument unsuccessfully made by the plaintiff in *Carroll*). Finally, the court observed that, while those contracts were formed by renters and rental companies, the statute made members of the general public—those who might be injured by the rental car operator's negligence—third-party beneficiaries of the statute's protections. Thus, persons injured by operation of the rented car, no matter where injured (and no matter where domiciled), could in effect "enforce" the contract, one of whose provisions was the Connecticut statute.

None of this compels the conclusion that *Daniels' U–Drive* was a "contract" case rather than a "tort" case. The difference between regarding the statute in *Daniels' U–Drive* as directly imposing an independent duty on rental car companies, rather than an instance of vicarious liability derivative of the renter's negligence, seems just a matter of semantics. Not surprisingly, the *Daniels' U–Drive* decision met with considerable scholarly criticism. Yet the analysis in *Daniels' U–Drive* may actually be more discerning than the approach taken by the First Restatement characterization rule, which was applied in *Venuto v. Robinson*. If you are skeptical about regarding the Connecticut statute as being somehow "incorporated" as a provision in the parties' rental agreement, consider that Daniels' U–Haul probably would have incorporated into their own business model the yearly costs likely to be imposed on them by operation of the statute. (They would, of course, have an incentive not to rent to careless drivers, just as the court in *Daniels' U–Drive* suggested.) It is equally likely that such anticipated costs would be reflected in the rates charged for rental cars. Unless Daniels' U–

Drive charged different rates to drivers remaining at all times in Connecticut from those charged to drivers who might drive out of state, there is every reason to view the statutorily imposed liability as an element of the agreement reached by Daniels' and those renting from them, even if the parties to the contract hadn't actually "negotiated" over that term. If this is true, then it makes sense (even under territorial principles) to apply the law of the state where that agreement was reached, even though the plaintiff in the lawsuit was not himself a party to the contract. The court in *Daniels' U–Drive*, by inquiring at least provisionally into the purposes of the Connecticut legislature,[28] evinced an awareness that such an inquiry can shed light on the question of which state's law it is really more sensible to apply. The opinion thus foreshadowed the more full-fledged "interest analysis" of a later generation.

"Purposivism" in Legal Analysis and the Different Meanings of the Same Legal Term in Different Contexts. The situation in *Venuto*, discussed above, also alerts us to a general danger to which jurisdiction-selecting approaches are vulnerable: the acontextual interpretation of words and phrases having legal significance. Having determined that New Jersey law should apply, the Third Circuit in *Venuto* examined the matter and found that New Jersey law (unlike North Carolina law) defined the relationship represented by the one between the trucker and the company as one of employee and employer. Since the definition of "employee" (as distinguished from "independent contractor"), however, has implications for many areas of law—taxation and the law of employee benefits come to mind—it might be useful to know for what specific legal *purposes* New Jersey lawmakers (whether legislature or courts) had defined the term "employee" and distinguished it from "independent contractor." Like many legal terms, the word "employee" is both a word used in the real world (albeit with a somewhat indeterminate meaning) and a legal construct—a word whose legal meaning is derived from its use under a given legal rule. As Legal Realist Walter Wheeler Cook once wrote, "The tendency to assume that a word which appears in two or more legal rules, and so in connection with more than one purpose, has and should have precisely the same scope in all of them, runs all through legal discussions. It has all the tenacity of original sin and must constantly be guarded against."[29] The idea here is that if the

---

28. "The purpose of the statute was not primarily to give the injured person a right of recovery against the tortious operator of the car, but to protect the safety of the traffic upon highways by providing an incentive to him who rented motor vehicles to rent them to competent and careful operators, by making him liable for damage resulting from the tortious operation of the rented vehicles." *Daniels' U–Drive*, 108 Conn. at 333, 143 A. at 164.

29. W.W. COOK, THE LOGICAL AND LEGAL BASIS OF THE CONFLICT OF LAWS 159 (1942).

relevant New Jersey cases had deemed the actors like the trucker to be "employees" in cases involving entitlement to employee benefits, or in cases involving the tax liabilities of employers, it would make little sense simply to assume that the same definition of "employee" must apply in the very different context of determining whether vicarious liability should attach in accident cases. It would be more sensible to make an independent judgment concerning the purposes lying behind states' different rules with respect to vicarious liability and determine whether application of each state's law would subserve those purposes.

As it happens, the New Jersey cases relied on by the Third Circuit in *Venuto* for New Jersey's definition of "employee" did involve questions of vicarious liability, so the Third Circuit was not guilty of Cook's version of "original sin." Cook's admonition is nevertheless a salutary one. His insistence on consulting the purposes behind legal rules and definitions when rendering a choice-of-law decision not only prefigured later "interest-oriented" approaches to choice of law; it is characteristic of the "purposivist" approach to statutory interpretation and legal analysis that has come to prominence in American legal thought since the mid-twentieth century.

2. *Substance and Procedure*

A particularly important example of the characterization problem deserves its own discussion: The line between substance and procedure. We know that, generally speaking, courts apply the rules of the forum governing the process of litigation, and that is how it should be; it would be intolerable if courts had to familiarize themselves with the procedural rules of all the state judicial systems and apply them in different cases. So the forum will apply its own "procedural" rules, even when the applicable choice-of-law rule indicates that the law of a different state should supply the rule of decision for "substantive" issues. This rule was, of course, reflected in the First Restatement. At the same time, we're all wearily familiar with the fact that the distinction between "procedure" and "substance" is not a precise one. The forum will apply its own rules concerning, say, the time period within which the defendant must respond to the complaint; that's pretty obviously a "procedural" issue. By contrast, whether a particular kind of contract (such as a covenant not to compete) is enforceable is obviously a substantive legal question, and will not be automatically governed by forum law (that is, the appropriate choice-of-law rule will refer to the state whose law is to be applied). The real problems arise when a particular issue seems to fall in the middle, and is not self-evidently either "substantive" or "procedural."

Consider, for example, the question of burden of proof with respect to a particular element of the plaintiff's claim. In *Shaps v. Provident Life & Accident Insurance Co.* (Fla. 2002),[30] Shaps had purchased a disability insurance policy while domiciled in New York, but had since moved to Florida. While still in New York, she had made a successful claim on the policy, which the insurer nevertheless ceased paying after about a year because it had determined that Shaps was no longer disabled under the terms of the policy. After moving to Florida, Shaps sued the insurer in the Florida courts to resume payments on the policy. Florida employs a *lex loci contracti* rule in contract enforcement matters, which in this case referred to New York law in case of any conflict. A principal difference between New York and Florida law in this instance, however, was that New York placed on the policyholder the burden of proving that she had remained disabled at the time that the insurer stopped paying benefits; Florida law placed on the insurer the burden of proving that Shaps had *not* been disabled at the time. Citing Florida precedents indicating that "substantive law prescribes duties and rights and procedural law concerns the means and methods to apply and enforce those duties and rights," the Florida Supreme Court in *Shaps* held that the "burden of proof" was "procedural" and that Florida law (*lex fori*) must govern. This was good for the policyholder, not so good for the insurer, whose contractual relationship with the insured, after all, had been conducted in New York, not Florida.

Perhaps the "burden of proof" sounds "procedural" in nature, but in the *Shaps* case it certainly mattered a lot to the parties. Of course, in the abstract, the location of the burden of proof *always* matters; it's easier, other things being equal, to win a case if the risk of the jury's being in doubt about a crucial issue rests on the adversary. But *Shaps* concretely illustrates just how consequential that question can be. Consider the difficulty of making proof concerning the extent of a person's disability at a particular time several years in the past. Often in such cases, credible evidence will be scarce. If there is little for the jury to go on, the judge's instruction to the jury to find against the party having the burden of proof if they are in doubt may have real bite. It is obvious from this example that characterization of an issue as "procedural" or "substantive" often has significant consequences, and it's also clear that there is no simple test for determining the proper characterization of issues that fall into the gray area. The facts that Shaps was, at the time of the suit, a Florida domiciliary and the insurer was not may have had as much to do with the Florida Supreme

---

30. 826 So.2d 250 (Fla. 2002). *See also Shaps v. Provident Life & Accident* *Insurance Co.*, 317 F.3d 1326 (11th Cir. 2003).

Court's ruling as did any purely analytical test for determining whether an issue is substantive or procedural.

A famous California Supreme Court opinion authored by Justice Roger Traynor, an important figure in the development of conflicts principles in the 1950s and 1960s, illustrates the substance-procedure dilemma even more vividly. In *Grant v. McAuliffe* (Cal. 1953),[31] the plaintiffs, California domiciliaries, were injured in Arizona when a car in which they were occupants collided with another car, driven by a man (named Pullen) who was also a California domiciliary. Pullen died before the three plaintiffs could bring suit; afterward, they sued Pullen's estate in California court to recover for the injuries they had suffered. The resulting conflict of laws concerned an arcane area of law dealing with "survival of actions." Under Arizona law at the time, a tort action that had not been commenced prior to the death of the defendant was "abated"—meaning that the cause of action died with the decedent. Under California law, by contrast, such a claim survived the decedent and could be brought against his estate.

Since the accident had taken place in Arizona, that state's law would ordinarily govern substantive aspects of the tort claim (such as the applicable standard of care) under the rule of *lex loci delicti*. However, this particular issue—survival of the cause of action—was somewhat trickier. In the minds of most nonlawyers, the issue seems as "substantive" as an issue can be; it's the difference between having no case and being able to maintain the action and at least have a chance at winning it. On the other hand, as the archaic phrase "abatement of the cause of action" implies, the traditional common-law rule of abatement did not mean that the tortfeasor's acts lost their wrongful character once he died, or that the plaintiffs no longer had suffered a harm calling for compensation. The rule spoke more to the common law's preference that the decedent's estate be settled without being depleted by such claims. Whether that makes the survival question one of "procedure" or one of "substance" is anybody's guess. The scholarly critics of the First Restatement approach would have argued that it is precisely these kinds of metaphysical inquiries that should be discarded, in favor of a choice-of-law analysis that gets closer to the heart of the matter: Which state has the real interest in this case?

Justice Traynor, faced with considerable precedent suggesting that survival of actions was a matter of "substance," and thus an issue that should be governed by *lex loci delicti* (Arizona law), nevertheless finessed the question (to put it politely) and held that it was instead a matter of "procedure," to be governed by the law of the forum—California. The result was that the action survived

31. 41 Cal.2d 859, 264 P.2d 944 (1953).

Pullen's death and could be maintained by the three plaintiffs. Justice Traynor's opinion, though a bit on the clever side, was more than simply judicial legerdemain in the deployment of the terms "procedure" and "substance"; it was an influential display of judicial dissatisfaction with the rigidity of traditional *lex loci* approaches to choice of law. Traynor was well aware, as any judge would be, that the case involved alleged wrongdoing by a California domiciliary and injuries suffered by California domiciliaries. He failed to see what purpose would be served by application to this dispute among Californians of an Arizona rule—which would supplant California's policy of compensation—whose misty common-law origins appeared to be connected with the administration of decedents' estates.[32] Realistically, Traynor probably believed, not that the question of survival of actions should generally be governed by *lex fori* (which was the consequence of calling the issue "procedural"), but that in this particular case, all sense and reason militated in favor of furthering the thoroughly *substantive* policies of California law (in particular, compensation of California domiciliaries and administration of a California domiciliary's estate). The need, however, that Traynor perceived to maintain continuity with the traditional First Restatement approach to choice of law led him to frame his analysis in terms of substance and procedure, and to reach the result he thought appropriate by designating the issue of survival of actions as "procedural" in nature. Some contemporary scholars criticized Traynor's opinion in *Grant* quite severely,[33] but in retrospect it appears to have been a sensible solution.

Right vs. Remedy. One species of the substance-procedure distinction concerns the treatment of judicial *remedies*. An old legal tradition holds that the remedy imposed by the law in cases where a right has been violated is to be distinguished from the right itself. At a basic analytic level, this is obviously correct; the question of whether you have been wronged is a separate question from the question of what remedy the law provides for your injury. But what significance, if any, should this distinction have for choice of law? Under the territorial approach, some courts assimilated the right-

---

32. Interestingly, a different kind of characterization move might have served Traynor's purposes just as well in *Grant v. McAuliffe*: One might have conceded that the key issue *was*, in fact, "substantive" in nature, but that it spoke to the law of administration of decedents' estates, not to the law of torts. This might have led to the conclusion that the law of the state of the decedent's estate should apply—in this case, California. Traynor did gesture in this direction in his opinion in *Grant*, 41 Cal.2d at 866, 264 P.2d at 949, but ultimately rested the decision on characterization of the issue as "procedural."

33. *See, e.g.,* James D. Sumner, Jr., *Choice of Law Governing Survival of Actions,* 9 HASTINGS LAW JOURNAL 128, 142 (1958). Professor Sumner's critique of *Grant v. McAuliffe* was in turn subjected to withering criticism in Brainerd Currie, *Survival of Actions: Adjudication Versus Automation in the Conflict of Laws,* 10 STANFORD LAW REVIEW 205 (1958).

remedy distinction to the substance-procedure distinction, regarding questions of remedy as matters of "procedure" and thus to be governed by the law of the forum. Thus the substantive rule of decision would be governed by the law of the locus while the remedy would be governed by the law of the forum, and obviously in a particular case the locus and the forum might not be the same. So far as "equitable" remedies, and others not traditionally recognized under the common law, are concerned, this principle was not only reasonable but an inescapable consequence of basic legal premises. Courts do not enter injunctions or order other kinds of specific relief solely because that would be the ordinary practice of a court in another state.[34]

By contrast, the notion that the question of money damages is invariably governed by the law of the forum makes less sense under modern conditions. Again, this particular conflicts issue would have been unlikely to arise prior to the statutory innovations of the late nineteenth and early twentieth centuries, which not only created new causes of action and modified old ones, but also defined and limited the scope of damage remedies for many causes of action. Since two states might, for example, create a statutory cause of action for wrongful death, but specify different principles for awarding damages in cases of liability, conflicts of law inevitably arose. This is what happened in one of the better-known decisions concerning remedies and choice of law, *Kilberg v. Northeast Airlines, Inc.* (N.Y. 1961).[35] The decedent flew from New York City to Massachusetts, having purchased his ticket in New York. When the plane crashed in Massachusetts, the administrator of the decedent's estate sued in New York court. Both New York and Massachusetts had statutes providing a cause of action for wrongful death, but Massachusetts law limited recovery in such cases to $15,000, while New York law did not limit recovery. The New York Court of Appeals, hewing to the basic premises of the territorial approach, acknowledged that the claim was governed by Massachusetts law, the place of the accident, but it was reluctant to rule that the available damages were limited to those provided by Massachusetts law. The court ended up applying New York law with respect to damages; one of the theories on which it based its decision is that the question of damages "pertains to the remedy, rather than the right," and as such could be treated as a matter of procedure, to be governed by the law of the forum.

Even on the premises of the First Restatement, *Kilberg* was highly questionable, and within a year the New York Court of

34. *See* the discussion of the U.S. Supreme Court's decision in *Baker v. General Motors Corp.* (1998) in Chapter 5.

35. 9 N.Y.2d 34, 211 N.Y.S.2d 133, 172 N.E.2d 526 (1961).

Appeals had repudiated its "right-vs.-remedy" reasoning.[36] The problem here goes beyond the sensible observation that, for most litigants, the remedy in a case is really what matters to them, and is far from being a mere "procedural" matter. When a statute both creates a cause of action and specifies the remedy to be provided in cases of liability, it is difficult to deny that the statute as a whole embodies a coherent and undifferentiated statement of the state's policy. To take the one without the other is largely to write a new statute. It is understandable that the New York Court of Appeals would have bridled at the notion of having to award what by 1961 was an unreasonably parsimonious damage remedy to the survivors of a person who had apparently been a New York domiciliary,[37] and that it would struggle to escape the dictates of the territorial approach in such a case. But the device of characterizing the damage limitation issue as one of "remedy," and hence of "procedure," is an artifact of the rigid rules of the *lex loci* system. As we will see, post-territorial choice-of-law approaches claim to take courts out of such straitjackets, by making the identification of states' interests in the application of their law an explicit part of the choice-of-law analysis.

Statutes of Limitations. We have observed that the "substance-procedure" distinction is a special instance of the "characterization" problem. The statute of limitations is itself a special illustration of the substance-procedure distinction in the context of choice of law.[38] While our discussion of "escape devices" thus far has been by way of indicating some of the limitations of the territorial approach, we'll take this opportunity to say a bit about how courts today deal with choice-of-law problems involving the statute of limitations.

There are limitations periods for most causes of action, whether those causes of action arise under statutes or are recognized by the common law. Every litigator understands the importance of the applicable limitations period to the success of a cause of action: She knows that if the statute of limitations has run prior to the commencement of the lawsuit, her client's claim will fail (and, if

---

36. *Davenport v. Webb*, 11 N.Y.2d 392, 230 N.Y.S.2d 17, 183 N.E.2d 902 (1962). The Court of Appeals in *Kilberg* had rested its decision on an alternative ground—that Massachusetts's statutory damage limitation violated New York public policy and should therefore not be applied. This rationale was also vulnerable, especially since the court then substituted New York law on the question (a dubious move when applying the "public policy" rationale). The "public policy exception" is discussed at greater length later in this chapter.

37. It is often assumed in discussions of *Kilberg* that the plaintiff and the decedent were domiciliaries of New York, and this is probably true, but that fact does not appear from the court's opinion.

38. Those who have studied the "*Erie* problem" will be at least passingly familiar with the ill-fated quest to categorize statutes of limitations as "substantive" or "procedural."

she is to blame, she may be liable for malpractice), and calling it a question of "procedure" rather than "substance" is not going to be consoling to her client. Therefore, the ancient common-law truism that the running of the statute of limitation does not extinguish the cause of action, but merely "suspends the remedy," means nothing to her. Understanding the centrality of the applicable limitations period to the success of the claim, she might naturally assume that the same state that supplies the substantive law governing her client's cause of action should also supply the statute of limitations. That, certainly, would be the simple and logical way to think about it; and sometimes it actually works out that way. Unfortunately, choice of law with respect to limitations periods has a more bewildering history than this, and even today the state of the law on this question is far from simple.

The Traditional View: *Lex Fori*. Traditionally, the conflicts rule with respect to statutes of limitations was that the law of the forum, not necessarily law of the locus, supplies the limitations rule in case of a conflict. The likely reason for this is that, historically, a principal justification for statutes of limitations is that the forum should have the authority to determine how and when its courts are to be employed for the adjudication of disputes. The limitations period is (at least in part) about regulating the flow of litigation in a state's courts, and in particular to ensure that courts do not have to decide cases in which the evidence may have grown stale and memories have become unreliable. To be sure, statutes of limitations also have another widely recognized purpose—to protect individuals from the assertion against them of old, stale claims. Traditionally, though, its rationale has been more about courts than about private parties. The statute of limitations itself certainly says nothing "substantive" about what kinds of harms give rise to a cause of action or subject a person to liability. After all, the fact that a state statute requires a negligence action to be brought within, say, two years of the plaintiff's knowledge of his injury doesn't mean that, after expiration of the limitations period, the defendant's act has ceased to be wrongful, or that he has a cherished substantive right to cause such mayhem as he pleases so long as no one sues him for it within two years.

Once increased mobility and liberalized rules of personal jurisdiction made it easier for plaintiffs to choose from more than one possible forum, however, the traditional *lex fori* rule for limitations periods (giving rise to the possibility that the limitation rule and the cause of action might come from different states) created serious incentives for forum shopping. For example, let's hypothesize that, in the *Carroll* case, the laws of Mississippi and Alabama were reversed: Mississippi has abrogated the fellow servant rule, while Alabama has retained it. Let's also assume that the Mississippi limitations period was two years for a tort action, the Alabama limitations period was three years, and the plaintiff sued two years and six months after the accident occurred. If the *lex fori* rule for limitations periods is applied, the plaintiff cannot maintain an action in the Mississippi courts, but can do so in the Alabama courts even though Mississippi substantive law applies to the lawsuit. If we further alter the facts to say that the plaintiff was a Mississippi (not Alabama) domiciliary, it becomes clearer that the choice to sue in Alabama court is a strategic option available to plaintiff simply by virtue of (1) the defendant's susceptibility to suit there (*i.e.* personal jurisdiction), (2) Alabama's longer limitations period, and (3) the *lex fori* rule for limitations periods. Under the *lex loci delicti* principle for the substantive cause of action, the plaintiff would get the benefit of Mississippi tort law, but the *lex fori* rule for limitations periods would enable him to escape the Mississippi limitations period by suing in Alabama.

When the Limitations Period "Conditions the Substantive Right." Even during the heyday of the territorial theory, judges and commentators were troubled by these unsatisfactory consequences of the *lex fori* rule for statutes of limitation, and were aware that such limitations periods frequently have more than merely "procedural" effect. Thus, a line of doctrine emerged that, if the limitations period clearly "conditioned the right" established by the statutory cause of action, the limitations period should be supplied by the law of the same state that supplied the cause of action under the applicable *lex loci* rule. In practice, this usually amounted to saying that, if the limitations period specifically appeared in the same statute that created the cause of action, the two should "go together" in any conflicts situation. Even, though, if the limitations period were not literally in the same statute, it could be regarded as "going with" the cause of action if the statutory scheme as a whole made it clear that the two were intended to go together. In a famous statement of this principle, Justice Holmes noted:

> It is true that ... the ordinary limitations of actions are treated as laws of procedure, and as belonging to the *lex fori*, as affecting the remedy only, and not the right. But in cases where it has been possible to escape from that qualification by a reasonable distinction, courts have been willing to treat limitations of time as standing like other limitations, and cutting down the defendant's liability wherever he is sued. The common case is where a statute creates a new liability, and in the same section or in the same act limits the time within which it can be enforced, whether using words of condition or not.... But the fact that the limitation is contained in the same section or the same statute is material only as bearing on

construction. It is merely a ground for saying that the limitation goes to the right created, and accompanies the obligation everywhere. The same conclusion would be reached if the limitation was in a different statute, provided it was directed to the newly created liability so specifically as to warrant saying that it qualified the right.[39]

Accordingly, the First Restatement prescribed that, while ordinarily the statute of limitations would be governed by the *lex fori*, the limitations period would "go with" the cause of action under the circumstances described by Justice Holmes. In the variation on *Carroll* hypothesized in the previous paragraph, the Mississippi statute of limitations would operate to bar Carroll's claim even if it were brought in an Alabama court, so long as that limitations period were specified in the same Mississippi statute that created the cause of action itself.

With the advent of choice-of-law methodologies that depart from the strict territorial premises of the First Restatement, different approaches to conflicts with respect to statutes of limitations have emerged. Let's consider the three most important of these approaches.

The Second Restatement. We haven't said much about it yet, but the reason we refer to the 1934 Restatement as the "First Restatement" is that there is a Restatement (Second) of Conflict of Laws, promulgated in 1971. As you'll learn in the next chapter, the general approach to choice of law taken by the Second Restatement is that the law of the state having the "most significant relationship" to the dispute should apply. This basic principle applies to conflicts involving statutes of limitations as it does to other conflicts. However, the Second Restatement goes on to say:

> In general, unless the exceptional circumstances of the case make such a result unreasonable: (1) The forum will apply its own statute of limitations barring the claim; (2) The forum will apply its own statute of limitations permitting the claim unless (a) maintenance of the claim would serve no substantial interest of the forum; and (b) the claim would be barred under the statute of limitations of a state having a more significant relationship to the parties and the occurrence.[40]

The upshot of this Byzantine provision seems to be that the forum is to apply its own statute of limitations to a case that is otherwise governed by the substantive law of another state if its own limitations period is *shorter* than that of the other state; but it ordinarily should not do so if its limitations period is *longer* than that of the other state. This provision seems to embody a general preference

---

39. *Davis v. Mills*, 194 U.S. 451, 454 (1904).

40. Restatement (Second) of Conflict of Laws, § 142 (Supp. 1988).

for the barring of claims, which may seem to the reader a rather hard-hearted approach. In this respect the Second Restatement embodies, as it does in so many other instances,[41] an effort to appease both modernists and traditionalists in the choice-of-law debate: It modifies the traditional *lex fori* view to the extent of permitting a *shorter* limitations period than the forum's to apply when a different state has a "more significant relationship" to the dispute (in which case that other state will almost certainly apply the substantive rule of decision in the case), but it acknowledges the very traditional rule that forum law must supply the ultimate authority for determining whether a claim can be maintained in the courts of the forum.

The Uniform Conflict of Laws–Limitations Act (1982). As of 2009, this Uniform Act had been adopted by seven (7) states (Arkansas, Colorado, Montana, North Dakota, Oregon, Washington, and Nebraska). In pertinent part, it reads as follows:

§ 2.   Conflict of Laws; Limitation Periods.

  (a) Except as provided by Section 4, if a claim is substantively based:

     (1) upon the law of one other state, the limitation period of that state applies; or

     (2) upon the law of more than one state, the limitation period of one of those states chosen by the law of conflict of laws of this State, applies.

  (b) The limitation period of this State applies to all other claims.

This seems essentially to mean that statutes of limitations are considered to be "substantive," and are taken from the state that provides the substantive law for the dispute.

Interest Analysis. As we'll see in greater detail in the next chapter, an influential choice-of-law methodology known as "interest analysis" suggests that forum law should apply in conflicts situations, *except* when (1) the forum has no cognizable interest in having its law applied to the case, and (2) another state *does* have a cognizable interest in having its law applied. Under interest analysis, a conflict involving the limitations periods supplied by two (or more) states is resolved using this approach just as would any other conflict. We might imagine that, where limitations periods are concerned, the forum will *always* have a cognizable interest—the interest in keeping its courts free of old claims or those that are difficult to resolve confidently because of the erosion of memories and other evidence. Since, in the purest form of interest analysis,

---

41. For further elaboration of this notion, see the more extensive discus- sion of the Second Restatement in Chap- ter 2.

the existence of a legitimate interest on the part of the forum in the application of its own law is a sufficient condition for concluding that forum law should apply, all conflicts involving limitations periods should be governed by forum law. In reality, the number of states that have adopted interest analysis in anything like this pure a form is extremely small. There are, though, a few cases in which such an analysis has been applied to limitations periods.

Borrowing and Tolling Statutes. To this mix should be added the "borrowing statutes" that exist in something more than half the states. These statutes, most of which were enacted many years ago, were mostly efforts to specify that the forum will apply the limitations period of the state where the cause of action arose or "accrued." (Under the older legal mind-set that underlies the territorial approach to choice of law, to say that a cause of action "arose" or "accrued" in a particular place was tantamount to saying that any resulting legal dispute should be governed by the law of that state.) They thus attempted, commendably, to limit the operation of the *lex fori* principle in conflicts over limitations periods. One example is Nevada's ancient borrowing statute, dating from the later nineteenth century:

> When a cause of action has arisen in another state, or in a foreign country, and by the laws thereof an action thereon cannot there be maintained against a person by reason of the lapse of time, an action thereon shall not be maintained against him in this State, except in favor of a citizen thereof who has held the cause of action from the time it accrued.[42]

The strange final clause of this borrowing statute suggests some of the numerous questions of interpretation and application that are raised by these antiquated laws. We won't delve further into these.[43] We will, however, mention a final statutory wrinkle that can complicate conflicts even further in the arena of statutes of limitations: "tolling" statutes. You are probably at least passingly familiar with the notion that certain events can "toll"—that is, "stop the clock" on—the running of the statute of limitations on a particular claim. Most tolling statutes are concerned, at a minimum, with one such type of event: the absence of the defendant from the state in which the claim arose from the jurisdiction. The idea is that the otherwise applicable statute of limitations should not deprive the plaintiff of a claim just because the defendant has made himself unamenable to suit in the state. Many of these tolling statutes (which are usually of ancient vintage) are less important than they once were, since under today's relaxed standards for

---

42. Nev. Rev. Stat. 11.020.

43. One question you might consider, however, is this: Should a state's choice-of-law reference to the statute of limitations of another state include that other state's borrowing statute as part of the bargain?

personal jurisdiction, the defendant's absence from the forum does not necessarily make him un-suable there. Nevertheless, it is certainly possible for a defendant to place himself beyond service of process, and in such cases a tolling statute keeps the plaintiff from losing his claim as a result.

What does this have to do with conflicts? One answer is that it may sometimes be unclear whether a state's borrowing statute contemplates application not only of another state's limitations period, but also of that other state's tolling statute, which may differ from the forum's in some significant way.[44] The moral of the story: When considering the problem of a limitations period in a case with multistate connections, be sure to research the relevant borrowing and tolling statutes, if any.

3. Renvoi

As we have seen, the rule in American conflicts law is that the forum applies its own rules of choice of law. This, of course, will lead in certain cases to the application of foreign law. But just what does it mean for the forum to "apply foreign law"? One answer, which has been assumed in all of our analysis thus far, is that the forum applies the other state's substantive or "internal" law. If, in a tort case, there is a conflict between State A and State B concerning the applicable standard of care (say, negligence vs. strict liability), and the forum's choice-of-law rule directs the court to the law of State B, the forum simply applies State B's law concerning standard of care—which is clearly "substantive" law. But an alternative view might be that, when the forum's choice-of-law rule directs it to apply the law of State B, that reference is to the "whole" law of State B, which includes that state's choice-of-law rules. As you can imagine, reference to State B's choice-of-law rules could make the problem more complicated; those rules, applied by the forum, could point to the law of yet another state, or even back to the forum. Any time the choice-of-law rule of the forum differs from the corresponding choice-of-law rule used by the jurisdiction to which the forum's choice-of-law rule points in the first instance, the question of whether the reference is to the "internal" or to the "whole" law of that state will have obvious consequences. The term *"renvoi"* (a French word that most American conflicts scholars pronounce "RON-voy," although any native French speaker would be aghast at this) refers to this problem of whether and how to apply the "whole" law of a foreign state, including its choice-of-law rules.

---

44. For a famous if idiosyncratic case raising these issues, see *West v. Theis*, 15 Idaho 167, 96 P. 932 (1908). A disproportionate number of the strange legal problems created by the operation of borrowing and tolling statutes seem to emerge from the Western states.

The first and most important point to understand is that *renvoi* plays but a small role in domestic American conflicts law. In the vast majority of cases, references to foreign law made by the forum's choice-of-law rules are to the "internal" law of the foreign state, meaning its substantive rule of decision. By and large, American conflicts law does not mess around with applying foreign choice-of-law rules. That is good news, because application of foreign conflicts rules would further complicate an already intricate problem. In addition, the majority of American conflicts theorists have rejected the *renvoi* principle. For example, Joseph Beale, architect of the "vested rights" theory rationalizing the territorial approach to conflicts, rejected it. Since, on his view, the location of certain events at certain times fixed the parties' *substantive* rights pursuant to the law of that place, there was no reason for the forum to consider that state's conflicts rules; the choice-of-law reference should simply be to that state's substantive law. Proponents of a more "modern," interest-oriented approach to choice of law, which will be discussed in the next chapter, likewise have rejected the *renvoi* principle. Since, in their view, what matters is the "interest" a state has in having its substantive law (reflecting its overall "policy") applied in a particular case, any reference to foreign law should be to that internal law, not the "whole" law of that state.

Nevertheless, on occasion one will find the forum applying foreign choice-of-law rules; sometimes we can even say that there is good reason for doing this. And for many years (although not recently) jurists debated the problem of *renvoi* quite hotly; it seems to lie at the core of more general theoretical disputes about conflicts law. As Larry Kramer has said, "To solve the problem of the renvoi ... one must understand what exactly it means to 'choose' a foreign law."[45] So it's worth taking a few moments to understand what is at stake in deciding whether a reference to foreign law should be to the "internal" (substantive) or to the "whole" law (including choice-of-law rules) of that jurisdiction.

Application of the *renvoi* principle might make sense, for example, if we thought that the goal of the forum in applying foreign law was to mimic, as precisely as possible, what a court of that foreign state would do if it were deciding the case. If State B's own choice-of-law rule would point to the law of another state (perhaps the forum itself), the only way for the forum (State A) to replicate the way in which Court B would decide the case would be to apply the "whole law" of State B, including its choice-of-law rule.[46] By contrast, if the goal of the forum's choice-of-law decision

---

45. Kramer, *Return of the Renvoi*, 66 N.Y.U. L. Rev. 979, 983 (1991).

46. Some have argued that application of the *renvoi* principle would diminis either to vindicate the private substantive rights of the parties (under Beale's theory) or to effectuate the substantive policies of the state whose law is chosen (under interest analysis), then it makes more sense to avoid reference to the foreign state's choice-of-law rule.

The *renvoi* idea might not have retained the interest that it has, at least for scholars of American conflicts law, were it not for the picturesque (and mind-bending) logical problems to which it can lead. The simplest variation occurs when a case is brought in State A, whose choice-of-law principles point to application of the law of State B. State B's choice-of-law rule, however, points to application of the law of State A. If we employ the *renvoi* principle, and each successive choice-of-law reference includes the "whole law" of the chosen state, we have a problem of infinite regress: We would be pushed from State A, to State B, back to State A, and so on.

One might think that such a scenario arises solely in the diseased minds of conflicts professors seeking to torment their students, but a famous actual case from 1926 illustrates the problem. (One knows that one is dealing with a truly arcane legal concept when one has to resort to a case from 1926 to illustrate it.) In *In re Annesley*,[47] an Englishman died intestate while domiciled in France. The conflict in this case concerned whether English or French law should govern disposition of the decedent's personal property. England's choice-of-law rule referred to French law (law of the decedent's last known domicile). France's choice-of-law rule referred to English law (law of the decedent's nationality). As it happens, prior French case law also indicated that, had the case been brought there, the French court's choice-of-law reference would have been to "whole" law of England. The case, brought in English court, thus presented the theoretical possibility of infinite regress, should the English court's choice-of-law reference be to the whole of French law. The English court "solved" the problem by accepting French law's reference back to the "whole" of English law, which then pointed back to internal French law, which was applied to the case. There is, however, no especially compelling justification for the English court's having decided to terminate the

ish forum shopping. That is, if *renvoi* is not observed—that is, if references to foreign law are only to their substantive or "internal" law, as is generally the case today in American conflicts law—litigants can shop for a favorable forum if they can predict how the possible forums' choice-of-law rules will operate. Supposedly, reference by the forum to the "whole law" of the other state would mitigate this "forum shopping" problem. So long, however, as different states have different choice-of-law rules, one cannot escape disuniformity in the results different courts would reach in a specific case, even when *renvoi* principles are used.

47. 1 Ch. 692 (1926).

renvoi game precisely where it did; its decision was purely a practical one.

While *renvoi* plays a respected role in the conflicts law of some other countries, it is generally rejected in the United States. The First Restatement (1934) generally rejected *renvoi*, in accord with the views of its Reporter, Joseph Beale, but it did identify two exceptions: questions of title to land, and questions concerning "the validity of a decree of divorce." Is there a justification for these exceptions? Today, we'd be unlikely to find the justification for treating these two, and only these two, situations differently to be compelling, but recall that traditional legal doctrine regarded real property as being completely and exclusively within the sovereign power of the state in which it was situated. Apparently this militates in favor of the forum's deciding the case precisely as the courts of the locus would, which thus would require application of the choice-of-law rules of the locus. As for marriage and divorce, Beale explained that it was especially desirable that the marital status of an individual be treated uniformly throughout the country, and he thought that reference to the whole law of the marital domicile would promote this. The Second Restatement more or less rejects *renvoi* altogether, not even referring to the two exceptions identified by the First Restatement.

Today, most of the handful of *renvoi* cases that arise in state courts in the United States concern the settlement of estates. Of these, quite a few involve claims that the law of a foreign country should apply, because some part of the decedent's estate is situated there. The *renvoi* problem is less likely to arise in an estate matter where there are multistate elements but no connection with a foreign country; many states in the United States have borrowing or reception statutes that function to resolve interstate conflicts in estate cases.

Why does the topic of *"renvoi"* appear here (as it does in many casebooks) under the rubric of "Escape Devices"? Because, from time to time, an American court will apply *renvoi* concepts to reach a result that it prefers and that differs from the reference that would result from the otherwise applicable choice-of-law principle. Rarely do such courts justify these rulings, apart from the observation that the customary reference to the foreign state's internal law alone would result in an outcome that the courts of that state, applying a different choice-of-law rule, would not have reached had the case been brought there. Of course, since the whole *renvoi* problem only arises if the forum's original choice-of-law reference is to the other state's law, the outcome of these manipulations can only be to apply the forum's substantive law. For example, in

Braxton v. Anco Electric, Inc. (N.C. 1991),[48] the plaintiff, a North Carolina domiciliary, was injured in a construction site accident in Virginia. The defendant employer was a North Carolina corporation. Under North Carolina workers compensation law, the injured worker was not barred from seeking a judicial remedy, while under Virginia law, he was. At this time the North Carolina courts still employed the *lex loci delicti* rule for torts; Virginia law applied the law of the state where the plaintiff was employed and received workers compensation benefits. The Supreme Court of North Carolina applied North Carolina law and found for the plaintiff, resting its decision partly on application of the *renvoi* doctrine. It gave no persuasive explanation as to why *renvoi* should be deployed here; it noted only that a Virginia Court would have applied North Carolina law, as though that were not a possibility in *any* case in which the choice-of-law rules of the two interested states would point to different states. One way of justifying the result, if not the reasoning, in *Braxton* would have been a more general criticism of the *lex loci delicti* rule and the objectionable result to which it pointed in this particular case. But the North Carolina Supreme Court evidently preferred not to cast such thoroughgoing doubt on the territorial approach. The court's partial reliance on *renvoi* reasoning was a classic example of the use of *renvoi* as an "escape device."

The *Braxton* case demonstrates that, while *renvoi* is largely an anomaly in American conflicts law, courts and litigants still occasionally find ways of inserting it into the choice-of-law analysis. For that reason it is well to be aware of its presence, lurking in the shadows of American conflicts law.

4. Public Policy

The most controversial of the "devices" by which courts have avoided the application of foreign law to which the applicable *lex loci* rule would otherwise have directed them is the principle that the forum will not apply foreign law that outrages the public policy of the forum. This principle is a revealing one, for a number of reasons. First, it brings us face to face with the reality that the forum's decision to apply foreign law in appropriate cases is, at bottom, a matter of the forum's sovereign prerogative, as Joseph Story's "comity" approach suggests. Even those, such as Professor Beale, who were most eager to ground the system of choice of law on a set of rules that the forum was somehow *obliged* to apply, could not deny that, ultimately, the forum was entitled to decline to enforce foreign law that violated the forum's strongly held public policy. A simple, if anachronistic, example: Suppose that the law of the forum regards contracts for gambling as illegal and unenforcea-

48. 330 N.C. 124, 409 S.E.2d 914 (1991).

ble. Now suppose that two forum domiciliaries travel to another state, which regards such agreements as enforceable, purely for the purpose of signing the contract there. The parties then return to the forum and, after a dispute arises, one sues the other there; the defendant defends on the ground that the contract is unenforceable. Even if the forum's choice-of-law rule is *lex loci contracti*, which should result in the contract's being enforced, it would not be surprising if the forum declined to apply the other state's law, because to do so would result in a brazen end-run around the forum's public policy.

Of course, the foregoing example also illustrates the rigidity and occasional manipulability of the *lex loci* principle. Jurisdiction-selecting rules (like those of the traditional *lex loci* approach) and the availability of a "public policy exception" go hand in hand as a practical matter, even though they are difficult to reconcile conceptually. When push comes to shove, the forum will not lightly tolerate the use of its courts to effectuate legal results that the forum itself has condemned. The "public policy exception" is a quixotic attempt to package this basic reality in doctrinal terms and incorporate it into the *lex loci* system itself. Note that, under more "modern" choice-of-law methodologies that attempt to resolve conflicts at least partly by reference to the interests of the relevant states, there is no need for an "exception" based on public policy; such policy considerations form an important part of the choice-of-law calculus itself.

Obviously, the "public policy exception" is discomfiting for those, like Beale, who sought to make the territorial approach a universal, self-consistent system that imposed an *obligation* on the forum to apply foreign law where appropriate. The real practical problem with the "public policy exception" under the traditional approach, however, is that, when applied too liberally, it can authorize courts to characterize virtually any rule of forum law as embodying "strongly held policy," resulting in the nonapplication of foreign law whenever it differs from that of the forum and the relevant *lex loci* rule points to it. This would make a mockery of the *lex loci* principle. In our earlier example, we could understand why the forum might regard its no-gambling-contracts rule as expressing a very strong policy of the forum. But, to embroider the hypothetical somewhat, suppose the parties went to the other state to form an ordinary contract (not in violation of the forum's policy), but communicated there by mail rather than in person. If the forum uses the "mailbox rule" for determining when and whether a contract was actually formed, and the other state uses a different rule, would the forum really be justified in declining to apply the other state's rule even though the applicable *lex loci contracti* rule would point there in the case of a conflict? It's hard to imagine the "mailbox rule" expressing a strongly held forum policy; it's just a rule to govern contract formation because we need a rule. Although this is admittedly a fanciful example, courts have at times been very tempted to apply the "strong public policy" label to forum law in questionable cases—*especially* when forum law is expressed in a statute. It is, after all, easy to regard statutes as embodying deeply considered and strongly held convictions about what is best for the people of the state. From there it is a short and tempting step to applying that characterization to *all* of the forum's statutes, or at least to a lot of them, and even to the forum's common-law rules.

In the best-known discussion of the "public policy exception," *Loucks v. Standard Oil Co. of New York* (N.Y. 1918),[49] Judge Benjamin Cardozo gave a salutary warning against overzealous application by the forum of the "public policy exception" to avoid application of foreign law. In *Loucks*, a New York resident was killed in Massachusetts by a vehicle operated by employees of Standard Oil (a New York corporation). Both New York and Massachusetts had enacted statutes recognizing a cause of action for wrongful death; the Massachusetts law, however, capped damages at $10,000, which the New York statute did not.[50] The traditional *lex loci* rule, of course, pointed to Massachusetts law. It was argued that the New York courts should decline to apply the Massachusetts law, because its cap on damages violated New York's strongly held policy of full compensation for wrongful death. Cardozo rejected the argument in memorable terms:

> We are not so provincial as to say that every solution of a problem is wrong because we deal with it otherwise at home. . . . The courts are not free to refuse to enforce a foreign right at the pleasure of the judges, to suit the individual notion of expediency or fairness. They do not close their doors, unless help would violate some fundamental principle of justice, some prevalent conception of good morals, some deep-rooted tradition of the common weal. . . . [T]here is nothing in the Massachusetts statute that outrages the public policy of New York.[51]

This regularly quoted statement is easy enough to comprehend. Since, however, some of the oddities of *Loucks* are not always explained in the casebooks that excerpt the case, a few words of clarification are in order. First, *Loucks* involved a wrongful death statute. The common law had not recognized such a cause of action. Wrongful death statutes were, in the second half of the nineteenth century, perhaps the most controversial example of legislation that

49. 224 N.Y. 99, 120 N.E. 198 (1918).

50. Actually, we earlier discussed this very conflict in our treatment of the *Kilberg* case, in connection with the issue of treating damage limitations as a question of "remedy" for choice-of-law purposes.

51. 224 N.Y. at 111, 120 N.E. at 201, 202.

altered common-law rights and duties, at least until worker's compensation statutes came along.[52] Whereas common-law personal injury claims had long been regarded as "transitory"—enforceable in any court, even outside the state where the accident had occurred—courts were much more reticent about giving these wrongful death statutes "extraterritorial" application. Some courts, however, had devised an expedient doctrine according to which they would indeed enforce the rights created by another state's wrongful death statute so long as the forum itself had a statute that was "substantially similar" to the other state's. In his *Loucks* opinion, Cardozo had acknowledged that the New York and Massachusetts wrongful death statutes were not "substantially similar," but he rejected the notion that that alone should result in the failure to give the plaintiff a remedy under Massachusetts law.

Second, this early-twentieth-century uncertainty about the extraterritorial application of wrongful death statutes, together with an understanding of now-obsolete conceptions of jurisdiction and choice of law that prevailed at the time of *Loucks*, helps explain the parties' litigation strategy and how the "public policy" issue arose in the case. Many readers of *Loucks* assume that it must have been the *plaintiffs* who argued against application of the Massachusetts statute (to which *lex loci delicti* pointed, since the accident occurred there), since it limited damages while the New York statute did not. But it was actually the *defendants* who made the argument. To Cardozo and his juristic contemporaries, the consequence of refusing to apply Massachusetts law was not the substitution and application of New York law; it was dismissal of the case for lack of jurisdiction.[53] Prevailing conceptions of the *lex loci* system, with its mandatory choice-of-law references, did not admit of the possibility that the law of a *different* state (such as the forum) could rush in to fill the void if "public policy" barred enforcement of the otherwise applicable foreign law; either *lex loci delicti* were to be applied, or the case must be dismissed. The defendant Standard Oil attempted to exploit this fact in raising the "public policy" argument. Under then-existing principles of personal jurisdiction, Standard Oil might not have been amenable to suit in Massachusetts; and, in any event, it might well have been expensive and difficult for the plaintiffs (New York residents) to sue Standard Oil there. Had Cardozo accepted Standard Oil's "public policy" argument, the

---

52. Another example was employers' liability acts that, among other things, abrogated or modified common-law defenses to actions for personal injuries in industrial accidents. The attitude toward such statutes on the part of courts is illustrated in the *Carroll* case, discussed earlier in this Chapter.

53. As Cardozo framed the issue, "We must decide whether the difference [between Massachusetts and New York law] is a sufficient reason for declining jurisdiction." *Loucks*, 224 N.Y. at 106, 120 N.E. at 200.

plaintiffs might well have been left without a remedy despite the fact that *both* Massachusetts and New York recognized a cause of action for wrongful death. (Perhaps this fact influenced Cardozo's disposition of the "public policy" argument.)

Finally, though Cardozo's treatment of the public policy issue in *Loucks* was refreshingly pragmatic, his opinion remained very much under the sway of the contemporary "vested rights" approach to choice of law. He spoke of the "foreign right" held by the plaintiffs by virtue of the decedent's death in Massachusetts as a species of "property." This is rather different from the language one would likely find today in judicial opinions concerning choice of law, where a state's prerogative to have its law applied, rather than enforcement of a "right" that a party has picked up during her travels, is the coin of the realm.

An excellent example of how much the basic legal conceptions concerning jurisdiction and choice of law have changed since the early twentieth century is to compare the *Loucks* decision with *Kilberg v. Northeast Airlines, Inc.* (N.Y. 1961),[54] also decided by the New York Court of Appeals, which we discussed in a previous section in connection with the right-remedy distinction. The basic framework of the *Kilberg* case is uncannily similar to that in *Loucks*. In *Kilberg*, a man (who was apparently a New York resident) was killed when a plane he had boarded in New York City crashed in Massachusetts. The Massachusetts legislature had by this time raised its damage limit in wrongful death cases to a princely $15,000, while New York again had no such limitation. The decedent's estate sued the airline in New York court. The Court of Appeals noted that (as in the *Loucks*) case the traditional *lex loci delicti* rule (which it had yet to abandon in tort cases) pointed to the application of Massachusetts law. This time, however, it declined to apply the Massachusetts damage limitation, not only because it characterized the damages limitation as a question of "remedy" to be governed by *lex fori* (as discussed above), but also because application of Massachusetts law would violate New York's strong public policy. The court made a weak effort to distinguish the *Loucks* decision.

The significance of comparing *Kilberg* with *Loucks* is not just that the court in *Kilberg* reached the opposite conclusion on the "public policy" question from what Cardozo had decided in *Loucks*, but also that the court in *Kilberg* no longer believed, as Cardozo had, that the alternative to applying Massachusetts law was dismissal of the case for lack of jurisdiction. The court simply applied New York's (uncapped) damages rule. The legal notion that the decedent's estate could enforce only the "vested right" that the

54. 9 N.Y.2d 34, 211 N.Y.S.2d 133, 172 N.E.2d 526 (1961).

decedent had acquired by suffering a fatal accident in Massachusetts had by 1961 passed from the scene; now the question was whether New York had the right to apply its *own* law, notwithstanding the reference to Massachusetts law made by the usual *lex loci* rule, given the nature and intensity of New York's public policy. Of course, under these circumstances it was the *plaintiff* (unlike in *Loucks*) who argued against application of Massachusetts law, believing that the alternative was application of the more favorable New York law on damages.

Although *Loucks* and *Kilberg* reached diametrically opposed results on the "public policy" question despite the similarity of the facts of the cases, one can argue that both were correctly decided, or at least surmise why the court in *Kilberg* came out so differently on the question. Between 1918 and 1961 Massachusetts had raised the damage limit for wrongful death cases by all of $5000. If $10,000 had seemed to some in 1918 an ungenerous award for death caused in an automobile accident, $15,000 may have seemed in 1961 to be downright indefensible as a maximum award for death caused in a commercial airline crash. Thus one could reasonably say (perhaps also taking into account that by 1960 the cause of action for wrongful death no longer seemed novel to anyone) that what had not been an outrage against New York public policy in 1918 had become one by 1961. Nevertheless, what is really revealed by comparing *Loucks* and *Kilberg* is that the conceptual underpinnings of the territorial approach had substantially lost their grip on courts and scholars, although the husk remained. (As we'll see in Chapter 2, the New York Court of Appeals during the 1950s had, in other kinds of cases, begun to depart in certain ways from *lex loci* rules.) Proper application of that older approach should have required the *Kilberg* court to dismiss the case for lack of jurisdiction once it determined that it would not apply the Massachusetts damage-limitation provision. But, increasingly, courts were not concerning themselves with such theoretical niceties; choice of law was no longer about enforcing rights that had vested under the *only* applicable law, but about "choosing" the law that (for good reasons or bad) appeared to be the most appropriate.

In connection with *Kilberg*, we should note that there can be something dubious about a court's applying foreign law in accordance with the applicable *lex loci* rule for the underlying cause of action, while refusing to give effect to that foreign law with respect to another legal issue in the case that may be closely related to the cause of action. To avoid any confusion here, it is clear that American conflicts generally accepts the concept of *depeçage*—the possibility of applying the laws of different states to different issues in the same case. But that does not mean that it is proper for a court to apply foreign law for the purpose of giving the plaintiff a cause of action, but to refuse, through use of the "public policy" exception or some other device, to recognize a legal defense that that same foreign law gives the defendant in the same case. It is one thing, as in our "gambling contract" example, for the forum to decline to apply a cause of action based on foreign law for breach when the forum reprehends such contracts. The result is, or should be, the end of the litigation on that contract, and if the court is conceiving the matter correctly, the dismissal should be on jurisdictional grounds: Let the parties litigate somewhere else. It is a different matter, however, for a court to "pick and choose" among the various parts of foreign law, applying those portions that appeal to it and disregarding the rest. As Justice Brandeis wrote for the Court in 1930, "A state may, on occasion, decline to enforce a foreign cause of action. In so doing, it merely denies a remedy, leaving unimpaired the plaintiff's substantive right, so that he is free to enforce it elsewhere. But to refuse to give effect to a substantive defense under the applicable law of another state ... subjects the defendant to irremediable liability. This may not be done."[55]

Here's a hypothetical, based on the *Carroll* case, to illustrate the point: Assume that Carroll (the Alabama worker) had actually been killed in the railroad crash in Mississippi, which, as, in the real case, was caused by the negligence of another worker. Let's also assume the railroad was incorporated in Mississippi and was a domiciliary of that state rather than of Alabama, in the actual case. Finally, let's assume that Mississippi has a wrongful death statute, but that Alabama does not. Carroll's widow brings a claim in Alabama court, seeking damages for the wrongful death of her husband. The railroad defends on the ground that the "fellow servant rule" still applies under Mississippi law, and that doctrine applies just as much to wrongful death claims as to ordinary negligence claims. The Alabama court applies the Mississippi wrongful death statute, as the traditional *lex loci* rule would direct it to; but as to the railroad's "fellow servant" defense under Mississippi law, the Alabama regards it as violating Alabama's "strong public policy" (recall that Alabama's employers' liability act had abrogated the fellow servant rule). So what the Alabama court has done in this hypothetical is to apply Mississippi law to vindicate a claim for wrongful death (by one of its domiciliaries) that Alabama law does not itself recognize; but when the defendant raises a defense, also based on Mississippi law, the Alabama court refuses to recognize it and instead, in effect, applies Alabama law abrogating the fellow servant rule defense. Moreover, it's obvious

55. *Bradford Electric Light Co. v. Clapper*, 286 U.S. 145, 160 (1932), discussed at greater length in Chapter 4.

that had the case been brought in the courts of Mississippi, the railroad's fellow servant defense would have been recognized and the plaintiff would have lost.

It would be hard to defend this disposition of the case by the Alabama courts. What the New York Court of Appeals did in *Kilberg*, though, wasn't all that different. The Court of Appeals took the cause of action from Massachusetts, as required by the *lex loci* rule, but it refused to apply the Massachusetts damages limitation, instead applying New York's own damages rule. The impropriety seems less acute in *Kilberg* than in the *Carroll*-based hypothetical, because in *Kilberg* both New York and Massachusetts recognized a cause of action for wrongful death. Still, the basic premises of the territorial approach didn't even permit serious consideration of applying New York law as to the cause of action. As we will see, today a New York court, applying a conflicts methodology focused on identifying governmental interests, might well hold in the *Kilberg* situation simply that New York law ought to apply with respect to all the issues.

Is the "Public Policy Exception" Unconstitutional? Professor (as he then was) Larry Kramer has argued that the "public policy" exception is, at its heart, unconstitutional. Although his argument is too complex to cover in detail here, the essence of it is that, under our federal system, animated by the Privileges and Immunities and Full Faith and Credit Clauses in Article IV, a state should not be able to discriminate against foreign-created rights simply on the ground that it disagrees, even intensely, with the policies that those rights express.[56] There is quite a bit to be said for this argument, but it isn't likely to become the law of the land anytime soon. In the meantime, the "public policy exception" is still part of the law wherever courts continue to apply *lex loci* principles. If the "public policy" doctrine is often a defensible, even salutary assertion of the forum's sovereign prerogative, it can also be a crutch on which courts rely to avoid application of foreign law.[57]

C. Pleading and Proving Foreign Law

Many conflicts casebooks include a brief section on this topic, and invariably they feature it in their chapter on the traditional

56. Larry Kramer, *Same–Sex Marriage, Conflict of Laws, and the Unconstitutional Public Policy Exception*, 106 YALE LAW JOURNAL 1965 (1997). As the title of the article suggests, Kramer's argument was motivated by his view that states ought not be able to refuse to recognize the rights held by same-sex couples married under the laws of states that recognize same-sex marriage.

57. A classic article on vagaries of the "public policy exception" and the dangers of its excessive use is Monrad G. Paulsen & Michael I. Sovern, *"Public Policy" in the Conflict of Laws*, 56 COLUMBIA LAW REVIEW 969 (1956).

territorial approach to choice of law, just as we are doing here. More than anything else, consideration of this issue sheds a little light on some of the conceptual foundations of choice of law, particularly under the territorial approach, so it's worth taking a look at. It isn't something, though, that merits a huge amount of your time.

As is by now obvious, the application by courts of foreign law—that is, the law of another jurisdiction—to a dispute is a frequent and unremarkable thing. Thus far we've assumed that courts can apply foreign law with pretty much the same ease as forum law. Yet the identification, interpretation, and application of foreign law can sometimes be more challenging for a court than is the application of forum law.

The conflicts scholar Brainerd Currie once observed that the application of forum law, which courts presumably know and understand better than they do the law of other jurisdictions, is the "natural and normal" thing for a court to do, and that there should therefore be a presumption that forum law applies in any individual case, to be displaced by foreign law only if there are very good reasons for doing so. To some extent, Currie's observation was reflected in a traditional conflicts rule: A plaintiff basing her claim on foreign law was required to allege the content of that foreign law in her complaint, and (assuming the parties disagreed about the content of that law) she had the burden of proving it as well. This, of course, differs from our understanding of how the governing law functions in a case where there are no "foreign" elements and there is no dispute that forum law applies. In that conventional situation, we require the plaintiff to allege the "facts" that underlie her cause of action, not the law itself; the court is assumed to "know" the law, or at least to be able to identify, interpret, and apply it without its having been specifically discussed in the pleadings. Any dispute between the parties concerning the identification and interpretation of the governing law will ordinarily be determined on a pretrial motion, such as a demurrer (or motion pursuant to Fed. R. Civ. P. 12(b)(6), in the federal courts) or a motion for summary judgment.

By contrast, traditional conflicts theory held that, where the cause of action was alleged to have arisen under foreign law,[58] a plaintiff who failed to allege the content of that foreign law in her complaint had, for that reason alone, failed to state a cause of

---

58. Don't forget that, in most discussions of conflicts law, the term "foreign" simply refers to any state that is not the forum. That frequently means that the law of a state of the U.S. is "foreign law" for purposes of the conflicts analysis. The phrase doesn't necessarily refer to the law of a foreign country, although of course sometimes it can. In this book, it will be clear from the context whether the word "foreign" is being used to refer to a foreign country, or simply to a state that is not the forum.

action. (Conversely, a defendant's affirmative defense based on foreign law would, upon motion, be deemed legally insufficient if the content of the foreign law were not alleged.) This distinctive treatment of legal contentions founded on foreign law reflected the stylized way in which traditional theory conceptualized choice-of-law problems. In his effort to systematize the territorial approach to choice of law, Joseph Beale explained that, where a court applied foreign law, it was actually treating the content of foreign law as a "fact." A court did not "choose" foreign law to apply, as law; it enforced the "vested rights" acquired by parties by virtue of the *facts* that particular things had occurred in particular places where foreign law governed, and the *fact* of such rights having been acquired was established by pleading and proving the content of the foreign law (as well as the facts that the party had acted in the relevant place at the relevant time). Thus, the failure to plead the content of the law of the jurisdiction where the plaintiff had acquired his "vested right" should result in dismissal of the complaint, just as with any other failure to allege an element of the cause of action.

The notion that courts cannot be presumed to know the content of foreign law, and that the parties therefore assume the responsibility for advising the court of it, made sense two hundred years ago, when comprehensive law libraries were rare and a court's access to the statute books and reported decisions of another jurisdiction was spotty at best. It may even make sense in some cases today involving the laws of foreign countries, especially those whose basic legal concepts differ in important ways from our own. But it has long since ceased to make sense in the context of the American union, where the laws of the different states have a great deal in common and where it is not difficult for a court of one U.S. state to ascertain the law of another. Moreover, today we *do* think of courts "choosing" among different sources of governing law when deciding conflicts questions; even contemporary proponents of territorial approaches to choice of law no longer accept the "vested rights" theory. Therefore, in the federal judicial system and in the systems of all fifty states, judges are entitled to take "judicial notice" of the laws of other states. Parties seeking to rely on foreign law—and here we mean the law of another state of the United States—ordinarily are not obliged to allege the content of that law in the pleadings, and in any event the content of that foreign law will rarely if ever be in doubt. Any legal dispute about the applicability and substance of foreign law will normally be raised by motion, frequently of the pre-answer variety.

The law of foreign countries, however, is usually treated differently. For example, Fed. R. Civ. P. 44.1 provides that, in cases brought in federal court,

[a] party who intends to raise an issue about a foreign country's law must give notice by a pleading or other writing. In
determining foreign law, the court may consider any relevant
material or source, including testimony, whether or not submitted by a party or admissible under the Federal Rules of
Evidence. The court's determination must be treated as a
ruling on a question of law.

This provision essentially avoids metaphysical inquiries concerning
whether or not foreign law is a "fact." On the one hand, far from
presuming that the judge is a guru who "knows" the content of a
foreign country's law, the rule empowers her to solicit the assistance of the parties in developing evidence concerning that content.
Parties frequently introduce the testimony of experts to establish
the substance of foreign country law. On the other hand, the rule
specifies that the court's ruling on the matter will be "treated as a
ruling on a question of law." This is merely a practical way of
saying that the matter is one for the judge, not the factfinder; that
it will not be subject to the evidentiary rules that normally apply to
the trial of facts; and that the issue will be subject to *de novo*
review on appeal.

A frequently cited example of the older approach to the problem of pleading foreign law is *Walton v. Arabian American Oil Co.*
(2d Cir. 1956).[59] *Walton* is something of a mess, and a decision that
Brainerd Currie subjected to sharp criticism, but it does serve to
illustrate the old approach to the treatment of foreign law. Walton,
a domiciliary of Arkansas, was injured while in Saudi Arabia when
a truck owned by the Arab–American Oil Co. ("Aramco"), driven by
an Aramco employee, struck his car. Walton sued Aramco in the
Federal District Court for the Southern District of New York.
Under the law of most if not all states in the United States, the
questions of negligence and vicarious liability would have been
fairly simply determined, but the prevailing *lex loci* rule dictated
that the law of Saudi Arabia should apply. It was therefore necessary to know what the substance of Saudi Arabian law on the
matter was. The plaintiff, however, included nothing in the complaint about the relevant Saudi Arabian law, and declined to
respond when the court gave him a further opportunity to provide
it. It's not clear why the plaintiff's counsel did not take up the
court's suggestion. Presumably, Saudi Arabian law was unfavorable
to the plaintiff's position, perhaps on the question of vicarious
liability; perhaps counsel simply hoped things would turn out better
if he professed ignorance of the law's substance, in the manner of a
person who turns his back on a rock thrown at him, on the theory
that the rock will be unable to find him if his back is turned. Or,
perhaps, plaintiff lacked the resources necessary to make a thor-

59.   233 F.2d 541 (2d Cir. 1956).

ough inquiry into the relevant Saudi Arabian legal principles. In any case, the federal district court, holding that the content of the relevant Saudi Arabian law constituted a necessary element of the claim, dismissed the complaint on Fed. R. Civ. P. 12(b)(6) grounds. The Second Circuit affirmed.

Walton looks peculiar, but it is easier to criticize the courts' ruling than to explain what it should have done instead. Even if we discard the formalistic notion that foreign law is a "fact" to be pleaded and proved like other facts, we still need to decide what should happen when the court is unable to inform itself of the content of the foreign law which, according to the applicable choice-of-law reference, should apply. Today, one can imagine a court, not in thrall to the territorial approach, simply "defaulting" to the law of another state—usually, the law of the forum—simply because of the inability to determine the content of Saudi Arabian law. Brainerd Currie, whose theories (as we shall see) embraced a strong bias in favor of the application of forum law, recommended this approach to *Walton*.[60] Such a result, however, was not possible for one truly committed to the *lex loci* system (as Currie assuredly was not), which designated *lex loci delicti* and no other law as the permissible choice-of-law reference; there was no "second best" law to apply. Another possibility might be for the court to dismiss the case on jurisdictional grounds, once it had determined it was unable to determine the law of Saudia Arabia. The fact of the matter is that the traditional territorial theory doesn't have a very good answer to the problem in *Walton*. Today, a similarly situated court would be more likely to devote greater energy to identifying the substance of the relevant foreign law, perhaps by appointing a special master to assist it, or relying on the testimony of experts hired by the parties. Rare today is the case in which the party seeking the benefit of foreign law, perhaps with the assistance of the court, is unable to produce evidence of the content of that law, even though it may be contested or countered by the adversary.

And, in fact, those frustrated by the failure of anyone in *Walton* to favor us with the content of Saudi American law regarding vicarious liability should find their frustration alleviated by the decision of a U.S. District Court in *Chadwick v. Aramco* (D.Del.

---

60. Brainerd Currie, *On the Displacement of the Law of the Forum*, 58 COLUMBIA LAW REVIEW 964, 1002 (1958). Larry Kramer, rejecting this solution to *Walton*, argues that the entire problem has been made unnecessarily complex; one should simply determine, on a 12(b)(6) motion, whether any state has a legitimate interest in the application of its law giving the plaintiff a recovery; if not, the 12(b)(6) motion should be granted. Larry Kramer, *Interest Analysis and the Presumption of Forum Law*, 56 UNIVERSITY OF CHICAGO LAW REVIEW 1301 (1989). In any case, a post-territorial, interest-based conflicts analysis would be likely to determine that the proper choice-of-law reference would be, if anything, to the law of some American state, since both plaintiff and defendant were domiciliaries of a state of the United States.

1987),[61] a perfect companion to *Walton* that illustrates a more rational approach to the problem. In *Chadwick*, a Florida domiciliary employed in Saudi Arabia by Aramco sued the company for damages based on the negligent medical treatment of him in Saudi Arabia by a physician employed by a company that had contracted with Aramco to provide medical services for particular employees. One of the contested issues, as in *Walton*, was whether the physician's negligence should be imputed to Aramco under the principles of vicarious liability. The Federal District Court, applying Delaware's choice-of-law rules, held that Delaware continue to use the *lex loci delicti* rule for conflicts in tort cases; that the question of vicarious liability should thus be governed by the law of Saudi Arabia; that the law of Saudi Arabia did not recognize the principle of vicarious liability; and that therefore the plaintiff's claim must be dismissed on 12(b)(6) grounds. The court applied Fed. R. Civ. P. 44.1, quoted above, concerning the determination of the content of the law of a foreign country, and it relied for its conclusion on an affidavit of an expert (presumably hired by the defendant) on the content of Saudi Arabian law. In what today seems an overly lighthearted reference to the *Shari'a*, upon which substantial parts of Saudi Arabian law rest, the court began its opinion by stating, "This case is governed by what the Angel Gabriel said to the Prophet Mohammad in the Seventh Century A.D."

* * * *

We've focused in this chapter on identifying the characteristic features, and conceptual underpinnings, of the traditional or *"lex loci"* approach to choice of law. While we've indicated that that approach has been subjected to many kinds of criticisms, the fact is that *lex loci* ideas remain important in many parts of American conflicts law. Nevertheless, a relentless academic and juristic critique in the mid-twentieth century of the First Restatement, and of the *lex loci* ideas that underlay it, led to the emergence of other choice-of-law methodologies that differ from the traditional approach in significant ways. To that critique, and to the ensuing sea change in conflicts law, we now turn.

61.   656 F.Supp. 857 (D.Del. 1987).

Chapter 2

MODERN APPROACHES
TO CHOICE OF LAW

A. The Scholarly Critique of the Territorial Approach

Our discussion of the territorial approach to choice of law in Chapter 1 identified some of the difficulties it raises, but since (as we'll see) all approaches to choice of law have problems, this alone isn't enough to discredit the territorial theory altogether. The *lex loci* idea has been around for hundreds of years, and is still the dominant framework for resolving conflicts in legal systems outside the United States. It would be the height of arrogance to suggest that judges, lawyers, jurisprudes, and entire legal systems have been in thrall to an intellectually bankrupt or legally indefensible approach to conflicts. Yet, beginning in the 1920s, the territorial approach was subjected to vehement attack by scholars and some judges, and it has been, to a substantial degree, supplanted by choice-of-law methodologies resting on different premises. Why?

One reason is that some jurists, principally Professor Joseph Beale, had attempted to elevate the territorial approach to an all-embracing, theoretically grounded system that must determine and explain the resolution of all conflicts problems. It is essential to distinguish the general idea of *lex loci* as simply one practical approach to the choice-of-problem, from Beale's elaborate systemization of it, based on the concept of "vested rights." Beale's enterprise was in keeping with a broader-based effort by legal scholars in the late nineteenth and early twentieth centuries to reduce many areas of the law to complete, self-consistent systems. The efforts of Harvard Law School Professor and Dean Christopher Columbus Langdell to establish law as a "science" by crystallizing such fields as contract law into a few principles, from which the results in new cases could be deduced, is the best-known example. Professor Beale's attempt to provide such a foundation for a complete system of conflicts principles may have been the most ambitious and most learned of all these efforts. His labors resulted in numerous scholarly articles, a casebook, a three-volume treatise on

Conflicts, and the First Restatement (1934), for which he was the Principal Reporter and on which he was the dominant influence.

Had Beale not mounted this ambitious effort at producing what amounted to a "unified field theory" of conflict of laws, the general attack on the territorial theory might have been more gradual and certainly less venomous. The emerging school of Legal Realism found Beale and the First Restatement to be an inviting target for its general critique of "legal formalism" and the pretensions of law to be based on a set of principles divorced from social and political considerations. Some critics of Beale ridiculed the concept of "vested rights" as a fiction with little basis in people's actual behavior. Others noted that the particular references specified by the *lex loci* rules were contestable if not arbitrary, and could hardly be regarded as the result of a deductive system based on objective first principles. David Cavers, Beale's younger colleague at Harvard Law School, criticized the notion (implicit in a jurisdiction-selecting theory like Beale's) that the "content" of the governing law should be "irrelevant" to a functioning choice-of-law methodology. All of these criticisms had particular bite in an era in which formal intellectual systems of all kinds were under attack by a new generation of reform-minded scholars.[1]

Although the scholarly criticisms of the territorial approach to choice of law have unquestionably been influential in the development of American conflicts law in the twentieth century and beyond, it was not until *courts* began to demonstrate dissatisfaction with the tyranny of the traditional *lex loci* rules that the shape of conflicts law began to change in earnest. As Beale's critics often pointed out, the all-embracing system comprehended by the First Restatement had never accurately described the pattern of actual conflicts decisions by courts, and probably never would. Courts dissatisfied with particular outcomes determined by application of *lex loci* rules found ways, often using the "escape devices" described in Chapter 1, of evading those outcomes. For a time, these "escapes" departed from the results ordained by the *lex loci* approach without overtly repudiating the territorial system as a whole. Beginning in the 1950s, however, something a bit different began happening: Some courts made choice-of-law rulings that (explicitly or implicitly) questioned the very premises underlying the *lex loci* approach and that suggested different ways of solving conflicts problems. Among the pioneers were Justice (later Chief Justice) Roger Traynor of the California Supreme Court and, especially, Judge (later Chief Judge) Stanley Fuld of the New York Court of Appeals.

1. EDWARD A. PURCELL, JR., THE CRISIS OF DEMOCRATIC THEORY: SCIENTIFIC NATURALISM AND THE PROBLEM OF VALUE (1973).

B. New York and the "Center of Gravity" Approach: *Auten* and *Haag*

Two New York Court of Appeals decisions in 1954 and 1961 pointed the way to a different approach. In *Auten v. Auten* (N.Y. 1954),[2] the plaintiff ex-wife had been married in England and lived there until her husband deserted her, moved to New York, obtained an *ex parte* divorce, and remarried. The abandoned wife made a trip to New York, seeking a settlement, and concluded a separation agreement with her ex-husband. The agreement provided that he would pay her a monthly stipend; it also stipulated that neither party would sue the other in any court over matters relating to the separation, divorce, or the husband's remarriage. When the husband failed to make his monthly stipend as scheduled, the wife sued for divorce in England on the ground of adultery. That proceeding went nowhere, and she subsequently brought suit against him in New York court for recovery of the stipend amounts she was owed. He defended on the ground that her institution of the divorce proceeding in England constituted a repudiation of the separation agreement, so that he was relieved of his obligation under the agreement to pay her the stipend. New York law, at least on one interpretation, would have vindicated the husband's position on this point; the substance of English law on the point was ambiguous but may have vindicated her position.

The conventional *lex loci* approach would likely have held that the law of New York, where the separation agreement was concluded, should govern. This would not have led to a very palatable result, in light of the defendant's alleged adultery, his admitted abandonment of his wife, and his efforts to evade even his modest financial obligation to his abandoned and impecunious spouse. Of course, a timely exercise in characterization (for example by viewing the dispute as being "about" the marriage and thus governed by the law of the marital domicile), or, perhaps, application of the public policy exception, could have led to the opposite conclusion. The Court of Appeals, to its credit, did not bother with these expedients. It simply held that recent New York decisions on related conflicts issues had been moving in the direction of an approach that Judge Fuld labeled as the "center of gravity" or the "grouping of contacts" theory. "Under this theory," according to Judge Fuld, "the courts, instead of regarding as conclusive the parties' intention or the place of making or performance, lay emphasis rather upon the law of the place 'which has the most significant contacts with the matter in dispute.' "[3] The Court of

---

2. 308 N.Y. 155, 124 N.E.2d 99 (1954).

3. 308 N.Y. at 160, 124 N.E.2d at 101–02, *quoting Rubin v. Irving a Trust Co.,* 305 N.Y. 288, 305, 113 N.E.2d 424, 431 (1953).

Appeals then concluded that the contacts with England were clearly more significant than those with New York, and that the court below had erred in granting the defendant summary judgment under New York law.

The court's application of the "most significant contacts" or "center of gravity" idea had (as Judge Fuld noted) been foreshadowed by some earlier New York decisions, and it did not represent a legal or intellectual revolution. Scholars in the conflicts field had long played with the same idea. Nevertheless, the decision in *Auten* is something of a landmark in the development of American choice of law. The emphasis on "contacts" suggested a more fluid, case-specific approach to the choice-of-law problem than that embodied by the *lex loci* system, and it necessarily implied that more than one jurisdiction might have a plausible claim to the application of its law, with the "choice" to be resolved by an assessment of the specific facts (contacts) revealed by the case. The contrast with the First Restatement approach is stark. The First Restatement produces a categorical, bright-line answer to a conflicts problem; the *Auten* approach requires a relative assessment of contacts. This more fluid approach is in keeping with the general tenor of much of modern American law, which tends to favor "balancing" and "reasonableness" tests over bright-line rules. Moreover, it promises to reduce the judicial compulsion to seek refuge in "escape devices," since the "contacts" assessment presumably will enable the court to reach a sensible result with no need for subterfuges. To be sure, the *Auten* approach does not mandate an explicit inquiry into the substance of the competing laws or into the purposes behind them, as some more recent choice-of-law methodologies do. In that respect, it is not a sharp break with the premises underlying the First Restatement. Otherwise, though, it is.

As unobjectionable as the phrase "more significant contacts" may appear—who, really, would dispute the notion that the law of the state with the most significant connections to a dispute should apply?—it is, upon reflection, a rather blunt instrument. *Auten* tells us nothing, at least nothing explicit, about how to rank particular contacts in terms of relevance or substantiality. The result in *Auten* itself seems quite acceptable, but, in reaching it, Judge Fuld itemized contacts with England that ranged from the important to the trivial. It is true, as Judge Fuld pointed out, that the parties had lived in England as husband and wife for fourteen years, which was certainly an important contact. But he also mentioned, among other things, that the separation agreement provided that the ex-husband could visit the children "if he should go to England." This perhaps helped establish the fact, which no one disputed, that the ex-wife continued to live in England, but it hardly constituted an additional English "contact" of any significance. In the end, the significance of a particular contact with a jurisdiction is largely a function of the importance that the jurisdiction itself, as expressed by its substantive law, attaches to it. That was the ultimate point of scholars later associated with the "interest analysis" approach to conflicts; if, say, the ex-wife's domicile in England should be regarded as a particularly important contact with England, it is largely because England has a rule of law that reflects that country's policy with respect to English domiciliaries in a position like that of Mrs. Auten. The court in *Auten* did not engage these issues in its treatment of contacts.

Some of the problems with the "grouping of contacts" approach were revealed more vividly when the New York Court of Appeals decided *Haag v. Barnes* (N.Y. 1961)[4] seven years later. Although *Haag* was not precisely "on all fours" with *Auten*, there were some interesting similarities. The facts in *Haag* seem straight out of an episode of the TV series *Mad Men*, with Don Draper cast as the defendant. Ms. Haag worked as a legal secretary in New York City; Mr. Barnes, a Chicago businessman, hired her through a temp agency to work with him on one of his business trips to New York. The relationship between Mr. Barnes and Ms. Haag "ripened into friendship," and soon thereafter into what a later generation might term a friendship with benefits (accruing more, it seems in retrospect, to Mr. Barnes than to Ms. Haag). When Ms. Haag became pregnant, she traveled to Chicago, where Mr. Barnes refused to see her, but through his attorney he paid for the delivery of her child in a Chicago hospital. After the birth of her child, she went back to New York, returning to Chicago (at the direction of Mr. Barnes's attorney) to execute an agreement with Mr. Barnes according to which he would provide financial support for the child until the child reached sixteen years of age. The agreement also specified that it did not constitute an admission that Mr. Barnes was the father of the child, and it released him from further legal claims with respect to the support of the child. It also provided that any disputes under the contract were to be governed by Illinois law.

Eventually, Ms. Haag returned to New York City. Some time thereafter she brought a paternity proceeding in New York court against Mr. Barnes, seemingly in an effort to obtain a judicial order of support (greater than that which she was receiving) pursuant to New York domestic relations law. He moved to dismiss the case on the ground that the support agreement he had made with her should be enforced and that it barred litigation by Ms. Barnes on the question of support. Putting to one side the agreement's choice-

---

4. 9 N.Y.2d 554, 216 N.Y.S.2d 65, 175 N.E.2d 441 (1961).

of-law provision, the case involved a conflict of laws: Illinois law regarded the agreement as effective to bar any future litigation over support. New York law required such an agreement to be court-approved in order to be given effect to bar future litigation; it would therefore have regarded that contractual provision as unenforceable. The New York Court of Appeals, with the opinion again being written by Judge Fuld, applied Illinois law and ruled in favor of Mr. Barnes.

The Court of Appeals in *Haag*, which chose not to rest its decision on the agreement's choice-of-law provision, proceeded to decide the case under the "grouping-of-contacts" theory that had been deployed in *Auten*. Its conclusion that the Illinois contacts clearly preponderated over those with New York is somewhat surprising. The similarities between *Haag* and *Auten* were not superficial. In both *Haag* and *Auten* the man left a relationship in which he had fathered a child. In both cases, the woman traveled temporarily to the man's domicile to execute an agreement providing for her (or her child's) support. There, perhaps, the similarities end. One can't help thinking that the Court was influenced by its perception—shaped in part by contemporary cultural norms that may be less in evidence today—of the equities in the two cases. Mr. Barnes may or may not have been a cad—one hesitates to judge based on the sparse reported facts—but Mr. Auten seems to have been the genuine article. He had abandoned his wife, removed to a distant realm, obtained an *ex parte* divorce, and failed to make even the meager stipend payments called for by his agreement with Mrs. Auten. By contrast, Mr. Barnes, according to the court, had over a period of years paid Ms. Haag $30,000, a "sum[] far in excess of his agreement." (Of course, it is possible that a New York domestic relations court, applying New York law, would have found that amount to be inadequate and ordered greater support.) Something about the court's opinion in *Haag* suggests a certain sympathy for Mr. Barnes and a slight coolness toward the position of Ms. Haag (who, after all, had alleged that Mr. Barnes had seduced her with promises to divorce his wife and to marry Ms. Haag). Perhaps the Don Drapers of the world had a cultural stature in 1961 that is difficult to appreciate in 2010.

The real point, though, is the way in which the Court in *Haag* used the "contacts" idea to reach the conclusion that Illinois law should apply. Judge Fuld considered that "the New York contacts are of far less weight and significance" than those with Illinois. Sober analysis does not support him in this conclusion. His enumeration of the contacts with Illinois suggested the ease with which one contact can morph, like cells, into several. For example, he placed emphasis, not only on the fact that the support agreement had been executed by the parties in Chicago, but also on the fact that the attorneys for both sides were from Chicago, as though there were some independent significance to be ascribed to Ms. Haag's having hired local counsel to assist her once she came to Chicago to negotiate the agreement. After noting that Mr. Barnes resided and had his place of business in Illinois, Judge Fuld thought the fact that Mr. Barnes's payments under the agreement were and would be "made from Chicago" somehow added weight to the connections with Illinois. (He did not add that the payments were "received in New York.") Perhaps most questionable, he emphasized the fact that the child had been born in Chicago—without mentioning that it was Mr. Barnes's attorney who had instructed Ms. Haag to have her child in a Chicago hospital.[5] (Astonishingly, Ms. Haag did not take choice-of-law considerations into account when deciding to abide by this instruction.) By contrast, Judge Fuld found the fact that Ms. Haag and her child resided in New York to be relevant but insufficient to match the Illinois contacts he had enumerated. It goes without saying that the *locus assignatione* did not help Ms. Haag's contacts score, either.

The analysis by the New York Court of Appeals in *Haag v. Barnes* was not an especially good advertisement for the new "grouping of contacts" method. The case suggested that simply "counting contacts," without any metric for assessing the relative significance of particular contacts, was too crude an approach. It also suggested that the assessment of contacts is just as vulnerable to judicial manipulation as had been the "escape devices" of yore. Even as *Auten* and *Haag* were being decided, however, scholars were at work on a more discriminating treatment of "contacts" as a constituent of choice-of-law analysis that attempted to link the relevant contacts with the policies of the states where those contacts existed. Nevertheless, the "grouping of contacts" approach featured in *Auten* and *Haag*, despite its flaws, was both an important break from traditional conflicts law and a way-station to the methodologies that have made substantial inroads on conflicts law today.

C. Interest Analysis: The Currie Approach

"Interest analysis," as an alternative to the traditional territorial approach to choice of law, is indelibly associated with the name

---

5. Whether Mr. Barnes's attorney had the conflict-of-laws problem in mind when issuing this instruction to Ms. Haag is a matter of speculation, and perhaps a bit far-fetched. It would not have been unthinkable, however, for an alert attorney to advise a client to create as many contacts as possible with the jurisdiction having the more favorable law, in the wake of the *Auten* decision and its emphasis on contacts. Surely, in any case, Mr. Barnes's attorney would have known about New York law on child support when advising Mr. Barnes on how to deal with Ms. Haag. Perhaps Mr. Barnes's unwillingness to treat with Ms. Haag anywhere but in Chicago reflected a larger legal strategy on the part of his counsel.

of Brainerd Currie, the legal scholar who argued earliest and most forcefully for a choice-of-law methodology based on a systematic assessment of the interests of the concerned states that might be implicated in a particular dispute. Currie's scholarship (published in the 1950s and 1960s), while brilliant and creative in its own right, built on criticisms that other scholars, principally of the Legal Realist mentality, had been leveling at the traditional approach for more than a generation. It is rare in the United States for a single legal scholar to have influenced, not only academic discourse, but even the reasoning of courts, to the degree that Currie's work has.

It is possible that today's casebooks and treatises on conflicts of laws in the United States slightly overemphasize Currie's ideas. Although debates over those ideas have permeated conflicts scholarship from the 1950s to the present day, "interest analysis" as Currie conceived it has been adopted only by a very small number of state courts. The conflicts opinions of high courts in such states as New York and California (which, concededly, were themselves influenced by Currie's writings) have loomed as large in the development of "modern" conflicts principles as anything written by Currie himself. Moreover, the Second Restatement, discussed below, is the preferred choice-of-law methodology in many more states than is interest analysis as such. Nevertheless, since an understanding of interest analysis can illuminate all the "modern" theories of choice of law, including the Second Restatement, it is important to explore the basic ideas that underlay Currie's approach.

1. Choice of Law as an Exercise in Interpretation and Construction

Currie wrote at a time when, unlike in the nineteenth century, rules of decision that had been created by *statute* had become ubiquitous. Moreover, as signaled by the decision of the U.S. Supreme Court in *Erie R.R. v. Tompkins* (1938),[6] no longer were rules of decision created under the common law meaningfully different from rules of decision created by statute. Unlike Beale and other scholars proceeding from nineteenth-century assumptions about the nature of law, Currie did not think that giving a state statute "extraterritorial" effect—that is, applying it to conduct occurring outside the state—violated a basic limitation on the political authority of states, nor did he think that such statutes should be presumed to apply only within the territorial boundaries

---

6. 304 U.S. 64 (1938).

of the state. He simply observed that most statutes—for example, the Alabama Employers' Liability Act at issue in *Carroll*—said nothing about their territorial scope. Moreover, common-law rules of decision had the same feature: The rights and duties they specified were not, generally speaking, defined in terms of the territorial limits of the state. For example, the common-law "fellow servant rule" that prevailed in Mississippi at the time of the *Carroll* case did not say, "Employers shall be held harmless for the negligence of their employees that injure other employees if and only if the injury is incurred in Mississippi." Of course, the traditional *lex loci* approach to conflicts effectively treated the Mississippi and Alabama rules as having precisely that territorial scope; but it was that traditional choice-of-law approach that Currie (and his critical predecessors) rejected.

To Currie, then, the kind of conflict represented by the *Carroll* case was precisely that—a *conflict* between two rules of decision, neither of them limited by its terms to events occurring within the state, and both presumptively applicable to the case at hand. The existence of a *conflict* of laws, and the consequent need to make a *choice* of law, could not be wished away by categorical *lex loci* rules that suggested that in any case only one of the competing laws could legitimately be said to apply. They *both* "applied." The question was what tools of legal analysis could and should be deployed to determine which law should prevail in the individual case.

Currie's answer was to use tools of statutory construction and interpretation that were familiar from their use in purely domestic cases. Just as questions concerning the proper scope and meaning of a statute in a wholly domestic context often required courts to use such devices as "legislative history" or "policy analysis" to resolve ambiguities,[7] something similar could be done to resolve interstate conflicts of laws. In a sense, one could ask with respect to each of the laws in a conflicts situation, "Does the history and evident 'policy' lying behind this law suggest that it should apply to this particular case that involves multistate elements?" For Currie, this amounted to making some commonsense inferences about when, in a particular case having multistate elements, a state's legitimate "interests" were actually implicated. If, in an individual case, the answer were "no" with respect to one of the laws (but not the other), it made sense as a matter of statutory interpretation to

---

7. Moreover, courts sometimes have to resolve what might be called a "domestic conflict"—where two rules of law operative in a single jurisdiction seem to lead to different results, requiring a determination of which rule should govern. *See Chesny v. Marek*, 720 F.2d 474 (7th Cir. 1983), *rev'd*, 473 U.S. 1 (1985) (resolving "conflict" between Fed. R. Civ. P. 68 and 42 U.S.C. § 1988). The point is that these problems are solved using conventional principles of statutory interpretation.

apply the other. These situations Currie called "false conflicts." For example, Currie would probably have concluded that the interests of the state of Mississippi were not meaningfully implicated in the *Carroll* case, because the plaintiff and defendant were both Alabama domiciliaries and the negligence apparently occurred in Alabama (although the injury was suffered in Mississippi). Alabama law should therefore apply, in contrast to the actual decision in *Carroll*.

The Emphasis on Domiciliary Interests. Currie's ideas bore the mark of their time, and some of his basic views about the nature of law and lawmaking would not have been widely shared by nineteenth-century jurists (and certainly not by Joseph Beale). First, Currie took it virtually as a given that, in enacting a statute, state legislators were principally concerned with the effect of the state law on domiciliaries, and only secondarily with the benefits or burdens it might place on nondomiciliaries. Similarly, although statutes regulating people's behavior were not intrinsically barred from extraterritorial effect, they might be presumed to be concerned principally with behavior taking place within the state. Such presumptions concerning legislative "purposes" or "interests" helped in determining the proper scope of state laws in cases involving multistate connections. These ideas reflected a conception of state lawmaking as protective and regulatory—as establishing *policies* for the governance of human behavior—and not simply a way of enforcing private rights. It's very much a twentieth- (and twenty-first-) century view of governance. By contrast, Beale's conception of choice of law as a way of enforcing "vested rights," to be vindicated in any court in the world, reflected a very different view of law than the notion that legislators are presumed to concern themselves with their own domiciliaries above all.

The Presumption That Forum Law Should Apply. Second, Currie obviously accepted the basic idea that courts must sometimes apply foreign law, but he believed that even in conflicts cases the displacement of forum law by foreign law should be the exception, justified only by very good reasons. As observed by one of the most distinguished expositors and refiners of interest analysis, "The question we are trying to answer in choice of law cases is not 'whose law is to be applied?' . . . Instead, our question could better be phrased as 'under what circumstances is a departure from local law justified?' "[8] Currie believed that application of forum law was in most situations the "normal and natural" thing for courts to do,

---

8. Herma Hill Kay, *The Use of Comparative Impairment to Resolve True Conflicts: An Evaluation of the California Experience*, 68 CALIFORNIA LAW REVIEW 577, 617 (1980) Professor Kay here uses the term "local law" instead of "forum law," in order to avoid some of the ideological baggage that had attached to the latter term during the many years of academic debate over Currie's interest analysis approach.

and that application of foreign law should be reserved for the relatively uncommon and anomalous case. In part he justified this view by observing that the judiciary forms part of the governing structure of the state, and that one of the considerations that should govern the behavior of state courts is their responsibility to carry into effect clear state policy, unless application of foreign law is clearly called for. In effect, he believed that there should be a presumption that forum law applies, and that presumption could be overcome in conflicts cases only by a demonstration that the interests of the forum were not implicated and that the interests of another state were. These ideas are dramatically different from those of Joseph Beale, whose "vested rights" theory presumed that courts are not principally concerned with vindicating state policy or the interests of domiciliaries, but with the enforcement of vested rights, wherever and by whomever obtained. The difference between Beale and Currie is nothing less than the difference between an older common-law view of law as enforcing the rights and duties of private parties, and a later view of law as expressing the legitimate policy of the state.

"Purposive" Legal Analysis Versus Formal, Categorical Rules. One of Currie's most telling, and most passionately articulated points, concerned what he called the "imperative" quality of the First Restatement approach—that is, its categorical identification of the "correct" choice-of-law reference without a case-specific consideration of the facts and the policies expressed by the laws competing for recognition. By the time Currie was writing in the 1950s and 1960s, it had become an accepted feature of American law that courts should attempt to interpret and apply constitutions and statutes in the way best calculated to give effect to their purposes. Often this involves a contextual reading of the statute, an examination of the evident intent of the legislature, an understanding of the legal status quo that the statute has displaced, and so on. By the 1950s, even the strictest textualist would not have argued that statutes should be interpreted with complete "blindness" to these contextualizing factors; that had been one of the lessons of the movements for "sociological jurisprudence" and "legal realism" earlier in the century. Yet, complained Currie, the jurisdiction-selecting rules of the First Restatement applied the "blindness" technique to precisely the situation where prudence and attention to context were most insistently required: in the sensitive task of adjusting the interests of states that had responded to a particular social problem with different legal rules. Because he regarded the choice-of-law problem generally as a clash between competing social policies, he found unacceptable the theoretically "blind" stance of "mandatory" jurisdiction-selecting rules such as those found in the First Restatement.

2. Identification of False and True Conflicts: The Heart of Interest Analysis

False Conflicts. Currie went beyond most prior critics of the First Restatement and the territorial approach by explaining how his interest-oriented approach would operate in practice. Most scholars today, whether they like or dislike Currie's approach, agree that his most fruitful insight lies in the identification of what he called "false conflicts."[9] By deploying the analysis of state "interests" as described above, Currie believed that, in many situations seemingly raising a conflict of laws, one could demonstrate that only one of the states would see its legitimate interests advanced by application of its law. If application of the other state's law would do nothing to advance that state's "interests," Currie reasoned, then there was in no meaningful sense a "conflict" between the two laws; application of the law of the one state whose interests could be advanced should be the obvious solution. The situation presented a "false conflict."

The approach Currie would have taken to the *Carroll* case, as discussed above, illustrates his conception of a false conflict. Currie would have seen both the Mississippi and Alabama laws as *prima facie* "applying" to the situation, because neither law was, by its terms, restricted to a particular territory or to domiciliaries of a particular state. But further analysis of the ultimate goals behind the respective laws indicates that Mississippi's interests would not be advanced in any meaningful way by application of its law; presumably its "fellow servant rule" was designed principally to protect *Mississippi* corporations from liability (or, perhaps, to encourage Mississippi employees to take affirmative steps for their own safety and protection). By contrast, application of Alabama law in the case could be seen as advancing at least two, perhaps three, distinct interests of Alabama: (1) to provide compensation for an Alabama worker and domiciliary; (2) to impose a standard of due care on Alabama corporations and their employees; and (3) to regulate the behavior of companies operating on Alabama soil, by encouraging them to monitor the potentially injurious behavior of their employees. With the respective state interests articulated in this way, the problem could be seen as a "false conflict," with Alabama being the only one of the two states whose interests would be advanced by application of its law.

---

9. It is important to be clear about what Currie meant by the phrase "false conflict." It does *not* mean that application of either of the two laws competing for recognition in a particular case would lead to the same result. Rather, as is spelled out in the text, Currie used the term "false conflict" to describe a situation in which the two laws do, at a formal level, "conflict" with one another, but in which the analysis of state interests reveals that only one of the states has a cognizable interest that would be advanced by application of its law.

True Conflicts and *Lex Fori*. If there is such a thing as a "false conflict," there must be such a thing as a "true conflict." For Currie, a "true conflict" was one in which the interests of each state would be advanced by application of its law. This situation can be illustrated by a small variation on the facts in *Carroll*. Suppose the railroad in *Carroll* had been a Mississippi corporation rather than an Alabama corporation. In that case, Currie would probably have credited Mississippi with an "interest" that would have been advanced by application of Mississippi's fellow-servant rule: Mississippi's desire to shield Mississippi corporations from excessive liability caused by its employees' negligence. When one counterposes that interest with the state interest underlying Alabama's liability rule, in providing compensation for its domiciliaries, we have what Currie called a "true conflict": cognizable[10] interests on both sides.

Currie's method of resolving such "true conflicts" was simply to apply forum law. This, of course, was one of the more controversial of Currie's proposals. He acknowledged that, analytically, this resolution of true conflicts was not especially satisfying, but it followed from his view that the forum's own law, as the law best known and most "native" to courts, should be the presumptive choice-of-law reference, to be displaced only when there existed very good reason for doing so; state courts had no business advancing another state's interests at the expense of the forum's. It also reflected Currie's belief that the forum should not attempt to "weigh" the interests of the competing states in an attempt to determine which should prevail over the other; he insisted that this was an improper task for courts. Once it was determined that each state had at least some cognizable interest, a true conflict existed, and forum law should be applied. Of course, Currie's *lex fori* solution to true conflicts was anathema to those who regarded the role of courts as being a neutral umpire in resolving conflicts, not as having a particular obligation to vindicate forum law and policy. Moreover, it appeared to be a direct invitation to forum shopping, at least where courts in all the interested states used the "interest analysis" methodology for conflicts: In any "true conflict," a plaintiff could obtain the benefit of whichever state's rule was more advantageous to her by suing in the courts of that state.

The "Unprovided–For" Case. Finally, the concepts of "false" and "true" conflicts, defined in terms of whether the relevant states would have their legitimate interests advanced by application of their law, implies that in some cases *neither* state would have its interests so advanced. Currie referred to this scenar-

---

10. In this book, I use the term "cognizable" simply to refer to state interests that most interest analysts would agree should "count" as legitimate interests.

io as the "unprovided-for case," a phrase as awkward as the concept it represents. The "unprovided-for case" can be illustrated by yet another variation on the facts in *Carroll*. Suppose that the plaintiff in *Carroll*, the injured employee, had been a Mississippi domiciliary, that the railroad was an Alabama corporation, and the negligence actually occurred in Mississippi. (Diagram the contacts and the relevant state interests; it helps.) While the proper allocation of "interests" in such a case is always subject to debate, one could argue that *neither* Alabama nor Mississippi had a cognizable interest in having its law applied in this circumstance. Alabama's liability-imposing rule, on this reasoning, is meant to protect Alabama plaintiffs, and secondarily to regulate behavior that occurs on Alabama territory. Mississippi's fellow-servant rule, on the other hand, is meant to protect the interests of Mississippi corporations. None of these interests would be served by application of the respective state's law, since there is no Alabama plaintiff, no Mississippi corporation, and no negligence or injury in Alabama. There are no interests to advance, and it is thus an "unprovided-for case." How should we deal with this situation? Currie, not surprisingly, specified that in such an instance forum law should be applied.

The concept of the "unprovided-for case" is obviously problematic. It underscores a confusion or ambiguity that can easily arise when considering the interest analysis idea. Currie, of course, began with the observation that, in an apparent conflicts situation, the law of both states "applied" *prima facie* (in general, the laws did not specify any geographical limitation); interest analysis was a way of applying principles of interpretation and construction to resolve what is, in conventional parlance, a conflict of laws. But, having identified a false conflict, it is an easy (though questionable) step to the conclusion that the law of the state lacking a cognizable interest actually *doesn't* "apply" in the particular case. This seems confusing. A conflict of laws that interest analysis deems to be a "false conflict" is still a conflict of laws, isn't it?

The usual theoretical explanation for this difficulty rests on the notion that a law's application to a purely domestic situation, and its application to a dispute featuring multistate elements, are two distinct legal questions. Obviously the law of a state should be interpreted as applying to a dispute whose elements are all domestic to that state; that seems to be less an exercise in interpretation than a belaboring of the obvious. But the foundation of the "interest analysis" idea is that one can't give an authoritative account in the abstract of whether and how that law should apply in multistate situations; the law's meaning, the nature of its application, in a particular multistate situation can only be determined by an analysis of the nature of the dispute's connections with the forum and with another state, the law of the other state, and the policies or "interests" of the respective states that are implicated *in that case* by the particular connections with them. Only when rendering that analysis in the individual case can we give a proper account of what the state's law actually *means* in the context of a case raising those particular facts. Thus, application of the state's law in a wholly domestic case and its application in a case with multistate elements are distinct exercises in interpretation of the state's law.

This distinction between the law's meaning in a wholly domestic situation and its meaning in a multistate situation thus makes it is possible to say that the law "applies" *prima facie* in the multistate situation, but can ultimately be determined to have no sensible application in the particular multistate case because none of the state's legitimate interests would be served. By extension, it makes sense to say that this can be true of *both* states in a particular case, leading to the "unprovided-for case." But, however impressive in its abstract reasoning, this construct seems somehow unreal. It implies that, in the situation represented by the "unprovided-for" case, there is *no* law that really governs of its own force, and that the respective legislatures in the two states would regard this as a satisfactory outcome. Few scholars (and fewer courts) have found this explanation to be palatable. Some have concluded from the awkwardness of Currie's treatment of the "unprovided-for case" that interest analysis as a whole rests on a shaky conceptual foundation.

No Judicial Balancing of Interests to Resolve "True Conflict" Cases. It is interesting to observe that, for Currie, the existence (or not) of a cognizable state interest was tantamount to an "on-off" switch; either a state has such an interest in the application of its law in a particular situation, or it does not. If both of the states whose laws compete for application in a particular case have such an interest, then a true conflict exists, and the solution is to apply forum law. Currie rejected the notion that a court might assess the relative strength of a state's interests, or the *degree* to which those interests were implicated in an individual case, in order to determine which of two concededly interested states had, on the whole, the better claim to application of its state's law. Courts, he wrote, ought not to be entrusted with weighing or balancing state interests as they might be implicated in a particular dispute; that was more of legislative task than a judicial one. This is a particularly notable feature of Currie's approach, since one of the principal criticisms that has been made of interest analysis is that the task of identifying state "interests" is itself highly subjective, enmeshing courts in calculations concerning legislative purposes and what "counts" as such a purpose. In one sense, then, Currie's approach contemplates a large role for courts in identifying congnizable state interests, while it frowns on the notion that courts should engage in the intrinsically "legislative" enterprise of balancing those interests.

3. Criticisms of the Currie Approach

Currie's "interest analysis" is unquestionably a scholarly *tour de force*, drawing effectively on history, political science, and the insights of Legal Realism. His critique of the concepts underlying the First Restatement approach was razor-sharp, and (unlike some others) he met the challenge of offering a full-blown system of choice of law to replace it. Moreover, most scholars, even those who reject interest analysis, agree that it avoids some of the weaknesses of the traditional approach. Under interest analysis, there is no need for characterization of a dispute, and thus for the kinds of evasions in which courts sometimes engage when performing that task; interest analysis simply requires an assessment of the purposes underlying state law, and of the degree to which they are implicated in a particular case, regardless of how we "characterize" the issue. There is, similarly, no need for a "public policy exception"; by definition, interest analysis incorporates considerations of the respective states' policies. And, of course, interest analysis requires no arbitrary specification of particular events (such as "place of the accident") as being of crucial importance. Interest analysis takes place aboveboard; when it is employed, the policy-based reasons for choice-of-law decisions are not submerged beneath seemingly neutral jurisdiction-selecting rules and escape devices. Currie was a brilliant writer, and it is no diminution of his achievement to say that he was an extremely effective polemicist. Although it is important not to diminish the importance of the choice-of-law ideas of judges and other scholars of his generation, his influence is easy to see even in modern conflicts methodologies that differ from his own. Still, his version of interest analysis has been vulnerable to criticism, and some of those criticisms have been telling.

Predictability and Ad Hoc Approaches to Choice of Law. At the most general level, there remain many who believe that the jurisdiction-selecting approach represented by the First Restatement is preferable to the kind of *ad hoc*, case-by-case analysis that is required by the "interest" approach. When every conflicts problem calls for an investigation into whether the relevant states' cognizable interests are implicated under *this* particular set of circumstances, there is little room for *ex ante* predictability and certainty, or meaningful generalizations to govern those conflicts. Even if one concedes that the degree to which the jurisdiction-selecting, territorial approach of the First Restatement promotes predictability and certainty is overstated, certain jurists believe there is something about reducing every conflicts problem to an on-the-fly judicial calculation of the interests at stake that is anti-thetical to the nature of "law." This objection is closely connected to the general suspicion that courts, once licensed to perform this kind of analysis, will become "judicial policymakers," ascribing interests to states in order to reach the results that they want. Even if judges applying jurisdiction-selecting rules often do the same thing, for example by resorting to the "escape devices," there may be something to be said for a system of choice-of-law rules that at least has the *appearance* of coherence and universality.

Lex Fori and the Problem of Forum Shopping. As noted in Chapter 1, the prospect of forum shopping can arise any time a case can be brought in more than one state and those states use different choice-of-law methodologies. Moreover, conflicts scholars today are somewhat less mortified by the specter of forum shopping than were Beale and other architects of the First Restatement approach, who thought that widespread forum shopping would derogate from the systemic integrity of the *lex loci* method. Never-theless, *lex fori*, which is the solution that Currie devised for both true conflicts and unprovided-for cases, seems a particularly direct invitation to forum shopping: Where each (or neither) of the relevant states has a cognizable interest, most parties will wish to litigate in the state whose law is favorable to them. For this and other reasons, the *lex fori* approach to true conflicts strikes some jurists as heavy-handed and unsatisfying. Of course, one can adopt a form of interest analysis without necessarily adopting the *lex fori* rule for true conflicts; to attack the *lex fori* rule for true conflicts is not necessarily to attach interest analysis as such. Below we discuss some other ways of resolving true conflicts.

The Problem of Identifying State Interests. This is where the most serious objections to interest analysis lie. Analytically, Currie's "interest analysis" rests on premises concerning the na-ture of lawmaking, and the nature of statutory interpretation, that are at least arguable. The ascription of "interests" to states is closely related to the idea of legislative "purpose" or "intent," and the identification of legislative purposes is a notoriously slippery task. When dozens or hundreds of legislators vote on a measure, the concept of a unitary legislative "purpose" may be something of a chimera. Moreover, it may be sensible in many cases to speak of legislative purpose concerning a statute as it applies purely domes-tically, but that may say little about what the legislative purpose or intent is with respect to multistate situations in which there is a conflict with another state's law. As Currie himself recognized, legislatures don't typically concern themselves with these questions of extraterritorial application when enacting a law; they are focused on what the policy should be for their own state.

It is the specific interests, however, that Currie tended to ascribe to all legislatures that have generated the most criticism. One particularly controversial feature of interest analysis and its ascription of interests to states is its emphasis on *domiciliary* interests. For example, Currie thought it sensible, even obvious, to presume that when a state legislature enacts a "protective" statute, such as the Alabama Employers' Liability Act at issue in *Carroll*, it is concerned with protecting its own domiciliaries; it has no generally cognizable interest in protecting the domiciliaries of other states. Currie not only believed that legislatures do, as a matter of fact, concern themselves first and foremost with forum domiciliaries and forum activities; at times he appeared to suggest that this is the way in which a healthy politics *should* work. So he attributed these interests to legislatures in a somewhat conclusory fashion, without doing much empirical work to determine what kinds of purposes may actually underlie particular statutes. Thus Currie would not have credited the possibility that the Alabama legislature wanted to protect domiciliaries (industrial workers) of states other than Alabama when it enacted its Employers' Liability Act, or at least that such interests might carry some weight in a choice-of-law analysis. These assumptions, of course, nettled adherents of the traditional approach to choice of law, who believed that courts dealing with conflicts of law were obliged to enforce the "vested rights" of parties, wherever and by whomever acquired, and not indulge in the provincial and self-seeking assumption that states were more "interested" in the welfare of their domiciliaries than in that of other people. In fact, some argued that such a systematic preference for domiciliary interests in the identification and crediting of state interests violated the Privileges and Immunities Clause of the U.S. Constitution.[11]

Even those critics not wedded to the traditional approach, however, found Currie's allocations of interests to be at times somewhat artificial and factitious. It was not simply that Currie emphasized domiciliary interests; in some cases his characterization (remember that word) of the very nature of the state's policy was arbitrary. For example, Currie used the famous case of *Milliken v. Pratt* (Mass. 1878) (discussed in Chapter 1) as a canvass upon which to portray his ideas about state interests; he discussed a number of hypothetical variations on the facts of *Milliken*, suggesting for instance that were Mrs. Pratt to have been a domiciliary of Maine, there was little reason to apply Massachusetts law voiding

---

11. This contention is taken up in greater detail in Chapter 4. Currie anticipated this objection, co-authoring an article with Herma Hill Kay (then writing as Herma Hill Schreter), a distinguished conflicts scholar in her own right, ad- dressing the Privileges and Immunities argument. Brainerd Currie & Herma Hill Schreter, *Unconstitutional Discrimination in the Conflict of Laws: Privilege and Immunities*, 69 YALE LAW JOURNAL 1323 (1960).

the contract (as predicted by the *lex loci contracti* rule) simply because the contract had been made in Massachusetts. The purpose of Massachusetts's law disabling married women from making enforceable contracts, according to Currie, was to protect the married women of Massachusetts, and in this variation Mrs. Pratt was not a Massachusetts domiciliary. But, as Professor Lea Brilmayer pointed out in an important critique of interest analysis, the Massachusetts rule could just as easily be regarded as regulatory in nature, not simply protective: It created a disincentive for merchants to form contracts with married women, putatively on the ground that Massachusetts merchants, at least, shouldn't "overreach" in that manner. One could thus identify in the law an interest in regulating the behavior of Massachusetts merchants, which would be vindicated by voiding their contracts with married women regardless of what state the woman hailed from. "Treating married women's contract statutes as protective rather than regulatory seems arbitrary—they are both," according to Professor Brilmayer.[12] The same problem emerges in many other cases purporting to apply interest analysis, where the nature of the state interests involved can plausibly be stated in more than one way.

Comparing Statutory and Common–Law Rules of Decision. Another problem raised by interest analysis concerns the analysis of rules of decision created by the common law rather than by statute. It is at least intelligible to speak of state "interests," in the sense of a state policy, being reflected in a statute. Statutes do, after all, express a policy of some sort. It is less persuasive, however, to characterize common-law principles in this way, and frequently it is a common-law rule of decision, rather than a statute, that stands on one or both sides of a conflict of laws. (In *Carroll*, for example, the Mississippi "fellow servant rule" was a common-law principle.) It is true that by the time Currie began writing in the 1950s, it had become conventional to regard rules of decision created by the common law as standing on the same plane as statutes; both are considered to be expressions of the positive law of the state. Moreover, some scholars today regard many common-law rules of the eighteenth and nineteenth centuries as reflecting sophisticated judicial understandings concerning efficiency and economic growth—an exercise in statecraft and lawmaking. Nevertheless, it is awkward to think of ancient common-law principles as embodying state "policy" in the same way that statutes do, much less as being focused on state domiciliaries. After all, many of

12. Lea Brilmayer, *Interest Analysis and the Myth of Legislative Intent*, 78 Michigan Law Review 392, 405 (1980). In reality, the Massachusetts rule disabling married women from making contracts was a product of the common law, not legislation, so Brilmayer's phrase "married women's contract statutes" is ahistorical. However, Currie's commentary on *Milliken v. Pratt* had itself cast the problem in terms of legislative purpose, so Brilmayer's characterization is apt.

our most venerable common-rule rules emerged from traditional status relationships and customary practices, not from distinct "policies" associated with individual states.

The potential awkwardness of applying "interest analysis" without distinguishing between statutory and common-law rules of decision emerges more clearly when there is a conflict pitting one against the other—particularly where the statutory rule of one state is simply the abrogation of the same traditional common-law rule that remains the law in the other state. Consider one of our variations on the *Carroll* scenario: The injured worker is a Mississippi domiciliary, the railroad is an Alabama corporation, the negligent act takes place in Mississippi, and the case is brought in Alabama court. As we saw earlier, Currie would probably have regarded this as an "unprovided-for case": With no Alabama beneficiary to protect, and no behavior within Alabama to regulate, the interests underlying the Alabama statute would not be advanced by applying it; with no Mississippi defendant to shield from liability, the interests underlying the Mississippi common-law fellow-servant rule cannot be advanced by application of that rule. It appears to be an "unprovided-for case," and Currie's theory mandates application of forum law—here, Alabama's employers liability act, abrogating the fellow-servant rule and imposing liability on the defendant—in such an instance.

But how much sense does this really make? On Currie's own assumptions concerning state interests, Alabama's statute has no real claim to application here, since there is no Alabama plaintiff and no relevant behavior within Alabama. Isn't there a possible alternative to the *non sequitur*, called for by Currie's "unprovided-for case" analysis, that neither state "cares" and that the Alabama statute must therefore be applied? One alternative would be to observe that the Alabama statute was enacted against the background of an existing common-law rule—to wit, that an injured employee may not recover from the employer for the negligence of a fellow employee. Why not assume that, since analysis of the relevant interests reveals that Alabama's interests *in application of its statute* are not implicated here, we should default to what would otherwise be the common-law rule—the fellow-servant rule? However one illustrates or resolves it, the interests underlying a common-law rule and the interests underlying a statute that abrogates it may in some sense be incommensurable—that is, difficult to compare on the same plane.

These are but a few of the analytic problems unleashed by interest analysis. Of course, there has never been a choice-of-law methodology that was not vulnerable to intellectual critique on a number of grounds. Determining the merits of interest analysis vis-à-vis other approaches is best done by examining its operation in actual cases.

D. Identifying False Conflicts in New York: Guest Statutes and Beyond

A number of scholars have concluded that the traditional First Restatement approach is weakest, and the interest analysis approach correspondingly superior, for one particular kind of case: the situation illustrated by *Carroll*, in which both plaintiff and defendant are domiciliaries of State A, but in which the location of the event deemed crucial by the relevant *lex loci* rule is State B. The result in *Carroll* seems troubling to us because Alabama's employer liability act is denied effect despite the fact that both plaintiff and defendant were Alabama domiciliaries, and even the negligent behavior occurred at least in part in Alabama. The choice-of-law result ordained by Currie's method seems far more defensible in such a case. Interest analysis will reveal many common-domicile cases to be instances of "false conflicts," and the identification of false conflicts is the most persuasive contribution of interest analysis. The question, though, is whether the advantages of interest analysis extend beyond such "common-domicile" cases. It has been argued that one might simply refine the traditional, jurisdiction-selecting approach to provide a *lex loci* rule, incorporating considerations of party domicile, for certain common-domicile cases.

Some of the vagaries of interest analysis, in particular the nature of certain common-domicile cases, are revealed in the choice-of-law jurisprudence over the past 50 years of the New York Court of Appeals, which along with the California Supreme Court was the first court to prove hospitable to the basic premises of interest analysis. (The Court of Appeals, of course, had already indicated its willingness to depart from the traditional approach in the *Auten* and *Haag* cases, discussed above, although prior to 1963 it had not done so in tort cases.) The line of New York cases in the 1960s and 1970s involving the application of foreign "guest statutes" has become something of a set piece in the study of conflicts, although now a rather academic one, since guest statutes in the United States, like the precious gem Turquoise, are now found only in three states. Nevertheless, the principles announced in those "guest statute" cases continue to guide the New York courts in the resolution of conflicts, so it is worth briefly synopsizing them.

1. Guest Statutes in the New York Courts: Babcock, Dym, *and* Tooker

A "guest statute" is a law that bars or limits recovery by a passenger in an automobile against the driver of the automobile for injuries caused by the driver's negligence. Although, as we shall see, the "purpose" of such laws can always be debated, many claim that the basic idea underlying them is the fear that in many cases, the driver and passenger may (because of their pre-existing relationship) collude in litigation, with the driver putting up only a tepid defense, so that recovery can be had from the insurer.[13] This, so the argument goes, can redound to the detriment not only of the insurer, but also of policyholders who may have to absorb the cost of such liability judgments through higher premiums. In the 1960s and 1970s, Ontario, part of which abuts western New York, had such a guest statute in place, while New York did not.

In *Babcock v. Jackson* (N.Y. 1963),[14] the plaintiff passenger was injured when the defendant driver crashed the car while on a weekend visit to Ontario. The plaintiff and defendant were neighbors and New York domiciliaries. The defendant's car was garaged, registered, and insured in New York. The traditional *lex loci delicti* rule, of course, would have required application of Ontario's guest statute, barring recovery. The New York Court of Appeals chose to abandon the *lex loci delicti* rule for such cases, and held that New York law (imposing liability on the defendant) should apply. The Court observed that Ontario's guest statute was concerned with preventing collusion that would redound to the detriment of Ontario policyholders, an interest not implicated by the facts of the case since the parties, the insurer, and (presumably) the insurer's policyholders were New Yorkers, and the automobile was garaged and insured in New York. At the same time, New York's interests in compensating New York injured parties and establishing standards of care for New York drivers were clearly implicated. Of the two states, only New York had a cognizable interest in the application of its law. It was a classic case of a "false conflict" as Currie had defined the term.

Even this limited departure from traditional principles was met with some criticism, and the subsequent history of the "guest statute" problem in the New York courts was surprisingly contentious. That history revealed, for example, that not everyone agreed on the purpose underlying guest statutes in general and Ontario's in particular. In a second case, *Dym v. Gordon* (N.Y. 1965),[15] the plaintiff-passenger and defendant-driver were again both New York domiciliaries, but the accident took place in Colorado, where the parties had gone to college. Colorado had a guest statute, which

---

13. The history of guest statutes in the United States does not support the idea that they were originally founded on a desire to prevent collusion against insurance companies. For purposes of this discussion, and so as not to upset the applecart, we will indulge the assumption that they were.

14. 12 N.Y.2d 473, 240 N.Y.S.2d 743, 191 N.E.2d 279 (1963).

15. 16 N.Y.2d 120, 262 N.Y.S.2d 463, 209 N.E.2d 792 (1965).

differed from Ontario's in permitting the passenger to recover in cases of "gross negligence." The New York Court of Appeals assessed the purposes of the Colorado guest statute differently from how it had assessed the purposes of the Ontario statute; it regarded the Colorado statute as reflecting not only a desire to avoid collusion against insurers but also a policy of subordinating the claims of "ungrateful guests" to those of other parties in other vehicles who might also have been injured. Since there did exist such injured third parties in the case who happened to be Colorado domiciliaries, there was no false conflict as in *Babcock*; Colorado's guest statute served to protect the Colorado victims. The Court of Appeals ended up applying Colorado law to bar the plaintiff's claim. Some years later the vagaries of identifying the "purposes" underlying guest statutes were further underscored by a suggestion that enactment of the Ontario guest statute had been motivated as much by the Ontario Prime Minister's pique at having been sued by two "ungrateful" hitchhikers he had picked up (who sued him after they were injured in an accident) as by any concern with collusion and insurance rates.

In yet a third case, *Tooker v. Lopez* (N.Y. 1969),[16] the New York Court of Appeals overruled its decision in *Dym v. Gordon*. The facts were similar to those in *Dym v. Gordon*; the passenger and driver, both of whom died in an auto accident in Michigan, were New York domiciliaries who had gone to Michigan to attend college. The decedent driver's car had been garaged and insured in New York. Michigan's guest statute was similar to Colorado's in that it permitted recovery in cases of the driver's "willful misconduct" or "gross negligence." The Court in *Tooker* held that New York law should apply, permitting the passenger's estate to sue the driver's estate. In doing so, the Court rejected the "teleological" characterization of the guest statute's purposes that had held sway in *Dym v. Gordon*; the Michigan statute was about preventing collusion, not about subordinating the claims of "ungrateful guests" to those of other injured parties. (There was, in fact, a Michigan domiciliary injured in the accident, which would seemingly have militated in favor of the application of Michigan law had *Dym v. Gordon* been followed.) Since no Michigan insurer was involved so far as the relationship between Tooker and Lopez was concerned, this was again, as in *Babcock*, a false conflict and New York law should apply.

The New York cases from *Babcock* to *Tooker* did not only suggest the difficulty of attaining consensus on the real "purpose" of guest statutes. It also revealed a diversity of views on the significance to be attributed to commonality of domicile in a state

16. 24 N.Y.2d 569, 301 N.Y.S.2d 519, 249 N.E.2d 394 (1969).

different from the state of injury. Dissenting in *Tooker*, Judge Breitel argued that not all instances of common domicile presented the same problem. Breitel agreed with the decision in *Babcock*, because the happenstance that the accident in that case occurred in Ontario rather than at some other place (namely, in New York) during the weekend trip had no independent significance or connection with the relationship among the parties; it was "wholly adventitious," and therefore application of Ontario law to this dispute which otherwise concerned only New York would be arbitrary and pointless. But in both *Dym* and *Tooker*, the driver and passenger had not merely gone on a day trip to an adjacent state, as in *Babcock*, but had relocated for a substantial period of time to another state to attend college. The fact that the automobile accident occurred in that state was not "adventitious,"[17] but rather an unsurprising detail given that they had chosen to spend nine months out of the year there. Moreover, in both *Dym* and *Tooker* the *relationship* between the parties had originated in the state where they attended college; they had not even known each other in New York. In Judge Breitel's eyes, then, the fact in *Dym* and *Tooker* of the parties' common domicile in New York was not as decisive a consideration for purposes of the choice-of-law question as it had been in *Babcock*; the driver and passenger in both *Dym* and *Tooker* had knowingly associated themselves for a substantial period of time with the state of their college education, and application of that state's law to litigation arising out of an accident taking place there was in no sense arbitrary.

Babcock, *Dym*, and *Tooker* all featured disputes in which the state of wrong and injury, which would have been the customary reference under the territorial approach, differed from the state of common domicile of the plaintiff and defendant (or the decedents). This configuration of parties and events is often thought to present the best advertisement for the Currie approach; it is much like the *Carroll* situation, in which the court's selection of the law of the place of injury, with no meaningful consideration of the law of the state of common domicile, seems arbitrary. Yet the New York "guest statute" cases reveal that application of interest analysis even to the common-domicile situation is not free from problems. First, of course, the New York Court of Appeals could not agree in the three cases on the proper characterization of the interests underlying the relevant guest statute: In *Dym*, the notion that such students are intended to subordinate the claims of "ungrateful guests" to claims made by more deserving victims temporarily held

---

17. The word "adventitious" is defined by the *Merriam–Webster Online Dictionary* as "not inherent or innate," or "arising or occurring sporadically or in other than the usual location." http://www.merriam-webster.com/dictionary/ADVENTITIOUS (last visited December 7, 2009).

sway. Second, Judge Breitel's dissent in *Tooker* observed that, realistically, the fact of common domicile may be more relevant in some situations than in others. Conventional principles governing the law of domicile (which was largely developed in areas of law lying outside conflict of laws as such) would treat the domicile of the parties in *Tooker* as New York rather than Michigan, because the young women presumably had not evidenced an intention to relocate permanently from New York. But shouldn't the several months' residence in Michigan of the young women in *Tooker* lead us to ascribe less significance to their New York "domicile" than to the New York domicile of the parties in *Babcock* or *Carroll*—or, at least, to ascribe *some* interest to Michigan, which presumably has some concern for students enrolled for months at a time at its educational institutions, even if they formally remain "domiciliaries" of another state?

Finally, *Tooker* itself raised an uncomfortable problem not directly present in *Babcock* (or, for that matter, *Carroll*), since another woman, a Michigan domiciliary, had also been injured in the fatal crash and was also a plaintiff in the case. The reasoning of the majority in *Tooker* implied that, unlike the survivors of the New York passenger, the Michigan woman would not be able to recover for her injuries since there was no reason to give her the protection of New York law. One result of elevating domiciliary interests at the expense of the locus interests that animated the territorial system is that people who are similarly situated, apart from their domicile, can easily receive different choice-of-law outcomes (and thus different substantive outcomes) from one another. Defenders of interest analysis commonly point out that this situation is a consequence, not of conflicts law, but of American federalism, in which rules of law frequently vary from state to state. A passenger-victim in a "guest-statute" state will do less well in litigation against the driver in a dispute wholly domestic to that state, than will a passenger-victim in a "no-guest-statute" state where the dispute is wholly domestic to *that* state. We seem to accept that reality without great protest, even if the auto accidents in the two cases are otherwise very similar. But where there is a single accident, and the legal outcomes for the two victims differ solely because of their domicile, it seems a bit more troubling. This is particularly the case when, as in *Tooker*, it is the forum domiciliaries who are reaping benefits denied to those who live elsewhere.

2. *Contiguous–Border Torts and the "Neumeier Rules"*

Conflicts of laws arising from activities occurring near the borders of contiguous states whose laws differ in relevant respects, as in *Babcock*, are sure to surface periodically. (In fact, some scholars who acknowledge the importance of assessing state interests in choice of law believe that cross-border torts present a distinct problem, precisely because they are predictable and recurrent, thus making patterns of judicial decisions in such cases a potential source of interstate friction.) It should have been especially obvious that, so long as Ontario had a guest statute and New York did not, variations on the *Babcock v. Jackson* scenario would continue to come before the New York courts (if not those of Ontario). In *Neumeier v. Kuehner* (N.Y. 1972),[18] Chief Judge Fuld, who had played a large role in the reorientation of New York conflicts law, sought to distill from the prior guest statute cases a series of three basic rules to govern such conflicts. What is significant about the court's adoption of the "*Neumeier* rules" is that they reflect a desire to return to a set of quasi-territorial "rules" specifically for the guest statute situation, whereas *Babcock v. Jackson* had seemingly represented a reaction against the jurisdiction-selecting approach of the First Restatement.

In *Neumeier*, the decedent driver had been a resident of Buffalo, New York; the decedent passenger had been a resident of Ontario. (Thus this was not a common-domicile case.) The driver drove to Ontario, picked up the passenger there, and drove on with him to another destination in Ontario. On the way there, they collided with a train, and were both instantly killed. The passenger's estate brought suit against the driver's estate. As in *Babcock*, *Dym*, and *Tooker*, the accident occurred outside of New York, and traditional *lex loci* principles would have resulted in application of Ontario's guest statute, barring recovery.

If one focuses on domiciliary interests, however, the facts of *Neumeier* were more complex than those in the preceding cases. In *Neumeier*, the plaintiff's decedent (like the plaintiff herself) had been a domiciliary of Ontario. On the other hand, the defendant's decedent (like the defendant herself) had been a domiciliary of New York, and presumably (the court did not say) his car was garaged and insured there. In fact, if one were to look at the case through Currie's lenses, one might categorize it as an "unprovided-for" case: If Ontario's guest statute were characterized as intended to protect Ontario insurers and their policyholders from collusive claims, Ontario did not have a policy for the situation raised by *Neumeier*. By the same token, if one regards New York's liability policy as designed (1) to protect New York plaintiffs and (2) to regulate behavior on New York roads, one might conclude that New York's policy is not implicated on the facts of *Neumeier*, either. In any case, the court concluded that Ontario's guest statute should apply. In coming to this conclusion, Chief Justice Fuld announced

18. 31 N.Y.2d 121, 335 N.Y.S.2d 64, 286 N.E.2d 454 (1972).

the three "*Neumeier* rules" that should apply thenceforth in conflicts cases involving foreign guest statutes:

1. When the guest-passenger and the host-driver are domiciled in the same state, and the car is there registered, the law of that state should control and determine the standard of care which the host owes to his guest.

2. When the driver's conduct occurred in the state of his domicile and that state does not cast him in liability for that conduct, he should not be held liable by reason of the fact that liability would be imposed upon him under the tort law of the state of the victim's domicile. Conversely, when the guest was injured in the state of his own domicile and its law permits recovery, the driver who has come into that state should not—in the absence of special circumstances—be permitted to interpose the law of his state as a defense.

3. In other situations, when the passenger and the driver are domiciled in different states, the rule is necessarily less categorical. Normally, the applicable rule of decision will be that of the state where the accident occurred but not if it can be shown that displacing that normally applicable rule will advance the relevant substantive law purposes without impairing the smooth working of the multi-state system or producing great uncertainty for litigants.[19]

Neumeier Rule #1, then, explains the results in *Babcock* and *Tooker* (although one may question whether those cases actually concerned "standard of care" at all). The facts of *Neumeier* itself fit into Rule #3. The court held that the law of Ontario—the place where the accident occurred—should therefore apply because it had not been shown that New York's connection with the controversy was sufficient to justify displacing the rule of l*ex loci delicti.* The result in *Neumeier* might superficially appear to be a gesture of comity in the direction of Ontario, since the court applied Ontario law. The significance of that gesture, though, was undoubtedly lost on Ontario, not to mention her plaintiff, since the result was to deprive the Ontario plaintiff of a remedy (albeit in accordance with Ontario law) and to immunize the New York defendant from liability. It is one of the ambitions of those favoring an "interest analysis" approach to choice of law to demonstrate that courts are capable of deferring at times to foreign law and do not invariably find a way to apply forum law. But the real issue may be whether courts applying interest analysis have a predilection for favoring

19. *Neumeier*, 31 N.Y.2d at 128, 335 N.Y.S.2d at 70, 286 N.E.2d at 457– 58. Chief Judge Fuld had earlier pro- posed these rules in his concurring opinion in the *Tooker* case.

forum *residents*, not just forum law. The result in *Neumeier* does nothing to dispel that concern.

3.   Conduct Regulation and Loss Distribution: Beyond Guest Statutes

Neumeier more or less brought to an end the New York courts' saga of guest statutes and choice of law.[20] Although that saga had begun in *Babcock* with an analysis that bore all the hallmarks of interest analysis, the "*Neumeier* rules" suggested that, at least for guest statute cases, *ad hoc* interest analysis should eventually give way to choice-of-law rules for those particular situations. With the decline of guest statutes, the question became whether the "*Neumeier* rules" ought to govern conflicts in other kinds of tort cases as well, or whether a case-by-case assessment of interests was called for. Of course, the *Neumeier* rules could not simply be transposed uncritically to other areas. All legal rules that pertain to what we call "tort law" do not address the same problems or serve the same purposes. That had been one of the insights of the First Restatement's critics.

In fact, a comparison of the laws competing for application in the guest statute cases themselves confirms that different legal rules can be addressed to different problems. For example, New York's basic law of negligence and wrongful death establishes a standard of care for wrongdoers and a policy of compensation for victims. We wouldn't, though, say that Ontario's guest statute simply embodies a different policy with respect to the same questions; in particular, we wouldn't say that the guest statute reflects a policy that a driver should be entitled to drive negligently so long as her only victim is the passenger in her car. One might say instead that the guest statute reflects a decision by Ontario to allocate the loss in such cases to the passenger, rather than to insurers and their policyholders—not because compensation of victims and regulation of the behavior of drivers are bad ideas, but because Ontario thinks those policies should be subordinated to the policy of eliminating the collusion incentive. Following this reasoning, Ontario's guest statute could be characterized as a "loss-distribution" rule, whereas New York's negligence rule is "conduct-regulating" and compensatory in purpose. You'll notice that we have here used the word "characterize," a term and concept that loomed large in the *lex loci* approach. Just as characterization of the dispute helps determine the proper *lex loci* rule, and thus the choice-of-law reference, in the territorial system, characterization of legal rules and their purposes can influence the ascription of

---

20. Cases concerning guest statutes and conflicts were heard by courts in several other states as well.

interests, and thus the outcomes in particular cases, under interest analysis.

Consider *Schultz v. Boy Scouts of America, Inc.* (N.Y. 1985),[21] one of the most important conflicts cases decided by the New York Court of Appeals in the wake of the guest statute cases. Cristopher and Richard Schultz, young teenage boys residing in New Jersey, were sexually molested by Edmond Coakeley, a Franciscan Brother who was their teacher at Catholic school and Scoutmaster of their Boy Scout troop. Much of the molestation took place on scouting trips in the state of New York, although Cristopher was also subjected to molestation in New Jersey. Cristopher ultimately committed suicide. His parents sued the Roman Catholic Archdiocese of Newark (which operated the boys' school) in New Jersey court, but the suit was dismissed because the Archdiocese had tort immunity under New Jersey law. The parents then sued the Boy Scouts, the Franciscan Brothers, and others for personal injuries to themselves and to Richard, and for Cristopher's wrongful death, in New York court. The Boy Scouts of America were at the time considered a domiciliary of New Jersey, while Franciscan Brothers was considered to be domiciled in Ohio. New Jersey recognized the legal doctrine of charitable immunity, while New York did not. The question was whether the plaintiffs' claims against the Boy Scouts and the Franciscan Brothers were barred by the doctrine of charitable immunity. Let's focus first on the claims against the Boy Scouts.

When applying an interest-oriented choice-of-law analysis in a case, it's helpful to ask first how the case would have come out using the traditional, territorial approach. Here, that would depend on how the dispute were characterized: If we regard the problem as one of tort law, then (assuming for simplicity's sake that the wrongful acts, and consequent injuries, took place in New York) it is likely that New York law would apply and that the suit brought by the Schultzes would not be barred. If, instead, we regard the issue as one of status or capacity to sue and be sued, it could be argued that, at least in the case of the Boy Scouts, the law of the domicile (New Jersey) should apply and the suit should be barred. Obviously, under the *lex loci* approach, a lot would ride on how one characterizes the issue. In any case, though, the New York guest statute cases, culminating in *Neumeier v. Kuehner*, had established that a different kind of analysis was in order.

If we assume that the "*Neumeier* rules" as such should be applied in all kinds of tort cases, not just those involving guest statutes, the first *Neumeier* rule would seem to govern in *Schultz*: Both the Schultzes and the Boy Scouts were domiciled in New

---

21.   65 N.Y.2d 189, 491 N.Y.S.2d 90, 480 N.E.2d 679 (1985).

Jersey. Therefore, according to *Neumeier* Rule #1, the law of the common domicile should apply, which would result in the dismissal of the case on charitable immunity grounds. The Court of Appeals, however, noted that the structure of the *Schultz* case made it a "reverse-*Babcock*" situation, because (unlike in *Babcock*) the law of the common domicile did not protect the plaintiffs while the law of the place of injury did. Arguably, the court in *Neumeier*, in devising Rule #1, may not have this "reverse-*Babcock*" scenario in mind. The Court of Appeals in *Schultz* thus recognized that it might be appropriate to conduct an independent choice-of-law analysis, based on interest-analysis principles, rather than just blindly apply *Neumeier* rule #1.

Resorting to basic interest analysis, the Court found that *Schultz* presented a false conflict and that New Jersey had the only cognizable interests at stake. Of particular importance in this holding was the Court's conclusion that New York's legitimate deterrence interests would not be served by application of its "nonimmunity" rule. Viewing the competing rules of law—New Jersey's immunity rule and New York's "nonimmunity" rule—as loss-distributing rather than conduct-regulating, the Court saw the location of the wrongful behavior in New York as making no difference to the outcome. New Jersey, as the domicile of both the plaintiffs and the Boy Scouts, had a cognizable interest in the allocation of loss as between them; New York had no such interest since New York presumably has no policy of loss allocation for non-domiciliaries.[22] The result in *Schultz* accords with our intuition that, in general, it is sensible to apply the law of the common domicile in a conflicts case. Moreover, in light of the plaintiffs' earlier failure in the New Jersey courts, a decision in their favor in the New York courts (albeit against different defendants) might have seemed to be a reward for forum-shopping. Nevertheless, a closer look at *Schultz* suggests that the matter is not so simple.

The Court's reasoning in *Schultz* exposes some of the weaknesses of interest analysis, particular its categorical way of assessing interests. In principle, of course, there is some merit to

---

22. Note that one feature of the *Schultz* decision is that it resulted not only in the application of New Jersey law, but also in a decision favorable to a New Jersey domiciliary. Of course, this latter fact says nothing especially compelling about the willingness of the New York Court of Appeals to defer to the interests of New Jersey, because (1) there was no New York domiciliary in the case to favor, and (2) the decision was also *unfavorable* to New Jersey domiciliaries (the plaintiffs). As Professor Douglas Laycock has stated in criticism of the domiciliary emphasis of interest analysis, "A state does not disprove its brazen desire to favor residents by deferring in cases where it has no opportunity to favor a resident. I will believe that one state is deferring to others when deference imposes costs as well as benefits." Douglas Laycock, *Equal Citizens of Equal and Territorial States: The Constitutional Foundations of Choice of Law*, 92 COLUMBIA LAW REVIEW 249, 284 (1992).

distinguishing analytically between loss-allocating and behavior-regulating rules, and for applying the law of the common domicile where the issue clearly is one of loss allocation. One hypothetical example might be the rule of joint and several liability. If the wrongful behavior occurs in State A while all of the defendants reside in State B, and State B provides for joint and several liability while State A does not, it makes sense to say that State B's rule on joint and several liability should apply. That rule does allocate loss among the several defendants, and, while the rule may also operate to benefit a plaintiff (by making it easier for him to obtain compensation from a single defendant), its application can be clearly distinguished from the question of the wrongfulness of the defendants' behavior, as to which application of the law of State A might well be called for since the behavior occurred there.

The conflict over immunity rules in *Schultz*, however, seems different. To characterize the New York rule as a "nonimmunity" rule, thus placing it on the same plane with New Jersey's immunity rule for purposes of assessing the relative interests involved, is worse than arbitrary; it serves to conceal the real nature of New York's interest in the application of its law. New York does not really have a law of "nonimmunity" for charitable organizations; one might as well characterize the entire law of negligence in New York as a "nonimmunity" rule, in the sense that those to whom its law of negligence applies are not "immune" from the liability it imposes. Rather, in the absence of an immunity rule, what New York has to offer in this case is law that imposes liability on persons and organizations for negligent hiring, supervision, and training. That law is, if anything, a "conduct-regulating" rule. If one takes seriously the distinction between conduct-regulating and loss-allocating rules, what we have here is a comparison between apples and oranges. New Jersey's interest here may be in allocating loss as between the plaintiffs and the charitable organizations that the state has determined should be shielded from damage awards, but New York's interest lies in imposing its duty of reasonable care on those acting within its borders (as well as, of course, protecting its domiciliaries, of which there were none in this case).[23]

---

23. In keeping with its conception of New York's law as reflecting a "nonimmunity" rule, the Court in *Schultz* took up, only to dismiss, two putative arguments concerning the presence of a cognizable interest on the part of New York: (1) an interest in "protect[ing] medical creditors who provided services to injured parties in the locus State," and (2) an interest in "prevent[ing] injured tort victims from becoming public wards in the locus State." However strong or weak one regards those two putative interests, it is hard to see why they pertain more to the "loss-allocating" than to the "conduct-regulating" dimension of the New York rule.

The most tangible analytic payoff of the interest approach is the identification of false conflicts. A court deploying interest analysis will usually be happiest when it can characterize a conflict as "false," because that avoids the need to favor one state's interest over the other's: Only one state has one. No court wants to be confronted with "true conflicts" because there is no very satisfying way of resolving them, least of all Currie's *lex fori* solution. But this preference can operate as an incentive to find a particular conflict to be "false" when it really isn't. The court's ultimate conclusion in *Schultz* that New Jersey law should apply is, of course, defensible. After all, the parties were all New Jersey domiciliaries, and the New Jersey courts had already denied the plaintiffs a remedy in their case against the Archdiocese. It would, perhaps, have appeared disrespectful to New Jersey for the New York Court of Appeals now to apply New York law and override New Jersey's immunity rule. But *Schultz* was not a false conflict; it pitted New York's law imposing liability against New Jersey's law shielding the defendants from liability. The interests of both states were implicated. The more direct route to the Court's decision to apply New Jersey law would have been simply to say that, under the circumstances, New Jersey's interest in allocating losses among its domiciliaries should prevail over New York's interest in regulating the behavior of people acting within its borders.

Or consider another analysis, which leads to the opposite conclusion: New Jersey's law relevant to the *Schultz* case consists not only of an immunity rule, but also a background principle favoring compensation to plaintiffs injured by negligent behavior, to which the principle of immunity is a limited exception. New Jersey's charitable immunity rule represents a decision by New Jersey that, faced with the policy of compensation to injured domiciliaries on the one hand and the desire to promote charitable organizational activity on the other, the balance will be struck in favor of the latter. It is not, however, a repudiation of the principle of compensation for plaintiff domiciliaries. New Jersey takes no pleasure in denying a remedy to the plaintiffs in *Schultz*. Therefore, while application of New Jersey law would further no policy of New York (and in fact would negate New York's policy of regulating behavior within the state), application of New York law would at least vindicate New Jersey's policy of compensation. According to this calculus, New York law should be applied because that solution (unlike the alternative) would advance a cognizable interest of each state.[24] Some might balk at this attribution to New Jersey of a default compensation policy as well as a specific immunity policy, since, in a case wholly domestic to New Jersey, it is clear that the

24. This analysis bears a strong resemblance to the doctrine of "comparative impairment," discussed in the next section.

governing law would result in immunity and no compensation. If one, though, takes seriously the notion of identifying state interests, it does not seem inappropriate to take New Jersey's compensation interest into account.[25]

Since *Schultz*, the New York Court of Appeals has continued to deal with the problem of interest analysis in conflicts cases.[26] Its decisions from 1963 to the present constitute the most ambitious and coherent effort by any single state high court to apply the insights of interest analysis to conflicts problems. Those decisions illustrate both the possibilities and limits of the methodology.

E.   Resolving True Conflicts

1.   *Currie's Approach*

As noted, Currie recommended that, in a case featuring a "true conflict," the forum should simply apply forum law. This stance was partly a function of Currie's antipathy for the notion that judges could make comparative assessments of state interests by "balancing" them. It seems surprising that Currie would be so adamant on this point, given his comfort with courts' assessment of state interests for the purpose of determining whether a conflict were false or true (or "unprovided for"). In any case, though, Currie was not especially troubled by the use of *lex fori* as a default or "tiebreaker" solution, because he believed in general that the law of the forum should be the presumptive choice-of-law reference, to be displaced only for very good reasons. However, courts—even those sufficiently persuaded by interest analysis to deploy it to describe conflicts as "true" or "false"—have generally been reluctant to adopt Currie's *lex fori* solution for true conflicts.[27] That

---

25. Close readers of the *Schultz* case will note an additional unsatisfying part of that decision: the Court of Appeals's offhand ruling that the second defendant, Franciscan Brothers, should also receive the benefit of New Jersey's charitable immunity rule. The Franciscan Brothers were domiciled in Ohio, which recognized the doctrine of charitable immunity only in part: There was no immunity for claims of negligence in hiring and supervision. In something of a *non sequitur*, the Court of Appeals stated, "For this reason, no doubt, defendant Franciscan Brothers does not claim Ohio law governs and the choice is between the law of New York and the law of New Jersey," and it simply assumed that since New Jersey was the choice-of-law reference for the Boy Scouts, the same answer must be provided for the claims against the Franciscan Brothers. Regardless of what law the Franciscan Brothers may have "claimed" should apply, the true "choice" as to the claims against them was between the law of New York (place of injury) and the law of Ohio (place of domicile), neither of which provided for immunity under the circumstances of the case. Perhaps the Court of Appeals regarded as unpalatable the prospect of ruling that the Boy Scouts could escape liability but that the Franciscan Brothers could not.

26. *Cooney v. Osgood Machinery, Inc.*, 81 N.Y.2d 66, 595 N.Y.S.2d 919, 612 N.E.2d 277 (1993), an important case decided after *Schultz*, is discussed in Chapter 3, in a section dealing with conflicts in product liability cases.

27. For a (somewhat notorious) exception, see *Lilienthal v. Kaufman*, 239 Or. 1, 395 P.2d 543 (1964).

solution sounds, perhaps, a bit too self-seeking for most judges to espouse openly.

Moderate and Restrained Interpretation. This, though, was not all that Currie had to say about true conflicts. He recognized that identification of a false conflict was a happier outcome of the choice-of-law analysis than identification of a true conflict; it was better to conclude that only one state had a legitimate interest in the application of its law than that a choice between the two laws was necessary, especially if the instrument for doing so was going to be as blunt as the *lex fori* expedient: "[T]o assert a conflict between the interests of the forum and the foreign state is a serious matter."[28] He therefore urged that a court applying interest analysis have a "second look" at the interest of the forum, to determine whether it was truly implicated by the facts of the case, before concluding that a true conflict was at hand. This second look amounted to "a more moderate and restrained interpretation both of the [forum's] policy and of the circumstances in which it must be applied to effectuate the forum's legitimate purpose." Thus true conflicts, and unnecessary disparagement of foreign law, might be avoided in some cases.

Of course, Currie's injunction referred only to the court's assessment of the interests of the forum, not to its assessment of the interests of the other potentially interested state(s); courts certainly have no business giving a "moderate and restrained interpretation" of the interests of another state when dealing with a conflicts problem. This "one-way" quality of the "second look" idea is understandable, since one of the criticisms leveled at Currie's approach was its unwonted predilection for the application of forum law. Of course, one can justly ask whether this advocacy of "moderate and restrained interpretation" doesn't amount to a weakening of the "on-off" quality of interest identification, and in reality involve the court in a process of balancing of interests.[29] Nevertheless, "moderate and restrained interpretation" is an important part of Currie's overall theory, suggesting that courts should avoid unnecessary disrespect for foreign law by means of the *lex fori* solution for true conflicts.

28. Brainerd Currie, *The Disinterested Third State*, 28 LAW & CONTEMPORARY PROBLEMS 754, 757 (1963).

29. Currie professed to find a "brilliant" example of "moderate and restrained interpretation" in Justice Traynor's opinion in *Bernkrant v. Fowler*, 55 Cal.2d 588, 12 Cal.Rptr. 266, 360 P.2d 906 (1961). Although Justice Traynor did not use the language of interest analysis as such in *Bernkrant*, he did find his way to applying Nevada rather than foreign law in this somewhat odd case. It could be said that Traynor was rather modest in his assessment of California's interest in the case, which to Currie was a demonstration that courts were indeed capable of applying what amounted to interest analysis without undue inflation of the forum's interests.

2. Comparative Impairment

Many people who are otherwise attracted to Currie's version of "interest analysis" find it difficult to accept his proposal to resolve true conflicts by automatically applying forum law. The problem is not only that the automatic application of forum law in such situations can seem a crude solution. Another complaint is that the "on-off switch" method of identifying state interests—either a cognizable interest exists or it doesn't—leaves no room for comparing the intensity or weight of the interests asserted by, or (more accurately) imputed to, the interested states. Perhaps we can soften the rigidity of Currie's approach to true conflicts by going beyond mere identification of interests, to comparing them in weight and in the intensity with which they are held.

This is the virtue of a variant of interest analysis that has come to be known as "comparative impairment." This approach to choice of law, which thus far has been adopted only in California (and which has had only limited and erratic application even there), was the brainchild of William Baxter, an antitrust scholar whose economic acumen informed his brief foray into the scholarly world of conflict of laws.[30] "Comparative impairment," with its roots in game theory and public choice, is the conflicts methodology that has proved most congenial to scholars who favor economic analysis of legal rules. In the view of the author (who is not such a scholar), comparative impairment is in principle the most discerning of the various approaches to resolving true conflicts. In practice, however, it has not fared particularly well, partly because judicial decisions in the one state that purports to use the method—California—have lacked the nuance that Baxter demonstrated in describing it.

In his seminal law review article, Baxter proposed that, when contemplating how to deal with instances of what Currie would term a true conflict, we envision a negotiation between policymakers of the forum and those of the foreign state over proper resolution of all the disputes that might arise out of their conflicting legal rules. Just as negotiators concerning a treaty or interstate compact would attempt to provide for a wide variety of contingencies, and could be expected to give ground on one issue in return for concessions on another, the hypothetical state negotiators concerning possible conflicts of laws in a wide variety of factual scenarios could be thought of as doing the same thing. While Baxter followed Currie's analysis so far as identification and resolution of "false conflicts" was concerned, he recommended a more flexible approach

30. William F. Baxter, *Choice of Law and the Federal System*, 16 STANFORD LAW REVIEW 1 (1963).

to the treatment of state interests in cases where a true conflict might exist:

> The question "Will the social objective underlying [a state's] rule be furthered by the application of the rule in cases like the present one?" need not necessarily be answered "Yes" or "No"; the answer will often be, "Yes, to some extent." The extent to which the purpose underlying a rule will be furthered by application or impaired by nonapplication to cases of a particular category may be regarded as the measure of the rule's pertinence and of the state's interest in the rule's application to cases within the category. Normative resolution of real conflicts cases is possible where one of the assertedly applicable rules is more pertinent to the case than the competing rule.[31]

That is, one can envision negotiators on behalf of each state making rational judgments as to how essential it is to vindication of their state's interests that its rule be applied in a particular case, and that this could serve as the basis for "progress" in the negotiation such that we could legitimately posit that one of the states would yield ground—*i.e.* consent to the nonapplication of its law—in that particular case, on the theory that in some other hypothetical conflict that might arise, the other state could be expected to do the same.

As Baxter put it, "Implicit in the principle is an assertion that a court can and should go beyond a determination whether a state has *any* governmental interest in the application of its internal law—that a court can and should determine which state's internal objective will be least impaired by subordination in cases like the one before it."[32] Hence the term "comparative impairment": The methodology contemplates that, in cases of true conflict, the law of the state whose cognizable interest would be more impaired by nonapplication of its law should be applied. The key to understanding the "comparative impairment" idea is that its analogy to a political negotiation between states does not envision a negotiation solely as to the conflict at issue in the particular case. Rather, the negotiation that the "comparative impairment" idea posits, as an analogy to the court's task of resolving a conflict, is one in which it is plausible to speculate that one state might yield (despite the existence of an interest) in one case on the theory that its interest is less than the other state's, and that the other side will yield in some other, future conflict in which the reverse is true. Obviously, the interstate political negotiation is a fiction, an "ideal type"; there could never be an actual negotiation between states that

---

31. *Id.* at 9.

32. *Id.* at 18 (emphasis in the original).

accounted for all possible fact patterns that might lead to disputes containing connections to both states—let alone the millions of such negotiations that would be necessarily to cover the potential disputes between all pairs of the 50 states. The negotiation analogy, though, does dramatize the notion that a government interest, rather than being either completely implicated or not at all implicated in a case, can at times be "somewhat implicated," and that mutual recognition of this fact by the courts of the interested states can help to resolve true conflicts.

California is the one state to have adopted these "comparative impairment" principles for use in conflicts cases. (Note that California courts only apply this method in tort cases, and tend to apply some version of Second Restatement principles in contract cases.) That California has been willing to make such a move in its law of conflicts is not surprising, as the California Supreme Court, under the intellectual leadership of Justice Roger Traynor, was one of the first state courts openly to question the merits of *lex loci* principles in the 1950s and 1960s. Two cases from the 1970s illustrate the "comparative impairment" analysis in action. *Bernhard v. Harrah's Club* (Cal. 1976)[33] raised a classic conflict in policies between the states of California and Nevada. At the time, California imposed liability on tavern owners and other suppliers of alcoholic beverages for injuries caused to third parties by consumers of such beverages inappropriately served them by the tavern (that is, when it was apparent the consumer was already intoxicated). For rather obvious reasons, Nevada, whose economy relies substantially on the health of its casino industry, has no such law. Two California residents drove to Harrah's in Nevada, where they were served alcoholic beverages, allegedly even after their state of intoxication was obvious. They drove home, and after crossing the border back into California, they negligently collided with a California motorcyclist, who was severely injured. Of possible interest are the additional facts that Harrah's regularly advertised for and solicited business in California, and that the casino was reasonably close to the California border; Harrah's undoubtedly counted among its patrons a substantial number of Californians, and this was certainly not an accident.

Conventional analysis of the policies of both California and Nevada makes it obvious that each had a strong interest in having its law apply to this case. At a minimum, California's liability rule sought to protect the safety of its residents on the roads of California, and that interest was clearly implicated in this situation. Conversely, Nevada, by immunizing casinos from dram shop liability, was in part acting to provide economic protection for a vital

33. 16 Cal.3d 313, 128 Cal.Rptr. 215, 546 P.2d 719 (1976).

sector of its economy; this interest, too, was clearly implicated in this case. (In analyzing the conflicts problem it is important to remember that the plaintiff was the California motorcyclist, not the California residents who imbibed the alcohol in Nevada and caused the accident in California.) Currie's *lex fori* approach for such true conflicts, of course, would result in the application of California law. But what should be the result if Baxter's "comparative impairment" approach is applied? Can one say that California holds its resident-protective liability policy more intensely than Nevada holds its casino-protective nonliability policy, or vice versa?

Here is how the California Supreme Court applied the "comparative impairment" method in *Bernhard*:

> It seems clear that California cannot reasonably effectuate its policy if it does not extend its regulation to include out-of-state tavern keepers such as defendant who regularly and purposely sell intoxicating beverages to California residents in places and under conditions in which it is reasonably certain these residents will return to California and act therein while still in an intoxicated state. California's interest would be very significantly impaired if its policy were not applied to defendant.

> Since the act of selling alcoholic beverages to obviously intoxicated persons is already proscribed in Nevada,[a] the application of California's rule of civil liability would not impose an entirely new duty requiring the ability to distinguish between California residents and other patrons. Rather the imposition of such liability involves an increased economic exposure, which, at least for businesses which actively solicit extensive California patronage, is a foreseeable and coverable business expense. Moreover, Nevada's interest in protecting its tavern keepers from civil liability of a boundless and unrestricted nature will not be significantly impaired when as in the instant case liability is imposed only on those tavern keepers who actively solicit California business.

> Therefore . . . , we conclude that California has an important and abiding interest in applying its rule of decision to the case at bench, that the policy of this state would be more significantly impaired if such rule were not applied and that the trial court erred in not applying California law.

Bernhard (like everything else in conflicts law) has been criticized, and one might ask whether application of "comparative impairment" ideas in that case constituted mere window dressing, reaching the same result that would have been reached by Currie's

---

a. The court is here referring to the fact that, under Nevada law, criminal liability attaches to tavern keepers who serve intoxicants to persons already drunk, although there is no civil "dram shop" liability.—C.S.

lex fori rule for true conflicts or, for that matter, by any court eager to apply forum law or to find for a forum domiciliary. One could further ask whether the Nevada courts, even if applying the same conflicts methodology (which they do not), would have been likely to reach the same result. As Professor Herma Hill Kay has demonstrated, the court in *Bernhard* purported to apply Baxter's modification of Currie's interest approach but misunderstood both of them.[34]

Yet the California Supreme Court's gesture toward a quasi-economic analysis, primitive though it is, does at least acknowledge some of the interests at stake. The facts of *Bernhard* dramatize the unwieldiness of trying to identify and assess state interests where the consequences of actions within a state, and the occasions for effectuating policies established by that state, do not necessarily respect state lines. The court was certainly correct to observe that Harrah's pervasive efforts to reach out to California residents ought to play some role in the analysis, and that Nevada casinos that knowingly rely on a substantial amount of business from California patrons (or, more precisely, those who may subsequently injure California domiciliaries) can reasonably insure against exposure to liability. Perhaps, on that theory, Nevada and its casinos truly are better situated to absorb the blow of nonapplication of Nevada's casino-protective law than is California and its innocent residents like the motorcyclist injured in *Bernhard*. On the other hand, Nevada *has* declared a policy of protecting Nevada casinos, whether they solicit California business or not, and it is doubtful that Nevada policymakers (not to say the state's casinos) would be much consoled by the court's observation that Nevada's "real" policy of shielding casinos generally from dram shop liability would not be "significantly impaired" by large liability judgments only against casinos that "actively solicit California business."

In the end, no off-the-cuff economic analysis by a court dealing with an individual conflicts problem is going to be a very persuasive justification for its decision, no matter what result it reaches. If states were actually in the habit of negotiating interstate agreements concerning the outcome of private lawsuits raising major issues of state policy, as the "comparative impairment" approach asks us to imagine, the *Bernhard* situation would seem to be a natural example for one of the subjects of such a negotiation: two adjacent states, with clearly conflicting legal rules embodying strongly held policies, concerning a type of multistate dispute that is likely to recur from time to time. In that respect, Baxter's

34. Herma Hill Kay, *The Use of Comparative Impairment to Resolve True Conflicts: An Evaluation of the California Experience*, 68 CALIFORNIA LAW REVIEW 577, 582–86 (1980). Among other things, Baxter in his article did not actually propose that state courts adopt the "comparative impairment" approach; his discussion was directed more to the possible role of federal courts in resolving true conflicts.

metaphor of an interstate negotiation seems quite apt. But it may be too much to expect the California Supreme Court, in carrying out this analysis, to speak for Nevada's overall interests in quite the way that Nevada would speak for herself in such a negotiation. In deciding *Bernhard* and applying California law to the benefit of a forum domiciliary and the detriment of a Nevada casino, the California Supreme Court obviously offered no concessions to Nevada law in some putative future case as compensation.[35] Application of California law in *Bernhard* does not appear to be any less acceptable than applying Nevada law would have been; the question is whether the court's application of the comparative impairment idea made its ruling more analytically persuasive.

On the other hand, the California Supreme Court did, in a subsequent case, demonstrate that the "comparative impairment" method need not invariably lead to the application of forum law. In *Offshore Rental Co. v. Continental Oil Co.* (Cal. 1978),[36] a California corporation sent a high-ranking executive of the company to Continental's Louisiana facilities to negotiate an agreement. While he was there, he was injured due to the negligence of one of Continental's employees. Offshore sued Continental under an old California statute making actionable "[a]ny injury to a servant which affects his ability to serve his master," which had been interpreted as applying to corporate employees. Louisiana law did not recognize such a corporate cause of action for injuries negligently inflicted on corporate employees. The California Supreme Court applied the "comparative impairment" method and held that Louisiana law should apply. Since the injury took place in Louisiana and the injured party was an executive of a California corporation, the court concluded that the interests of both California and Louisiana were implicated by the dispute. The court concluded that California policy would be less seriously impaired by the nonapplication of its law than would be the case with Louisiana. Its conclusion rested largely on its observation that the California legal rule conferring a cause of action on corporations for injuries to a "key employee" was "archaic" and different from the law of most other states; no California court had even considered the statutory provision for many years. Since there was little evidence that California was strongly committed to enforcement of this archaic statute, the California Supreme Court held that California policy would be less grievously impaired by application of the Louisiana rule than Louisiana policy would be by application of the California rule.

35. *Nevada v. Hall*, 440 U.S. 410 (1979), discussed in Chapter 4, suggests that such forbearance by the California courts was not forthcoming as a general matter.

36. 22 Cal.3d 157, 148 Cal.Rptr. 867, 583 P.2d 721 (1978).

No one can be outraged by the conclusion that Louisiana law should apply in *Offshore Rental*; the Court's modesty in applying foreign law and in denying a remedy to a California party seems commendable. The question is whether the court's use of the "comparative impairment" concept convincingly explains that result. In one sense, it does. The court's disparagement of the California rule as strange and archaic implied that "real" California policy would not be much impaired by failure to apply it. On the other hand, if the court was going to regard California's interests as so attenuated in *Offshore Rental*, why not simply call the case a false conflict? There doesn't seem to be a great deal of difference between the court's assessment of the California rule in *Offshore Rental* and what Currie called "moderate and restrained interpretation" of forum law.

This observation, however, begets another question. The fear and suspicion that courts may manipulate the choice-of-law process in order to favor forum law (and, at times, forum domiciliaries) loom large in criticism of virtually all conflicts methodologies. But does a court risk running afoul of basic principles when it errs in the other direction? Whether engaging in "moderate and restrained interpretation" of forum law, or disparaging forum law in order to make room for the application of foreign law as in *Offshore Rental*, a court may appear to be assuming something of a legislative task. Let's assume that the California statute, "archaic" though it might be, does clearly confer a cause of action on a corporation when one of its "key employees" is injured due to the negligence of another. If the California Supreme Court were to decline to apply this state statute in a case wholly domestic to California, simply on the ground that it was "archaic" and different from how other states treat the issue, the court would probably stand accused of usurping a legislative prerogative. Of course, in the multistate situation, the situation is somewhat different, because of the need to recognize the prerogatives of foreign law. But is a court somehow more entitled to disparage forum law in a conflicts situation than in a wholly domestic situation? Would the "comparative impairment" approach justify a court in disparaging the law of the *other* state as archaic and anomalous?

The general principle underlying the comparative impairment approach is sound: When each state has a cognizable interest in the application of its law, it stands to reason that, in an individual case, one state's investment may be less intense than the other's. Judicial assessments of comparative "impairment" in individual cases, however, may not be convincing to all involved. Of course, one of the oddities of the governmental interest approach to choice of law is that we rarely hear from the states themselves as to how they would measure the intensity of their interest in the application of their respective laws in a particular case; that task is left to the parties, whose sole incentive is not to vindicate state policy but to win a case. How "California" and "Nevada," respectively, actually feel about the *Bernhard* decision, for example, may not map perfectly on to the way that Bernhard and Harrah's, respectively, felt about it. In any event, although California still purports to follow the comparative impairment approach for conflicts in tort cases, the courts there have not been particularly consistent in its application. No other state has formally adopted it.

3. Other Solutions: "Principles of Preference" and "Shared Policies"

There is a discernible life-cycle in the reaction against territorial theories of choice of law and the move toward more "interest"-oriented approaches. Both courts and scholars, after some experience with interest analysis in a series of decisions, will be tempted to distill from those decisions a set of rules, for conflicts that are likely to arise with some frequency, that will obviate the need for a wholly case-by-case analysis. One example of this (discussed above) is the *"Neumeier* Rules," devised by the New York Court of Appeals to govern future guest statute cases. The New York Court of Appeals later extended the *Neumeier* rules to other kinds of tort problems. In addition, even some scholars hospitable to interest analysis recognize that it is desirable to have "true conflicts" decided by something less arbitrary than Currie's *lex fori* solution, and that perhaps there is a middle way between remorseless application of *lex loci* rules and a completely *ad hoc* approach. As the late David Cavers, one of the most erudite twentieth-century scholars of choice of law, wrote, "We may have to accept the adequately articulated *ad hoc* decision as an interim substitute, but we should persevere in the search for rules or principles which would determine when the law of a state which served one purpose should be preferred to the law of another state which served a different purpose." Hence the search for rules to resolve various kinds of true conflicts.

Cavers and "Principles of Preference." Professor Cavers himself proposed one of the most ambitious rule-based approaches to true conflicts, which he called "principles of preference." While ably defended and carefully thought out, these principles were fairly complex, and they were not easy to state succinctly. For example, Cavers proposed as one such principle of preference:

> Where the liability laws of the state of injury set a *higher* standard of conduct or of financial protection against injury than the laws of the state where the person causing the injury has acted or had his home, the laws of the state of injury should determine the standard and the protection applicable to

the case, at least where the person injured was not so related to the person causing the injury that the question should be relegated to the law governing their relationship.

Like all of Cavers's principles of preference, this one presumed that there was a true conflict—that each relevant state had a plausible interest in the application of its law. He illustrated this principle using a variation on *Grant v. McAuliffe* (Cal. 1953) (discussed in Chapter 1), which had involved the fatal car accident in Arizona in which both the victims and the wrongdoer had been Californians, and in which Arizona (unlike California) had a rule of abatement, according to which the cause of action "abated" with the death of the tortfeasor. In his hypothetical, Cavers changed the facts to provide that the accident occurred in California and that the alleged tortfeasor was actually a domiciliary of Arizona. Cavers argued, in accordance with the principle he had proposed, that California law should apply, even in an Arizona court: "Californians should not be put in jeopardy in California simply because an Arizonian, mounted in one of those death-dealing four-wheeled mechanical contrivances that are made in Michigan, had come into California from a state whose law provides a lower standard of financial protection than does California's."[37]

Here is another of Cavers's proposed principles, also addressed to torts:

> Where the law of a state in which a relationship has its seat has imposed a standard of conduct or of financial protection on one party to that relationship for the benefit of the other party which is higher than the like standard imposed by the state of injury, the law of the former state should determine the standard of conduct or of financial protection applicable to the case for the benefit of the party protected by that state's law.[38]

Cavers explained these and his several other principles of preference at length, using among his examples hypothetical variations of several famous cases (*Grant v. McAuliffe, Haumschild v. Continental Casualty Co., Kilberg v. Northeast Airlines, Babcock v. Jackson*) that we have earlier discussed. Some, but not all, of Cavers's principles of preference tended to favor territorial solutions, and in defending these principles, Cavers restated the case for territorial rules on the ground that "customary attitudes toward law" tended

---

37. David F. Cavers, The Choice-of-Law Process 142 (1965) (footnote omitted). Cavers noted that Brainerd Currie had considered the same hypothetical in an earlier article and had concluded (in accordance with Currie's *lex fori* solution in true conflict situations) that an Arizona court should apply Arizona law, a conclusion that Cavers deprecated.

38. *Id.* at 166. Cavers cited *Haumschild v. Continental Casualty Co.* (Wis. 1959) and *Babcock v. Jackson* (N.Y. 1963) as illustrations of this principle, although he conceded that these might not even be true conflicts to begin with.

to align with them. It's unclear if he was referring to "attitudes" that have themselves been shaped by the historical emphasis on territoriality, or an innate human intuition about the importance of place. In any case, elegantly articulated and explained though they are, Cavers's principles of preference have not made a deep imprint in the case law.[39] What is notable about Cavers's proposal is that the scholar who decades earlier had issued one of the most influential critiques of jurisdiction-selecting choice-of-law rules[40] clearly hoped that, with experience, the *ad hoc* approaches that replaced them could ultimately give way, at least in part, to a more nuanced set of rules—rules that more often than not will reflect a territorialist mind-set.

Kramer, Shared Policies, and "Policy–Selecting Rules." Larry Kramer, the most articulate expositor of interest analysis in the 1980s and 1990s, proposed in a series of law review articles a refinement of comparative impairment as a solution to true conflicts. Kramer observed that even a conflict of laws between two states on a specific issue can appear against the background of a more global policy that the two states actually share. (One example might be our discussion of *Schultz v. Boy Scouts of America* above, where we noted that *both* New York and New Jersey had a general policy of compensating victims for negligently inflicted injuries, although New Jersey law had an overlay of "charitable immunity" for cases brought against licensed charities.) Building on Baxter's image of an interstate negotiation and the game-theoretic assumptions on which it is based, Kramer hypothesized that a set of choice-of-law rules (more precisely, tie-breaking rules for true conflicts) could legitimately take account of such shared policies for particular types of situations. The result would be to systematically advance these larger shared goals over the long haul, resulting in a collective judicial approach that is more reciprocal and less conflictual than simple case-by-case adjudication. According to Kramer, "Because the conflicting interests underlying specific laws will presumably balance out over time and many cases, choosing the law that consistently advances the shared policy ... yields a marginal benefit to both states."[41]

Assessing the merits of Kramer's approach requires a lengthier set of illustrations than we can set forth here. One example would

---

39. One exception is *Cipolla v. Shaposka*, 439 Pa. 563, 267 A.2d 854 (1970), a guest statute case in which the host and guest were domiciliaries of different states. The Supreme Court of Pennsylvania relied in part on one of Cavers's "principles of preference" in holding that the guest statute of Delaware, domicile of the host, should govern.

40. David F. Cavers, *A Critique of the Choice-of-Law Problem*, 47 HARVARD LAW REVIEW 173 (1933).

41. Larry Kramer, *Return of the Renvoi*, 66 NEW YORK UNIVERSITY LAW REVIEW 979, 1021 (1991).

be that, since all states share a policy that generally favors the enforcement of contracts, a true conflict in a contract enforcement case in which one state's statute of frauds would make the contract unenforceable and the other's would not should result in selection of the law that would enforce the contract. Another example, as suggested in our previous discussion of *Schultz v. Boy Scouts of America*, would be that where the law of both states favors compensation of negligent injured persons, but only one state provides legal immunity for the particular defendant in the case, the general rule of compensation should prevail in case of a true conflict. The most important point to be gleaned from this brief discussion of it is that, like Baxter's original treatment of "comparative impairment," it underscores the fact that a state may have relevant "interests" in a given case that go beyond the specific interest in having its legal rule applied in this particular case; perhaps consideration of larger policies and longer-term goals should also figure in the conversation.

F.   Territoriality Redux?

In the face of all the esoterica about "true" and "false" conflicts, "comparative impairment," "principles of preference," and "policy-selecting rules," some courts and scholars have advocated a return to the good old jurisdiction-selecting rules of the territorial variety. And, of course, many had never been enchanted by interest analysis to begin with. Much of this criticism by jurists, not only of interest analysis but also of other modern approaches such as the Second Restatement (considered below), has focused on their *ad hoc* nature, turning Conflict of Laws into a "veritable playpen for judicial policymakers," in the acidulous judgment of one state supreme court justice.[42] Others argued that the century-long assault on the *lex loci* approach had understated its advantages and even its consonance with basic human intuitions about justice and sovereignty. In this view, one could recognize the advantages of *lex loci* rules in avoiding the subjectivity of more *ad hoc* approaches, without adopting Joseph Beale's elaborate and flawed theoretical justification for them. Of course, those who had rejected the territorial approach reminded their adversaries that courts had never been consistent in their application of territorial principles even during the supposed heyday of the *lex loci* approach. And so it went. The entire debate over domestic choice of law in the United States essentially collapsed of its own weight in the 1990s, as conflicts scholars found more interesting things to write about and courts demonstrated that, on the whole, they were not all that

42. *Paul v. National Life,* 177 W.Va. 427, 429, 352 S.E.2d 550, 551 (1986) (Neely, J.)

interested in theoretical, systemic coherence when deciding conflicts cases. This may explain why the Restatement (Second) of Conflict of Laws (the "Second Restatement"), to be considered in the next section, has proved so popular among courts in resolving conflicts of laws.

G. The Second Restatement: The "Most Significant Relationship"

Coinciding roughly with the period during which Brainerd Currie produced his groundbreaking scholarship on interest analysis, the American Law Institute drafted, discussed, and finally promulgated the Second Restatement of Conflict of Laws. Dissatisfaction with some of the outmoded provisions of the First Restatement led the ALI to begin drafting a new Restatement in the early 1950s. The first draft proved so controversial, and invited so many disparate calls for its revision or even its withdrawal, that it was nearly twenty years before the Restatement (Second) of Conflict of Laws was finally promulgated in 1971. Specific provisions of the Second Restatement have been revised since then, but the Second Restatement remains fundamentally what it was when first published. As with any Restatement, its provisions become law only when, and to the extent that, individual states adopt them. But it has been widely adopted: The Second Restatement has become the source cited most often by courts rendering choice-of-law decisions.

Early drafts of the Second Restatement reflected the substantial criticisms that had been made of the older territorial approach to choice of law and embodied some commitment to the kind of "contacts" ideas that the New York Court of Appeals brought to the forefront in its decision in *Auten v. Auten* (1954). These early efforts, however, evoked opposition both from those who thought they went too far in repudiating the territorial idea and those who thought they did not go far enough. The result is that the Second Restatement—at least the part of it that concerns choice of law—seems a hybrid of older and more modern approaches. Its organizing concept—that conflicts should be resolved by application of the law of the state having the "most significant relationship" to the dispute—seems on the surface to reject the jurisdiction-selecting approach of the First Restatement. Like the decisions of the New York Court of Appeals in *Auten* and *Haag*, it suggests that an examination of the facts of the individual case, rather than a process of categorization followed by application of a predefined *lex loci* rule, is necessary. But this gesture away from the jurisdiction-selecting approach is counterbalanced by a mélange of provisions that seek to establish "presumptive" choice-of-law references for particular kinds of cases. Those presumptive rules have all the hallmarks of a jurisdiction-selecting approach, especially since many of the presumptive rules are territorial in nature. The result is an overall approach that many scholars have disparaged as being "all things to all people,"[43] but that many courts seem to like precisely because it allows for so much flexibility in the resolution of particular choice-of-law problems.

We'll start our treatment of the Second Restatement with a discussion of its approach in tort cases.

1. Torts

The First Level of Analysis: § 6 and Basic Principles. So what is it that the Second Restatement says? Its overarching, umbrella provision on choice of law implies that strict jurisdiction-selecting provisions are no longer the order of the day:

§ 6. Choice-of-Law Principles

(1) A court, subject to constitutional restrictions, will follow a statutory directive of its own state on choice of law.

(2) When there is no such directive, the factors relevant to the choice of the applicable rule of law include

   (a) the needs of the interstate and international systems,

   (b) the relevant policies of the forum,

   (c) the relevant policies of other interested states and the relative interests of those states in the determination of the particular issue,

   (d) the protection of justified expectations,

   (e) the basic policies underlying the particular field of law,

   (f) certainty, predictability and uniformity of result, and

   (g) ease in the determination and application of the law to be applied.

Without further guidance, this list of factors, more extensive and less concrete than those emphasized by Currie (who was mostly interested in factors (b) and (c)), would present courts with a rather frustrating task. There is nothing to indicate how to rank these factors in importance; some of the factors, such as (a) and (e), seem mystifying when stated in the abstract. The list of factors is not even exclusive; presumably some other factors might come into play in certain kinds of conflicts, but it's not clear what those might be. The Second Restatement did, of course, provide ample commentary on § 6(2), in an effort to supply a more complete account of the meaning of the various factors and how they might be analyzed in

---

43. Douglas Laycock, *Equal Citizens of Equal and Territorial States: The Constitutional Foundations of Choice of Law*, 92 COLUMBIA LAW REVIEW 249, 253 (1992) ("[t]rying to be all things to all people," the Second Restatement "produced mush").

particular kinds of cases. But § 6 remains more a statement of the general aspirations of a good choice-of-law methodology than a helpful heuristic for resolving actual conflicts.

A Second Level of Analysis: The General Principle in Tort Cases. The Second Restatement, however, does move to a second level, in provisions that state and refine the "most significant relationship" concept for particular areas of the law. Thus, for torts we have the following general provision:

§ 145. The General Principle in Tort Cases

(1) The rights and liabilities of the parties with respect to an issue in tort are determined by the local law of the state which, with respect to that issue, has the most significant relationship to the occurrence and the parties under the principles stated in § 6.

(2) Contacts to be taken into account in applying the principles of § 6 to determine the law applicable to an issue include:

    (a) the place where the injury occurred,

    (b) the place where the conduct causing the injury occurred,

    (c) the domicil, residence, nationality, place of incorporation and place of business of the parties, and

    (d) the place where the relationship, if any, between the parties is centered.

These contacts are to be evaluated according to their relative importance with respect to the particular issue.

Considered by itself, § 145 does seem to get us somewhere. Whereas the "most significant contacts" test applied by the New York Court of Appeals in *Auten* and *Haag* gave little consideration to what kinds of contacts should matter, § 145 gives a non-exclusive list for tort cases: (a) place of injury, (b) place of conduct, (c) domicile, and (d) the "seat of the relationship." In other words, § 145(2) gives us a sense of where the "most significant relationship" is likely to be in the majority of tort cases. By mentioning both locus and domicile, § 145(2) gives comfort to both advocates and opponents of the territorial approach. (Note that (d) reflects, to some extent, the view of Judge Breitel in his dissent in *Tooker v. Lopez*, because it ascribes independent significance to the "seat" of a relationship—a consideration that neither Beale nor Currie emphasized.) Of course, the list of contacts is not exclusive, again implying that there might other kinds of contacts that should matter in a particular situation, but it at least provides guidance beyond that which § 145(1) alone would give.

However, the relationship between the calculus envisioned by § 145 and the "general principles" of § 6 is very unclear. Which provision should play more of a role in identifying the state with the "most significant relationship" in a tort case—§ 6 or § 145(2)? If the principles itemized in § 6 cast doubt on the appropriateness of applying the law of the state that would otherwise be chosen under § 145(2), what is the purpose of the latter provision? One can imagine, for example, that the respective interests of the forum and another state, mentioned in § 6(2)(b) and § 6(2)(c), in a particular tort case might counsel the consideration of contacts other than those (locus, domicile, "seat" of relationship) referenced in § 145(2). In that case, § 145(2) would be simply a starting point to get one thinking about the contacts that are likely to be significant. The Second Restatement leaves courts very much at large concerning the interaction between § 6 and § 145 in tort cases.

A Third Level of Analysis: Presumptive Rules. Finally, though, the Second Restatement provides yet a third point of reference for choice of law in tort cases: a lengthy series of "presumptive rules" for specific types of tort issues. Essentially, these are guesses or predictions by the drafters concerning which state is likely to be the one with the "most significant relationship" to a particular dispute with respect to a particular issue in most cases. Here are a couple of examples of such "presumptive rules":

§ 156. Tortious Character of Conduct.

(1) The law selected by application of the rule of § 145 determines whether the actor's conduct was tortious.

(2) The applicable law will usually be the local law of the state where the injury occurred.

* * * *

§ 166. Imputed Negligence.

(1) The law selected by application of the rule of § 145 determines the circumstances in which a person is barred from recovery by the negligence of another.

(2) The applicable law will usually be the local law of the state where the injury occurred.

The word "usually," of course, suggests that the presumptions established by such rules as § 156 and § 166 can be rebutted.

In some situations, by the way, the Second Restatement refrains from specifying a presumptive rule:

§ 167. Survival of Actions.

The law selected by application of the rule of § 145 determines whether a claim for damages for a tort survives the death of the tortfeasor or of the injured person.

No presumptive rule is offered for this situation. Note that this is the provision that would have applied in *Grant v. McAuliffe* (Cal.

1953)[44] had the Second Restatement been in effect there at that time. The Reporter's Comment to § 167 reveals that, while the weight of authority in state courts at the time of the Second Restatement's publication (1971) favored application of the law of the place of conduct and injury, the drafters (no doubt sympathetic to Justice Traynor's instincts in *Grant v. McAuliffe*) declined to make that a presumptive rule, "in view of the growing realization that all issues in tort need not be governed by a single law."

"Presumptive rules" such as those set forth in § 156 and § 166 (and in a great many other sections of the Second Restatement) can be a helpful starting point for analysis, and are no doubt a relief to those leery of *ad hoc* choice-of-law determinations that attempt to assess a variety of factors and "contacts" in each individual case. As such, of course, they augur a return to jurisdiction-selecting rules, whose tyranny supposedly was one of the original motive forces behind the Second Restatement project. While not all of Second Restatement's presumptive rules for torts refer to *lex loci delicti*, § 156 and § 166 do, and in this respect they are not untypical.

In effect, provisions like § 156 and § 166 offer courts the following instructions for resolution of tort conflicts:

— Apply the law of the state that has the "most significant relationship" to the dispute. For many (but not all) of the rules, this will be the law of the state where the injury occurred.

— But sometimes the state referenced by this presumptive rule won't really be the state that has the "most significant relationship" to the dispute. So you need to perform the analysis spelled out in § 145 (under the watchful influence, of course, of the factors mentioned in § 6) anyway. In the end, you're supposed to apply the law of the state that has the "most significant relationship" to the dispute.

If you have to perform the "most significant relationship" inquiry anyway, it would seem that the presumptions embodied in the presumptive rules aren't doing much analytic work. A lot, then, will depend on the real role of the presumptive rules. If the specific rules are only "presumptive" and can be displaced by selection of another state's law under § 6 and § 145, just how strong should the presumption be? How deferential should courts be to the presumptive rules? The Second Restatement, despite its wealth of examples illustrating how the rules should operate, doesn't give much guidance on these questions. As a result, courts differ considerably in their treatment of the presumptive rules. A court eager to

44. Discussed in Chapter 1.

avoid extended analysis of the considerations in § 6 and of the contacts itemized in § 145 can simply apply the relevant presumptive rule with little effort at testing the presumption.[45] More often, courts merely pay lip service to the presumptive rules, taking the opportunity offered by § 6 and § 145 to apply the law that seems to them most appropriate, which will often be different from that referenced by the presumptive rule. Courts' overall predilection for the latter approach is consistent with the basic reason for the Second Restatement's popularity with judges: It is "flexible," which is a euphemistic way of saying that it places a great deal of discretion in the hands of courts making choice-of-law determinations.

A useful illustration of a court's application of the Second Restatement in a tort case is *Phillips v. General Motors Corp.* (Mont. 2000).[46] It is difficult to say that *Phillips* is "typical," since courts have used the loose-jointed Second Restatement in so many ways, but it does represent one court's effort to apply the Second Restatement in a coherent way. The Byrds were involved in a fatal auto accident in Kansas in 1997. Three of them died as a result, and one child was seriously injured. At the time of the accident, the Byrds were domiciliaries of Montana. Their pickup truck, made by General Motors, had been purchased, used, by Mr. Byrd in North Carolina in 1995. GM, of course, is headquartered in Michigan. Thus, Kansas, Montana, North Carolina, and Michigan all had some plausible connection with the dispute. The issues as to which there was a potential conflict of laws were several; of particular importance were limitations that the law of Kansas (the place of the accident) placed on recovery of compensatory damages for noneconomic harm and of punitive damages, both of which can be very important elements of recovery in a product liability case involving wrongful death. The law of Montana (the state of the Byrds' domicile at the time of the accident) did not limit recovery of

---

45. Some courts, evincing general hostility to even the partial modification of the territorial approach embodied by the Second Restatement, go even farther. In *Spinozzi v. ITT Sheraton Corp.*, 174 F.3d 842 (7th Cir. 1999), an Illinois domiciliary was injured, allegedly because of the negligence of defendant's employee, in a Mexican hotel. Mexican law made contributory negligence a complete defense; Illinois uses the "comparative negligence" approach. The plaintiff brought a diversity action in federal court in Illinois, which required the application of Illinois's choice-of-law methodology, which happened to be the Second Restatement. Chief Judge Posner, openly expressing distaste for the "nebulous" nature of non-jurisdiction-select-

ing approaches, professed to find in § 145 a "spectral" re-emergence, phoenix-like, of the *lex loci delicti* rule. Not only did Chief Judge Posner abjure any effort at testing the presumptive reference, he did not even bother to identify the correct presumptive rule (§ 164, which governs contributory fault). A federal court sitting in diversity is required to apply the choice-of-law rules of the state in which it sits (see Chapter 7, below). It is difficult, though, to imagine the Illinois courts expressing such obvious disdain for a choice-of-law methodology that they themselves had adopted to govern tort conflicts in their state.

46. 298 Mont. 438, 995 P.2d 1002 (2000).

noneconomic and punitive damages as Kansas law did. The Montana court concluded that Montana law should apply.

Let us focus first on the *structure* of the court's analysis. The court made the obligatory reference to some of the relevant specific rules, including § 171 (damages). (Oddly, the court did not mention § 175, concerning actions for wrongful death, although this was perhaps defensible because, as to the damages issue, § 171 would have superseded § 175.) Since § 171 does not evince a preference for the law of the locus, simply referencing the "most significant relationship" mantra of § 145, it does not advance the analysis very much. The court understandably went on to assess § 6 and § 145. It is, though, evident that the court was utterly uninterested even in the presumptive rules it deigned to mention, since the court never even stated what the substance of any of those rules is. The court then proceed to consider each of the seven factors identified in § 6(2). It treated the second and third of these factors—"the relevant policies of the forum" and "the relevant policies of other interested states and the relative interests of those states in the determination of the particular issue"—together, and it was in the course of this discussion that it folded in its consideration of the contacts itemized in § 145 (place of injury, domicile of the parties, etc.). Thus, the court's analytic strategy was to (1) cite but essentially ignore the potentially applicable presumptive rules; (2) proceed to a *seriatim* discussion of the considerations mentioned in § 6(2); and (3) analyze the contacts listed in § 145 as part of its discussion of § 6(2)(b) and § 6(2)(c), the "interest" provisions of § 6. Whatever one thinks of this approach to the analysis, it is not surprising that some courts would adopt it, in the absence of further guidance from the Second Restatement itself.

Nor should anyone be surprised that, after all the smoke had cleared, the court concluded that Montana law should apply, with the result that the interests of those who had at the time of the accident been Montana domiciliaries were protected; there were no limitations on noneconomic and punitive damages. As with so many conflicts cases, on a purely impressionistic basis it's hard to argue that this result is less defensible than any other that might have been reached. It is equally hard, however, to take seriously the notion the Montana Supreme Court's formulaic and often conclusory analysis of § 6 and § 145 compels that result.

One example will suffice to illustrate the point. The court in *Phillips* asserted flatly that "the purpose of a state's product liability laws is to protect and provide compensation to its residents and regulate the sale of products within its borders." Thus, the interests underlying Kansas's law limiting punitive damages were not implicated in the case. This general statement regarding the interests lying behind a state's law on product liability may be fair enough, although it would seem that a law specifically *limiting* punitive damages could better be characterized as protecting sellers, not consumers. (How can a limitation on punitive damages "provide compensation to" anyone? Even laws allowing for unlimited punitive damages are meant to serve deterrent, not compensatory, interests.) But when it came to assessing the interests underlying Montana's law, which does not limit punitive damages, the court found that those interests were indeed implicated, because "punitive damages serve to punish and deter conduct deemed wrongful—in this case, placing a defective product into the stream of commerce which subsequently injured a Montana resident." Since GM is a Michigan corporation and its truck was sold in 1985 in North Carolina, coming there into the possession of the Byrds ten years later, before they actually became Montana residents, this distinction between the interests of Kansas and the interests of Montana makes little sense. It would seem that the interests lying behind laws on punitive damages, whether limited or unlimited, would be implicated where the state is the state of manufacture or the state into which the defendant delivers the product, not where the state is one into which a subsequent purchaser happens to have brought the product years later. The question of the plaintiffs' domicile, if it does not coincide with the state into which the manufacturer delivered the product, should be irrelevant to specifically punitive or deterrent interests.

It is not necessary to give a blow-by-blow account of the court's lengthy opinion in *Phillips* to conclude that the Second Restatement left the field wide open for the court to turn a case in which at least two states, if not more, had plausible interests into a case where all the considerations tilted either in the direction of Montana or in no particular direction at all. This, after all, has always been the goal of most courts deciding conflicts cases—to find a choice-of-law reference that is not only correct, but also decisively correct. Paradoxically, the Second Restatement, by giving a seat at the table to all views on proper conflicts methodology and often providing cover for more than one possible outcome, makes possible analyses like that in *Phillips*, in which all factors can be made to point in one direction.

2. Contracts

The Second Restatement's treatment of conflicts in contract cases largely mirrors the pattern in torts, and doesn't require extensive independent treatment. The same three-level analysis applies; the first level, of course, consists of § 6. Just as § 145 represents the "general principle" for tort cases, § 188 does the same for contract cases:

§ 188. Law Governing Contract Issues in Absence of Effective Choice by the Parties

(1) The rights and duties of the parties with respect to an issue in contract are determined by the local law of the state which, with respect to that issue, has the most significant relationship to the transaction and the parties under the principles stated in § 6.

(2) In the absence of an effective choice of law by the parties (see § 187) the contacts to be taken into account in applying the principles of § 6 to determine the law applicable to an issue include:

    (a) the place of contracting;

    (b) the place of negotiation of the contract;

    (c) the place of performance;

    (d) the location of the subject matter of the contract, and

    (e) the domicil, residence, nationality, place of incorporation and place of business of the parties.

These contacts are to be evaluated according to their relative importance with respect to the particular issue.

(3) If the place of negotiating the contract and the place of performance are in the same state, the local law of this state will usually be applied, except as otherwise provided in §§ 189–199 and 203.

(§ 187, concerning the treatment of contractual choice-of-law clauses, is discussed in Chapter 3.) As with § 145, § 188(2) nods in the direction of both the territorial theory and interest analysis by itemizing both the place of the contract and domicile as contacts to be considered (among others). Moreover, § 187(3) serves as a kind of *über*-presumptive rule, specifying that the *lex loci contracti* will usually apply if it is the same place where the contract was negotiated. This presumption thus does not kick in when the signing of a contract in a particular place is an isolated fact bearing no larger significance, as Currie warned against in his series of hypotheticals based on *Milliken v. Pratt*. And, as with torts, § 188 is supplemented with a series of presumptive rules applying to specific types of contracts and specific types of contract issues.

A somewhat larger number of states have adopted the Second Restatement for conflicts in contract cases than have done so for conflicts in tort cases. In general, conflicts in contract cases, whatever methodology is used, produces less controversy than conflicts in tort cases. The widespread use of choice-of-law clauses in contracts, at least by sophisticated economic actors, is one reason for this. Another reason is that large areas of commercial law are governed by the Uniform Commercial Code, which includes its own choice-of-law principles and which in any case is designed to provide a substantial measure of uniformity to commercial law. This is not to say that conflicts in contract law do not frequently arise, because they do, particularly with respect to matters of contract interpretation. It is simply that, in general, differences between the states in the law of personal injury (particularly in such areas as product liability, mass torts, medical malpractice, measure of damages, etc.) speak to more intensely held views of public policy than do such legal differences as may exist with respect to contract interpretation and enforcement. So, even if courts applying the Second Restatement to contract cases may be engaged in a collective enterprise that is no more coherent in its outcomes and analysis than is the case with respect to torts, the Second Restatement contracts cases tend to provoke less severe criticism, even from scholars who specialize in Severe Criticism.

H. The Better Law

Yes, there is a choice-of-law methodology known colloquially as the "better law" approach. It all sounds so simple. The court, faced with a conflict of laws, solves the problem by choosing ... the "better" of the laws competing for recognition. However, in reality the methodology is neither as inane in conception nor as simple to apply as this description makes it sound.

The "better law" methodology is actually based on the scholarly ideas of Professor Robert A. Leflar, who in 1966 published two important articles on the subject of "choice-influencing considerations" in American conflicts law.[47] Leflar was engaged in an enterprise that had occupied many scholars throughout the twentieth century, including those who during the 1950s and 1960s were in the process of drafting the Second Restatement: identification of a list of general factors and purposes that should govern a court making a conflicts ruling. Beale, for example, had also compiled such a list of considerations, but simply concluded that the territorial, jurisdiction-selecting approach best subserved those purposes. Leflar, by contrast, set out his list of factors as a guide to which courts could directly refer in making their rulings—as, in essence, a choice-of-law methodology in itself. The identification of these "choice-influencing considerations" was, in Leflar's rendering, both a normative and a descriptive enterprise. Leflar argued that these were the crucial considerations that *should* govern choice-of-law determinations, but to a certain extent Leflar identified these particular considerations because his study of thousands of conflicts

---

47. Robert A. Leflar, *Choice–Influencing Considerations in Conflicts Law,* 41 NEW YORK UNIVERSITY LAW REVIEW 267 (1966); Robert A. Leflar, *Conflicts Law:*

cases convinced him that these *were* what had mattered in the past and would continue to matter to courts making such rulings, no matter how much we might wish otherwise.

Leflar's five "choice-influencing considerations" were these:

(1) Predictability of Results;

(2) Maintenance of Interstate and International Order;

(3) Simplification of the Judicial Task;

(4) Advancement of the Forum's Governmental Interests;

(5) Application of the Better Rule of Law.

(The first four of these can be found, albeit in restated form, in § 6 of the Second Restatement.) To Leflar, these considerations did not constitute a heuristic that could or should be applied in mechanical fashion, but rather were principles that ought to inform the forum's ultimate decision on choice of law. In his two articles, Leflar supplied a wealth of hypothetical examples (several based on actual decided cases) to illustrate the meaning of these considerations and how they had played out, or might play out, in litigation. Leflar's approach merits mention here and in most conflicts casebooks because the courts of Minnesota, Wisconsin, Rhode Island, New Hampshire, and Arkansas have actually adopted his approach as their choice-of-law methodology, at least for certain types of cases.

Both the hypothetical illustrations given by Leflar in his articles and the actual conflicts decisions rendered by the courts in the states where his methodology has been adopted suggest that, in many if not most cases, the analysis boils down to considerations (4) and (5). (1) "Predictability of Results," for example, proved mostly irrelevant in tort cases.[48] The emphasis on predictability can be a helpful guide in contracts cases, but it's a principle that most modern approaches to choice of law recognize, for example in their hospitality to choice-of-law clauses. In fact, the age-old emphasis on vindicating "what the parties would have intended" is itself based on the idea that the promotion of predictability is an important consideration. (2) "Maintenance of Interstate and International Order," a criterion that most people find rather vague (and which also appears in the Second Restatement), seemed simply to suggest that the forum should not "ruffle feathers" by being too unseemly in the disregard of foreign law. Therefore, it verges on circularity, since the point of the choice-influencing considerations is to guide a court toward a reasonable choice-of-law ruling, and the more rea-

More on Choice–Influencing Considerations, 54 California Law Review 1584 (1966).

48. In fact, the statement that considerations of predictability do not matter in choice of law with respect to torts because "people do not plan to have accidents," which has been made by both courts and scholars, is too facile. If one believes (not everyone does) that there are some choice-of-law references in tort situations that accord better than others with people's general intuitions, than the use of those references will promote a kind of predictability.

sonable the ruling is, the less it will ruffle feathers. (3) "Simplification of the Judicial Task" helps explain why courts should apply
their own rules of procedure, but beyond that almost always results
in a conclusion that the forum can apply forum law and foreign law
with about equal ease, at least in domestic cases.

Consideration (4) constitutes a recognition, echoed by Currie
although rejected by Beale and other scholars who consider avoidance of forum-shopping among the high priorities of any choice-of-
law methodology, that "a court has a natural and largely justifiable
primary concern with advancement of the governmental interests
of its own state."[49] Courts, in this view, are not simply neutral
tribunals that should be equally indifferent to the interests of the
forum and the foreign jurisdiction; they are, in part, governing
institutions whose sovereign power is limited and defined by the
jurisdiction in which they sit. This suggests that a refined assessment of whether forum interests would be advanced by application
of its law should form a legitimate part of the choice-of-law process.
Interestingly, whereas Currie's "interest analysis" specified that
the interests of foreign state as well as that of the forum should be
assessed when determining whether a "true" or a "false" conflict is
present, Leflar's consideration (4) speaks only of the forum's interests.[50] This reminds us that Leflar's choice-influencing considerations are all rooted in what courts have done and what courts can
be expected to do; courts dealing with conflicts problems have
invariably been attentive to the interests of the forum because it *is*
the forum, but tend to be attentive to the claims of another state's
interests mostly out of reciprocity considerations (*i.e.* enlightened
self-interest).

In the end, courts applying Leflar's approach have largely
boiled the problem down to consideration (5), the "better rule of
law," which is why the phrase "the better law" has come to be
shorthand for the overall methodology. Leflar somewhat ruefully
acknowledged the likelihood that courts would, in general, tend to
find that forum law was "better." In fact, this is a natural consequence of the observation in consideration (4) that courts are
naturally interested in vindication of the forum's policy. Yet Leflar
made clear, much as Cardozo had indicated in his discussion of the
public policy exception, that "better" must mean something more
than "different." Designating one of the competing laws as the
"better law" was most appropriate when the other law was an
anachronistic relic, or was dramatically out of step with the law of
most other jurisdictions, or, perhaps, struck the court as licensing a

49. Leflar, *Choice–Influencing Considerations, supra* n.47.

50. At the same time, of course,
Currie's recommended solution for "true
conflicts," application of forum law, did
express an important preference for forum interests.

particularly unjust result.[51] In fact, overzealous preference for forum law might run afoul of consideration (2), since brazen disregard for foreign law could cause undesirable interstate friction. Moreover, Leflar hastened to emphasize that courts should not hesitate to regard foreign (not just forum) law as "better" in appropriate cases. Needless to say, these counsels of moderation and restraint have not always been honored in the observance. Still, courts have at times also indicated a sense of proportion in their application of the "better law" approach.

Minnesota, one of the handful of states to have adopted Leflar's "better law" approach as its choice-of-law methodology, offers an interesting example. In *Hague v. Allstate Insurance Co.* (Minn. 1978),[52] considered at greater length in Chapter 4 (concerning constitutional limitations on choice of law), a Wisconsin motorcyclist was killed in an accident in Wisconsin. He had been employed for 15 years prior to the accident across the border in Minnesota. His auto insurance policy (which covered three autos owned by him, although not his motorcycle) provided $15,000 in uninsured motorist coverage. Minnesota law would have permitted "stacking" of the uninsured motorist coverage to provide for a total of $45,000 in benefits, while Wisconsin law would have rejected "stacking" and limited coverage to $15,000. The decedent's widow (who, after the accident but prior to initiating litigation, had moved to Minnesota) sued in Minnesota court for a declaration that Minnesota law applied and that stacking would be allowed. The Minnesota Supreme Court, applying the "better law" approach, agreed with the plaintiff and held that Minnesota law applied, although the connections with Minnesota were attenuated and those with Wisconsin appeared considerably stronger. Among other reasons, the Minnesota Supreme Court considered the Minnesota rule to be "better" because "it requires the cost of accidents with uninsured motorists to be spread more broadly through insurance premiums than does the Wisconsin rule." The Minnesota Supreme Court's application of the "better law" approach in this case has been widely criticized for its transparent effort to arrive at the application of forum law.[53]

51. One might notice the parallels here with *Offshore Rental Co. v. Continental Oil Co.*, 22 Cal.3d 157, 148 Cal. Rptr. 867, 583 P.2d 721 (1978), discussed above in connection with the "comparative impairment" approach for resolving true conflicts. California's odd "key employee" rule in *Offshore Rental* not only fit Leflar's conception of when another law could legitimately be regarded as "better"; it also illustrated that the analysis could sometimes result in the forum's choice of foreign rather than forum law.

52. *Hague v. Allstate Ins. Co.*, 289 N.W.2d 43 (Minn. 1978), *aff'd*, 449 U.S. 302 (1981).

53. Note that, while one could characterize the Minnesota Supreme Court's analysis as expressing (1) a preference for forum law, it could equally well be described as expressing (2) a preference for a Minnesota domiciliary or (3) a preference for policyholders in insurance cases, or any and all of these. Or, for that matter, an objective, good-faith effort to apply the law and reach the legal-

Even Justice Stevens, who voted with the majority in the U.S. Supreme Court to sustain the constitutionality of the application of forum law in *Hague*, complained that the Minnesota Supreme Court's decision was "plainly unsound as a matter of normal conflicts law."[54]

Yet in a more recent but similar case, the Minnesota Supreme Court has exhibited a more even-handed approach. In *Jepson v. General Casualty Co. of Wisconsin* (Minn. 1994),[55] the plaintiff, a Minnesota resident at the time, was injured in Arizona while a passenger in an automobile. He had owned a business in North Dakota, which had purchased an insurance policy covering seven vehicles (six of which were registered in North Dakota and none in Minnesota). Evidently, the premiums charged for this North Dakota policy were lower than had the policy been purchased in Minnesota. As in *Hague*, Minnesota law permitted "stacking," while North Dakota law did not; and, like Ms. Hague, Jepson argued that the Minnesota courts should apply the Minnesota rule. The Minnesota Supreme Court rejected his argument. In its application of the "better law" approach, it gave considerations (1)–(4) more genuine reflection than many courts have. In fact, it found that considerations both of predictability and of "interstate order" militated in favor of the application of North Dakota law. The court drily observed that the forum-shopping ambitions of the plaintiff (who was by now an Arizona resident) were rather obvious. Most significant, though, it disdained the predilection for finding that forum law was "better law" that had seemed implicit in its *Hague* decision and some other Minnesota decisions: "Sometimes different laws are neither better nor worse in an objective way, just different." It rejected the notion that "forum law [must] always be the better law" and it held that North Dakota law, not Minnesota law, should apply.

While not all courts have applied the "better law" approach with the same sense of proportion as that demonstrated by the Minnesota Supreme Court's decision in its decision in *Jepson*, that case does suggest that the Leflar approach need not be a recipe for *ad hoc* provincialism, pure and simple. If the "better law" approach nevertheless seems to leave courts pretty much at large in making their choice-of-law rulings, remember that this is no less true for the Second Restatement and, in the eyes of many, interest analysis. In fact, one might say that Leflar's candid acknowledgment of the priority of forum law at least makes concrete what the Second

ly correct result. We have no calculus for determining which of these characterizations best describes the court's decision.

54. *Allstate Ins. Co. v. Hague*, 449 U.S. 302, 324 (1981) (Stevens, J., concurring).

55. 513 N.W.2d 467 (Minn.1994).

Restatement largely obscures. Leflar's "choice-influencing considerations" remain the conflicts methodology in several states, so it is well to be aware of that methodology's basic premises.

I. Does It Matter?

The "modern" choice-of-law methods described in this chapter have one very important thing in common: They are not the First Restatement. One hallmark of their collective departure from the territorial approach is their somewhat reduced emphasis on *locus* and a corresponding concern with domicile, a move that would have dismayed Joseph Beale. The real question, though, is how much the modern methods actually differ from one another. At the conceptual level, of course, it's easy to see some differences. Proponents of interest analysis, of course, rue the ghost of territoriality that seems to animate much of the Second Restatement. "Comparative impairment" embraces an approach to true conflicts that Brainerd Currie would not have accepted. Devotees of the Second Restatement may find Leflar's "Better Law" approach to be too open in its investigation of the substantive merits of the laws competing for recognition. But the proof of the pudding is in the actual decisions of the courts. Empirical studies are few and the portrait they draw is radically incomplete, but preliminary indications from the work that has been done thus far suggest that cases tend to come out pretty much the same way regardless of whether interest analysis, the Second Restatement, or the "Better Law" approach is used.

Whether this hypothesis (perhaps a bit deflating to theorists of the domestic choice-of-law process) would survive rigorous empirical scrutiny remains to be seen. But its general tenor would not surprise critics of the "choice-of-law revolution" that began over half a century ago. Their common quarrel with *all* of the post-territorialist methodologies was their licensing of *ad hoc* judicial policymaking in conflicts cases, substituting vague and contested concepts like "interests" and "contacts" for the disciplining hand of concrete *lex loci* rules. Whichever post-territorialist method they use, courts tend to turn its flexibility to their advantage in reaching results that simply make sense to them. Juristic argument concerning the domestic choice-of-law process has entered a lull; when the next great cycle of debates over American conflicts law arrives, it would not be surprising to see a revival of territorialism, even as the principle of territoriality slowly ebbs on the global stage.

Chapter 3

A FEW AREAS OF MODERN INTEREST

For the most part, Chapters 1 and 2 focused on identifying and fleshing out the choice-of-law methodologies that have predominated in the theory and practice of American conflicts law. We've considered the problem of conflicts as it arises in specific substantive areas of the law, but only as a way of helping us understand the basic conflicts approaches. And a number of our illustrative cases concerned specific substantive problems that you're not likely to find today; very few states have "guest statutes" any longer, the right of married women to make and enforce contracts is recognized in every state, and the "fellow servant rule" is now an ancient relic. In this chapter we'll take a very brief look at a handful of examples of choice-of-law problems that are more likely to arise, even if only episodically, in contemporary American law. We're just skimming the surface here; we want to give you a truer view of the current landscape than emerges from the first two chapters.

A. A View of the Landscape

Having explored the basic conflicts approaches, students usually are interested in knowing how widely used the different approaches are. Devising an accurate portrait of the choice-of-law methodologies employed by the various states is a hazardous undertaking at best. Some states use different methodologies for different types of legal problems. Some state courts may claim to be using one methodology (say, the Second Restatement), while the results they reach suggest they are in reality applying another (say, *lex loci*). Some state courts change their basic choice-of-law approach without troubling to say so explicitly. Sometimes, different courts in the same state may apply different methodologies, and occasionally even the state's highest court seems unaware of some of its own choice-of-law precedents.

There is one place to turn for a timely and accurate scorecard of the conflicts landscape: Dean Symeon Symeonides's *Annual Choice-of-Law Survey*, published each year in the *American Journal of Comparative Law*. His most recent survey, covering cases decided through the end of 2009, concludes that almost half the states now use (or profess to use) the Second Restatement in tort cases, and that almost the same number use the Second Restatement for contract cases (these two groups overlap, but are not identical).[1] No other conflicts methodology garners the support of nearly as large a number of states. Dean Symeonides's survey, while summarizing and analyzing the year's most important conflicts cases of all types, includes only torts and contracts when presenting in table format the different states' approaches. Torts and contracts together account for the largest number of conflicts rulings, and cases involving them tend to feature the courts' closest analyses of the state's law of conflicts. Certain other types of conflicts will often be governed by traditional conflicts rules (real and personal property) or statutory solutions (trusts and estates and domestic relations). But be sure always to check the state's case law concerning conflicts of the type you are researching.

B.   Statutory Solutions to Choice of Law

All the cases on choice of law that we saw in Chapters 1 and 2—and, for that matter, virtually all such American cases that we will see elsewhere in this book—feature courts applying conflicts principles in common-law fashion. That is, the forum's law of choice of law in these cases is to be found in case law, not in statutes. That has been the case from the earliest days of the Republic. One historical exception is Louisiana; consistent with the civil-law roots of Louisiana law, the choice-of-law rules of that state are codified. And, as noted at the end of this section, Oregon has recently codified its law of choice of law in the areas of contracts, torts, and other non-contractual obligations.

Is there an argument to be made that more states should codify their choice-of-law rules in statutes? On the surface, it is hard to see why this would promise any improvement in the results reached by courts in deciding conflicts cases. The real debate in American conflicts law is not over whether the law of choice of law should be embodied in common law or in statutes, but whether that law should be rule-based, as in the *lex loci* method, or more of an *approach*, in which (as with interest analysis or the Second Restatement) a more explicitly *ad hoc* process is used. Either method could as easily be specified by a statute as by decisional law, and it wouldn't seem to make a great deal of difference either way. In other words, the desirability of a statutory approach is largely a function of what the statute would say. Moreover, the First and

---

1. Symeon C. Symeonides, *Choice of Law in the American Courts in 2009: Twenty–Third Annual Survey*, 58 AMERI- CAN JOURNAL OF COMPARATIVE LAW (forthcoming 2010). For citations to the entire series of *Annual Surveys*, see *id.* at n.1.

Second Restatements are themselves in the nature of codifications, so any state whose courts profess to adopt one or the other *in toto* would in effect be applying law that is "statutory" in form, if not in the process by which it was promulgated. And it's clear that courts, faced with codified rules or principles such as are embodied in the Restatements, will be in practice little more constrained than in the application of non-codified principles.

Of course, there are many examples of statutes that govern conflicts with respect to particular kinds of issues. For example, in Chapter 1, we discussed borrowing statutes in connection with statutory limitations periods. These statutes direct the forum to apply a foreign statute of limitations in certain circumstances, even if the forum would ordinarily apply *lex fori* for its limitations principle. Another example is the choice-of-law provisions of the Uniform Commercial Code, discussed later in this Chapter. We also discuss, later in this Chapter, the problem of conflicts in auto insurance cases; some of these conflicts are governed by state statutory provisions. Questions of probate and testamentary succession can generate many problems of both choice of law and recognition of judgments, for example because conventional doctrine holds that most such questions are governed by the law of the decedent's domicile, but that *lex loci rei sitae* must have final authority over real property located outside the domicile. Most states have statutes that deal with some (but far from all) of the conflicts problems that can arise in the probate context. Section 2–506 of the Uniform Probate Code, which has been in adopted in about 20 states, provides:

> A written will is valid if executed in compliance with [other sections of the Code dealing with execution] or if its execution complies with the law at the time of execution of the place where the will is executed, or of the law of the place where at the time of execution or at the time of death the testator is domiciled, has a place of abode, or is a national.[2]

One state that has recently embarked on a project to codify large parts, if not all, of its law of choice of law is Oregon. In 2001, the state enacted a statute codifying a set of conflicts rules for contract disputes. And on January 1, 2010, a second statute, specifying conflicts rules for torts and other non-contractual claims, went into effect in Oregon. This statute was drafted by Dean Symeon C. Symeonides and Professor James A.R Nafziger of Willamette University College of Law.[3] The statute embodies assumptions drawn from both older and new approaches to conflicts. For

---

2.   Uniform Probate Code, § 2–506 (2004).

3.   *See* Symeon C. Symeonides, *Oregon's New Choice-of-Law Codification* *for Tort Conflicts: An Exegesis*, 88 OREGON LAW REVIEW (forthcoming 2010).

example, it accepts the "characterization" process and provides that characterization is to be governed by the law of the forum. It specifies *lex loci*-type rules for a variety of tort scenarios defined by the domicile of the parties, the location of the wrong, and so on. But in a section of the statute dealing with "residual" scenarios–those not falling within the specified scenarios for which *lex loci* rules are provided–it indicates that "the rights and liabilities of the parties with regard to disputed issues in a non-contractual claim are governed by the law of the state whose contacts with the parties and the dispute and whose policies on the disputed issues make application of the state's law the most appropriate for those issues."[4] The statute identifies a number of general factors, not unlike those found in § 145 of the Second Restatement, to be taken into account in making this determination.

The Oregon statute is surprisingly and impressively compact. It will be interesting to see the experience of Oregon courts in applying it unfold and to compare the results with those that obtained under the more conventional non-statutory conflicts rules in those courts.

C. The "Rule of Validation," Party Autonomy, and Enforcement of Contractual Choice-of-Law Provisions

In Chapter 1, we considered the case of *Milliken v. Pratt*, as an example of how the traditional territorial choice-of-law approach treats conflicts in contract cases, using the rule of *lex loci contracti*. In Chapter 2, we briefly considered how some "modern" choice-of-law methodologies deal with such contract conflicts. In practice, though, the legal issues raised by contract disputes are not all of a piece. In particular, issues of contract *validity* are roughly distinguishable from issues of contract *interpretation*. The traditional conflicts rule for questions of contract validity was to apply the law of the place where the contract was made, and for questions of contract interpretation (which tends to embrace questions surrounding the performance of the contract), the usual rule was to apply the law of place of performance. Obviously, these two places often were different.

Today, legal disputes concerning the validity of a contract are less common than disputes concerning interpretation and performance. But it's important to explore the problem of choice of law as it arises in the context of conflicts concerning the validity of a contract, because the way in which courts have resolved this problem says a lot about the nature of conflicts law in general. Of

---

4. Section 9, reprinted in *id.* at 72.

particular importance is the degree to which conflicts doctrine approves and even encourages the power of the parties to select, in their contract, the law to govern any disputes over the contract.

Enforcement of Contracts: Private Prerogative or State Policy? The basic conceptions underlying our law of contract differ in some important ways from the conceptions underlying, say, the modern law of torts. Today, we regard tort law as an expression of public policy. When tort law varies from state to state, we are apt to say that those differences reflect differences in public policy concerning such things as the standard of care to which people must adhere; the extent to which persons should be made whole for their losses; what role deterrence should play in tort law; to what extent the goal of tort law is to provide social insurance and regulation of risk; and so on. Those values and policies are expressed in the *state's* positive rules of tort law; we don't, by and large, confer on private parties the power to determine for themselves (or by agreement) what their duties of due care are. Certainly, as you know from tort law, the ability of parties to "contract out" of their basic duties under tort law is very limited.

Historically and philosophically, contract law rests on somewhat different premises. The basic principle that common-law courts will enforce private agreements is not simply a "rule of positive law" that some jurisdictions recognize and others do not, in the way that some jurisdictions recognize limitations on punitive damages and others do not. It is a basic principle of Anglo–American jurisprudence that, historically at least, finds its source in the customs and practices of private parties, not in the sovereign prerogative of the state to set social policy. This conception of contract law, emphasizing the intentions and preferences of the parties, underlay the development of the basic *lex loci contracti* principle for conflicts of law in contract matters. The late-eighteenth-century conflicts decisions by Lord Mansfield grounded the *lex loci contracti* rule largely on his observation that the parties ordinarily could be presumed to have *intended* that the law of the place of the contract would govern any disputes that might arise.

At the same time, despite its foundation in principles of private preference, English and American law never supposed that courts were bound to enforce all private contracts, no matter what they specified. To use only the most extreme example, a court would not enforce a contract for murder. In a sense, of course, such a principle did prioritize a kind of "social policy" over private preference. Some contracts are void and unenforceable because the state reprehends them. Thus, the law governing contract validity has always had something of a double character: There is a strong disposition in English and American law to enforce agreements reached by private parties, but the enforceability of such agreements does raise legitimate questions of state policy, and the state is empowered to make certain kinds of contracts illegal or unenforceable. Both party autonomy and state regulatory authority have their claims in the law of contract.

This double character can emerge vividly in the law of conflicts with respect to contract validity issues. While every state regards contracts to commit crimes as unenforceable, there are other kinds of contracts that some but not all states may regard as unenforceable. In the nineteenth century, several states barred the enforcement of contracts regarding speculation in futures, as a kind of gambling. Today, a few states bar or limit the enforcement of covenants not to compete.[5] Such prohibitions constitute an expression of social or economic policy, not the proscription of a universal moral wrong. The question is how conflicts law should respond to this situation when a contract has meaningful connections with two states, one of which regards the contract as enforceable and the other does not.

The "Rule of Validation." Let's first take up the question of how this question should be answered in a situation where there is no choice-of-law provision in the contract, and the law of one of the two interested states regards a particular provision of the contract as unenforceable. On the surface, this seems to be a conventional conflicts problem, to be resolved by whatever choice-of-law methodology or rule is provided by the law of the forum. Thus, the *lex loci* approach might dictate that the dispute should be governed by the law of the place where the contract was made; interest analysis would require a discriminating analysis of the purposes lying behind the respective states' rules; and so on. On this view, if one of the states bars the enforcement of the particular contractual provision involved (say, a noncompete covenant), and application of the forum's choice-of-law method leads to that state, then that provision should not be enforced by the forum. However, it's possible to take another view of the situation. If one credits the notion that parties usually intend for their contracts to be valid and enforceable—as one ancient authority put it, "The parties cannot be presumed to have contemplated a law which would defeat their engagements"[6]—why not simply apply *whichever* of the two laws would result in enforcement of the agreement?

5. A covenant not to compete or "non-compete clause" is a contractual provision binding a party (generally, an employee) not to engage in professional activity in competition with the other party (usually, the employer). Frequently these provisions are designed to keep the employee from working for a competitor, or setting up his own business in the same field, for a period of time after his employment with the original employer comes to an end.

6. Sir Robert Phillimore, Commentaries Upon International Law IV: 528 (3d ed. 1889). Incidentally, this homily brings to mind the case of *Milliken v. Pratt* (Mass. 1878), discussed in Chapter

This approach, which courts have occasionally applied, is sometimes called the "rule of validation." Clearly it represents a substantive bias in favor of the enforcement of agreements, even those regarded as unenforceable by the state that might otherwise supply the governing rule of decision, and it places considerable emphasis on the presumed intentions of the parties to the contract. If you like the "rule of validation," you probably are favorable toward the dimension of contract law that stresses the importance of validating party intentions (actual or presumed), rather than the prerogative of states to determine, as a matter of policy, which contracts are enforceable and which are not. Try pushing this idea a little farther: If you like the approach specified by the rule of validation, why not have a conflicts rule for such contract validity issues that says that the contract will be held valid and enforceable if the law of *any* jurisdiction, whether connected with the dispute or not, would regard it as enforceable? Why should the inquiry be limited to those states having a plausible connection with the dispute? Answering these questions will help clarify for you the extent to which you regard the intentions of private parties, rather than state regulation of contractual arrangements, as paramount.[7]

Enforcement of Contractual Choice-of-Law Provisions. The more relevant, real-world conflicts problem that arises in this context concerns the effect and enforceability of choice-of-law clauses. Today, business organizations and other persons and entities with competent legal representation will often insert choice-of-law provisions into their agreements. The insertion of a choice-of-law provision can provide a measure of certainty in case of a dispute and perhaps result in the application of a body of substantive law that is better developed and better fitted to the contract's subject matter than another state's law would be. (More disturbingly, where the choice-of-law provision is part of an adhesive contract in which one party has substantially greater bargaining power, it can subject the other party to a significant disadvantage in the case of a dispute.) The principal question is whether such choice-of-law provisions are generally enforceable, and if so to what extent. The short answer is that such provisions are generally enforceable; federal law regards them as presumptively enforceable, and the

1, in which Massachusetts law held that married women's contracts are unenforceable. Should Mrs. Pratt have been able to execute the guaranty and then rely on her state's law to invalidate the agreement? The "rule of validation" would say no.

7. The "rule of validation" plays a role in Larry Kramer's proposal, discussed in Chapter 2, that a recognition of "shared policies" can serve as the basis of an approach to resolving true conflicts. Kramer argues that, since all states have an underlying commitment to the enforcement of agreements, conflicts between states as to the enforcement of a particular kind of agreement can be resolved with a minimum of long-term friction by recourse to that general rule of enforcement.

states have predominantly (though not universally) taken the same position. As with other kinds of contractual provisions, it is the law of contract that in the first instance determines whether a choice-of-law provision should regarded as unenforceable, based on unconscionability or some other reason. But the law of conflicts also has to take a position on whether the law supplied by a choice-of-law provision should govern conflicts to which it applies, because the effect of validating the provision will often be to displace the law that, according to governing choice-of-law principles, would otherwise apply.

Jurists schooled in traditional conflicts theory found it difficult to credit the notion that the parties could choose the law to be applied. This is not surprising, since Beale and others saw *lex loci* rules as recognizing "vested rights" whose authority was independent of, and anterior to, any efforts of private parties to alter them. In a famous passage, Judge Learned Hand stated:

> People cannot by agreement substitute the law of another place; they may of course incorporate any provisions they wish into their agreements—a statute like anything else—and when they do, courts will try to make sense out of the whole, so far as they can. *But an agreement is not a contract, except as the law says it shall be*, and to try to make it one is to pull on one's bootstraps. Some law must impose the obligation, and the parties have nothing whatever to do with that; no more than with whether their acts are torts or crimes.[8]

This passage, particularly its italicized portion, dramatizes one side of what I have called the "double character" of contract. If Judge Hand is correct—and, in light of modern law's presumption that all law is positive law, his point seems well taken—there is something illegitimate about the power of private parties to supplant the legal rights recognized by *lex loci* (or other conflicts) rules by agreeing on a choice-of-law provision. There is a cart-before-the-horse quality (or, in Judge Hand's preferred metaphor, "pulling on one's bootstraps") to saying that a contract is valid because a particular provision in the contract says, albeit indirectly (by selecting the law of a validating jurisdiction), that it is valid. If the parties cannot expect to have a court enforce a contractual provision stating, "This contract is valid and enforceable," despite governing law to the contrary, why should they be able to do the same thing indirectly, by inserting a choice-of-law clause?

On the other hand, Hand's analogy between choice-of-law provisions that operate to displace the law concerning contract

---

8. *E. Gerli & Co. v. Cunard S.S. Co.*, 48 F.2d 115, 117 (2d Cir. 1931) (emphasis added).

validity that is identified by the applicable conflicts rule, and those that purport to determine whether the parties' "acts are torts or crimes," may be too facile. Earlier conflicts theories less committed to dogmatic conceptions of vested rights, such as those of Lord Mansfield and Justice Joseph Story, saw choice of law in the area of contract validity as being more rooted in party intention. That's not what criminal law or the law of torts is about.

Whatever the conceptual power of Judge Hand's argument, modern realities make it an impractical basis for determining the validity of choice-of-law provisions. The efficiencies to be realized through the use and enforcement of such provisions are too valuable to forgo. Knowing that such provisions are presumptively enforceable, parties can make substantial use of them to clarify the legal background for their transactions, and thus avoid litigation over many conflicts questions. Most, though not all, states regard such clauses as presumptively enforceable. And, more often than not, choice-of-law clauses operate to clarify matters of performance and interpretation, rather than fundamental questions of enforceability at all.

But some nagging questions do remain. Assuming that choice-of-law provisions are, as a general matter, enforceable, is there any requirement that the jurisdiction whose law is chosen have a meaningful connection with the transaction? Why may the parties not choose *any* law that will regard their agreement as enforceable? And (to return to Judge Hand's point) consider this example: If the parties are both domiciliaries of a state that regards their contract as legally usurious, and thus unenforceable, and the contract is made and to be performed there—in a word, if the case is wholly domestic to that state—it's obvious that the parties cannot insert into their contract a provision stating, "The rate of interest specified in this contract is valid and this contract is enforceable, notwithstanding the law of this state." At least, that is, they can't expect such a provision to be enforced. But if the parties can't do that, why should they be able to insert a choice-of-law provision that simply selects the law of a state that does not regard the contract as unlawfully usurious?

Section 187 of the Second Restatement. The conflicts rule that you are likely to encounter most often in this context is § 187 of the Second Restatement, concerning the enforceability of choice-of-law provisions. (More states have adopted the Second Restatement, or some version of its basic rules, for contracts conflicts than any other choice-of-law approach.)

Section 187 distinguishes between choice-of-law clauses concerning an issue "which the parties could have resolved by an explicit provision in their agreement directed to that issue," and choice-of-law clauses concerning issues that the parties could not have so resolved. In essence, this is a distinction between matters of contract interpretation and matters of contract validity. Generally speaking, a state's rules with respect to contract interpretation are "default rules"; parties to a transaction are entitled to "contract around" such rules if they wish, by including a specific provision to that effect, because the default rule is merely a convenience in order to prevent perpetual relitigation of common contract interpretation problems, rather than a statement of substantive state policy concerning what contracts are valid or not. Suppose, for example, that the case law in the state where a contract was made indicates that, in the absence of a specific provision to the contrary, delivery of the contracted-for goods within a reasonable time after the date specified in the contract will constitute substantial performance. The parties may specify in the contract, however, that *any* lateness beyond the date specified in the contract will result in a breach of the agreement. The parties have thus contracted around the state's default rule. The "substantial performance" issue is clearly one "which the parties could have resolved by an explicit provision in their agreement directed to that issue."

Section 187(1) states that if, instead of including in the contract the explicit provision concerning lateness of delivery and breach, the parties include a provision directing that disputes over performance will be governed by the law of State B, which (unlike State A) provides as its default rule that any lateness beyond the specified due date will constitute a breach, that choice-of-law provision will be enforced. Moreover, the parties can choose the law of *any* state to apply to such disputes, even a state that has no apparent connection to the transaction. This all makes sense. If the parties are free to incorporate a provision that directly supplants the local "default rule," there seems no reason why they may not accomplish the same end by designating the law of some state whose application would achieve the same result. The sovereignty of the state whose law is "ousted" by this process is not offended, because that state contemplates that its default rules for contract interpretation can be altered anyway, by choice of the parties.

Section 187(2), however, which concerns choice-of-law provisions governing an issue "which the parties could *not* have resolved by an explicit provision in their agreement directed to that issue," necessarily takes a different approach. Section 187(2) is primarily concerned with questions of contract validity. (For the sake of simplicity, we have been using fairly obvious, heavy-handed examples, such as contracts for murder, that are void in their entirety. Questions of contract validity, however, can also pertain to specific provisions of a contract, such as acceleration provisions or other provisos that state law might regard as unconscionable or otherwise unenforceable.) For these situations, § 187(2) provides that choice-of-law clauses are enforceable, "unless either

"(a) the chosen state has no substantial relationship to the parties or the transaction and there is no other reasonable basis for the parties' choice, or

"(b) application of the law of the chosen state would be contrary to a fundamental policy of a state which has a materially greater interest than the chosen state in the determination of the particular issue and which, under the rule of § 188, would be the state of the applicable law in the absence of an effective choice of law by the parties."

As we attempt to make sense of § 187(2), let's remember two things. First, of course, the enforcement of a choice-of-law clause only arises as an issue if its operation would displace the law that would be selected by operation of the otherwise applicable choice-of-law rule. From a conflicts perspective, that's the only situation that really interests us where a choice-of-law clause is concerned. Second, the "otherwise applicable choice-of-law rule" contemplated by § 187(2) is § 188, the Second Restatement's basic choice-of-law provision for contract conflicts. Note, though, that a state might conceivably follow § 187 for issues concerning choice-of-law agreements, even though it has not adopted the Second Restatement more generally or § 188 in particular for contracts conflicts. In such a case, the law potentially displaced by the choice-of-law provision would be that chosen by whatever choice-of-law rule is usually applied by the forum for contracts conflicts, be it *lex loci contracti* or something else.

As you can see, § 187(2) struggles to reconcile the principle of party autonomy with the prerogative of the state to regulate contracts. Presumptively such choice-of-law provisions are enforceable, even with respect to issues of contract validity, which is a strong gesture in the direction of party autonomy and the ability of parties to "contract around" even state rules that reflect important policy choices. Section 187(2) obviously does not give much credit to Judge Hand's concerns about the "bootstrapping" nature of such choice-of-law agreements. In subsections (a) and (b), however, § 187(2) cuts back on such party autonomy, and recognizes important state interests that must be respected before those provisions can be given effect. So, for example, party autonomy in its purest form (short of allowing the parties to create state law in their contracts) would allow the parties to select the law of *any* jurisdiction that might provide them a favorable ruling concerning the contract's validity; but § 187(2)(a) significantly limits this, by requiring either that the state whose law is chosen by the parties have a "substantial relationship to the parties or the transaction" or that there be some "other reasonable basis" for the selection of that state.

What interests are served by this provision that are not accounted for in § 187(2)(b) (discussed in the next paragraph)? Perhaps it is merely that some contractual choice-of-law references are too unseemly, too "unreasonable," too blatant an effort to avoid the operation of otherwise valid and applicable state law. Section 187(2)(a) says that a Nevada domiciliary and a California domiciliary may not specify that the validity of the contract itself will be governed by the law of Alaska, if Alaska has no "substantial relationship" to the transaction and there aren't any other good reasons for the choice of Alaska law. (The fact that, in this hypothetical, Alaska law would validate the contract does not by itself qualify as a good enough reason.)

Subsection (b) is perhaps more to the point, if a bit wordy. This provision addresses more directly the concerns raised by *ousting* the otherwise applicable law of a state by means of a choice-of-law provision. Section 187(2)(b) seeks to protect the state from such "ouster" of its law—namely, by invalidating the choice-of-law provision—but only under specified circumstances. First, of course, that state must have been the ordinary choice-of-law reference under § 188; otherwise we cannot intelligibly speak of "ouster." Second, the issue as to which such "ouster" is effectuated by the choice-of-law provision must concern a "fundamental policy" of the state, which the contractual choice of another state's law subverts. The subverted policy must be one that really matters to the state. Third, the state not only must be the one that application of § 188 would have pointed to; it *also* has to have a "materially greater interest" in the matter than the state whose law the parties have chosen. That is, even though the contractually chosen state may not have been the one to which § 188 would have referred, the choice can still be valid under § 187(2) if the interest in the matter of the "ousted" state isn't "materially greater" than that of the state chosen by the parties. If, say, the state chosen by the parties would have been a "close second" or at least a plausible candidate for selection using § 188, the contractual choice might still be valid under § 187(2).[9] Note that all three of the criteria mentioned in this paragraph (and in § 187(2)(b)) must be satisfied if § 187(2)(b) is to invalidate the choice-of-law provision.

---

9. This "materially greater interest" part of § 187(2)(b) thus seems to have some conceptual overlap with § 187(2)(a), which requires that the state whose law is contractually chosen have a "substantial relationship" with the matter (or that there be some other "reasonable basis" for the choice).

DeSantis v. Wackenhut Corp. An interesting example of § 187 in action is *DeSantis v. Wackenhut Corp.* (Tex. 1990),[10] a decision by the Supreme Court of Texas concerning the enforceability of a covenant not to compete that had been placed in an employment contract. Wackenhut, a company incorporated and headquartered in Florida, hired DeSantis to work at its Houston office. As part of the employment contract, DeSantis covenanted that, after leaving the employment of Wackenhut, he would refrain for two years from engaging in a competing business throughout a large part of Texas. The contract also provided that any disputes concerning the interpretation or performance of the contract would be governed by Florida law. DeSantis subsequently resigned from Wackenhut after their relationship had soured, and he proceeded to establish a competing business in the Houston area. Wackenhut sued DeSantis in the Texas courts, seeking damages and enforcement of the noncompete agreement. As the Supreme Court of Texas held, Texas law made the noncompete covenant unenforceable. But the court further had to determine whether the choice-of-law provision (referring to Florida law) should be enforced, since Florida law regarded the noncompete agreement as fully enforceable. Texas follows the Second Restatement, including § 187, when resolving conflicts in contract cases.

The Supreme Court of Texas held that the choice-of-law clause was unenforceable; that Texas law should govern the dispute; and that the noncompete provision was consequently unenforceable. (Be sure to distinguish the question of the enforceability of the choice-of-law provision from the question of the enforceability of the noncompete covenant; the latter, of course, depended on the former in *DeSantis*.) As discussed above, the validity of the noncompete covenant was *not* an issue that the parties could definitively have resolved simply by including the covenant in the contract; parties typically cannot establish the validity of their own contractual provisions in this way. Therefore, § 187(1) did not serve to validate the choice-of-law provision. (This, of course, doesn't mean that the choice-of-law provision might not have been valid and enforceable with respect to *other* issues as to which a conflict might arise, such as disputed questions of interpretation.) Therefore, it was necessary for the court to turn to § 187(2). First, of course, the court had to determine which state had the "most significant relationship" to the transaction under § 188 of the Second Restatement, in order to determine whether enforcement of the choice-of-law provision would even make a difference. Not unreasonably, the court held that Texas, as the place where the services by DeSantis were to be performed pursuant to his contract with Wackenhut, was the state with the most significant relationship to the transaction, and that

10.   793 S.W.2d 670 (Tex. 1990).

Texas law would apply in the absence of the choice-of-law clause. Of course, § 187(2)(a) provided no basis for invalidating the choice-of-law provision; obviously Florida, the state where Wackenhut was headquartered, had a "substantial relationship" to the transaction. So, on to § 187(2)(b).

The Texas Supreme Court explained, in one short paragraph, that not only did Texas have the "most significant relationship" to the dispute under § 188; it also had a "materially greater interest" in the matter than Florida. Central to its conclusion on this point was that its assertion that "[a]t stake here is whether a Texas resident can leave one Texas job to start a competing Texas business," an interest the court found materially greater than Florida's interest in "protecting a national business headquartered in that state."[11] Finally, the court considered whether Texas law holding noncompete covenants to be void constituted a "fundamental policy" that would be contravened by enforcing the choice-of-law provision and applying Florida law. Although the court conceded the difficulty of making metaphysical inquiries into whether a policy is "fundamental" or not for purposes of § 187(2), it ultimately concluded that Texas's policy was "fundamental" in this sense. Therefore, under § 187(2)(b), the choice-of-law clause was unenforceable, and Texas law was applied, meaning that the noncompete covenant was likewise held unenforceable, resulting in dismissal of Wackenhut's claim.

The *DeSantis* decision demonstrates how, as with so many Second Restatement provisions, § 187 leaves courts pretty much free to determine whether or not a contractual choice-of-law provision should be enforced. Although the text of § 187 suggests that the strong bias is toward enforcement of such provisions, the subjective criteria identified in both § 187(1) and § 187(2) for determining whether one of the exceptions applies leaves considerable room for decisions not to enforce. More than that, however, § 187 suggests that neither party autonomy nor state regulatory authority is the sole point of departure in devising a conflicts principle for choice-of-law clauses. Party autonomy is favored insofar as such clauses are permitted to oust the ordinary choice-of-law reference at all, but it is clear that at some point the authority of a state having the clearly superior interest in the dispute must prevail, at least where a matter of "fundamental policy" is concerned.[12]

---

11. 793 S.W.2d at 679.

12. One might note, of course, that noncompete covenants are distinctive (though hardly unique) in that they operate to limit the contractual freedom of those who agree to them. Thus one could see the action of the Texas Supreme Court in *DeSantis* as, somewhat paradoxically, violating party autonomy in order to protect party autonomy.

Party Autonomy, Efficiency, and the New Law Merchant. A few scholars have argued that conflicts law should give contracting parties more leeway than § 187 does to determine the law under which their disputes should be settled. Some of these arguments are framed explicitly in terms of economic efficiency and rest in part on a more general objection to the inefficiencies created by overregulation of economic transactions.[13] Others hearken back to an age in which a general "law merchant" thrived, according to which an international community of traders developed norms of mercantile practice and custom, independent of (or incorporated into) the positive law of the sovereign state.[14] This latter vision is reminiscent of that which produced the Uniform Commercial Code, which today contains choice-of-law provisions of its own. (These, of course, become part of state law when adopted as such by a state.) To the extent that choice-of-law clauses and mandatory arbitration provisions are enforceable—that is to say, to a substantial extent—this space of detachment from individual state regulation already exists, especially with sophisticated parties dealing in international transactions. Since, however, the law of conflict of laws is today considered to be the law of the state (in particular, the law of the forum), it is unlikely that conflicts law will leave the field entirely to the discretion of private parties in the near future.

D. Conflict of Laws and the Uniform Commercial Code

Some form of the Uniform Commercial Code has been adopted in every state in the United States. Among the UCC's provisions are several that concern choice of law. As such, these are probably the most heavily litigated statutory provisions on choice of law in the United States. The UCC, of course, aims for substantial uniformity throughout the United States in the law governing the commercial transactions to which it applies. The fact, though, that the UCC has been adopted in every state does not eliminate all conflicts problems in cases arising under its provisions. Some states have adopted the UCC with changes to some of its provisions. The UCC has been revised on occasion, and not all states have adopted the changes at the same time. International transactions subject to the UCC will likely feature one or more parties from states where the UCC is not in force. So conflicts will arise from time to time, and the UCC includes some provisions that attempt to provide for them.

Choice-of-Law Provisions Under the UCC and the Lost Promise of Proposed § 1–301. Of principal importance is the

---

13. *See, e.g.,* Larry E. Ribstein, *Choosing Law by Contract,* 18 JOURNAL OF CORPORATION LAW 245 (1993).

14. Friedrich K. Juenger, *American Conflicts Scholarship and the New Law*

Merchant, 28 VANDERBILT JOURNAL OF TRANSNATIONAL LAW 487 (1995).

UCC's basic provision on the parties' power to choose the applicable law by means of a choice-of-law provision. Prior to the most recent proposed revision to Article I of the UCC, this question was governed by § 1–105, which provides as follows:

> Except as provided hereafter in this section, when a transaction bears a reasonable relation to this state and also to another state or nation the parties may agree that the law either of this state or of such other state or nation shall govern their rights and duties. Failing such agreement this Act applies to transactions bearing an appropriate relation to this state.

This is actually a bit more restrictive of party autonomy than § 187 of the Second Restatement, and the general tendency in the last few decades has been to promote *greater* party autonomy in the selection of governing law. Thus, in the most recent revision of Article I, the American Law Institute proposed a new § 1–301 to replace § 1–105. Not to bury the lead: Before describing § 1–301, we have to tell you that, with the exception of the Virgin Islands, even those states and territories that have adopted revised Article I have balked at § 1–301, and have either refused to adopt it or have simply replaced its language with that of old § 1–105. It appears that proposed § 1–301 will not see the light of day in any states. But let's discuss it briefly anyway.

Section 1–301 favors the enforceability of choice-of-law clauses to a greater extent than does § 187 of the Second Restatement. In particular, § 1–301 does *not* require that the state whose law is chosen by the parties have a reasonable relationship to the parties or to the dispute. It does provide that such a provision not be enforced if to apply it would be contrary to a fundamental policy of a state whose law would otherwise apply to the dispute. But if that is not the case, then the choice-of-law provision will be enforced even if the state whose law is chosen bears no reasonable relation to the transaction.

With respect to questions of contract interpretation and other matters as to which state law is usually regarded as supplying "default rules," this provision is unremarkable. However, it does also serve to empower parties engaged in a strictly local transaction to evade local law regarding the *validity* of certain contracts, so long as the local law is not deemed to embody a "fundamental policy" of the state. This is about as far as we have seen a body of law go in permitting the parties essentially to "make their own law" by means of a choice-of-law agreement. In this sense, the provision is in harmony with the original vision of the UCC, which was partly to bring commercial law into accord with the customs and practices of the commercial community, somewhat like the old law merchant.

There is, however, one significant qualification of the autonomy conferred on the contracting parties by § 1–301: If one of the parties is a "consumer," the state whose law is chosen must bear a "reasonable relation" to the transaction, and the law chosen must not serve to deprive the consumer of the protective law of his state of residence, or, in the case of a sale of goods, of the protective law of the state where the consumer makes the contract or takes delivery of the goods (assuming that that is different from the state of his residence). Even with this qualification, though, § 1–301 is significantly more protective of party autonomy in the selection of governing law than its predecessor, § 1–105. But, as noted above, this may all be academic, at least for the time being.

Other Conflicts Provisions. The UCC, sensibly, provides that the state's normal conflicts rules should apply in the absence of a choice by the parties. Those "normal conflicts rules," however, presumably include a series of other conflicts provisions specified by the UCC for particular situations. This is not a book on the UCC, so we will avoid going into these other provisions, concerning letters of credit, bulk sales, certificates of title, investment securities, and so on. However, we will note that of particular importance are the conflict-of-laws provisions in Article 9 of the UCC, which concerns secured transactions and whose latest revision has been in effect in all states since January 1, 2002. These provisions are found at §§ 9–301 through 9–307 and govern conflicts with respect to security interests in personal property and fixtures.[15]

E.   Insurance Conflicts

The law of insurance is itself a vast and complex subject, so it is not surprising that it can generate difficult conflicts problems. Insurance policies frequently contain a choice-of-law provision, and often these will resolve any conflicts that arise. This may not always be the case, however. Insurance is one area in which legislatures in a number of states have actually provided for statutory conflicts rules, and usually these efforts have been designed to ensure that the law of the forum will apply in cases where the policyholder is a forum domiciliary or where there are other contacts with the forum. For example, a Texas statute provides:

> Any contract of insurance payable to any citizen or inhabitant of this State by any insurance company or corporation doing business within this State shall be held to be a contract made and entered into under and by virtue of the laws of this State relating to insurance, and governed thereby, notwithstanding such policy or contract of insurance may provide that the

---

15. An excellent discussion of these provisions can be found in RUSSELL J.   WEINTRAUB, COMMENTARY ON THE CONFLICT OF LAWS 602–18 (5th ed. 2006).

contract was executed and the premiums and policy (in case it becomes a demand) should be payable without this State, or at the home office of the company or corporation issuing the same.[16]

This provision, like similar statutes in a number of other states, dates from the early twentieth century, when populist resentment of large insurance corporations was, if anything, greater than today. The Texas courts have since offered a narrow interpretation of this statute, limiting its application to situations when the particular insurance policy was issued in the course of the insurer's business conducted in Texas. The point, however, is that there are similar statutes in a number of states, and that they frequently will direct the application of forum law in cases of insurance disputes with multistate contacts. In some cases these statutes trump any effort by the parties (realistically, the insurance company) to select the governing law in the insurance contract itself.

The various forms of *liability* insurance are particularly apt to make for choice-of-law trouble, however, because by definition such policies are triggered by events that involve third parties, who often are in effect beneficiaries of the policies. (Obviously, benefits under liability policies only attach when the policyholder is actually or putatively deemed legally liable to another person.) There can thus be three (if not more) distinct parties with interests to account for when analyzing the conflicts that can result. As we will see in Chapter 4, several of the important twentieth-century Supreme Court cases concerning constitutional limits on choice of law have involved liability insurance matters.

Not surprisingly, automobile insurance policies regularly produce knotty conflicts problems. Obviously, not every state follows the same substantive law principles with respect to auto insurance. Presumably many disputes that involve solely the policyholder and the underwriter will be governed by the law selected in the policy agreement (or, the law of the forum, as per the statutes described above if one exists in the forum). But many auto insurance conflicts are not this simple. Since somewhat fewer than half of the states in the United States provide for some variant of no-fault liability in auto accident cases, and since the laws of even those states differ significantly from one another in numerous respects, many kinds of conflicts can easily arise. Some, even if not resolved by a choice-of-law provision in the agreement, are resolved by state statutes that determine the territorial reach of policies issued to domiciliaries. But even these expedients do not provide for all situations, especially those involving out-of-state accidents with uninsured motorists.[17]

---

16. Tex. Ins. Code Art. 21.42 (Vernon 2005).

17. For an example, see *Kurent v. Farmers Insurance of Columbus, Inc.*, 62 Ohio St.3d 242, 581 N.E.2d 533 (1991).

There are pervasive differences in state law concerning mandatory policy limits for uninsured motorist coverage, the availability of "stacking" coverage (*i.e.* the ability to aggregate policy limits for each car on which the insured has a policy), and many other issues. In the absence of a specific statutory provision governing such conflicts, the forum's own choice-of-law methodology will come to the fore—and among the first issues is likely to be whether the case should be "characterized" as one of tort or one of contract.

F. Conflicts in Products Liability Litigation: Two Examples

Generally speaking, the law of products liability falls under the umbrella of tort law; therefore much of what we have said in Chapters 1 and 2 concerning choice of law in tort cases is relevant to products liability conflicts. But some of the structural complications that seem especially common in the products liability area can produce distinctive conflicts problems that are worth looking at briefly in their own right. Products liability cases frequently involve products that move through a complex chain of distribution, raising issues of joint and several liability whose specific legal treatment may vary from state to state. In addition, some products can produce injuries many years after their original manufacture and distribution; in such a situation conflicts of laws concerning the applicable periods of limitation and repose may be crucial. The interaction of product liability law with procedural rules governing party joinder and limitations periods can create difficult conflicts problems. Perhaps the central dilemma of these cases is that it is often impossible to square resolution of the conflict with any hope of vindicating the reasonable intentions of the parties when they first became involved in the transaction.

Contribution Rules and Joint and Several Liability. One example is *Cooney v. Osgood Machinery, Inc.* (1993),[18] a decision of the New York Court of Appeals that was mentioned briefly in Chapter 2. As you will recall from that chapter, by 1993 New York had come to employ the *"Neumeier* rules," a set of principles distilled from the early "guest statute" cases, to resolve certain kinds of conflicts in tort cases. *Cooney* illustrates just how complex these cases can be. In the late 1950s, Osgood Machinery, acting as a New York sales agent for a Buffalo company, procured a piece of industrial machinery (a "bending roll") from the manufacturer of the machinery. Osgood assisted in setting up and installing the machine for the Buffalo company. The ownership and location of the bending roll from 1961–1969 was shrouded in mystery by the

---

18.   81 N.Y.2d 66, 595 N.Y.S.2d 919, 612 N.E.2d 277 (1993).

time *Cooney* was decided, but we do know that in 1969 the roll was purchased by a Missouri corporation, Mueller Co. Mueller installed it in its Missouri plant and "modified it by adding a foot switch." While working at the Mueller plant, Cooney (a Missouri resident) was injured by the bending roll, perhaps by a malfunction of the foot switch.

Cooney sought and received workers' compensation benefits in Missouri. Missouri law provides that the recovery of such benefits thereafter releases the employer from any further liability. But Cooney then brought a products liability action in New York court against Osgood, the sales agent that had initially arranged for purchase (by the Buffalo company) of the bending roll in New York back in the late 1950s. (Note that Osgood almost certainly had no knowledge of the subsequent sale of the bending roll to Mueller in Missouri.) From Osgood's perspective, Mueller was a joint tortfeasor; after all, Cooney was Mueller's employee when injured and Cooney had made a successful workers' compensation claim. So Osgood asserted a third-party contribution claim against Mueller, seeking to implead Mueller as a third-party defendant in Cooney's New York lawsuit. Here, though, the conflict-of-laws issue reared its head. The Missouri workers' compensation statute mentioned above shields employers in the Mueller's situation from contribution claims, just as it exempts them from direct claims by employees who have received workers' compensation benefits. By contrast, New York law permits the assertion of contribution claims against employers under similar circumstances. In *Cooney*, the New York Court of Appeals was called upon to determine which state's law should apply to the contribution issue, and, consequently, whether the contribution claim could be asserted against Mueller in the New York proceeding.

The Court of Appeals was able to reach an intelligible and defensible result, using the "*Neumeier* rules." But first observe the odd circumstances here. It is difficult to imagine an example of a conflicts problem in which the relevant parties are more remote from another, or from a crucial event in the series of transactions leading to the dispute. Osgood had served as a sales agent in the late 1950s in connection with the sale of the bending roll to a New York company; although the later sale of the machine to a Missouri company was, in a tenuous and abstract way, "foreseeable," Osgood obviously had nothing to do with that and could hardly have anticipated in 1958 that a Missouri worker employed by a Missouri firm would be injured by the machine twenty years later. Similarly, from all that appears, Mueller knew nothing about the original sale of the machine in the late 1950s and would have been surprised to learn that, in resolving the dispute over Cooney's injury pursuant to the Missouri workers' compensation process, it remained vulnerable to a contribution claim in New York court as provided by New York law. The vagaries of product liability law, which can subject a manufacturer, distributor, or retailer to liability over wide expanses of time and space with respect to products that have changed hands (perhaps more than once), here combine with the complexities of workers' compensation law and quasi-procedural issues concerning indemnification, contribution, and third-party claims to create a conflicts problem in which it is impossible to vindicate the reasonable expectations of all the parties.

The Court of Appeals first observed that, as in *Schultz v. Boy Scouts of America* (N.Y. 1985), discussed in Chapter 2, the rule in dispute was "loss-allocating" rather than "conduct-regulating." Since the parties (Mueller and Osgood) were domiciled in different states, and local law favored the domiciliary in each case, *Neumeier* Rule #2 was applicable. This would have led to application of the law of the place of injury—that is, Missouri. However, the Court of Appeals, rather than applying the rule reflexively and ending the analysis at that point, tested its conclusion by working through the problem using the principles of interest analysis. The Court of Appeals conceded that Cooney presented a "true conflict": Missouri's no-contribution rule protected Mueller (a Missouri domiciliary), and New York's contribution rule protected Osgood (a New York domiciliary). The Court of Appeals explained that the better resolution of this true conflict was to apply Missouri law, which would indeed have been the reference under *Neumeier* Rule #2. Interestingly, the court placed considerable emphasis in reaching this result on the protection of reasonable expectations, something that we stated at the outset could not be done very well. While the application of Missouri law would accord with the reasonable expectations of Mueller, a Missouri domiciliary, the same obviously could not be said of Osgood, a New York domiciliary for whom the ultimate arrival of the "bending roll" in Missouri was in no real way foreseeable. The Court of Appeals, though, noted that establishment of the "contribution" rule in New York did not in any case occur until 1972, at least fourteen years after Osgood's participation in the bending roll saga. Since Osgood could no more have reasonably expected in 1958 to be the beneficiary of contribution principles under New York law than it could have expected to be subjected to Missouri law concerning contribution, the injustice of any violation of its realistic expectations through application of Missouri law was attenuated.

Limitations Periods and Statutes of Repose. Cooney involved the application of New York choice-of-law principles (seemingly a hybrid of the "*Neumeier* Rules" and interest analysis) to resolve a conflict concerning the effect of a workers' contribution payout on the operation of the doctrine of contribution. This is only one of many kinds of conflicts that can arise in the product liability arena. For example, in Chapter 2 we saw the case of *Phillips v. General Motors Corp.*, in which the Supreme Court of Montana applied the Second Restatement to the issue of limitations on compensatory and punitive damages in product liability actions. One final example we'll examine here concerns conflicts between the rules of different states with respect to limitations periods for product liability cases.

Gantes v. Kason Corp. (N.J. 1996)[19] raises important conflicts issues with respect not only to product liability, but also to statutes of limitations and to the definition of interests pursuant to governmental interest analysis. In *Gantes*, a Georgia domiciliary was killed when a machine that she was operating allegedly malfunctioned. The manufacturer of the machine was a New Jersey domiciliary. The manufacturer had originally sold the machine to a Pennsylvania company; its route to its ultimate destination in Georgia was not described in the court's opinion. The decedent's representative brought a wrongful-death action in New Jersey court. The lawsuit was within New Jersey's two-year statute of limitations; but it fell outside Georgia's statute of repose, which was ten years. The task of the New Jersey Supreme Court in Gantes was to determine whether New Jersey's two-year limitations period or Georgia's ten-year "repose" period should apply. Applying interest analysis, the court determined that only New Jersey had an interest in the application of its law. It thus ruled that the New Jersey limitations period should apply, that the Georgia statute of repose should not apply, and that therefore the suit could be maintained.

Gantes reveals many of the difficulties in applying interest analysis. The court treated the question as a conflict between New Jersey and Georgia law and assumed that only one of those laws could apply. However, a statute of limitations and a statute of repose are two different things, and may constitute an "apples and oranges" comparison. A statute of limitations places a duty on the injured party, once she has discovered her injury, to prosecute her claim within the limitations period. Compliance with the statute of limitations thus remains within the putative plaintiff's control. A statute of repose, however, places a time limit on the putative defendant's exposure to liability, regardless of whether and when a person is injured due to negligence in the product's manufacture or design; Georgia's statute of repose barred the commencement of any product-liability action more than ten years after the product's first sale for use or consumption. Thus, it functions to protect the manufacturers to which it applies, but, assuming that Georgia also

19. 145 N.J. 478, 679 A.2d 106 (1996).

has a statute of limitations, the statute of repose has much less to do with influencing the behavior of potential plaintiffs.

It was thus inapt for the New Jersey Supreme Court simply to view the New Jersey statute of limitations and the Georgia statute of repose as mutually exclusive alternatives. Had it investigated the matter more thoroughly, it would have found that Georgia also has a statute of limitations that governs product liability actions. Moreover, as the court specifically stated, New Jersey does not have a statute of repose that applies to manufacturers (although it does have a statute of repose applicable to certain other matters). A more accurate framing of the problem would have been, first, to determine whether the New Jersey or the Georgia *limitations* period should apply (assuming there was a conflict between them); and, second, to determine whether New Jersey law (no specified period) and Georgia law (ten years) with respect to *repose* should apply.

In the event, however, the New Jersey Supreme Court, observing more generically that application of New Jersey law would permit the plaintiff to proceed, while application of Georgia law would not, proceeded to compare apples and oranges. The apple in this case was New Jersey's two-year statute of limitations. The interests we usually associate with a limitations period are (1) to protect the forum from having to adjudicate stale claims, (2) to free potential defendants from indefinite fear of liability, and (assuming that this is a different interest) (3) to encourage potential plaintiffs to bring their claims promptly. Moreover, most applications of interest analysis would stress that (2) refers principally to "potential defendants domiciled in the state" and that (3) refers principally to "potential plaintiffs" domiciled in the state. On this basis, to conclude that New Jersey had a cognizable interest in the application of its two-year limitations period is a tricky endeavor. There was no New Jersey plaintiff (or decedent) in *Gantes*. The defendant, to be sure, was a New Jersey manufacturer. But presumably the defendant-protective "interest" served by a limitations period comes into being only after the limitations period has expired; allowance of the plaintiff's claim by application of a limitations period that has not yet expired serves no interest of the defendant. Similarly, application of New Jersey's two-year limitations period could not vindicate the forum's interest in keeping stale claims out of its courts; how could that interest be served by a decision that *permits* the claim to remain in the New Jersey courts? It is difficult to see precisely how the interests of New Jersey would be advanced by application of its law in *Gantes*.

The New Jersey Supreme Court finessed this problem by referring back to the deterrent interests served by its substantive law of product liability:

We conclude that this State has a strong interest in encouraging the manufacture and distribution of safe products for the public and, conversely, in deterring the manufacture and distribution of unsafe products within the state. That interest is furthered through the recognition of claims and the imposition of liability based on principles of strict products-liability law.... New Jersey in this case has a cognizable and substantial interest in deterrence that would be furthered by the application of its statute of limitations.[20]

One difficulty with this reasoning is that, as the court all but conceded, the substantive law on the product liability question likely would be that of Georgia. (New Jersey case law had determined that compensation rather than deterrence interests were the principal interests to be served by product liability law.) The court seemed to be saying that deterrence considerations that were secondary in assessing the states' interest in the application of their substantive law of product liability should be decisive in characterizing New Jersey's interest in application of its statute of limitations.[21] The court seemed to be on more solid ground in holding that Georgia had no real interest in the application of its statute of repose. According to its own courts, the purposes lying behind the statute of repose were to stabilize insurance underwriting, presumably for the benefit of both Georgia insurers and Georgia manufacturers, neither of which appeared to be involved in *Gantes*, and to keep stale claims out of Georgia courts.

If the court in *Gantes* was serious about applying interest analysis—and New Jersey has since abandoned interest analysis as its choice-of-law methodology—it might have made more sense to view *Gantes* as an "unprovided-for" case. Georgia had no Georgia manufacturer or insurer to protect with its statute of repose; New Jersey had no plaintiff (or decedent) to protect with its statute of limitations (viewed in this case as the rule more protective of the plaintiff's ability to maintain an action), and court-protective and defendant-protective dimensions of its limitations rule were not implicated in the case. A more discriminating analysis of interests, discussed above, would have actually compared the two state's periods of repose (Georgia: ten years; New Jersey: forever). Perhaps

---

20. *Gantes*, 145 N.J. at 490, 492–93, 679 A.2d at 111–12, 113.

21. The dissent in *Gantes* argued that application of New Jersey's statute of limitations would actually *disserve* one important New Jersey interest—protecting its manufacturers from large liabilities. Since New Jersey's limitations period had not yet expired when the suit was initiated, this argument does not seem strong. In effect, the dissent appeared to argue that the court should recognize a New Jersey interest (the interest in not discouraging manufacturers from doing business in New Jersey by subjecting them to suits there that would not have been entertained by courts in the place where the product was used) that was not reflected in any actual New Jersey law relevant to the case.

such an analysis would result in a false conflict, if one were to regard New Jersey's "non-repose" rule as part of a larger interest in subjecting its own manufacturers to a rigorous regime of product liability. Either way, given the premises of interest analysis, ultimate application of New Jersey law (as the tiebreaker in case of an "unprovided-for" case, or as the law of the only state with a cognizable interest) does not seem to be an outlandish result. Unfortunately, the New Jersey Supreme Court reached this result through an unpersuasive assessment of the forum's interests.

G. Complex Litigation

The phrase "complex litigation" can mean a number of things; it's more of a descriptive term than a legal one. For example, simply the fact that modern procedure contemplates the use of party joinder to an extent never recognized by the common law can give rise to problems of "complex litigation," because the addition of third-party plaintiffs and defendants, intervenors, and the like can produce difficult questions of jurisdiction, *res judicata*, and other procedural issues. For our purposes, the problem of "complex litigation" mostly concerns the fact that the presence of multiple parties, either domiciled in or with significant connections to different states, can drastically exacerbate choice-of-law problems that are difficult enough to begin with. A standard example is an airline crash in which numerous passengers, domiciled in a variety of states, are killed. Of course, in such a case, there may be multiple defendants as well: the airline, the designer and manufacturer of the airplane, and so on. There are many examples of complex litigation, but our standard examples will be the "mass tort" typified by an airline crash or widespread consumption of a disease-causing product (so-called "toxic torts").

Let's start by identifying a few realities about the American legal system that help give the complex litigation problem its basic character. First, multiple plaintiffs claiming to have been legally harmed by the action of a defendant are generally not obliged to bring their claims together in a single proceeding; each plaintiff has the right to bring her claim at the time of her choosing (assuming she files within the applicable limitations period, of course). Second, each plaintiff asserting a claim has an independent responsibility to demonstrate that the jurisdictional prerequisites for adjudication of her claim in the court in which she has sued have been met. These long-cherished principles of civil adjudication—better suited, perhaps, for an earlier age that knew nothing of complex litigation or the easy permeability of state lines—can make the efficient and equitable resolution of complex litigation more difficult. Third, the effect of these principles is mitigated to some extent for cases in federal court by the adoption of procedural rules that permit federal district courts to participate in consolidating, in a single federal district court, pretrial proceedings of several actual or foreseeable lawsuits arising out of a common act or set of acts by the defendant(s). This does not obviate the requirement that ultimate *trial* of each claim must accord with the basic principles mentioned above, leaving open the possibility of numerous trials in different places, but it can simplify the pretrial process, which after all is notoriously the part of American litigation that consumes the most resources and to which the parties direct their greatest energies.

These observations lead to a fourth, and very important, reality of much complex litigation: To a greater degree than "normal" litigation, there are a variety of pressures in the kinds of complex litigation we are considering here for the parties to settle. In cases in which the total potential liability of the defendant(s) is enormous, the available fund will likely be insufficient to completely compensate all plaintiffs; most plaintiffs, as well as the legal system itself, will have a strong incentive to reach a collectively fair settlement rather than witness a series of separate trials that could result in the complete depletion of the funds available to defray the judgments for all wronged plaintiffs. At the same time, defendants are often likely to prefer a settlement, over which they can exert some control, to the random and unpredictable results (not to mention the expense) of multiple trials. And most federal judges handling complex litigation in which numerous cases have been consolidated for pretrial purposes have good reason to prefer that the parties reach a settlement if at all possible.

One consequence of all this is that the resolution of pretrial issues—rulings on evidence, on discovery, on summary judgment, and so one—can assume vast importance in the parties' evolving calculations of their likelihood of succeeding at trial and of the value of their claims. Obviously such rulings regularly perform the same function in more simple litigation, but with the monetary stakes as high and the uncertainty as great as they are in the mass tort situation, those rulings are magnified in importance. Frequently one of these pretrial issues is choice of law. In mass tort cases, the legal issues as to which conflicts among state law are likely to arise include the availability of punitive damages and the availability and measurement of noneconomic damages. Other issues less likely to arise include the applicable standard of care, various forms of immunity, timeliness of claims, and the availability of damages for loss of consortium. The questions of punitive damages and compensatory damages for noneconomic loss, however, are the most consequential issues.

Let us focus on litigation in federal court for the moment, using as an example the case of *In re Air Crash Disaster Near*

Chicago, Illinois on May 25, 1979 (7th Cir. 1981).[22] A total of 273 persons were killed in the crash of an American Airlines jet. One hundred and eighteen separate wrongful death actions were filed in five different states and Puerto Rico; many of these were originally filed in state court and later removed to federal court. By order of the Federal Judicial Panel on Multidistrict Litigation, these 118 cases were consolidated and transferred to a single federal court, the Federal District Court for the Northern District of Illinois, for pretrial purposes only. Among the plaintiffs and decedents were residents of ten different states, Puerto Rico, and three foreign countries. Of course, wrongful death actions arise under state law, and the law of wrongful death (particularly with respect to the scope of recoverable damages) is not the same in all states, so each individual case raised the possibility of a significant conflict.

Moreover, even though federal law provides for consolidation for pretrial purposes, the court into which the case is transferred must apply the law that would be applied by the transferor courts to the claims originally filed there, including their law of choice of law.[23] That means that, in the *Air Crash* case, the Federal District Court for the Northern District of Illinois was, in theory, bound to make choice-of-law rulings using the choice-of-law rules of the six different jurisdictions, applying the rules appertaining to each of the six jurisdictions from which the cases had been temporarily transferred. A diversity of conflicts approaches, including *lex loci*, the Second Restatement, interest analysis, and comparative impairment, were represented by those six jurisdictions, so the court's task was genuinely complex. Of course, the court was not required to make choice-of-law rulings for each of the 118 cases that had initially been filed. The facts that (1) claims had originated only in six jurisdictions, (2) plaintiffs collectively represented a maximum of fourteen jurisdictions, and (3) the conflicts were confined to a few (albeit crucial) issues, substantially limited the choice-of-law mayhem with which the district court was faced. Still, mayhem there was.

The principal issue as to which there was a conflict of laws in the *Air Crash* case was whether punitive damages would be permitted. There were two defendants in the case (American Airlines and McDonnell Douglas), yielding a total of four states (the principal place of business and the place of alleged misconduct for each defendant) with a cognizable connection to the dispute: Missouri, New York, Oklahoma, and Hawai'i. In addition, the court regarded Illinois, the place of the accident, as having a plausible interest in the case. However, the court determined that, with respect to

---

22. 644 F.2d 594 (7th Cir. 1981).

23. As we will see in Chapter 7, federal courts sitting in diversity must apply the choice-of-law rules of the state in which they sit.

punitive damages, whose allowance is based on deterrence (rather than compensation) interests, and whose disallowance is based on a desire to relieve defendants of excess liability, the states of domicile of the victims or of their survivors did *not* have a cognizable connection with the dispute. Nor did the states of incorporation of the defendants. The analysis was somewhat simplified by the fact that there were only two variations on the substantive legal question presented: (1) punitive damages available, and (2) punitive damages not available. And the court had to perform the choice-of-analysis separately for each of several different methodologies represented among the six states in which claims had been originally filed: the Second Restatement, comparative impairment, interest analysis, and *lex loci*. Each analysis would have to be performed separately with respect to the claims asserted against each of the two defendants.

With two defendants and cases consolidated from federal districts in six different states, this tapestry required as many as twelve distinct inquiries into the choice-of-law problem. Anyone hopeful of arriving at a result in which these twelve inquiries would all yield the same state's substantive law on punitive damages would notice that one state among the five identified above was common to all of the individual actions: Illinois, the place of the accident. (Because the principal place of business and the place of alleged wrongdoing were different for each of the two defendants, none of those states was connected with each of the original lawsuits.) And, after a lengthy analysis, the Seventh Circuit in the *Air Crash* case found that each of the choice-of-law methodologies pointed to Illinois law on punitive damages. (Illinois disallows such punitives.)

The Seventh Circuit's choice-of-law analysis was a serious and thoughtful one. Nevertheless, it is doubtful that, were one to disaggregate the twelve different permutations, return the cases to their original places of filing, and instruct the original courts to perform the applicable choice-of-law analysis, the separate inquiries would all magically result in the application of Illinois law. Plainly the Seventh Circuit was much troubled, not only by the notion of permitting punitive damages for claims made by some plaintiffs and not for claims brought by others, but also by the prospect of permitting punitives for claims brought against one of the defendants and not for those brought against the other defendant. (Since the nature of the wrongful behavior, if any, attaching to the two defendants would have been different, it's not clear why the Seventh Circuit should have been disturbed by the latter scenario.) That is no doubt why the court's decision resulted in the application of a single source of law to the punitive damages question. The ultimate selection of Illinois law for any single one of the 118 claims in the case is not intuitively outlandish (although one could certainly argue that another jurisdiction would have a better claim to application of its law, and part of the court's analysis has been called a "grotesque distortion" by one conflicts scholar); what is highly questionable is whether the Seventh Circuit applied the various choice-of-law methodologies with a genuine commitment to the distinctive premises underlying those methodologies.

A more notorious example of the same kind of reasoning is the pretrial ruling on choice of law in the *Agent Orange* litigation, which had been consolidated for pretrial purposes into a single proceeding before Federal District Judge Jack Weinstein. The Agent Orange litigation was even more complex, as it was a "dispersed" rather than a "single-event" tort, for which many of the plaintiffs were certified as a class. Somewhat in the manner of the Seventh Circuit in the *Air Crash* case, Judge Weinstein determined that each of the choice-of-law methodologies represented among the courts from which the original cases were consolidated would result in selection of the same law to govern the legal questions as to which there was a conflict of laws. However, Judge Weinstein did not identify which state's law this would be; instead, his analysis of the respective choice-of-law methodologies led him to conclude that each would gravitate toward selection of what he called a "national consensus law" on the questions as to which there was a conflict. Judge Weinstein's analysis was obviously influenced by his strong belief that there should be a single, preferably federal, substantive law to govern the questions in this sprawling case, whether based on federal common law owing to the distinctive federal interest in a matter whose victims were primarily members of the U.S. armed forces and their families (a suggestion the Second Circuit had earlier rebuffed), or based on Congressional enactment, which had not taken place.

One consequence, and perhaps the principal intended consequence, of Judge Weinstein's Svengali-like reference to "national consensus law" was that it gave him somewhat greater leverage in inducing the parties to settle. Even after Judge Weinstein's decision on choice of law, the parties could not know what substantive law would apply in the case. This undoubtedly helped influence the parties to settle the case, as eventually happened. The settlement was ultimately upheld by the Second Circuit, which nevertheless carefully distanced itself from the implications of Judge Weinstein's "national consensus law" ruling.

The problem of choice of law in complex litigation presents far more issues than can be discussed at length here. These include the different considerations raised by dispersed and single-event torts; the relationship between choice of law and the certification requirements for class actions under Fed. R. Civ. P. 23; whether it should be of paramount importance to designate a single source of substantive law to govern conflicts in these cases; whether Congress should enact a federal statute to deal with these matters; and many others. The complex litigation problem highlights some of the difficulties created by our legal system's commitment to federalism and by the fact that these tort questions are usually governed by state law.[24] Proper treatment of mass tort actions, with respect not only to choice of law but also to a variety of other procedural and substantive matters, has engaged the energies of scholars, of the American Law Institute and its Complex Litigation Project, and of Congress, which has enlarged federal jurisdiction for certain class actions and for certain non-class litigation arising from single-event torts. A comprehensive strategy for dealing with choice-of-law issues in complex litigation, however, remains for the moment beyond our grasp.

H. Conflicts in Cyberspace

As with many other areas of law, the expanding hegemony of the Internet has created some major challenges for conflicts doctrine. This is hardly the first technological development to have had major implications for choice of law, and some have argued that the advent of "cyberspace" creates problems that are structurally no different from those that conflicts doctrine has previously demonstrated itself capable of handling. To take an elementary example, both contract law and conflicts law adapted without great difficulty to the invention of telegraphy and telephony, simply by devising rules of contract law to govern offer and acceptance and conflicts rules to determine the "place" of contracting. Closer to home, innovations in communication long predating the Internet have made determining the "location" of intangible assets—such as bank accounts and shares of stock—somewhat more complex than when "property" by and large referred to tangible things. To some extent, however, "cyberspace" presents a complication that is different in kind from previous innovations, because, in the words of scholars David Post and David Johnson, "events on the Net occur everywhere but nowhere in particular." Telephonic transactions generally take place between two identifiable points in space, but the posting of material on the web does not respect spatial boundaries.

---

24. As we will see more clearly in Chapter 7, the choice-of-law and consolidation complexities in this area are generated partly by the rule in *Klaxon Co. v. Stentor Electric Mfg. Co.*, 313 U.S. 487 (1941), that federal courts sitting in diversity must apply the choice-of-law rules of the states in which they sit, and the rule in *Van Dusen v. Barrack*, 376 U.S. 612 (1964), which requires a "transferee" court in the federal system to apply the law of the "transferor" court in the case of a transfer pursuant to 28 U.S.C. § 1404(a).

Whether these realities constitute "cyberspace" as a unique domain that should be governed by its own rules and presumptively free from the rules of particular sovereigns is something of a metaphysical question, and not our concern here. It's enough to note that the Internet can pose difficulties for jurisdiction-selecting choice-of-law rules that are based on territorial principles. For example, a territorial approach might lay emphasis on the physical *location* of a web server hosting a website whose posted material is alleged to violate the law. But, as Post and Johnson note:

> The notion that the effects of an activity taking place on [a] Web site radiate from a physical location over a geographic map in concentric circles of decreasing intensity, however sensible that may be in the nonvirtual world, is incoherent when applied to Cyberspace. A Web site physically located in Brazil ... has no more of an effect on individuals in Brazil than does a Web site physically located in Belgium or Belize that is accessible in Brazil.

Application of the law where the server is located, which has been a natural choice-of-law solution in some situations, thus seems less well supported than a similar approach to "nonvirtual" events; the fact of the server's physical location bears little relation to the interests and values that may be involved. At the same time, legal disputes ultimately do concern the claims of actual individuals or organizational entities to have been injured at the hands of other individuals or organizational entities. Law has never proved incapable of designating the *place* where individuals act or are domiciled, and, although identifying those places with respect to organizational entities is sometime based on fictions, the same is true for organizations. There is a difference between saying that it can be difficult to "localize" the significant events of a transaction for purposes of choice of law, which is true not only for the Internet but also for earlier technologies, and saying that cyberspace is a place to which traditional conceptions of sovereignty and regulatory authority should not apply at all.

Consider the application to internet transactions of the choice-of-law methodologies with which we've become familiar. Interestingly, the difficulties may be greater with respect to the traditional *lex loci* rules than with respect to modern approaches such as the Second Restatement and interest analysis. For example, if a conflicts issue arises in a dispute with respect to an e-commerce transaction, determining which state has the most significant relationship to the dispute, or the degree to which the legitimate interests of a state are implicated, is little different in kind from the equivalent inquiry with respect to non-Internet disputes. The fact that the Internet is "everywhere and nowhere" may enlarge the number of sovereign jurisdictions that may claim to have an interest—for example, consumers all over the world may be affected by information posted on a website—but that does not make it especially hard to determine whether, in a particular lawsuit brought by a particular plaintiff against a particular defendant, one state or another has a cognizable connection with the dispute. California has a legitimate interest in the welfare of California consumers, Illinois has a legitimate interest in the behavior of those operating web-based businesses from that state, and so on. *Lex loci* rules, however, by definition place emphasis on *place* or "locus," and the realm of cyberspace can at times confound our notion of "where something happens."

Consider, for example, the problem of defamation. If the online edition of *Barron's* magazine publishes a statement that the plaintiff alleges is defamatory, should the law governing the case be that of the state where the server "hosting" the article is located, that of the state where the plaintiff resides, or that of the state wherever the article might be accessed and read? To some extent, this problem is merely an extension of the age-old problem of choice of law in defamation cases, but the advent of Internet publication and immediate worldwide accessibility can push the problem to the outer limits. In *Dow Jones & Co. Inc. v. Gutnick* (Australia 2002),[25] the High Court of Australia held that an Australian domiciliary was entitled not only to sue Dow Jones in Australia court over the *Barron's* article mentioned above, but also to have Australian law govern the dispute. The choice-of-law ruling was especially consequential because, had the case been governed by American law, it is likely that the First Amendment would have precluded a finding of liability, since the plaintiff was a public figure. It's worth noting that, whereas the online version of Barron's had over 550,000 subscribers worldwide at the time, only about 1700 had been paid for with Australia-based credit cards. (Only five copies of the print edition of Barron's had been sent for distribution in Australia.)

Enforcing any ensuing judgment in the United States, where Dow Jones presumably has its assets, is another story. The problem of enforcing foreign libel judgments in U.S. courts is discussed in Chapter 8. The dim prospects of enforcement undoubtedly help account for the fact that Gutnick and Dow Jones ultimately settled the case for about $580,000.

25. [2002] HCA 56 (High Court of Australia, 2002).

Chapter 4

CONSTITUTIONAL LIMITATIONS ON CHOICE OF LAW

In previous chapters we have seen that, from time to time, courts make rulings on choice of law that seem downright dubious, at least as applications of the particular choice-of-law methodology they are purporting to employ. Invariably the result of these rulings is to apply forum law or, sometimes, to protect a forum domiciliary, even if the forum's connections with the dispute are slight compared with those of another state. In extreme cases, this may appear to be an illegitimate effort to favor forum law and/or domiciliaries. Does the U.S. Constitution place any limitations on the power of a court to apply forum law in the case of a conflict?[1]

The answer is that such constitutional limitations do exist, and occasionally the U.S. Supreme Court has found that a court has exceeded them; but those limitations are, in reality, quite minimal. Only in extreme cases will a court's ruling on choice of law violate the Constitution. Only if there are no plausible or "cognizable" connections between the forum and the dispute, or if a party could not reasonably have anticipated the application of forum law, will a court be constitutionally barred from applying that law to the dispute. The two constitutional provisions on which the Court has relied in setting limits on choice-of-law determinations by courts are the Due Process Clause of the Fourteenth Amendment, and the Full Faith and Credit Clause found in Article IV, § 1.

The constitutional analysis of choice of law bears some resemblance to the corresponding analysis of the constitutional power of courts to assert personal jurisdiction over defendants in civil cases. In both situations, the analysis emphasizes the significance and quantum of "contacts"; in personal jurisdiction, it is the contacts between the forum and the defendant that matters, while, in choice of law, it is the contacts between the forum and the underlying dispute that matters. And in each context, both (1) fairness to

---

1. The constitutional limitations discussed in this Chapter conceivably could apply when a court inappropriately applies the law of *any* state. However, since the problem almost always is the application of forum law by a court, this Chapter uses "the application of forum law" as a shorthand for the judicial practices that can come under constitutional scrutiny under the principles discussed herein.

151

individuals and (2) recognition of the prerogatives of other states play a role in the constitutional analysis. Nevertheless, the constitutional considerations with respect to choice of law and personal jurisdiction are not identical, so do not confuse or equate the two.

A. Due Process

The Supreme Court did not make any decisive statements on the constitutional limitations on choice of law until well into the twentieth century.[2] Its first such pronouncement, in the leading case of *Home Insurance Co. v. Dick* (1930),[3] declared that the Due Process Clause of the Fourteenth Amendment limits a court's power to apply the law of the forum to a dispute.

1. The Dick Case

In *Dick*, the Court established that a state may not, consistently with the Due Process clause, apply forum law in a case to the detriment of a party who had no meaningful connections with the forum. One Bonner, a resident of Mexico, had purchased a boat from a Mexican seller for use in Mexican waters; Bonner then purchased an accident insurance policy from a Mexican insurer, under a contract that required any claims for loss brought under the policy to be made within one (1) year of the loss. The Mexican insurer contracted with two New York insurance companies for reinsurance of the risk. Bonner then sold the boat to Dick, a Texas resident. The boat was subsequently lost in Mexican waters, and Dick failed to make a claim under the policy until more than a year had elapsed.

A Texas law, however, made any limitation provision in insurance contracts unenforceable if it specified that the claim had to be made within a period of less than two years. Dick therefore brought an action against the Mexican insurer in Texas state court, establishing *in rem* jurisdiction by garnishing the debt allegedly owed the insurer by the New York reinsurers, who had a agent in Texas.[4] The question was whether it was constitutional for the Texas court to apply Texas law, voiding the contract's one-year limitation period for claims. An affirmative answer to this question would mean that Dick had a cause of action against the Mexican insurer that could validly be adjudicated in the Texas court, and that

2. There were a few earlier cases that raised that issue, without rendering clear rules on the matter. *See, e.g., New York Life Insurance Co. v. Head*, 234 U.S. 149 (1914).

3. 281 U.S. 397 (1930).

4. The quaint notion that the insurer's debt to the reinsurer constituted attachable "property" that traveled with the reinsurers wherever they might be found was a consequence of the Court's decision in *Harris v. Balk*, 198 U.S. 215 (1905), which was subsequently overruled by the Court in *Shaffer v. Heitner*, 433 U.S. 186 (1977).

garnishment of the debt held by the New York reinsurers was sufficient to establish *in rem* jurisdiction in the Texas court. (It was this alleged deprivation of property belonging to the New York reinsurers that underlay their constitutional challenge, although the party that would ultimately be held liable to Dick was the Mexican insurer.)

In an opinion by Justice Brandeis, the Supreme Court held that the Texas court's application of Texas law violated the Due Process Clause of the Fourteenth Amendment:

> [N]othing in any way relating to the policy sued on, or to the contracts of reinsurance, was ever done or required to be done in Texas. All acts relating to the making of the policy were done in Mexico. All in relation to the making of the contracts of reinsurance were done there or in New York. And, likewise, all things in regard to performance were to be done outside of Texas. Neither the Texas laws nor the Texas courts were invoked for any purpose, except by Dick in the bringing of this suit. The fact that Dick's permanent residence was in Texas is without significance. At all times here material he was physically present and acting in Mexico. Texas was therefore without power to affect the terms of contracts so made. Its attempt to impose a greater obligation than that agreed upon and to seize property in payment of the imposed obligation violates the guaranty against deprivation of property without due process of law.[5]

For all that appeared, the Mexican insurer had not, at the time of its agreement with the Mexican resident Bonner, contemplated that Texas and its laws would have any connection with any ensuing controversy. Bonner's subsequent assignment of the boat to the Texas resident Dick, even if done with the Mexican insurer's knowledge, did not alter this fact. The Mexican insurer, having entered into an agreement (valid and enforceable under Mexican law) with a Mexican resident to insure a Mexican risk, had a Due Process right not to have the law of another state, with which it had no cognizable connection, applied so as to void a bargained-for provision of the contract that protected its interests.[6] By extension,

---

5. *Dick*, 281 U.S. at 407–08.

6. The procedural setting of *Dick* was complex, and closer examination of the case suggests that the Mexican insurer's lack of awareness of Texas's potential involvement may have been more formal than real. The insurer was likely aware of the substitution of Dick (who conducted activities in both Texas and Mexico) for Bonner as policyholder; it likewise may have understood that the New York reinsurers with whom it contracted did business in Texas. Moreover, one might venture that, by virtue of its geographic proximity to Mexico, application of Texas law presented less of a surprise to the Mexican insurer than application of the law of, say, Utah. However, then-prevailing understandings of choice of law, based on formal "vested rights" ideas, would not have regarded these as legitimate consider-the New York reinsurers had a Due Process right not to have their property seized as a way of initiating litigation as to which the laws of Texas were relied on for establishing liability.

Dick has come to stand for "the proposition that if a State has only an insignificant contact with the parties and the occurrence or transaction, application of its law is unconstitutional."[7] A closer look at Justice Brandeis's opinion in *Dick* suggests that he had no such broad principle in mind, although that principle may proceed logically enough from his analysis. He may not even have thought of *Dick* as a case about "conflict of laws" as such. Brandeis nowhere in his opinion refers to "conflict of laws," "choice of law," "law of the forum," "*lex loci*," or any of the conventional terms in use by jurists at the time when discussing the law of conflicts. What seems essential to Brandeis is Texas's "attempt to impose a greater obligation than that agreed upon and to seize property in payment of the imposed obligation."[8] "[D]eprivation of property without due process of law" are the words used by Brandeis. This is the language of "substantive due process" and the rights of contract and property, *circa* 1930. The opinion does not appear to go beyond this to establish general limitations on state courts' constitutional power to apply forum law to a case, and previous opinions by Brandeis suggest that he opposed subjecting choice of law to constitutional limitations under the Due Process Clause.[9]

Nevertheless, after decades of judicial interpretation and academic commentary, *Dick* does now stand for the proposition that the Due Process Clause forbids a state from applying forum law if the forum has no connections , or only minimal connections, to the dispute. This general principle remains good law,[10] although, as discussed below, the Court has ceased to distinguish very carefully between the limits placed on state courts' choice of law by the Due Process Clause and those placed on those courts by the Full Faith and Credit Clause. It is now rare to see a case raising a due process argument against application of forum law that does not also raise a full faith and credit argument, and the Court has tended to merge the two Clauses in its analysis. Precisely for this reason, however, it is important to understand the distinct values the Due Process

---

ations. The facts of *Dick* offered the Court an opportunity to establish that a court could not constitutionally apply the law of a state (practically speaking, the forum) to the disadvantage of a party that, *ex ante*, could not reasonably have expected that state's law to apply.

   7. *Allstate Insurance Co. v. Hague*, 449 U.S. 302, 310–11 (1981) (footnote omitted) (discussing *Dick*).

   8. *Dick*, 281 U.S. at 408.

   9. *See Kryger v. Wilson*, 242 U.S. 171, 176 (1916); *New York Life Ins. Co. v. Dodge*, 246 U.S. 357, 377, 382 (1918) (Brandeis, J., dissenting).

   10. The Supreme Court has cited *Dick* approvingly in a number of its most recent important decisions on the Constitution and choice of law. *See, e.g., Allstate Insurance. v. Hague*, 449 U.S. at 309–11; *Phillips Petroleum Co. v. Shutts*, 472 U.S. 797, 820 (1985).

limitation on choice of law protects, and under what conditions the courts will find that such a limitation has been violated.

2. Values Protected by the Due Process Clause: Fairness to Individuals, Reasonable Foreseeability, and Protection from "Unfair Surprise"

The Due Process Clause (unlike the Full Faith and Credit Clause) protects the rights of *individuals*. It is only by virtue of a violation of the constitutionally protected interests of an individual that a due process violation may be found. As applied to the problem of choice of law, the Due Process clause bars a state court from applying the law of a state whose law a party, at the time of the original transaction, *could not reasonably have foreseen* applying in a subsequent dispute. To do so would amount to *unfair surprise* to that party. This emphasis on foreseeability and surprise (which also appears in the Court's modern analysis of the limits on personal jurisdiction under the "minimum contacts" standard) was not made explicit in the *Dick* case. But subsequent decisions by the Supreme Court have made clear that these are the basic criteria for determining the constitutionality under the Due Process Clause of a state court's application of forum law.

Although the Texas court's application of Texas law was held unconstitutional in *Dick*, in practice the Supreme Court has since the 1930s rarely applied the *Dick* Due Process principle to invalidate a particular application of forum law by a state court. We will postpone further discussion of this post–1930s case law until after we have considered the role of the Full Faith and Credit Clause in this area. But one aspect of the Court's cases applying the *Dick* principle should be noted. At times the Court has appeared to give particularly short shrift to the Due Process challenges raised by corporate businesses having a regional or national market. The thinking appears to be that, if a company *generally* does substantial business in the forum, it is fair to subject it to forum law even in a case in which the *particular* transaction had little or no connection with the forum ultimately selected by the plaintiff for litigation. A corporation engaged in substantial business throughout the country, so the thinking goes, naturally will expect to be subjected *at some point* to the legal requirements of any particular state. Needless to say, this attitude facilitates forum shopping, for example in product liability cases where the plaintiff may need to search for a forum whose law includes a favorable statute of limitations.[11]

---

11. This was in fact the situation considered by the Court in both *Watson v. Employers Liab. Assur. Corp.*, 348 U.S. 66 (1954), and *Clay v. Sun Ins.* *Office, Ltd.*, 377 U.S. 179 (1964), in which the Court raised the "doing business" idea. *Watson* and *Clay* are discussed later in this Chapter.

It is difficult to say whether this *"quid pro quo"* rationale—so called because it seems to say to the defendant, "You do a lot of business in our state and get the protection of our laws *generally*, so it's only fair that we can apply our law to you in *this* case"—is simply a way of determining whether there has in fact been "unfair surprise" to the defendant in the application of forum law, or is a separate and independent criterion alongside the "unfair surprise" criterion. Frankly, it not easy to imagine a situation in which the application of forum law would satisfy one but not the other criterion. It is probably best to view this *"quid pro quo"* argument as window dressing for the already preconceived determination in a particular case that the forum has not violated the Due Process Clause in applying its own law.

B. Full Faith and Credit

There has never been serious doubt that Article IV, § 1, the Full Faith & Credit Clause of the Constitution, and its principal implementing statute, 28 U.S.C. § 1738, together require state courts to give effect to the *judgments* rendered by sister-state courts.[12] It is less obvious from the language of the Clause and the history of its adoption that it applies to choice of law. Scholars have debated for generations over whether the Clause as adopted in the original Constitution was intended to apply to choice-of-law problems.[13] Today, however, that debate is largely of academic interest, since the Supreme Court has long held that the Clause does place limits on the power of courts to apply forum law. The premise underlying this principle is that, when a court unjustifiably applies forum law, it is failing to apply the law of another state that has a greater claim to application; the forum is therefore failing to give "full faith and credit" to that other state's law.

In *Dick*, discussed above, the Full Faith and Credit Clause played no part in the decision. This is usually explained by the fact that the Clause does not require a state to accord full faith and credit to the laws or judgments of a foreign country, and in *Dick* it was Mexico's law that was displaced by the Texas court's application of Texas law in the case.[14] In a series of decisions in the 1930s,

---

12. This subject is treated at length in Chapter 5. At one time, some jurists argued that the Clause only required a state court to consider a sister-state judgment as *evidence* of the matters decided therein, rather than as definitively establishing those matters, but that view has long since been discarded.

13. *Compare* Kurt H. Nadelmann, *Full Faith and Credit to Judgments and Public Acts: A Historical–Analytical Re-*

appraisal, 56 MICHIGAN LAW REVIEW 33 (1957), *with* Douglas Laycock, *Equal Citizens of Equal and Territorial States: The Constitutional Foundations of Choice of Law*, 92 COLUMBIA LAW REVIEW 249, 290–310 (1992).

14. Actually, the reason that the Full Faith and Credit Clause was not discussed in *Dick* is more basic. The Court simply did not view the problem in the case as the failure to apply the

however, the Supreme Court made clear that the Clause does indeed limit state courts' choice of law. It is significant, both for historical and analytical reasons, that all three of these cases involved the application of workers' compensation laws, a statutory innovation of the early twentieth century.

1. The 1930s Cases on Full Faith and Credit and Choice of Law

Clapper (1932). In *Bradford Elec. Light Co. v. Clapper* (1932),[15] a Vermont employee of a Vermont company was sent by the company to New Hampshire to make repairs to an electrical installation there. The employee was electrocuted while performing the work in New Hampshire. Both New Hampshire and Vermont had workers' compensation statutes, but they differed in at least one important detail: New Hampshire law permitted the injured party (or his survivor) the option of submitting his claim to the state's workers' compensation tribunal or commencing a traditional common-law action against the employer in state court. Vermont law, by contrast, limited the employee (or survivor) to his remedy pursuant to the state's workers' compensation statute. Clapper's widow sued the company for wrongful death in New Hampshire state court, which upheld her right to do so under New Hampshire law. The Supreme Court, again speaking through Justice Brandeis, held that the application of New Hampshire law violated the Full Faith and Credit Clause.

Clapper has been superseded by later cases, and indeed Justice Brandeis's opinion is somewhat perplexing. Conventional choice-of-law theory at the time would have regarded *lex loci delicti*—in this case, New Hampshire—as at least the presumptive (if not the definitive) choice-of-law reference in this case of wrongful death.[16] The Court thus appeared to be condemning as unconstitutional a result that would have seemed unremarkable under the First Restatement. But Brandeis thought, not unreasonably, that if ever a state's worker's compensation law ought to be entitled to application, it is when the employer and employee both reside in the state (here, Vermont) and have created their contractual relationship there. Characterization of the issue as one of a contract that implicitly incorporated the Vermont worker's compensation rules

law of Mexico, where the contract was made and under which the one-year provision would have been valid; the problem was the application of the law of a state with no real connections to the transaction so as to nullify a contractual provision agreed to by the parties, which was valid under the laws of the place where the contract was made and to be performed.

15. 286 U.S. 145 (1932).

16. The First Restatement, promulgated two years after *Clapper*, stated that "the place of wrong" governed the question of whether the plaintiff had a cause of action in tort. Restatement (First) of Torts (1934), § 384.

assisted Brandeis in reaching this result: "If . . . the employee or his representative were free to disregard the law of Vermont and his contract, the effectiveness of the Vermont Act would be gravely impaired."[17] (One might reply to this by observing that, by sending the decedent to New Hampshire to perform work there, it was the employer and not the employee or his widow who had introduced New Hampshire into the picture.) In this analysis, however, Brandeis gave short shrift to the argument that New Hampshire, as well, had a legitimate interest in regulating the behavior of a company operating within the state and alleged to have acted wrongfully there. Thus, while application of Vermont law might well be defensible (and certainly constitutional) as a matter of choice-of-law theory, the Court's conclusion that it was constitutionally *compelled* by the Full Faith and Credit Clause seems questionable.[18]

Alaska Packers (1935). In *Alaska Packers Assoc. v. Industrial Accident Commission* (1935),[19] the Court changed course in another workers' compensation case, whose facts were somewhat analogous to those in *Clapper*. In *Alaska Packers*, the employee, a nonresident alien, was sent by his California employer to Alaska to perform canning work pursuant to an employment contract that they had formed in California. The employee was injured while working in Alaska, but, rather than invoking Alaska's workers' compensation process, he commenced a workers' compensation action in California after his return to that state. After an award was made pursuant to the California workers' compensation statute and upheld in the courts of that state, the California employer appealed to the Supreme Court on the ground that application of California's workers' compensation law instead of Alaska's violated the Full Faith and Credit Clause. The scenario in *Alaska Packers*

---

17. *Clapper*, 286 U.S. at 159. By emphasizing that the "residence" of both employer and employee was Vermont, Brandeis anticipated the emphasis on domicile associated with later, interest-based methodologies of choice of law. Incidentally, it's well known that Brandeis personally favored workers' compensation statutes as a policy for dealing with industrial accidents and that he regarded the option of choosing to sue in court, as under the New Hampshire law, as a threat to the efficacy of the administrative remedy. This view seems to have influenced his approach to the *Clapper* case.

18. *Clapper*, incidentally, makes for a very interesting study under interest analysis. Vermont's workers' compensation clearly was meant (1) to provide a swift administrative remedy for Vermont workers and (2) to provide Vermont employers with a streamlined process in cases of injury, enabling them to rationalize the costs associated with their employees' injuries. The particular New Hampshire rule at issue, by contrast, was the provision giving injured workers the option of suing in court or invoking the administrative process. If one concludes that New Hampshire's interest with respect to that provision pertained only to New Hampshire employers and employees, interest analysis might yield a false conflict and a conclusion that Vermont law should apply. But this, of course, does not necessarily speak to the *constitutionality* of applying New Hampshire law.

19. 294 U.S. 532 (1935).

differed in some particulars from that in *Clapper*. In *Clapper* both employer and employee were residents of Vermont, whereas in *Alaska Packers* only the employer was a California domiciliary.[20] Moreover, in *Clapper* most of the employee's work (though not the work that led to his death) took place in Vermont, while in *Alaska Packers* none of the employee's work, apparently, took place in California. Thus the connections in *Clapper* with Vermont were somewhat more substantial than the connection in *Alaska Packers* with California. Nevertheless, one might think that the reasoning in *Clapper* should have made *Alaska Packers* an easy case: If the application of Vermont law was constitutionally *required* in *Clapper*, surely the application of California law in *Alaska Packers* was constitutionally *permissible*.

But in *Alaska Packers*, Justice Stone (speaking for the Court) took the opportunity to reorient the constitutional analysis. Stone observed that, as in *Clapper*, *both* of the states involved had at least some plausible claim to the application of its own law—Alaska, because it was the place of injury, and California, because it was the employer's place of residence and the seat of the parties' contractual relationship. He noted, in a well-known passage, that a "rigid and literal enforcement of the full faith and credit clause, without regard to the statute of the forum, would lead to the absurd result that, wherever the conflict arises, the statute of each state must be enforced in the courts of the other, but cannot be in its own."[21] Stone's opinion upheld the application of California law without making it a constitutional requirement, and without denigrating the undoubted interest that Alaska might have in its law's application. He concluded that a cognizable interest such as California's was sufficient under the Full Faith and Credit Clause to justify application of forum law, unless the interest of another state was significantly greater than that of the forum. Such was not the case in *Alaska Packers*, he concluded. Stone's analysis implicitly accepted the possibility that the tribunals of either state might legitimately apply the law of the forum—a candid acknowledgment that the incentives for forum shopping such a situation created

---

20. Practically speaking, it was perhaps less relevant that the employee in *Alaska Packers* was not a California resident than that he was not an *Alaska* resident. As Justice Stone's opinion recounted, he was a seasonal worker in the Alaska fisheries, who would have had great difficulty initiating a case in the Alaska workers' compensation tribunal once he had returned to California to receive his pay. To have argued that the application of California law in his case would have been unconstitutional, while application of Vermont law was constitutionally compelled in *Clapper*, simply because the employee in *Alaska Packers* was not a California resident, would have been perverse.

21. *Alaska Packers*, 294 U.S. at 547.

might be a necessary evil, or at least one that the Constitution did not reprove.

Pacific Employers **(1939).** By the time of *Pacific Employers v. Industrial Acc. Comm'n* (1939),[22] yet another workers' compensation case, Justice Stone had come to the view that even this constitutional condition on the application of forum law—the requirement that the interest of another state not be significantly greater than that of the forum—was an impractical doctrine, because it would require courts (including the Supreme Court) to make comparative judgments in numerous cases about the relative substantiality of state "interests." While courts regularly do this today in making basic choice-of-law rulings, it is a far more serious matter to make determinations of *constitutionality* turn on such a subjective and imprecise calculus. The facts of *Pacific Employers* constituted another variation on the workers' compensation scenario, again rather like the situation in *Clapper*: The employer and employee were both Massachusetts residents; the employer sent the employee to California to work temporarily on a project; the employee was injured in the course of his employment in California and sought an award from the California workers' compensation commission; the employer appealed the ensuing award on the ground that failure to observe and apply the Massachusetts workers' compensation statute violated the Full Faith and Credit Clause.

Literally speaking, *Clapper* (which had not been overruled in *Alaska Packers*) could certainly be read as requiring the application of Massachusetts's workers' compensation law. But the Court in *Alaska Packers* had implicitly rejected the *Clapper* approach in favor of one more hospitable to the application of forum law, and in *Pacific Employers* the Court upheld the constitutionality of the application of California's workers' compensation law (while making a valiant but unpersuasive effort to distinguish *Clapper*). Moreover, Stone held for the Court that, for the forum to apply its own law, it was constitutionally sufficient that the forum have a plausible or "cognizable" interest in application of its law to the dispute (which was certainly the case in *Pacific Employers* itself).[23] Once this were determined to be the case, no further inquiry would be undertaken into the relative substantiality of another state's interest, and the demands of the Full Faith and Credit Clause would be satisfied. This basic holding, which went beyond even *Alaska Packers* in its reluctance to invalidate the forum's application of its own law, remains good law today.

22.   306 U.S. 493 (1939).

23.   "[T]he full faith and credit clause does not require one state to substitute for its own statute, applicable to persons and events within it, the conflicting statute of another state, even though that statute is of controlling force in the courts of the state of its enactment with respect to the same persons and events." *Pacific Employers*, 306 U.S. at 502.

2. The Continuing Relevance of Pacific Employers

The essential holding of *Pacific Employers* remains a foundational principle today in the constitutional analysis of choice of law: A state court does not violate the Full Faith and Credit Clause when it applies forum law, so long as the forum has sufficient connections with the dispute to give it a cognizable "interest" in its resolution. The Court's decisions in *Alaska Packers* and *Pacific Employers* may not seem extraordinary today, but they represented a shrewd recognition of and adaptation to the changing nature of American law, and they influenced the development of new ideas about choice of law. Supreme Court decisions through *Clapper* had evinced a constitutional squeamishness about what was deemed the "extraterritorial" application of state statutes; to many jurists, such extraterritorial application of the forum's statute to events in another state seemed to be an illegitimate exercise of the forum's "political" jurisdiction. But Stone's opinions in *Alaska Packers* and *Pacific Employers* recognized that, in an age of increased regulation, widespread statutory modification (as with workers' compensation schemes) of traditional common-law principles, state-by-state variations in legal rules, and geographic mobility, it was impractical to place rigid constitutional limits on "extraterritorial application of state law" even if one could define precisely what that phrase meant. Moreover, his opinions recognized that state laws like those at issue in the workers' compensation cases embody governmental *policies*—policies that states are presumptively entitled to see vindicated in cases where those policies are implicated. Thus, although *Alaska Packers* and *Pacific Employers* were decisions about the Full Faith and Credit Clause and not about conflicts methodology as such, they constituted a powerful (and precocious) validation of the idea that governmental interests are a legitimate consideration in choice of law.

Although *Pacific Employers* attempted to narrow the circumstances under which the application of forum law would violate the Full Faith and Credit Clause, it remains necessary to determine in individual cases whether the forum does in fact have the requisite interest in the case to justify application of its law under the Clause. Moreover, since the decision in *Pacific Employers*, the Supreme Court has steadily merged the Due Process and Full Faith and Credit analyses in its discussion of individual cases raising constitutional questions concerning choice of law, so that it is no longer possible clearly to demarcate precisely which clause is doing which work in the analysis. In any case, as discussed below, it apparently takes quite an extreme case for the Court to find that a state lacks the requisite connection with a dispute to justify applying its own law to it. The Court has simply concluded that the power of state courts to apply forum law is subject only to very modest limitations.

C. Due Process and Full Faith and Credit, Merged

Together, the Due Process principle of *Dick* and the Full Faith and Credit principle of *Pacific Employers* continue to govern the question of constitutional limitations on choice of law. It remains the case that a court may apply forum law if and only if (1) such application is not fundamentally unfair to a party (due process) and (2) the forum has a constitutionally sufficient interest in the application of its own law (Full Faith and Credit). However, since the 1930s the doctrine has evolved in some important ways. First, the Supreme Court has lost sight of the fact that the Due Process and Full Faith and Credit Clauses are distinct provisions and address different constitutional concerns in the choice-of-law context. In its most recent decisions on the matter, the Court has rendered opinions that are basically in accord with the principles set out by *Dick* and *Pacific Employers*, but that no longer bother to explain how much of the work is being done by the Due Process Clause and how much by the Full Faith and Credit Clause.

Second, the Court's decisions since 1939 have helped to indicate just what counts as impermissible unfairness (due process), and what counts as an adequate connection between the forum and the underlying transaction (full faith and credit). For example, the Court's decisions suggest that a party to whose detriment forum law has been applied will have difficulty establishing that it has been subjected to "unfair surprise," particularly if the party is a business corporation with even a modest degree of business outside its state of principal activity. "Unfair surprise" could be taken to mean that a party would not reasonably have expected forum law to be applied with respect to the particular transaction being litigated; at times, however, the Court has suggested it is constitutionally sufficient if the party could reasonably have expected that *some* dispute involving its activities would, some day, end up triggering the interests of the forum and thus leading to the application of forum law.

1. Implementing Dick *and* Pacific Employers*: The* Watson *and* Clay *Cases*

For example, in *Watson v. Employers Liab. Assur. Corp.* (1954),[24] the defendant insurer, a Massachusetts corporation, issued a liability insurance policy to an Illinois maker of hair products. The contract included a clause, valid and enforceable under both Massachusetts and Illinois law, providing that a consumer injured by one of the company's hair products could not maintain a "direct action" against the insurer (that is, no action could be brought

---

24.   348 U.S. 66 (1954).

directly against the insurer prior to an adjudication of the hair product company's liability, if any, to the consumer). A Louisiana resident used, and was injured by, one of the company's products and brought a direct action against the insurer in Louisiana court. Louisiana law regarded contractual "anti-direct-action" provisions as void and unenforceable. After the case was removed to federal court, the lower federal courts ruled that the complaint against the insurer should be dismissed because application of Louisiana law would violate the Due Process and Full Faith and Credit Clauses. The Supreme Court reversed, holding that application of Louisiana law was constitutional. The Court emphasized that the insurance policy was designed to cover judgments of liability wherever in the United States they might be entered, and that the hair product company (and presumably, the insurer) knew that its goods were likely to be used in all 50 states. Moreover, under *Pacific Employers*, Louisiana had a clear interest in the protection of its domiciliaries. These facts were sufficient to justify the application of Louisiana law to permit the direct action.[25]

In *Clay v. Sun Ins. Office, Ltd.* (1964),[26] a resident of Illinois purchased a liability policy from a British insurer. The policy included a clause requiring claims to be filed within twelve months of the loss (a provision that was enforceable under the law of both Illinois and England). After purchasing the policy, the insured moved to Florida, whose law regarded such limitation clauses as unenforceable. When the insured sued in Florida court to recover on a claim under the policy that it had brought after the twelve-month period had expired, the insurer contended that application of Florida law to invalidate the contractual limitation provision violated its constitutional rights. The Supreme Court rejected that contention, noting, " 'In this very case the policy was sold to Clay with

---

25. It is useful to compare *Watson* with *Hartford Acc. & Indem. Co. v. Delta & Pine Land Co.*, 292 U.S. 143 (1934), yet another case involving insurance. In *Delta & Pine*, a Tennessee business contracted for insurance to cover employee defalcations "in any position, anywhere"; the policy explicitly required that any claim be brought within 15 months of the offending employee's embezzlement. The business subsequently moved its main operations to Mississippi, where one of its employees embezzled funds. Mississippi had a statute that prohibited enforcement of the 15–month limitation period in the policy. The insured filed a claim after the fifteen-month period had expired, and sued the insurer on the policy. Doubtless the insured's relocation to Mississippi was known to the insurer; and the possibility of such relocation was reasonably foreseeable at the time the policy was issued, not least because of the words "in any position, anywhere" in the contract. Nevertheless, the Supreme Court, on the authority of *Home Ins. Co. v. Dick*, ruled that the Constitution forbade the application of Mississippi law to nullify the contractual 15–month limitation. It is clear that, by the time of *Watson*, the Court had moved to a much more forgiving attitude concerning the constitutionality of applying forum law. Although the Court in *Watson* sought to distinguish *Delta & Pine* rather than overrule it, it is safe to say that *Delta & Pine* is no longer good law.

26. 377 U.S. 179 (1964).

knowledge that he could take his property anywhere in the world he saw fit without losing the protection of his insurance.... Particularly since the company was licensed to do business in Florida, it must have known it might be sued there.' "[27] This reasoning suggests that, at least for a company that does business in a number of states, application of the law of a state that was not necessarily within the contemplation of the parties at the time they entered into their transaction may nevertheless comport with the Due Process Clause (as well as the Full Faith and Credit Clause). Although the result in *Clay* does not seem particularly tragic, the notion that the plaintiff, by an expedient post-transaction relocation to another state, might legitimately obtain the benefit of a more favorable law is an important indication of how reluctant the Court is to restrict the power of states to apply forum law.

2. *The Modern Cases:* Hague *and* Shutts

The most important decision by the Supreme Court since *Pacific Employers* on the Constitution and choice of law is *Allstate Ins. Co. v. Hague* (1981).[28] This decision revealed how minimal the constitutional limitations really are and how reluctant the Court is to embark on a quest to enforce them more rigorously. In *Hague*, the decedent was killed in a motorcycle accident in Wisconsin, near the border with Minnesota. He and his wife had lived in Wisconsin, although he had worked for the preceding fifteen years on the Minnesota side of the border. After the accident, but prior to the lawsuit, his widow moved to Minnesota, where she remarried and settled. Her late husband had owned three vehicles while they resided in Wisconsin, each with an insurance policy that included uninsured motorist coverage to a maximum of $15,000. Minnesota law permitted "stacking" of the three so as to provide a total of $45,000 in coverage; Wisconsin law did not. The widow brought an action in Minnesota court seeking a declaration that she was entitled to "stack" the policies and receive $45,000 from Allstate. The Minnesota court, applying the "better law" choice-of-law methodology, held that Minnesota law applied and that the plaintiff was permitted to stack the policies. The Minnesota Supreme Court upheld against constitutional challenge the application of Minnesota law to the dispute. In a 5–3 decision, the U.S. Supreme Court affirmed and found no constitutional violation in the Minnesota courts' application of Minnesota law.

---

27. *Clay*, 377 U.S. at 182, *quoting Clay v. Sun Ins. Office, Ltd.*, 363 U.S. 207, 221 (1960) (Black, J., dissenting).

28. 449 U.S. 302 (1981). The Minnesota Supreme Court's decision in

Hague is discussed in Chapter 2, in connection with the "better law" approach to choice-of-law questions.

In his plurality opinion, Justice Brennan asserted that Minnesota's connections with the parties and to the accident were "obviously significant"—although they have not seemed so obvious to everyone. The first of three significant connections itemized by Justice Brennan was that the decedent had been a "member of the Minnesota workforce" for 15 years prior to his death. Although the decedent had not been traveling to or from work when the accident occurred in the state of Wisconsin, Justice Brennan regarded this as "a very important contact." The second significant connection was that Allstate, the defendant, did a great deal of business in Minnesota (although of course the decedent had not been a Minnesota domiciliary at the time he obtained his policy from Allstate, or indeed at any time thereafter up to the time of his death). This precluded any suggestion of unfair surprise to the defendant, since Allstate must have known that Minnesota law would apply to *some* transactions in which it was involved there (and presumably factored that possibility into the calculation of its rates). The third significant connection was that the plaintiff, decedent's widow, had moved to Minnesota after her husband's death but prior to her institution of litigation. Minnesota's concern for the welfare of its domiciliaries gave that state a legitimate interest in the resolution of the dispute, even though the plaintiff had not resided in Minnesota at the time the cause of action arose. These considerations led Justice Brennan to conclude that the application of Minnesota law violated neither the Due Process Clause nor the Full Faith and Credit Clause.

Commentators have criticized the *Hague* decision rather severely. Even Justice Stevens in his concurrence acknowledged that the choice-of-law determination made by the Minnesota courts was "plainly unsound as a matter of normal conflicts law," although he did not think it amounted to a violation of the Constitution.[29] Justice Brennan's itemization, one might say his exaggerated assessment, of the three contacts with Minnesota has struck almost everyone as unconvincing. And yet, as measured against the general principles announced in *Dick*, *Pacific Employers*, and succeeding cases, *Hague* does not seem wrongly decided. Allstate was undoubtedly aware that the decedent commuted each working day to and from Minnesota, and for all Allstate knew an auto accident involving the decedent was as likely to occur in Minnesota as in Wisconsin. Although the application of Minnesota law in this particular case may have upset some of Allstate's actuarial assumptions, it

---

29. *Allstate*, 449 U.S. at 324 (Stevens, J., concurring in the judgment). The terms "unsound" and "normal conflicts law" reveal the lingering sense that certain conflicts holdings can be "right" and others "wrong," even though they violate neither the Constitution nor state law. It is difficult to know what else would make the Minnesota courts' ruling "unsound," other than its deviation from what the critic thinks would be the "sound" result.

could hardly be said that it amounted to "unfair surprise." More-over, the extensive amount of business done by Allstate in Minneso-ta provides a *"quid pro quo"* justification for the application of Minnesota law—Allstate could not complain of the application of Minnesota law, given the large amount of business it does there and the "protection" it thereby receives from Minnesota law. Finally, so long as one assumes that the plaintiff's relocation to Minnesota was not fraudulent, Minnesota's interest in her welfare as a domiciliary at the time of the suit is, under *Pacific Employers*, a cognizable connection with the parties and thus a sufficient condition for the application of Minnesota law. Perhaps Justice Stevens had the correct perspective on *Hague*: What is vexing about the Minnesota courts' application of Minnesota law is that it is intellectually indefensible under *any* plausible choice-of-law theory (other than *lex fori*)—not that it violated anyone's constitutional rights or exceeded Minnesota's power under the Constitution. Bad choice-of-law reasoning does not violate the Constitution unless it passes the boundaries set by *Dick* and *Pacific Employers*.

As it happens, in 1985 the Supreme Court was presented with a case in which it did, in fact, find that the limits of *Dick* and *Pacific Employers* had been reached and passed. In *Phillips Petro-leum v. Shutts* (1985),[30] Phillips Petroleum had leased mineral rights from over 30,000 individuals, and agreed to pay them royal-ties on its profits from sales of oil and gas. On a number of occasions, Phillips raised its oil and gas prices, actions that required final approval from the Federal Power Commission ["FPC"] (now the Federal Energy Regulatory Commission). Phillips was permit-ted to charge the higher prices while its application was pending before the FPC, but (based on the fact that it would have to refund retroactively the revenue obtained due to those increases if the FPC ultimately ruled against the increases) it did not pay increased royalties to the lessors until the FPC approved the price increases. When the increases were approved, Phillips did not pay interest on the deferred royalty increases to the lessors. A class action was brought in Kansas court on behalf of a large number of the lessors. The Kansas courts applied Kansas law to the entire case, "notwith-standing that over 99% of the gas leases and some 97% of the plaintiffs in the case had no apparent connection to the State of Kansas except for this lawsuit."[31]

One can understand why the Kansas courts were eager to apply a single source of substantive law to the case (wholly apart from the question of whether that law should be *Kansas* law). The prospect of making separate choice-of-law determinations for reso-

---

30. 472 U.S. 797 (1985).   **31.** *Shutts*, 472 U.S. at 814–15 (footnote omitted).

lution of claims brought by 30,000 plaintiffs residing in all 50 states, concerning land located in eleven states, was daunting; application of a single source of law to all the claims would simplify the task considerably. On the other hand, the selection of Kansas law as that single source was difficult to justify, even under the generous standard of *Hague*, when for many of the claims the only connection with Kansas was the fact of the lawsuit itself. Without at all questioning the ruling in *Hague*, the Supreme Court drew the line at the situation in *Shutts*. It was unconstitutional for the Kansas courts to apply Kansas law to claims with which Kansas had no significant contacts. While the Court again made little effort to distinguish clearly between the Due Process and Full Faith and Credit components of the constitutional test, it stressed the "arbitrariness and unfairness" of applying Kansas law. *Shutts* certainly makes sense as a Full Faith and Credit decision, at least as to those claimants whose leases had nothing to do with Kansas.

Shutts represents the only occasion since the 1930s on which the Supreme Court has struck down as unconstitutional a state court's application of forum law. Interestingly, however, the *Shutts* litigation came before the Court once more, when on remand the Kansas courts applied the state's own statute of limitations, the longest in the nation, to all of the plaintiffs' claims, even though (*per Shutts*) Kansas substantive law could not constitutionally be applied to many of those claims. In an opinion by Justice Scalia, the Court in *Sun Oil v. Wortman* (1988)[32] held that this was not unconstitutional. The Court's reasoning was that, since statutes of limitations had traditionally been regarded as "procedural," and thus subject to the law of the forum, there was nothing in the Constitution to bar such a practice, despite the fact that the modern view on statutes of limitations often regards those limitations as being "substantive" in nature, or at least that they should be determined by the law of the state whose law supplies the underlying case of action. Neither the Due Process Clause nor the Full Faith and Credit Clause was offended by the Kansas Supreme Court's decision.

Perhaps the *reductio ad absurdum* of the reasoning in *Sun Oil* came in a case that combined the *Sun Oil* principle with the holding of *Van Dusen v. Barrack* (1964)[33] that, where a case in federal court has been transferred from one judicial district to another under 28 U.S.C. § 1404(a) (allowing transfer for "the convenience of parties and witnesses"), the law of the "transferor court" should apply to questions thereafter arising in the transferee court. In *Ferens v. John Deere Co.* (1990),[34] a Pennsylvania

---

32. 486 U.S. 717 (1988).   **34.** 494 U.S. 516 (1990).
33. 376 U.S. 612 (1964).

resident was injured in Pennsylvania while using the defendant's machinery, but did not sue until after Pennsylvania's two-year limitations period had expired. The plaintiff brought his claim in federal district court in Mississippi, whose limitations period is six years. Although the defendant was a Delaware corporation with its principal place of business in Illinois, personal jurisdiction was ruled valid in Mississippi on the ground that the defendant did business there. The *plaintiff* then moved to transfer the case to a federal district court in Pennsylvania under 28 U.S.C. § 1404(a). The motion was granted, and the Supreme Court ruled that, pursuant to *Van Dusen v. Barrack*, Mississippi's six-year limitations period must be applied by the federal court in Pennsylvania. It is difficult to imagine a more flagrant instance of forum shopping. But the specter of forum shopping—which, of course, is also made possible by the very fact that the choice-of-law rules of different states differ from one another—does not necessarily amount to unconstitutionality.

3. *Full Faith and Credit, National Unity, and Sovereign Immunity*

The rationale underlying the Full Faith and Credit Clause, limited though the Clause's impact might be on choice of law, is that a state court's unwarranted disregard for the legal prerogatives of a sister state threatens the interest in national unity. It is that sister state's interests and dignity that are harmed, to the detriment of national harmony, when the Full Faith and Credit Clause is violated. Realistically, however, it's difficult to believe that in cases like *Allstate v. Hague*, the state (Wisconsin) whose law was not applied cares very much. Most of the cases discussing the impact of the Full Faith and Credit Clause on choice of law feature a private litigant claiming to defend the constitutional prerogatives of the state whose law was not applied, all so that party may obtain a more advantageous result in the case. That does not mean that the Clause's purposes shouldn't be given effect in such cases, or that states don't sometimes "care" when their law has been disregarded, but it does suggest that litigation over the Clause's impact on choice of law often emerges from the self-serving interests of a private litigant rather than the protestations of a state itself.

There are conflicts cases, however, in which a state's sovereign interests are implicated more directly, and here the application of the basic principles of *Pacific Employers* and *Allstate v. Hague* is trickier. In *Nevada v. Hall* (1979),[35] a Nevada state employee acting within the scope of his employment was driving in California when his auto collided with another, causing severe injuries to two

---

35. 440 U.S. 410 (1979).

California residents in the other vehicle. The California residents sued the State of Nevada (as well as the deceased driver's estate and the University of Nevada, for which he had worked) in California state court. The State of Nevada moved to quash the complaint on the ground that the state's statutory waiver of sovereign immunity permitted only suits brought against it in its own courts. When that contention proved unsuccessful, Nevada asserted, on the basis of a number of arguments including Full Faith and Credit, that the California court was required to apply that part of the Nevada statute that limited recovery in such actions against the state to $25,000. California law provided that another state could be sued in California courts with no dollar limitation, and an award for the plaintiffs of over a million dollars was upheld by the California courts. On appeal, the Supreme Court affirmed, ruling that nothing in the Constitution barred the California courts from applying forum law permitting a suit against another state, and declining to apply the other state's statutory cap on damages.

Nevada v. Hall was not all about choice of law and Full Faith and Credit. Nevada's first argument was that the Constitution recognizes the principle of state sovereign immunity, permitting a state to be sued in the courts of another state only with the first state's consent. Discussion of that contention, which the Court rejected, is outside the scope of this book. Beyond that, however, Nevada also argued that Full Faith and Credit required the California courts to apply Nevada law limiting the state's liability to $25,000. Conventional analysis based on *Pacific Employers* would suggest that this argument was weak; California certainly had a significant interest in the case, since plaintiffs were California domiciliaries and the accident had occurred in California. But does the fact that the suit had been brought against the state itself change things? Even if (as the Court ruled) sovereign immunity principles as such did not bar the California courts from hearing the suit, might not the presence of a sister state as a defendant implicate Full Faith and Credit values (promotion of interstate harmony, for example) to a greater degree than do cases between private parties?

The Court suggested that liability for state employees involved in automobile accidents did not compromise "core" aspects of state sovereignty so as to require reversal based on the Full Faith and Credit Clause: "California's exercise of jurisdiction in this case poses no substantial threat to our constitutional system of cooperative federalism. Suits involving traffic accidents occurring outside of Nevada could hardly interfere with Nevada's capacity to fulfill its own sovereign responsibilities."[36] As has been well pointed out, however, large damage awards (whatever the cause of action and

---

36. 440 U.S. at 424 n.24.

the subject matter of the lawsuit) are another matter; a state like Nevada might well consider that such judgments, if large and frequent enough, could "interfere with [its] capacity to fulfill its own sovereign responsibilities." At the same time, of course, it might equally well be a threat to interstate harmony, and thus to the values protected by the Full Faith and Credit Clause, were California compelled to apply Nevada law in the case. In any event, the Supreme Court rejected Nevada's Full Faith and Credit arguments.

Twenty-four years later, in *Franchise Tax Board v. Hyatt* (2003),[37] the shoe was truly on the other foot. The California Franchise Tax Board performed an audit of Hyatt, a one-time resident of California who had moved to Nevada. The tax board was investigating the possibility that Hyatt had, on an earlier California tax return, falsely claimed to have relocated from California to Nevada earlier than he actually had. When the California tax board, at the conclusion of its audit, assessed additional California tax liabilities for the period in question and imposed civil penalties for fraud, Hyatt filed suit against the tax board in Nevada court, claiming that during the course of the audit agents of the tax board had committed several torts against him, some intentional, some based on a negligence theory. A California statute grants the tax board and its employees immunity from suit for injuries caused in the course of assessing or collecting taxes. Nevada law likewise provides immunity for such agencies and employees, except that such immunity does not extend to intentional torts. The Nevada Supreme Court ordered dismissal of those of Hyatt's claims that were based on a negligence theory, but permitted his suit to go forward on the intentional tort claims. The U.S. Supreme Court affirmed, holding that it did not violate the Full Faith Credit Clause (or any other constitutional provision) for Nevada to apply its nonimmunity rule—or, to put it more precisely, to decline to apply California's immunity rule—under the circumstances of the case.

The basic structure of the *Hyatt* litigation was similar to that of *Nevada v. Hall* (with the roles of Nevada and California reversed). The tax board, however, strenuously attempted to distinguish *Nevada v. Hall* by arguing that taxation and tax collection, unlike the traffic accident at issue in *Hall*, involve "core" attributes of state sovereignty. (The passage quoted above from the Court's opinion in *Hall* was something of an invitation to the making of this argument.) The Court, though, declined to embark on the task of differentiating "core" from "non-core" state functions. Like *Hall*, *Hyatt* seems an easy case if one likens the case to the problems in *Pacific Employers* and *Allstate v. Hague*: Nevada

37.   538 U.S. 488 (2003).

certainly had the requisite connection with the dispute to justify application of its law under the Full Faith and Credit Clause. It is the element of state sovereignty, emerging from the fact that it was a California state agency that had been sued, that makes the question a harder one. And the Court in *Hyatt*, as in *Hall*, declined to hold that the forum was required to apply the law of the defendant state. It is interesting to note that the Court praised the Nevada Supreme Court for having "sensitively applied principles of comity with a healthy regard for California's sovereign status."[38] After all, the Nevada Supreme Court did recognize the tax board's immunity for the non-intentional torts. One wonders, though, whether the U.S. Supreme Court's decision would have been any different had the Nevada Supreme Court exhibited less "sensitivity" and a less "healthy regard for California's sovereign status," and simply applied Nevada's nonimmunity rule. Perhaps what impressed the Court about the Nevada Supreme Court's analysis is that, with respect to the non-intentional torts, as to which Nevada like California provides immunity, the state high court maintained an evenhanded attitude: It did not subject the California tax board to liability in its courts under conditions in which a Nevada state agency would be immune.

* * *

Putting aside the sovereign immunity cases as a separate category, *Allstate v. Hague* remains the basic standard for the constitutional limitations on choice of law. Only in the unusual situation where the forum state has no meaningful connection with the underlying claim will the state court's application of forum law be unconstitutional. The liberality of this standard is no doubt attributable to the fact that the U.S. Supreme Court does not wish to make the constitutionality of state courts' choice-of-law rulings (and assessment of the significance of a given state's connection with a particular dispute) a perpetually litigated issue that will require regular intervention by the Court.

Most of the cases discussed in this chapter thus far have involved statutes of limitations, state regulation of insurance policies, or workers' compensation. The obvious exception is *Shutts*, and the distinguishing feature of that case is the presence of a nationwide class action, which plainly presents a great challenge to the application of conventional choice-of-law methodologies. It is not surprising that these rather idiosyncratic problems have been the ones that have pushed the Court to define its constitutional approach to questions of choice of law. It is worth speculating, though, as to what other kinds of conflicts cases might raise new constitutional issues in the future. When states embody drastically

38. 538 U.S. at 499.

different social policies in their respective laws, "extraterritorial" application of one of those laws may raise serious objections. For example, suppose a state gives to the parents of a minor child a cause of action against a physician for performing an abortion on the minor without giving the parents notification as per the state's law. If the forum applies this law in a case against a physician residing in another state that does not require parental consent, might the physician's Due Process rights (or his state's Full Faith and Credit prerogatives) be violated? The point of this hypothetical is to suggest that, as you consider possible future variations on *Dick, Pacific Employers, Hague,* and *Shutts,* it is possible that *substantive law* conflicts (as opposed to such issues as limitations periods) will be the next frontier for the constitutional limitations on choice of law—but only if they speak to policies that citizens believe to be of fundamental importance.

D. The Privileges & Immunities Clause and the Problem of Discrimination in Choice of Law

The short of the matter is that the Privileges and Immunities Clause in Article IV, § 2 of the Constitution[39] does not figure in contemporary doctrine concerning constitutional limits on choice of law; the Supreme Court has never held that the Clause is relevant to the question. So you can stop reading here, proceed to the next section, and no one will be the wiser. Nevertheless, the Clause's proscription, at least in certain circumstances, of discrimination by a state against out-of-state residents would seem to have relevance for interest-based choice-of-law methodologies that place particular emphasis on domiciliary interests.[40] It's worth exploring that issue for a moment.

The Privileges and Immunities Clause reads: "The Citizens of each State shall be entitled to all Privileges and Immunities of Citizens in the Several States." Understood literally, the Clause might appear to bar states from conferring any benefits on in-state residents that it does not also offer to out-of-state residents (or, conversely, from imposing burdens on out-of-state residents that it does not also impose on in-state residents). But the Clause has

---

39. For purposes of the following discussion, the phrase "Privileges and Immunities Clause" refers to the Clause in Article IV of the Constitution. The "Privileges or Immunities Clause" in § 1 of the Fourteenth Amendment is not relevant to choice of law.

40. A classic article on this subject is Brainerd Currie & Herma Hill Schret-

er, *Unconstitutional Discrimination in the Conflict of Laws: Privileges and Immunities,* 69 YALE LAW JOURNAL 1323 (1960). A different perspective is provided in Douglas Laycock, *Equal Citizens of Equal and Territorial States: The Constitutional Foundations of Choice of Law,* 92 COLUMBIA LAW REVIEW 249, 261–88 (1992).

never been read so sweepingly; only discriminations with respect to privileges or immunities whose even-handed application "bear[s] upon the vitality of the Nation as a single entity,"[41] or that trench on a "fundamental right,"[42] bring the Clause into play. Moreover, the "vitality of the nation as a single entity" seems to be implicated principally in cases where the regulated activity is economic or business-related in nature—a situation that raises some of the same "national economy" interests one finds underlying the Dormant Commerce Clause. For example, the Court has struck down under the Privileges and Immunities Clause a New Hampshire statute limiting admission to the state bar to residents of New Hampshire; but it has upheld a Montana law that charged non-residents a higher fee for an elk-hunting license than residents.[43] The facts that the practice of law plays a "role in the national economy," and that it serves fundamental interests such as legal representation for those seeking to vindicate constitutional rights, were decisive in distinguishing the two cases.

The Privileges and Immunities Clause would seem relevant to the problem of choice of law because so many states now employ choice-of-law methodologies that explicitly identify domiciliary interests as among those that a court may legitimately take into account when solving a conflicts problem. Brainerd Currie's "interest analysis," discussed in Chapter 2, is the most vivid example, but the widely employed Second Restatement likewise recommends that the "policies" of the domiciliary state(s) be taken into account in choice-of-law determinations.[44] If a party's domicile becomes the decisive, or even a significant, factor in determining the choice of law in a particular case, the prospect of differential treatment of domiciliaries and nondomiciliaries—and, perhaps, discrimination against the latter—arises. When, as is frequently the case, the victorious party is a *forum* domiciliary, the inference that the forum resident has been favored becomes even stronger. In many instances, the non-domiciliary who thereby loses the case will have suffered an injury to an important interest, perhaps one that ordinarily would be recognized as cognizable under the Court's Privileges and Immunities jurisprudence.

41. *Baldwin v. Fish and Game Commission of Montana*, 436 U.S. 371, 383 (1978).

42. *Supreme Court of New Hampshire v. Piper*, 470 U.S. 274 (1985).

43. *Piper, supra* n. 42; *Baldwin, supra* n. 41.

44. Restatement (Second) of Conflict of Laws § 6. In this respect, the Second Restatement differs from Currie's approach because the Second Restatement also makes interstate harmony and the needs of the interstate system important considerations. Currie did not emphasize these factors to the same degree, and in fact believed that excessive even-handedness on the part of the forum so as to avoid privileging the forum's interests in the welfare of its own domiciliaries could amount to an unwarranted failure to

An example posited by Professor Douglas Laycock illustrates the point:[45]

> Suppose there are two acquaintances, Mary from Maryland and Del from Delaware. They go out together on occasion, and they take turns driving. One night, with Mary driving, they get into a wreck, and Del is hurt. Another night, with Del driving, they get into another wreck, and Mary is hurt.... Mary sues [Del] in Delaware. Del files a permissive counterclaim for his own injuries in the other wreck.... Finally, suppose that Delaware has a guest statute and Maryland does not.... [Laycock proceeds to analyze the problem using "interest analysis."] On Mary's claim against Del, Del wins. He is protected by the guest statute; Delaware has an interest in applying the statute to protect him; and the Delaware court has no reason ... to subordinate Delaware's interest to Maryland's. On Del's claim against Mary, Del also wins. Delaware has no interest in applying its guest statute to protect Mary, and Maryland has not attempted to protect her, so this is a false conflict. Delaware is free to pursue its interest in compensating Del. The bottom line is that Mary has to pay Del, but Del need not pay Mary....

Laycock used this admittedly stylized example to illustrate what he regarded as the unconstitutionally discriminatory features built into the very premises of interest analysis. Mary, the "out-of-stater," was denied the benefits of Delaware's guest statute that accrued to Del, the "in-stater." The usual rejoinder to this argument by defenders of interest analysis is that, so long as each party is given the "benefits" of his own state's law, there is really nothing discriminatory about this situation. Which characterization of the situation is more accurate? It really depends on what you think it means, in the choice-of-law context, for the forum to treat non-residents and residents equally. One view of such equal treatment is that, so long as the interests of the non-resident's *state* in the application of its law are given their proper due in the analysis—perhaps even resulting in application of that state's law—there is no discrimination, no matter which party that law protects. So long as there is no discrimination against the non-forum state's *law* (whatever its content), no one has reason to complain. The other view, though, focuses on the substantive outcome: If a nonresident, as a result of an interest-based choice-of-law ruling, is made to suffer a worse result than would a resident in identical circumstances, this is in itself discriminatory, regardless of which state is supplying the rule of decision. What matters, on this view, is

give effect to the forum's substantive policies.

45. Laycock, *Equal Citizens of Equal and Territorial States, supra* n. 40, at 276 (footnote omitted).

discrimination in substantive result against the non-resident, not discrimination against the law of her state.[46] There's no simple answer to the question of which, if either, of these two perspectives on the matter is the proper one.

Although the possibility that interest-based approaches might bring into play Privileges and Immunities Clause concerns has engaged scholars almost since Currie announced his "interest analysis,"[47] the U.S. Supreme Court gave the idea some unexpected (and surely unwitting) support in its 1975 decision in *Austin v. New Hampshire*, which, it is important to note, was not specifically about choice of law.[48] At the time *Austin* was decided, New Hampshire imposed no income tax on its residents. It did, however, tax the income earned in New Hampshire of *nonresidents* (such as Maine residents who commuted to work in New Hampshire). To ease the effects of this seeming discrimination, New Hampshire implemented a series of tax credits that provided the following: (1) If the nonresident's home state did not credit the nonresident for the New Hampshire tax, that tax would not be imposed by New Hampshire; and (2) New Hampshire would tax the nonresident at a rate no higher than that imposed by the nonresident's home state. Thus, the upshot of this tax regime was that New Hampshire applied its own tax rate (zero, as it happens) to the New Hampshire income of its own residents, and the tax rate of the nonresident's home state to the New Hampshire income of nonresidents. It is another instance of how the existence *vel non* of "discrimination" depends on the axis along which one chooses to measure it: So far as tax liability is concerned, New Hampshire (in theory) was

---

46. This point is illustrated by a comparison, perhaps more realistic than Laycock's example, of two similar cases whose essential factual difference lies in the changed domicile of one of the parties: *Babcock v. Jackson* (N.Y.1963) and *Neumeier v. Kuehner* (N.Y.1972), "guest statute" cases discussed at some length in Chapter 2. In *Babcock*, the New York Court of Appeals applied New York law (which included no "guest statute") to a case, arising out of an accident that took place in Ontario, in which both the driver and passenger were New York domiciliaries. In *Neumeier*, the accident again occurred in Ontario, but this time the passenger was an Ontario domiciliary (the driver was again a New York domiciliary). The New York Court of Appeals applied Ontario's guest statute, barring the plaintiff's claim. From one perspective—the perspective usually taken by proponents of interest analysis—the court's ruling in *Neumeier* represents a

commendable and cosmopolitan willingness to apply foreign law where that state's interests may be implicated. However, *Neumeier* did result in an Ontario plaintiff's being denied the right to pursue a negligence claim against a New York defendant in the New York courts, whereas in *Babcock* the New York plaintiff's right to pursue such a claim was protected. Structurally, the only salient difference between the two cases was that in *Babcock* a New York plaintiff was involved, and in *Neumeier* an Ontario plaintiff was involved. It is easy to see why some find this situation, which is a wholly unremarkable result if one accepts the premises of interest analysis, troubling and perhaps difficult to square with the Constitution.

47. *See* Currie & Schreter, *Unconstitutional Discrimination in the Conflict of Laws, supra* n. 40.

48. 420 U.S. 656 (1975).

treating the nonresident no differently from how that person's home state would treat her; but New Hampshire was certainly treating that nonresident differently from how it treated residents.

In *Austin*, the U.S. Supreme Court ruled that New Hampshire's tax regime violated the Privileges and Immunities Clause:

> The Privileges and Immunities Clause, *by making noncitizenship or nonresidence an improper basis for locating a special burden*, implicates not only the individual's right to nondiscriminatory treatment but also, perhaps more so, the structural balance essential to the concept of federalism. Since nonresidents are not represented in the taxing State's legislative halls ..., judicial acquiescence in taxation schemes that burden them particularly would remit them to such redress as they could secure through their own State; but "to prevent [retaliation] was one of the chief ends sought to be accomplished by the adoption of the Constitution." ...

> Against this background establishing a rule of substantial equality of treatment for the citizens of the taxing State and nonresident taxpayers, the New Hampshire Commuters Income Tax cannot be sustained.... [T]he argument advanced in favor of the tax is that the ultimate burden it imposes is 'not more onerous in effect,' ... on nonresidents because their total state tax liability is unchanged once the tax credit they receive from their State of residence is taken into account.... While this argument has an initial appeal it cannot be squared with the underlying policy of comity to which the Privileges and Immunities Clause commits us.[49]

The Court's opinion in *Austin* said nothing about choice of law. However, the operation of the New Hampshire tax regime struck down in *Austin* suggests an analogy to interest-oriented approaches to choice of law. *Prima facie*, the New Hampshire system accorded a 0% tax rate to residents but denied the benefit of that rate to nonresident "commuters" who worked in New Hampshire. Instead, New Hampshire applied the tax rate specified by the nonresident's state's law. This situation maps fairly well onto the situation presented by a choice-of-law problem: Under interest analysis, the nonapplication of forum law to benefit a nondomiciliary is sometimes defended on the ground that considerations of "comity" militate in favor of leaving room for the application of the other state's law—even if it that law isn't favorable to that state's domiciliary. *Austin* presents the same situation because New Hampshire was giving Maine domiciliaries the "benefit" of their

49. *Austin*, 420 U.S. at 662, 665–66 (emphasis supplied, footnotes and citations omitted).

own state's law—the higher tax rate of their state. If the New Hampshire tax scheme was struck down as unconstitutional in *Austin*, so the argument goes, interest analysis (with its emphasis on domiciliary interests) should fall as well.[50]

Nevertheless, this argument has never been entertained seriously by courts, and certainly not by the U.S. Supreme Court. After all, since *Pacific Employers* (1939), the mere presence of a plausible state interest as a basis for applying forum law is sufficient to satisfy the Full Faith and Credit Clause, and for even longer the Court has made clear that plausible domiciliary interests qualify. It would be odd if the Privileges and Immunities Clause were to invalidate that which the Full Faith and Credit Clause legitimates. Beyond that, analogizing choice of law to the *Austin* decision and its invocation of the Privileges and Immunities Clause would enmesh courts in metaphysical inquiries as to when the application of forum law to a resident's claim or defense amounts to a "benefit" that is being denied to non-residents. Is every application of forum law to a resident, while denying its application in otherwise identical cases to a nonresident, improperly discriminatory? Does the law have to be one that is unambiguously "favorable" to the party to whom it is applied? Since a state's laws can, as applied in an individual case, disadvantage a resident quite as often as it benefits her, it is hard to say that the *general* emphasis placed on domiciliary interests by interest analysis is inherently discriminatory. It is only in the pattern of individual choice-of-law rulings made by courts applying this methodology that one can hope to discern impermissible bias, and it is simply too cumbersome to analyze all these cases as a way of determining whether particular applications of interest analysis amount to unconstitutional discrimination under the Privileges & Immunities Clause.

E.   Other Constitutional Provisions

Although rarely understood as such, other constitutional provisions and doctrines themselves embody what appear to be choice-of-law principles. For example, the Supremacy Clause obliges courts (not to mention other governmental actors) to give effect to federal law when it comes into conflict with state law. In these situations, the Supremacy Clause functions as a sort of constitutional choice-of-law rule. The Commerce Clause, particularly in its "dormant" aspect, operates to displace certain state laws affecting interstate commerce, even if the competing federal policy is a "non-policy." The general doctrine of pre-emption embodies some of the same ideas. And the "*Erie* doctrine," to be discussed in Chapter 7, is

---

50. The argument paraphrased here is presented in John Hart Ely, *Choice of Law and the State's Interest in* *Protecting Its Own*, 23 WILLIAM & MARY LAW REVIEW 173 (1981).

often (if somewhat inaccurately) regarded as addressing a conflicts problem, by dictating the application of state (rather than federal) law in certain cases falling within the federal courts' diversity jurisdiction. Some conflicts problems potentially involving the law of foreign sovereigns can trigger separation-of-powers concerns—in particular, the increasingly important problem of the extraterritorial application of U.S. law.

Nevertheless, the constitutional limitations on the domestic choice-of-law methodologies are supplied by the Due Process and Full Faith and Credit Clauses. This is what conflicts casebooks have in mind in their chapters entitled "Constitutional Limitations on Choice of Law."

F. The Obligation to Provide a Forum

The overriding purpose of the Full Faith and Credit Clause is to promote a certain kind of interstate harmony by limiting the power of states blatantly to disregard the legitimate interests of sister states through unwarranted failure to apply their laws and to recognize their judgments. In the context of choice of law, as has been discussed above, this means that a court may not apply forum law when the forum has no plausible connection with the dispute. But the seeming disregard of foreign law can arise in a different kind of situation as well: Can a state refuse to provide a forum in which a particular foreign cause of action can be adjudicated? Can it simply bar particular foreign-created causes of action from vindication in its courts of general jurisdiction? In many cases, such action by a state would disparage foreign law quite as brazenly as would a state court's application of forum law where the forum had little connection with the dispute. It is today unusual to find states barring their courts wholesale from hearing particular foreign causes of action. But the situation arose more frequently earlier in the twentieth century, when states were sometimes more resistant to the extraterritorial application of statutorily created causes of action. Analysis of those earlier cases sheds light more generally on the limits the Constitution places on the power of state courts to refuse to apply foreign law.

1. Hughes v. Fetter *(1951)*

Undoubtedly it would violate the Full Faith and Credit Clause for a state simply to bar wholesale the application of *any* foreign law in any cases heard by its courts; it would be hard to imagine an act more hostile to the value of "interstate harmony" the Clause is meant to promote. But a more difficult situation is presented if a state declares that it will not permit a particular foreign-created cause of action to be enforced in its courts. In the important case of

Hughes v. Fetter (1951),[51] Wisconsin had enacted a wrongful death statute that created a cause of action for wrongful death, but only as to accidents that took place within the state. In itself, this limitation was perfectly constitutional; a state has no constitutional obligation to create a cause of action that covers all possible situations. However, in *Hughes*, the Wisconsin Supreme Court interpreted this statute also to bar the adjudication in Wisconsin courts of claims, based on the wrongful death statutes of *other* states, arising out of deaths that occurred outside Wisconsin. A Wisconsin resident was killed in an automobile accident that took place in Illinois, and his survivor sued the other driver, also a Wisconsin resident, for wrongful death. The plaintiff could not proceed under Wisconsin's wrongful death statute, since the accident had not taken place in Wisconsin, so she invoked the wrongful death statute of Illinois. In terms of traditional *lex loci* conceptions, this made sense, since the accident had taken place in Illinois. Nevertheless, the Wisconsin Supreme Court ruled that the survivor's wrongful death claim under Illinois law could not be vindicated in the state's courts. Notably, the decision did not amount merely to a dismissal of the claim for lack of jurisdiction, but constituted a dismissal on the merits, making the matter *res judicata* as to any other suit the plaintiff might bring, in Wisconsin or any other state. The Supreme Court ruled that the Wisconsin statute, as thus interpreted and applied by the Wisconsin courts, violated the Full Faith and Credit Clause.

While the exclusion of a foreign cause of action from a state's courts might well appear to embody the hostility to the interests of foreign states that the Full Faith and Credit Clause disapproves, the Supreme Court's decision in *Hughes v. Fetter* is at first glance somewhat puzzling. The Wisconsin Supreme Court's decision seemed defensible in light of the traditional "public policy" exception to then-prevailing *lex loci delicti* ideas. That court reasoned that the Wisconsin statute's limitation to deaths occurring within the state itself expressed a strong public policy against the imposition of liability arising out of deaths caused outside the state, regardless of which state supplied the cause of action; application of another state's law in order to give plaintiff a remedy for a death occurring elsewhere would be an end-run around that policy. The fact that both plaintiff and defendant were residents of Wisconsin may even have fortified the court's view that the state's own residents should not be able to skirt the state's policy in this way. Moreover, if the Wisconsin court had simply chosen to apply Wisconsin law to the case—which, although unorthodox under the prevailing *lex loci* approach, would today seem uncontroversial under such cases as *Babcock v. Jackson*—the outcome presumably

51. 341 U.S. 609 (1951).

would have been dismissal of the plaintiff's claim (the accident had not occurred in Wisconsin as required by the statute); and Supreme Court decisions such as *Alaska Packers* and *Pacific Employers* would have suggested that such an outcome was constitutional, since Wisconsin certainly had an interest in applying its law.

Is there any difference between these (presumably constitutional) ways of deciding the case, and the application of a Wisconsin rule that simply declares generally that foreign causes of action for wrongful death based on deaths in another state will not be vindicated in Wisconsin courts? The answer seems to lie in Justice Black's observation in *Hughes* that Wisconsin "has no real feeling of antagonism against wrongful death suits in general" (as evidenced by the fact that Wisconsin did have a wrongful death statute of its own, albeit not applicable in this particular situation). Underlying this casual observation is the intuition that, under the Full Faith and Credit Clause, a state's refusal to apply foreign law must not be based simply on the fact that it *is* foreign. The reasoning in *Hughes* implies that, had Wisconsin not itself recognized a cause of action for wrongful death under its own laws, refusal to assume jurisdiction over wrongful death claims arising under the laws of other states would have been unassailable under the Full Faith and Credit Clause; Wisconsin would have been treating foreign wrongful death claims precisely as it treated wrongful death claims purporting to arise under forum law. More to the point, it would certainly have been constitutional under *Pacifica Employers* for Wisconsin to have applied its own law to the dispute, since both the plaintiff and defendants were residents of that state. But instead, Wisconsin simply declared that no wrongful death claim arising under the laws of any other state could be adjudicated in its courts. This, according to the Court in *Hughes*, was an impermissible derogation of the interests of other states.

Hughes remains good law, and is still cited from time to time, although in the opinion of this author the majority's opinion is unpersuasive. It was simply a case in which the Wisconsin courts identified and vindicated the state's strong policy that a remedy for wrongful death should accrue only for those deaths occurring within the state. *Contra* Justice Black, Wisconsin *did* have a "real feeling of antagonism" against wrongful death claims—that is, toward those claims arising out of injuries that had occurred outside the state—judging, at least, from its statute limiting recovery to those situations. Perhaps Justice Black was reluctant to credit such a policy, finding it less comprehensible than a policy against, say, the enforcement of a contract the state found to be immoral. To him it was a case of two states having wrongful death statutes, in which the courts of one state refused to apply the foreign state's statute (though directed to do so by the forum's usual *lex loci* rule) seemingly for no reason other than the fact that it *was* foreign. In this author's view, the real problem in *Hughes*—a problem that also arises in the more modern applications of the "public policy" exception—was the dismissal of the plaintiff's claim on the merits, in effect by applying forum law. Had the plaintiff been left free to pursue his claim elsewhere (a disposition that should also be the proper ruling when the "public policy exception" is applied), the Wisconsin Supreme court's decision in *Hughes* would have seemed unremarkable.

As it stands, the reasoning of *Hughes* does raise the question of whether the "public policy exception," at least in extreme cases, violates the Full Faith and Credit Clause.[52] As we have seen, while recognition of such an exception is probably a practical necessity in jurisdiction-selecting choice-of-law methodologies such as the First Restatement, the "public policy" doctrine can often be little more than a convenient rationalization for a court's applying forum law when its usual choice-of-law rule would point clearly to foreign law.[53] Such provincialism can seem as destructive of Full Faith and Credit ideals as what the Supreme Court thought the Wisconsin courts had done in *Hughes*. Yet the "public policy" exception has never itself been held unconstitutional. Perhaps it is the very fact that application of the exception is based on substantive considerations—a strong aversion to the content of the foreign law in the particular case—rather than rejection of foreign law simply because it is foreign, that accounts for this. So long as the basic constitutional requirements of *Pacifica Employers* are met, a state can constitutionally decline to apply foreign law on policy grounds, but it cannot do so when no reason appears for the refusal other than that the law is that of another state.

2.   Tennessee Coal, Iron & R.R. Co. v. George *(1914)*

Hughes was a case in which a state supposedly refused to enforce a foreign-created cause of action. What about the obverse situation, in which a state establishes a cause of action but provides that it may not be enforced in the tribunals of any other state? In *Tennessee Coal, Iron & R.R. Co. v. George* (1914),[54] plaintiff, a railroad worker, sued the defendant railroad in a Georgia court for an injury he had suffered while working for the defendant in

---

52. This is the argument made by Larry Kramer in his article *Same-Sex Marriage, Conflict of Laws, and the Unconstitutional Public Policy Exception*, 106 YALE LAW JOURNAL 1965 (1997).

53. While early application of the "public policy exception" usually resulted in jurisdictional dismissals that in theory allowed the plaintiff to re-file in

another court, many dismissals on "public policy" grounds have been on the merits, meaning that the forum's substantive distaste for the otherwise applicable foreign law resulted in the complete loss of plaintiff's claim. The constitutionality of such rulings seems difficult to justify.

54.   233 U.S. 354 (1914).

Alabama. He sought recovery pursuant to an Alabama statute that made the employer liable to the employee for injuries caused by defects in the defendant's machinery. The Alabama statute also, however, provided that "all actions under [the statute] must be brought in a court of competent jurisdiction within the state of Alabama, and not elsewhere." The defendant argued that it was a violation of the Full Faith and Credit Clause for the Georgia courts to decline to enforce this latter provision, and to proceed to adjudicate the case based on the substantive portion of the Alabama statute. The Supreme Court disagreed, holding that Alabama could not bar the courts of other states from vindicating rights created by Alabama law. While some "remedial" provisions, such as a limitations period specifically enacted as part of the statute creating the cause of actions, might be so integral to the claim itself that the foreign court might be compelled to apply it, Alabama's "venue" provision was not: "[V]enue is no part of the right" created by the Alabama law.

George can only be understood in the light of the conceptual premises underlying conflict-of-laws reasoning at the time the case was decided. First, of course, it was axiomatic that the law of Alabama (the *loci delicti*) was the proper choice-of-law reference; even if Georgia law also recognized the no-fault vicarious liability principle embodied in the Alabama rule, the Georgia court must apply Alabama law, not its own. Second, and closely related, the theory underlying this then-prevailing *lex loci* principle was the "vested rights" idea. The Supreme Court emphasized that the Alabama cause of action was "transitory," which was another way of saying that by virtue of his injury in Alabama under the circumstances of the case, plaintiff had acquired a right to compensation that must be recognized in courts everywhere. The Court did not think that Alabama could create a right, based on a personal injury, that by its very nature was "transitory," and at the same time declare it to be "non-transitory"—unenforceable outside Alabama. A right was a right, enforceable anywhere once created.

The understanding of choice of law that generally prevails today makes it unlikely that the Court would look at the problem the same way today. We do not generally speak of "transitory" causes of action and distinguish them from other foreign-created rules of decision, so far as choice of law is concerned. And (as illustrated by the modern treatment of conflicts issues with respect to statutes of limitations, discussed in Chapter 1) the analysis today does not concern itself with whether the disputed question (venue or anything else) is "part of the right." Courts simply apply foreign law whenever application of the forum's choice-of-law methodology instructs them to do so. How, then, would a case like *George* be decided were it to arise today? Since there are few modern examples of a state's creating a civil cause of action enforceable only in courts of the forum, one can't really say; although the conceptual rationale underlying *George* no longer holds water, *George* remains good law, and will probably continue to do so in the absence of a dispute raising the same issue. It is, though, easy today to think of state-created rules of law whose enforcement the state might legitimately wish to confine to its own *administrative* tribunals. Administrative rules and processes such as those embodied in state workers' compensation schemes (which often differ from one another) constitute an important example. While the Supreme Court has decided that a state generally has constitutional authority to apply another state's workers' compensation law,[55] the practical reality is that states do generally respect the desires of sister states to confine adjudications of such laws to their own specialized tribunals.

55. *Crider v. Zurich Ins. Co.*, 380 U.S. 39 (1965).

Chapter 5

RECOGNITION OF JUDGMENTS

"Recognition of Judgments" is, after choice of law, the most important general topic in the modern conflict-of-laws class. Of course, many conflicts students will already have encountered the topic of "judgments" in their first-year class in Civil Procedure, as part of the study of res judicata (claim preclusion) and collateral estoppel (issue preclusion). All problems of recognition of judgments involve an effort by a party to deploy the results of Case A *preclusively* (*i.e.* to prevent relitigation by the adversary) in a subsequent Case B.

When both Case A and Case B are heard by the courts of a single state, there is no conflicts problem. Recognition of judgments becomes a topic of interest to Conflict of Laws, however, when the court deciding Case B is from a state different from that in which Case A was decided. This problem has come to be known as "interjurisdictional preclusion" (or, sometimes, "interstate preclusion"), and it is the subject of this chapter. As you will see, the study of interjurisdictional preclusion requires a careful understanding of the Full Faith and Credit Clause of the U.S. Constitution.

Before turning to the problem of interjurisdictional preclusion, we'll review the general principles governing recognition of judgments. Although most students will have encountered these principles in a general way in their first-year Civil Procedure class, this section will discuss them in considerable detail because (1) you more than likely have forgotten them and (2) an understanding of them is crucial to an appropriate understanding of the problem of interjurisdictional preclusion and Full Faith and Credit. The following discussion of basic principles of preclusion assumes that both the first and the second case in any preclusion situation are heard in courts of the same state; the preclusion problem is wholly "domestic" to one state. Then, when we turn in the second half of the Chapter to interjurisdictional preclusion and Full Faith and Credit, the two cases will pertain to two different states.

Note that, in most of the remainder of this Chapter, I will use the terms "Case A" and "Case B" to refer to the first and second, respectively, of two lawsuits. Similarly, "Court A" refers to the court that hears and decides "Case A," and likewise for "Court B." When, later in the Chapter, we turn to the question of interjurisdictional preclusion, the two lawsuits in our examples invariably will have been brought in two different states. In this context, "State A" (as in "the law of State A") and "State B" will refer respectively to these two states. Sometimes, as is traditional, "Court A" is called the "rendering court," and "Court B" is called the "recognition court." The foregoing conventions are simple and intuitive and should cause no confusion.

A. The Basics of Claim and Issue Preclusion: A Review

1. The Terminology of Preclusion

The terminology that courts use when referring to problems of judgments and their recognition can be confusing and inconsistent. The general area of Judgments is variously referred to as Prior (or Former) Adjudication, Respect for Judgments, Recognition of Judgments, Res Judicata, and Preclusion. Moreover, the general field of Judgments embraces two different doctrines, the doctrine of *claim preclusion* and the doctrine of *issue preclusion*, each of which terms also have a number of synonyms. The traditional term for claim preclusion is *res judicata*, and sometimes in older cases one will find more exotic terms such as "estoppel by judgment" and "merger and bar." The traditional term for issue preclusion is "collateral estoppel," and occasionally as "estoppel by verdict."

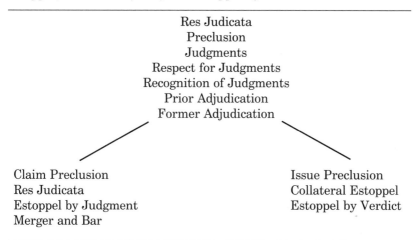

Res Judicata
Preclusion
Judgments
Respect for Judgments
Recognition of Judgments
Prior Adjudication
Former Adjudication

Claim Preclusion
Res Judicata
Estoppel by Judgment
Merger and Bar

Issue Preclusion
Collateral Estoppel
Estoppel by Verdict

Figure 1

As indicated by the title of this chapter, the umbrella term I will most often use to refer to the entire topic is "Recognition of

Judgments," or, simply, "Judgments." I will also use the modern terms "claim preclusion" and "issue preclusion," although on occasion I will have to use their respective synonyms of *"res judicata"* and "collateral estoppel." These are the terms most commonly in use today; on occasion, especially when reading a case that was decided or a treatise that was published prior to the 1960s, you may encounter one of the older and less familiar terms.

2. Claim Preclusion

At its most basic, the idea of claim preclusion (or *res judicata*) is both simple and obvious: Once a claim brought by P against D has been finally adjudicated, that should be the end of the matter. In fact, that is the literal English translation of *"res judicata"*: "The matter has been adjudicated." If P loses the case, she should not be permitted to bring a second action against D raising the same claim; if D loses the case, he should not be able to relitigate his liability on that claim in a second proceeding. One bite at the apple is all that the judicial system can and should permit.

Almost all claim preclusion problems, however, are at least somewhat more complicated than this easy case, and many are much more complicated. The real questions arise when the claims brought by P against D in Case A and Case B, respectively, are nominally different, but may be so related to one another that adjudication of the first claim in Case A should bar litigation of the second claim in a subsequent proceeding. For example, one might consider P to be barred from raising a claim against D in Case B, when P clearly had the opportunity to do so (but abstained from doing so) in Case A. In the examples that follow, assume that both Case A and Case B are heard in the courts of the same state.

Example 1: Pat and David are involved in an automobile accident. Pat sues David in Case A for personal injuries requiring medical care. After that case is litigated to a conclusion, she brings a second lawsuit, Case B, based on the damage to her automobile as a result of the same accident. Should final adjudication of the first claim preclude a subsequent lawsuit on the second claim? (Note that this question can arise whether or not Pat was victorious in Case A.) In this instance, the claim in Case B is essentially the same claim in Case A, based on the identical set of circumstances; the only difference is that the relief sought by Pat—the nature and measure of the harm she has suffered—is different in the two cases.

Example 2: Depending on the ingenuity of plaintiff's lawyer, a given set of facts could be stated as either a contract claim or a tort claim. Some product liability cases, for instance, could be characterized as a breach-of-warranty (contract) claim as well as a tort claim. Since what one must prove to prevail on a breach-of-warranty claim is somewhat different from what one must prove to prevail on a tort claim, the two claims are, at least formally, "different." Should the plaintiff be permitted to bring two separate cases based on the same set of facts, one framed as a breach-of-warranty claim and the other as a tort claim? Unlike the situation in Example 1, here the claims in Case A and Case B are, at least nominally, different ones (tort versus contract). As in Example 1, though, the two claims arise out of the same set of events.

Example 3: Finally, consider a more difficult case: The City of Denver has towed Pat's car because of a parking violation.[1] Pat, disputing the city's justification for towing (and retaining) her car, brings a common-law "replevin" action against the city, as she might do against any private individual she claims was wrongfully holding her property. She also, though, believes that the towing of her car was a violation of the Due Process Clause of the Fourteenth Amendment, because she was given no notice or hearing prior to the towing of her car concerning the imminent deprivation of her property, and the city is a state actor.[2] Can she bring the replevin claim and the Fourteenth Amendment claim against the City of Denver in separate proceedings, or will principles of claim preclusion require that she bring both claims in one proceeding? In this instance, it is clear that Pat has brought two entirely distinct claims in the two cases. And, unlike in the previous examples, the "set of circumstances"—that is, the facts that will have to be proved—to establish each of the two claims will be somewhat different, although they will clearly overlap. For example, to prevail on the replevin claim, Pat will have to show that the City acted *wrongfully* in towing the car, whereas in her constitutional claim she would only have to show that the car was towed (whether rightfully or wrongfully) prior to her receiving any notice from the City. Still, one can imagine an argument that the two claims are sufficiently similar that they should have been brought together in a single proceeding, and that Pat's failure to bring the constitutional claim in her first lawsuit should bar her from ever bringing it in a subsequent proceeding.

Example 4. The first three examples involved the possibility that a *plaintiff* in a second case could be barred by the doctrine of claim preclusion from asserting a particular claim. But consider the

---

1. This example is loosely based on the decision in *Frier v. City of Vandalia*, 770 F.2d 699 (7th Cir. 1985).

2. Many readers will be inclined to view Pat's constitutional claim regarding the lack of notice and a prior hearing as weak; the notion that the police should track down a car's owner and conduct a formal hearing prior to towing her car when she allegedly is illegally parked seems a bit fanciful. But the question of claim preclusion precedes any examination of the merits of Pat's constitutional claim; if we determine that that claim is barred by the doctrine of claim preclusion, there is no need even to assess whether that claim has any substantive merit.

following scenario, based on the facts of Example 3: The City of Denver fails to appear in Pat's replevin action, and a default judgment is entered in Pat's favor. The City continues to keep Pat's car. Pat then initiates a second lawsuit, seeking to enforce the judgment (that is, to require the City to return the car to Pat and to comply with any other remedial orders made by the first court). May the City now appear in the second suit and contest the merits of Pat's replevin suit—to argue, for example, that its detention of Pat's car was legally justified? Almost certainly not. (This example assumes that the City had no legitimate objection to the jurisdiction of the court in the first case.) This, too, is an example of claim preclusion in operation, although in this case it is working to bar a *defendant* rather than a plaintiff from litigating the merits of a claim. If it seems odd to use the term "claim preclusion" to characterize a situation in which it is the defendant who is being barred from litigating, perhaps the older term *"res judicata"* will better fit the situation; since Pat's claim has already been adjudicated (albeit via a default judgment) in Case A, the City should not be able to litigate the merits of that claim in Case B.

a.   The Claim Preclusion Principle Defined

Many other, even more complicated, examples could be given. For now, though, let's consider the basic principles of claim preclusion that would help determine how the four examples mentioned above should be resolved. The basic rule, roughly stated, is that *a valid final judgment rendered on the merits in a case brought by P against D bars relitigation of the same claim between the same parties in a subsequent proceeding.*

The three key criteria, then, for the operation of claim preclusion in Case B are that:

(1) The claim in Case B is the "same" as that adjudicated in Case A.

(2) The parties in Case B are the "same" as those in Case A.

(3) The judgment reached in Case A must have been "on the merits."

We've put quotation marks around key terms in each of these criteria, because each of these requirements is, in practice, more complicated than might appear from the basic definition.

i.   The "Same Claim"

The first criterion for claim preclusion, as stated above, is that the same *claim* be involved in the two cases. But if this statement were read literally, problems of claim preclusion would rarely arise. As noted above, few parties attempt to raise the *identical* claim in a second case after it has already been adjudicated. Neither Example

2 nor Example 3 above involved such a trivial situation. The real question is: *When* should two claims that have been brought in two separate proceedings be considered "the same" for purposes of claim preclusion? Courts answered this question differently 100 years ago from how, by and large, they answer it today; moreover, even today the laws of the different states vary on this question. You should be aware of the different legal "tests" that courts of different states have devised for determining whether two claims are "the same" for purposes of claim preclusion.

The Modern Test: Same Conduct, Transaction or Occurrence. This is the test that one finds most often today (although different jurisdictions may express the test in slightly different ways), and the clear trend among the states is toward the adoption of this test. It is favored, for example, by the Restatement (Second) of Judgments. The essence of this test is that *if the claim in Case B arose out of the same set of events on which the claim in Case A was based, then adjudication of the initial claim in Case A precludes the parties from litigating the second claim in a subsequent Case B.* We can call this the "same transaction" test—shorthand for "same conduct, transaction, or occurrence."

Thus, for instance, in Example 1 above, it's pretty obvious that Pat's claim for damage to her automobile in Case B should be barred; clearly the events (the auto accident) underlying the two claims are nearly identical. She had her chance in Case A, and there seems no good reason to give her another one (unless there are exceptional circumstances, such as when the damage to her automobile only comes to light after she has litigated her initial claim based on damage to her person).

Likewise, in Example 2, it appears that the "same transaction" test would operate to bar Pat's tort claim in Case B; whether she styles it a breach-of-warranty claim or a product liability claim, the dispute is really about the accident and the injuries Pat suffered as a result of it. True, a few of the details that would be relevant to a breach-of-warranty claim would be less important in a product liability claim. In the warranty claim, there might be greater emphasis on the specific warnings or promises that the defendant did or did not make than there would be in the product liability claim. Nevertheless, courts today are likely to regard these possible differences as unimportant for purposes of claim preclusion, and bar Pat from bringing the tort claim in a second case after having lost the breach-of-warranty claim in the first case (or vice versa).

This modern "transactional" test has become popular with courts because the concept underlying it is simple and sensible: The plaintiff should bring all claims arising out of a single set of events that are reasonably available to her in a single proceeding, or else lose the omitted claims forever. The "transactional" test is thus more efficient than permitting claims to be "split" or to be spread out over two or more proceedings. For courts concerned about the size of their dockets and the drain that repetitive litigation places on the judicial system's resources, this is a considerable advantage. Moreover, it is quite a burden on defendants to subject them to repetitive litigation based on a single set of events. The downside of the transactional test is that there is no universally accepted formula for determining just when two sets of events should count as "the same transaction." In many instances reasonable people could disagree, and the question sometimes seems to reduce to a metaphysical inquiry into when two situations are "the same" or "different." Nevertheless, it is the sort of judgment call that courts are called upon to render all the time.

Thus, for instance, how should Example 3, the one involving the towing of Pat's car, be decided using the "transactional" test? One could argue that Pat's replevin claim is "about" the episode involving the towing of her car, including where and whether she was lawfully parked, while her constitutional claim is "about" the City's failure to notify her prior to towing her car. It probably makes sense to say that the two claims do arise out of the same set of events, but it's not easy to "prove" that that's the right answer; it's more of an intuition that many but not all people will share. We could plow through many dozens of reported decisions in a variety of contexts, in which courts attempt to determine what constitutes the "same transaction" for purposes of claim preclusion, without learning very much about how to define the term more generally. Perhaps the most instructive observation one can make is this: The more eager the court in Case B is to promote litigation efficiency, and to avoid hearing unnecessary claims—and many courts today are motivated by precisely these concerns—the more likely it will, in close cases, determine that the sets of circumstances underlying the claims in Case A and Case B are, in fact, the "same."[3]

It is worth emphasizing that even the modern "same transaction" test for claim preclusion does not require a plaintiff to bring all claims she may have against a given defendant in a single proceeding, if those claims do not arise out of the same set of circumstances. In some situations where parties have an ongoing relationship, it is not unrealistic to imagine their getting into legal disputes widely separated by time and circumstance. If one wanted to devise a claim preclusion principle that promoted litigation

3. Devotees of civil procedure will observe that the "transactional" test is not limited to the claim preclusion context. In federal practice, for example, similar tests can be found in such areas as permissive joinder of parties (Fed. R. Civ. P. 20), the relation-back doctrine (Fed. R. Civ. P. 15(c)), and supplemental jurisdiction (28 U.S.C. § 1367). The pervasiveness in modern civil procedure of this emphasis on "transactional" tests reflects a policy of efficiency in civil litigation that the rigid rules of older common-law practice often subverted.

efficiency even more than the "same transaction" test, one could require that the plaintiff bring *all* claims she has against a given defendant in a single proceeding, no matter when and where the claims arose. But, under current law, no principle of claim preclusion requires the plaintiff to bring a claim against the defendant based on a transaction in 2005 in a proceeding in which she has raised a claim against the defendant based on an entirely different transaction in 2008. (Of course, the statute of limitations may provide an independent incentive for the plaintiff to bring even unrelated claims against the defendant in a single proceeding.)

Older Common–Law Tests: Same Evidence, Primary Right, Etc. The common law was traditionally less hospitable to the operation of claim preclusion than courts are today. There was no "same transaction" test prior to the latter part of the twentieth century; the rules governing claim preclusion were, instead, a logical outgrowth of the generally rigid limits the common law placed on pleading. Since, for example, old (*i.e.* pre–1900) common-law practice simply did not permit a plaintiff to bring both a contract and a tort claim in the same proceeding, the omission of one or the other from Case A did not, and could not, mean that the plaintiff was barred from bringing the omitted claim in a subsequent Case B. To paraphrase Mae West, "same transaction" had nothing to do with it.[4] As the rules of common-law procedure were reformed in the nineteenth and twentieth centuries, offering more liberal opportunity for joinder of parties and claims in a single proceeding, courts slowly developed rules that gave greater scope for operation of the doctrine of claim preclusion.

Thus, for example, the California courts developed a test for claim preclusion, which they still purport to apply, based on what they called the "primary right" theory.[5] It is a doctrine too arcane to describe here, steeped as it is in older common-law concepts, but in general it sweeps less broadly (*i.e.* bars fewer claims) than does the "transactional" test. A few states continue to adhere to what is called the "same evidence" test, which holds that claim preclusion should apply only when "the same evidence would sustain both" the claim in Case A and the claim in Case B.[6] In theory, application of this test would mean that claim preclusion should not apply in Example 3, above, because the evidence required to sustain Pat's

4. This observation reminds us of a more general proposition about claim preclusion: Preclusion cannot fairly operate where there was no opportunity, or an inadequate opportunity, to raise the omitted claim in the first proceeding. In this sense the law of claim preclusion has developed in tandem with the rules governing pleading; as joinder of claims has become more easily available, claim preclusion has been given greater scope.

5. *See Mycogen Corp. v. Monsanto Co.*, 28 Cal.4th 888, 904, 123 Cal.Rptr.2d 432, 443–44, 51 P.3d 297, 306–07 (2002).

6. Friedenthal, Kane & Miller, Civil Procedure 664 (4th ed. 2005).

replevin claim is somewhat different from what would be required to sustain her constitutional claim. This is a good example of how the "same transaction" test for claim preclusion and older, narrower tests can produce different results. The "same transaction" test probably would bar Pat's constitutional claim in the same Case B, but, as the diagram below illustrates, the facts needed to prove the two claims do not overlap entirely, and so application of the "same evidence" test might well result in Pat's being permitted to bring her constitutional claim in a second case.

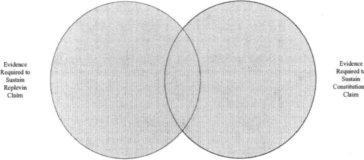

Evidence Required to Sustain Replevin Claim

Evidence Required to Sustain Constitutional Claim

Figure 2

When you get right down to it, this older "same evidence" test doesn't seem much different from a test for claim preclusion that would bar litigation only of a claim identical to that which was adjudicated in Case A. But in reality, even those state courts that purport to adhere to the "same evidence" test are increasingly applying it in a way that makes it indistinguishable from the "transactional" test. Since not all states have formally adopted the "transactional" test, litigators need to determine carefully which test for claim preclusion a given state applies. But, whatever the test in a given state may be called, the transactional approach has become the practice in the great majority of states. *Note to aspiring (or current) litigators*: Beware of courts that purport to follow the "same evidence" or other older test but apply it in a way that is indistinguishable from the more broadly sweeping "transactional" test. When planning litigation in a "Case A" situation, a savvy litigator must take account of the potential *res judicata* consequences of omitting possibly available claims in Case A.

ii.   The "Same Parties"

The second criterion for claim preclusion is that the parties in Case A and Case B must be the same in order for claim preclusion to operate. Put more formally, claim preclusion will not operate unless the claim in Case B is between the same parties, or their privies, as the claim brought in Case A. **This is a bedrock requirement for the operation of claim preclusion.** (Importantly, it is not always a requirement for *issue* preclusion, as discussed below.) The meaning of "same parties" is a bit more firmly fixed than that of the term "same claim." In each of the examples above, for instance, it is clear that the parties in Case A and Case B are the same: Pat is the plaintiff in all the cases, David is the defendant in each of the cases in Examples 1 and 2, and the City of Denver is the defendant in Examples 3 and 4. In Example 1 and 2, had Case A been styled *Pat v. David* and Case B styled *Nestor v. David*, where Pat and Nestor are different people, claim preclusion could not operate in Case B because of the "same parties" requirement, even if the claims in both cases seemed to arise out of the same general set of events.

Nevertheless, in some cases it can be challenging to determine whether the parties in the two cases are really the "same." In particular, the related doctrines of (1) *privity* and (2) *representation* are important to understanding the "same parties" idea.

Privity. Sometimes it is appropriate for claim preclusion to operate in Case B even when the party asserting it, or the party against whom it is being asserted, is not *literally* the same party as was present in Case A. Such is the case when the party in Case B (against whom the adversary wants to assert a claim preclusion argument) is "in privity with" (or is "a privy of") the party who was present in Case A. A classic example of privity is succession to ownership of real property. Suppose David owns a small house on some land that he also owns. David's neighbor, Miranda, has through long use acquired an *easement* right to use David's driveway (which is technically part of David's land) as a passageway to her own garage. In fact, the two of them once had a dispute about Miranda's use of the driveway, resulting in a lawsuit for ejectment brought by David against Miranda (Case A), in which the court held that Miranda had in fact acquired an easement by virtue of David's long acquiescence in her use of the driveway. In other words, David lost Case A. David then sells his house and the accompanying land to Ezekiel. Unless a specific arrangement (involving Miranda's consent) to the contrary has been made, David's conveyance of the house and land to Ezekiel will include all encumbrances on it, including Miranda's legally adjudicated easement right. If Ezekiel now sues Miranda (Case B) in ejectment to keep her from using the driveway (which is, indeed, now owned by Ezekiel), she can move for summary judgment based on claim preclusion. Although the plaintiffs in *David v. Miranda* and *Ezekiel v. Miranda* are literally different people, Ezekiel, as successor in interest to David, is *in privity* with him so far as rights and liabilities growing out of the property is concerned. For that reason, claim preclusion would be properly applied to bar Ezekiel's claim even though, for most legal purposes, he is completely independent of David. This makes sense; there is no reason for Miranda to have to relitigate the question of her easement right every time her neighbor's property changes hands.[7]

Another clear example of the privity concept concerns the administrator of an estate. If a creditor sued the decedent during his lifetime to recover a debt, and received a judgment (Case A) in his favor, in many states he may sue the estate (which, depending on the rules of the particular state, may be personified by the administrator or executor, who is the nominal party in any posthumous litigation) to recover the judgment he received (Case B) if the debtor died in the interim.[8] The administrator cannot relitigate the merits of the debt claim simply because his name is different from that of the deceased. The administrator is in privity with the decedent for these purposes. The lesson of this example and many others that might be given is that the general requirement that Case A and Case B feature the "same parties" should not permit relitigation of what is really the same claim, simply because of a change in the party's name that is merely formal. Whether we regard the "privity" concept as an exception to the "same parties" requirement, or simply as a legal fiction whereby the decedent and the administrator are regarded as the "same party," does not matter very much. It is simply a necessary and commonsense part of the doctrine of claim preclusion.

The privity concept is limited in scope. It does not apply simply to any two parties who happen to have common interests. Each spouse in a marriage, for example, has independent legal personality and is generally not regarded as being in privity with the other for purposes of preclusion. So, for example, if the spouses are both injured in an automobile accident caused by a third party, the husband can wait until the outcome of his wife's lawsuit against the third party before bringing his own lawsuit against the third party. Of course, one can devise many hypotheticals featuring more difficult problems, such as leaseholds held by tenants in common, where sorting out the degree to which parties are in "privity" with

---

7. The discussion of privity in this section focuses on its application in the area of claim preclusion. The concept of privity, however, also plays a role in issue preclusion, which is discussed below. With respect to both claim preclusion and issue preclusion, the question can arise as to whether a party who was not formally present in Case A, but who has a particular kind of relationship with a party who *was* present, should be bound by the judgment in Case A. For an example of the way in which this question can arise in the context of issue preclusion, see the discussion of *Martin v. Wilks*, below.

8. Or, at any rate, if the creditor is unable to recover in Case B, it will be the result of some independent legal rule governing the estate's liability for debts incurred prior to the owner's death, not because "privity" between the administrator and the decedent is lacking.

one another for purposes of preclusion can be complex. The emphasis here is on the basic illustrations of the concept, so we'll avoid the messier examples for now.

Representation. The general shape of the doctrine of privity is thus reasonably clear. That is less true, however, of a concept to which the doctrine of privity is closely related—the concept of *representation*. It is a good idea to become comfortable with the concept of representation and to understand the important role that it plays in preclusion doctrine.

The very legitimacy of regarding a person as legally bound by an adjudication of her rights rests on the notion that her legal interests have been adequately represented in that legal proceeding. This is one of the most basic principles of due process of law. The general requirement that a party have been present *as a party* (that is, not just sitting in the courtroom, or otherwise generally aware of the pendency of the litigation) in Case A in order for her to suffer the effects of claim or issue preclusion in Case B reflects this idea; if a person is a formal party in a case, she can be expected to protect her own interests and it is fair to assume that she will do so. The concept of representation sometimes reaches farther than this, however, and can occasionally justify regarding an individual or entity as legally bound by the outcome of an adjudication even though, technically speaking, she was not a party to it.

For example, suppose that a trade association is formed that includes as members all the major manufacturers of widgets. Call it the Widget Trade Association ["WTA"]. One of its purposes is to represent the interests of the industry as a whole—to lobby Congress and state legislatures, interact with administrative agencies, and to sue in court. WTA sues the Environmental Protection Agency in federal court, challenging the legality of a regulation issued by the EPA. If WTA loses this case on the merits, may American Widgets, Inc. ["AWI"], an individual company that is a member of WTA, sue the EPA in a second case, raising the same challenge to the same regulation? The answer is almost certainly "no." Claim preclusion will bar AWI's claim, even though AWI was not, literally speaking, a party in the first case. The very mission of WTA, the trade association, is to represent the interests of its members. There is no reason to give AWI two bites at the apple— first through WTA's suit, then through its own. AWI's interests were adequately represented in Case A. (In fact, if we regarded AWI as entitled to bring its own suit once WTA had lost, logically we would have to permit *every* member of the WTA to bring its own suit, since each individual member is legally distinct from every other.) This is not, properly considered, an example of "privity," although courts occasionally make the mistake of calling it that. Whatever we call it, the basic point should be clear: AWI will be barred from litigating its legal challenge in Case B as surely as if it had been the plaintiff in the first case. And the reason is that its interests have been adequately *represented* in the earlier cases brought by WTA.

The widget trade association example is a pretty simple one. Other situations may present greater difficulties. Because of crowded dockets and the perception that traditional doctrine sometimes gives nominally different parties the opportunity to litigate what is really the same claim more than once, courts have been tempted to expand the "representation" idea to cover more situations. But in *Taylor v. Sturgell* (2008),[9] the Supreme Court cast a cold eye on at least one such move by lower federal courts. In *Taylor*, the Court ruled that the doctrine of "virtual representation," which had been developed by some lower federal courts, has no place in federal preclusion law. In *Taylor*, Herrick, an antique airplane enthusiast wishing to restore a 1930s aircraft, made a Freedom of Information Act ["FOIA"] request seeking information from the Federal Aviation Administration ["FAA"] concerning the plane's technical specifications. The FAA denied the request; when Herrick then sued the FAA in the Federal District Court for the District of Wyoming, that court, whose decision was upheld by the Tenth Circuit, ruled against Herrick.

Taylor, a second antique airplane enthusiast who was well acquainted with Herrick, then brought a second FOIA request, seeking the same information. Upon denial of the request by the FAA, Taylor sued in the Federal District Court for the District of Columbia. That court, affirmed by the D.C. Circuit, held that Taylor's interests had been "virtually represented" by Herrick in the first case, and that Taylor's FOIA claim was thus barred by claim preclusion. The D.C. Circuit emphasized a number of factors in ruling that Taylor's claim was barred, including the facts that Herrick and Taylor employed the same lawyer and that Taylor used in his suit some documents that had been obtained by Herrick in the course of his own litigation. While the D.C. Circuit did not suggest that there had been outright collusion between Herrick and Taylor in order to obtain two chances at litigating the FOIA request, it is clear that the court was concerned about the ease with which a FOIA request concerning specific materials of interest to a potentially large number of people could be litigated over and over.

The Supreme Court, however, reversed the D.C. Circuit and rejected the notion of "virtual representation" that the D.C. Circuit and some other federal courts had articulated. The Court acknowledged that some exceptions to the usual "same parties" requirement do exist, where there is "adequate representation" of the

9. 128 S.Ct. 2161 (2008).

interests of the unnamed party (the party in Case B) in Case A. However, "virtual representation," as defined variously by federal courts, is not synonymous with "adequate representation." The Court disapproved the "fluid" test applied by the D.C. Circuit, according to which such subjective factors as the "close relationship" between the parties in Case A and Case B and "tactical maneuvering" on the second plaintiff's part to avoid the preclusive effects of Case A would play a role in determining whether the second plaintiff's claim should be barred. The Court, noting that the lower courts in the case had misread previous Supreme Court decisions on claim preclusion and "adequate representation," declined to expand the scope of exceptions to the usual "same parties" requirement, especially those based on loose, multi-factor balancing tests such as that applied by the D.C. Circuit. The Court thus reaffirmed the traditional commitment of the federal judiciary to the bedrock principle that no person may be bound by a judgment to which she was not a party.

One should not overstate the gravity of the *Taylor* decision. The D.C. Circuit was understandably concerned about the possible proliferation of FOIA requests concerning a single document that would be licensed by remorseless application of the traditional rule. But remember that the doctrine of *stare decisis* is a fairly reliable safeguard against this kind of danger, at least where the two cases are brought in the same jurisdiction.[10] Although this was not the case in *Taylor*—the D.C. Circuit is not literally bound by the precedents of the Eighth Circuit—in most situations the chances are good that the reasoning given by the federal court in Case A for denying a FOIA request will be relied on by the courts in another federal circuit should the same kind of legal question arise in a second case.[11] In addition, the Supreme Court's ruling in *Taylor*

---

10. Note also that the concept of "standing to sue" serves as an independent limitation on the ability of distinct individuals to multiply lawsuits against the same defendant raising essentially the same legal issue. A potential litigant in a second lawsuit, at least in the federal courts, must show that she has an independent cognizable legal interest in the outcome of the case, and isn't just seeking a ruling on behalf of someone else.

11. In this connection, it is instructive to understand precisely why the *Taylor* litigation arose as it did. When the Eighth Circuit ruled against Herrick in the first case, it specifically withheld judgment on two legal issues that Herrick had not properly raised on appeal, and that the court implied *might* have

been a basis for granting Herrick's FOIA request. For example, the FAA based its denial of Herrick's request partly on the fact that Fairchild, manufacturer of the plane at issue, expressed its objection to disclosure of the information sought. Many years previously, Fairchild had declined to object to a different party's request for information, perhaps suggesting "waiver" of any objection it might proffer to a subsequent request like Herrick's. Assuming that such a "waiver" can and did occur, there are questions as to whether it can later be withdrawn by the manufacturer, and if so whether such a withdrawal had to have been made *prior* to Herrick's FOIA request (not just in response to it) in order to be legally effective. The Eighth Circuit pointed out that it was

concerned the preclusive effect of a federal court decision in a federal-question case (FOIA); the Court's ruling was thus a statement of federal common law. It is by no means clear that the decision bears upon the legitimacy of the "virtual representation" idea as it may be applied by state judiciaries, at least with respect to state-law claims.[12]

Difference Between "Privity" and "Representation." It may appear from the foregoing discussion that the concepts of "privity" and "representation" are basically the same. Not so; they are related but distinct. "Privity" involves a situation in which one party, in the eyes of the law, succeeds to certain rights and liabilities of another, because of a formal legal relationship between them that has been effectuated either contractually or by operation of law. In the "representation" situation, the second party still retains her own independent rights and liabilities, but the first party is legally regarded as representing the second party's legal interests in a lawsuit with respect to those rights and liabilities.

Is the "Same Parties" Requirement for Claim Preclusion Too Forgiving? Many people believe that our judicial system is a bit too tolerant of litigation that seems duplicative because the plaintiff in the second case could easily have "joined" an earlier lawsuit that determined the same issue. For example, each of the injured parties in an accident is, technically, entitled to bring her own separate lawsuit, although frequently strategic considerations will militate in favor of some or all of the victims' bringing their claims in one proceeding. Some courts and scholars have proposed placing more of a responsibility on claimants who can easily join a pending lawsuit to do so, on pain of having their claims barred. However one views this situation, our system still regards the prerogative of each distinct plaintiff to bring her case independently as a basic principle. The concepts of privity and representation go only a small distance in limiting that prerogative.

iii.   A "Judgment on the Merits"

An additional condition for the operation of claim preclusion is that the judgment reached in Case A have been "on the merits." A

not considering such issues due to Herrick's failure to have raised them properly, thus strongly implying that actual consideration of them might have led to a different result. This vitiated to some extent the possible force of *stare decisis* in Taylor's subsequent lawsuit; he could now raise the issues on which the Eighth Circuit had reserved judgment in Herrick's case. Although the Supreme Court did not base its decision in *Taylor* on this distinctive feature of the case, it

helps explain (1) why Taylor believed it appropriate to bring a second FOIA action and (2) why the Court's holding in *Taylor*, maintaining the status quo in federal preclusion law, is unexceptionable.

12. The Court made reference in *Taylor* to the basic due-process norms inherent in the "representation" requirement, but its holding was not itself based on the Constitution.

case should not be given what we call "preclusive effect" if the adjudication was on some basis short of being "on the merits." The problem is to figure out what this means in practice.

The phrase "on the merits," while having a certain intuitively understandable meaning, is more of a legal conclusion than a useful heuristic. The obvious cases are—well, they're obvious. A case that has been litigated to a conclusion, with the jury rendering a verdict, the court entering judgment, and the judgment upheld on appeal, clearly is a judgment "on the merits"; there is no reason not to apply the principles of claim preclusion, assuming the other criteria for the doctrine have been met. At the other extreme is a dismissal for lack of subject matter jurisdiction in Case A. Clearly such a dismissal should not operate preclusively to bar the plaintiff from bringing the case again in the proper court; therefore, we regard that dismissal as *not* being "on the merits." Lying between these two examples are more difficult cases, and it is challenging to give a simple, reliable test for determining just which kinds of adjudications should be regarded as being "on the merits" for purposes of claim preclusion. The most realistic general statement we can make is a rather circular one: If the disposition in the first case is of the type that we think *ought* be given preclusive effect—*i.e.* if it's a situation in which the plaintiff or defendant, having lost the first case, should not get another chance to litigate it—then we regard the disposition as being "on the merits," and thus having claim-preclusive effect. Another way of phrasing it is that, if permitting the plaintiff or defendant a second opportunity would defeat the purpose of the ruling that caused her to lose the first case, then that ruling in the first case should be regarded as being "on the merits."

Summary judgment is typically regarded as a judgment on the merits; the summary judgment device would be robbed of much of its usefulness if the plaintiff, having had her case dismissed on summary judgment, could just start over again with another lawsuit. Similarly, dismissal of a complaint for failure to state a claim upon which relief can be granted (in federal procedure, Fed. R. Civ. P. 12(b)(6)) is, for purposes of claim preclusion, regarded as a judgment on the merits, even though in formal terms such a dismissal says only that the allegations in the complaint do not state a cause of action.[13] It would be unreasonable to permit

13. The norm in federal practice is that plaintiff should be given leave to file one amended complaint upon dismissal under Fed. R. Civ. P. 12(b)(6). The doctrine of claim preclusion will not bar this. If she declines that opportunity, however, or the amended complaint is likewise dismissed, any further attempt to bring her claim will thereafter be barred on claim preclusion grounds.

One can easily find oneself wading into metaphysical waters when assessing whether and to what extent various dispositions of cases, including judgment after jury trial, really are "on the merits." For example, an order of summary judgment against the plaintiff doesn't

plaintiffs to file the same claim over and over again with no preclusion consequences. The same is obviously true (with respect to either plaintiffs or defendants) for directed verdicts and judgments notwithstanding the verdict (collectively known in federal practice as judgments as a matter of law). In all these situations, there has been a substantive legal determination that a party's claim should or should not proceed. Permitting the plaintiff to begin again with a second lawsuit would be daft.

What about default judgments? That these are judgments on the merits—that they "count" for purposes of claim preclusion—follows from the general rule of thumb that, if the purpose of the procedural device would be subverted by permitting the party to relitigate the claim, then claim preclusion should apply. The purpose of a default judgment (assuming that jurisdiction is proper and that there has been adequate notice to the defendant) is to create a strong disincentive for the defendant simply to ignore a lawsuit brought against him; to make that disincentive effective, he must be barred from ever litigating the claim in a future proceeding. A contrary rule would make the default judgment largely a useless device, requiring the plaintiff to file lawsuit after lawsuit until the defendant felt moved to respond. (Thus, claim preclusion operates in this context by barring the defendant from contesting the case "on the merits" in Case B if he defaulted in Case A.)

Another example of dispositions that are not "on the merits" in any literal way, but that really must be given claim-preclusive effect in order to be effective, relates to the sanctions that may be imposed on attorneys and parties for litigation misbehavior. Under the Federal Rules of Civil Procedure, the district court may, in extreme cases, choose as a sanction for violations of Rule 11, Rule 26(g), or Rule 37 one that amounts to deciding a claim in favor of the adverse party.[14] In order to make these sanctions effective, the adjudications of the underlying claim that they effectuate must be

literally say, "What the plaintiff alleged didn't actually happen"; usually, it is simply a statement that the plaintiff has not at this point produced evidence sufficient to entitle a jury to find for him. A 12(b)(6) dismissal says even less about "what happened"; it's just about the insufficiency of what the plaintiff alleged, an insufficiency that might have as much to do with his lawyer's skill as with what "really happened." Even a jury verdict can be seen simply as the jury's assessment of the evidence presented, not an authoritative historical account of the "actual facts." Nevertheless, claim preclusion is concerned with how our system of adjudication should operate, not with getting all the facts right. So the requirement that the result in Case A have been "on the merits" is

concerned first and foremost with what kinds of dispositions should be given claim-preclusive effect in order to make the litigation system rational and efficient.

14. For example, one possible sanction for violation of Rule 11 is to strike a claim from the complaint. Although the phrase "dismissal of the claim" is not used, striking a claim from the complaint amounts to precisely the same thing. Another possible sanction, sometimes employed in cases of discovery abuse by a defendant, is to deem the allegations to which the discovery dispute is relevant to be admitted. In some cases this could lead immediately to judgment for the adverse party.

given claim-preclusive effect in subsequent proceedings. Finally, dismissal for failure to prosecute a claim—what in the federal system is known as "involuntary dismissal" pursuant to Fed. R. Civ. P. 41—must be given claim-preclusive effect so that there are real consequences for the plaintiff in initiating a lawsuit and then not bothering to show up to litigate the case further. This is simply the obverse of the default judgment situation. All of these examples involve the application of claim preclusion where the substantive merits of the claim were never really adjudicated. A default judgment, for example, tells us nothing about whether the plaintiff ought to have "won" had the case been contested by the defendant and litigated in the usual way. But, for purposes of claim preclusion, all these adjudications are considered to be "on the merits."

b. Some Additional Issues

The Law of Claim Preclusion Applied in Federal Courts. As we've observed, the law of preclusion governing cases heard in a state's courts is state law—usually, judge-made law. The federal law of preclusion is, by and large, a matter of federal common law (that is, the governing principles have been developed by the federal courts themselves rather than set forth in statutes or supplied by state law). For causes of action arising under federal law, preclusion principles developed and articulated by the federal courts, such as the "same transaction" test for claim preclusion, govern. For state-law claims heard by federal courts sitting in diversity, the source of preclusion law is a trickier question: It too is federal common law, but the content of that federal common law is that, where the federal court in Case A is sitting in diversity, the preclusion effects of its judgments will be governed by the preclusion law of the state in which it sits.[15]

Claim Preclusion as Deployed Against a Defendant: The Problem of Enforcement of Judgments. Most, though not all, illustrations of claim preclusion involve a defendant who seeks to bar the plaintiff in Case B from litigating claims that were brought (unsuccessfully), or that were not brought at all, in Case A. However, claim preclusion can sometimes inure to the benefit of a plaintiff who *prevailed* on a claim in Case A.[16] Usually this occurs when a

---

15. *Semtek International Inc. v. Lockheed Martin Corp.*, 531 U.S. 497 (2001).

16. To be precise, when using the term "plaintiff" in this context we really mean "claimant." Usually the plaintiff and the claimant are one and the same, but not always. When, for example, a counterclaim is available to a defendant, she is considered a "claimant" with respect to that counterclaim, although she is still, technically, the "defendant" in the case. It is important to know that claim preclusion principles can apply, depending on the rules in a particular jurisdiction, not only to garden-variety claims brought by the plaintiff but to certain other claims that are raised, or

plaintiff who was successful in Case A seeks to "enforce" the judgment in order to collect from the defendant.

Enforcement of a judgment, especially when sought in the same jurisdiction that rendered the initial judgment, often involves merely a ministerial act without requiring a new judicial proceeding. That's not to say that it is always simple or easy for the successful claimant to get satisfaction; sometimes it requires garnishment of the defendant's wages or some other method of enforcement involving law enforcement officials. But, when sought in the same jurisdiction, enforcement generally doesn't require the initiation of a new lawsuit. Traditional doctrine, by contrast, holds that when enforcement is sought in a jurisdiction different from the one in which the judgment was obtained (perhaps because State B is where the defendant's assets are located), the original judgment must be "reduced to a judgment" in the second state prior to any attempt to enforce it there. Reducing the State A judgment to a judgment in State B, while frequently a simple task, is a judicial proceeding involving the same parties as Case A and permits the defendant to appear and raise any objections he may have. He may not, however, raise any issues that speak to the merits of the original claim. This fact is usually treated as an illustration of claim preclusion; the enforcement proceeding is thought of as raising the "same claim" as that on which the plaintiff prevailed in Case A.

This is the principal example of a successful *plaintiff* deploying claim preclusion principles in a subsequent proceeding. By far the most common use of claim preclusion is by a defendant in Case B against a plaintiff who was *unsuccessful* in Case A, and that is the situation in most of the examples given here.

Claim Preclusion Principles as Applied to Counterclaims and Other Kinds of Claims. Students of federal civil procedure will be familiar with Fed. R. Civ. P. 13 and the doctrine of "compulsory counterclaims." A counterclaim is a claim for relief asserted by the defendant against the plaintiff. The doctrine of compulsory counterclaims is in part a special instance of the doctrine of claim preclusion. In federal courts, if the defendant fails to raise as a counterclaim in Case A a claim available to him against the plaintiff that arises out of the "same transaction or occurrence" as the plaintiff's claim, he is barred from raising that claim, whether as a plaintiff or otherwise, against the adverse party in a subsequent proceeding. (This is, of course, simply the "same transaction" test that many states use for claim preclusion more generally.) Some states have the same or a similar rule for counter-

that could have been raised, in the first proceeding. But the rules are complex and vary from state to state, so be sure to familiarize yourself with the relevant state's joinder and preclusion rules in an individual case.

claims; some do not.[17] The point to be stressed here is that the compulsory counterclaim issue is, at bottom, a claim preclusion issue; the "same transaction" test that applies in the federal courts requires that counsel for the defendant be alert, lest she lose forever claims that her client might have against the adverse party, simply by omitting them from the answer. The treatment, for purposes of preclusion, in *state* courts of claims in Case B that should have been raised in Case A, but were not, will depend on the law of State A—namely, the conditions (if any) under which the law of State A regards counterclaims as compulsory.

The Federal Rules of Civil Procedure make available, under prescribed circumstances, certain other kinds of claims: cross-claims, in which one plaintiff raises a claim against another plaintiff or one defendant raises a claim against another defendant; third-party claims, in which a defendant asserts a claim against a new "third-party" defendant; claims brought against existing parties by a third-party defendant who has been brought into the case; and claims brought by the original plaintiff against a third-party defendant. In general, the parties entitled to make such claims are *not* barred from asserting them later in another proceeding, should they elect not to raise them. For example, there is no "compulsory cross-claim" doctrine. The federal rulesmakers and the federal courts evidently have decided that the availability of these more exotic varieties of party and claim joinder should not subject unsuspecting parties to the claim-preclusive consequences of failing to exploit them in Case A. As always, there may be variations among the states in the procedural rules that they employ concerning the kinds of claims that can be raised in a proceeding, and the preclusion consequences (if any) of omitting them.

An Exceptionally Brief Note on Subject Matter Jurisdiction and Claim Preclusion in the Federal Courts. As you've no doubt learned elsewhere, all claims brought by a plaintiff in a proceeding in federal court must have an independent basis of federal jurisdiction; those that do not must arise out of the same set of circumstances (*i.e.* form part of the "same case or controversy") as a claim brought by the plaintiff that *does* have such an independent basis of federal jurisdiction, in order to be within the jurisdiction of the federal court. (This is the principle of "supplemental jurisdiction." *See* 28 U.S.C. § 1367.) We're not going to explore these jurisdictional issues as such. But there is one point worth making here about the interaction between federal subject matter jurisdiction and claim preclusion in the federal courts. The test for whether supplemental jurisdiction exists for a claim not indepen-

---

17. Terminology can also differ from state to state. For example, what are called "counterclaims" in federal civil practice are called "cross-claims" in California practice.

dently supported by federal jurisdiction—that it be part of the "same case or controversy" as a claim that does have an independent basis of federal jurisdiction—is, practically speaking, pretty much identical to the test ("same transaction or occurrence") used in the federal courts (and in many states, of course) for determining whether a claim will be barred under claim preclusion principles if omitted from Case A. In theory, a claim lacking an independent basis of federal jurisdiction that is omitted in Case A should be barred in Case B under precisely the same circumstances in which the *inclusion* of that claim in Case A would be regarded as within the supplemental jurisdiction of the federal courts. And it would be obviously unfair for such a claim actually to be ruled *outside* the federal court's supplemental jurisdiction in Case A, and then barred by claim preclusion principles when the plaintiff subsequently tried to raise it in Case B. It would be perverse to tell the plaintiff first that he *can't* raise the claim in Case A, and later tell him that he *should have* raised the claim in Case A.

This general observation reminds us that this basic "same transaction" (or "same case or controversy") inquiry for preclusion could actually arise for the first time at one of two distinct moments: (1) at the threshold of Case A, when the plaintiff attempted to convince the federal court that his nonfederal[18] claim formed part of the "same case or controversy" as his federal claim and thus fell within the federal court's supplemental jurisdiction; or (2) in Case B, when the plaintiff argues that his omission of the nonfederal claim in Case A should not bar him from raising the claim in this Case B, because it did not arise out of the "same transaction or occurrence" as the federal claim he did bring in Case A. (The same observation could be made in a slightly more complicated way in the case of counterclaims, where it is the *defendant* in Case A who might have raised a nonfederal counterclaim in Case A, or who might instead have raised it for the first time as a plaintiff in Case B.)

In strict theory, the analysis of the problem should be identical whether it arises in the first scenario (in Case A itself) or in the second scenario (in Case B), because it's the same problem: Do the two claims arise out of the same transaction or occurrence? Some empirical investigations of limited scope, however, have suggested that, in practice, courts are less likely to find that the nonfederal claim arose out of the same set of events as the federal claim brought in Case A when the matter is raised for the first time in

---

18. In this paragraph in the text, the term "nonfederal" is used synonymously with the more cumbersome phrase "not independently supported by federal jurisdiction." Likewise, the term "federal" used in the next sentence in the text is, in this context only, synonymous with "independently supported by federal jurisdiction."

Case B than they are when the matter is raised in Case A itself. Why? Because the stakes are higher for the claimant when the matter is decided in Case B. In that context, the court is determining whether the claim omitted from Case A should be barred altogether—a rather dismal prospect for the claimant. When the matter arises and is determined in Case A, it is usually for the purpose of determining whether the federal court in Case A has (supplemental) jurisdiction to hear the nonfederal claim that the claimant is trying to raise. A negative answer to this question is less devastating to the claimant, since he doesn't automatically lose the claim forever but retains the ability to raise it later in the proper court.

3. *Issue Preclusion*

The operation of issue preclusion bars a party from relitigating a particular issue that was determined in a previous action to which she was a party. The general rule governing issue preclusion (also called "collateral estoppel") is stated by the Restatement (Second) of Judgments:

> When an issue of fact or law is actually litigated and determined by a valid and final judgment, and the determination is essential to the judgment, the determination is conclusive in a subsequent action between the parties, whether on the same or a different claim.[19]

While the law governing issue preclusion varies among the states as to some specific points, the broad principle articulated by the Restatement is in operation everywhere. Apart from the requirement that the first judgment have been "valid and final," which applies to all instances of preclusion, we can break down the basic requirements for the operation of issue preclusion as follows:

— The issue as to which relitigation is now sought to be barred must be the same as that decided in the earlier proceeding.

— The issue must have been "actually litigated and determined" in the earlier proceeding.

— The issue must have been "essential to the judgment" in the first case.

In addition, there is an important fourth requirement that is not specifically mentioned in § 27 of the Restatement (it is covered in later sections), but which is everywhere recognized as part of the doctrine of issue (as well as claim) preclusion:

19. Restatement (Second) of Judgments § 27.

— The party against whom issue preclusion is asserted must have had a "full and fair opportunity" to litigate the issue in Case A.

This last requirement is, in part, a restatement of the bedrock principle of *res judicata*: Preclusion of any kind may not operate to the detriment of a party who was not present *as a party* in the first proceeding. While this principle holds for claim preclusion (subject to the doctrines of "privity" and "representation" discussed earlier) as well, it is especially important to keep this in mind with respect to issue preclusion because, in many states, issue preclusion can be *invoked* by a party who was *not* a party in the earlier case. The fourth requirement above, however, goes even beyond the "bedrock principle" mentioned above and, as explained below, limits the operation of issue preclusion when a party was technically present in Case A but other features of the litigation in that case would make it unfair or inappropriate to have the judgment in that case bind her as to a particular issue.

a.   The Same Issue: What Is an "Issue"?

Whether the issue as to which preclusion of relitigation is now sought is the same as the issue decided in the earlier case is often simple to determine. A basic example is where the driver of a car has allegedly, through his own negligence, caused injuries to two pedestrians in one accident. As we know, the injured persons are not required to sue together. Assume that one of them sues the driver and obtains a judgment after a jury trial. It is easy to see that, among other things, the driver's negligence (in, say, running a red light) with respect to that particular accident must have been conclusively established as a result of the judgment. We know this even if the jury returned only a general ("black box") verdict in favor of the plaintiff; negligence (breach of a duty of due care) is plainly an element of a personal injury claim, and logically one could not have obtained a judgment on such a claim without establishing all of the elements of that claim. If the other injured person then sues the driver in a second proceeding, the defendant can be barred from relitigating the question of his own negligence with respect to the accident.[20] The "issue"—his negligence—is clearly the same in both cases.

This is an easy example to understand because the "issue" is a legal element of the cause of action in both Case A and Case B.

---

20. This example assumes that nonmutual collateral estoppel—the doctrine that permits a party in Case B who was not a party in Case A to receive the benefit of issue preclusion in Case B, so long as the party against whom it is asserted was a party in Case A—applies in the jurisdiction. That doctrine will be discussed later in this Chapter. The focus of this particular example is on whether the *issue* is actually the same in the two cases.

Sometimes, the "issue" is simply a *fact* that is relevant to both cases. For instance, building on the same example, one finding in the first case may have been that the defendant lacked a valid driver's license at the time of the accident. (To simplify the problem, assume that Case A was a bench trial and that the lack of a valid driver's license was an explicit finding of fact made by the judge. Or, perhaps, the fact was not disputed by the defendant.) This, too, would be an "issue" that the defendant could be barred from relitigating in a subsequent case brought by the other injured party.

There are cases in which determining whether the issue is the "same" can be more difficult. We'll forgo further exploration of these more difficult situations.[21] For present purposes it is sufficient to understand the basic point that the issue in the two cases needs to be the same in order for issue preclusion to operate.

b. Actually Litigated and Determined

The requirement that an issue have been "actually litigated and determined" in order for issue preclusion to operate seems reasonable if not obvious, but in practice it can raise some difficult questions. In particular, it constitutes one of the critical differences between claim preclusion and issue preclusion.

Default Judgments, Involuntary Dismissals. We saw above that there are a variety of circumstances in which a judgment on the merits can be entered against or in favor of a party without there having been actual litigation or determination of some or all essential parts of the claim. A default judgment entered against the no-show defendant is the plainest example. Involuntary dismissal for failure to prosecute is another example, with the no-show

---

21. One possibility could arise when Case B is in another state, raising the topic of "interjurisdictional preclusion" that is the subject of the latter part of this Chapter. Suppose State A regards driving over the speed limit to be negligence *per se*, while State B does not, leaving such matters to the factfinder. In Case A, arising out of an auto accident, the plaintiff sues the defendant. Court A concludes that the law of State A should apply, and the jury finds that the defendant had been driving over the speed limit, thus leading automatically under State A's negligence *per se* rule that the defendant had been negligent. The plaintiff in Case A obtains a verdict and a judgment. Now, a second plaintiff injured in the same accident sues the same defendant in a court in State B. The court in State B holds that the law of State B, including its rule that driving over the speed limit is not negligence *per se*, should be applied in this Case B. The plaintiff (assuming that the doctrine of nonmutuality applies in State A) certainly can successfully use the doctrine of issue preclusion to estop the defendant from relitigating the question of whether he was driving over the speed limit; it's clearly the same "issue" in both cases. But can the defendant also be estopped from relitigating in Case B the larger question of his negligence? Many courts would say no. Since his "negligence" was adjudicated under a legal principle that State B (whose law, by the terms of this hypothetical, is to apply in this Case B) does not recognize, it is not really the same "issue" as that confronting the court in Case B.

plaintiff this time suffering the consequences. In both of these situations, claim preclusion will work to the detriment of the no-show party: In the default judgment situation, the defendant cannot seek to contest the merits of the plaintiff's claim if the latter seeks enforcement of the judgment in a second proceeding; in the involuntary dismissal situation, the plaintiff cannot bring a second case raising the same claim he so improvidently abandoned in the first case. The law regards claim preclusion as being fully operative in both circumstances because parties should suffer the consequences of ignoring legitimately commenced ongoing litigation, which wastes the time and resources of both the court and the adverse party.

Not so with issue preclusion, at least according to traditional doctrine. Unlike claim preclusion, the conventional law of issue preclusion requires that the issue with respect to which preclusion of relitigation is sought have been *actually* litigated and determined in the first proceeding. The default judgment provides an especially clear example. Let us build an example on the framework of the case, hypothesized above, in which Pat's automobile had been towed by the City of Denver, and the City fails to appear. Default judgment is entered against the City. Now Pat brings a second lawsuit (Case B) against the City, basing his claim on the Fourteenth Amendment's Due Process Clause and 42 U.S.C. § 1983, on the theory that no constitutionally adequate hearing had been held by the City. The fact that Pat actually owned the car (or, to be super-precise, had some legally cognizable possessory interest in it) is a logically necessary part of both the replevin and constitutional claims; that "issue" is common to both claims. Does the default judgment rendered in favor of Pat in Case A mean that, should the City finally show up and litigate in Case B, it is barred from litigating the issue of whether Pat actually owned the car? No. Because that issue was never litigated and determined in Case A, issue preclusion may not operate. The City may litigate the issue of Pat's actual ownership of the car in Case B.[22]

Similar reasoning applies to the case of involuntary dismissal. Suppose Pat files his replevin action against the City of Denver and, after the City files its answer, Pat takes no further action in the case. The court dismisses the claim on the ground that Pat failed to prosecute the claim, and enters judgment in favor of the City. Suppose further that Colorado (in whose courts both cases are heard) follows the narrow "same evidence" test for claim preclu-

---

22. Do not confuse this hypothetical with one in which Case B is Pat's effort to *enforce* the default judgment she obtained in Case A on her replevin claim. This latter scenario is an occasion for the application of *claim preclusion* principles, and the City would not be permitted to litigate in the Case B enforcement proceeding issues concerning the "merits" of the replevin claim, including Pat's actual ownership of the car.

sion. Now, in Case B, Pat sues the City again, this time raising his constitutional claim under 42 U.S.C. § 1983. May the City move for summary judgment, arguing that issue preclusion bars Pat from litigating and establishing in Case B that he was the owner of the automobile? Well, the City can make whatever motions it wants, but the court should deny this one. The issue of the car's ownership was not actually litigated and determined in Case A.[23]

Determining Which Issues the Jury Actually Decided. Closer consideration of the involuntary dismissal example leads to a different illustration of the "actually litigated and determined" principle. That illustration is based on the following reality about litigation: When Case A is litigated to a conclusion and judgment is entered for plaintiff, it is logically necessary that plaintiff have prevailed on all the elements of the claim. However, if judgment is entered for defendant, it is not necessarily the case that plaintiff *failed* to make her case on all elements of the claim. Failure on merely one element is enough to result in judgment for defendant. Therefore, depending on what issues were resolved prior to trial and what disputed issues were given to the jury to decide, we may not be able to infer from the jury's verdict for the defendant just which particular issues the jury decided adversely to the plaintiff. This dilemma is particularly acute when the jury returns the traditional "black box" general verdict in which the jury says merely "verdict for defendant," as distinguished from a special verdict and/or answers to specific interrogatories, or a bench trial in which the judge-factfinder makes specific findings of fact. If we cannot infer with logical precision that a jury verdict amounts to resolution of a particular issue adversely to the plaintiff, we cannot say that that issue was "actually litigated and determined" for purposes of issue preclusion in a subsequent proceeding.

Suppose that, instead of dismissal for failure to prosecute, Pat lost his replevin suit in Case A because the case went to a jury, which returned a general verdict against him. Judgment for the City is entered and upheld on appeal. Now Pat brings his second lawsuit under § 1983, based on his constitutional argument. (Again assume that Colorado uses the "same evidence" test for claim preclusion, so that this second claim is not barred by claim preclusion.) May the City move for partial summary judgment aiming to bar Pat from establishing that he was the owner of the automobile?

23. It should be noted here that, while "actually litigated and determined" remains a requirement for the application of issue preclusion, courts have begun to express some impatience with that requirement in the "default judgment" and "failure to prosecute" situations described in the text, as well in cases where default was prescribed as a sanction for litigation misbehavior. With judicial resources at a premium, courts are not apt to be pleased if a party who fails to appear in a case later asserts the right to litigate one of the issues he has already forgone the opportunity of contesting.

Under most circumstances, no. Because the jury's verdict may have rested on the unpersuasiveness of Pat's evidence on any one of a number of issues—whether Pat owned the car, whether the car was actually towed, whether the car was still in the possession of the city, etc.—we cannot "know" whether the jury actually concluded that he did not own the car, that is, whether that issue was "actually litigated and determined." Issue preclusion would be inappropriate in Case B.

Of course, not all general verdicts are so opaque. Pretrial or pre-verdict motions may have removed issues from dispute, narrowing the disputed issues considerably. Sometimes a case will go to the jury to resolve a single issue, in which case the verdict can serve as a basis for issue preclusion with respect to that issue. In some cases the judge may instruct the jury to answer specific interrogatories or to render a special verdict, which will produce findings that are specific enough to lay the basis for issue preclusion in a later case. Bench trials usually involve specific findings of fact and conclusions of law by the trial judge, and these too may serve as the basis for issue preclusion. In such instances, we usually are comfortable saying whether a particular issue has been "actually litigated and determined" in Case A.

c.   Essential to the Judgment

The requirement that determination of an issue have been "essential" to the judgment in Case A in order for issue preclusion to operate in Case B can raise some difficult issues. A classic example concerns the old doctrine of contributory negligence, which (unlike today's comparative negligence approach) operated to bar plaintiff's negligence claim if she had been at all negligent herself. If in Case A the court finds that *both* the plaintiff and defendant had been negligent in an auto accident, resulting in a judgment for the defendant, issue preclusion will *not* bar relitigation in a later case of the question of whether the defendant had been negligent in the accident. Court A's determination that the defendant had been negligent was obviously not essential to the judgment in Case A; that determination was not even logically related to the judgment. Moreover, the defendant in Case A, being the victor, would have had no opportunity to appeal the determination that he had been negligent, and it seems inappropriate to give issue-preclusive effect to such a determination.[24]

But what about a case in which the plaintiff loses for two independent reasons, each of which is an adequate reason for holding against her? For example, suppose we alter the example in the previous paragraph and hypothesize that, in Case A, the court

---

24. *Cambria v. Jeffery*, 307 Mass. 49, 29 N.E.2d 555 (1940).

found against the plaintiff both because she had been contributorily negligent and because her injuries had not been caused by the accident. If in Case B the same plaintiff sues another defendant for personal injuries arising out of the same accident, should the finding of the plaintiff's contributory negligence in Case A be given issue-preclusive effect in Case B? One can envision several possible answers to the question: (1) Both of the previously determined issues should be given issue-preclusive effect; (2) neither should; or (3) only one of them should. We can dismiss (3) because it is difficult to see how giving one and not the other determination preclusive effect could be justified. The first Restatement of Judgments opted for (1). The Restatement (Second) of Judgments opted for (2); it based this view on the notions that (a) a court finding against a party on two independent grounds may be less inclined to be as rigorous in its explanation of each individual ground than in a case where it rests its decision on only one ground, and (b) the more independent grounds on which the plaintiff loses, the less incentive she will have to appeal the decision to a higher court. Moreover, even if there is an appeal, the appellate court in Case A will often affirm on only one of the grounds relied on by the trial court. A determination as to which the losing party may be unable to obtain effective appellate review does not, in the eyes of the Second Restatement of Judgments, deserve full issue-preclusive effect. Thus, reasoned the Second Restatement, neither of the two (or more) grounds should be regarded as "essential to the judgment," and neither should be given issue-preclusive effect.[25]

Today, though, this is not the predominant view, and the solution recommended by the First Restatement of Judgments is more widely followed. Many courts now treat the question on a case-by-case basis, and, if they are convinced that Court A considered the issues carefully and that the parties had a full and fair opportunity to litigate them, conclude that determinations as to those issues should both be given issue-preclusive effect even if either one would serve as an adequate and independent basis for the judgment. In such cases, then, *both* determinations will be regarded as "essential to the judgment" and thus eligible for issue-preclusive treatment in Case B.[26] Of course, in order for this to be the case, the court in Case A must have clearly determined both issues. Sometimes it can be difficult to tell whether the court's assertions in Case A concerning an alternative ground for decision is a formal holding, or is rather simply dictum (in which case it should not be given issue-preclusive effect). It's important, there-

---

25. Restatement (Second) of Judgments § 27, comment i. The Reporters cited the decision in *Halpern v. Schwartz*, 426 F.2d 102 (2d Cir. 1970), in support of their view.

26. *See, e.g., Jean Alexander Cosmetics, Inc. v. L'Oreal USA, Inc.*, 458 F.3d 244, 249–57 (3d Cir. 2006).

fore, to ascertain whether Court A has in fact made a formal determination as to each issue for which issue-preclusive effect is being sought in Case B.

d.   Nonmutuality in Issue Preclusion

The Concept of Nonmutuality. As discussed above, the operation of claim preclusion in Case B requires that the parties in that case be the same as those in Case A—subject to the usual qualifications concerning the doctrines of privity and representation. For a long time, this requirement of "same parties" applied to issue preclusion as well: Not only the party against whom issue preclusion was being sought in Case B, but also the party seeking to take advantage of issue preclusion, had to have been a party in Case A. This is no longer the case in most states; "mutuality of parties" is no longer a predicate in those states for the operation of issue preclusion.[27] It is still true that the party *against* whom preclusion is sought must have been a party in Case A—this is a basic requirement of due process—but in most states a party in Case B who did not participate in Case A may move to preclude the adverse party from relitigating an issue decided in Case A, assuming the other requirements for issue preclusion have been met. This doctrine has traditionally been called "nonmutual collateral estoppel," but "nonmutual issue preclusion" would be just as appropriate and fits better with the modern move to the "preclusion" terminology.

The "multiple-claimant" scenario is the classic illustration of nonmutuality. Multiple passengers injured in one automobile accident need not bring their claims against the wrongdoer together in a single proceeding. If Passenger #1 prevails against the defendant in Case A, thus establishing the defendant's negligence, Passenger #2 can then file her own lawsuit and move on issue preclusion grounds to prevent the defendant from relitigating the question of his own negligence in Case B. (Formally, Passenger #2 would make a motion for summary judgment or some analogous motion, arguing that, under the doctrine of issue preclusion, she is entitled as a matter of law to prevail on the particular issue.) This is a clear example of nonmutual collateral estoppel because Passenger #2, the "precluder" in Case B, did not participate in Case A. (Of course, this would only resolve the question of the defendant's negligence; Passenger #2 would still have to establish the extent of her own injuries, and perhaps questions of causation.)

Why "Mutuality" Was Once a Requirement for Issue Preclusion. Most judges, attorneys, legal scholars, and law stu-

---

27. For a good account of state law on the mutuality requirement in issue preclusion, up to date as of mid–2009, see Steven P. Nonkes, Note, *Reducing* *the Unfair Effects of Nonmutual Issue Preclusion Through Damages Limits*, 94 Cornell Law Review 1459, 1467–68 (2009).

dents see the doctrine of nonmutuality as obviously correct and wonder why mutuality was ever a requirement for issue preclusion. "No satisfactory rationalization," said Justice Roger Traynor in the decision that removed the mutuality requirement for issue preclusion in California, "has been advanced for the requirement of mutuality. Just why a party who was not bound by a previous action should be [prevented] from asserting it as [preclusive] against a party who was bound by it is difficult to comprehend."[28] This is not quite correct. The demise of the mutuality requirement, like many twentieth-century changes in civil procedure (such as adoption of the broad-sweeping "same transaction" test for claim preclusion), reflects a profound though historically gradual change in the prevailing conception of the nature and purposes of civil litigation. The modern conception conceives the dispute between the parties as concerning a real-life event or set of events, which a lawsuit should resolve to the extent possible, adjudicating the interested parties' claims and establishing "the facts" necessary to resolve those claims. Modern procedural rules that facilitate joinder of parties and claims, establish "same transaction" tests for claim preclusion and other doctrines, and remove the requirement of mutuality from issue preclusion, reflect this conception.

A more traditional, if now antiquated, view of civil litigation regards the lawsuit solely as a means of determining whether one party has been harmed by another and should now be compensated, using the limited and specific procedures set out by private law to determine this. Ultimately, this approach to civil litigation seeks to restore the *status quo* between the parties to the case, rather than officially to establish "historical facts" for purposes of future litigation or to conserve judicial resources by adjudicating the rights and liabilities of a variety of possible claimants.[29] The traditional paucity of procedural devices for joining claims and parties in one proceeding, and the narrow scope for operation of claim and issue preclusion (including the doctrine of mutuality), reflected this older conception of civil litigation. In this view, the "issues" decided in Case A are not historical facts designed to govern future proceedings, but formal conclusions necessary to determine whether *this* defendant invaded *this* plaintiff's rights and must compensate her in order to restore the *status quo* between *them*. The issues decided in Case A are (on this view) relevant only to the dispute between the parties in Case A; they have no bearing on what some other person might raise as a claim against one of these parties in a

---

28. *Bernhard v. Bank of America Nat. Trust & Savings Ass'n,* 19 Cal.2d 807, 812, 122 P.2d 892, 895 (1942).

29. The sociologist Martin Shapiro famously captured this view by observing that "it must be remembered that the basic aim of a trial is to resolve a conflict or impose social controls, not to find the facts." Martin Shapiro, Courts: A Comparative and Political Analysis 44 (1981).

subsequent case. This older approach to civil litigation at least partly explains why the doctrine of mutuality prevailed with respect to issue preclusion. Most observers and participants now find this view of civil litigation to be quaint, not to say ill adapted to the realities of civil litigation in a world of limited resources and widespread litigiousness. That is why nonmutuality is now the rule for issue preclusion in most jurisdictions.

Nonmutuality and Efficiency; "Offensive" and "Defensive" Uses of Issue Preclusion. But is the doctrine of nonmutuality actually more "efficient" overall than the doctrine of nonmutuality that it replaced? That is, does it reduce litigation (assuming that that is what we want)? Assessing the efficiency effects of the nonmutuality doctrine requires separate analysis of what are known, respectively, as "offensive" and "defensive" uses of issue preclusion. (The terms "offensive" and "defensive" in this context are not legal terms as such, but simply help to distinguish the different kinds of circumstances in which nonmutual collateral estoppel can operate.) "Offensive nonmutual collateral estoppel" occurs when there are multiple claimants and a single defendant, and a claimant in Case B seeks to use an earlier claimant's successful litigation against the defendant to preclude the defendant from relitigating issues decided adversely to it in Case A. The "multiple-claimant" situation epitomized by the multi-passenger accident is a clear illustration; later claimants can use issue preclusion *offensively* against the defendant in subsequent cases.

"Defensive nonmutual collateral estoppel" occurs when a single claimant serially sues more than one defendant, and the claimant's loss in Case A enables a different defendant in Case B to preclude the claimant from relitigating issues decided adversely to him in Case A. An example would be a plaintiff claiming to hold a patent on a device or process that he believes several companies are infringing. If Case A results in a legal determination that the claimant does not even hold a valid patent, future defendants sued by the plaintiff on similar claims can use the doctrine of nonmutual issue preclusion *defensively* to prevent the plaintiff from relitigating the validity of his patent. The key feature distinguishing offensive from defensive uses of issue preclusion is not simply that plaintiffs typically use the former and defendants typically use the latter (although that is true), but that offensive nonmutual collateral estoppel typically applies when there are multiple claimants who serially sue a single defendant, while with defensive nonmutual collateral estoppel there is a single claimant who serially sues more than one defendant. In all cases of issue preclusion, of course, the party against whom preclusion is asserted must have been a party in the earlier case.

The U.S. Supreme Court took a major step toward recognition of the doctrine of nonmutuality in federal question cases heard in the federal courts when it decided *Blonder–Tongue Laboratories, Inc. v. University of Illinois Foundation* (1971),[30] a case involving the patent situation discussed above as an example of defensive nonmutual collateral estoppel. In *Blonder–Tongue*, the Court held that the unsuccessful patent plaintiff in Case A was estopped from suing another alleged infringer in Case B, because in Case A the plaintiff had been found not to possess a valid patent. The Court examined the subject of nonmutuality in earnest in *Parklane Hosiery v. Shore* (1979),[31] the decision in which it adopted, as a matter of federal common law, the doctrine of nonmutuality for civil litigation in federal court cases based on federal question jurisdiction. In *Parklane Hosiery*, the United States civilly sued the defendant in federal court under the securities fraud laws, based on alleged misbehavior by the company's officers and directors. When a final judgment was entered against the company, a group of private plaintiffs sued the defendant in a second proceeding in federal court, based on the same cause of action and the same set of events.[32] The plaintiffs in Case B moved for partial summary judgment, based on the argument that the company should not be able to relitigate the question of the officers' and directors' misdeeds, established in Case A. This was an attempt to deploy offensive nonmutual collateral estoppel: same defendant, same set of events, new claimants.

The Supreme Court, which had not yet established the doctrine of nonmutuality for issue preclusion in the federal courts in this kind of situation, considered the possible effects of establishing such a doctrine. The Court observed that the doctrine of nonmutuality might in fact create an incentive for potential plaintiffs in the multiple-claimant (offensive) situation to "sit on the sidelines"— that is, to wait until one individual plaintiff pursued a successful case against the defendant, at which point the sideline-sitter(s) could begin another proceeding against the defendant and reap the benefits of nonmutual collateral estoppel. Since it would seemingly

---

30. 402 U.S. 313 (1971).

31. 439 U.S. 322 (1979).

32. In reality, the private lawsuit, which I have here denominated as Case B, was filed prior to the government's lawsuit. The plaintiffs in the private case, however, waited until disposition of the government's case before moving for summary judgment. Therefore, it better serves our purposes here to describe the private lawsuit as Case B. Incidentally, the sequence of events in

Parkland Hosiery illustrates the *modus operandi* of many plaintiffs' lawyers working in the antitrust and securities fraud fields. Nothing pleases such attorneys more than the discovery that the government has initiated civil or criminal proceedings against a corporate defendant or officers and directors in these areas, because a judgment or settlement favorable to the government can open the door for private litigation against the same defendant(s) and effective use of preclusion doctrines.

be more "efficient" for the claims arising from a single set of events to be resolved in as small a number of judicial proceedings as possible, this incentive would seem to militate against the efficiency of nonmutuality, at least in the "offensive" context.[33] Despite its concern with the possibility of producing more litigation, the Court concluded that nonmutuality should be the rule for issue preclusion in the federal courts exercising their federal question jurisdiction,[34] whether in the "offensive" or the "defensive" context. The courts in most states have come to a similar conclusion with respect to the law of their own states.

Nonmutuality and the "Multiple–Claimant Anomaly." In coming to its decision in *Parklane Hosiery*, the Court (like those state courts that have discarded the mutuality requirement for issue preclusion) implicitly rejected an argument first made by the redoubtable Brainerd Currie, one that cast at least theoretical doubt on the legitimacy of nonmutuality in the multi-claimant situation.[35] Currie generalized the problem of multiple claimants, positing a situation in which a large number of persons were injured by a single defendant. (Currie hypothesized a railroad crash, in which 50 individuals were injured, but many mass torts would illustrate the problem just as well.) In this extreme hypothetical, the first 25 passengers each sued the defendant individually, and the defendant received a jury verdict in each case. The defendant, of course, could not exploit any of its victories by precluding each new plaintiff from relitigating certain issues, because no one can be bound by a judgment in a case to which one was not a party. As soon as plaintiff #26 won a verdict, however, each of the remaining passengers could sue the defendant as a group and prevent the defendant from relitigating such issues as negligence and causation. The asymmetry created by the fact that one or more of the multiple claimants can exploit the preclusion consequences of the success of a previous claimant, but that the defendant may not exploit the preclusion consequences of *its* success against new claimants, appears to facilitate an unfair result.

---

33. The Court distinguished the defensive use of nonmutual collateral estoppel, using the patent case decided in *Blonder–Tongue* as an illustration; a patent claimant, faced with the prospect that a single case against a single defendant could yield an adverse ruling that future possible defendants could use preclusively to quickly terminate later cases brought against them by the plaintiff, would lack the incentive to sue individual defendants serially and would be more likely to sue all possible defendants in a single proceeding. That's what the Court speculated, anyway; whether it is a realistic speculation is subject to debate.

34. The emphasis here on "federal question" cases is important. In diversity cases, the federal courts employ state issue preclusion rules, pursuant to the "*Erie* Doctrine," which is treated in Chapter 7.

35. Brainerd Currie, *Mutuality of Collateral Estoppel: Limits of the Bern-*

Currie's emphasis was not so much on the unfairness to the defendant in this example, but on the concern, highlighted by the example, that the operation of nonmutual collateral estoppel could multiply an incorrect outcome, compounding the mistakes that any litigation system will inevitably produce from time to time. When 25 consecutive plaintiffs all lose their cases and the 26th wins, it is reasonable to infer that the 26th case was an "anomaly"—that the jury engaged in flawed reasoning or that some mistake was made at trial, producing an erroneous outcome. But it is also reasonably probable that, in any series of 50 cases or some other large number, a few anomalies will occur. Moreover, reasoned Currie, if we assume that in any such series of cases an anomaly is likely to show up somewhere, there is no reason to believe that the anomaly will not result in the *first*, rather than the 26th, case—or at least in some case nearer the beginning than the 26th. If it does, then nonmutuality can result in incorrect awards for upwards of fifty plaintiffs, even though none really should have received one. There is a risk, then, that nonmutuality in multiple-claimant situations can produce incorrect outcomes and work substantial injustice. Moreover, since most applications of issue preclusion involve not 50 but two or perhaps three proceedings, the fact that the judgment in the first case might be incorrect suggests that the entire doctrine of nonmutuality might be ill founded.

Currie's argument was clever, but it has not persuaded courts to eschew the doctrine of nonmutuality. The structure of Currie's hypothetical was stylized, unlikely to arise often in practice in precisely the way he posited (although multiple-claimant situations are certainly common).[36] Moreover, the entire edifice of the law of preclusion (if not the litigation system itself) rests on the presumption that, generally speaking, adjudications of disputes reach correct results and may legitimately serve to terminate further litigation with respect to the same claims and issues. The problem of nonmutual collateral estoppel where multiple claimants exploit the preclusion consequences of the first successful case presents the specter of preclusion on a larger and more dramatic scale, but the basic problem is the same as in any "normal" Case A–Case B situation. To dispense with the doctrine of nonmutuality altogether, because of the theoretical possibility of occasional authorship of incorrect results in a particular situation, would be to throw out the proverbial baby with the bathwater.

Nevertheless, the argument made by Currie has in fact been given partial recognition by the general rule in the multi-claimant situation that, if inconsistent outcomes have *already* been rendered

---

hard *Doctrine,* 9 Stanford Law Review 281 (1957).

36. *But see State Farm Fire & Cas. Co. v. Century Home Components, Inc.,* 275 Or. 97, 550 P.2d 1185 (1976).

in cases brought by individual claimants against a defendant, a subsequent claimant may not preclude the defendant from relitigating issues that were established by the successful one of the previous claimants.[37] Strictly as a matter of logic, it is not obvious why the existence of outstanding inconsistent judgments should make a difference to the legitimacy of giving effect to nonmutuality, since the mere possibility of such inconsistencies or anomalies exists in *any* multi-claimant situation. In reality, however, it is easy to see why the actual existence of previous inconsistent judgments matters. It is simply too unseemly to permit a new claimant to pick and choose among previous adjudications and exploit the one that works to her advantage, while the defendant can make no hay from the previous adjudication in her favor.

The Unavailability of "Procedural Opportunities" in Case A. Currie's invocation of the "multiple-claimant anomaly" is not the only concern that has been expressed about the wholesale adoption of the nonmutuality principle. Some have argued that nonmutuality can lead to unfair results in other ways. In *Parklane Hosiery* itself, for example, the defendant argued that assertion against it of nonmutual collateral estoppel would be unfair because trial by jury, which was available to it in Case B, had not been available to it in Case A.[38] To permit the application of nonmutual collateral estoppel would be to give preclusive effect, to resolve an issue in a proceeding (Case B) in which the defendant would otherwise have the right to a jury, to a determination that had been made in a proceeding (Case A) where no such trial right had been available to the defendant. The Supreme Court in *Parklane Hosiery* rejected this argument. It acknowledged that, as a general matter, courts should be careful not to give issue-preclusive effect to determinations made in proceedings where important procedural protections were denied to the losing party that he would be entitled to assert in Case B; but the availability or unavailability of jury trial does not systematically inure to the benefit of either the plaintiff or the defendant in civil litigation, so the absence of jury trial in Case A in *Parklane Hosiery* was not a reason for denying issue-preclusive effect to the determinations made in Case A. This and other possible objections to nonmutuality are considered below in the section entitled "The Limits of Preclusion," because they are not necessarily confined to cases of nonmutuality, but rather may suggest limitations on the doctrine of preclusion more generally. The point to be made here is simply that the doctrine of nonmutu-

---

37. Restatement (Second) of Judgments § 29(4) and comment f; *State Farm, supra* n. 36.

38. Because the government in its suit in *Parklane Hosiery* had sought only injunctive relief, the defendant was not entitled to demand a jury trial under the securities laws. A private lawsuit seeking money damages, as in Case B, did entitle the defendant to a jury.

ality may at first glance appear to be an appealing approach to issue preclusion, but there are reasons to be cautious in its application.

e. Nonmutuality, Complex and Public Law Litigation, and Class Actions

The vagaries of claim and issue preclusion frequently present attorneys with important long-term strategic questions at the outset of litigation. Depending on the preclusion rules operating in the forum, plaintiffs' counsel must consider that the assertion of one cause of action may serve to bar her from bringing, in a subsequent case, other related claims that she omits. In jurisdictions that recognize the doctrine of compulsory counterclaims, defendants' counsel similarly must be careful not to unwittingly forfeit possible claims against the plaintiff. Since jurisdictions can vary in their preclusion rules, those differences might in some cases even affect the plaintiff's choice of forum where the courts of more than one state would have jurisdiction.

Complex and "Public Law" Litigation. As noted above, the operation of nonmutual collateral estoppel presents a particular risk for defendants where multiple potential claimants loom. This is largely the problem of complex litigation—the large-scale lawsuit, often involving multiple parties, which has become a widespread phenomenon in the litigation world during the last half-century. Whereas the archetypal private lawsuit envisioned by the pre-World War II common law was an action brought by one individual against another for money damages, the scale of cognizable legal injuries that can be wrought by the actions of governments and large corporations has greatly expanded, so that a given set of events can give rise to potential claims on the part of many people. If the telephone company illegally and surreptitiously adds a small charge to everyone's monthly bill, then millions of individuals may have a cause of action against the company, all arising out of a single instance of misfeasance. Airline crashes, toxic torts, and other episodic disasters can likewise give rise to causes of action on the part of numerous and sometimes innumerable plaintiffs. Many of the most important changes to the rules of civil procedure during the last 75 years have been designed to facilitate and streamline the process by which such complex litigation can be resolved.

Precisely because there are so many potential claimants arising out of such events, adjudication of even one of the potential claims can have a broader impact than we customarily associate with the garden-variety civil lawsuit. Even when the defendant in such cases is nominally "private" and the cause of action is drawn from the traditional "private law" areas of tort, contract, or property, the scale of the dispute makes it obvious that its implications are far from being merely private. For example, if a single plaintiff sues a major automobile company over injuries suffered because of an alleged design defect causing a particular model's engine to explode upon contact with the vehicle's rear bumper, others injured in accidents involving the same model will be eagerly awaiting the results. There may be a significant number of people hoping to take "preclusive advantage" of the first successful plaintiff's victory to prevent the auto manufacturer from relitigating certain issues in their own lawsuits. (This is one reason why defendants in such cases often seek to make the settlements they reach with individual plaintiffs confidential.) Moreover, since the question of automobile safety is of widespread interest to the public, the results of the first lawsuit, and the way in which it is litigated, can seem almost to carry the weight of a major decision on public policy.

Consider this hypothetical example: A private company is suspected of contaminating, over a long period of time, the drinking water of a city neighborhood with toxic chemicals. A resident of that neighborhood is diagnosed with a rare disease, which has been associated with exposure to one of the chemicals. The resident dies from the disease, and his widow brings a wrongful death suit against the company. In defending the action, the defendant has more to think about than simply winning this case. If the case is litigated to a conclusion, and judgment is entered for the plaintiff, it is likely that issues related to the defendant's wrongful behavior will be conclusively established. If others develop symptoms of the rare disease, they will probably sue the defendant and seek to prevent the defendant from relitigating some or all of these issues, based on issue preclusion. This is one incentive defendants have for settling such cases. Now assume that the case, rather than being settled, results in a substantial money judgment for the plaintiff. The defendant takes an appeal. The plaintiff, eager to recover her judgment and worried that the judgment may be reversed on appeal, indicates a willingness to settle the case with the defendant for an amount that is substantial but that is smaller than the judgment. The defendant is also willing to settle on these terms, but only if the plaintiff agrees that the trial court's judgment be vacated. (Sometimes the parties will even agree to a "stipulated reversal," which results in judgment, as a formal matter, actually being entered in favor of the defendant.) Should such settlement agreements be approved by the courts? Consider that one consequence of the settlement will be that other potential plaintiffs will no longer be able to bar the defendant from relitigating certain questions in subsequent lawsuits. Should this larger interest in the conclusive determination of certain issues in the first case play any role in determining the propriety of such settlements?[39]

39. For a discussion of this issue, see Steven R. Harmon, Comment, *Un-* *settling Settlements: Should Stipulated Reversals Be Allowed to Trump Judg-*

Finally, consider the interaction of preclusion doctrines with what has generally become known as "public law litigation." Since the 1960s, the use of litigation as a means of effecting political and social change has become familiar (although it is, perhaps, less widely celebrated today than it once was). Such litigation has been deployed as a means of desegregating public institutions, improving conditions of confinement in prisons and mental institutions, and otherwise forcing changes in policy on governments. As Abram Chayes noted over 30 years ago in an influential article, such public law litigation has features that differ from traditional private-law litigation, even though in both situations the same formal device of litigation is employed.[40] For example, in public law litigation, the relief sought is often prospective, in the form of an injunction, rather than restorative (which is the usual goal of money damages). Moreover, by its very nature the outcome of public law litigation can affect many who are not technically parties to the case. Changes in government policy, even if by way of injunction, often have lasting and unpredictable effects. For example, a judicial order desegregating a school district's public school system will dramatically affect people and institutions, present and future, who are not formal parties to the lawsuit. Finally, the "public law" of public law litigation frequently is constitutional law, the most politically contested area of law in our society. Unlike, say, personal injury litigation, which is based on longstanding principles of private law that are unlikely to change dramatically anytime soon, the content of constitutional rights and duties can change with a single U.S. Supreme Court decision. This means that the preclusive effect of certain cases involving "public law" issues may be less secure than that of other kinds of rulings.

Martin v. Wilks (1989). All of these issues came to the fore in *Martin v. Wilks* (1989),[41] an important Supreme Court decision illustrating several of the complexities of conventional preclusion doctrine as applied to public law litigation. In the early 1970s, a group of Black firefighters brought an employment discrimination claim in federal district court against the City of Birmingham and the Jefferson County Personnel Board, alleging that the city's fire department had engaged in a pattern and practice of racial discrimination in its hiring and promotion practices. The City and the Board each settled with the plaintiffs; the parties entered into a consent decree that required the fire department to set and implement certain goals for the hiring and promotion of Black firefight-

ments' Collateral Estoppel Effects Under Neary?, 85 CALIFORNIA LAW REVIEW 479 (1997).

40. Abram Chayes, *The Role of the Judge in Public Law Litigation*, 89 HARVARD LAW REVIEW 1281 (1976).

41. 490 U.S. 755 (1989).

ers. The consent decrees were approved by the federal district court, and the court's approval of them constituted an official adjudication that the adoption of the goals for hiring and promoting Black firefighters were legal and constitutional. Several years later, a group of white firefighters sued the City and the Board in federal court, arguing that the fire department had discriminated against them by passing them over in promotion decisions, using the guidelines specified in the consent decree in the original case. The City defended on the ground that it had simply been relying on the decree (and on the approval of its terms by the district court) in the first case. In effect, the City was arguing that the new plaintiffs, the white firefighters, should be barred by issue preclusion from relitigating the question of the legality of the guidelines set forth in the original consent decree. The Supreme Court ruled against the City, holding that the new plaintiffs must be permitted their day in court to challenge the legality of the department's hiring and promotion practices.

In terms of conventional preclusion doctrine, *Martin v. Wilks* was a fairly easy case. As we have emphasized, due process prohibits a person from having his rights conclusively determined in a proceeding to which he was not a party. The white firefighters had not been parties in the first proceeding. Therefore any rulings in the first case concerning the legality of the provisions embodied in the consent decree could not be conclusive as against them. Although the white firefighters—let us assume for the moment that those we are calling the "white firefighters" were capable of becoming parties during the first suit—had had an opportunity to intervene in the first case, they had not done so.[42] The Court in *Martin v. Wilks* upheld the traditional rule that there is no duty to intervene in a case or risk having one's rights conclusively adjudicated. If plaintiffs in Case A wish to insure against the possibility of later challenges to the results of the case, said the Court, they may invoke the liberal joinder provisions of the Federal Rules of Civil Procedure to join those parties on whom the adjudication will be binding.[43] In other words, the burden of ensuring that the results of a case will bind outsiders to the case rests on the parties who are already in the case.

While the formal doctrine applied in *Martin v. Wilks* was uncontroversial, the facts of the case illustrate that the no-duty-to-

42. In fact, a group of white firefighters sought to intervene in the first case, but their petition to intervene was denied by the court as untimely. It is thus technically correct to say that they had had an opportunity to intervene in the first case, but had failed to exercise it.

43. The relevant joinder device would have been Fed R. Civ. P. 19, governing joinder of "necessary and indispensable parties" at the behest of a party already in the case.

intervene (even where it would be very easy to do so) rule may have unique and disruptive effects in the context of multi-party public law litigation. On the one hand, the fact that much public law litigation will end up affecting many who are not parties (for example, by diverting resources to the fire department that might be used for other public purposes, or by making it more difficult for white firefighters to be promoted) is all the more reason to take care that the rights of absentees are not conclusively determined without meaningful opportunity for participation. At the same time, however, the very purpose of such public law litigation frequently is to bring public policy into accord with constitutional or other legal standards, not simply for the moment or for the sole benefit of the present plaintiffs, but for the foreseeable future. If the no-duty-to-intervene rule is applied to such litigation, the results of such litigation must remain provisional so long as there are persons, not parties in the present case, with standing to challenge them in a second lawsuit. The opportunity to join parties at the outset will not always be an effective solution for the plaintiffs; in many cases it may be difficult for them to identify in advance all persons who might ultimately have their interests affected by resolution of the first suit.

While these arguments are not sufficient reason to dispense entirely with the requirement that no one may have his rights conclusively determined by a proceeding to which she is not a party, they might suggest the propriety of a rule that at least would impose a duty to intervene on the part of those who are fully aware of the pendency of litigation, who know or reasonably could be expected to know that their legal interests might be affected by the outcome of the litigation, and who could easily intervene under the rules of the forum. In fact, Congress, overruling the specific holding in *Martin v. Wilks*, enacted a principle much like this in the Civil Rights Act of 1991, providing that in employment discrimination cases involving consent decrees, those with actual notice of the pendency of the first case and the opportunity to intervene may not challenge the terms of the decree in a later proceeding, even if they never officially became "parties" in the original lawsuit. For the most part, however, there remains no "duty to intervene" in civil litigation in most situations, whether or not involving "public law" litigation.

It is worth understanding how and why the problem in *Martin v. Wilks* arose in the way it did. The prospective relief granted as part of the consent decree had continuing impact on numerous people, including the white firefighters seeking to be hired or promoted. And, crucially, between the time that the consent judgment in the first case became final and initiation of the second lawsuit, the Supreme Court had begun to give indications that the kind of race-specific remedies that were embodied in the consent decree might be inconsistent with the Fourteenth Amendment's Equal Protection Clause. Thus there had been a discernible "change in the law," or at least some uncertainty about the constitutionality in the 1980s of what had been constitutional at the time of the original consent decree.[44] Moreover, the setting of *Martin v. Wilks* was a bit unusual in that the issue as to which preclusion was sought was not the determination in Case A that the Black plaintiffs' rights had been violated, but the constitutional validity of the remedy provided by the agreed-upon and judicially approved consent decree. Although the consent decree was technically an adjudication, one can see why such a decree makes the application of preclusion more questionable than would a more conventional adjudication: The issue of the legality and constitutionality of the agreed-upon race-conscious remedy may not have been "actually litigated and determined" in the sense of a genuine adversary contest. The City and the Board in Case A were not in any sense "representatives" of the white firefighters, and may have been motivated more by a desire to reach an agreement with the plaintiffs than anything else.[45]

All of this underscores the fact that *Martin v. Wilks* fits the model of wide-ranging, multiple-party, "public law" litigation that we have contrasted with the traditional, garden-variety, "A vs. B" private lawsuit on which it is modeled. Had Case A involved only a single plaintiff, raising an issue of private law such as a tort or contract dispute, it's unlikely that the remedy provided him would have remained in operation for a period of years, or that its legality would have been called into question by a later judicial decision. Preclusion principles clearly raise some distinct issues in the context of complex litigation, particularly where "public law" litigation is involved.

Class Actions and Group Litigation. The problem of preclusion and class actions is discussed in greater detail near the end

---

44. The reason that this is important for understanding *Martin v. Wilks* is that, in an ordinary case and under ordinary circumstances, even permitting the white firefighters to proceed with their claim in Case B in the same federal district court might be expected to result in dismissal on *stare decisis* grounds—the governing precedent being the district court's implicit upholding in Case A of the constitutionality of the race-specific remedies. But with new constitutional doubts about such decrees having been sown by the Supreme Court in the interim, this could no longer be assumed.

45. Note that, had the "white firefighters" actually been parties in Case A, an interesting question concerning the doctrine of representation might have arisen in any subsequent effort in Case B by white firefighters to challenge the legality of the consent decree ultimately entered. Can "white firefighters" in the early 1970s be regarded as legally representing the interests of "white firefighters" in the mid-1980s, such that preclusion can operate? The question raises issues about group identity and the reification of race that go well beyond our subject here.

of this Chapter in connection with interjurisdictional preclusion and Full Faith and Credit, an area where the complexities of applying preclusion doctrine to class actions are most vividly on display. For now, let us simply observe that the class-action device, as useful as it is, can have powerful and sometimes unanticipated preclusion consequences—in particular, for potential claimants. Fed. R. Civ. P. 23 and analogous state rules provide in a variety of circumstances for the certification of a plaintiff class (or, in theory, a defendant class, but this rarely occurs), making the class-action device a potent means of aggregating monetary claims, obtaining injunctive relief that protects a large number of people, or otherwise facilitating large-scale adjudication that could not realistically be achieved were the class device not available. The flip side of this, of course, is that all members of a certified class who do not "opt out" of the litigation are bound by the results of the class action. Since in many situations it will be impractical to notify all members of a plaintiff class—they are too numerous and widely dispersed—of the pending litigation, many such members will have their rights determined by a proceeding of which they had no actual knowledge.

The legitimacy of this situation rests heavily on the concept of "representation" at which we looked earlier in this chapter when discussing the meaning of the term "the same parties." Fed. R. Civ. P. 23 requires, as a condition of judicial certification of a proposed plaintiff class, that the named plaintiffs "will fairly and adequately protect the interests of the class."[46] There is no other theory on which the rights of absent members of the plaintiff class can justifiably be conclusively determined by a class action; otherwise our "bedrock principle" of preclusion—that no one should be bound by the results of a proceeding to which she was not a party—would be violated. This makes it all the more imperative that a judge, when certifying a class, be scrupulous in determining that the named plaintiffs will "fairly and adequately protect" the interests of absent class members. How might the named plaintiffs fail in this responsibility in a particular case? For example, by agreeing to a settlement of the case that privileges their own financial interests (say, by minimizing the costs they, as named plaintiffs, might have to incur by further litigation of the case) over those of absent plaintiffs. At times, unfortunately, judicial care in making such judgments by way of certifying such classes has been more in evidence in some cases than in others, particularly in some state

---

46. Fed. R. Civ. P. 23(a)(4). This requirement is to be distinguished from what is usually called the "representativeness" requirement for class actions—that "the claims or defenses of the representative parties [be] typical of the claims or defenses of the class." Fed. R. Civ. P. 23(a)(3). In speaking here of the "representation" concept, I am referring instead to Fed. R. Civ. P. 23(a)(4), concerning the ability of the named plaintiffs to protect the interests of the members of the class as a whole.

courts. These problems are discussed further below, in our treatment of interjurisdictional preclusion.

Here is an example of how the "representation" idea intersects with preclusion in group litigation, albeit in the context of what is known as a "shareholder's derivative suit" rather than a class action as such. Fed. R. Civ. P. 23.1 permits one or more shareholders to bring a lawsuit, on behalf of the corporation and all its shareholders, to enforce a right of the corporation that the corporation itself is failing to enforce. (Often these derivative actions are brought against the corporation's own officers and directors, helping to explain why the "corporation" has not itself acted to enforce the rights being asserted). Just as with class actions, the results of the derivative action are binding on all the corporation's shareholders. And, just as with class actions, the federal rule requires that the named plaintiff(s) adequately represent the interests of other shareholders: "The derivative action may not be maintained if it appears that the plaintiff does not fairly and adequately represent the interests of shareholders or members who are similarly situated in enforcing the right of the corporation or association." Fed. R. Civ. P. 23.1(a). In *Saylor v. Lindsley* (2d Cir. 1968),[47] a shareholder had brought a derivative action in federal court against some of the corporation's directors. When confronted with a New York legal requirement that he post a security bond with the federal district court, he abandoned the lawsuit, without bothering to dismiss it voluntarily. The court subsequently entered judgment for the defendants under Fed. R. Civ. P. 41(b), governing involuntary dismissal in the federal court. When a different shareholder brought the same claim (based on the same alleged malfeasance) against the directors in the same federal district court a few years later, that court dismissed the case on the ground of *res judicata*; the earlier lawsuit had conclusively determined the rights of all the corporation's shareholders arising out of the alleged malfeasance.

The Second Circuit reversed. Although it justified its conclusion in part on its assertion that the involuntary dismissal in Case A should not qualify as "an adjudication upon the merits," that conclusion was questionable in light of the fact that, in general, involuntary dismissals (as specified by Fed. R. Civ. P. 41(b) itself) must be given *res judicata* effect if they are to constitute a useful device. Rather, what really seemed to move the court is that the plaintiff in Case A had not "fairly and adequately represented the interests of the shareholders" when he simply dropped his lawsuit like a hot potato without bothering to dismiss it voluntarily. (Unlike Fed. R. Civ. P. 23, Fed. R. Civ. P. 23.1 does not require "certification" by the court of the derivative action, meaning that it

---

47.   391 F.2d 965 (2d Cir. 1968).

would be legitimate to attack the "representativeness" of the plaintiff in Case A collaterally, in Case B, since the adequacy of his representation would not have been actually litigated and determined in Case A.) *Saylor* is probably best read as a case about the "adequate representation" requirement of the derivative suit rule, and it illustrates what we have said more generally about representation and preclusion in group litigation.

4. The Limits of Preclusion

There are some situations in which preclusion should not be permitted to apply, although the conventional criteria for applying it have been met. The law of preclusion is, for the most part, state law, and the principles governing these "exceptions" to the operation of preclusion are not precisely identical in all states. However, the Restatement (Second) of Judgments, frequently relied on by state courts, gives a helpful analysis of what these exceptions might be.[48]

"Differences in the Quality or Extensiveness of the Procedures ..." In the context of claim preclusion, consider the basic facts of Pat's claim against the City of Denver for the towing of her car, with one change in facts: Assume both cases were brought in Colorado state court. If Colorado uses the "same transaction" test for claim preclusion, Pat would be barred from bringing a constitutional claim against the city in Case B, if she had already litigated in Case A a replevin claim against the City that arose from the same set of events. It would be unfair, however, to bar Pat from raising her constitutional claim in Case A had the first replevin action been litigated in a specialized Colorado court that did not have jurisdiction to hear constitutional claims. Simply stated, one cannot be precluded from raising a claim in Case B if the court in Case A had no jurisdiction to consider that claim. This notion is encapsulated in the more general requirement, applicable in all instances of preclusion, that a party against whom claim or issue preclusion is sought must have had a full and fair opportunity to litigate the claim or issue in Case A.

We can expand on this principle to suggest a further limitation on preclusion: If the litigation rules applicable in Court A are meaningfully different from those in Court B, normal preclusion rules might not apply. Here, "meaningfully different" means that the difference in the applicable rules and procedures available in the two cases may have a real effect on the party's ability to

---

48. Restatement (Second) of Judgments § 28. Section 28 is concerned with limitations on the operation of issue preclusion. Some analogous discussion of limitations on the operation of claim preclusion can be found in § 20 and § 26.

establish her case. The concept is set forth in § 28 of the Restatement (Second) of Judgments:

> Although an issue is actually litigated and determined by a valid and final judgment, and the determination is essential to the judgment, relitigation of the issue in a subsequent action between the parties is not precluded in the following circumstances: ...
>
> (3) A new determination of the issue is warranted by differences in the quality or extensiveness of the procedures followed in the two courts or by factors relating to the allocation of jurisdiction between them.

To illustrate, let's again build on Pat's car-towing saga. Suppose that the tribunal in Case A, the replevin case, did permit Pat to raise any constitutional claims she might have. However, suppose also that that tribunal has relatively informal procedures, such that there is no ability to depose witnesses, or even to be represented by counsel.[49] Should Pat's omission of her constitutional claim from this proceeding bar her from raising it in Case B in a state court of general jurisdiction, with its full panoply of procedural devices and protections, since the replevin and constitutional claims arose out of the same transaction? Probably not. In particular, Pat's legal inability to be represented by counsel in Case A militates strongly against application of the normal preclusion rules in Case B; it's hard to say that Pat had a "full and fair opportunity" to litigate the constitutional claim in Case A.

One variation on the "different procedures" idea that invariably finds its way into law-school hypotheticals concerns differences in the standard of proof that is used in Case A and Case B. This is particularly relevant where a party seeks to use the results of a criminal proceeding in a later civil proceeding, or vice versa. For example, if the defendant is sued in Case A for wrongful death and loses the case, can he be precluded in a subsequent criminal prosecution from contesting issues that were decided adversely to him in the wrongful-death proceeding? Under most circumstances, the answer will be no. The disputed factual issues in the wrongful-death action will most likely have been determined using a "preponderance of the evidence" standard; determinations made adversely to the defendant under that standard do not translate into equivalent determinations under the higher standard of "beyond a reasonable doubt." Of course, the defendant is in a bleaker position if the criminal case comes first and he is convicted. In principle, the

---

49. Although this example is a hypothetical, not necessarily based on an actual court that is recognized under Colorado law, the scenario is not fanciful. Many local courts, such as small claims courts, have abbreviated procedures and may disallow the use of lawyers.

difference in the standard of proof will now work, if at all, to his detriment should he be sued for wrongful death; there is no reason to fail to give preclusive effect to determinations made (adversely to the defendant) pursuant to a "beyond a reasonable doubt" standard in a proceeding where the standard of proof will be lower.

Inconsistent Outstanding Judgments. Some other exceptions to the operation of preclusion arise specifically in the context of nonmutual collateral estoppel, where the possibility of multiple claimants exists. The "multiple-claimant anomaly" has already been discussed. The Restatement (Second) of Judgments, while generally accepting the principle of nonmutuality, opines that when there are outstanding inconsistent judgments, nonmutual collateral estoppel should not be applied in a subsequent case.[50] How far this principle extends—that is, how many successful lawsuits have to have been brought before the existence of one outstanding unsuccessful case will no longer bar the application of nonmutual collateral estoppel—is anybody's guess. It is not a question that has been extensively litigated.

Insufficient Incentive to Litigate Vigorously in Case A. Another example, which again is found more often in law school hypotheticals than in actual reported decisions, revolves around a defendant's incentive, or lack thereof, aggressively to litigate a small claim when a second claimant with a much larger claim lurks, unbeknownst to the defendant, as a potential plaintiff in a second case. The idea is that if the driver of an automobile injures two pedestrians, one of whom sues the driver for $500, the driver may have insufficient incentive to litigate aggressively and may with little resistance allow the plaintiff to recover her $500. Now the second injured passenger sues the driver for $5 million and seeks to bar the driver from relitigating the question of his own negligence. Some have suggested that it would be inappropriate to allow nonmutual collateral estoppel to operate against the defendant in this situation. Perhaps; but it is not a principle that has left much of a footprint in the reported cases. Defendants are more likely to settle a small case than to allow the plaintiff to march off, unimpeded, with a judgment. (Note that, in these multiple-claimant situations, a default judgment in one case will not give rise to the application of nonmutual collateral estoppel in a second case because issue preclusion requires that an issue have been "actually litigated and determined," which is not the case in a default judgment.)

Those interested in further discussion of the possible exceptions to the operation of preclusion should consult §§ 28–29 of the Restatement (Second) of Judgments.

---

50. Restatement (Second) of Judgments § 29(4). Section 29 deals generally with nonmutuality in issue preclusion.

No Issue Preclusion Against the United States. We'll conclude our discussion of limits on the operation of preclusion with a final exception to the usual rules of preclusion: Issue preclusion, generally speaking, is not available against the federal government. Let's explain how and why this is a tricky issue. Again, the situation giving rise to this principle is that in which there are multiple claimants. Virtually by definition, government actions affect many people. When one claimant successfully sues the federal government, others may follow suit (literally, figuratively speaking) and seek to preclude the government from re-litigating issues decided adversely to it in the first proceeding. As we've discussed above in connection with the "multiple-claimant anomaly," in general (apart from the problem of inconsistent outstanding judgments), the theoretical possibility of "anomalies" is not a sufficient reason for us to keep subsequent plaintiffs from being able to employ issue preclusion against the defendant. Rigorous application of the doctrines of claim and issue preclusion is acceptable, partly because a losing party in Case A can seek appellate review of that decision. In multiple-claimant situations, the risk that egregiously incorrect decisions will be "reproduced" by means of issue preclusion is attenuated by the likelihood that such decisions will be corrected on appeal.

But things are a little different when the federal government is the defendant. A decision adverse to the government in a case brought by one of many potential claimants can be rendered by any of the almost 100 federal district courts in the country. It is both impracticable and undesirable for the government to appeal all unfavorable rulings. More than with private litigants, the federal government's decisions to appeal adverse rulings (usually made by the Office of the Solicitor General in the Department of Justice) are made with an eye toward long-term strategic considerations concerning allocation of departmental resources, the importance of the legal issue relative to others, the likelihood of success on the merits, and so on. There are many reasons why a given administration might choose not to appeal such a case, wholly apart from its view of the merits. If the success of a single claimant could serve as the basis for a multitude of other lawsuits in which the government would be precluded from re-litigating key issues, the government would have to strongly consider appealing the initial claimant's victory regardless of other considerations. Because the federal government differs in these respects from private litigants, it is inappropriate for issue preclusion to apply against the federal government in multiple-claimant situations.[51]

---

51. The logic of the foregoing argument might suggest that issue preclusion *should* legitimately apply where the government in fact has received effective appellate review, perhaps all the way to the Supreme Court, in Case A. The Supreme Court, however, has never announced such a principle.

The leading case in this area is *United States v. Mendoza* (1984).[52] During World War II, Congress enacted a temporary modification of the naturalization laws that liberalized naturalization requirements for noncitizens who had served honorably in the U.S. Armed Forces during the war. Residents of the Philippines were eligible, but in 1945 the government of the Philippines asked the United States to suspend the liberalized nationalization requirements for residents of the Philippines, because it feared an exodus of Filipino nationals to the United States just as the Philippines had achieved national independence. Moreover, even during the period prior to revocation of the naturalization policy, the U.S. had failed to keep in the Philippines, for all but a few months of the program's duration, an immigration officer who could administer naturalization proceedings. The window of opportunity for naturalization according to the relaxed requirements was thus cut short prematurely, keeping some Filipinos who wished to take advantage of the program from being able to do so. In the 1970s a group of such Filipinos successfully sued the United States in Federal District Court, claiming that their Due Process rights had been violated and that they were entitled to consideration for naturalization. This decision was not appealed by the United States. Subsequently Mendoza (not a party in the first lawsuit), a Filipino national who had served in a military capacity for the U.S. during World War II, sued the U.S. in Federal District Court, claiming a right to naturalization and seeking to bar the U.S. from contesting issues decided adversely to it in the earlier proceeding. The Supreme Court held that Mendoza could not make use of nonmutual collateral estoppel against the United States, even though the doctrine could ordinarily be applied against a private party under analogous circumstances:

> We hold ... that nonmutual offensive collateral estoppel simply does not apply against the government in such a way as to preclude relitigation of issues such as those involved in this case. The conduct of government litigation in the courts of the United States is sufficiently different from the conduct of private civil litigation in those courts so that what might otherwise be economy interests underlying a broad application of collateral estoppel are outweighed by the constraints which peculiarly affect the government.[53]

And there the matter rests.

5. The Difference Between Preclusion and Precedent

Discussion of the complexities of issue preclusion in such cases as *Martin v. Wilks* and *United States v. Mendoza* suggests the

52.   464 U.S. 154 (1984).

53.   *Mendoza*, 464 U.S. at 162–63 (footnote omitted).

importance of keeping carefully in mind the distinction between *preclusion* and *precedent*. Preclusion of any kind *always* requires that the party against whom it is being asserted in Case B (or her privy) must have been a party in Case A. No one may be bound by a judgment to which she was not a party. There is obviously no such requirement for the operation of precedent and the principle of *stare decisis*. The doctrine of precedent holds that a court should follow the legal principles that it, or a court of superior authority in the same jurisdiction, has announced in earlier cases. For *stare decisis* to operate, it does not matter whether the parties in Case B are the same as in Case A. By the same token, of course, a second pre-eminent difference between preclusion and precedent is that the doctrine of preclusion is (subject to the various exceptions already mentioned) a strict one; Court B has no *ad hoc* discretion to refuse to apply the principles of preclusion.

Precedent and *stare decisis*, by contrast, constitute a looser, more amorphous principle. The doctrine holds that a court *should* follow its own precedents, but does not bar a court from re-examining and possibly overruling them when changed circumstances or a strong conviction that the earlier holding was incorrect suggest that it should. (Moreover, it's well known that courts seeking to avoid the *stare decisis* effect of an earlier ruling can exercise considerable creativity in distinguishing the present case from the earlier one. This is a very important practical limitation on operation of the *stare decisis* principle.) Finally, application of the doctrine of precedent requires an understanding of the jurisdictional reach of a particular court's holdings and the authority that superior courts have over inferior courts. The U.S. Supreme Court's holdings are binding as precedent throughout the country, and (at a formal level at least) no lower federal court can qualify or overrule them. A holding by a federal district court, by contrast, is binding precedent only within that federal district.[54]

Had the Supreme Court not barred the use of issue preclusion in *Mendoza*, conventional preclusion doctrine would have permitted other claimants to sue the United States in any federal district court and to have barred the United States from relitigating certain issues relevant to the citizenship claims. Because of the *Mendoza* decision, issue preclusion was unavailable. But the *Mendoza* decision would not, technically speaking, keep later claimants suing in the same federal district from being able to argue that the *precedent* of the original district court holding—that Filipino nationals in the same circumstances as the original claimant position were

---

54. Even this principle is qualified somewhat by the fact that different district courts within a district may decide the identical issue differently.

entitled to naturalization—should be followed. In *Martin v. Wilks*, to take another example, the Supreme Court explained why the white firefighters in Case B could not be *precluded* from litigating the legality of the consent order reached in Case A. But that would not mean that the City of Birmingham, sued in Case B by the white firefighters in the same Federal District Court that had rendered the decree in Case A, could not argue that that court's precedent (Case A itself) should result in a ruling on the merits in favor of the City in Case B. Of course, in each of these two examples, there might be reasons for the district court in Case B to limit the reach of its relevant precedent, or distinguish it. But it is sufficient here simply to see that the concepts of "preclusion" and "precedent" represent different ideas.

B. Interjurisdictional Preclusion and Full Faith and Credit

Now, at last, we turn to claim and issue preclusion specifically as those concepts relate to the subject of Conflict of Laws. As noted at the beginning of this Chapter, problems of claim and issue preclusion always involve a Case A and a Case B (where "A" is the first case and "B" is the second case); the question is whether, and to what extent, matters determined in Case A are barred from relitigation in Case B. Where both Case A and Case B are heard in the courts of the same state, the various preclusion issues obviously are governed by that state's law. Claim and issue preclusion, and the general subject of recognition of judgments, become matters of interest to Conflict of Laws when Case A and Case B, respectively, are heard by the courts of *different* states. To what extent are the courts of State B obliged to give effect to the judgments rendered by the courts of State A? In general, this problem is known as *interjurisdictional preclusion*. The basic doctrine governing the problem is that of *full faith and credit*. These are the central topics of the remainder of this Chapter.

1. Full Faith and Credit: Article IV and 28 U.S.C. § 1738

The way in which the courts of State B treat the judgments of courts of State A implicates questions of state sovereignty in our federal system. On the one hand, for the courts of State B to be *compelled*, against their wishes, to recognize and give effect to the judgments of the courts of State A might seem to violate the sovereignty of State B. On the other hand, for the judgments of the courts of State A simply to be ignored by the courts of State B—*i.e.*, to allow the parties to relitigate a claim or issue in Court B whose relitigation would clearly be barred by preclusion principles in the courts of State A were the second case to have been brought there—is to disrespect the sovereign prerogatives of State A. Is

Court B's decision to recognize Court A's judgments, and give them some sort of "effect," simply a matter of courtesy (sometimes called "comity"), or is there some legally imposed duty on Court B to treat those judgments in a particular way?

The Full Faith and Credit Clause ["FFC Clause"] of the U.S. Constitution, together with the Congressional statutes implementing it, 28 U.S.C. § 1738 *et seq.*, answers this question. In particular, the FFC Clause requires state courts to give "full faith and credit" to the judgments of sister states: "Full Faith and Credit shall be given in each State to the ... judicial Proceedings of every other State."[55] Precisely what it means to give "full faith and credit" can sometimes be uncertain, but, at a minimum, the FFC Clause clearly prohibits the courts of State B from ignoring—from failing to give *any* binding effect to—the judgments of the courts of State A. The FFC Clause thus serves as a rule in favor of interjurisdictional recognition of judgments, imposing a constitutional duty of recognition on the courts of State B.

It is interesting to contrast this situation from that which obtains in the international sphere. There is no "super-constitution" imposing a legally enforceable duty on the judicial tribunals of one nation-state to give legal effect to, or even to recognize, the judgments of another. There is no "Full Faith and Credit Clause" of the world. The signatories to certain bilateral or multilateral treaties or conventions may submit themselves to such duties, and the courts of one nation-state may in individual cases give effect to foreign judgments based on comity or on practical considerations, but in the absence of such an agreement the tribunals of one state have no positive legal duty to recognize foreign judgments. By contrast, within the domain of the U.S. legal system, the FFC Clause imposes a constitutional duty of recognition on all the states of the United States.

This duty of recognition with respect to judicial judgments is more rigid, and admits of far less discretion and subjectivity, than one finds in the area of choice of law. We saw, for example, in Chapter 4, that, where choice of law is concerned, a state court has considerable leeway to decline to apply foreign law on grounds of the forum's strongly held public policy, even if the applicable choice-of-law rule would ordinarily refer to that foreign law. The U.S. Constitution (including the FFC Clause) imposes only minimal limitations on courts making such choice-of-law rulings. Does a similar situation obtain with interjurisdictional preclusion—that is, when it is a foreign *judgment* and not a foreign *rule of decision* that the forum is being asked to recognize? May a state court decline to recognize and enforce a sister-state judgment when to do so would

---

55.   U.S. Const. art. iv, § 1.

violate the forum's strongly held public policy? What if the decision of the rendering court is plainly wrong, even outrageously so—can the recognition court decline to enforce it?

2.   The Basic Doctrine: Fauntleroy v. Lum

The answer to all these questions is "no." As the Supreme Court stated in 1998, "A court may be guided by the forum State's 'public policy' in determining the *law* applicable to a controversy.... But our decisions support no roving 'public policy exception' to the full faith and credit due *judgments*."[56] The command of the Full Faith and Credit Clause in this respect is firm. This is not to say that there are *no* occasions on which a court may decline to enforce the judgment of a sister-state court. As explained further below, no credit is due a judgment rendered by a court that lacked jurisdiction over the defendant, and there may be other narrow exceptions to the full faith and credit requirement. But concerns about violation of the "policy" of the forum are not a legitimate basis for declining enforcement of a sister-state judgment.

Fauntleroy v. Lum (1908). This point was made clear by the Supreme Court in *Fauntleroy v. Lum* (1908),[57] one of the Court's leading cases on full faith and credit to judgments. In *Fauntleroy*, two residents of Mississippi entered into a futures contract in Mississippi. A Mississippi statute prohibited the making of such agreements, and prohibited its courts from enforcing them.[58] One of the parties, claiming he was owed money by the other as a result of the contract, brought his claim to arbitration in Mississippi, and received a ruling from the arbitrator in his favor. He then brought an action against his alleged debtor in the courts of Missouri to recover the amount of the arbitration award. The Missouri court— overlooking or disregarding the fact that the law of the state (Mississippi) in which the contract had been made and performed prohibited such contracts and their enforcement—permitted the case to go forward, and a jury found for the creditor. The creditor assigned the judgment to his attorney, who immediately sued in the courts of Mississippi to recover on it. (The assignee mostly likely resorted to the courts of Mississippi for enforcement because that is where the debtor and/or his property were.)

This sequence of events in effect meant that, if the Mississippi court were now compelled by the FFC Clause to enforce the

---

56. *Baker v. General Motors Corp.*, 522 U.S. 222, 233 (1998) (citations and footnotes omitted) (emphasis in the original).

57.   210 U.S. 230 (1908).

58.   Futures contracts, which are today familiar on the floors of "futures exchanges," are agreements to buy or sell a particular commodity or financial instrument for a fixed price in the future. In the nineteenth century, they were often thought of as a form of gambling (as indeed they are) and were prohibited by some states.

Missouri judgment, the Mississippi creditor would be able to enforce his futures contract in a Mississippi court, despite the fact that Mississippi law would have barred the court from enforcing it had the action on the contract been brought there initially. The Mississippi courts understandably did not like this idea very much. The Missouri courts had clearly gone astray in enforcing the arbitration award, since those courts should have applied Mississippi law barring enforcement of the original contract. Nevertheless, the U.S. Supreme Court held that enforcement by the Mississippi courts of the Missouri judgment was required by the FFC Clause and the full faith and credit statute. Occasional imposition on the recognition state (State B) of the kind of "mistake" made by the Missouri court here was, in the Court's view, a small but necessary price to pay for firm and consistent enforcement of the FFC Clause's duty of recognition.

At first glance, it might appear that the sequence of events in *Fauntleroy*, together with the Court's rigid rule on full faith and credit to judgments, would enable parties to subvert the laws and policies of State A, which clearly should govern in a case brought in that state's courts, simply by resorting instead to the courts of State B, obtaining a judgment disregarding or misapplying State A's law, and taking the resulting judgment to State A for judicial enforcement there. There is little reason, however, to believe that such situations are likely often to arise. First, as the Court pointed out in *Fauntleroy*, it can be presumed that courts will not often "get it wrong" in the spectacular way that the Missouri court did in *Fauntleroy*: "Mistakes will be rare."[59] In the vast majority of situations, the courts of State A will not foolishly or brazenly decline to apply the law of State B when that is unquestionably called for. (Actually, since constitutional standards for choice of law are so minimal, the fact that it will be rare for Court A to err so badly in failing to apply the law of State B that it amounts to a violation of the Constitution might not be saying very much.)

Second, there is a safeguard against such situations in the fact that the losing party in the first case can appeal the decision through the appellate courts of that state; any egregious "mistakes" made by the trial court would stand a good chance of being corrected on appeal, eliminating the problem of interstate recognition of "clearly wrong" judgments. In fact, the firm rule on interjurisdictional preclusion and Full Faith and Credit announced in *Fauntleroy* is based largely on the notion that it is more efficient, and more respectful of state sovereignty, to rely on intrastate appellate review of the original judgment for correction of incorrect judgments than to permit the withholding of recognition by a sister state. Imagine the confusion if the courts of State B could regularly

---

59. *Fauntleroy*, 210 U.S. at 237–38.

decline to recognize the rulings of sister states on the ground that Court A—in the opinion of Court B—got its choice-of-law decision "wrong."

Whose Preclusion Rule Should Govern? *Fauntleroy*, then, makes clear that the Full Faith and Credit rule requiring the courts of State B to recognize the judgments of the courts of State A is a firm one. However, precisely what it means to "recognize" a judgment—or to give it full faith and credit—may not be so clear. Simply ignoring the judgment of a sister state—acting as though it did not exist—is obviously impermissible. But there are more difficult problems, based on the fact that different states may have different rules for claim or issue preclusion. For purposes of preclusion, must the courts of State B treat the judgments of the courts of State A precisely as the latter would had the case been brought there? Or may they apply State B's own rules of preclusion, potentially reaching a different result than would have ensued had the second case been brought in State A? Such a situation might arise, for example, when State A uses the "same transaction" test for claim preclusion while State B uses the "same evidence" test. In some cases, the operation of preclusion would depend on which test were used. For example, in Pat's never-ending tale of *The Car That Would Be Towed*, a Colorado court applying the "same transaction" test would regard her constitutional claim in Case B as precluded by the fact that she had litigated her replevin claim to a conclusion in an earlier Case A in a Colorado court. But if Case B were heard in the courts of a state that applies the "same evidence" test, her constitutional claim could be heard in Case B if the court in that case considered itself free to apply State B's own rule for claim preclusion.

The clear answer is that, when faced with a judgment rendered by Court A, Court B must employ the preclusion rules of State A. What "full faith and credit" means, then, is that Court B must give the judgment of Court A the *same effect* that a court of State A would, meaning that the preclusion law of State A must govern in Case B. Many might regard this as intuitively correct, but the text of the FFC Clause does not clearly establish the principle, and this is where the full faith and credit *statute* comes in. The FFC Clause says only that "Full Faith and Credit" must be given, but does not say that this means that Court B must decide the second case the same way that a court of State A would. However, the principal implementing statute of the FFC Clause, 28 U.S.C. § 1738, leaves little room for doubt on this point: "The records and judicial proceedings of any court of any ... State, Territory, or Possession, ... shall have the *same* full faith and credit in every court within the United States and its Territories and Possessions as they have by law or usage in the courts of such State, Territory, or Possession from which they are taken.''[60] So the rule is that, where the applicable preclusion rules of States A and B differ, Court B must use the preclusion rule of State A—that is, it must give the judgment of Court A the same effect that courts of State A would give it.

As Professor Howard M. Erichson has cogently explained, this would be the sensible rule even if 28 U.S.C. § 1738 did not clearly resolve the question.[61] His argument is based on the practical needs and expectations of the litigating parties. If the courts of State B were free to employ that state's preclusion rule instead of State A's, the parties in Case A would be uncertain about the binding effect and security of the judgment reached in that case. At the time of the first lawsuit, no one could know for certain where a subsequent proceeding might be brought raising preclusion issues; in some potential "recognition" states, the preclusion rule might differ from that of State A. Such uncertainty might well affect the plaintiff's choice of forum, or even her desire to bring the first case at all, and it might affect the defendant's strategic choices within that first litigation as well. Far better, at least from the perspective of the practical litigant, to have a rule requiring that the preclusion rules of State A be applied in any subsequent proceeding raising preclusion issues, so that the parties can know at the outset what the preclusion consequences of the first lawsuit, if any, will be. This rule promotes the kind of certainty that benefits litigants and the litigation system in general.

The Law of Full Faith and Credit is Federal Law. It is very important to see that the *source* of the rule that State A's preclusion rule should govern is not the law of State A, but federal law—namely, 28 U.S.C. § 1738. State A provides the substance of the preclusion rule ("same evidence," "same transaction," or whatever it may happen to be), but it is *federal* law that tells us that State A's preclusion rule is the one that must govern problems of interjurisdictional preclusion. What this means is that no state has independent power directly to determine the interjurisdictional effect of its own judgments. Thus, for example, if State A uses the "same evidence" rule for claim preclusion, neither the law nor the courts of State A may provide that its judgment will bar all subsequent claims between the parties brought in courts of other states that arise out of the same transaction as the original claim. In other words, a hypothetical statute reading, "The judgments of the courts of this state will be *res judicata* with respect to all other claims brought in a court of this state that would be based on the same evidence as the one adjudicated, but shall be *res judicata* with

60. 28 U.S.C. § 1738 (emphasis added).

61. Howard M. Erichson, *Interjurisdictional Preclusion*, 96 MICHIGAN LAW REVIEW 945 (1998).

respect to all claims brought in a court of another state that arose out of the same transaction as the one adjudicated," would be ineffective as beyond the state's power—pre-empted, in fact, by 28 U.S.C. § 1738. The interstate effect of the judgment is a matter of federal law, based on the full-faith-and-credit principle. Of course, the interstate effect of its courts' judgments is indirectly determined by State A's preclusion rules, but only as a result of federal law on full faith and credit.

What if Case B Is Heard by a Federal Court? The careful reader will observe that the text of the FFC Clause does not make crystal-clear that the duty to give full faith and credit to state-court judgments that is imposed by the Clause rests on federal as well as state courts: "Full Faith and Credit shall be given in each State to the ... judicial Proceedings of every other State." Lest there be any ambiguity about this, however, 28 U.S.C. § 1738 makes it very clear that federal courts must give such full faith and credit to state-court judgments: "The records and judicial proceedings of any court of any ... State, Territory, or Possession, ... shall have the *same* full faith and credit *in every court within the United States and its Territories and Possessions* ..." (emphasis added) Congress has clear authority to impose this duty on federal courts, not only because of the FFC Clause itself, but pursuant to Congress's power to regulate the jurisdiction and procedures of the federal courts under Article III.

What if the Judgment in Case A Was Rendered by a Federal Court? Neither the FFC Clause nor 28 U.S.C. § 1738 creates any obligation to recognize a judgment of a *federal* court; this much is clear from the text of the two provisions. Can a state court therefore decline to recognize a judgment rendered by a federal court on a matter of federal law? The answer, everyone seems to agree, is "no," but it's surprising how difficult it is to find clear authority on that point. Some have suggested that the Supremacy Clause is authority for the proposition, but interpreting the Supremacy Clause to apply to the decisions of the federal courts seems awkward. Perhaps the duty of state courts to recognize federal-court judgments on matters of federal law can simply be inferred from the federal structure ... or perhaps this is one of those rare occasions in law on which one can answer the question by saying, "It's just not done." Finally, if the federal court in Case A was sitting in diversity, both state and federal courts must give the judgment in such a case the effect that the courts of the state in which (Federal) Court A was sitting would give it.

3. *Interjurisdictional Recognition and the Role of State Interests*

We've emphasized that the full-faith-and-credit principle means something different in the domain of choice of law from what it means in the domain of recognition of judgments. The foregoing discussion, however, illustrates how the problem of inter-jurisdictional preclusion is, in at least one sense, a problem of choice of law. That is, the rule (embodied in the full faith and credit statute, 28 U.S.C. § 1738) that Court B must apply the preclusion rule of State A is really a choice-of-law rule directing Court B to apply the law of State A. While judges and scholars rarely discuss the problem in these terms, the rule of § 1738 does amount in effect to a choice-of-law rule.

When we conceive problem in this way, we can see that, were it not for § 1738, there might be some situations in which application of **State B**'s preclusion rule would be justified, and perhaps even preferable to State A's preclusion rule. Recall from Chapter 2, concerning choice of law, that many "modern" approaches to choice of law call for an examination of the interested states' policies or "interests" in carrying out the choice-of-law analysis. As Professor Erichson's analysis suggests, in most litigation contexts the prac-tical approach is for Court B to apply the preclusion law of State A, in order to promote the reasonable expectations of the parties and to protect the integrity of Court A's judgments. But some situations may raise greater difficulties. In *Yarborough v. Yarborough* (1933),[62] the Yarboroughs were divorced in a proceeding in Georgia state court. The court granted the divorce and made an award of "permanent alimony," which included a lump sum of $1750 to be put in trust for the Yarboroughs' daughter Sadie to provide for her "support, education, and other needs." Under the law of Georgia, this award of "permanent alimony" was final and non-modifiable. A year later, Sadie, now sixteen years old and living with her grandfather in South Carolina, brought a suit against Mr. Yarbor-ough in South Carolina state court, seeking additional financial support for her education, as she now wished to attend college. Mr. Yarborough unsuccessfully asserted as a defense the earlier Georgia judgment, arguing that it should preclude any further claims by Sadie for additional support. The South Carolina court made an award in Sadie's favor of $50 monthly, which was upheld by the state supreme court.

Conventional doctrine as established in *Fauntleroy v. Lum* would suggest that full faith and credit to the judgment of the Georgia courts required that Sadie's petition for financial support be denied. That is indeed how the U.S. Supreme Court ruled in *Yarborough*. Because Georgia law regarded the initial award of "permanent alimony" as final and non-modifiable (which is, in a

62.   290 U.S. 202 (1933).

sense, a rule of preclusion, directing that there should be no further litigation concerning Mr. Yarborough's support obligations), a Georgia court would have regarded the question of Sadie's support as *res judicata*, and would on that basis have denied any request for further support. Thus, full faith and credit required South Carolina to rule the same way. This is in accord with *Fauntleroy v. Lum*, § 1738, and the principle that Court B must apply the preclusion rules of State A. But, as Justice Stone pointed out in his dissent in *Yarborough*, the question of child support raises special issues not necessarily found in conventional litigation. The adequacy of a given level of child support is by nature a dynamic thing, depending on changing circumstances. (That is why, today, the law of every state provides that a child support order is presumptively modifiable.) Moreover, South Carolina might have a different public policy concerning the support and maintenance of minor children than Georgia, and, after all, South Carolina was by this time Sadie's home. There was something disturbing, suggested Justice Stone, about conferring on a Georgia judgment the power to preclude any effort by South Carolina to effectuate its child support policies with respect to a minor currently living in that state.

The crux of the *Yarborough* case was that Georgia law made its "permanent alimony" decrees final and non-modifiable, while South Carolina law provided that its courts should retain continuing jurisdiction over its support decrees, so that they could be modified as circumstances might require. In effect, what the case presented was a conflict between Georgia's "preclusion rule" for this kind of case (the decree is final and non-modifiable) and South Carolina's (the decree is modifiable). Although Justice Stone did not use the phrase "interest analysis," he appeared to argue that South Carolina had a stronger interest in application of its preclusion rule (modifiability) than Georgia had in application of its rule, since South Carolina was now Sadie's domicile. Note that, while Justice Stone's solution would result in Court B's treating the judgment of Court A differently from how the courts of State A would treat it, it could equally well be said that Court B would be treating the judgment of Court A precisely as Court B treats its own judgments. Many have found Justice Stone's dissent to be persuasive, but in *Yarborough* the standard rule prevailed: South Carolina must treat the earlier Georgia judgment as a Georgia court would have.

Although Justice Stone's argument in *Yarborough* did not convince a majority of the Court, it does raise the question as to whether there are situations in which Court B's claim to application of its own state's preclusion rule might be particularly strong. If there are such situations, they may fall into a fairly distinct category. For the most part, they involve situations in which it is customary for courts to maintain continuing jurisdiction with respect to some changing state of affairs. The law of domestic relations, involving awards of support and custody that are usually modifiable, would be the clearest example.[63] Such cases of "continuing jurisdiction" typically involve remedies that are equitable in nature. One would rarely if ever see the need for continuing jurisdiction in the typical common-law claim for money damages, where a final compensatory award in Case A is generally the end of the matter. Perhaps what really gave rise to the *Yarborough* case was Georgia's rather unusual preclusion rule (no longer in effect) excluding Sadie's support award from future modification. One would be hard pressed to see a similar case arise today. In any case, though, it remains (unconcise) hornbook law that full faith and credit requires application of the rendering state's rule of preclusion.

4. Workers' Compensation: An Exception to Full Faith and Credit?

Most of the cases and examples we use to illustrate conflicts principles are conventional or "garden-variety" *in personam* cases of "A versus B," heard by a state trial court of general jurisdiction and involving traditional private law causes of action for money damages. Our leading case on full faith and credit, *Fauntleroy v. Lum*, is a good example: It concerned enforcement of a simple common-law judgment for contract damages. Many of the more difficult issues in preclusion, however, involve interstate recognition of non-traditional remedies, or of judgments rendered by administrative tribunals that typically apply only the forum's rules of law. One area in which interjurisdictional preclusion has caused particular difficulty is that of workers' compensation.

As you may have noticed in Chapter 4, some of the most important Supreme Court decisions setting out the constitutional limitations on state courts' power to apply forum law have been workers' compensation cases.[64] The first state workers' compensation[65] statutes, enacted toward the beginning of the twentieth century, differed markedly from the traditional common-law approach to workplace injuries, and the various state statutes also differed from one another in numerous ways. It was therefore inevitable that workers' compensation would create conflicts problems because many cases of workplace injury implicate the interests

---

63. The complex and difficult questions of recognition of spousal and child support orders are treated at length in Chapter 6.

64. Examples include *Bradford Elec. Light Co. v. Clapper*, 286 U.S. 145 (1932); *Alaska Packers Assoc. v. Indus-*

trial Accident Commission, 294 U.S. 532 (1935); and *Pacific Employers v. Industrial Accident Commission*, 306 U.S. 493 (1939).

65. Prior to the 1970s, "workers' compensation" was typically known as "workmen's compensation."

of more than one state. The domicile of the employer, the domicile of the employee, the place of injury, and the place where the employment agreement was reached, each of which could be relevant to determining which state's scheme should apply in a particular case, will not refer to the same state in all cases. The *Alaska Packers* (1935) and *Pacific Employers* (1939) decisions made clear that state tribunals have wide constitutional latitude to apply forum law in awarding workers' compensation benefits. This gave the injured worker, in cases with multistate connections, some freedom to choose the forum for adjudication of his workers' compensation claim—a valuable option where one of the interested states might provide more generous benefits than the others, or at least proved to be a more convenient forum in which to litigate.

But what if the worker sought and received an award from a workers' compensation tribunal in one of the interested states, and then discovered that the available benefits were actually higher in a different state with which his employment also had a connection? Could he then initiate a workers' compensation proceeding in the second state to receive the difference in benefits? Or would the award in the first proceeding be *res judicata*, barring him from bringing a subsequent claim anywhere else? In *Thomas v. Washington Gas Light Co.* (1980),[66] the U.S. Supreme Court held that the FFC Clause and 28 U.S.C. § 1738 did *not* bar the second workers' compensation proceeding in this kind of situation. In *Thomas*, the worker was a resident of the District of Columbia and was hired to work there by a D.C. company. While thus employed, he was sent on a job to Virginia, where he sustained a back injury. Upon application, he received a workers' compensation award from the Virginia Industrial Commission. Years later, he sought an additional workers' compensation award from the D.C. Department of Labor. His employer, which was officially a party in the proceedings and for which adverse workers' compensation awards would have important consequences, argued that full faith and credit required denial of an additional award in the D.C. tribunal. The Supreme Court, though, ruled that the worker was not barred by full faith and credit from receiving an additional award from the D.C. tribunal.

Thomas has been widely criticized. It seems wasteful and inefficient to permit a claimant to invoke the machinery of more than one state's workers' compensation tribunal to obtain an award for a single workplace injury. At first glance, it does not seem unjust to ask that the claimant determine in advance which, of the tribunals that *Pacific Employers* would permit to apply forum law, will provide the most generous benefits and to make that the forum

---

66.   448 U.S. 261 (1980).

for his claim (although of course not all workers will have expert legal counsel). After the result in *Thomas*, it seems that there is nothing the employer can do to avoid having to participate in more than one proceeding if the worker is able to make two successive claims as the plaintiff in *Thomas* did. And there seems to be more than a hint of disrespect for the first state's tribunal in refusing to confer finality on its award. Moreover, the Court's reasoning in *Thomas* was confusing and in some respects unpersuasive. For example, it engaged in an assessment of the cognizable "interests" Virginia had in seeing that its award was final and not augmented by any supplementary award by another state's tribunal, which interests the Court regarded as insufficient to militate against permitting the worker to initiate a second proceeding in D.C. This framing of the analysis was inapt. Full faith and credit to judgments is not, as we have seen, a matter of assessing the relative "interests" of the rendering and recognition fora. That is an inquiry more appropriate to choice of law than to recognition of judgments.[67] And, although we cannot get into the nitty-gritty details here, the Court's handling of some of its own precedents on the issue was confusing.

Nevertheless, as an interpretation of the FFC Clause and 28 U.S.C. § 1738, *Thomas* is defensible if not necessarily compelling. First, of course, we should be clear that Thomas did not receive a "double" award, since the D.C. award would only have brought his total compensation to the level he would have received had he brought his claim there initially. Similarly, as the Supreme Court pointed out, Thomas's employer could not reasonably have expected that Thomas would not bring his claim in the D.C. tribunal to begin with, so (apart from the possible expenses of its participation in a second administrative proceeding) it had no cognizable interest in limiting Thomas to the amount of the initial award.

But, more to the point, does the result in *Thomas* violate the basic full-faith-and-credit principle that questions of interjurisdictional preclusion should be governed by the preclusion rule of State A? Not really. It is true, of course, that Virginia law would not have permitted Thomas to obtain a supplemental award in a second proceeding *in Virginia's workers' compensation tribunal*; the first Virginia award would have been, for those purposes, *res judicata*. It might therefore appear that the D.C. tribunal should reach the same result in the second case. However, as the Court pointed out in *Thomas*, the full-faith-and-credit principle as applied to interjurisdictional preclusion rests on the assumption that the tribunal in Case A has the authority to determine all of the matters that a

---

67. These and other criticisms of the decision in *Thomas* can be found in Stewart E. Sterk, *Full Faith and Credit, More or Less, to Judgments: Doubts* *About* Thomas v. Washington Gas Light Co., 69 GEORGETOWN LAW JOURNAL 1329 (1981).

second tribunal hearing the case would. (Thus, for example, in *Fauntleroy v. Lum* there was nothing to prevent the Missouri court in Case A from properly interpreting and applying Mississippi law to hold the futures contract unenforceable, even though it failed to do so; full faith and credit therefore barred the Mississippi courts from refusing to recognize and enforce the Missouri judgment.) In *Thomas*, however, the Virginia tribunal was bound to apply Virginia law, and Virginia law only, in determining the award to be made to Thomas. It could not consider the schedule of rates and the other rules that D.C. law provided for its own workers' compensation awards.

Therefore, it is somewhat beside the point to say that Virginia would have barred a second proceeding by Thomas had he brought it there. Thomas would not, and could not, have brought at any point a workers' compensation claim in Virginia asking for benefits based on D.C. workers' compensation law and procedure; and the reasons he could not do so have nothing to do with preclusion. State workers' compensation tribunals simply do not apply the law and procedures of the workers' compensation regimes in other states. For this reason, the Court's conclusion that full faith and credit did not prevent the D.C. tribunal from making a supplementary award is analytically defensible. Moreover, one should not conclude from *Thomas* that workers' compensation is an "exception" to full faith and credit; the Court in *Thomas* simply held that full faith and credit did not require what Thomas's D.C. employer claimed it requires.

What, then, makes *Thomas* seem like a strange and difficult case? The answer is that the conventional analysis of interjurisdictional preclusion and full faith and credit does not easily fit the administrative adjudication model represented by state workers' compensation regimes. Because workers' compensation tribunals do not apply the rules of other states for the determination of awards, a second claim brought before a different state's tribunal is not really the "same claim" as the first. To be sure, Justice White argued in dissent in *Thomas* that the workers' compensation situation, in which the first tribunal in effect can apply only the rules of the forum, is no different in principle from, say, a mandatory choice-of-law rule that directs the forum to apply the law of the place of injury, which in many workers' compensation cases would be the same as forum law. Since such choice-of-law rules are, by and large, constitutional—requiring the courts of other states to give effect to the judgments reached by courts applying those rules—D.C.'s full-faith-and-credit obligation in *Thomas* should likewise not be vitiated by the fact that the Virginia workers' compensation tribunal could apply only Virginia law.

While there is some force to Justice White's observation, his hypothetical choice-of-law rule is not conceptually identical to the restrictions placed on a state workers' compensation tribunal. The choice-of-law rules that govern courts of general jurisdiction, at least as they are understood today, are not "jurisdictional"—that is, they do not speak to the *power* of a court. By contrast, the rules specified in statutes setting up state workers' compensation regimes *are* jurisdictional—these rules strictly limit the kinds of cases that the tribunal may hear, and the principles that they may apply. Moreover, as we saw in our discussion of *Hughes v. Fetter* (1951) in Chapter 4, there certainly are constitutional limitations on the ability of a state to forbid its courts from hearing foreign-created causes of action. Recall one of the situations we hypothesized concerning Pat's car-towing case to illustrate the limits on preclusion doctrine. We said that, in Pat's first lawsuit in Colorado court, she was not even permitted to raise her constitutional claim because that court lacked jurisdiction to hear it; under such circumstances, her later lawsuit in a Colorado court of general jurisdiction obviously should not result in a holding that she is barred from raising her constitutional claim now. Similarly, in *Thomas*, the Virginia tribunal lacked jurisdiction to hear the D.C. workers' compensation claim (based on D.C. rules) that Thomas sought to raise in the second proceeding in D.C. If that is so, the principle of full faith and credit should not bar the second proceeding.

In spite of all this formal analysis, it's quite understandable that some would regard the result in *Thomas* as being a bit troubling, because the prospect of multiple administrative proceedings for any injured worker who can see advantage in doing so seems rather inefficient. And there is something to be said for the principle of *finality*—the notion that an employer can regard the question of workers' compensation for a single injured worker as subject to the principle of "one and done." Does *Thomas* have implications that go beyond workers' compensation cases? Probably not too many. *Thomas* does not hold that full faith and credit does not apply to the rulings of administrative tribunals generally. It is common for issues determined in administrative proceedings to be given *res judicata* effect, and full faith and credit would require tribunals in other states to give those rulings the same effect. For example, had a Virginia workers' compensation tribunal determined that Thomas had worked for a certain number of hours in a given year, it's likely that full faith and credit would require a D.C. tribunal to bar relitigation of that question in a subsequent proceeding. It is safest to read *Thomas* as being limited to the fairly distinctive situation of workers' compensation, where more than one state's tribunal will often be available.

5. Full Faith and Credit to Judgments Rendered Without Jurisdiction

Our discussion of *Fauntleroy v. Lum* emphasized that full faith and credit to judgments is a firm command. There is, however, an important exception to the rule of full faith and credit: Full faith and credit does not require recognition of judgments that have been rendered in a case in which the first court lacked jurisdiction over the defendant. You may already be familiar with this principle from its application in *Pennoyer v. Neff* (1877).[68] *Pennoyer* not only established that the U.S. Constitution limits the power of state courts to assert personal jurisdiction over nonresident defendants; it established that the recognition court need not, and in fact may not, give effect to judgments rendered without such jurisdiction. While the constitutional standards of *Pennoyer* for the exercise of personal jurisdiction have mostly been superseded, the full-faith-and-credit portion of *Pennoyer* remains good law.

The *Pennoyer* principle as it relates to judgments rendered without personal jurisdiction is pretty simple to understand. If Court A had no power over the defendant, enforcement or recognition of its judgment against her by Court B would seem to be clearly illegitimate. The full faith and credit obligation does not run this far. Despite the simplicity of the general principle, however, a number of more difficult questions lurk below the surface. For example, what kinds of defects in a judicial proceeding count as "jurisdictional" (and thus exempt the judgment from the full faith and credit obligation)? And does the absence of *subject matter* jurisdiction render a judgment unenforceable in the same way that the absence of *personal* jurisdiction does?

General appearance, special appearance, and default judgments. If, in Case A, the defendant defaults (*i.e.* fails to respond to the complaint in timely fashion or to "appear" in the action), a default judgment will likely be entered against her. It is important to understand that not all default judgments constitute judgments rendered without personal jurisdiction; quite the contrary. If that were the case, the default judgment would be a useless device. The availability, in appropriate cases, of a default judgment that is enforceable in a second proceeding is an essential tool for motivating a properly sued defendant to appear in the case and not simply ignore it. It is true, of course, that the possibility for abuse of the default judgment device exists, where the defendant fails to appear simply because she has never been notified of the proceeding or has no connection with the (perhaps distant) forum. A major purpose of the principle that full faith or credit should be denied a judgment in a case where the defendant was not subject to the

---

68. 95 U.S. 714 (1877).

court's jurisdiction is to permit the defendant to attack, in a second (or "collateral") proceeding brought by the plaintiff to collect on the judgment, the legitimacy of the judgment in the first case on grounds of lack of personal jurisdiction.

But what about a defendant in Case A who (1) knows full well that she has been sued, *i.e.* she has been properly served, but who (2) believes that, under current law, the court lacks jurisdiction to render a personal judgment against her? She could simply fail to appear in the case, have a default judgment entered against her, and wait until a second lawsuit to enforce the judgment before appearing to attack "collaterally" that judgment on grounds of lack of personal jurisdiction. But that is risky business. When a defendant defaults, the *only* ground on which she is permitted to attack, in a collateral proceeding, the judgment in the first case is lack of jurisdiction; by failing to appear in the first case, she in effect waives any opportunity to contest the merits of the lawsuit. Most defendants presented with the situation described in this paragraph, then, would prefer to challenge the court's jurisdiction in the first case itself.

But does such a defendant, by challenging the court's jurisdiction, *ipso facto consent* to the court's jurisdiction by participating in the proceeding? No. All state trial courts of general jurisdiction permit (as do the Federal Rules of Civil Procedure) a defendant to make what is called a "special appearance" strictly for the purpose of challenging the court's jurisdiction over her. (The precise terminology for this process varies from state to state; in California, for example, rather than saying that the defendant makes a "special appearance," the rules require the defendant to file a "motion to quash.") If a defendant makes such a special appearance and is successful in her challenge to personal jurisdiction, the case will be dismissed. If her challenge to personal jurisdiction is denied, then— depending on the rules of the specific state—she may have the choice of (1) proceeding to litigate the case on the merits, or (2) appealing the denial of her challenge to personal jurisdiction. (In federal court, the defendant who unsuccessfully challenges the court's jurisdiction over her ordinarily cannot appeal that ruling immediately; she must litigate the case on the merits, leaving appeal of the jurisdictional ruling until after a final judgment has been entered—or, of course, she can choose to default.) Simply defaulting at this point is not much of an option, since the question of the court's jurisdiction is *res judicata* and no other defense could be raised by the defendant in a collateral proceeding.

One point of this excursus on default judgments is to illustrate that, while Court A's jurisdiction over the defendant may ordinarily be raised by the defendant in a collateral proceeding, this is not the case where the question of jurisdiction was *actually litigated and determined* by Court A. If the defendant makes no appearance, special or otherwise, in the first proceeding, then the court's power to enter an *in personam* judgment against her may be raised in a second proceeding, because the question of personal jurisdiction was never actually litigated and determined in the first case. But if the defendant makes a special appearance in the first case, and Court A rules that personal jurisdiction over her is proper, the defendant is not entitled to collaterally attack Court A's jurisdiction over her. This is true whether the dispute over personal jurisdiction in Case A concerned a question of fact or a question over proper application of the legal principles governing personal jurisdiction.

So, for example, consider an admittedly fanciful hypothetical based on the important personal jurisdiction case of *Burnham v. Superior Court* (1990).[69] In *Burnham*, the California courts asserted jurisdiction over the defendant based on personal service made upon him while he was briefly and temporarily in California, although his connections with California were otherwise quite limited. According to the theory under which the Supreme Court plurality upheld the constitutionality of jurisdiction over Mr. Burnham, the fact that the lawsuit was initiated, and the defendant served, while he was present in California was crucial to the outcome. Suppose, however, that Mr. Burnham challenged personal jurisdiction in the California court, claiming that personal service had been made on him not while he within the state of California, but while he was in the state of Nevada. If the California court were to hold, as a matter of *fact*, that service had indeed been made in California, and that Mr. Burnham was therefore subject to the court's jurisdiction, that ruling would have issue-preclusive effect in any subsequent proceeding, including—as a result of full faith and credit—any enforcement action brought in another state. Thus, even if Mr. Burnham defaulted in Case A after the court's adverse ruling on personal jurisdiction, he could not collaterally attack the court's jurisdiction in a subsequent proceeding. This is in marked contrast to the situation in which the defendant makes no appearance whatever in the first case.

The result would be the same if, instead of claiming that he had been served in Nevada rather than in California, Mr. Burnham made a special appearance in the first case and argued that mere in-state service in California, in the absence of other "minimum contacts," was insufficient to permit the assertion of personal jurisdiction over him in a California court. We know, assuming that Justice Scalia's plurality opinion in the actual *Burnham* case is governing law, that Mr. Burnham's legal argument would fail. Were the California court thus to overrule Mr. Burnham's challenge to

69.   495 U.S. 604 (1990).

its jurisdiction, Mr. Burnham would again be unable to raise that challenge collaterally in a subsequent proceeding, because the question had been litigated and determined in Case A. Again, the court's ruling on the point would be *res judicata*—entitled to issue-preclusive effect in other states as per the FFC Clause—even though its ruling was a "legal" rather than a "factual" one.

Lack of Fair Notice. Under current law, the question of personal jurisdiction—the sheer power of a court to render a personal judgment against the defendant—is distinct from the question of whether the defendant has had constitutionally adequate notice of the proceeding. Both constitutional personal jurisdiction and constitutionally adequate notice must be satisfied. There are cases in which notice to the defendant has been exemplary, complying with the Constitution and the process set out by the state's own judicial code or rules of procedure, but in which personal jurisdiction is clearly lacking because the defendant has no contacts at all with the forum. As we have seen, no full faith and credit is due to a (default) judgment reached in such a case. But there are also cases in which personal jurisdiction over the defendant is clearly proper (as when the defendant is a citizen and resident of the state in which the case is brought), but in which notice to the defendant is clearly inadequate or lacking altogether. Even though this defect is not always termed a problem of "jurisdiction," full faith and credit clearly does not require, or even permit, enforcement of such a judgment by Court B. It is obviously unacceptable to enforce a judgment rendered in a case in which the defendant did not receive constitutionally adequate notice; recognition (in the sense of enforcement) is not only not required by full faith and credit, but positively forbidden by due process.[70]

What About a Failure of Subject Matter Jurisdiction in Case A? Most of the conventional examples illustrating the principle that full faith and credit is not due a judgment rendered without jurisdiction involve personal jurisdiction. Students naturally want to know if the principle applies in the same way when what was lacking in Case A was *subject matter*, rather than personal, jurisdiction. The answer to this question is murkier than it should be. Most students first encounter the concept of subject matter jurisdiction specifically in the context of the federal courts. They learn that the subject matter jurisdiction of the federal courts is strictly limited by Article III of the U.S. Constitution and by applicable federal statutes. It is a natural, and in fact a correct,

---

70. What if the asserted defect in the notice received by the defendant in Case A is not that it failed constitutional standards, but simply did not comply with State A's own rules for service of process? If the notice accorded the defendant in Case A complied with constitutional standards, it's unlikely that the departure from State's prescribed method of service would justify denying full faith and credit to the judgment ultimately entered in Case A.

inference from this principle that a judgment by a federal court rendered without federal jurisdiction (which is an infrequent thing, since both litigants and the federal courts themselves are generally fastidious about raising and determining the question of the court's subject matter jurisdiction) should not be enforced by another court. If the Constitution places such emphasis on limiting the power of the federal courts, surely it must preclude the recognition of federal court judgments violating those limits. But this is not really a problem of full faith and credit as such. Neither the FFC Clause nor 28 U.S.C. § 1738 concerns the respect that should be given judgments rendered by *federal* courts; the full faith and credit principle is addressed to the respect due to judgments rendered by *state* courts. It simply follows from Article III itself that no federal court judgment violating those jurisdictional limits can be enforced in another proceeding. Of course, collateral inquiry into the subject jurisdiction of the federal court in Case A is foreclosed if the question of federal subject matter jurisdiction was raised and resolved in Case A.

Subject matter jurisdiction, however, refers to more than just the jurisdiction of federal courts. In all state judicial systems, subject matter jurisdiction is allocated among different courts: trial courts of general jurisdiction, specialized courts like small claims and probate courts, trial courts whose jurisdiction may be defined by the amount in controversy, and so on. These allocations of subject matter jurisdiction among the courts in a state, important though they are, do not usually rise to the same level of constitutional gravity as do the limitations on federal jurisdiction. The subject matter jurisdiction of the federal courts is limited because the limited nature of federal power is a constitutional priority; the subject matter jurisdiction of the various courts of a state (putting aside the degree to which Congress may have conferred exclusive jurisdiction on federal courts to hear claims arising under certain parts of federal law) is usually just a decision by a state concerning how it wishes to allocate its judicial resources. May a court in State B inquire into the niceties of the rules governing subject matter jurisdiction of the courts of State A—thus, for example, whether the trial court in State A properly assumed jurisdiction over a case that should instead have gone to that state's small claims court— and on that basis deny full faith and credit to Court A's judgment?

Problems like these don't arise very often, and when they do they can be resolved by application of three familiar principles. (1) A defendant who makes a general appearance in Case A and who fails to challenge the court's subject matter jurisdiction (for example, to argue that the case instead should have been heard by the small claims court) can be said to have waived his objection. (This is not true for the subject matter jurisdiction in federal courts, but is generally true in the state courts.) (2) A defendant who does challenge Court A's subject matter jurisdiction, and whose challenge is rejected by the court, may not collaterally attack that court's jurisdiction in a subsequent proceeding; issue preclusion will apply, because the issue of Court A's jurisdiction was actually litigated and determined in Case A. (Remember that there is rarely any unfairness in this situation, because the defendant at some point will have had the opportunity to appeal Court A's rejection of his jurisdictional challenge through the courts of State A.) (3) So far as interstate recognition of the judgment by Court A is concerned, Court B should refuse to recognize the judgment rendered by Court A allegedly in violation of the limitations on its subject matter jurisdiction if and only if another court in State A would do so. Principles (1) and (2) are principles that would be recognized by the preclusion law of virtually every state; principle (3) is simply a special instance of the full-faith-and-credit rule of 28 U.S.C. § 1738 that the recognition state should apply the preclusion rule of the rendering state.

Recognition Due a State–Court Judgment With Respect to a Claim Arising Under Federal Law Over Which Federal Courts Have Exclusive Jurisdiction. As noted, principle (3) above is but a restatement of the full-faith-and-credit notion that, in an interjurisdictional preclusion situation, Court B should apply the preclusion rule of State A. Oddly, this is so firm a rule that the U.S. Supreme Court has applied it even in cases where the defect in Court A's subject matter jurisdiction was not its violation of a state rule allocating jurisdiction among the state's courts, but its incorrect assumption of jurisdiction over a claim arising under *federal* law that falls within the exclusive jurisdiction of the federal courts. Even if Court B is a federal court, it must treat Court A's judgment in this situation in the same way that State A's own courts would. Thus, in *Marrese v. American Academy of Orthopaedic Surgeons* (1985),[71] the plaintiffs in Case A brought a state-law claim in state court against the defendant, which had denied the plaintiffs' applications for membership in the Academy. When they lost that case, they filed another suit (Case B) against the defendant in federal court, raising a claim under the federal antitrust laws, over which the federal courts have exclusive jurisdiction. The defendant raised the defense of claim preclusion, based on the plaintiffs' failure to raise the antitrust claim in Case A. This should have been easy, right? One would think that the plaintiffs could not be precluded from asserting a claim in Case B by virtue of its omission in Case A if, as in this case, Court A would not have jurisdiction over that claim.

71.   470 U.S. 373 (1985).

But the Supreme Court in *Marrese* found the matter less simple than that. It ruled that, under 28 U.S.C. § 1738, the federal court in Case B must first determine whether the preclusion law of State A would regard the federal antitrust claim as precluded by virtue of its omission from Case A, despite the state court's lack of authority to hear such a claim—that is, whether a court of that state, hearing Case B, would regard the claim as barred. Although, as it happened, the preclusion law of the state in this case did *not* provide for *res judicata* in such a situation, the Supreme Court's analysis left open the possibility that, in another situation, a state's preclusion rule might, consistently with full faith and credit, provide for preclusion in this situation, and that a federal court in Case B would have to abide by that rule. This seems surprising: A principle that we have tended to regard as simple fairness—that a party may not be precluded from raising a claim in Case B that the court in Case A had no authority to hear—is evidently not required by the U.S. Constitution. As we will see, this particular chicken *has* come home to roost, as a more recent Supreme Court decision has featured a state preclusion rule that did, apparently, give preclusive effect to a state-court decision concerning a federal claim over which federal courts have exclusive jurisdiction—and the federal court in Case B was required to apply that preclusion rule.

Durfee v. Duke. Many casebooks include the Supreme Court's decision in *Durfee v. Duke* (1963)[72] as an illustration of the problems raised by the claimed lack of subject matter jurisdiction in Case A as a reason for denying interstate recognition in Case B. *Durfee* involved a question of title to land that was situated at the bottom of the Missouri River, lying between Nebraska and Missouri. The plaintiffs in Case A, alleging title to the land, brought a state quiet-title action, naming another claimant as the defendant, in Nebraska court. Under traditional principles, the Nebraska court would have jurisdiction to decide the matter only if the land was "in" Nebraska. Although we customarily think that the location of land—whether it is situated in one state or another—isn't subject to much doubt, the situation in *Durfee* was different: The actual "location" of the land in question depended, as a matter of law, on the course of the Missouri River, and in particular on whether a change that had occurred in the river's course had been caused by what engineers call "avulsion" or by what they call "accretion." The Nebraska courts in Case A determined that the change in the river's course had been caused by avulsion and that therefore the land was in Nebraska; it further held that the land belonged to the plaintiff. The defendant subsequently brought an action (Case B) against the original plaintiffs in Missouri court, raising the same issue—title to the land. The question was whether full faith and

72. 375 U.S. 106 (1963).

credit barred the Missouri court in Case B from inquiring into the question of title and the factual issues (avulsion, accretion, etc.) underlying it.[73] The Supreme Court held that the court in Case B was so barred, because the question of the Nebraska court's subject matter jurisdiction had been actually litigated and determined in Case A and thus was *res judicata*.

Durfee v. Duke is a bit of a tangle. What gives the case its distinctive character is the traditional rule that only the state in which real property is situated has the authority to determine questions of title to it. For centuries, the dogma (though never actually treated as a *constitutional* principle in American law) was regarded as a first principle of sovereignty, a shield against unwarranted intrusions by other states or nations. This seems to invest the question of the Nebraska court's jurisdiction over the case with more significance than would be the case if the subject matter jurisdiction issue in Case A concerned, say, whether that court was the proper one under Nebraska's own rules for allocating jurisdiction among her courts. Add to this the fact that a state court may have just a bit of incentive to find that the land *is* within its borders. Perhaps the importance of ensuring that no court exceed its authority by adjudicating upon land situated outside its borders should trump the usual full faith and credit rule, and permit a second court to decide the question anew.

In any case, these considerations were not determinative for the Court in *Durfee*, and its decision is probably the right one. After all, a court must have jurisdiction to determine its own jurisdiction, and to fail to regard the Nebraska's jurisdictional determination as *res judicata* would be to make the issue of the land's location endlessly litigable. Moreover, the notion that only the state in which land is situated has authority to adjudicate upon it is no longer quite the sacred cow it once was; certainly our discussion of choice of law with respect to matters of real property suggests that other states may at times have interests in the matter that are worthy of recognition. Finally, our discussion of the relationship of *personal* jurisdiction to full faith and credit presents us with an illuminating analogy. Obviously, under *Pennoyer v. Neff* a judgment rendered by a court lacking personal jurisdiction over the defendant is not entitled to full faith and credit; but an actual finding by the court in Case A has jurisdiction over the defendant is itself *res judicata*, protected from re-examination by the principle of issue preclusion. The situation in *Durfee* is analogous, since the Nebraska

---

73. In fact, Case B, originally filed in Missouri state court, was removed to Federal District Court by the defendants in Case B. Since this makes no difference in the analysis, we will refer to the "Missouri court" when discussing Case B.

court did in fact determine that the land was in Nebraska and it therefore had jurisdiction.[74]

6. *Full Faith and Credit, Real Property, and Jurisdiction*

We just saw that full faith and credit does not require (or even permit) recognition and enforcement of judgments that were rendered without personal jurisdiction over the defendant.[75] This is the principal exception to the otherwise firm rule that full faith and credit is due to judgments of sister states. As *Fauntleroy v. Lum* tells us, even a mistake by Court A concerning which state's law should be applied does not justify Court B in refusing to recognize and give effect to Court A's judgment.

There is one type of case, however, that seems at first glance to constitute an exception to this basic rule. That is the case in which Court A renders a ruling concerning real property that is situated outside State A. A number of older cases held that such rulings need not be treated as *res judicata* (*i.e.* need not be extended full faith and credit) in a later case in the courts of State B (usually, the state where the real property is located). In some of these cases, it might appear that Court A's error, and the reason for denying its judgment full faith and credit, was its application of the "wrong" substantive law (usually, forum law) to the matter; if so, this appears to be contrary to the holding in *Fauntleroy v. Lum*. Upon further review, however, the real foundation for these older rulings is the absence of *jurisdiction* in Case A. As noted in our discussion of *Durfee v. Duke*, traditional common-law doctrine held that no court could legitimately assert jurisdiction over real property situated outside the state's boundaries. Seen in this light, these earlier cases are not anomalous, but simply examples of the previously described principle that full faith and credit is not due to judgments rendered without jurisdiction.

A famous, if antique, example of this principle is the U.S. Supreme Court's decision in *Clarke v. Clarke* (1900).[76] The Clarke family lived in South Carolina; Mrs. Clarke owned real property in

74. The Court in *Durfee v. Duke* did not deny that the course of the Missouri River at the relevant place might one day change. But the course of the river was relevant only to the legitimate jurisdiction of the Nebraska courts at the time the lawsuit was brought. Once it is accepted that that court properly had jurisdiction, the substantive determination of title must be *res judicata*.

75. When we speak of judgments "rendered without personal jurisdiction over the defendant," we mean cases in which the assertion of jurisdiction over the defendant violates constitutional limits on personal jurisdiction, such as those established by the "minimum contacts" principle of *International Shoe* (1945) and subsequent Supreme Court decisions. One can, of course, hypothesize a case in which those constitutional limits were satisfied, but the local long-arm statute was not. Full faith and credit would likely be due to the judgment in this latter situation, where personal jurisdiction in the first case would at least have been constitutional.

76. 178 U.S. 186 (1900).

Connecticut. Mrs. Clarke died; her will provided that the real property in Connecticut be divided equally among her husband and her two daughters. One of the daughters died shortly thereafter. Mr. Clarke, as executor of his late wife's estate, sued in South Carolina court, seeking an order permitting him to sell the Connecticut land. The South Carolina court ruled that Mrs. Clarke's will had worked an "equitable conversion" of the Connecticut land into personal property, meaning that Mr. Clarke had authority to sell it as part of the estate. Mr. Clarke, armed with this ruling, filed a suit in the courts of Connecticut (where the land was located) as administrator of his late daughter's estate, to determine the disposition of her share of the Connecticut land. Under South Carolina law, pursuant to the South Carolina courts' determination that there had been an equitable conversion of the Connecticut land into personalty, the land would be divided between Mr. Clarke and his surviving daughter; under Connecticut law, the whole thing would go to his surviving daughter. The Connecticut courts applied Connecticut law, giving the property to the surviving daughter. In Mr. Clarke's view, this ruling failed to give full faith and credit to the South Carolina judgment. He appealed to the U.S. Supreme Court.

The Supreme Court affirmed, holding that the Connecticut court need not give full faith and credit to the South Carolina court's ruling that the will had converted the Connecticut land into personalty (and that it would in fact be improper to do so). The Court gave a number of reasons for this conclusion, but central to its holding was that the South Carolina court was not empowered to render a final judgment, entitled to full faith and credit in other states, concerning rights in real property situated in Connecticut (or anywhere else outside South Carolina). One might be tempted to view the problem as an error in the South Carolina's choice of law; it should have applied Connecticut, rather than South Carolina, law concerning the question of equitable conversion. If so, *Fauntleroy v. Lum* tells us that this error would in no way vitiate the Connecticut courts' obligation to enforce the judgment. But the case is really about *jurisdiction*, not choice of law. The traditional theory held that South Carolina had no authority to render a binding judgment with respect to real property in Connecticut; therefore no full faith and credit was due.[77]

77. One of the notable things about the *Clarke* case is that it illustrates some fancy footwork by Mr. Clarke, or by his lawyer, none of which casts an especially attractive light on Mr. Clarke. Understanding that the courts of South Carolina (whose law on distribution of his wife's estate was more favorable to his interests than Connecticut's) could not render a binding judgment that operated directly on the land in Connecticut, he attempted to accomplish the same thing by seeking an equitable ruling from the South Carolina courts concerning the meaning of the will (which allegedly "converted" the real property into personal property), and then sought to have the Connecticut courts recognize

The principle that only the courts of a state in which real property is situated have jurisdiction to make binding judgments concerning rights in that property is a hoary one, rooted in older conceptions of sovereignty and the exclusive power of a state to regulate affairs within its borders. The historical relationship of land to power in Anglo–American jurisprudence has given that jurisdictional principle particular purchase. That principle, however, is out of keeping with American law's more recent acknowledgment that legal disputes, whatever their subject, frequently implicate the interests of persons in multiple jurisdictions, as well as the legitimate interests of the states themselves. Even if we use a *lex loci* principle to resolve the choice-of-law issues, we regard courts anywhere in the United States as having authority—judicial jurisdiction—to resolve tort and contract disputes, so long as personal jurisdiction over the defendant is satisfied. The notion that real property is "special" (this is sometimes termed the "land taboo"), and thus requires special jurisdictional rules, because of its traditional connection to sovereignty, has diminishing appeal. Choice-of-law rules, which do still tend to favor the *lex loci rei sitae* in real property cases even in jurisdictions otherwise committed to an interest-oriented approach, can be relied on to avoid unwonted disrespect for the law and policy of the locus.

Courts are thus less likely today to apply rigid jurisdictional limits on their ability to adjudicate cases involving rights in real property located elsewhere. Nevertheless, most Conflicts casebooks include at least a couple of older cases illustrating the traditional, sometimes maddeningly arcane, reasoning concerning the "land taboo" and its approach to jurisdiction in cases involving real property. Rather than attempt to explicate these strange-sounding older cases, let us simply observe that, even today, a lawyer who deals with land title questions does have to be scrupulous about inquiring into the kinds of judicial judgments that may in the past have cast a "cloud" upon title to that land. This includes examination of prior decrees that may have ordered a conveyance of the land, without necessarily purporting directly to affect title to the land. The theory here is that a judicial decree ordering the *conveyance* of land (situated outside the forum) by one person to another would be presumptively valid and subject to full faith and credit obligations elsewhere, since it does not directly affect *title*; whereas a judicial determination purporting to decide who has title to the land (situated outside the jurisdiction) might be regarded as *not* entitled to recognition elsewhere. Yes, it really is that esoteric. Since the encumbrances and "clouds" on title to real property can

and enforce that ruling as to the property located there, by way of the Full Faith and Credit Clause.

reach back decades if not much longer, lawyers inquiring into the security of title to such property still need to account for these niceties, even though modern-day legal rules may have made these questions a bit simpler to resolve.[78]

7. Full Faith and Credit to Equitable Decrees

Law and Equity. Until the mid-twentieth century, American law, like the English legal system from which it was mostly derived, maintained a fairly clear distinction between "law" and "equity." Actions at "law" referred to causes of action that had traditionally been heard by the courts of common law, exemplified by the time-honored action for money damages based on a civil wrong: a tort, breach of contract, or damage to property rights. Many of the examples given in this book are based on such common-law actions for damages; they are the simplest cases and they best illustrate the points about choice of law or recognition of judgments that we are trying to demonstrate.

English and early American jurisprudence has also provided us, however, with a second, distinct stream of legal doctrine: the decisions of courts of equity. Historically, courts exercising equity jurisdiction have dealt with claims for relief that did not fit easily into the common-law formulas establishing rights and remedies for the private law areas of contract, tort, and property. The term "equity" itself suggests that the purpose of equitable jurisdiction was to provide a measure of justice when the technical requirements of the common law did not support a remedy, although over time "equity" evolved simply into a repository of legal principles alongside those of the common law, rather than a source of "justice." Well into the twentieth century, courts of equity were distinct from courts of law in many states. Today, the formal distinction between law and equity has largely disappeared from American law; for example, in an effort to abolish the distinction in the federal courts, Fed. R. Civ. P. 2 provides, "There is one form of action—the civil action."

The historical distinction between law and equity continues to echo, however, in a variety of legal contexts, even in jurisdictions that (like most) have formally abolished the distinction so far as the jurisdiction of courts is concerned. The distinction is particularly relevant where the *remedies* that courts may order as a result of a finding of liability are concerned. The hallmark of the traditional "action at law" was the remedy of money damages. But today we are familiar with other kinds of remedies that courts regularly

---

78. One of the famous cases raising such issues is *Fall v. Eastin*, 215 U.S. 1 (1909). Brainerd Currie discussed *Fall v. Eastin*, and the general problems facing lawyers dealing with decrees affecting land, in his article *Full Faith and Credit to Foreign Land Decrees*, 21 University of Chicago Law Review 620 (1954).

impose—in particular, the *injunction*, which typically orders a party to do or to refrain from doing something. Familiar as it is today, the injunction was not originally conceived as a remedy that common-law courts might impose in the ordinary common-law cases they were empowered to hear. The roots of the injunction as a remedy lie in the powers asserted by courts of equity. Thus, one often hears the injunction described as an "equitable remedy." With the functions of law and equity courts now merged in most states in a single system of courts, trial courts of general jurisdiction (and many other courts of first instance) regularly grant injunctive relief in appropriate cases, as well as the more traditional imposition of money damages. Their power to do so is not generally subject to debate.

Traditional Mechanisms for Enforcing Money Judgments. All this is a preface to the observation that interjurisdictional recognition and enforcement of conventional awards of money damages pursuant to a finding of liability do not generally cause much difficulty. Court A holds that the defendant is liable to the plaintiff, and that the defendant is indebted to the plaintiff in the amount of $1000. If the defendant fails to pay the judgment, and she has no property in State A but some property in State B whose sale could be used to defray the judgment, it may become necessary for the plaintiff to seek enforcement of the judgment in a court of State B. Traditional doctrine required plaintiff first to "reduce" the judgment of Court A to a judgment in a court of State B. Both claim preclusion and full faith and credit would be at work in such an action to reduce the judgment to a State B judgment; Court B would be required by full faith and credit to "recognize" the State A judgment, and principles of claim preclusion (recognized by every state) would bar the defendant from being able to contest the case on the merits in the Court B action. After reduction of the judgment to a judgment in State B, the plaintiff could then initiate the enforcement mechanism provided generally by State B for enforcement of its own money-damage judgments—traditionally, by seeking a writ from Court B instructing a law enforcement officer in that state to seize the defendant's property in that state and sell it at auction, with the amount of the plaintiff's judgment ($1000) being paid to him with part or all of the proceeds.

Many states have simplified this two-stage process by merging reduction and enforcement into one proceeding, and the general process of enforcing judgments has become somewhat less quaint (for example, judicial orders "freezing" or "attaching" or "sequestering" a person's assets situated within the state are quite common).[79] Nevertheless, the picturesque nineteenth-century image of

79. Most states have adopted, in whole or in part, the Uniform Enforce- ment of Foreign Judgments Act, which greatly simplifies interstate enforcement

the local sheriff seizing the defendant's property and selling it at auction does capture the traditional conception of interjurisdictional enforcement of money judgments: First reduce the judgment of Court A to a judgment in State B, then make use of State B's enforcement processes.

So far, so good. In practical effect, one might say that the conventional money-damage remedy of Court A travels to State B along with the liability judgment of Court A—although it is necessary to follow State B's own procedures for enforcement of that remedy. Certainly all states have some such procedure. More difficult questions arise, however, when the remedy provided by Court A consists of an injunction ordering the defendant (or someone else) to do or to refrain from doing something. To what extent does full faith and credit require courts in states other than State A to enforce such an injunction according to its terms? Court A can, in many circumstances, order a party to refrain from certain actions no matter where she may be. But does full faith and credit require that courts in other states enforce that order to the letter if it becomes necessary for someone to attempt to enforce it?

***Baker v. General Motors* (1998).** Generally, the answer is "no." Of course, states, in the interest of comity and reciprocity, may choose to devise rules that will provide for the enforcement of certain kinds of foreign judicial orders (such as support orders). But mechanisms of enforcing a judgment do not automatically "travel with" a judgment to another state by way of the full faith and credit principle the way that the judgment itself does, as the U.S. Supreme Court announced in *Baker v. General Motors Corp.* (1998).[80] Ronald Elwell, a longtime employee of General Motors, became involved in a dispute with the company over the terms of his retirement and began testifying as an expert on behalf of plaintiffs in product liability actions against GM. When Elwell ultimately sued GM in Michigan state court for wrongful discharge, the parties reached a settlement that included a permanent injunction forbidding him from testifying as an expert against GM in future product liability cases. The injunction was not geographically limited. Subsequently, the Bakers brought a wrongful death action against GM in federal court in Missouri, based on their mother's death in an auto accident involving a GM automobile. The Bakers sought Elwell's testimony as an expert, and GM sought to block Elwell from testifying by moving to enforce the injunction that had been entered as a result of the settlement in the earlier case. Although the Federal District Court permitted Elwell to testify, the

of money judgments and provides that a foreign judgment properly registered in the judgment debtor's state, with proper notice to the debtor, will be enforced as if it were a judgment of the forum.

80. 522 U.S. 222 (1998).

Court of Appeals reversed, holding that, as a matter of full faith and credit, the Michigan court's injunction should be enforced by the District Court. The Supreme Court reversed, holding that the District Court was not bound to enforce the injunction and that Elwell could therefore testify.

The essence of the Court's holding can be found in the following passage: "Full faith and credit ... does not mean that States must adopt the practices of other States regarding the time, manner, and mechanisms for enforcing judgments. Enforcement measures do not travel with the sister state judgment as preclusive effects do; such measures remain subject to the even-handed control of forum law." Why should this be so? The Court seemed to find the answer in traditional notions of sovereignty, noting that historically "[o]rders commanding action or inaction have been denied enforcement in a sister State when they purported to accomplish an official act within the exclusive province of that other State or interfered with litigation over which the ordering State had no authority." Applying these ideas to the *Baker* litigation, the Court held that the District Court in Missouri was not bound to apply the Michigan state court injunction according to its terms. The state of Missouri may have its own way of giving effect to orders such as the injunction imposed on Elwell by the Michigan court; the FFC Clause does not require Missouri to do it the way Michigan would do it.

Although the general proposition announced in *Baker* may seem reasonable enough,[81] its application to the *Baker* litigation itself raises some questions. What would the District Court in Missouri have done had the earlier litigation in *Elwell v. GM* been conducted in Missouri, rather than Michigan, state court? Isn't it likely that Missouri law and judicial practice would have provided for the enforcement of the injunction in its own courts? The Supreme Court mentioned in *Baker* that the interjurisdictional enforcement of enforcement measures "remain[s] subject to the even-handed control of forum law." Does this mean that the Full Faith and Credit Clause requires Missouri courts (and the Federal

---

81. In concurrence, Justice Kennedy offered an alternative justification for the result in *Baker*: Since the Bakers themselves had not been parties in the Elwell litigation that had resulted in the Michigan injunction, they could not themselves be precluded in their own lawsuit from contesting the enforcement of that injunction. This argument seems to prove too much, however. As a practical matter, injunctive remedies frequently affect persons not present before the court. As non-parties in the first case, such persons might have a claim to relitigate the questions of fact and law that underlay the judgment resulting in the injunction, but only if they had standing to do so. The Bakers obviously had no standing to litigate the issues underlying the original dispute between Elwell and GM. The court-approved remedy as a result of that earlier litigation was, legally speaking, a matter of concern to Elwell and GM, not to other persons who might be peripherally affected by the obligations assumed by Elwell as a result of the injunction.

District Court in Missouri) to accord foreign enforcement measures (like injunctions) the same effect that they would give to the enforcement measures issued by their own courts?

Little effort was made in the *Baker* decision to determine whether Missouri's treatment of foreign and domestic injunctions was, in the Court's words, "even-handed," for example by examining Missouri law to see how the courts of Missouri treat injunctions entered by other Missouri courts. One might think that discrimination against foreign-issued injunctions would be likely to produce the kind of interstate "friction" against which the Full Faith and Credit Clause was designed to guard. One can agree that different states specify different procedural mechanisms for enforcing judicial decrees, and that no state is obliged to follow the procedures of another state, while also observing that the recognition state should not treat foreign injunctions differently from those issued by its own courts. In any case, the Court in *Baker* did not probe these matters in much depth. The upshot of the holding is simply that the Full Faith and Credit Clause does not oblige states to *enforce* (as opposed to *recognize*) the judgments of a sister state in the manner specified by that sister state's law.

Anti-suit injunctions. A type of injunction the enforcement of which is particularly likely to provoke resistance from a sister state is the anti-suit injunction—an injunction barring the parties before the court from continuing litigation in another jurisdiction.[82] Such an injunction is presumptively enforceable by the court that issued it. But, as Justice Ginsburg pointed out in her majority opinion in *Baker*, state courts have not generally regarded themselves bound by full faith and credit to enforce such injunctions when they have been entered by a court of a sister state. (That is not to say that a court may not *choose* to enforce such an injunction, as an expression of prudence or comity.) It appears to follow from the reasoning in *Baker* that the Court has ratified that position. In extreme cases, of course, this could lead to a chaotic situation in which rival courts enjoin the conduct of litigation between the parties in the other court, with no supervening principle available to resolve the conflict. The principle of full faith and credit, evidently, is not robust enough to resolve this situation definitively. At some point reliance simply has to be placed on the willingness of one court or the other to yield.

8. Congress's Power to Legislate Pursuant to the Full Faith and Credit Clause and the Problem of "Partial Repeal" of § 1738

The Implementation Clause of Article IV, § 1. One of the mysteries of the Full Faith and Credit Clause is the scope of the

---

82. This situation arises from time to time in the area of child custody determinations. See Chapter 6.

power conferred on Congress by the second clause of Art. IV, § 1 of the Constitution, which provides that "Congress may by general Laws prescribe ... the Effect" of judgments rendered by a state court. Section 1738 of Title 28 is the most important of Congress's exercise of this power. As we've seen, this statute prescribes that the effect given by Court B to Court A's judgment must be the same effect that another court in State A would give to the earlier judgment. But how far does the Congressional power to "prescribe ... the Effect" of state-court judgments go? Although the statute's wording suggests that the power is plenary, surely Congress cannot exercise it so as to provide that state-court judgments must or need be given *no* effect. That would nullify one of the FFC Clause's principal purposes. The task, then, is one of line-drawing; when Congress exercises the power granted to it by the FFC Clause, it must do so in a way that does not render the overall purposes of the FFC Clause wholly void. Moreover, the Clause itself requires that Congress, in exercising its power, do so by enacting "general Laws." Historical reconstruction of the common meaning of the phrase "general Laws" in 1788 suggests that, at a minimum, the Clause bars Congress from altering the full-faith-and-credit obligations only with respect to a particular case or individual, by enactment of a "private bill." Presumably it also bars Congress from creating full-faith-and-credit rules that apply to some states but not others. Beyond that, the effect of the "general Laws" requirement is uncertain.

At present these issues are largely academic ones, because Congress has exercised its power under the FFC Clause on only a few occasions. Over the years, a number of scholars have argued that Congress has made insufficient use of its powers under the FFC Clause.[83] Some, for example, have suggested that enactment of a uniform choice-of-law methodology, to be used in all states, would be both a desirable and constitutional exercise of Congressional power pursuant to the Clause. But Congress has generally limited itself to the general FFC implementation statute and a few provisions modifying the full-faith-and-credit obligation in specific instances. In addition to 28 U.S.C. § 1738 itself, Congress has enacted detailed statutes governing interstate recognition and enforcement of child custody and child support decrees, which have presented notorious difficulties. These Congressional enactments have almost universally been regarded as reasonable exercises of Congress's power, and constitutional challenges to them based on the FFC Clause were quickly overruled. Section 1738C of Title 28, however, which forms part of the federal Defense of Marriage Act

---

83. *See, e.g.,* Brainerd Currie, *Full Faith and Credit, Chiefly to Judgments:*   *A Role for Congress,* 1964 SUPREME COURT REVIEW 89.

["DOMA"], discussed at greater length in Chapter 6, presents more complex problems. Sections 1738A and 1738B are efforts to provide a procedural road map for interstate enforcement of child custody and child support decrees, respectively, in order to minimize the likelihood of conflicting decrees in specific cases and to bring some semblance of order and stability to what had sometimes become judicial wars over jurisdiction. Section 1738C, however, does something like the opposite; to the extent that it relieves states of the obligation of giving effect to certain sister-state judgments, it actually *undermines* the national uniformity in recognition of those judgments that the FFC Clause was designed to ensure.

The Question of "Partial Repeal." Since Congress, empowered by the FFC Clause, has enacted 28 U.S.C. § 1738, it obviously can amend and even repeal that statute. Both the chances and the advisability of *total* repeal are slight, but it is certainly within Congress's power to subordinate the principle of full faith and credit to other interests in particular situations where other federal interests may be involved. For example, § 1738C can itself be seen as an explicit partial repeal of § 1738, because it absolves the states of certain full-faith-and-credit obligations with respect to certain incidents of same-sex marriage that might otherwise be mandatory pursuant to § 1738.

In *Allen v. McCurry* (1980),[84] the U.S. Supreme Court considered whether 42 U.S.C. § 1983 should be read as effecting partial repeal of 28 U.S.C. § 1738. The facts of *Allen* illustrate well the way in which application of issue preclusion principles can be particularly troubling in some instances. McCurry was arrested for possession of heroin by police in St. Louis, Missouri after a search and seizure of evidence at his home that McCurry contended was in violation of the Fourth Amendment. At a suppression hearing, McCurry's Fourth Amendment argument was rejected, and he was subsequently convicted. McCurry later brought a civil suit against the police in Federal District Court based on 42 U.S.C. § 1983, alleging again that his Fourth Amendment rights had been violated by the search and seizure. The police officers argued that issue preclusion barred McCurry from litigating this point, since it had already been determined adversely to him in the state-court suppression hearing. The Supreme Court agreed with this argument, holding that McCurry's § 1983 claim was barred by principles of issue preclusion.

Ordinary principles of issue preclusion and full faith and credit would appear to support the Court's holding. McCurry did raise the Fourth Amendment issue in his earlier case; his contention was

---

84.   449 U.S. 90 (1980).

resolved adversely to him; and § 1738 requires federal courts to give full faith and credit to the judgments of state courts. The circumstances in *McCurry*, however, suggest there may be reason to pause before concluding as the Court did. When a criminal defendant is arraigned on a serious charge, a motion for suppression of evidence is one of the numerous tactics that his (no doubt harried) lawyer will consider. In determining whether to make such a motion and, if so, how to frame it, the lawyer will take into account many strategic considerations, but the motion's effect on his client's later ability to bring a § 1983 action will probably not be one of them. In fact, in many if not most situations, it would border on ineffective assistance of counsel not to raise a suppression argument if it stands even a modest chance of resulting in the suppression of important evidence against the defendant. To introduce into this calculus the possibility that the defendant will forfeit a potentially meritorious cause of action by making an unsuccessful suppression motion seems inconsistent with the constitutional protections generally afforded criminal defendants in felony cases. It is one thing to build the doctrine of preclusion around the notion that the parties engaged in civil litigation in Case A can be expected to consider the effects of their litigation choices on their ability to litigate claims and issues in a future Case B. It is quite another to assume that criminal defendants and their attorneys should be expected to frame their litigation strategies with an eye to civil causes of action that might be brought by the defendant in the future.

The problem of using the results of the state criminal proceedings to preclude the defendant in Case A from bringing a § 1983 claim in Case B assumes greater poignancy when one considers the origins of the cause of action that is now codified at 42 U.S.C. § 1983. When first enacted in 1871, the statute was a response to the complete breakdown in even-handed administration of criminal justice in the South after the Civil War. States and localities in the South rarely brought criminal prosecutions when Blacks were subjected to terror and violence after the war; Blacks themselves often received what is politely known as "summary justice" if they were suspected of crimes. Since § 1983 was thus conceived in the crucible of the complete failure of criminal justice processes in the South, one might argue that there is, at least historically, something discordant about according the results of those processes *res judicata* effect in later federal court proceedings featuring the criminal defendant's § 1983 claim that his constitutional rights were denied in the state proceedings.

But to argue, as the defendant (and the dissenting Justices) did in *Allen v. McCurry*, that these considerations should lead to the conclusion that § 1983 "partially repeals" § 1738, and that full faith and credit does not require that state-court criminal proceedings be given preclusive effect in subsequent § 1983 litigation, is an uphill battle. Obviously, the text of § 1983 says nothing about preclusion. (In fact, it would be very surprising it if did. A predecessor statute to § 1738 was on the books in 1871, but the drafters of § 1983 could hardly be expected to have concerned themselves, one way or another, with the statute's effect on the full-faith-and-credit obligations due state criminal proceedings.) Depending on one's particular approach to statutory interpretation, perhaps one could argue that the considerations described in the previous two paragraphs should have led the Court to "read into" § 1983 a repeal of § 1738 that was not explicit in the statute's text. But the Court in *Allen v. McCurry* examined the history of the enactment of § 1983, as well the Court's own precedents interpreting the statute, and found no reason to conclude that § 1983 silently effectuated a "partial repeal" of § 1738. An important part of the Court's reasoning was that, whereas a suspicion of the integrity of state criminal processes may legitimately have been one of the motives for the original enactment of § 1983, it is no longer acceptable for federal courts to presume that those state processes warrant such suspicion. The Court was thus unwilling to find a "partial repeal" of § 1738 in § 1983.

Class Actions, Interjurisdictional Preclusion, § 1738, and Adequacy of Representation. *Allen v. McCurry* is consistent with the Supreme Court's general reluctance to limit the preclusive effect in federal courts of state-court judgments, even if the result is to bar the plaintiff in Case B from raising a cause of action under the federal civil-rights laws. Another example of the same attitude is *Marrese v. American Academy of Orthopaedic Surgeons* (1974), discussed above. In that case, the Court held that the interjurisdictional preclusive effect of a state-court judgment with respect to a federal claim over which federal courts have exclusive jurisdiction is governed, under § 1738, by State A's law of preclusion. Thus, the Court rejected the notion that the exclusive jurisdiction in the federal courts over certain federal claims might absolve the federal courts of the duty to give effect to state-court judgments improperly adjudicating such claims. One might expect that no state would have a preclusion rule giving *res judicata* effect to judgments of its courts ruling on federal claims over which jurisdiction lies exclusively in the federal courts, but *Matsushita Electric Industrial Co. v. Epstein* (1996)[85] proved otherwise. In *Matsushita*, the Supreme Court dealt with a complex case treating the doctrines of full faith and credit and interjurisdictional preclusion with respect to class-action lawsuits. The results of the Court's decision in *Matsushita* are so striking, if not shocking, that they deserve brief consideration here. A brief overview of the interplay

85.   516 U.S. 367 (1996).

between class action procedure and interjurisdictional preclusion is necessary to cast the issues in *Matsushita* in bolder relief.

As mentioned earlier in this chapter, one of the essential attributes of the modern class action is that a final judgment reached in a case in which a class has been certified should bind class members in roughly the same way that a judgment involving individual plaintiffs will bind them. Ordinarily, when a plaintiff class has been certified and has prevailed against the defendant on a given cause of action, an individual member of the class (assuming she did not opt out of the class action) may not thereafter maintain an action against the same defendant on the same cause of action. Without such a preclusion principle, the class-action device would be of limited use, not to mention fundamentally unfair to defendants. But problems of fairness to class members remain. Because it will often not be possible to provide for actual notice to all class members—constitutional standards require only that notice be "practicable under the circumstances"—it is crucial that there be a process by which it can be assured that absent (and perhaps unreachable) members of the class will have their interests adequately represented in the litigation. The procedural requirements set out by Fed. R. Civ. P. 23 were designed to provide the constitutionally necessary safeguards.[86] Courts have relied on rigorous application of the stated requirements for certification of (and subsequent prosecution) of class actions under Fed. R. Civ. P. 23(b)(3)—constitutionally adequate notice, opportunity for members of the plaintiff class to opt out of the class, adequacy of representation of the class by the named plaintiffs—to ensure that the risk of unfairness is acceptably small.[87]

The question of "adequacy of representation" with respect to absent class members has in recent years become more pressing, particularly where questions of full faith and credit and interjurisdictional preclusion are concerned. There are several reasons for this, but of particular importance are the conflicts of interest, particularly those between some or all of the plaintiff class and class counsel, that can arise where class *settlement* is a possibility.[88]

---

86. For a helpful overview of the basic principles of Fed. R. Civ. P. 23, see *Amchem Products, Inc. v. Windsor*, 521 U.S. 591, 613–17 (1997). Although Rule 23 has been amended in some particulars since *Amchem* was decided, the basic points made in *Amchem* concerning that rule remain valid.

87. In *Phillips Petroleum Co. v. Shutts*, 472 U.S. 797 (1985), the United States Supreme Court set out standards concerning when absent class members may constitutionally be bound by the outcome of class litigation.

88. In an important decision in 1997, *Amchem Products, Inc. v. Windsor, supra* n.86, the Supreme Court made clear that federal district courts must be rigorous in applying the class certification requirements specified in Fed. R. Civ. P. 23, including when a class is being certified solely for the purposes of possible settlement.

When a class action is settled, class counsel may be awarded attorneys' fees by the court as a percentage of the recovery or "economic benefit" achieved on behalf of the class; alternatively, the defendant may agree to pay a fixed amount in attorneys' fees as part of the settlement itself.[89] In non-class litigation, the temptations this scenario may present the lawyer to act in a self-serving way is at least theoretically tolerable because an individual client can monitor lawyer behavior and assume responsibility for litigation decisions, including the decision to settle. By contrast, in class litigation, absent class members cannot monitor lawyer behavior in the same way. In addition, because named plaintiffs in class actions frequently (and legally) receive an extra fee for their services, they may lack the incentive to oppose self-serving attorneys in their choice of strategy.

This situation creates some strategic incentives for defendants faced with the possibility of multiple class actions in different jurisdictions. Such a defendant may attempt to exploit a particular class counsel's desire to recover attorney's fees by seeking to conclude an early settlement on terms that protect the defendant from any additional exposure to liability but that may enrich class counsel at the expense of some or all of the plaintiff class. The situation has been well described by legal scholars Marcel Kahan and Linda Silberman:

> In a multijurisdictional or multicourt setting, two additional problems aggravate the danger of self-serving actions by class attorneys: the "plaintiff shopping" or "lawyer shopping" problem and the "forum shopping" problem. The plaintiff/lawyer shopping problem arises when a second competing class action covering the same or a related set of claims is filed (or, for that matter, when a class attorney is worried that a competing action *may* be filed). When there are competing class actions, the outcome of the action that is concluded first is binding on the whole class. Because judges typically award attorneys' fees predominantly to the lawyers who act as class counsel in their courts, each set of competing lawyers has a strong financial incentive to bring its action to a speedy conclusion. Defendants, well aware of these incentives, can thus go plaintiff and lawyer shopping: By indicating that they will deal with class counsel

---

89. Technically, the "adequacy of representation" that is required for the certification of any class action refers to the adequacy with which the named plaintiffs will represent the interests of all members of the class. Nevertheless, the line between the adequacy provided by the *named plaintiffs* and that provided by *class counsel* has been substantially blurred in the case law. Allegations of inadequate representation are addressed as often to the conflicts on the part of class *counsel* as to the conflicts on the part of named plaintiffs who do not

who is willing to settle for the least, they implicitly create a "reverse auction" in which competing class lawyers "underbid" each other in order to have their own action settled first and earn attorneys' fees.[90]

Of course, it is the *court* that bears ultimate responsibility both for certifying a class and for approving any settlement that may be reached. Much depends on the firmness with which courts enforce the "adequacy of representation" standard when certifying a class. Unfortunately, in the 1980s and 1990s, the courts of some states developed reputations (deserved or otherwise) for being far less rigorous than others in observing the predicates for certification of a class, and consequently far more willing to certify a class, in particular for purposes of settlement. Although the Supreme Court in 1997 made it clear that "adequacy of representation" was a factor to be taken very seriously in the certification of a class in federal court, it left open an important question: Whether the impropriety of class certification (based on inadequacy of representation or other factors under Fed. R. Civ. P. 23) might be attacked *collaterally*, in a separate proceeding subsequently brought by members of the original class on the same or related claims against the same defendant(s).

That is a question of particular interest in connection with class actions and interjurisdictional preclusion. If a state court in Case A is too casual about certifying a class and holding that there is adequacy of representation for purposes of a class settlement, must the courts of other states regard the question of adequacy of representation as *res judicata*? The assumption generally has been that judicially approved class settlements, so long as the process of class certification and settlement met Due Process standards, could *not* be collaterally attacked on such grounds as inadequacy of representation of some or all of the class's absent members. Since Court A has made a specific finding that representation was adequate, conventional principles would dictate that the issue has been "actually litigated and determined" and thus entitled to full faith and credit. In recent years, however, some "recognition" courts, bothered by attempts to enforce *res judicata* principles arising out of class settlements in other states where "adequacy of representation" has seemed particularly dubious, have begun to bridle at this suggestion.[91]

share all the interests and incentives of the absent plaintiffs.

90. Marcel Kahan & Linda Silberman, *The Inadequate Search for "Adequacy" in Class Actions: A Critique of* Epstein v. MCA, Inc., 73 NEW YORK UNIVERSITY LAW REVIEW 765, 775 (1998). Kahan and Silberman go on to describe the

"forum shopping" part of the equation, noting that the courts of some states have developed reputations for failing to insist on true adequacy of representation when certifying a class.

91. *See, e.g., Stephenson v. Dow Chemical*, 273 F.3d 249 (2d Cir. 2001),

Matsushita **(1996).** Something like the unseemly activity described above by Kahan and Silberman appears to have taken place in the *Matsushita* case. MCA shareholders brought a class action in Delaware court, based on alleged violations of Delaware state law in the purchase of MCA by Matsushita. A parallel class action proceeding was instituted in federal court, raising federal claims (under the securities laws) over which the federal courts have exclusive subject matter jurisdiction. Class counsel in the Delaware court thereupon concluded a quick settlement that purported to extinguish *all* claims the plaintiff class might have against the defendants, even the federal claims over which Delaware state courts have no subject matter jurisdiction and which remained part of the parallel federal court proceeding. The Delaware courts approved the class settlement. The defendants, returning to federal court, argued that that proceeding should be dismissed, because the judicially approved settlement in the Delaware case was *res judicata* pursuant to § 1738 as to all claims in the federal proceeding, including the federal claims that lay exclusively within federal jurisdiction. The U.S. Court of Appeals for the Ninth Circuit rejected the argument as to the federal claims, holding that no such *res judicata* effect should be given as to claims over which the Delaware courts had no jurisdiction. The Supreme Court, relying in part on the *Marrese* decision, ruled that the Delaware litigation should be given preclusive effect in the federal litigation, barring even the federal claims from litigation in the federal court.

At a strictly doctrinal level, the Court's decision in *Matsushita* was consistent with *Marrese*, which had held that, under § 1738, the rendering court's preclusion rule must apply to determine the preclusive effect of its judgment even as to claims over which it has no jurisdiction. The Court also found that Delaware does in fact recognize a rule of preclusion according to which a Delaware court's judgment with respect to federal claims over which it has no jurisdiction is *res judicata* in a subsequent proceeding brought in Delaware court. This somewhat surprising finding has been criticized as a misreading of Delaware law, but, assuming the Court was correct in its finding, *Marrese* would appear to require dismissal of

aff'd by a divided court and vacated on other grounds, 539 U.S. 111 (2003); State v. Homeside Lending, Inc., 175 Vt. 239, 826 A.2d 997 (2003). The Homeside Lending decision is but one of the opinions generated by one of the most notorious class action episodes on record. According to the Vermont Supreme Court in Homeside Lending, plaintiff's counsel negotiated and received judicial approval from the Alabama courts for a settlement that ended up costing some members of the plaintiff class more in attorney's fees than it provided for them in an award of damages. For discussions, see Homeside Lending; Susan P. Koniak & George M. Cohen, Under Cloak of Settlement, 82 VIRGINIA LAW REVIEW 1051, 1057–84 (1996); Kamilewicz v. Bank of Boston Corp., 100 F.3d 1348, 1349–52 (7th Cir. 1996) (Easterbrook, J., dissenting from denial of rehearing en banc).

the federal litigation on *res judicata* grounds. Referencing the concept of "partial repeal" of § 1738, the Court concluded that nothing in the federal securities statute sued on by the plaintiff class suggested that it operated as such a partial repeal.

The Court's decision in *Matsushita*, however, obscured some of the practical realities of the litigation, which illustrate the incentives for self-dealing in class-action practice in the multi-jurisdictional context described previously. The parallel state and federal proceedings suggest a competition between different class counsel for control of the case. The settlement reached by class counsel and the defendants in the Delaware Court of Chancery was so meager in its provision for the plaintiff class that the Vice Chancellor initially refused to approve it. A settlement slightly more favorable to the plaintiff class was later approved by the Vice Chancellor, although he expressed considerable reluctance and acknowledged the possibility that there may have been "collusion" between class counsel and the defendants. In assessing all of this, one must ask what the benefit was to the plaintiff class in having the litigation brought in Delaware court to begin with. As the Ninth Circuit pointed out on remand from the Supreme Court, litigating in a court with no jurisdiction to hear the potential federal claims)— which presumably were not without value (and certainly were stronger than the state-law claims)—meant that the plaintiffs lost all bargaining power for purposes of settlement that they might have held in the form of the federal claims. There was no credible threat to the defendants that going to trial in Delaware might result in a large judgment on the federal claims, precisely because the Delaware courts had no jurisdiction to hear such claims. This made it likely that any settlement of the case would be meager, and raises the suspicion that class counsel in the Delaware case either began the case, or came to view it, as one that would have to be settled quickly if counsel were to realize much in the way of financial benefits.

The real heart of the problem in *Matsushita*, then, was not the Court's application of the rather odd *Marrese* doctrine, nor its reading of Delaware preclusion law, but an issue that the Court studiously avoided deciding: whether adequacy of representation of the plaintiff class in the Delaware litigation could be collaterally attacked in the federal court proceeding. In a separate opinion, Justice Ginsburg observed that the majority's ruling left open that question on remand. After the case was remanded by the Supreme Court, the Ninth Circuit held that the Delaware class settlement was not binding in a separate federal action brought by absent class members who claimed that their interests had not been adequately represented in the Delaware proceeding. The panel's decision was far-reaching. It not only held that Due Process requires that absent plaintiffs in the federal proceeding be able to avoid the *res judicata* effect of the Delaware proceeding by collaterally contesting the propriety of the Delaware court's ruling that class counsel and the named plaintiffs would adequately protect the interests of the class; it indicated that *adequacy of representation in fact* was itself a Due Process requirement, and that plaintiffs in the federal proceeding should be able to resist the *res judicata* effect of the Delaware settlement by demonstrating that class counsel's actual behavior *subsequent to* certification of the class revealed inadequate representation.[92]

Within two years, however, a reconstituted panel of the Ninth Circuit, rehearing the case, vacated the first panel's opinion and ruled that adequacy of representation in the Delaware proceeding could not be challenged collaterally in the federal court, and that therefore the federal plaintiffs' claims were barred by *res judicata*.[93] The long and sorry *Matsushita* saga in the federal courts was over. The Supreme Court has never ruled on whether collateral attack with respect to adequacy of representation in a class suit is permitted.

92. *Epstein v. MCA, Inc.*, 126 F.3d 1235 (9th Cir. 1997), *vacated and superseded*, 179 F.3d 641 (9th Cir. 1999).

93. *Epstein v. MCA, Inc.*, 179 F.3d 641 (9th Cir. 1999).

Chapter 6

CONFLICT OF LAWS AND DOMESTIC RELATIONS

"If there is one thing that the people are entitled to expect from their lawmakers, it is rules of law that will enable individuals to tell whether they are married and, if so, to whom. Today many people who have simply lived in more than one state do not know, and the most learned lawyer cannot advise them with any confidence."

— Justice Jackson, dissenting in *Estin v. Estin* (1948)[1]

Family law has long presented difficult problems for conflict of laws. Marriage, divorce, child custody, and child support, as well as issues of estate law that are ancillary to the law of domestic relations, can be enormously complex even when multiple jurisdictions are not involved; when they are, conventional conflicts principles often seem poorly adapted to the problems raised. Most of the important conflicts problems involving family law pertain to recognition of judgments, rather than choice of law. The judgments rendered by courts dealing with domestic relations issues are not always as "neat and clean" as judgments that pertain to traditional common-law actions for damages; the interjurisdictional effect of divorces or custody or support decrees can raise unexpected difficulties.

A. Marriage

Marriage is Not a Judgment. The advent of legal recognition for same-sex marriage in some states has brought to the fore age-old questions concerning interjurisdictional recognition of marriage and its legal incidents.[2] Actions by state legislatures and courts establishing the legality of same-sex marriage[3] have pro-

---

1. 334 U.S. 541, 553 (1948) (Jackson, J., dissenting).

2. By "incidents" we mean legal rights and duties that attach specifically because of one's married status, such as tax liabilities, hospital visitation rights under state law, and many others.

3. As of this writing, five states (as well as Washington, D.C.) have legalized same-sex marriage celebrated within their borders: Massachusetts, Connecticut, Iowa, Vermont, and New Hampshire. The question of full faith and credit and same-sex marriage, however, really began to receive attention as a

voked a wide-ranging discussion concerning whether such marriages are entitled to interstate recognition by virtue of the full faith and credit principle, and Congress has even enacted a statute purporting to exempt states from this obligation. Much of this discussion, however, has overlooked the fact that full faith and credit has only a limited role to play in the context of marriage, because *marriage is not a judgment*. In the United States, divorces, which are granted by courts, are considered to be judgments, but the celebration of a legal marriage is not. (One reason for this is that divorces are often contested, requiring a dispute resolution mechanism, whereas marriages presumably take place by consent of both spouses.) For that reason, the obligation of full faith and credit to judgments does not apply to marriages as such. Of course, interjurisdictional recognition of marriages has for centuries been a concern of courts and other governmental bodies all over the world, since the legal rules concerning marriage have often varied from one jurisdiction to another; but the Full Faith and Credit ["FFC"] Clause, even as to marriages and disputes that take place entirely within the United States, has, by and large, not been the legal mechanism for resolving these questions of recognition.

The Principle of *Lex Loci Celebrationis*. Historically, certain variations among jurisdictions in the law of marriage have been more consequential than others. For example, the minimum age at which one may legally marry without parental consent is not uniform throughout the United States.[4] In some states in the United States, it is legal to marry one's first cousin, but in others it is not. Some legal systems recognize the doctrine of plural marriage, sometimes called "polygamy."[5] Until disconcertingly late in the twentieth century, numerous states not only refused to recognize the legality of interracial marriage, but also made miscegenation—defined variously as sex between whites and non-whites, or cohabitation of a white person with a non-white person—a crime.[6]

result of the Hawai'i Supreme Court's decision in *Baehr v. Lewin*, 74 Haw. 530, 852 P.2d 44 (1993), which suggested that the right to same-sex marriage might be constitutionally guaranteed under the Equal Protection Clause of the Fourteenth Amendment. Before this issue could be conclusively adjudicated, the voters of Hawai'i approved an amendment to the state constitution barring legalization in the state of same-sex marriage.

4. In most states, the minimum age is 18 years. In Mississippi, it is 21 years.

5. For example, some nation-states that follow Islamic law with respect to

marriage issues generally recognize plural marriage, though only for men.

6. Laws prohibiting interracial marriage were declared unconstitutional by the U.S. Supreme Court in *Loving v. Virginia*, 388 U.S. 1 (1967). *Loving* was in fact a case involving interstate recognition of interracial marriage, as the Lovings had been married in the District of Columbia and then had returned to Virginia, whose law criminalized interracial co-habitation. The U.S. Supreme Court assessed the constitutionality of the Virginia statute directly, rather than constitutionally requiring recognition of the Lovings' Virginia marriage under the FFC Clause.

And, to take the most recent example, at least five states have, as of this writing, altered their laws to recognize same-sex marriage, while most states still do not.

Long before the founding of the American republic, the jurists of civil-law nations developed a basic principle to deal with such conflicts of laws: "Marriages valid where celebrated are valid everywhere" (this is essentially a rule of *lex loci celebrationis* for questions of a marriage's validity). Observation of this principle meant that the forum would often recognize a marriage performed outside the forum as legal and valid, even though forum law did not itself recognize such a union as legal. Like all traditional conflicts principles, this one assumed that the forum retained authority to disregard it in cases where recognition might threaten public order or undermine the forum's fundamental policy. The idea was that, all in all, it will ordinarily be better for the forum to recognize marriages valid where performed, even if they are not valid under forum law; enormous disruptions might arise if, for example, a couple's children were regarded as legitimate in one place but not in another. Provincial or reflexive disregard of the law of the place of the marriage was discouraged. But the forum remained entitled to place limits on this principle; it was not obliged to recognize a marriage under laws it regarded as repugnant to the forum's fundamental norms.

Throughout American history, the *lex loci celebrationis* principle has functioned as a rule of reason; courts have exercised a pragmatic discretion in applying it. Usually, for example, the rights of a married couple relocating from their place of marriage to a state whose law prohibited the marriage on account of the "degrees of consanguinity" (an archaic phrase referring to the closeness of blood relatives) would be recognized by the new state in case of a dispute. Rarely did it seem to a court that public order or morality would be threatened simply by recognition, say, of a foreign marriage between first cousins where the *lex loci celebrationis* sanctioned such a marriage. Interestingly, even plural marriages legally performed outside the United States have occasionally been recognized by state courts for particular purposes, such as distribution of assets in cases of intestacy. It is not necessarily a threat to the forum's public policy to permit a claim in the forum by one of the widows, where the decedent, having been married to two women under the laws of their common domicile, happened to have real property in the forum whose disposition could only there be authoritatively adjudicated.

Historically, the practical line of demarcation between recognition and non-recognition has often been whether the couple had lived for a substantial period in the place of celebration and later relocated to the forum with the intention of remaining there; or, instead, had transiently relocated from the forum to a state with friendlier laws simply to evade the forum's interdiction of their marriage, only to return to the forum. Courts have by and large been more willing to recognize the legality of foreign marriages in the former situation than in the latter, which they are apt to see as an "end-run" around the forum's laws pertaining to marriage. This rough dichotomy today remains an important point of departure, as state courts assess the degree to which same-sex marriages valid where celebrated should be recognized elsewhere.[7] As with the historical illustrations of marriage laws that differ from state to state, courts can be expected to be especially unwilling to exercise their discretion to recognize same-sex marriages performed elsewhere if the parties were forum residents and simply evaded forum law by making a transient appearance in the other state purely in order to become legally married, then returning to the forum.

Recognition of the "Incidents" of Marriage; DOMA. As mentioned, because the consecration of a marriage or the conferral of civil union status is not a "judgment," the forum is not bound by full faith and credit to legally recognize same-sex marriages *qua* marriages—that is, to treat such married couples as possessing the identical rights and liabilities as those held by couples (traditionally, opposite-sex couples) married under the laws of the forum. But that doesn't prevent the courts of any particular state that has not legalized same-sex marriage from *choosing* to recognize same-sex marriages performed elsewhere if they wish (unless barred by forum law from doing so). They simply aren't constitutionally obliged to. Moreover, to observe that there is no FFC obligation to recognize such marriages lock, stock, and barrel is to focus on a bit of an abstraction—the idea of a marriage *qua* marriage. So far as *law* is concerned, the real meaning of marriage consists in the legal rights and duties that appertain to it. (So far as *people* are concerned, of course, the mere fact of conferring the word "marriage" equally on same-sex and heterosexual unions also matters a great deal.)

One doesn't often see cases in which a same-sex couple who have been legally married in another state seek a simple declaratory judgment that they are considered to be legally married in the forum (although, of course, most if not all such couples would

---

7. The dichotomy is well illustrated by the history in the United States of recognition by the forum of marriages performed elsewhere that violated forum anti-miscegenation laws. One is naturally reluctant to cite laws that were based on notions of racial purity and racial subordination, and that today are clearly unconstitutional, as good illustrations of contemporary doctrine. Nevertheless, the miscegenation cases do serve as a precursor of the recognition problems raised by same-sex marriage. *See* Andrew Koppelman, *Same-Sex Marriage and Public Policy: The Miscegenation Precedents*, 16 Quinnipiac Law Review 105 (1996).

prefer that their status not change from place to place). Instead, the forum typically considers the legal status of the couple, and the question of interstate recognition, in the context of litigation over what are called the "incidents" of marriage. These are legal issues that are technically ancillary to the fact of marriage itself but that depend on an assessment of whether the couple is legally married (or were at the time the legal rights at issue were supposed to have come into being). There are many such issues. One obvious example is tax liability under the federal income tax laws; another is distribution of assets upon death in case of intestacy. Most states limit visitation rights, in case of hospitalization, to close family members (notably, the hospitalized person's spouse); whether the forum chooses to recognize a foreign-performed same-sex marriage as valid within the forum for purposes of visitation rights can obviously be a question of great importance to individual couples. These are only a few of the conflicts problems that can arise with respect to the incidents of marriage.

Some of the legal entitlements or liabilities mentioned in the foregoing paragraph arise directly from the fact of a legal marriage, and do not usually come into being as the result of litigation. Since there has not been a *judgment* in these situations, full faith and credit has little role to play. The fact, for example, that a same-sex married couple cannot file a joint federal income tax return is a direct consequence of a federal statute. Similarly, if a same-sex spouse were to be denied visitation rights in the forum (although entitled to those rights in the state of celebration), she might conceivably challenge the denial in court, but there is no real full-faith-and-credit issue because there is no prior judgment to which to refer. But some incidents of marriage might well have previously been the subject of litigation in the state where the marriage was performed, and interjurisdictional enforcement of the ensuing judgment might then bring the full-faith-and-credit principle into play.

A good example is the cause of action, recognized in some form in all the states, for wrongful death. This brings us all the way back to the beginning of Chapter 1, where we itemized as one of our paradigm examples of a conflicts problem the auto accident—due to the negligence of Patricia, an Alabama domiciliary—that ended the life of Edward, who had been married to Philip under the law of Massachusetts. Among the statutory beneficiaries of wrongful death statutes—those who have standing to bring such a claim and for whose benefit any award is made—is the surviving spouse. Unless state law has provided otherwise, the term "spouse" in these statutes will have one meaning in states that recognize same-sex marriage and another meaning in other states. Assume that Philip brought a successful wrongful-death case in Massachusetts court against Patricia, the Alabama driver whose negligent driving had caused Edward's death. Must the courts of Alabama, where Patricia has assets that can be used to pay the judgment, recognize and enforce the Massachusetts judgment when Philip brings it to Alabama for enforcement? Ordinary principles of full faith and credit would suggest that the answer is "yes." As the Supreme Court said in another context in *Baker v. General Motors* (1998), discussed in Chapter 5, there is no "roving public-policy exception" to Alabama's full-faith-and-credit obligation to give the Massachusetts judgment the same preclusive effect that a Massachusetts court would. And, in our example, a bona fide *judgment* in favor of Philip has been rendered by the Massachusetts courts. Alabama should not be able to disregard that judgment simply because it is based on a Massachusetts law whose policy Alabama disfavors.

However, Congress, in the Defense of Marriage Act ["DOMA"], part of which is codified at 28 U.S.C. § 1738C, appears to have relieved Alabama of the obligation of recognition and enforcement in this situation. To the extent that DOMA purports simply to absolve states of the obligation to recognize same-sex marriages *as such* that have been performed in another state, the statute is gratuitous; such marriages in themselves are not judgments and would not in any case trigger the FFC Clause's mandate concerning interjurisdictional recognition of judgments. But DOMA nevertheless has considerable bite so far as same-sex marriage and full faith and credit are concerned, because the statute's language does appear to address states' obligation to respect *judgments* that depend in part on the marital status of the person in whose favor the judgment was rendered:

> No State, territory, or possession of the United States, or Indian tribe, shall be required to give effect to any public act, record, or judicial proceeding of any other State, territory, possession, or tribe respecting a relationship between persons of the same sex that is treated as a marriage under the laws of such other State, territory, possession, or tribe, *or a right or claim arising from such relationship.*[8]

The language "a right or claim arising from such relationship" seems to cover the wrongful death situation; Phillip's right to recover under Massachusetts wrongful death law is such a right. Thus, with respect to the example given above, DOMA appears to withdraw part of a state's full-faith-and-credit obligation that would otherwise exist. Alabama courts are not obliged to recognize or give effect to Phillip's Massachusetts judgment.

What we said above about marriages as such applies as well to the *incidents* of marriage: The fact that, as a result of DOMA, a state is not constitutionally *required* to recognize rights or claims

---

8. 28 U.S.C. § 1738C (emphasis added).

arising out of a same-sex marriage valid under the laws of another state does not mean that such a state might not *choose* to recognize those rights in an individual case. There certainly is no constitutional bar to its doing so. Some scholars have explained why, even without the FFC Clause, a state court should consider recognizing such marriages in particular situations, for particular purposes.[9] Even if a state court might view it as a violation of the forum's strongly held public policy to treat a same-sex couple to be "a married couple" for *all* purposes in the forum, the same court might not regard the recognition of, say, their spousal hospital visitation rights as an outrage upon the forum's public policy. Similarly, it would not be unthinkable for the Alabama courts to enforce Phillip's wrongful death judgment in our hypothetical, even though those courts are not *obliged* to enforce it. We are likely to see rapid developments in this area of the law as state courts consider whether and to what extent they should recognize same-sex marriages, or the incidents thereof, performed elsewhere.

It is understandable that, if all states were constitutionally required (which they are not) to recognize all marriages (including same-sex marriages) legally performed under the laws of another state, many people would object, and not just on the grounds of opposition to same-sex marriage. The use of the full-faith-and-credit principle, in effect, to determine state law concerning a social institution in which all states are deeply interested, and on which different states have different views, seems a strange and unwieldy way of making law for the forum. (We will see the same oddity arising in the context of full faith and credit to divorce decrees.) It does appear, though, that where bona fide judgments are concerned, as in the case of Phillip, Edward, and Patricia, there is less of a threat to the sovereignty of the forum in extending recognition.[10]

B. Divorce

Divorces in the United States, unlike marriages, *are* judicial judgments.[11] Most such divorce proceedings are styled *Spouse v.*

9. *See, e.g.,* Andrew Koppelman, *Interstate Recognition of Same–Sex Marriages and Civil Unions: A Handbook for Judges,* 153 UNIVERSITY OF PENNSYLVANIA LAW REVIEW 2143 (2005).

10. Dean Larry Kramer has argued that a refusal by the forum to give effect to a same-sex marriage legally consecrated in another state is unconstitutional. His reasoning, building on the Supreme Court's decision in *Hughes v. Fetter* (1951), discussed in Chapter 4, is that to refuse to give effect to the marriage amounts to a blanket refusal to apply foreign law in such cases, even when the forum's usual choice-of-law rules would point there. Kramer argues that, under

Hughes v. Fetter, to discriminate against foreign law purely because of the forum's distaste for its substance violates the FFC clause. Larry Kramer, *Same–Sex Marriage, Conflict of Laws, and the Unconstitutional Public Policy Exception,* 106 YALE LAW JOURNAL 1965 (1997). Kramer's analysis, which is quite persuasive as an argument against the constitutionality of the "public policy exception" to *lex loci* rules, is less so with respect to marriage as such, partly because it has been conventional for so long for the forum to apply *lex fori* to questions relating to marriage.

11. Well into the nineteenth century, divorces were sometimes granted by

Spouse. As one might imagine, there are numerous contexts in which the interjurisdictional effect of a divorce can easily arise. It's a free and rather mobile country, and people move about. For the status—married or divorced—of a person to change depending on what state she happens to be in at any given time could lead to intolerable confusion. To take only the example we mentioned earlier, the rights of the children of a person who has remarried can be seriously affected if the earlier divorce of one of her parents is now called into question, not to mention that the parent herself could be regarded as guilty of bigamy or criminal cohabitation.

The law of divorce, including the permissible grounds for divorce, has never been uniform throughout all the states. The general historical trend, however, has been expansion over time of the permissible grounds for divorce, and greater ease in the procuring of an uncontested divorce. Until the twentieth century, legal limitations on the grounds for divorce (whatever else might be said in their behalf or against them) made it difficult to dissolve an unhappy or oppressive marriage. Particularly poignant was the legal plight of an abandoned spouse (most often a woman): If an abandoning spouse could not be found and served with divorce papers, the stay-at-home spouse[12] might find it well-nigh impossible to obtain a divorce and to remarry.[13] As the legal historian Hendrik

"private bills" in state legislatures, but the responsibility for granting dissolutions of marriage has long since rested with courts.

12. The term "stay-at-home spouse" is something of a term of art in discussions of divorce and full faith and credit, although perhaps an unfortunate one given its similarity to the terms "stay-at-home mom" and "stay-at-home dad," which are better known in today's culture.

13. In his opinion for the Supreme Court in *Pennoyer v. Neff*, 95 U.S. 714 (1877), Justice Field made a discreet reference to this problem when he exempted from *Pennoyer's* constitutional threshold for personal jurisdiction

proceedings to determine the status of one of its citizens towards a nonresident which would be binding within the State, though made without service of process or personal notice to the nonresident. The jurisdiction which every State possesses to determine the civil status and capacities of all its inhabitants involves authority to prescribe the conditions on which proceedings affecting them may be commenced and carried on within its territory. The State, for example, has absolute right to prescribe the conditions upon which the marriage relation between its own citizens shall be created, and the causes for which it may be dissolved. One of the parties guilty of acts for which, by the law of the State, a dissolution may be granted may have removed to a State where no dissolution is permitted. The complaining party would, therefore, fail if a divorce were sought in the State of the defendant; and if application could not be made to the tribunals of the complainant's domicile in such case, and proceedings be there instituted without personal service of process or personal notice to the offending party, the injured citizen would be without redress.

95 U.S. at 734–35. Of course, the obverse scenario could arise as well; the abandoning spouse might seek an *ex*

Hartog has demonstrated, abandoned or simply unhappy spouses in the nineteenth century exhibited great resourcefulness in working around these legal constraints to create new lives for themselves.[14] Nevertheless, the vagaries of divorce law, nineteenth-century notions concerning the power of courts over absent defendants, and geographic mobility combined to place many married persons in legal straitjackets.

The emergence of a new legal landscape for divorce in the twentieth century was the product of two developments (both, of course, underwritten by larger cultural changes):

1. The substantive reform of divorce law in a number of states, in particular to include more liberal grounds for divorce.

2. The relaxation of conventional personal jurisdiction principles in divorce cases, so as to make *ex parte* divorce easier to obtain, and presumptively subject to interjurisdictional recognition pursuant to full faith and credit.

It is thus no exaggeration to say that full faith and credit and the complexities of our federal system have played an important, if secondary, role in the development of the law of divorce in the United States. The importance of interstate recognition problems was amplified by the fact that not all states substantially liberalized their divorce laws, and at any rate did not do so at the same pace; under these circumstances, problems of conflict of laws and, in particular, recognition of judgments, grew fruitful and multiplied.

1. Ex Parte *Divorce and Full Faith and Credit: The* Williams *Decisions*

"Williams I": Williams v. North Carolina (1942). The case that reoriented the doctrine governing interstate recognition of divorce decrees, moving it toward the situation that prevails today, was *Williams v. North Carolina* (1942).[15] Prior to the *Williams* decision, the Supreme Court had fashioned a confusing doctrine (formalized in its 1906 decision in *Haddock v. Haddock*[16]) concerning full faith and credit to judgments of divorces, in particular *ex parte* divorces (divorces that are rendered in the absence of one of the spouses). The Court in *Haddock* held that (1) because of the plenary authority of a state over marital relations for those within

---

parte divorce in the state to which he had removed.

14. HENDRIK HARTOG, MAN AND WIFE IN AMERICA: A HISTORY (2000).

15. 317 U.S. 287 (1942). I will refer to this decision as *"Williams I,"* as the Court decided a second important case

involving the same parties three years later, *Williams v. North Carolina*, 325 U.S. 226 (1945) [*"Williams II"*], discussed below. When it is unnecessary to distinguish the two decisions, I will refer to them collectively as *"Williams"*.

16. 201 U.S. 562 (1906).

its borders, divorce decrees rendered by its courts could not be directly questioned on due process grounds based on lack of jurisdiction; but that (2) such decrees, if collaterally determined to have been rendered without jurisdiction over an absent spouse, were not constitutionally entitled to full faith and credit. The first of these conclusions is difficult to square with the constitutional rules for personal jurisdiction established by *Pennoyer v. Neff* (1877), at least in spirit, but the Court finessed this issue by observing that divorce is by nature an *in rem* proceeding, and that the *"rem"*—the marriage—is present wherever either spouse may be at any given moment. (Moreover, as noted above, *Pennoyer* had specifically excluded divorce proceedings from the rules for personal jurisdiction laid down in that case.) The Court based the second conclusion on its view that to compel the enforcement in the forum of an *ex parte* divorce obtained outside the forum was an intrusion on the sovereignty of the forum. One logical consequence of the *Haddock* doctrine, then, was that a person conceivably could be considered legally married in one state but not another.

By the time the Supreme Court heard the *Williams I* case in 1942, matters had changed significantly even in the few decades since *Haddock*. Not only had more states liberalized their divorce laws, but a few states, notably Nevada, had established what in practical terms amounted to a market in no-fault divorce decrees, with modest residency requirements and several easy-to-satisfy grounds for dissolution.[17] Interstate travel, especially over long distances, was easier. Simply stated, more people were getting divorced—and, in particular, more were getting divorced under the laws of states different from those of their "true" domiciles. Under these circumstances, the *Haddock* doctrine threatened to throw the legal rights and status of a large number of people into chaos.

In *Williams I*, Otis Williams and Lillie Hendrix, each a resident of North Carolina and each married to someone else in that state, traveled to Las Vegas, Nevada in May 1940. After the six weeks prescribed by Nevada law to obtain residency requisite to receiving a divorce, each filed a petition for divorce. Neither of the "stay-at home" spouses appeared in the respective divorce proceedings in Nevada, although constructive (rather than personal) service was made on each of them. Both divorce petitions were granted by the Nevada courts, whereupon Williams and Hendrix were married in Las Vegas. They then returned to North Carolina, where they lived

---

17. Strictly speaking, the term "no-fault divorce" refers to a state divorce law that provides for divorce without the necessity of showing fault on the part of one of the parties—for example, when the petition for divorce is based on "irreconcilable differences." The first such statute was passed in California in 1970. I say that the Nevada laws of the 1940s often amounted to the equivalent of "no-fault divorce" because it was so easy to prove the grounds (though they were technically based on fault) for divorce.

openly as husband and wife. They were subsequently indicted in North Carolina for the criminal offense of bigamous cohabitation. Williams and Hendrix pleaded not guilty, and offered as evidence in their defense the divorce decrees they had obtained in Nevada. The North Carolina court, however, ruled that those decrees were not entitled to full faith and credit in North Carolina. Williams and Hendrix were then convicted and sentenced to state prison. After the North Carolina Supreme Court upheld the convictions, the defendants appealed to the U.S. Supreme Court.

The first thing to understand about the *Williams I* case is that the defendants were arguing that full faith and credit should extend to the Nevada *divorce* decrees, not to the marriage performed in that state. (Obviously, the validity of the divorce decrees was a prerequisite to the validity of the new marriage.) The second thing to recognize is that the divorces in the *Williams I* case had been granted *"ex parte"*: Neither of the "stay-at-home" spouses had consented to divorce, or even to appear in the divorce proceeding. (An *ex parte* divorce thus bears some resemblance to a default judgment.) Thus, *Williams I* does not, itself, deal with the interstate status of divorces to which both parties have actually consented and appeared in the action.

Finally, it should be clear that, if the standard for personal jurisdiction that *Pennoyer v. Neff* (a case that was still good law in 1942) had established generally for *in personam* proceedings were to have been applied in *Williams I*, the divorce decrees should neither have been valid within Nevada nor entitled to full faith and credit in North Carolina (or anywhere else). Neither of the stay-at-home spouses had been served in Nevada or, for all that appears, had ever been in Nevada. Neither had property in Nevada.[18] (Of course, *Pennoyer* had carved out an exception for divorce decrees, but it is hard to see why the unfairness to an absent defendant is necessarily less in the case of a divorce than in other kinds of cases.) Moreover, *Haddock v. Haddock*, while holding that an *ex parte* divorce decree could not be challenged directly for absence of personal jurisdiction under *Pennoyer*, had held that there was no full-faith-and-credit obligation to enforce such a decree. *Haddock* seemed to support North Carolina's position that it need not recognize the Nevada divorce decrees and could prosecute Williams and Hendrix for bigamous cohabitation.

In spite of this, the Supreme Court in *Williams I* overturned the bigamy convictions. It held that the assertion of jurisdiction by

---

18. If you're wondering whether the "minimum contacts" standard for jurisdiction established by the Supreme Court three years after *Williams I* might have validly created jurisdiction in Nevada, note that neither stay-at-home spouse had had any cognizable "contacts" with Nevada, apart from the unilateral actions of their spouses in traveling to Nevada.

the Nevada court to render the divorce decrees was itself constitutional and violated no one's due process rights; and that, therefore, the divorce decrees were entitled to recognition in North Carolina under the FFC Clause. The Court reasoned that unique considerations govern questions of jurisdiction in divorce proceedings, noting that, traditionally, it had been a sufficient condition for jurisdiction in a divorce case that the "marital domicile" be in the forum, and that "marital domicile" could follow the domicile of one of the parties to the marriage. Williams (and Hendrix) *had* in fact established "domicile" in Nevada, at least as defined by Nevada's requirement of six weeks' residence in Nevada; North Carolina had not contested this point. Thus, the divorce decrees, being in conformity with Nevada's jurisdictional requirements, were certainly valid in Nevada, and, stated the Court, full faith and credit required all other states to recognize their validity as well. *Williams I* thus overturned the holding in *Haddock v. Haddock*—at least, that part of *Haddock* which concerned full faith and credit to *ex parte* divorce decrees.

Practical policy considerations may have favored the result in *Williams I*, but the specific reasoning relied on by the Court is not compelling and probably convinced no one. There is no escaping the fact that the *ex parte* divorce decrees in *Williams* seem flagrantly inconsistent with basic principles of fairness to the absent party, unless one chooses to credit the contrived notion that the "marital domicile" exists wherever either spouse happens to be at any given time and that the courts in that place can therefore dissolve the marriage with no unfairness to the stay-at-home spouse. As Justice Jackson wrote in dissent, the Court's opinion in *Williams I* implied that "settled family relationships may be destroyed by a procedure that we would not recognize if the suit were one to collect a grocery bill."[19] *Haddock v. Haddock* notwithstanding, conventional understandings of due process and personal jurisdiction should have suggested that the divorce decrees were not even valid in Nevada (should anyone with standing wish to challenge them there); *a fortiori*, they were not entitled to recognition in North Carolina.

The practical reality, however, is that by 1942 people were obtaining "Nevada divorces," or at least divorces outside the *bona fide* marital domicile, in ever greater numbers. Some such divorces were *ex parte* and against the wishes of one of the spouses; some were consensual; either way, a great many of them were evasions of the law of the marital domicile. These realities placed the Court in a difficult position. The law of domestic relations has always been regarded as the example *par excellence* of a matter confined to the

---

19. *Williams I*, 317 U.S. at 316 (Jackson, J., dissenting) (footnote omitted).

power of the states. The Court was plainly reluctant to place *direct* constitutional limitations on the power of a state (such as Nevada) to grant a divorce pursuant to its own rules, for example by establishing minimum constitutional standards for the period of "residence" requisite to a valid divorce. Indeed, to this day, it has never done so. Once, however, the Court chose not to limit directly Nevada's power to grant divorces to Williams and Hendrix—meaning that Nevada's divorce decrees by definition must be valid within Nevada—denying full faith and credit to those decrees in other states (as the Court had done in *Haddock*) would permit the legal status of family relationships to vary from state to state. The Court obviously found this an unpalatable result. The majority in *Williams I* probably saw little to admire in the Nevada divorce industry or in the behavior of the defendants in that case. Nor did they likely care for the idea that one state, through its idiosyncratic divorce laws and procedures, should be able to thwart the domestic relations policy of another (if not *all* others, as Justice Jackson suggested in dissent). But the majority no doubt viewed the result in *Williams I* as the lesser of two evils.

"Williams II": *Williams v. North Carolina* **(1945).** Yet the Court's decision in *Williams I* proved not to be the end of the matter. In the original bigamy prosecutions brought against Williams and Hendrix, the North Carolina courts, relying on *Haddock v. Haddock*, had denied that full faith and credit bound the state to recognize the Nevada divorces; they had not denied the validity *within Nevada* of the divorces rendered therein or contested the fact of "residence" in Nevada that had underlain the Nevada divorce decrees. In his concurring opinion in *Williams I*, Justice Frankfurter gave a broad hint that the result in that case (which, among other things, overruled *Haddock*) might have been different had North Carolina argued that the defendants' "domicile" within Nevada, a prerequisite even under Nevada law for the validity of the divorce decrees, was really a sham (despite the fact that the Nevada courts had found it to be bona fide).[20] The State of North Carolina thereupon took up this broad hint, retried Williams and Hendrix for bigamous cohabitation, and secured their convictions. The result was yet another appeal to the Supreme Court. And, this time, in *Williams II*, the Court upheld the convictions.

How could the Court justify coming to a different result from that reached in *Williams I*? Justice Frankfurter's majority opinion

---

20. Note that the legal definition of "domicile," however else it might vary from state to state, almost always includes a finding that the person in question intends to remain in the forum, or (in some formulations) has the "nonintention" of leaving. It is this "fact," often attained by a *pro forma* recitation by the party that is then uncritically accepted by the court, that most rankled Frankfurter and others considering the problem of interstate recognition of such divorces.

in *Williams II* held that the North Carolina courts were free to determine whether the defendants had legitimately acquired "domicile" in Nevada—and thus whether the Nevada court had jurisdiction to render the divorce decrees—notwithstanding the recitations of the defendants in their respective divorce proceedings (and acceptance of those recitations by the Nevada tribunal) that they had resided in Nevada for the requisite six weeks *and* that they intended (which they plainly did not) to stay in Nevada indefinitely. Having determined that the defendants never really established domicile in Nevada, the North Carolina court could legitimately conclude that it was not bound by the Nevada decrees. The bigamy prosecutions and convictions were thus upheld in *Williams II*.

The Court's opinion in *Williams II* is as notable for what it did not hold as for what it did. Frankfurter, in his majority opinion, never suggested that the Nevada decrees were in themselves not valid or binding within the state of Nevada. His opinion only held that North Carolina could subsequently inquire into the question of domicile in Nevada and on that basis refuse to recognize the Nevada divorces. The inference was thus inescapable that, after *Williams II*, Williams and Hendrix were a married couple in Nevada, but cohabiting bigamists in North Carolina. While acknowledging this fact, Frankfurter suggested in his opinion that there was less evil in this potential instability in marital status than there was in denying North Carolina its sovereign power to inquire independently into the *bona fides* of the parties' domicile in Nevada.

The Court's reasoning in *Williams II* might appear, on the surface, to be glaringly inconsistent with at least one conventional principle of issue preclusion and full faith and credit. Generally, although we recognize that the absence of jurisdiction in Court A is a basis for denying recognition of the judgment in Court B, Court A's actual *finding* that it had jurisdiction is itself binding; that issue thus cannot be relitigated in Court B. The holding in *Williams II* seems inconsistent with that principle, since the Nevada court had actually *found* that Williams and Hendrix had attained the statutorily defined domicile and that the Nevada court thus had jurisdiction to render a divorce in each of their cases. Three factors, however, explain why the inconsistency of *Williams II* with that full-faith-and-credit principle may be more apparent than real. First, a basic requirement for the operation of issue preclusion is that the issue have been actually litigated and determined in Case A. The Nevada court may have "determined" that it had jurisdiction, but it is a stretch to say that the issue had actually been "litigated." Both divorce proceedings were *ex parte*; neither the stay-at-home spouse nor anyone else was present to contest the jurisdictional question (or, for that matter, anything else) in the

Nevada court. Without a genuinely adversarial proceeding, one can't really think of the issue as having been "litigated," and thus the argument for interjurisdictional preclusion pursuant to full-faith-and-credit principles is quite attenuated. Second, the State of North Carolina was not a party in the Nevada proceedings, and could legitimately argue that the issue of domicile should not be *res judicata* as to *it*.

Third, in emphasizing that "domicile" (formally defined in terms of "marital domicile") in the forum had traditionally been regarded as the basis for jurisdiction to render divorce decrees, Frankfurter's opinion pointed to one of those logical conundrums for which conflict of laws seems to be such fertile soil. In the usual personal jurisdiction/full faith and credit scenario typified by the analysis in *Pennoyer v. Neff*, the jurisdictional finding by Court A that precludes collateral inquiry by Court B is usually a question of fact. For example, Court A might have found as a matter of fact that the defendant was served while in State A, making personal jurisdiction appropriate. Court B might later disagree with Court A's conclusion regarding that fact, but it's not because states A and B have different definitions of what it means to be "served while in State A"; they don't. Court B may simply think the evidence shows that the defendant was not served in State A. But that matter is *res judicata* because of issue preclusion, and full faith and credit bars Court B from inquiring into the matter anew. Even the more amorphous standard of "minimum contacts" that governs modern personal jurisdiction is a uniform constitutional standard, not one left to the different definitions given it by different states.

In emphasizing that "domicile" in the forum had traditionally been regarded as the basis for jurisdiction to render divorce decrees, however, Frankfurter referred to a concept that is not really a fact (like having been served while in the state), but a legal conclusion. What it means to be "domiciled" in a state for purposes of divorce jurisdiction is determined by that particular state's law, not by a universally accepted dictionary definition; and different states obviously define "domicile" differently (and a given state might even define the term differently for different legal purposes). If all states (including North Carolina) agreed that six weeks' residence in a state, and the intention to remain there indefinitely, satisfied the legal definition of "domicile" for the purpose of rendering a divorce decree, then (putting aside the "actually litigated and determined" question) the Nevada court's factual finding that Williams and Hendrix had satisfied these criteria would, seemingly, be binding on North Carolina. But there is no such universally accepted legal definition of "domicile." To say that Nevada has power to grant a divorce decree only if the party is domiciled there—and that, if she is, the Nevada court's finding is entitled to recognition elsewhere—is simply to invite another question: Who decides when a person is "domiciled" in Nevada, and is the decider's conclusion binding on tribunals in other states?

Once we put the question this way, one could see the problem actually as one of choice of law (although the Court did not view it in these terms). We have a conflict between two legal rules, those belonging to Nevada and North Carolina respectively, concerning the legal meaning of "domicile"—just as we might have a conflict concerning what kind of behavior constitutes negligence *per se* or acceptance of a contractual offer. Seen in this light, the Nevada court would have been in the position of deciding, in the first instance, whether Nevada or North Carolina law should apply to whether Williams and Hendrix had established "residence" or "domicile" in Nevada. We might suspect that, in light of the lovebirds' long residence in North Carolina and the location there of their marriages, the natural conclusion is that the Nevada court should apply North Carolina law governing domicile for purposes of divorce—presumably resulting in a refusal to render the divorce decrees. Of course, courts do not do this; in divorce proceedings, they invariably apply forum law to such central issues as the permissible grounds for divorce and satisfaction of the requirement of domicile. But even if it were true that courts sometimes apply foreign law in certain cases to resolve these issues, and the Nevada court flagrantly failed to do so in the divorce proceedings, the *Fauntleroy v. Lum* principle would require North Carolina to recognize the decrees and give effect to them; a "wrong" choice-of-law ruling cannot be the subject of collateral attack.

Of course, the majority in *Williams II* did not see the problem in this light. While never stating either that "domicile" in the forum was a *constitutional* prerequisite for divorce jurisdiction, or that there was some universal or constitutional definition of "domicile," Frankfurter strongly implied that Nevada's finding of domicile for Williams and Hendrix was in some way sufficiently dubious as to entitle the North Carolina court to disregard it, and determine for itself whether or not there had been *bona fide* domicile in Nevada. Presumably Frankfurter did not mean to suggest that Court B can *always* inquire independently into the validity of domicile in Case A. But the line between "sufficiently dubious" and "not sufficiently dubious" was not made clear.

The Rule of *Lex Fori* in Divorce Cases. Why, by the way, do courts in divorce cases never apply foreign law to such basic substantive questions as the permissible grounds for divorce? Application of forum law in all divorce cases is obviously not constitutionally required under the forgiving standards of *Pacifica Employers* and *Allstate v. Hague*, and if the prospect of conferring full-faith-and-credit status on decrees like Nevada's in the *Williams* cases seems troubling, perhaps the most sensible way of dealing with the problem is to insist that the forum not apply forum divorce law in obviously inappropriate circumstances. One advantage of this approach would be to avoid the specter of couples who are considered to be married in one state but not in another. It does seem that, if the underlying concern in a case like *Williams* is the ousting of North Carolina's legitimate authority over the marital status of a North Carolina couple, it would be simpler to impose limitations at the Case A (choice-of-law) stage rather than wait until the Case B (recognition) stage to raise the question. Thus, for example, what if one applied to divorce cases the constitutional standards for choice of law? While the constitutional limits established by cases like *Allstate v. Hague* are admittedly rather minimal, one might argue that application by the forum of its own law when another state has a dramatically better claim to be the state of "marital domicile"[21] violates the Constitution.

The short if unsatisfying answer is that that is just not the way things are. First, the Court in *Pacific Employers* specifically disavowed a constitutional test that would call for a *comparison* of the claims of two states to have their law applied to a case, and focused simply on whether the forum has the requisite connections with the dispute to justify application of its law. If the widow's post-accident move from Wisconsin to Minnesota in *Allstate v. Hague* could serve as a legitimate basis for the application of Minnesota law, it is hard to envision the Court questioning the authority of a state to apply its law in a divorce proceeding where one or both spouses have had at least some period of residence in the forum. More generally, as noted at the outset of this discussion, the Court is undoubtedly very reluctant to intervene directly in the proceedings established by a state to govern dissolution of a marriage; it's the paradigmatic example of a legal matter that belongs to state and not federal authority. And, as the rather unexacting standards established by *Pacific Employers* and *Hague* suggest, the Court has no interest in arbitrating questions about the constitutional limits of choice of law on a regular basis. The law applied by state courts to divorce matters is invariably forum law, and there is little law suggesting what in the way of bona fide domicile might be constitutionally required in order for a court to assert divorce jurisdiction in a particular case.

21. It is important to add here that the concept of "marital domicile" no longer plays the important role it once did in many legal questions concerning domestic relations. The phenomenon of spouses (estranged or otherwise) living in different states has become widespread enough for the concept of "marital domicile" to be of doubtful utility. Moreover, criticism of the traditional (but now extinct) rule that the domicile of the wife is legally presumed to be that of the husband helped to discredit the larger concept of "marital domicile" in many contexts.

2. Divorce by Consent

As suggested by Justice Jackson's "grocery bill" observation in his dissent in *Williams I*, the *ex parte* nature of the Nevada divorce proceedings in *Williams* is at least part of what gave some Justices pause about giving those decrees interstate issue preclusive effect *via* full faith and credit. This fact has implications that go far beyond the *Williams* cases. When the divorce is *ex parte*, as in *Williams*, enforcement of the resulting decree does seem troubling, especially when the stay-at-home spouse apparently would not even be subject to the jurisdiction of the divorcing court under conventional personal jurisdiction principles. But what about divorce by *consent*, in which each of the parties to a marriage wants a divorce, but (owing to the narrow grounds for divorce in their state of residence) must travel out of the marital domicile to obtain one? Such a situation, while still likely to involve a rather feigned display of domicile in the jurisdiction granting the divorce, at least avoids the overtones of unfairness to a stay-at-home spouse that were present in the *Williams* litigation. In other words, in an uncontested divorce, the court quite clearly does not lack jurisdiction over the parties, since each is consenting to jurisdiction. Should such divorces be entitled to full faith and credit in the marital domicile, free of the qualifications created by *Williams II*?

Although *Williams II* did not itself concern a consensual divorce, a close reading of Justice Frankfurter's majority opinion in that case suggests his belief that even divorce by consent ought not necessarily result in a decree that other states, in particular the original state of marital domicile, are bound by full faith and credit to recognize. Our usual reason for denying full faith and credit to a judgment rendered without personal jurisdiction is that the interests of the defendant were not adequately represented; this concern underlies the foundational principle of the law of preclusion that no one may be bound by a judgment in a case to which she was not a party. This concern would seem not to be present in the case of divorce by consent. But to Frankfurter (and at least some of his concurring brethren), what was most troubling about the absence of a genuine "contest" in *either* an *ex parte* or a consensual divorce was the lack of representation of the interests of the *state* of the original marital domicile, particularly if one or both of the divorcing parties were to return to that domicile after a divorce rendered elsewhere. What seemed unacceptable to them in the *Williams* scenario was the subversion of North Carolina's strong social policy concerning marriage and divorce, through the simple expedient of its resident(s) removing transiently to another state and then returning with divorce decrees (and a marriage license) in hand. This prospect was, to them, as unseemly in the case of divorce by consent as it was in the case of *ex parte* divorce; in both situations there was no assurance that the interests of the state of erstwhile (and future) marital domicile would be fairly considered in the divorce proceeding held elsewhere.

Sherrer v. Sherrer (1948). And so it was that Frankfurter dissented in *Sherrer v. Sherrer* (1948),[22] in which the Supreme Court ruled that divorces obtained by consent must be accorded full faith and credit and recognized in all other states. The facts in *Sherrer* were complex, but the essence of them is that the Sherrers, whose marital domicile had been in Massachusetts, were divorced in a proceeding filed by Mrs. Sherrer in Florida, in which Mr. Sherrer was present and which he had the opportunity to contest (he did not in fact contest it). Later, Mr. Sherrer brought an action in Massachusetts probate court, seeking a decree declaring that his wife had deserted him, which declaration would have terminated many of her dower rights. The Massachusetts probate court issued the decree, finding that Mrs. Sherrer had never intended to remain in Florida and that therefore the Florida divorce decree was not entitled to full faith and credit. The Massachusetts court in effect treated the situation as in form identical to that in *Williams II*: It regarded the process by which Mrs. Sherrer had obtained the Florida divorce decree as an evasion of Massachusetts divorce law, and the court regarded itself as entitled to inquire into the *bona fides* of the domicile that Mrs. Sherrer had obtained in Florida as a prerequisite to invoking its divorce jurisdiction.

The Supreme Court overturned the ruling of the Massachusetts courts and held that those courts were required by full faith and credit to recognize the legitimacy of the Florida divorce decree. The Court stressed that, unlike the stay-at-home spouses in *Williams*, Mr. Sherrer had appeared in the Florida proceeding and had had an opportunity to contest it. Therefore, there was no reason why full faith and credit should not apply. The facts of *Sherrer* were, admittedly, a bit unusual. Mr. Sherrer's "appearance" in the Florida proceeding seems to have been tepid and ambivalent, and the decree was rendered pursuant to a stipulation concerning custody arrangements and a deposition; Mr. Sherrer was never asked any questions on the record concerning domicile or, indeed, the merits of the divorce case. It is also less clear in this case than in *Williams* that Mrs. Sherrer (and her new husband) never intended to remain in Florida. Nevertheless, the doctrinal significance of the *Sherrer* decision is that divorce by consent is to be accorded full faith and credit—even when rendered by a court of a state in which the residence of the divorcing parties appears in retrospect to have been merely transient—so long as that period of

22. 334 U.S. 343 (1948).

residence at least resembles something that could reasonably be called "domicile."

Sherrer revealed that, unlike Frankfurter and the one other Justice who joined his dissent in that case, most of the Court regarded the holding in *Williams II* to be founded on the absence in that case of a genuine opportunity for the stay-at-home spouses to appear and to contest the divorce actions—not on the absence in those actions of meaningful representation of the interests of North Carolina. Justice Frankfurter might well be correct that *Sherrer* not only licensed sham divorces—based on declarations of intent to remain "which, in any other type of litigation, would be regarded as perjury, but which is not so regarded where divorce is involved because ladies and gentlemen indulge in it"[23]—but also, by means of the full faith and credit principle, forced their legal consequences upon states that had the greatest legitimate interest in the matter. But the Court has, probably understandably, preferred to look the other way.

If we step back a moment from the *Williams* and *Sherrer* cases and look at them in the context of the history and fundamental purposes of the Full Faith and Credit Clause, we can better understand the force of Justice Frankfurter's position. At the time the Constitution, with its FFC Clause guaranteeing interstate recognition of judgments, was ratified, the legal issue to which that guarantee was most obviously directed was judgments for debt. Debtors could remove to another state, perhaps their original home state, and escape the effect of judgments that had been rendered in favor of their creditors. In some cases, the courts of State B displayed little interest in protecting the judgment creditor's rights. The FFC Clause was designed largely to put a stop to this situation. The point here is that the Clause was drafted and ratified in an environment in which there was little variation among the states regarding fundamental legal rules. Probably no one present at the 1787 Convention seriously doubted that enforcement by one state's courts of judgments for debt rendered by the courts of another was a desirable legal principle, if not a moral obligation. The law of debt was common law shared by all the states, and its basic premises did not differ from state to state. Full faith and credit was not about enforcing judgments based on state law that was highly idiosyncratic or that differed in fundamental ways from the law of the forum.

The significance of the full-faith-and-credit principle had changed by the 1940s. Major differences among the laws of the states had long since become ubiquitous, including laws that might result in judicial judgments concerning such sensitive matters of state "policy" as divorce. Those differences were both real and

23. *Sherrer*, 334 U.S. at 367 (Frankfurter, J., dissenting).

legitimate. In the context of divorce, the FFC Clause could now seem to operate as a way of permitting the policy of an easy-divorce state to trump the law of a tough-divorce state, at least as to those domiciliaries of the latter willing to travel to the tribunals of the former.[24] Decisions like *Williams I* and *Sherrer v. Sherrer* thus implicated the Supreme Court, albeit indirectly, in the *de facto* regulation of norms of divorce law, perhaps *the* area that has usually been regarded as the exclusive province of the states. This was obviously not a scenario envisioned by those who had drafted and ratified the FFC Clause. One can thus understand why Justice Frankfurter (and others) might be disturbed by the uncritical application of full-faith-and-credit principles in the divorce cases, even if one disagrees with his conclusion that the state is like a "party" whose interests must be represented in the divorce proceeding if its results are to be given *res judicata* effect elsewhere.

What has rendered Frankfurter's position anachronistic is not any fundamental error in his reasoning, but the fact that state laws regarding divorce, while still exhibiting important differences from state to state, have gravitated toward the no-fault approach for consensual divorces. *Williams II* remains good law, so in cases of nonconsensual *ex parte* divorce, the state of the stay-at-home spouse still technically has the constitutional authority to relitigate, if it cares to do so, the question of the divorcing state's power to render the decree based on the absence of bona fide domicile. But the public as a whole does not care about these things as much as it once did, at least to the degree that would motivate local or state authorities to resist recognition of foreign divorces (by, for example, initiating prosecutions for bigamy). Of course, these questions still matter to some individuals. Not infrequently one sees disaffected spouses racing to courthouses in different states in order to obtain a divorce on more favorable terms than the other might. But, if anything, this simply reflects the now-general understanding that full-faith-and-credit obligations will attach to whichever court's decision is rendered first. The Court's decisions in *Williams I* and *Sherrer* did not cause liberalization in the laws and norms governing divorce in the United States, but rather reflected a realistic assessment of the interests involved and a sense of the direction in which divorce law was headed.

A Constitutional Standard for Domicile Prerequisite to Divorce Decrees? As we observed, the Court in *Williams II* did not deny that the divorces obtained by Williams and Hendrix in Nevada were in themselves valid and entitled to enforcement

24. Some may respond to the statement in the text by disparaging the value or legitimacy of divorce laws that limit the grounds of divorce, making it difficult to obtain. However that may be, that argument concerns the substantive law of divorce, not the appropriate interpretation of the FFC Clause.

within Nevada. Thus, the Court has never placed constitutional limits on the power of a state to render a divorce decree enforceable within its own boundaries. Should it? Should a state be able to render a divorce decree based on one spouse's residence within the forum for one day, or one hour? Note that, both with divorces by consent and *ex parte* divorces, there usually will be no one with standing to appeal a divorce decree, so that any challenges to the divorce will invariably come by way of collateral attack. In any case, the Supreme Court has shown no interest in imposing such constitutional limits on state authority to render divorce decrees valid within the state; it is only in the full-faith-and-credit/interstate recognition context that it has (in *Williams II*) imposed some modest limitations on Court B's obligation to give effect to a divorce decree rendered elsewhere. Even in that context we don't have a clear sense of the circumstances—how "dubious" the finding of domicile in Case A has to be—that will justify Court B in reexamining the question of domicile in Case A.

The question of constitutional limits on the power of a court to render a divorce did, however, arise in one interesting decision by the U.S. Court of Appeals for the Third Circuit in the 1950s. In 1953, the U.S. Virgin Islands, an unincorporated territory of the United States, enacted a law providing for divorce jurisdiction in its courts after the plaintiff's continuous presence in the territory for six weeks.[25] The defendant did not even have to be present in the territory, although he either had to have been served personally or have made a general appearance in the proceeding. In *Alton v. Alton* (3d Cir. 1953),[26] the Third Circuit held that the legislation violated the Due Process Clause of the Fifth Amendment:

> Domestic relations are a matter of concern to the state where a person is domiciled. An attempt by another jurisdiction to affect the relation of a foreign domiciliary is unconstitutional even though both parties are in court and neither one raises

---

25. Rather than defining "domicile" as six weeks' continuous residence, the Virgin Islands statute stated that such residence would be *"prima facie* evidence of domicile." With no party present to contest a consensual divorce, this presumption would not in fact be rebutted. The statute was obviously an effort by the Virgin Islands to create a market there for "migratory divorces" sought by residents in the United States whose home states' divorce laws made obtaining one difficult. Since the U.S. Virgin Islands is a territory of the United States, full-faith-and-credit obligations attach to the judgments of their courts.

26. 207 F.2d 667 (3d Cir. 1953), *vacated as moot*, 347 U.S. 610 (1954). The procedural posture of the *Alton* case, which permitted the case to be appealed to the Third Circuit, was unusual. The wife traveled to the Virgin Islands and sought a divorce, which her husband did not contest, from the local district court there in accord with the Virgin Islands law described in the text. The court, unsatisfied with the evidence of domicile, refused to grant the divorce, and the wife appealed that decision to the Third Circuit.

the question. The question may well be asked as to what the lack of due process is. The defendant is not complaining. Nevertheless, if the jurisdiction for divorce continues to be based on domicile, as we think it does, we believe it to be lack of due process for one state to take to itself the readjustment of domestic relations between those domiciled elsewhere.

The Third Circuit offered, as an alternative basis for its holding, the fact that the Virgin Islands Organic Act did not authorize the Virgin Islands to enact legislation providing for the granting of divorces to parties domiciled elsewhere. On petition for writ of certiorari, the Supreme Court vacated the Third Circuit's judgment as moot because in the interim the husband had obtained a divorce in the courts of Connecticut. So the Third Circuit's holding in *Alton v. Alton* perished in the cradle.[27] This is about as far as the federal courts have gone in trying to establish federal constitutional limits on the power of courts outside the marital domicile to render a divorce to which both spouses have consented.

3. *Foreign Divorces Not Subject to Full Faith and Credit*

For a variety of reasons, the divorce laws of the state of New York remained stringent long after many other states had liberalized theirs. Even today, there is no "no-fault" or "irreconcilable differences" divorce in New York. Until 1966, adultery was the sole ground for divorce specified by New York law. So long as this situation prevailed, it was not uncommon for relatively well-to-do (and unadulterous) New York couples, seeking a divorce but unenthusiastic about satisfying even Nevada's undemanding residency requirement, to seek and receive so-called "Mexican divorces," and then to return to New York. At the time, it was possible to obtain a divorce in certain border cities in Mexico upon a showing of merely one day's residence by one party to the marriage. Of course, even putting aside whether *Williams I* would require foreign recognition of divorces obtained pursuant to a residence period of one day, a divorce obtained in Mexico or any other foreign country is not entitled to full faith and credit by the FFC Clause. The question

---

27. Judge Hastie, dissenting in *Alton v. Alton*, offered an interesting alternative to the majority's analysis. He denied that "domicile" was a constitutional prerequisite to the exercise of divorce jurisdiction, and he believed that any objections to personal jurisdiction in the Altons' divorce proceeding were resolved by the fact that both spouses had consented to appear in the case. But an additional question, he opined, was raised by whose substantive law of divorce should be applied in the Virgin Islands litigation: that of the Virgin Islands, whose connections with the parties was modest, or that of Connecticut, the state of marital domicile. *Alton*, 207 F.2d at 685 (Hastie, J., dissenting). Whether or not the application of forum (Virgin Islands) law would be unconstitutional is an interesting question. But the short answer to all of this is that state courts do not apply the substantive law of other states with respect to the permissible grounds for divorce.

nevertheless remained for courts in states like New York as to whether they should, as a matter of public policy, choose to recognize and give effect to such divorces. Note that one of the considerations that likely played an important role in *Williams I*—that it is highly undesirable to establish rules of law making a person married in one state and not in another—may have less force in the context of foreign divorces. Note also that, for the most part, we are speaking here of consensual divorces, so that the due process rights of stay-at-home spouses are not at issue. Over a period of many years, various lower New York courts had held, if sometimes reluctantly, that such "Mexican divorces"[28] should be recognized in New York, until the New York Court of Appeals in 1965 held explicitly in *Rosenstiel v. Rosenstiel* that "public policy" militated in favor of recognition—largely because of the number of people who had relied on the effectiveness of such divorces based on the earlier lower court decisions.[29] Courts in many other states have declined to recognize such divorces, and it is ironic (though hardly inexplicable) that the state whose divorce law is best known for its stringency is also the only state whose courts have unambiguously recognized so-called "quickie divorces" obtained outside the United States.

The problem raised by "quickie divorces" not subject to full faith and credit, and the recognition they should receive, is less pertinent now than in the past. Certainly, consensual divorces are easy enough to obtain in many states, and even states that retain stricter grounds for divorce usually are not highly motivated to bring the force of local law against domiciliaries who have returned after removing transiently to an "easier" jurisdiction to obtain a divorce. *Ex parte* divorces, particularly those imposed on unwilling spouses, can still lead to fierce legal battles and the occasional interjurisdictional recognition problem; but public policy has ceased to favor keeping an unhappy spouse in a marriage he or she no longer wants.

---

28. The phrase "Mexican divorce" no longer makes sense, since one-day divorces are no longer available under Mexican law. There are other choices, however. *See, e.g.*, Joseph B. Treaster, *A Weekend in Haiti Can Include a Divorce*, NEW YORK TIMES, July 12, 1986; Steely Dan, *Haitian Divorce*, from THE ROYAL SCAM (ABC/Dunhill 1976).

29. *Rosenstiel v. Rosenstiel*, 16 N.Y.2d 64, 262 N.Y.S.2d 86, 209 N.E.2d 709 (1965). The facts of Rosenstiel reveal another way in which collateral attack on an earlier divorce decree can arise: The defendant's second husband sought an annulment of their marriage,

based on his contention that the defendant's divorce in Mexico from her first husband was invalid because based on sham domicile there. The *Rosenstiel* decision was not without its critics. *See* David P. Currie, *Suitcase Divorce in the Conflict of Laws*: Simons, Rosenstiel, *and* Borax, 34 UNIVERSITY OF CHICAGO LAW REVIEW 26 (1966). Apart from the predictable observations about the evasion of New York divorce law and policy, critics noted that the "privilege" of a Mexican divorce was reserved for those New Yorkers wealthy enough to afford a trip to Mexico and a hotel stay of at least one night there.

4. Dissolution of Same–Sex Marriages and Civil Unions

Those states that have legalized same-sex marriage naturally provide for dissolution of such marriages—divorces—on the same grounds as are specified for opposite-sex marriages. A problem of interstate recognition might arise, however, if one or both spouses in a same-sex marriage that is valid under the laws of State A seeks a dissolution of that marriage in State B, which does not recognize same-sex marriage. Fundamentally, the problem reduces to whether and to what extent Court B will "recognize" the marriage itself, which of course the FFC Clause does not oblige them to do. Invariably, State B's law governing divorce applies to dissolution of "marriages"; if there is no legally cognizable marriage before Court B, there is nothing for the law of State B to dissolve. Court B could, of course, choose to recognize the same-sex marriage and adjudicate the divorce petition on that basis; alternatively, it could choose to recognize the same-sex marriage for purposes of divorce only, and adjudicate the divorce petition on that basis. Or Court B could decline jurisdiction over the divorce proceeding on the ground that state law provides for divorce proceedings only in the case of a legally recognized marriage. There is as yet little case law on this precise question. Legalization of same-sex marriage is still new, and presumably same-sex spouses seeking a divorce can resort to the tribunals of the state in which they were legally married.

An analogous problem has arisen, however, with attempts to dissolve same-sex "civil unions." A number of states have created the legal status of "civil union" in lieu of the status of marriage as such. Civil union statutes, which have been around longer than laws providing for legal same-sex marriage, usually provide that the benefits attaching to civil-union status are the same as those enjoyed by married couples. In some cases, a disaffected member of a same-sex union consecrated in State A has sought to attain a dissolution of that union under the divorce laws of State B, which does not itself recognize the legal institution of civil union. For example, in both *Rosengarten v. Downes* (Conn. 2002)[30] and *B.S. v. F.B.* (N.Y. Sup. Ct. 2009),[31] one member of a civil union that had been performed under the laws of Vermont (which legally sanctions such unions) sought dissolution under the divorce laws of another state which did not provide for civil unions. In both cases the courts determined that they lacked subject matter jurisdiction to entertain the divorce petitions, because forum law did not provide the court with jurisdiction to dissolve "civil unions." There is an interesting difference between the two decisions, however. In *Rosengarten*, the

---

30. 71 Conn.App. 372, 802 A.2d 170 (2002). An appeal in *Rosengarten* was eventually dismissed as moot upon the death of Rosengarten.

31. 25 Misc.3d 520, 883 N.Y.S.2d 458 (Sup.Ct. 2009).

Connecticut court relied in part on the fact that "the Connecticut legislature has not demonstrated a willingness to recognize civil unions." In *B.S. v. F.B.*, by contrast, an executive order has required New York officials to recognize same-sex *marriages*; the court's decision, therefore, rests much more on the simple textual observation that the divorce statute applies only to "married" persons. One possible inference from this is that the New York courts could assume subject matter jurisdiction in a divorce proceeding brought by a spouse in a same-sex *marriage* celebrated under the laws of another state, whereas the Connecticut courts are not likely to take that position.

Both *Rosengarten* and *B.S. v. F.B.* appear to involve partners who traveled to Vermont in order to celebrate a civil union there and then returned to their original state, where they sought to initiate a dissolution proceeding. If a similar situation arose in which a same-sex couple traveled briefly to another state solely for the purpose of being married there, it would not be surprising if courts in some states (such as Connecticut) were disinclined in such cases to choose to recognize such foreign marriages, even if only for the purpose of granting a divorce.

5. The Incidents of Marriage and "Divisible Divorce"

As often as not, divorce decrees include provisions for important matters that go beyond simple termination of a marriage. Spousal support (still known in some places as "alimony" or "maintenance"), division of property, child support, and child custody are the most common issues to arise. Moreover, the status of a marriage will affect many default rules of law concerning, for example, disposition of property upon death in case of intestacy and rights of dower. The question is whether the full-faith-and-credit principles set out by the *Williams* cases and by *Sherrer v. Sherrer* apply to these effects of a marriage's dissolution precisely as they do to the divorce itself. The answer is that they do not. The complexity of the issues—a product of the immense variety of the kinds of legal issues created by separation and divorce, multiplied by the confusing and inconsistent way in which the Supreme Court has treated the different full-faith-and-credit problems that have arisen in the area—can be overwhelming.

In *Estin v. Estin* (1948),[32] the Supreme Court held that a Nevada *ex parte* divorce decree, while entitled to full faith and credit in the New York courts, could not operate to terminate the obligations of one of the spouses to make monthly payments of alimony pursuant to a pre-existing New York separation decree. The precise reasoning of the Court in *Estin* is perhaps less impor-

---

32.   334 U.S. 541 (1948).

tant than the fact that the case established the principle of "divisible divorce." As per *Williams I*, New York was required by full faith and credit to recognize the Nevada divorce decree. In other words, the parties must be recognized as divorced in New York as well as Nevada. The Court, however, ruled that the same was not true of the decree as it respected the husband's previously established alimony obligations. Stripped to its essentials, the Court's reasoning was that a proceeding in which the "stay-at-home" spouse did not appear (and over whom the Nevada court would not have personal jurisdiction under conventional principles outside the divorce area) should not operate to determine conclusively that party's property rights (in this case, in her alimony award). Full faith and credit was not due to such a ruling. Taken by itself, this is a sensible observation: It accords with basic principles concerning full faith and credit and the authority of courts to determine the rights of persons over whom they do not have jurisdiction.[33] Since, however, *Estin* was decided against the backdrop of *Williams I*, which had upheld the authority of courts to render *ex parte* divorce decrees, the two cases together raised the prospect that a divorce decree could be considered, for purposes of full faith and credit, "half good and half bad," in the words of Justice Jackson—good for purposes of terminating the marriage, bad for purposes of settling alimony rights (and presumably other incidents of the marriage).

Actually, the Court's holding in *Estin* is a bit puzzling, since the Nevada decree itself said nothing about the husband's alimony obligations. The Court's analysis would have followed quite naturally had the Nevada divorce decree specifically included a provision setting Mr. Estin's monthly alimony obligations at zero, or some number different from that specified by the New York separation order, but such was not the case. The Court's analysis perhaps makes more sense in light of the fact that, under *New York* law at the time, a divorce decree evidently operated to terminate any alimony obligations that had been made pursuant to a prior separation order. As both Justice Jackson and Justice Frankfurter observed in their separate dissenting opinions, since *Williams I* re-

---

33. One logical problem created by the reasoning in *Estin*, however, is that it would appear to cast doubt on the constitutionality of Nevada's giving preclusive effect *within Nevada* to an order in an *ex parte* divorce case purporting to terminate a previous support order. Precisely because the Court in *Estin* assimilated the property-disposition aspects of a divorce decree to the usual rules for personal jurisdiction *in personam* cases, termination of property rights in an *ex parte* proceeding would appear to be, at least under the older *Pennoyer* standard for personal jurisdiction, unconstitutional, so long as the stay-at-home spouse was outside Nevada. Of course, to posit the existence of a *previous* support order rendered by a Nevada court suggests the kind of connections with Nevada on the part of the stay-at-home spouse that might validate personal jurisdiction under the current *International Shoe* standard. In any case, Nevada had not in fact provided that its divorce decrees operated to terminate pre-existing support obligations.

quired recognition of the Nevada divorce decree, the New York courts must give the Nevada divorce decree the same effect they would give a New York decree—presumably, an abrogation of the pre-existing support obligation ("New York ... may not ... discriminate against a Nevada decree granted to one there domiciled, and afford it less effect than it gives to a decree of its own with similar jurisdictional foundation"[34]). This assertion, though, is actually more debatable than it appears at first glance. Full faith and credit generally requires Court B, as per 28 U.S.C. § 1738, to give the judgments of Court A the same effect that they would have in State A, not the same effect that similar judgments rendered by courts of State B would have within that state. Would it not make as much sense to ask what effect Nevada gives *its own* divorce decrees with respect to pre-existing support obligations, and then require the New York courts to adhere to that? An answer to this question does not emerge from any of the opinions in *Estin v. Estin*. But, if in fact Nevada law did *not* state that a decree of divorce rendered by its courts automatically terminates the effect of a support order previously made by a Nevada court with respect to the same parties, then the result ordained by the Supreme Court in *Estin* makes sense and is consistent with full faith and credit and § 1738.

Because the Court's opinion in *Estin* placed considerable emphasis on the "property interest" held by Mrs. Estin in the New York support order, several important cases decided after *Estin* have turned on whether particular matters affected by an *ex parte* divorce decree qualify as a "property interest" such that the decree is entitled to no full faith and credit with respect to those matters. For example, certain spousal rights, whether created by common law or created by statute, can come into being upon marriage and terminate when the marriage has been dissolved. Others are treated as "inchoate," coming into being only upon the occurrence of some event such as the other spouse's death. Does full faith and credit require that an *ex parte* divorce, rendered by a court that lacks personal jurisdiction over the absent spouse, be given effect by other states not only as to the termination of the marriage but also as to the termination of rights that inhered in the marriage? *Kahn v. Kahn* (S.D.N.Y. 1992) is a dramatic illustration, not only of the implications of the *Estin* "divisible divorce" doctrine, but of the myriad problems of law and lawyering created by full-faith-and-credit doctrine after *Williams*.[35]

Alfred and Miriam Kahn were married in 1949. He subsequently became a professor at Columbia University, where he held a TIAA–CREF retirement annuity policy. The federal Retirement

---

34. 334 U.S. at 552 (Frankfurter, J., dissenting).

35. 801 F.Supp. 1237 (S.D.N.Y. 1992).

Equity Act of 1984, an amendment to ERISA, entitled his spouse to demand a joint and survivor annuity option upon his retirement and election to receive annuity benefits. Alfred Kahn filed for divorce from Miriam in 1974 in New York, but the court ruled he had not proved the grounds (cruel and inhuman treatment) for divorce under New York law. Instead, the court entered a separation order which, among other things, required him to pay Miriam $500 per week in support. In 1979, having moved to New Jersey, Alfred obtained an *ex parte* divorce there. When he retired and elected to receive annuity benefits in 1989, he chose a single life option, and Miriam sued in New York court to compel Alfred to select the joint and survivor annuity option. (The case, in which TIAA–CREF was also named as a defendant, was removed to federal district court.) The Federal District Court acknowledged that, while New York was bound to recognize the New Jersey divorce as such, under *Estin v. Estin* that divorce could not *ipso facto* terminate Miriam's property rights under New York law. Therefore, Miriam's entitlement to the $500 in weekly support survived the New Jersey divorce decree. But what about Miriam's right to compel Alfred to select the joint and survivor annuity option? The Court ruled that the New Jersey decree, which New York must respect, had brought to an end Miriam's status as a "spouse," and only a "spouse" had the right under the Retirement Equity Act to compel the selection by Alfred of the joint and survivor annuity option once he elected to receive benefits in 1989. Therefore, after the 1979 divorce Miriam no longer had the right to compel Alfred to select the joint and survivor annuity option.

To distinguish between Miriam's $500–per–week right to support and her right to joint benefits under Alfred's annuity policy might appear somewhat arbitrary, although the court's opinion (which acknowledged the harshness of the result) seems legally sound. More than that, however, *Kahn v. Kahn* underscores the very real hardships that can be worked by the Supreme Court's holding in *Williams* that *ex parte* divorces are entitled to full faith and credit. Miriam, who did not want to be divorced, prevailed in the divorce proceeding in New York, which was the marital domicile; the subsequent *ex parte* divorce operated to deprive her of a valuable benefit to which she would have been legally entitled had there been no divorce. While the possibility of such results may be a necessary price to pay for a constitutional doctrine that enables unhappy spouses to obtain divorces that are entitled to recognition everywhere in the country, it does demonstrate that the costs can be high for "stay-at-home" spouses.

C. Interstate Recognition of Child Custody Decrees

1. Full Faith and Credit and Domestic Child Custody Decrees

As we've seen, application of full-faith-and-credit principles to divorce decrees is awkward, even though such decrees are "judgments." The situation is even more difficult with respect to child custody decrees, which are also judgments. Unlike divorce decrees as such, custody orders are usually modifiable. The substantive law governing custody disputes in most states centers on the "best interests of the child" standard, and that is an inherently subjective paradigm on whose application reasonable people can disagree in many cases; in other words, it would be fatuous to suppose that all courts would agree on what result would emerge in an individual case from application of the "best interests of the child" standard for custody. Finally, questions of child custody in a marriage whose bonds have frayed usually provoke strong feelings and can move people to exercise self-help in defiance of the law.

Uncritical application of full-faith-and-credit principles might suggest that, whenever a court having jurisdiction over the matter issues a custody order, that order is binding on courts everywhere in the United States. But things cannot be that simple, because most custody orders are modifiable, in contemplation of the fact that circumstances can change and perhaps call for revision of the custody arrangement.[36] If we recall that 28 U.S.C. § 1738 requires state courts to give the judgment of a sister state the same effect that the sister state would give it, it would appear that so long as Court B (or C, or D) could establish jurisdiction over the child, it would have the same power to modify the original custody decree as would the Court A that originally issued it. The problem is that, consistent though this principle might be with conventional notions concerning interjurisdictional preclusion, it would permit a parent disappointed with the custody determination in Case A simply to remove the child to State B (or C, or D) and seek modification there. Unfortunately, that temptation is not always resisted. In the case of a very young child, a parent acting in defiance of Court A's ruling by removing the child to State B can quite possibly profit from the removal; if enough time passes before proceedings are initiated in Court B, the "best interests of the child" standard might lead that court to place the child (albeit reluctantly) in the custody of the wrongdoer, because most psychologists regard disruption in the stability of a very young child's relationship with his primary caregiver to be detrimental to the child's well-being. Sensible judicial resolution of custody disputes requires that most orders be presumptively modifiable upon changed circumstances; but the intrinsic modifiability of custody decrees, combined with conven-

---

36. This observation calls to mind the Supreme Court's decision in *Yarbor-* *ough v. Yarborough*, 290 U.S. 202 (1933), discussed in Chapter 5.

tional full-faith-and-credit theory, is an invitation to repetitive (and perhaps destructive) litigation.

There have been many legal efforts to ameliorate the effects of full-faith-and-credit doctrine in this area. For American lawyers dealing in custody matters, three statutes are crucial starting points in dealing with the problems of jurisdiction to render judgments in custody cases and interjurisdictional recognition of those judgments. These statutes are (1) the Uniform Child Custody Jurisdiction and Enforcement Act ["UCCJEA"], which is a revision of the similarly titled Uniform Child Custody Jurisdiction Act ["UCCJA"]; (2) the federal Parental Kidnapping Prevention Act ["PKPA"], part of which is codified at 28 U.S.C. § 1738A; and (3) the federal International Child Abduction Remedies Act, implementing the Hague Convention on the Civil Aspects of International Child Abduction.

The UCCJA. Let us begin with the UCCJA, which has largely been superseded by the UCCJEA. Uniform acts, of course, are promulgated by the National Conference of Commissioners on Uniform State Laws, and, as with any other statute, become law in a particular state only by specific enactment there. The UCCJA was promulgated in 1968 and was eventually adopted by all 50 states and the District of Columbia; its effectiveness depended heavily not only on its widespread adoption (since part of the problem to which it was addressed was lack of uniformity among the states in the exercise of jurisdiction to make, modify, and enforce custody decrees) but also on consistency from state to state in its interpretation. The UCCJA and UCCJEA manifestly do *not* purport to create substantive standards for child custody determinations. The first goal of the UCCJA was to clarify the basis on which a court could legitimately exercise initial jurisdiction in a custody matter. Under conventional notions of personal and subject matter jurisdiction, one parent's ability to remove a child to another state could enable him to litigate custody in a forum advantageous to himself, or could conceivably divest the child's real "home state" of jurisdiction to decide the matter. The UCCJA's jurisdiction provisions attempted to vest initial jurisdiction in the court that made the most overall sense, given its access to information about the child and the family. A second important goal of the UCCJA was to discourage simultaneous litigation of custody issues in courts of different states. The Uniform Act's jurisdiction provisions made initial jurisdiction possible in more than one state, but the Act provided that, once a court had assumed jurisdiction "substantially in conformity with" the Act's jurisdictional provisions, the courts of another state should not exercise jurisdiction in the matter, even if it would have been entitled to had the case come to that court first. (This provision did largely eliminate the specter of two courts battling simultaneously over the same custody issues, but it also created a clear incentive for a "race to the courthouse" by the individual parents seeking a favorable forum.)

A third goal, of course, was to provide clearer parameters for the conditions under which a court could modify the custody order of the court initially exercising jurisdiction. This provision attempted to refine the general full-faith-and-credit principle that any "new" court having jurisdiction over the child might freely modify the existing order so long as the initial court had power to do so as well. The Uniform Act specified instead that a second court should exercise jurisdiction to modify (assuming it possessed such jurisdiction pursuant to the Act's own jurisdictional requirements) *only* if the original court no longer had jurisdiction (for example, because of a permanent change in the child's location) or had explicitly declined to decline its jurisdiction to modify. The design here was to create a presumption that the court that initially assumed jurisdiction and entered the first custody order should have the exclusive authority to modify it. The Act, however, also provided for the identification of a new initial "custody court" once the family's ties with the original court were no longer sufficient to justify jurisdiction there. Other provisions of the Uniform Act encouraged communication among courts of different states concerning a particular custody matter and transfer of relevant evidence to the court exercising initial jurisdiction. Overall, the Act attempted to ensure that custody matters are handled by one court at a time, while making possible a change in that court when circumstances imperatively demanded it.

The UCCJA was a thoughtful effort to resolve a difficult problem, and its adoption by all 50 states and the District of Columbia promised at least some measure of clarity and rationality concerning jurisdiction to render, modify, and enforce child custody decrees. That promise remained to some extent unfulfilled, however, partly because the UCCJA provided for four (4) alternative bases for initial jurisdiction. The first of these bases was the child's "home state," a term whose meaning might be contested in particular cases but which in many situations has a clear, intuitive meaning;[37] other, alternative bases for jurisdiction included one defined by the "best interests of the child" standard, emergency jurisdiction based on imminent danger to the child, and a catch-all

---

37. The more recently enacted UC-CJEA provides this definition of "home state": "The state in which a child lived with a parent or a person acting as a parent for at least six consecutive months immediately before the commencement of a child custody proceeding." It is clear, then, that cases can easily arise in which no "home state" as thus defined exists, as in the case of a child whose parent(s) move from state to state for short periods of time.

provision in case none of the other three criteria could be satisfied. The Act did not privilege "home state" jurisdiction over the other possible bases for initial jurisdiction, and so a race to the courthouse (perhaps even involving kidnapping) still could result in jurisdiction's being vested in a court outside the child's "home state" even if that state might appear in other respects to be an inferior forum. Custody orders in such situations would be subject to recognition and enforcement under full-faith-and-credit principles, and of course the courts of any state that had adopted the UCCJA were bound not to modify the initial court order unless it could be said that that court no longer had jurisdiction as defined by the Act. In particular, the jurisdictional alternative based on subjective "best-interests-of-the-child" considerations gave courts wide latitude to find jurisdiction, and frequently enmeshed them in an analysis of the substantive question of custody as a way of determining jurisdiction—something the Uniform Act's drafters had clearly not intended. Before looking at how the UCCJEA attempts to ameliorate this and other problems with the UCCJA, we need to look briefly at the federal Parental Kidnapping Prevention Act.

The Federal Parental Kidnapping Prevention Act. Partly as a result of the problems created by the alternative bases for jurisdiction created by the UCCJA, Congress in 1981 enacted the Parental Kidnapping Prevention Act ["PKPA"], which amended 28 U.S.C. § 1738 with respect to state-court child-custody orders. The PKPA largely incorporated the Uniform Act's criteria concerning initial and modification jurisdiction and enforcement, with one crucial exception: It upheld mandatory interstate enforcement of custody orders entered by courts exercising "home state" jurisdiction, but provided only in very limited circumstances for full faith and credit to orders entered by courts exercising jurisdiction on one of the other bases specified in the Uniform Act. In other words, for purposes of full faith and credit, the PKPA privileged custody orders rendered by courts exercising "home state" jurisdiction over custody orders rendered by courts asserting jurisdiction on some other basis. Among other things, this made it possible in many cases for a "Court B" to deny recognition to, or to exercise modification jurisdiction with respect to, a standing custody order that had been rendered by a court outside the "home state" (assuming that such a home state existed). This in turn reduced some of the incentives to kidnapping (or certain other kinds of strategic litigation behavior) that the UCCJA's ecumenical definition of initial jurisdiction had created. Obviously, the PKPA could not and did not purport to establish the conditions under which a state court could assert jurisdiction in the first instance over a custody matter (this would seem to be beyond the constitutional authority of Congress), but it created a particular jurisdictional criterion—"home state" jurisdiction—for the kinds of orders that would henceforth be subject to full faith and credit.

The UCCJEA. The PKPA's prioritization of "home state" jurisdiction in custody matters was a salutary development, but it created an inconsistency with the UCCJA. This is one reason, though not the only one, why the National Conference of Commissioners on Uniform State Laws promulgated a new uniform law, the Uniform Child Custody Jurisdiction and Enforcement Act ["UCCJEA"] in 1997 to replace the UCCJA. The UCCJEA, like the PKPA, prioritizes "home state" jurisdiction, making clear that a court of a different state has jurisdiction only if no state qualifies as a "home state" or a court of the "home state" has declined jurisdiction. In addition, the UCCJEA removes the phrase "best interests of the child" from the provisions governing jurisdiction, so as to eliminate confusion between the jurisdictional and substantive analysis regarding custody. As of this writing, 48 states and the District of Columbia have adopted the UCCJEA; only Massachusetts and Vermont have not, and bills have been introduced in the legislatures of each of those states that would codify the UCCJEA.

The difficult questions raised with respect to both jurisdiction and enforcement by the UCCJEA are more numerous than can be itemized here. The bottom line is that a thorough understanding of both the UCCJEA and the PKPA is important for practitioners of family law. The important points to underscore here are these: Custody decrees are judgments, and thus fall within the ambit of full faith and credit, as implemented by Congress (for example, the PKPA, 28 U.S.C. § 1738A). The fact that many if not most custody decrees are modifiable, however, puts those decrees in a unique category and substantially complicates the problem of interstate recognition and enforcement. Even at the time of the initial legal proceeding, more than one state can plausibly claim an interest in the matter justifying assumption of jurisdiction by its courts; the significance of another state's interest can grow more plausible as time passes and the child's needs and even her location, as well as the circumstances of her parents, may change. Custody issues tend to arouse strong feelings in parents, and the possibility of concurrent jurisdiction can give rise to strategic behavior and even kidnapping as a way of securing a favorable ruling, so long as principles of concurrent power to modify prevail. The UCCJEA (supplanting the UCCJA) and the federal PKPA are efforts to rationalize the principles governing jurisdiction and interstate enforcement custody orders, such that incentives both to kidnap and to race to the courthouse may be reduced, and courts' obligations to yield to the jurisdiction that has already properly assumed power over the case are made firmer. Those laws do not eliminate what one scholar has called the "tragedy of the inter-state child,"[38] but they do provide something of a framework for judicial superintendence of this difficult problem.

2. *International Child Abduction: The Hague Convention*

Child abduction in the context of custody disputes is a problem of international dimension. The Hague Convention on the Civil Aspects of International Child Abduction, to which the United States is a signatory, attempts both to provide a remedy for international abductions in violation of pre-existing custody rights, and to deter such abductions by reducing the likelihood that an abductor can obtain a more favorable forum for a custody determination by removing the child to a different country. Of course, the Convention's provisions apply only in cases where both of the relevant countries have signed and implemented it. The United States has implemented the Hague Convention by enacting the International Child Abduction Remedies Act ["ICARA"], enforceable in American courts.

The "Remedy of Return." The Convention's centerpiece is its provision for a "remedy of return" in cases where a child has been abducted to another country in violation of a pre-existing custody determination. In the United States, the aggrieved parent files an application under the Convention in the state or federal court where the child is located. The "remedy of return" is a provisional remedy, in that proceedings under the convention are not intended to inquire substantively into the question of custody, but merely to determine whether the child should be returned to the jurisdiction from which he has been taken; moreover, formally speaking the "return" is to the jurisdiction, not to the "left-behind" parent as such, although in practice it may sometimes be difficult to distinguish between the two.

Return Under the Hague Convention and the Risk of Domestic Violence. Kidnapping as such is universally condemned, and at first glance it might seem difficult to argue with a "remedy of return" in cases covered by the Hague Convention. However, a number of difficult issues have arisen under the Convention. In particular, the questions of abduction and of the appropriate remedy can assume a different complexion when the abducting parent claims to have acted in order to rescue the child from domestic violence or abuse. Most likely, the general assumption behind the Convention when it was first drafted was that abductions were largely carried out by male parents and that women parents would be the ones mostly likely to seek a remedy under the

---

38. Anne B. Goldstein, *The Tragedy of the Interstate Child: A Critical Reexamination of the Uniform Child Custody* *Jurisdiction Act and the Parental Kidnapping Prevention Act*, 25 U.C. DAVIS LAW REVIEW 845 (1992).

Convention. In practice, the reverse has been true, with a large number of applicants for return being men whose wives or companions have removed the child to another country allegedly to escape violence or abuse at the hands of the male partner. Importantly, the Convention provides an exception to the presumptive "remedy of return" if "there is a grave risk that his or her return would expose the child to physical or psychological harm or otherwise place the child in an intolerable situation." Proper interpretation of this provision has been frequently litigated in American courts (and elsewhere) since implementation of the Convention.

The possibility of "grave risk" of physical or psychological harm to the child, making the remedy of return inappropriate in some cases, does not necessarily mean that the only alternative to return is denial of relief to the applicant altogether and leaving the child with the abducting parent. After all, invocation of the Convention by the left-behind parent rests on the fact that he has some sort of pre-existing custody right. (Needless to say, irrespective of the danger of violence or abuse at the hands of the left-behind parent, the Convention does not clothe abductions under any circumstances with legal legitimacy.) Accordingly, the Convention provides that return subject to "undertakings," or conditions, may be appropriate in certain circumstances; such undertakings might include, for example, an agreement that the child will be returned to the original country but not remanded to the custody of the left-behind parent, until a hearing is held by a tribunal of that original country concerning the allegations of abuse and the propriety of maintaining custody in the party remaining in that country. Here, as elsewhere, the Convention struggles to find a balance between (1) a substantive concern for the child's welfare and (2) a proper respect for the capacity of the original country's tribunals to ensure it. American courts applying the Convention have sometimes been faced with the uncomfortable question of determining whether returning the child to the tribunals of the original country will satisfactorily protect the child from the threat of violence or abuse.[39]

Moreover, determining whether there is in fact "a grave risk that his or her return would expose the child to physical or psychological harm or otherwise place the child in an intolerable situation" is often a vexed question. It is one thing to find the existence of such a "grave risk" where there is evidence of actual prior abuse of the child. But there can be more difficult situations, such as when the vulnerability to violence or abuse pertains more directly to the abducting parent (usually, the mother) than to the

---

39. *See, e.g., Van de Sande v. Van de Sande*, 431 F.3d 567, 572 (7th Cir. 2005) ("Concern with comity among nations argues for a narrow interpretation of the 'grave risk of harm' defense; but the safety of children is paramount").

child as such, and it is argued that the child may suffer irreparable psychological harm as a result of witnessing continued violence directed against the mother. The contention can be a plausible one in many cases, but resolving it will often be difficult and perhaps require expert psychological assessments. This can turn the proceeding under the Convention, generally designed to quickly make available a provisional remedy so that actual custody matters can be determined by the tribunals in the proper country, into something resembling a custody contest itself, featuring psychological testimony that delves into family dynamics and considerations of parental fitness. Some scholars have balked at this use of proceedings under the convention, while others regard it as sometimes necessary to give meaning to the "grave risk" exception to the remedy of return.[40] Because some cases clearly do feature the risk of violence and abuse to the mother, these questions concerning "return" proceedings under the Convention have become something of a battleground about law's treatment of domestic violence more generally.

"Custody Rights" and *Ne Exeat* Clauses. As noted, the Convention provides a "remedy of return" only in cases where abduction of the child has violated the "custody rights" of the left-behind parent. What qualifies as a "custody right"? In the United States, to say that a parent has "custody rights" usually means that the parent has been granted full or joint custody or custody subject to certain conditions. For example, "visitation rights" might not be regarded as a "custody right" as such. Outside the United States, the phrase "custody rights" can have a broader reach, and its use in the Convention could be read as providing the remedy of return even in some cases where the left-behind parent did not have a legally adjudicated right to custody. In particular, the use of so-called *"ne exeat"* clauses is fairly common in European and South American countries; these are orders that prohibit a custodial parent from removing a child from the jurisdiction, even though the other parent may have no right to custody as such.

When a *"ne exeat* clause" has been incorporated in a judicial order, does abduction constitute a violation of "custody rights" held by the non-custodial parent, such that the Convention's "remedy of return" will apply? There is a lot riding on this question. A court granting custody to one parent may well consider it important, for a variety of reasons, to assure that the other parent's rights of access to the child are respected as well. The *ne exeat* clause might,

---

40. *Compare* Linda Silberman, *The Hague Child Abduction Convention Turns Twenty: Gender Politics and Other Issues*, 33 NEW YORK UNIVERSITY JOURNAL OF INTERNATIONAL LAW AND POLICY 221, 239 (2000) (opposing this use of proceedings under the Convention) *with* Merle H. Weiner, *International Child Abduction and the Escape from Domestic Violence*, 69 FORDHAM LAW REVIEW 593, 662

in some cases, be part of a provisional order pending ultimate determination of the custody question. To deny outright the remedy of return after abduction in some of these cases might be to license subversion of the custody determination process altogether. On the other hand, the concepts of "custody" and of "access" do seem to be distinct from one another. A spirited, if not vehement, disagreement has sprung up among both courts and scholars concerning the relationship between the Convention's remedy of return and *"ne exeat"* clauses.[41] In fact, the U.S. Supreme Court is expected to rule on the question in a case it is hearing during the 2009–2010 term.[42]

D. Spousal and Child Support Orders

Both spousal support (also known as alimony or maintenance) and child support orders raise problems of interjurisdictional recognition and full faith and credit. In some respects the issue resembles that of child custody. In both support and custody situations, we have a *judgment* that is presumptively entitled to interstate recognition and enforcement as per the Full Faith and Credit clause. And both support and custody orders are frequently modifiable under the law of the rendering state; on a conventional reading of the FFC Clause, then, a court in State B would have power to modify the order on the same terms that the courts of State A could. As we have seen, the UCCJEA and the PKPA modify these principles in the context of child custody, placing limits on the power of a court in a second state to modify.

In practice, however, interstate recognition of support orders raises problems distinct from those in the custody context. Historically, the problem has been that of the "abandoning husband" (today the popular term seems to be "deadbeat dad"); having been ordered in State A as part of a divorce decree or other type of proceeding to provide spousal and/or child support, the husband removes to another jurisdiction, perhaps disappearing from sight altogether. But there doesn't have to have been actual "abandonment" or disappearance for the problem of interstate enforcement to arise; all we need is a spouse who is failing to make good on his support obligations and who now resides in a state different from that of the complaining spouse.

(2000) (regarding it as sometimes necessary).

41. *Compare* Linda Silberman, *Interpreting the Hague Abduction Convention: In Search of a Global Jurisprudence*, 38 U.C. DAVIS LAW REVIEW 1049, 1070 (2005) (*ne exeat* clauses do confer "custody rights" for purposes of the Convention) *with* Carol S. Bruch, *The*

Unmet Needs of Domestic Violence Victims and Their Children in Hague Child Abduction Convention Cases, 38 FAMILY LAW QUARTERLY 529, 539–40 (2004) (such clauses do not constitute such a "custody right").

42. *Abbott v. Abbott* (U.S. Supreme Court Docket No. 08–645) (argued January 12, 2010).

URESA/RURESA. In Chapter 5, concerning Recognition of Judgments, we spoke rather casually of the victor in Case A being able to enforce her judgment in State B, but this can be a very onerous task for a spouse seeking interstate enforcement of a support order. Not everyone has the resources to pursue enforcement litigation in another state. Early in the twentieth century, the Uniform Reciprocal Enforcement of Support Act ["URESA"] (later largely supplanted by the Revised Uniform Reciprocal Enforcement of Support Act ["RURESA"]), adopted by all the states, attempted to address the problem by making it possible for the obligee to enforce the obligor's support obligations by initiating a proceeding in Court A (the "obligee state"), whereupon Court A would transfer the relevant information to Court B (the "obligor state").[43] In theory, this would enable the obligee to enforce the support order without having to litigate directly in a distant forum. RURESA later provided an alternative mechanism by which the obligee (in most cases, the wife or mother) could simply register State A's support order in State B, without having to appear in a State B proceeding. These provisions ameliorated some of the difficulties that plagued spouses/parents in their efforts to enforce support orders in other states. In practice, however, URESA/RURESA gave rise to a new difficulty—the possibility of multiple outstanding support orders in different states, producing confusion with respect to support obligations and the proper jurisdiction of the relevant courts. Under URESA/RURESA, Court B, rather than simply providing enforcement or modification of an outstanding support order issued by Court A, frequently would conduct a support proceeding *de novo*. Since Court B's new order did not (and could not) terminate Court A's original order, multiple support orders would be legally operative.

The Uniform Interstate Family Support Act. The system established by URESA/RURESA has been gradually supplanted by a new uniform law, the Uniform Interstate Family Support Act ["UIFSA"], in combination with a number of federal laws. Beginning in the early 1990s, widespread concern over parental neglect of child support obligations, together with a change in national welfare policy, resulted in a series of federal laws regulating the establishment, modification, and enforcement of support orders. UIFSA, which has now been adopted by all the states, operates to localize in a single court jurisdiction to enter and modify support decrees, similar to what the UCCJA and UCCJEA have done for custody decrees. UIFSA, unlike URESA/RURESA, operates to implement a "single-order" approach to support orders with inter-

---

43. In this context, "obligor" refers to the spouse who has been ordered to make support payments; the "obligee" is the spouse or child in whose favor the order has been entered.

state implications, essentially eliminating the problem of multiple outstanding support orders. Carefully crafted procedures for registering orders in other states, together with a generous "long-arm" provision enabling the issuing court to maintain jurisdiction over an out-of-state spouse, are central to this single-order approach.

In 1996, Congress required all states to adopt the UIFSA as a condition of receiving block grants under the federal Temporary Aid for Needy Families assistance program. Moreover, in 1992 Congress added 28 U.S.C. § 1738B to the full-faith-and-credit statute, which does for support orders more or less what the Parental Kidnapping Prevention Act (adding § 1738A to the statute) did for child custody orders: It aligned federal full-faith-and-credit requirements with the relevant uniform state law setting forth the principles of initial and modification jurisdiction. The combination of the UIFSA and 18 U.S.C. § 1738B has imparted a modicum of order and coherence to the problem of the interstate status and effect of support orders. However, a few support orders made while URESA/RURESA still governed these issues remain outstanding; when these are "cleared out" of the system, the UIFSA and § 1738B will provide the structure for resolving all interstate issues with respect to child support.

Note that the UIFSA distinguishes in an important respect between orders for spousal support and orders for child support. Under the UIFSA, the court issuing a *spousal* support order (the "issuing court") has exclusive modification jurisdiction for the duration of the support obligation; no other court may modify the order. By contrast, it is possible for the issuing court to lose jurisdiction over an order for *child* support if none of the relevant persons—the obligor, the obligee, and the child—resides any longer in the state. Under these circumstances, another court can assume modification jurisdiction. This raises a choice-of-law question: Under the UIFSA, whose law should govern proceedings in a court of a state different from that of the issuing court?

Answering that question requires us to distinguish between *modification* and *enforcement* of the issuing court's order. The choice-of-law issue is simple where modification is concerned: In cases of spousal support, the problem essentially does not even exist, since the issuing court retains exclusive modification jurisdiction for the life of the order. With respect to child support orders, if a tribunal outside the issuing state properly concludes, pursuant to UIFSA's jurisdiction provisions, that the issuing state has lost exclusive modification jurisdiction, and that the forum can properly assert jurisdiction, forum law (which the statute refers to as "local law") will apply to subsequent modification. But enforcement is a different story (with respect to both spousal and child support orders): If the issuing court's order is simply registered in a new state for purposes of enforcement there, and the issuing court has not lost its exclusive modification jurisdiction, then the law of that issuing court, not that of the enforcement court (called the "responding court"), applies to an enforcement proceeding. What kinds of legal issues might raise a conflicts problem in this latter situation? One example arises when the laws of the issuing and responding states differ with respect to the age at which the legal duty to support a child terminates. If the issuing court's order requires (in accordance with the law of that state) that support payments continue until the child reaches the age of 21, the responding court must enforce that provision even if the local law of the forum holds that the duty of support ceases when the child reaches the age of 18.

Chapter 7

THE LAW APPLIED IN FEDERAL COURTS

Every lawyer, and every law student who has made it through law school far enough to take a class in Conflict of Laws, has heard of the *"Erie* doctrine." But, famous as it is, sometimes the topic is given only cursory treatment in such courses as Civil Procedure and Federal Courts. It's not uncommon for professors in upper-level courses of all kinds, when they teach a case that happens to involve an *"Erie* issue," to say, "Of course, you learned about *Erie* in your civil procedure class," when in fact you haven't.

So here it is—a discussion of *Erie* that is extensive enough to get you through a conversation at a cocktail party, but not so long that you will send other guests fleeing from the room.

A. The *"Erie* Doctrine": An Introduction

The phrases *"Erie* doctrine" or *"Erie* problem," which are ubiquitous in the literature on the federal courts, can be misleading. These are usually shorthand references to a constellation of problems concerning whether a federal court, hearing a case that falls within its diversity jurisdiction, should apply state or federal law to decide a particular issue in the case. These various problems, however, do not all raise identical issues, and it's important to treat them distinctly and separately. The material in this chapter will set out and explain those differences.

If you need a rough statement right away of what most people mean when referring to the *"Erie* doctrine," you could do worse than this: *With the exception of certain rules of "procedure," federal courts sitting in diversity must apply state law, including state decisional law, to the disputes they hear. The state law to be applied includes the choice-of-law rules of the state in which the court is sitting.* There is a lot more to the *"Erie* doctrine" than this, however, and some could justly criticize the italicized statement as imprecise. A richer definition of the doctrine will emerge the long way, through an examination of how the doctrine has developed. Before getting down to cases, let us identify a few general themes that will emerge in more detail in the subsequent discussion.

1. Why Discuss Erie in a Book on Conflict of Laws?

Because many of the cases described as falling within "the *Erie* doctrine" seem to present the question of whether state or federal law on a particular issue should be applied by a federal court sitting in diversity, it is natural to think of the problem as one of choice of law. For this reason—as well as the fact that, at some schools, *Erie* may not be systematically covered in any other class—it makes sense to include a chapter on the subject in this book. Keep in mind, though, that the *"Erie* problem" presents questions that are analytically quite different from the material on choice of law discussed in previous chapters. The relationship between federal and state law, which is what the *"Erie* problem" is largely about, is a different animal from the relationship between the laws of different states. Judges and scholars tend not to think of the general issue of "the law applied in federal courts" as a conflicts issue, although there are differences of opinion on the matter. At the same time, there are enough points of contact, both doctrinal and conceptual, between the *"Erie* problem" and the more conventional choice-of-law problem to make consideration of the former appropriate here.

2. The Three Broad Dimensions of the "Erie Doctrine"

Considered collectively, *Erie*, and the many subsequent Supreme Court cases decided on the authority of *Erie*, bring to the surface at least three large legal questions about our judicial system:

Jurisprudence. The *Erie* decision itself raised, in a stark way, whether in our legal system there is such a thing as "general law," belonging neither to the federal government nor to the states, on which federal courts can rely in deciding cases. The answer is "no." The *Erie* decision is thus an important marker of our legal system's decisive adoption of the view that all law applied by courts is the law of some sovereign state or nation. Of all the cases discussed in this chapter, only the original *Erie* decision really concerned itself with this question. Today, the presumption that there is no such thing as "general law" enforceable in our courts is so deeply ingrained that the question rarely arises anymore. Most *"Erie* questions" considered by courts today don't raise these jurisprudential questions.

Federalism. The second question, and the one with which the cases discussed in this chapter are most centrally concerned, is the relationship between state power and federal power. Simply stated: What do the fundamental principles of federalism— which govern the allocation of power between national power and that of the states—tell us about whether and when federal courts sitting in diversity may apply federal (as opposed to state) law to a particular issue?

Separation of Powers. A third question, which is somewhat less conspicuous in the cases than the second but which necessarily arises at certain points, concerns the relationship between the federal courts and Congress in determining the legitimate power of the federal courts to make and apply rules of law to govern the cases they hear. We know that federal courts—like all courts—at times make law; among other things, it is neither unusual nor particularly controversial for them to develop rules for the management and superintendence of litigation where Congress has not already done so for them. But does the provenance of a particular federal rule— that is, whether it was developed by the federal courts or was instead derived from an Act of Congress—matter in determining whether, in a particular diversity case, a federal rule should govern notwithstanding the existence of a conflicting state rule? Sometimes it may appear that a federal rule should prevail over a competing state rule only if the federal rule plausibly derives from an express or implied policy or invitation from Congress. If the second question speaks to the structural principles of "federalism," this third question brings principles of separation of powers into play.

3. *"Substance" vs. "Procedure"*

Most of the cases discussed in this Chapter, aside from the *Erie* decision itself, concerns the possible application in diversity cases of rules (whether state or federal) that sound as though they are "procedural" in nature, or least could reasonably be regarded as such. The categories of "substance" and "procedure" loom large in the jurisprudence of *Erie*, but, as you probably know from other areas of the law, those terms are imprecise and sometimes downright unhelpful. As the Supreme Court itself has noted, a bit drily, "Classification of a law as 'substantive' or 'procedural' for *Erie* purposes is sometimes a challenging endeavor."[1] We already know from our study of interest analysis in choice of law that *all* rules of law, even those that seem to be obviously "procedural," themselves reflect substantive policies; lawmakers presumably have reasons for establishing the procedural rules that they do. At the same time, we intuitively sense that there is a difference between rules of law (like tort or contract law) that govern people's behavior in the world outside the courts (that's "substance"), and rules of law (such as the time within which the defendant must answer the complaint)

---

1. *Gasperini v. Center for Humanities, Inc.*, 518 U.S. 415, 427 (1996) (foot-   note omitted).

that regulate the way in which litigation is to be managed in a particular court (that's "procedure"). In what follows we will frequently have to employ those terms at least provisionally, while recognizing that calling a particular rule "substantive" or "procedural" isn't by itself necessarily going to determine how a particular "*Erie* problem" should be resolved.

4. The Role of the Constitution in the "Erie Doctrine"

Another issue you will see discussed in the following pages is the precise role of the Constitution (as opposed to other sources of law, such as Congressional statutes) in determining the principles that the Supreme Court has announced in *Erie* and succeeding cases. The *Erie* decision itself was based on the Constitution, although it is only by careful analysis that one can explain just how and why the Constitution compelled the result in *Erie*. By contrast, it is much more difficult to say how the Court's decisions reached after *Erie*, and purporting to rely on that decision, have anything to do with the Constitution, even though the *results* of those decisions are all either correct or eminently defensible. Now, the average litigator may care less about whether the reasoning underlying one of the important "*Erie* cases" is based on the Constitution or on something else, than she does about the essential holding in the case (usually, whether a federal rule or a state rule should apply as to a particular issue in a diversity case). In trying to make sense of the doctrines discussed in this chapter, though, it really does help to understand the reasoning behind them (or at least the reasoning that we can use to rationalize them after the fact), and this requires an examination of the role that the Constitution plays in those doctrines.

5. Federal Courts Sitting in Diversity: Surrogates for State Courts or an Independent Judicial System?

The *Erie* problem forces us to consider and define the real function of the federal courts when they are acting pursuant to their "diversity" jurisdiction. Most scholars agree that the creation of diversity jurisdiction in the federal courts at the dawn of the republic was founded on the view that state courts could not always be relied on to treat litigants from other states fairly in their disputes with in-state residents. Thus, in cases where the parties are from different states, a so-called "neutral" forum should be made available—the federal courts.[2] There is also general agreement, however, that the availability of federal diversity jurisdiction

---

2. Few jurists believe that this worry about the potential bias against out-of-staters has much to commend it today. There have consequently been several attempts over the years to eliminate the diversity jurisdiction of the federal courts, although as yet none of them has been successful.

should not give parties (plaintiffs by bringing suit in federal court, defendants by removing a case there) an opportunity to obtain the benefit of *governing substantive law* that is different, and for them more favorable, than state law would be. That is, the choice of *forum* created by the existence of concurrent jurisdiction in cases where the parties are of diverse citizenship does not mean that the parties should have a choice of the *law* that governs their disputes. The incentive for forum shopping created by such a situation would be disrespectful of state law, and it could discriminate against similarly situated parties who, being citizens of the same state as their adversaries, don't have the right to litigate in federal court on their nonfederal claims.

In resolving the myriad of *"Erie* problems" that federal courts face every year, however, one must ask whether this distaste for forum shopping means that federal courts sitting in diversity should, to the maximum possible extent, simply seek to "stand in the shoes of" a state court when deciding a case. We don't want federal courts to be a place where someone can evade the essential results that would be reached had the case been heard in state court, but there's only so far we can go in having federal litigation precisely mimic what would take place were the case to be heard in state court. To take an obvious example, federal judges have life tenure, whereas many of their counterparts do not, a difference that could, in some untraceable way, influence how they would decide a particular case. More to the point, it would be odd to expect the federal courts to apply one set of procedural rules to govern federal question cases and another set (mimicking state rules) in diversity cases, simply because of a desire precisely to "match" the procedures of the state court in the diversity situation. At some point the interests of the federal courts as an independent judicial system, and of Congress in regulating the processes of those courts, may compete with or come to prevail over the revulsion against forum shopping and the prerogatives of state law. One's view as to whether the federal or the state rule should be applied in particular kinds of situations will depend to some extent on one's view concerning the character and *raison d'être* of federal courts sitting in diversity—as simple surrogates for state courts, as an independent system of tribunals possessed of a distinctly *federal* interest in the management of litigation in its courts, or as some combination of the two.

6. The Supreme Court's Messy Line of Decisions, and Not the Logically Consistent Theories of Legal Scholars, Are the Law

Despite numerous heroic attempts, no one can draw a line through all the Supreme Court's *"Erie* decisions" (much less the thousands of cases decided by lower federal courts) and come up with a pithy, coherent doctrinal formulation that explains all of the cases. The *"Erie* doctrine" is something of a muddle because the Supreme Court has largely made it up as it has gone along, stressing first one and then another of the essential values underlying *Erie*, encountering new problems that require refinement of the Court's earlier pronouncements. At the same time, legal scholars have for several decades argued over the true meaning of, and proper rationale for, *Erie* and subsequent decisions. Some of those analyses have been very discerning, and at times quite brilliant. This chapter's effort to give some sort of structure for understanding the doctrine as a whole has been strongly influenced by some of those scholarly analyses.[3] But remember that what the Court has done, or will do, is not the same as what a legal scholar said the Court has done, or should do. For better or worse, the Court has not provided us with a comprehensive and self-consistent line of cases, but those decisions, not the more intellectually satisfying summations of legal scholars, are what the modern-day litigator has to work with.

*7. The Vast Majority of "*Erie *Decisions" Have Been Rendered by the Lower Federal Courts, Not the Supreme Court*

There are, after all, federal courts other than the Supreme Court, and the thousands of holdings rendered by those courts on questions involving *Erie* numerically dwarf the handful of Supreme Court decisions. While the Court's decisions may provide the general framework for addressing questions concerning the law that should be applied by federal courts in diversity cases, most of the law concerning the vast array of knotty problems that can arise in this area is the work of the lower federal courts. The specific *"Erie* problems" apt to come up in legal practice are more likely to have been addressed in a prior Court of Appeals or District Court decision than in a decision by the Supreme Court.

B.   The Decision in *Erie R.R. v. Tompkins* (1938)

Let us proceed to the *Erie* decision itself. In *Erie R.R. Co. v. Tompkins* (1938),[4] a pedestrian was walking along the right-of-way adjoining a railroad track. A train passed through, and a swinging door that had been negligently left open struck the pedestrian and badly injured him. The pedestrian was a citizen of Pennsylvania, and the defendant railroad was a citizen of New York. The plaintiff was thus entitled to sue in Federal District Court, invoking its

---

3. Two famous scholarly treatments of *Erie* have particularly influenced the discussion in this chapter: John Hart Ely, *The Irrepressible Myth of* Erie, 87 HARVARD LAW REVIEW 693 (1974), and Peter Westen & Jeffrey S. Lehman, *Is There Life for* Erie *After the Death of Diversity?*, 78 MICHIGAN LAW REVIEW 311 (1980).

4.   304 U.S. 64 (1938).

diversity jurisdiction, and he did so. Previous decisions of the Pennsylvania state courts indicated that the plaintiff should legally be regarded as a "trespasser" and thus barred from recovering. The federal courts, however, had determined in a number of prior cases that the question of whether, under the circumstances in the case, plaintiff was to be regarded as a trespasser and barred from recovery was a question of "general law," not necessarily to be governed by the case law of the state, when the case was brought into a federal court on diversity grounds. The federal district court in *Erie* ruled that the question was one of "general law," and that, according to those "general law" principles, Tompkins was *not* a trespasser who should be barred from recovering. Obviously, had the case been heard by a Pennsylvania state court, Tompkins would have been out of luck. By suing in federal rather than Pennsylvania state court, Tompkins had succeeded in having applied to his case substantive law that was more favorable to him.

In an historic decision, one of the most famous in American law, the Supreme Court ruled in *Erie* that it was improper for the federal courts to have disregarded the Pennsylvania case law and to have invoked principles of "general law" to decide the case. The Court went further, holding that, when exercising its diversity jurisdiction, a federal court is governed not only by the applicable *statutory* law of the state in which the federal court is sitting (which had never been doubted), but also by the applicable *case* law of that state. The Court ruled that federal courts sitting in diversity have no authority to create or apply principles of "general law" that differ from applicable state rules of decision in diversity cases. The Court's decision in *Erie* overruled the venerable case of *Swift v. Tyson* (1842) and swept away a century or more of jurisprudence developed by federal courts and commentators who took for granted the propriety of the federal courts' reliance on "general law" principles (rather than state decisional law) to decide certain kinds of diversity cases.

C. What *Erie* Got Rid Of

One should disentangle two aspects of the *Erie* decision. The first, whose implications have been explored in the many "*Erie*" cases decided since 1938, is the Court's holding that, under the circumstances presented in the *Erie* case, state decisional law should provide the rule of decision. The second aspect, closely related to but distinct from the first, is that federal courts have no authority to apply rules of law drawn from some amorphous body of "general law," associated with no particular sovereign state or nation. Since students seem to find this latter part of *Erie*'s holding to be unremarkable—the concept of a court's applying "general law" does seem today to be an unfamiliar one—it's helpful to understand the age-old practice of federal courts that *Erie* disapproved. This in turn will help explain the reasoning of the *Erie* decision itself.

Article III, Diversity Jurisdiction, and the Rules of Decision Act. Article III of the Constitution empowers Congress to create lower federal courts and to confer on them jurisdiction to hear (among other things) cases between citizens of different states. This Congress did in the Judiciary Act of 1789. But Article III said nothing about what *law* should govern such disputes.[5] Resolution of this question, apparently, it likewise left to Congress (or, perhaps, to tacitly understood contemporary legal principles that scholars have found difficult to unearth). The Constitution had provided for diversity jurisdiction in the federal courts largely because of a concern that not all state courts could be relied upon to treat out-of-state litigants fairly, and that a federal forum would be more "neutral." Having created a neutral forum for such cases, it would not have been unthinkable for Congress also to provide its own rules of substantive law to govern such diversity cases;[6] but Congress chose a different, more expedient approach instead. In § 34 of the Judiciary Act of 1789, a provision that today is known as the Rules of Decision Act ["RDA"],[7] Congress provided:

> The laws of the several States, except where the Constitution, treaties, or statutes of the United States otherwise require or provide, shall be regarded as rules of decision in trials at

5. Students sometimes mistakenly think that Article III defines diversity jurisdiction as the power of a federal court to decide claims *based on state law* that are brought by a citizen of one state against a citizen of another state. Actually, both Article III and 28 U.S.C. § 1332 mention only the fact that the case must be one between citizens of different states. Whether "state law" (however defined) should govern such a dispute is a matter to be determined by reasoning from other sources of law (including the Rules of Decision Act, discussed below)—not from the constitutional and statutory definitions of the federal courts' diversity jurisdiction, which themselves say nothing about whether "state law" should govern such cases. After all, there is nothing in the Constitution or 28 U.S.C. § 1332 that explicitly prevents the law, say, of a foreign country from supplying the rule of decision in a federal court case brought by the citizen of one U.S. state against the citizen of another. Incidentally, if plaintiff's claim arises under federal law

in a case where the parties are citizens of different states, it is presumed that the federal court's jurisdiction is of the "federal question" variety, and the citizenship of the parties can be disregarded. We look to the possible "federal question" basis for jurisdiction before looking to the citizenship of the parties.

6. Some courts and commentators believe that it would have been unconstitutional for Congress to do this, but that conclusion seems hasty. It is sufficient to observe that it would have been both politically and practically infeasible for Congress to attempt to supply a comprehensive code of law for diversity cases.

7. The Rules of Decision Act is today codified, slightly reworded, at 28 U.S.C. § 1652. The Rules of Decision Act plays an important (if sometimes confusing) role in the basic line of "*Erie* cases," so you should attend to it carefully. In the discussion that follows, the phrases "§ 34 of the Judiciary Act of 1789" and "the Rules of Decision Act" are used interchangeably.

common law, in the courts of the United States, in cases where they apply.

The precise meaning of this provision has been debated ever since its enactment, but most agree that, at a minimum, it requires federal courts sitting in diversity to apply "the laws of the ... States ... in cases where they apply." (The phrase "in cases where they apply," which might seem to completely beg the question, can for the moment be taken to mean "in cases where they would apply if the case were to have been brought in state court.") Note, for what it is worth, that it is thus a *federal statute* that directs the federal courts to apply state law in such cases.

But what was encompassed within the phrase "the laws of the several States"? Clearly it includes applicable state *statutes*. If a state has a statute that purports to provide a rule of decision for that particular case (for example, a wrongful death statute), that state statute should apply in the federal court proceeding if jurisdiction is founded on diversity of citizenship. The federal court has no business consulting "general principles" or some other source of law besides that of the state; the state statute should govern. From the beginning, however, the word "laws" as used in § 34 of the Judiciary Act of 1789 was usually taken *not* to refer to substantive rules of decision that had emerged in common-law fashion through the decisions of state courts. If there were no state statute, then, the federal court sitting in diversity at times could, and in fact ought to, consult "general principles"—most often, the principles of the common law as understood by that court—for the proper rule of decision in the case.

This conclusion seemed sensible to most pre-Civil War judges and commentators for a number of reasons. One reason sometimes given is that the word "laws" as used in § 34 of the Judiciary Act of 1789 seems to be an awkward way of referring to common-law rules. Thus, the "law of California" includes rules of law that have been established by judicial decision, but the phrase "the laws of California" suggests, in the minds of most people, only codified laws. It is not clear, however, that this modern usage was conventional in 1789. Far more important was this fact: While today we do not regard the force and significance of common-law rules as fundamentally different from that of statutes—both are part of the positive law of the state—this was not the general understanding in 1789. The "common law" at that time was regarded not so much a determinate body of legal rules, as a decisional *process* by which courts consulted various authorities—previous cases (English as well as U.S. cases), jurisprudential writings, and sound reasoning and common sense—for evidence of what the law, the "right answer," on a particular question was. (This is what nineteenth-century jurists meant when they insisted that courts did not "make" law, but rather found or "discovered" it.) In addition, while courts well appreciated that the common-law process could generate different judicial holdings in different jurisdictions, since circumstances varied from state to state, in 1789 the conception still prevailed that the common law was a general repository of reason, experience, precedent, and common sense, not a body of determinate rules possessed by a particular state. Courts deciding common-law cases would, of course, follow their own precedents under the doctrine of *stare decisis*, but most jurists continued to distinguish rather sharply between the nature of the common law and the nature of statutory law. It would probably have seemed odd to them, in 1789 at any rate, to regard common-law judicial decisions as themselves embraced within the phrase "the laws of the several States."

Since § 34 of the Judiciary Act of 1789 thus did not specify what "law" federal courts should apply in diversity cases where there was no applicable state statute, federal courts tended to act in such cases as they supposed English and American common-law courts had long acted. They did not assume, as we do today, that *all* law applied by courts in any case must belong to a sovereign political unit (either a state or the United States); they considered themselves bound to consult a variety of sources of law, not all of them emanating from a sovereign state, each of which was relevant to particular kinds of cases.[8] Obviously, cases arising under federal law were governed by federal law, and, as we have seen, applicable state statutes should govern in diversity cases. But other *kinds* of disputes might be resolved by sources of law belonging to no particular sovereign. Cases arising out of armed conflict between nations, for example, might be governed by the laws of war, itself a species of the "law of nations." Cases involving relations and practices among commercial traders might be governed by a body of law known as the "law merchant," or, where activity on the high seas was concerned, maritime law. All of these bodies of law were what we might call "transcendental," or perhaps "transnational"; they were not the possession of any single sovereign state, and in diversity cases raising such issues the federal courts did not always consider themselves strictly bound by judicial decisions of the states in which they sat. To some extent, even "the common law" as such could be seen as embodying such transcendental legal principles.

At the same time, most federal courts sitting in diversity recognized that some legal questions, even when not governed by a state statute, were by nature "local" in their significance, and were

---

8. The discussion in the text relies on one of the best treatments of these historical questions: William A. Fletcher, *The General Common Law and Section* *34 of the Judiciary Act of 1789: The Example of Marine Insurance*, 97 HARVARD LAW REVIEW 1513, 1517ff. (1984).

committed to the legal and political power of the state in which they were localized. In such cases, the law that emerged from the state's own judicial decisions should govern. A clear example would be questions concerning real property situated within a state. In such cases, Federal courts sitting in diversity usually considered themselves bound by the principles that had been announced in the courts of the states in which they sat, because they were distinctively "local" questions—not questions of more universal or "general" interest that called for recourse to more "transcendental" bodies of legal principle.[9] (In fact, the term "local" as used in this context was closely related to the Latin phrase "*lex loci*," which is familiar to students of choice of law. Questions of "local" law were by and large those that, as of the early nineteenth century, had traditionally been governed by the *lex loci*.) It's important to note that, at the turn of the nineteenth century, differences between the "local" law of one state and that of others were not as widespread as they would later become, so the need for federal courts sitting in diversity to identify cases featuring a problem of "local" law did not recur frequently.

When a federal court sitting in diversity concluded that the question with which it was presented was not one of "local" law, and was not governed by a state statute, it was apt to conclude that the question was one of "general law." In the legal conception of the times, such "general law" as applied by federal courts, was not *federal* law; it was just "general" law. (For example, the fact that that a federal court sitting in diversity might think it appropriate to apply principles of "general law" to a case did not mean that the case fell within the "federal question" jurisdiction of the federal courts.) In fact, the assumption was that a federal court attempting to discern and apply general law in a diversity case was doing what all courts, including state courts, would or should do in the same situation. And this sometimes involved consulting sources or bodies of law like the law merchant or the law of nations.

D. Justice Story and *Swift v. Tyson* (1842)

When Justice Story wrote the Court's opinion in *Swift v. Tyson* (1842),[10] the case always taken to typify the practice that *Erie* forbade, he was not announcing any novel or surprising principles. *Swift*, a diversity case brought in federal court in New York, turned

---

9. For example, the question of what remedy (if any) was appropriate where a ship's cargo, intended for delivery pursuant to a mercantile agreement, was lost at sea was a question of interest to traders everywhere, not just those from Rhode Island; the answer should be supplied by the rules and customs of the law merchant, a transnational body of law. By contrast, the question of title to land in Rhode Island was a question of interest to Rhode Island, and not to other states.

10. 41 U.S. 1 (1842).

on an important if arcane point of commercial law: whether a pre-existing debt constituted valuable consideration for a bill of exchange, such that a holder in due course might take the bill free from any defects of which he had had no notice. In a cash-poor and credit-hungry economy, resolution of questions concerning the negotiability of such credit instruments as bills of exchange was important. So, in the view of many, was the task of devising rules for these matters that were uniform throughout the nation. Justice Story, a strong economic nationalist who rued the effects of a patchwork of state legal rules on such vital commercial questions, held in *Swift v. Tyson* that this question, of fundamental importance to the commercial community, was *not* merely of local dimension, to be governed by New York state decisions; it was a question of "general law" to be resolved by the federal court's reasoned distillation of principles drawn from commercial custom and practice and from the views of courts and commentators throughout the English-speaking world. (No New York statute applied to the question.) He specifically denied that the § 34 of the Judiciary Act of 1789 required the federal courts to follow the New York decisions in *Swift*. Based on this inquiry, Justice Story derived and applied a legal principle contrary to the one that had been suggested by the New York court decisions.

Swift v. Tyson is the canonical instance of a federal court's applying "general law," and declining to follow the rule established by the decisions of the courts of the state in which the federal court sat, in deciding a diversity case. It is also the U.S. Supreme Court's clearest statement of the doctrine, although only one of many cases in which the Court applied it. In Justice Story's conception, the rule he derived from the "general law" sources he consulted was not, strictly speaking, "federal" law, nor did it become such by virtue of its application in *Swift*; the question remained one of "general law," to which all courts, state and federal, should have recourse in rendering their common-law decisions in cases that were not governed by statute and were not "merely local" in nature. The New York courts themselves were not "bound" by the decision in *Swift*. The entire conception seems rather strange to us today, but in 1842 it lay in the legal and jurisprudential mainstream.

E.   What Was Wrong (Or Became Wrong) About *Swift v. Tyson*?

If the decision in *Swift* did not evoke great controversy at the time it was issued, how and why did it become anathema to the Supreme Court in 1938, resulting in its overruling in *Erie*? The reason often given is that, by the early twentieth century if not earlier, the conception of law on which *Swift* was based had become an anachronism. *Swift* assumed the existence of a body of "general law" applicable in U.S. courts that emanated from no sovereign entity, but whose content was distilled from the customs or practices of some transnational community (of merchants, for example, or of seafaring traders) as well as the views of eminent jurists and commentators, and which commended itself over the years to courts engaged in the process of reasoned analysis of legal disputes. To a legal culture increasingly under the sway of a more "positivist" conception of law—one in which law is the command of the sovereign state—such a view seemed quaint. It also seemed difficult to square with the notion of republican government, in which the elected representatives of the governed make the laws, not courts and certainly not vaguely defined transnational communities. We no longer credit the notion that law, at least the law that American courts apply in reaching decisions, can legitimately emanate from any source other than a sovereign state or nation.[11]

This jurisprudential explanation for the demise of *Swift* and "general law" is certainly part of the story, but it's not all of it. Equally important is that federal courts, in the century after *Swift* was decided, were not always careful to observe the boundary between questions of local law and questions of "general" law. They continued to assume the power to identify and apply principles of "general law" long after the concept of transnational communities of merchants, traders, etc. had ceased to have much meaning to lawyers and judges. By the late nineteenth century, some federal courts sitting in diversity were adding to the domain of "general law" large portions of the law of tort and even property—seemingly the paradigms of state or "local" issues—whose only justification for such treatment seemed to be that some federal judges did not care for the rules of law that had been adopted by state courts to govern those issues. This tendency was increasingly seen as a power grab by federal courts at the expense of the rightful powers of the states, their judiciaries, and their people. Moreover, by the late nineteenth century and well into the twentieth, many believed that the federal judiciary was more conservative and more resistant to change than the state judiciaries, and they sensed (whether accurately or not) that principles of "general law" derived by federal courts for use in diversity cases were more "conservative" than the corresponding principles adopted by state courts as part of their state's common law.

Perhaps the most salient weakness of the *Swift* doctrine to emerge by the 1920s was that, with the demise of the conception of law that had sustained it, the application of "general law" princi-

---

11. One sees echoes of this point in today's debates concerning whether customary international law may legitimately form the basis of a rule of deci-sion in the federal courts. *See Sosa v. Alvarez–Machain,* 542 U.S. 692, 739–49 (Scalia, J., dissenting).

ples by federal courts sitting in diversity seemed to facilitate the development of two distinct bodies of substantive law to govern wide areas of human behavior. Parties able to invoke the diversity jurisdiction of the federal courts could conceivably obtain the benefit of different substantive law from what would apply in state court. Considerable "forum-shopping" advantages accrued to those litigants best situated to exploit them.[12] When, during the first third of the twentieth century, the federal courts came under general attack as forces of political and economic reaction, the doctrine of *Swift v. Tyson* was one of the principal offenders in the eyes of reformers.[13] The decision in *Erie* was the culmination of these developments.

F. The Constitutional Basis of the *Erie* Decision

On what *legal* basis, then, did the Court in *Erie* rest in overruling *Swift v. Tyson* and determining that federal courts sitting in diversity were not to ignore state decisional law and instead consult principles of "general law"? As many have noted, the Court might have been able to reach the result that it did in *Erie* by re-examining Justice Story's interpretation of § 34 of the Judiciary Act of 1789 and ruling, contrary to what Story had said in *Swift*, that the word "laws" found therein encompassed state decisional law (whether the matter was one of a "local" or of a "general" nature).[14] This move was advocated by Justice Reed in

---

12. The example most frequently cited as the *reductio ad absurdum* of this situation is the case of *Black & White Taxicab & Transfer Co. v. Brown & Yellow Taxicab & Transfer Co.*, 276 U.S. 518 (1928). In the *Taxicab* case, the Louisville & Nashville Railroad had contracted with Brown & Yellow to give that company exclusive pick-up and drop-off privileges at one of its stations in Kentucky. Black & White wanted a piece of the action, and when they began picking up passengers at the station, Brown & Yellow sued for interference with its contractual rights. Kentucky case law viewed the exclusive privilege enjoyed by Brown & Yellow as void and unenforceable because contrary to the state's policy against exclusive or preferential arrangements in the conduct of business by a common carrier (the railroad). Both taxicab companies were, realistically, Kentucky companies; that's where they did their business. Prior to bringing its lawsuit, however, Brown & Yellow dissolved itself and reincorporated under the laws of Tennessee. It was therefore able to sue Black & White in

federal court, and when it did, the federal court (sitting in diversity) characterized the issue as one of "general law," not governed by Kentucky case law. It thereupon held that Brown & Yellow's exclusive contractual privilege was valid and enforceable under principles of "general law." Because Brown & Yellow's reincorporation in Tennessee had enabled it to obtain the benefit of governing law different from what the Kentucky courts would have applied, the U.S. Supreme Court's affirmance of this decision helped to discredit the *Swift* doctrine and the whole idea of "general law" (which Justice Holmes memorably caricatured in his dissent in the *Taxicab* case as "this outside thing to be found").

13. These developments are well described in EDWARD A. PURCELL, JR., BRANDEIS AND THE PROGRESSIVE CONSTITUTION: *ERIE*, THE JUDICIAL POWER, AND THE POLITICS OF THE FEDERAL COURTS IN TWENTIETH-CENTURY AMERICA 11–92 (2000).

14. In 1923, Charles Warren had published an article in the *Harvard Law Review* purporting to demonstrate,

his separate concurrence in *Erie*, partly because the decision in *Erie* would then have been one of *statutory* interpretation, and therefore would not unnecessarily limit Congress's constitutional power to adopt principles for the federal courts to follow in deciding diversity cases. If Congress were to disagree with the Court's decision in *Erie*, Justice Reed's approach would leave room for Congress simply to overrule the Court by amending the Rules of Decision Act to that effect. But Brandeis, though he professed to agree with Justice Reed's analysis of the statute, quite purposefully went beyond this purely statutory approach in his majority opinion; he clearly thought it vital to hold that the *Swift* doctrine was *unconstitutional*. Brandeis's approach has often been defended on *stare decisis* grounds: The Court is typically reluctant to overrule its prior decisions interpreting a Congressional statute, on the theory that long acquiescence by Congress in the interpretation should be regarded as vindication of it, and that in any case Congress retains the power to overrule the earlier decision if it wishes to. By contrast, only the Court can overrule a previous decision that was based on constitutional grounds, and the principle of *stare decisis* has perhaps less force under those circumstances. On this view, it would have been difficult to defend the *Erie* decision had it done no more than overrule *Swift*'s interpretation of the Rules of Decision Act, but a decision overruling *Swift* on constitutional grounds would be better justified.

There is some merit to this explanation, but the fact of the matter is that, wholly apart from the niceties of *stare decisis*, Brandeis (like the justices who joined his opinion) was determined to put *Erie* on a constitutional basis. He insisted that the federal courts' practice of disregarding state decisional law and applying "general law" to decide diversity cases violated the Constitution. What part of the Constitution, though, had that practice violated? As we've noted, Article III does not say what law—state, federal, or other—federal courts must apply in diversity cases, so Article III can't be the relevant constitutional provision. Brandeis suggested one possibility when he mentioned in *Erie* that the *Swift* doctrine had led to a kind of discrimination.[15] While he was correct about

---

based on an examination of some of the original sources, that § 34 had in fact been intended to make state decisional law binding on federal courts sitting in diversity. Charles Warren, *New Light on the History of the Federal Judiciary Act of 1789*, 37 HARVARD LAW REVIEW 49 (1923). Justice Brandeis cited Warren's article approvingly in his opinion for the Court in *Erie*. More recent scholarship has cast serious doubt on Warren's conclusions.

15. "*Swift v. Tyson* introduced grave discrimination by noncitizens against citizens. It made rights enjoyed under the unwritten 'general law' vary according to whether enforcement was sought in the state or in the federal court; and the privilege of selecting the court in which the right should be determined was conferred upon the noncitizen. Thus, the doctrine rendered impossible equal protection of the law." *Erie*, 304 U.S. at 74–75 (footnote omitted).

this, the discrimination was not the type of which we usually think when dealing with the constitutional requirement of equal protection, such as race or sex discrimination; it was discrimination between citizens and non-citizens of a particular state. For example, under the *Swift* doctrine, a citizen of a state who had been sued on a nonfederal claim by a co-citizen in state court could not remove to federal court, but a non-citizen sued in state court by the same plaintiff in another case raising identical issues *could* remove to federal court, potentially giving him an opportunity to obtain more favorable substantive law.[16] That circumstance, which many regard as at least unseemly, might well be a reason for criticizing the *Swift* doctrine. But it is difficult to argue that such "discrimination" between defendants who are co-citizens of the plaintiff and those who are not violates the Constitution,[17] and Brandeis's *Erie* opinion understandably did not really pursue the effort to demonstrate that it does. This suggests that his reference to "grave discrimination" was more rhetoric or "metaphor" (Professor Ely's word) than anything else.

Still, Brandeis must have had *something* in mind when he suggested that the federal courts had been engaged in an "unconstitutional course" pursuant to the *Swift* doctrine. Although his *Erie* opinion is not completely clear on the point, Brandeis appears to have rested his constitutional argument on the limited scope of the powers conferred on the federal government *generally* by the Constitution. Notably, he did not premise his argument on the notion that federal courts have no constitutional power whatever to make law. Such an assertion not only would have reflected a naïve view of what courts do, but also would have flown in the face of the

---

16. Defining the kinds of "discrimination" licensed by *Swift v. Tyson* is a tricky proposition. Probably the best description of this kind of discrimination was provided by Professor John Hart Ely, who referred to "the unfairness of subjecting a person involved in litigation with a citizen of a different state to a body of law different from that which applies when his next door neighbor is involved in similar litigation with a cocitizen." John Hart Ely, *The Irrepressible Myth of* Erie, 87 Harvard Law Review 693, 712 (1974). The discrimination in this formulation thus consists in the different results reached in *two* separate pieces of litigation. It is harder to see *Swift* as facilitating discrimination between the two parties in a single lawsuit, since the rules governing diversity jurisdiction do not systematically favor either in-staters or out-of-staters in their ability to select between state and

federal court in a given case. The only exception is the fact that in-state defendants in diversity cases are not permitted to remove to federal court—and any advantage that would give the out-of-state plaintiff in such a case in terms of the ability to choose one court or the other (and thus to choose more favorable law under the *Swift* regime) is a consequence of the removal statute, not of *Swift v. Tyson.*

17. Presumably, the relevant constitutional provision with respect to such discrimination would be the Fifth Amendment (not the Fourteenth Amendment, since we are speaking of actions by federal, not state, courts). But at the time *Erie* was decided, the Court had not yet ruled that Fourteenth Amendment principles of equal protection are embodied in the Fifth Amendment. *Cf. Bolling v. Sharpe,* 347 U.S. 497 (1954).

undoubted power of the federal courts to develop rules of law in aid, say, of their jurisdiction in admiralty, a widely conceded point. So it is not the mere fact that federal courts had been devising rules of law, or even that they had been devising rules of "general" law unconnected with any sovereign nation or state, that rendered their behavior unconstitutional. (There is nothing in the Constitution that declares that "law is the command of the sovereign," *i.e.* that only the positive law of a state or nation can be applied in the federal courts.) What is crucial is the *breadth* of the lawmaking power that the federal courts had assumed in cases like *Erie*, concerning matters that even Congress lacked power to regulate so comprehensively.

Brandeis observed in *Erie* that Article I of the Constitution limits, to enumerated categories, the power of *Congress* to make law; and he intimated that whatever power federal courts might possess to develop and apply rules of decision for diversity cases, that power surely had no greater scope than Congress's power under Article I to legislate. The federal courts had, in Brandeis's characterization, claimed a virtually unbounded power in diversity cases to identify and apply rules of "general law," with little or no attention to whether the cases in which they did so implicated a subject matter that Congress itself could constitutionally regulate. As Brandeis noted, this was not something that Congress itself had constitutional power to do: "Congress has no power to declare substantive rules of common law applicable in a State, whether they be local in their nature or 'general,' be they commercial law or a part of the law of torts."[18] Therefore the federal courts lacked the cognate power to exercise the broad lawmaking power that seemed to be licensed by *Swift*. Scholars sometimes call this the principle of "coextension"—the notion that the lawmaking power of federal courts is at most coextensive with that of Congress.

Brandeis's argument in *Erie* is persuasive, but it may be incomplete.[19] It is true that the erratic course taken by federal courts since *Swift* had led them to assume power to apply "general law" in a wide variety of fields, and that the earlier "local law"

---

18. *Erie*, 304 U.S. at 78.

19. In the first place, the passage quoted in the previous paragraph in the text seems oddly imprecise. Brandeis did not say that "Congress has no power to enact a statute governing torts or commercial law that does not reasonably fall within the power to regulate interstate commerce or some other one of Congress's enumerated powers," which would have been the simple approach. Instead, he said that "Congress has no power to declare substantive rules of common law applicable in a State." The very concept of Congress's enacting "substantive rules of common law" is difficult to visualize, if not a contradiction in terms: Isn't the one remaining distinguishing feature of "common law" the fact that it is *not* enacted by a legislature? It is unclear what significance should be ascribed to Brandeis's choice of wording; perhaps it is best explained as an effort not to unduly limit the power of Congress.

limitation, to which even Justice Story had adhered, had been steadily eroded. It is also true that Congress lacks power to enact a general code of common law for the federal courts that disrespects the boundaries prescribed in Article I. But consider more specifically the facts of the *Erie* case itself. It involved a tort allegedly committed by a carrier operating in interstate commerce. It was clear in 1938, as it is clear today, that Congress has the power to enact a federal statute to govern tort actions brought against common carriers engaged in interstate business. In fact, Congress had done something analogous in 1906, when it enacted the Federal Employers' Liability Act to govern lawsuits brought against interstate carriers for injuries to their *employees.* Suppose that the federal courts had, by the time of *Erie,* developed a set of "general law" principles specifically to govern torts allegedly committed by interstate carriers, and that the lower court in *Erie* had based its decision on this clearly demarcated area of "general" law. Such a course of action by the federal courts would not seem, *so far as subject matter is concerned,* to have exceeded the scope of lawmaking power conferred on Congress by Article I; the tort liability of interstate carriers is certainly a subject within the competence of the federal government. Yet the language of the *Erie* opinion, taken literally, suggests that this hypothetical assumption by the federal courts of lawmaking powers with specific reference to torts by carriers engaged in interstate commerce would be every bit as constitutionally objectionable as the actual course of action taken by the federal courts after *Swift.*

Therefore, the constitutional reasoning of Brandeis's opinion in *Erie* cannot be based *solely* on the notion that the lawmaking power of the federal courts is coextensive with that of Congress. An additional element is necessary. That element, based on the doctrine of separation of powers,[20] is that the federal courts should not "make law" *in advance of* any action or invitation by Congress, even with respect to subject matter areas that lie within Congress's competence pursuant to Article I. This is not a *wholesale* rejection of the power of federal courts to devise rules of law no matter what the circumstances. Even after *Erie,* as we will see, there are areas within the constitutional domain of the national government as to which the federal courts have legitimate power to "make law." And if there are such areas, there seems no reason to regard the application by federal courts of such rules of law specifically in diversity cases as *unconstitutional.* But if federal courts are to have such power, there must be a plausible connection with some policy established by Congress on the matter—an invitation to the federal

---

20. For a different view of this question, see Peter Westen & Jeffrey S. Lehman, *Is There Life for* Erie *After the Death of Diversity?,* 78 Michigan Law Review 311 (1980).

courts to devise rules of law on the matter, or at least rules that are in accord with Congress's stated policy. On this reasoning, if Congress has not enacted a statute to govern, say, the tort liability of interstate carriers—and has done nothing to indicate its wish that the federal judiciary devise such rules on their own—then the federal courts may not themselves do so. It is this combination of the principle of "coextension," *with* the notion that the federal courts should not devise rules of law in advance of any indication of Congress's policy on the matter, that warrants *Erie*'s far-reaching conclusion: Federal courts sitting in diversity are constitutionally barred, at least as to "substantive matters," from applying rules of law that conflict with applicable state law in the manner and on the scale that many federal courts did prior to *Erie*.[21]

G. Taking Stock of *Erie*

Before looking at some of the important cases that the Supreme Court has decided on the authority of *Erie*, let's make a few final observations about *Erie* itself.

Federal Courts Regularly "Make Law." First, it is important not to be misled by the denunciation of "judicial lawmaking" that has long accompanied criticism of the *Swift v. Tyson* doctrine. It is true that, in announcing and applying "general law" principles in the wake of *Swift*, the federal courts were engaged in a rather freewheeling enterprise that disrespected state law. But the notion that "lawmaking" by federal courts is presumptively illegitimate is simplistic. The practical and conceptual differences between what federal courts are doing when they interpret and apply federal statutes and what they do when purporting to declare and apply law in the absence of a statute are often exaggerated. After *Erie*, the power of federal courts to make "federal common law" is thought to be strictly limited; so far as the interpretation and application of federal law is concerned, the federal courts are pretty much supposed to stick to the Constitution, Acts of Congress, and other codified sources of federal law. But the judicial process of interpreting these codified sources of federal law often looks a lot like the process of developing common-law principles. Because

---

21. The wordy formulation in the text is attributable to the author's caution in stating the holding and rationale of *Erie* in as precise a way as possible. It would certainly be more concise to describe *Erie* as holding that "federal courts sitting in diversity are constitutionally bound, at least as to 'substantive matters,' to apply state decisional law." Yet it is doubtful that the actual application of state law (as opposed to the nonapplication of judicially-created rules of "general law") is *constitutionally* required. Rather, it is the federal Rules of Decision Act ("The laws of the several states ... shall be regarded as rules of decision ...") that appears to mandate the application of state law in the *Erie* situation. *See* Westen & Lehman, *Is There Life for Erie?*, *id.* at 315.

statutes *always* require interpretation, courts that apply them are constantly in the process of "making" law.

Sometimes, as with the Delphic words of the Sherman Act, Congress's command is so broad and indefinite that it virtually constitutes an invitation to the federal courts to supply, in the course of deciding litigated cases, much of the statute's detailed substantive content. Federal courts applying the Sherman Act are, literally speaking, engaged in application of a *statute*, but, after 120 years, much of the substantive meaning of the Act has been provided by the federal courts, acting in a manner not strikingly different from a common-law court. The point, again, is that the meaning of *Erie* resides not in a wholesale rejection of the idea that federal courts can make law, but rather in the notion that those lawmaking powers are subject to the important limitations imposed on the national government vis-à-vis the states by Article I, and on the federal judiciary in particular by the principle of separation of powers. As our reference to the Sherman Act suggests, assumption of lawmaking powers by the federal courts may seem less troubling if Congress, explicitly or implicitly, has actually invited those courts to supply, in common-law fashion, substantive principles (as to a subject that Congress itself has constitutional power to regulate).

No Constitutional "Enclaves" of Exclusive State Power. Second, it is common for jurists to suggest that the sin of the *Swift* doctrine, which the federal courts after *Erie* must scrupulously avoid, lies in the way that that doctrine empowered federal courts to invade substantive areas that lie exclusively within the control of the *states* under the Constitution. This statement is superficially appealing, but it conceals a potential misunderstanding about the Constitution's allocation of power between the federal government and the states. It is all too easy to infer from the statement that various categories of human activity—say, domestic relations, personal injuries, and so on—are constitutionally considered to be the exclusive province of the states. They are *"state* matters." But the Constitution does not explicitly define such matters as exclusive to the states. Rather, the content of what the Constitution leaves (exclusively or concurrently) to the residual power of the states is defined by the Constitution's explicit grants of limited authority to the national government, largely in Article I. As John Hart Ely famously and persuasively argued, there are no predefined "enclaves" of state authority; instead, there is what remains after certain portions of the traditional governmental powers have been withdrawn from the states and conferred on Congress.[22] Something

---

22. Admittedly, not all judges and scholars concur in this statement. Some argue, for example, that the Tenth Amendment protects certain sovereignty and dignitary interests on the part of the States that cannot be inferred simply from the limited allocation of authority to the federal government.

important rides on this seemingly theoretical point. There is a tendency to regard both *Erie,* and many of the cases decided on its authority, as involving a constitutional requirement that state law should supply the rule to be applied by federal courts in certain diversity situations. But in a number of the cases we will look at, it is more proper to say that the state rule should apply because Congress, which would have the power to provide a federal rule for the federal courts sitting in diversity, simply has chosen not to do so. It is downright misleading in these cases to think that the state rule applies because of some constitutional judgment that the issue is intrinsically a "state matter."

    Erie **is Not Really a "Choice-of-Law" Problem.** Third, and related, it is best not to think of the *"Erie* problem" (which, of course, takes many guises) as a conflict-of-laws or choice-of-law question. It is certainly not a matter of using either *lex loci* or ad hoc, "interest"-oriented methodologies to decide whether state or federal law should be applied with respect to a matter to be determined by a federal court sitting in diversity. If the concept of conflict of laws has any relevance to the *"Erie* problem," it resides in the fact that the Supremacy Clause (or, in some instances, the Rules of Decision Act) acts as a kind of "choice-of-law" rule for situations in which federal and state law conflict. As we will see, in many cases the real *"Erie* question" will be whether Congress has, consistently with its Constitutional powers, in fact provided a rule for use in a diversity case, and it is the Supremacy Clause that tells us that in such cases the federal rule must be applied, even in the face of a competing state rule.

H.   The *"Erie* Doctrine" After *Erie*: From *Klaxon* (1941) to *Walker* (1980)

    Thus far we have given an account of the holding in *Erie* and discussed that holding's relationship to the Constitution. Yet, of all the important cases decided since *Erie* that purport to be governed by *Erie,* few closely resemble the situation in the actual *Erie* case, where the question concerned the proper source of law concerning a matter belonging to the substantive law of torts. Virtually all the cases following *Erie* that you are likely to find in your casebook concern legal questions that might plausibly be regarded as "procedural" in nature. This is part of what gives the subject its sometimes puzzling quality—the sense that all the important problems seem to concern such arcana as rules governing the date on which a civil action is commenced or methods for service of process. The basic dilemma presented by this line of cases, stated in oversimplified terms, is this: On the one hand, *Erie* made clear that, apart from some exceptional situations, state decisional law as to matters of substance (for example, principles governing liability in tort) must govern federal courts sitting in diversity. On the other hand, it is unthinkable that such federal courts must apply state law to each and every issue that might arise in the case, such as the form of pleadings to be used or the time within which one must file a notice of appeal. Some legal issues just seem naturally to be governed by the rules devised specifically for the tribunal that is hearing the case. We tend to think of such issues as "procedural" in nature, to distinguish them from "substantive" issues. Unfortunately, this simple dichotomy has never proved to be the talisman one might hope it to be. Moreover, a close reading of these post-*Erie* cases suggests that not all issues lumped under the umbrella term "*Erie* problem" necessarily raise the same analytical problem that *Erie* itself did.

1. Klaxon v. Stentor *(1941)*

A very important case decided by the Supreme Court in the wake of *Erie* is *Klaxon v. Stentor* (1941).[23] In *Klaxon*, the Court ruled that, in diversity cases, a federal court must apply the choice-of-law rules of the state in which it sits. That is, the federal courts sitting in diversity may not develop and apply, in common-law fashion, their own choice-of-law principles concerning which state's substantive law should apply. (Note how the *Klaxon* rule differs from the traditional conflicts rule that the law of choice of law is the law of the forum.) Since lawsuits featuring citizens of different states not infrequently raise conflicts issues, the Court's holding in *Klaxon* is an important one. On the surface, its decision seems simple and sensible enough. One alternative—which, to be sure, some very eminent commentators have strongly advocated—would be for federal courts to develop and apply their own choice-of-law rules for diversity cases. Developing a nationally uniform set of rules in this manner would be a cumbersome and slow-moving process at best, and the Supreme Court presumably has little appetite for hearing and deciding several cases a year for the purpose of providing a uniform set of conflicts rules for federal courts sitting in diversity. In any case, the *Klaxon* rule is by now a venerable and firmly-implanted one: Federal courts sitting in diversity must apply the choice-of-law rules of the states in which they sit.

The harder question, however, is *why* this must be the answer—that is, what source of law dictates the result in *Klaxon*. Does the Constitution compel that result, as it did in *Erie*? The question of whose choice-of-law rule—state or federal—should apply in diversity cases differs in important ways from the tort-law question presented in the *Erie* case. Choice-of-law rules are somehow less "substantive" in nature than tort-law rules; that is why

23.   313 U.S. 487 (1941).

choice of law is governed by *lex fori* in ordinary conflicts cases. In particular, Congress almost certainly has the power to legislate choice-of-law rules for federal courts sitting in diversity cases, should it wish to do so. This is a big difference from the *Erie* case. Congress lacks constitutional power to provide a comprehensive code of tort law for federal courts sitting in diversity, but it would be odd to say that Congress can create lower federal courts, invest in them the authority to decide cases between citizens of different states, yet not have the power to provide for them choice-of-law rules to determine *which* state's substantive law should apply in those cases. A federal choice-of-law rule for such cases would not constitute disrespect for state law *per se*, since the ultimate result would still be the application of substantive state law.

It is true, of course, that Congress has not in fact provided such a set of choice-of-law rules, and we earlier considered that separation-of-powers principles might preclude the federal courts from beating Congress to the punch even as to matters that legitimately fall within national lawmaking authority. But, of all the subjects of lawmaking, choice of law is the one that historically has been regarded as perhaps *most* properly residing within the lawmaking domain of courts themselves. Virtually every state in the union relies on judicial rather than legislative action for the development of choice-of-law principles. There is simply no compelling reason to regard the development and application of choice-of-law rules for diversity cases as *constitutionally* forbidden to the federal courts. If *Klaxon* was correctly decided, it must be for reasons that differ from the reasoning on which *Erie* relied in holding that *Swift v. Tyson* had licensed an "unconstitutional course" of action by the federal courts.

The Court rested the result in *Klaxon* on a consideration that had loomed large in *Erie*: The impropriety (not to say the unseemliness) in our federal system of enabling a party to obtain different substantive outcomes in federal and state court, and thus to shop for the more favorable of the two forums, in diversity situations. Although the choice of forum will not always be as obvious and predictable for the party as it was, say, in *Erie* itself, it does remain possible that the choice-of-law rule devised by a federal court would, in a particular case, refer to the substantive law of a state different from that whose law would be chosen by the choice-of-law rule of the state in which the federal court is sitting. A party could rely on this fact in determining the court in which to litigate. Thus a forum-shopping opportunity might arise.

The Court stated in *Klaxon*, "Any other ruling would do violence to the principle of uniformity within a state upon which the [*Erie*] decision is based." It's very much a debatable question, though, whether the "principle of uniformity within a state" is really the "basis" for the *Erie* decision, especially since we regard *Erie* as a decision based on the Constitution. The Constitution bars Congress, and thus the federal courts, from legislating wholesale as to matters not confided to Congress by Article I or another part of the Constitution. Is this the same thing, though, as saying that the Constitution requires "uniformity within a state"? Is the *Constitution* offended when a party is able to choose between state and federal court based on the differing choice-of-law rules that would be available? After all, this is precisely the same forum-shopping opportunity that plaintiffs often exploit in deciding in which of two state courts to file. Unseemly forum-shopping opportunities may, as Brandeis noted in *Erie*, have been a highly undesirable consequence of the *Swift* doctrine. But, at bottom, *Erie* was correctly decided not simply because parallel judicial systems create forum-shopping opportunities, but because the Constitution confers no power on the federal government to make law on matters outside the limits specified therein. Still and all, the Supreme Court has never really divested itself of the notion that a desire not to promote forum-shopping as between state and federal court lies at the "core" of the *Erie* decision. This is the ambiguity in *Erie* and its progeny that still makes it important to pinpoint the core of the doctrine: Whether the "meaning" of *Erie* lies in the distaste for a party's ability to "choose" between two sources of law, or in a more concrete assessment of the allocation of the power to legislate as between the states and the federal government. Obviously this author opts for the latter account, but the Supreme Court (surely a more authoritative source) still places considerable emphasis on the former.

The result in *Klaxon*, however, does seem to be a practical one. Could one, then, offer a clearer rationale for the decision? Perhaps the most doctrinally satisfying approach would be to say that the federal courts do have the authority to develop federal common law on the matter of choice of law in diversity cases; and that the Supreme Court in *Klaxon* determined that, as a matter of federal common law, the choice-of-rule applied in such cases will be the rule that is applied by the courts of the state in which the federal court sits. Alternatively, one could reason that Congress has provided no law or clear policy on the question of which choice-of-law rules should govern federal courts sitting in diversity, and, in the absence of any Congressional rule on the subject, the Rules of Decision Act determines that state law should apply.[24] That is, one might say that Congress certainly has the constitutional authority

---

24. Another possible rationale is that the Supreme Court in *Klaxon* was merely exercising its inherent judicial powers to provide housekeeping rules for the federal judiciary. That would be an ironic rationale for a ruling that denied federal courts the authority to devise their own choice-of-law rules for diversity cases!

to provide choice-of-law rules for federal courts sitting in diversity, but that it has not done so, and therefore the federal courts should not do so in advance of any Congressional directive to that effect. One could then refer to the Rules of Decision Act as the authority establishing that state law should govern as to this choice-of-law question. Of course, the question is pretty much an academic one; the *Klaxon* decision says what it says, and it is the *Klaxon* rule that litigators need to know: Federal courts sitting in diversity apply the choice-of-law rules of the state in which they sit.

2. *Limitations Periods:* Guaranty Trust v. York *(1945)*

In *Guaranty Trust v. York* (1945),[25] a federal court sitting in diversity was faced with the question whether (1) a state statute of limitations that would bar plaintiff's claim, or (2) the federal equitable doctrine of laches, which would have permitted the plaintiff to proceed, should be applied to determine whether the plaintiff could maintain his suit based on a state-law claim. (The federal court was being asked to administer an equitable remedy, which is why the possible application of the equitable doctrine of laches was relevant.)[26] As with *Klaxon v. Stentor*, the issue "sounds" like a procedural one. A limitations period seems somehow distinct from the cause of action itself.[27] Yet we know from our study of statutes of limitations in choice of law that the matter is not so simple; not all states regard all such matters as governed by the law of the

---

25. 326 U.S. 99 (1945).

26. The procedural setting of *Guaranty Trust v. York* was more complex than sometimes appears from the decision as excerpted or summarized in casebooks. One might think that the outcome in *Guaranty Trust* should have been clear without even referring to the *Erie* decision; the state's limitations provision was embodied in a state *statute*, and, long before *Erie*, it had been generally recognized that applicable state *statutes* must govern in diversity cases, by command of the Rules of Decision Act. What distinguished the *Guaranty Trust* situation was the fact that the plaintiff was seeking a remedy that was equitable in nature; the power to hear cases "in equity" had been explicitly conferred on federal courts (in particular, what were then denominated the "circuit courts") in § 11 of the Judiciary Act of 1789. The Court conceived that the *Guaranty Trust* litigation presented a distinct problem, one in which the federal courts' undoubted equitable powers (and the availability of the doctrine of "laches," a traditional equitable principle for handling the problem of stale claims) were pitted against an applicable state

statute of limitations. It chose to analyze this problem through the prism of *Erie* and the basic principles that it believed *Erie* represented. For these reasons, it is something of an oversimplification to characterize *Guaranty Trust* as holding that, in diversity cases, the state's limitation period should govern, although that is usually what it is taken to mean. The distinctions between law and equity, and between the federal courts' legal and equitable powers, are no longer of much importance in the federal judiciary, so the precise circumstances that characterize the *Guaranty Trust* case would be unlikely to arise today.

27. Older authorities sometimes called procedural issues questions of "adjectival law." Though the term is archaic, it describes something important: "adjectival" conveys a sense of "adjunct to." The procedural rule is adjunct to, or is in aid of, or somehow qualifies, the substantive right. Thus a statute of limitations could be seen as "adjective to" the substantive cause of action.

forum, as would be the case if we could simply label limitations periods as "procedural." In *Guaranty Trust*, the Court, speaking through Justice Frankfurter, held that the state statute of limitations must govern. As with *Klaxon*, the result is palatable enough, while the rationale for the result seems elusive. Justice Frankfurter conspicuously avoided stating that the result in *Guaranty Trust* was *constitutionally* compelled. One reason for that, in consonance with our earlier discussion of *Klaxon*, is that Congress surely possesses the constitutional power to enact a comprehensive statute of limitations for cases, including diversity (or equity) cases, brought in the federal courts. However one characterizes the rationales generally underlying statutes of limitations, historically one of them has been the need to ensure that courts hear only cases for which the evidence is likely to be fresh, and to free those courts from the burden of hearing a plethora of "old" cases. If states can enact such statutes in aid of their own judiciaries, it is hard to see why Congress cannot do the same for the federal courts, whether the underlying cause of action is derived from state or federal (or some other) law. And if Congress has this power, it is not easy to see why the federal courts themselves might not constitutionally develop their own rules governing the staleness of claims, especially since *Guaranty Trust* specifically involved equitable powers that had plainly (and constitutionally) been conferred on the federal courts by Congress.[28]

So, if it's not the Constitution, what is the rationale on which *Guaranty Trust* is based? Justice Frankfurter in *Guaranty Trust* referenced the familiar forum-shopping bogeyman:

> In essence, the intent of [*Erie*] was to insure that, in all cases where a federal court is exercising jurisdiction solely because of the diversity of citizenship of the parties, the outcome of the litigation in the federal court should be substantially the same, so far as legal rules determine the outcome of a litigation, as it would be if tried in a State court. The nub of the policy that underlies [*Erie*] is that, for the same transaction, the accident of a suit by a nonresident litigant in a federal court, instead of in a State court a block away, should not lead to a substantially different result.

It is indeed true that the outcome for the parties in *Guaranty Trust* would differ dramatically depending on whether the state limitations rule or the federal "laches" principle applied. Thus was born the "outcome determinative" test for determining whether state or federal law should apply with respect to an issue in a diversity case: If application of one or the other rule would (other things being equal) substantially "determine" the outcome of the case, the state rule must apply.

28. *See* fn. 26.

Like *Klaxon, Guaranty Trust* is and probably always will be grouped with *Erie* as an example of the *"Erie* problem"; but, at the risk of repetition, let's be clear that *Erie* actually rests on a different rationale than do the two later cases. Brandeis quite explicitly rested the *Erie* decision on constitutional grounds, having to do with the lack of power in either Congress or the federal courts to develop, willy-nilly, substantive rules of tort law. *Klaxon* and *Guaranty Trust,* by contrast, rest on what Justice Frankfurter claimed was the "nub of the policy that underlies" *Erie*: avoidance of the kind of unseemly forum shopping that would be licensed by application of the federal rule in such situations. An alternative (though hardly definitive) rationale for *Guaranty Trust* would be that Congress, although it had conferred on the federal courts the power to grant traditional equitable *remedies,* had not itself expressed any policy concerning limitations on actions brought in federal diversity actions, and that in the absence of any federal rule on the subject, the Rules of Decision Act mandated the application of the state limitations period.

Anyway, whether Frankfurter could have done a more persuasive job of explaining the result in *Guaranty Trust* is not that important.[29] The more significant point is that, as it turned out, *Guaranty Trust*'s "outcome determinative" test did not prove to be a durable analytic tool. The reason is fairly obvious: Resolution of just about *any* difference between a state rule and a federal rule that the parties think it worthwhile to argue about can, in theory, "determine" the "outcome" of a federal diversity case. For example, if the state's rules require the entry of a default judgment under circumstances where the federal rules would not, what we have here (besides a failure to litigate) is an issue whose resolution will obviously "determine" the "outcome" of the case. If you find this example frivolous, consider that the law in some states provides a test for granting summary judgment, or for taking an interlocutory appeal,[30] that is significantly different from that which prevails in the federal courts. It is no joke to suggest that these differences can indeed be "outcome determinative," yet few would argue that the state rule in these situations must be applied

---

29. There is a reasonable, if not necessarily compelling, case to be made that *Guaranty Trust* was wrongly decided. Not only would the "laches" doctrine (or some other limitations principle) developed and applied by federal courts in equity cases have been within Congress's power to enact if it wished to; it could be seen as having been adopted by the federal courts at the implicit invitation of Congress in the Judiciary Act of 1789. One could therefore argue that the federal doctrine should prevail over a

contrary state rule by virtue of the Supremacy Clause.

30. For example, in federal practice, where the "final judgment rule" prevails, defendant's appeal of the denial of her motion to dismiss for lack of personal jurisdiction cannot be immediately appealed, while in California practice, the defendant ordinarily *must* immediately appeal the denial of the equivalent motion, or else lose any further ability to litigate the issue.

by federal courts sitting in diversity. Without more, the concept of "outcome determinativeness" alone cannot solve these problems.

3. *More Than Forum Shopping:* Byrd v. Blue Ridge *(1958)*

The Court moved in a somewhat different direction in *Byrd v. Blue Ridge Rural Elec. Co–Op., Inc.* (1958), often regarded as the first significant *"Erie"* decision by the Court after *Guaranty Trust*.[31] *Byrd* was a diversity action for personal injuries in which one of the main issues was whether the plaintiff was a "statutory employee" under state law, in which case he was limited to a worker's compensation remedy. Clearly the substantive "statutory employee" question was to be governed by state law, but a separate question was whether that factual question should be determined by the judge (as South Carolina decisions had said it should) or by the jury (as suggested by federal case law).[32] The Court held that, in this case, the "federal rule"—jury trial—must prevail.

To make sense of *Byrd*, first observe that Congress undoubtedly is constitutionally authorized to provide that trials in civil cases (including those founded on diversity) in the federal courts shall be by jury (although it hadn't exercised that power in this instance). Thus, as with *Klaxon* and *Guaranty Trust*, we are dealing with a problem somewhat different from that in *Erie* itself, where Congress assuredly did *not* have the constitutional power to provide a general code of tort law for all cases heard in federal court. The question then became the scope of the power of federal *courts* to provide for jury trial in this kind of case. In his opinion for the Court in *Byrd*, Justice Brennan struck a note in defense of federal power to superintend the workings of the federal judiciary that had not been heard in *Klaxon* or *Guaranty Trust*: "The federal system is an independent system for administering justice to litigants who properly invoke its jurisdiction. An essential characteristic of that system is the manner in which, in civil common-law actions, it distributes trial functions between judge and jury and ... assigns the decisions of disputed questions of fact to the jury."[33] This statement marks a subtle shift in emphasis from the observation of Justice Frankfurter in *Guaranty Trust* that great care should be taken to ensure that litigants not be able to obtain different results from filing in state and federal court.

31.   356 U.S. 525 (1958). The Court in 1949 had decided three cases in which it sought to elaborate on the meaning of the *Guaranty Trust* case: *Ragan v. Merchants Transfer & Warehouse Co.*, 337 U.S. 530 (1949); *Woods v. Interstate Realty Co.*, 337 U.S. 535 (1949); *Cohen v. Beneficial Industrial Loan Corp.*, 337 U.S. 541 (1949).

32.   Note that the Court in *Byrd* did not hold that the Seventh Amendment required a jury trial in such cases, which would have made the case much simpler and devoid of *"Erie"* considerations.

33.   356 U.S. at 537 (footnote and citations omitted).

Of course, the "valence" of jury trial—the likelihood that it will provide a given plaintiff with a more favorable result than would a bench trial—is far less predictable *ex ante* than is the fact that, as in *Guaranty Trust*, one limitations period will bar the plaintiff's claim while the other will not. One can certainly reconcile the reasoning in *Byrd* with that in *Guaranty Trust*, as the Court in *Byrd* did, by noting that the risk of forum shopping is less obvious in the *Byrd* situation. But the opinion in *Byrd* did go somewhat beyond the *Guaranty Trust* analysis, in noting that there are some prerogatives possessed by the federal judicial system that compete with the injunction in *Guaranty Trust* that, above all, federal courts sitting in diversity should fundamentally reach the same results that an equivalently situated state court would. To Justice Brennan in *Byrd*, what it means to be a functioning federal court includes the power to establish some legal rules, even in diversity cases, that might differ from what state law would provide.

Justice Brennan's comment on the prerogatives of the federal judicial system, however, does not by itself dictate that the federal jury trial rule should be applied in *Byrd*; having determined that the federal courts have the power to provide for jury trial in this kind of case, one still needs a reason for saying that that federal rule should prevail over the state rule. On this question, *Byrd* is less satisfying. At bottom, Justice Brennan relied on two rationales in determining that the federal "jury trial" rule should apply: (1) South Carolina's "judge trial" rule for determining whether the plaintiff was a "statutory employee" was not "bound up" with the underlying substantive cause of action in the way that the statute of limitations was "bound up" with the cause of action in *Guaranty Trust*, and (2) "[T]here is a strong federal policy against allowing state rules to disrupt the judge-jury relationship in the federal courts." The second of these rationales does little more than restate the problem (why should that "strong federal policy" prevail?), and the first is something of a variation on the "outcome determinativeness" test, which—as tests go—is itself not particularly "determinative." Moreover, it's hard to believe that, had South Carolina's "judge trial" rule been more "bound up" with the substantive cause of action—say, by being part of the same statute—*Byrd* would have been decided differently by the Court.

Perhaps the better explanation for the result in *Byrd* is that, once one determines that the federal "jury trial" rule at issue in *Byrd* is *in itself* a valid exercise of federal power—that it could legitimately be applied by a federal court in the absence of any conflict with a countervailing state rule—it must prevail over such a conflicting state rule. This would appear to be the command of the Supremacy Clause. On this reasoning, the real question in

Klaxon, *Guaranty Trust*, and *Byrd* would be whether in fact there *was* a valid and applicable "federal rule"—in particular, whether a given federal *judicial* practice was sufficiently settled and connected to an explicit command of Congress to justify saying that a valid "federal rule" was applicable. In *Klaxon*, as I suggested earlier, there was no general federal choice-of-law statute, or even evidence that Congress intended the federal courts to develop generally applicable choice-of-rules; the Rules of Decision Act (*not* the Constitution) would thus mandate application of the state choice-of-law rule, making the result in *Klaxon* correct. *Guaranty Trust* is slightly more difficult to explain using this rationale, because, while Congress had not enacted a statute of limitations applicable to the state cause of action in that case, it *had* conferred on the federal courts the general power to grant equitable remedies, which might be thought to have affirmed those courts' power to apply such equitable doctrines as laches. Our reasoning here might thus militate in favor of a different result than was actually reached in *Guaranty Trust*. Nevertheless, it seems more accurate to say that the laches doctrine applied by the lower federal court in *Guaranty Trust* couldn't really be connected with a federal policy explicitly established by Congress, and that, as in *Klaxon*, the Rules of Decision Act mandated application of the state statute of limitations, there being no relevant "federal rule" to compete with it.

What about *Byrd*? The federal "jury trial" rule at issue in that case was at bottom a creation of the federal courts themselves. One can argue that Justice Brennan both recognized the importance of attempting to connect that rule with some national legislative policy and was unsuccessful in doing so, thus making the outcome in *Byrd* incorrect. There was no *Congressional* statement concerning a federal policy of referring the "statutory employee" issue to a jury (hardly surprising, since the substantive "statutory employee" issue was a question of state law), but Justice Brennan tried to find such a policy in the *Constitution*. Justice Brennan noted that the "federal system ... assigns the decisions of disputed questions of fact to the jury" "*under the influence—if not the command—of the Seventh Amendment*" (emphasis added).

The italicized words, particularly the weasel word "influence," demonstrate why Justice Brennan's effort here was unavailing. In a footnote, Justice Brennan specifically disclaimed any consideration of the concrete question whether the Seventh Amendment in fact mandated the use of jury trial with respect to this "statutory employee" question. Whatever "influence" the Seventh Amendment can be said to have in a case where the Court has declined to say that it actually applies, this does not amount to either a Congressional or Constitutional rule or policy that grounds the federal courts' development of the "jury trial" rule for "statutory employee" issues. That is not to say that the federal courts may never develop such a rule in the absence of explicit Congressional authorization or invitation, but that, on the rationale proposed in this and the preceding paragraph, such a judicially-created rule must give way to a countervailing state rule in cases where they conflict. Thus, one could argue that *Byrd* was incorrectly decided. In confirming, however, that there are situations in which the federal judicial system has a strong claim to the application of its own rules in diversity cases, *Byrd* was a salutary corrective to the over-emphasis on uniformity and avoidance of forum-shopping that characterized the Court's opinions in *Klaxon* and *Guaranty Trust*.

    4. The Role of the Rules Enabling Act: Hanna v. Plumer *(1965)*

    The notion that, as to an issue that could reasonably be described as "procedural," an applicable federal rule must always prevail in diversity cases if it is in itself valid has never been adopted by the Supreme Court in an unqualified way, and some commentators reject the idea altogether. It would, in theory, open the door to some of the forum-shopping opportunities that exercised the Court so much in *Guaranty Trust*.[34] However, in *Hanna v. Plumer* (1965),[35] the Supreme Court's next important interpretation of *Erie*, the Court moved in the direction of precisely that notion. In *Hanna*, a diversity action originally brought in the U.S. District Court for the District of Massachusetts, the plaintiff sued the executor of the estate of the alleged wrongdoer, who had died after the events in questions. The plaintiff served the papers on the wife of the executor at their home. Fed. R. Civ. P. 4, which governs service of process in federal litigation, permits the summons and complaint to be served "by leaving copies thereof at [the defendant's] dwelling house or usual place of abode with some person of

---

34. A hypothetical example will suggest how the proposed rationale could lead to unpalatable results. Suppose Congress were to enact a one-year statute of limitations, to apply to all cases brought in federal court. Then suppose plaintiff, a citizen of New York, brought a claim against defendant, a citizen of California, in New York state court, based on a New York cause of action. (All the relevant events took place in New York, making New York the clear choice-of-law reference, and the events occurred two years ago.) The limitations period under New York's statute is six years. Defendant removes to federal court, as the removal statute entitles him to. The proposed rationale would appear to suggest that the federal court should dismiss the claim on statute-of-limitations grounds: Congress has constitutional power to devise a limitations period for cases (diversity or otherwise) brought in federal court; it has clearly exercised that power; and therefore that valid federal rule must apply, per the Supremacy Clause. Perhaps this particular disagreeable result could be avoided by noting that, since it is the "judicial housekeeping" aspect of the statute of limitations on which we relied in concluding that such a federal statute is within Congress's power to enact, dismissal should be rendered without prejudice to the claim's being brought again in state court—or simply be remanded to state court.

35. 380 U.S. 460 (1965).

suitable age and discretion then residing therein," while Massachusetts law, governing litigation in the state courts, required personal service upon the defendant. The federal district court held that the Massachusetts rule for service of process applied, and dismissed the action. The Supreme Court reversed.

Hanna introduces another element into the *"Erie* doctrine" mix: the federal Rules Enabling Act, under whose authority the Federal Rules of Civil Procedure (and numerous other rules governing litigation in the federal courts) are promulgated. In *Guaranty Trust* and *Byrd*, the federal rule that competed for application was in some sense "procedural," but in each case that federal rule had been created by the courts rather than Congress. By contrast, Fed. R. Civ. P. 4 (at issue in *Hanna*), if not an actual "statute" itself, is clearly the creature of a federal statute—the Rules Enabling Act. That Act itself specifies both the process for the promulgation of rules of procedure, and the important limitation that such rules must really be an attempt to regulate "procedure."[36] Noting this, Chief Justice Warren in his opinion for the Court in *Hanna* held that, so long as an applicable Federal Rule of Civil Procedure is in itself valid—which is to say that it is consistent with the Rules Enabling Act as well as the Constitution—it must apply in federal litigation, even in diversity cases where the state in which the federal court sits would apply a different rule in its own courts.

> When a situation is covered by one of the Federal Rules, the question facing the court is a far cry from the typical, relatively unguided *Erie* choice: the court has been instructed to apply the Federal Rule, and can refuse to do so only if the Advisory Committee, this Court and Congress erred in their prima facie judgment that the Rule in question transgresses neither the terms of the Enabling Act nor constitutional restrictions....
>
> [T]he opinion in *Erie*, which involved no Federal Rule and dealt with a question which was "substantive" in every traditional sense (whether the railroad owed a duty of care to Tompkins as a trespasser or a licensee), surely neither said nor implied that measures like Rule 4(d)(1) are unconstitutional. For the constitutional provision for a federal court system (augmented by the Necessary and Proper Clause) carries with it congressional power to make rules governing the practice and pleading in those courts, which in turn includes a power to regulate matters which, though falling within the uncertain area between substance and procedure, are rationally capable of classification as either.[37]

36. No rule promulgated pursuant to the Rules Enabling Act shall "abridge, enlarge or modify any substantive right." 28 U.S.C. § 2072(b).

37. *Hanna*, 380 U.S. at 471, 472.

The Court thus suggested that *Erie*, and succeeding cases like *Guaranty Trust*, did not even provide the appropriate test for the problem in *Hanna*. The mere validity of Rule 4 (under the Constitution and the Rules Enabling Act) was sufficient to dictate that it should prevail over the conflicting state rule. And even if the "outcome determinative" test of *Guaranty Trust* were the appropriate test, according to the Court in *Hanna*, that test must be understood in terms of the "twin aims" of *Erie*: "discouragement of forum-shopping and avoidance of inequitable administration of the laws." Unlike in *Guaranty Trust*, there simply was no reason to think that the availability in federal court of a method of service of process not provided by state law would substantially affect anyone's choice of a forum.

Hanna thus appeared to do two things. First, and most important, it strongly suggested that if a Federal Rule of Civil Procedure (indeed, any rule promulgated pursuant to the Rules Enabling Act) is valid under the Constitution and under the Rules Enabling Act, then it should apply in a federal diversity case even if it conflicts with an otherwise applicable state rule. Thus, *Erie*—"twin aims" and all—did not govern the case. The Court's separation of cases involving the Rules Enabling Act, in which conformity with the latter constitutes the proper test, into a separate category is both helpful and justified. If a federal rule promulgated pursuant to the Rules Enabling Act is valid in itself, it would appear that the Supremacy Clause would mandate its application in a diversity case in the face of a conflicting state rule.[38] However, *Hanna*, with its reference to those "twin aims," also reinforced the idea that in cases where *Erie does* provide the appropriate test—namely, cases in which the federal rule is, instead, judge-made—avoidance of forum shopping and of the unfairness attendant upon that situation constitutes the touchstone of that test. This somewhat modified "outcome determination" approach thus should lead to the application of state law in cases where the federal rule is *not* a rule that was promulgated pursuant to the Rules Enabling Act, and the difference between the state and federal rules would present a party with an obvious incentive to select one forum over the other.

What, though, if the federal rule is judge-made, and the difference between the state and federal rules does *not* present a party with an obvious incentive to select one forum over the other? This

---

38. As straightforward as the *Hanna* rule is, it does not necessarily cohere with every one of the Court's prior ruling in "*Erie* cases." In *Ragan v. Merchants Transfer & Warehouse Co.*, 337 U.S. 530 (1949), the Court had held that in a diversity action, the state's rule for determining when an action was commenced for purposes of the statute of limitations, rather than Fed. R. Civ. P. 3, should apply. The *Hanna* test seemingly would have produced a different result. The Court in *Hanna* made a somewhat weak effort to distinguish the decision in *Ragan*.

is the situation presented by *Byrd*. *Hanna*'s analysis does not provide a direct answer to the question.

5.   *Is There an "Unavoidable Conflict"?* Walker v. Armco Steel (1980)

Whatever their virtues or defects, *Klaxon*, *Guaranty Trust*, *Byrd*, and *Hanna* all proceed on the premise that both a state rule and a federal rule, each valid in its own right, applied on their face to a case heard by a federal court sitting in diversity, and that they conflicted. (This differs from the reasoning in the *Erie* case itself, where the Court determined that whatever "general law" (in contradistinction to the applicable state law) governing torts that the federal court might wish to apply did not, constitutionally speaking, even exist; thus there was no "conflict" between state and federal law.) By the same reasoning, if no federal rule even applies, there is no "conflict" and no real difficulty in concluding that the state rule applies. This was the Court's reasoning in *Walker v. Armco Steel Corp.* (1980).[39] In *Walker*, the plaintiff brought a tort claim, arising under Kansas law, in federal district court in Kansas. Kansas law provides that, for purposes of the applicable statute of limitations, it is *service* of the complaint on the defendant, and not mere filing of the complaint in court, that must be effectuated prior to the running of the statute. Seemingly by contrast, Fed. R. Civ. P. 3 states, "A civil action [in federal court] is commenced by filing a complaint with the court." The plaintiff in *Walker* filed his complaint with the federal court prior to running of the Kansas statute (which concededly applied to the case), but did not serve the complaint on the defendant until after the statute had run. Had the case been brought in state court in Kansas, then, clearly the claim would have been dismissed by reason of the statute of limitations.

Assuming that Fed. R. Civ. P. 3 constitutes, among other things, a rule for determining when the plaintiff has commenced an action in federal court for purposes of any *federal* limitations period that might apply (say, in a case in which the plaintiff's claim arises under federal law), there would appear to be in *Walker* a conflict between a state and a federal rule. If so, *Hanna* should have dictated that the federal rule should apply, meaning that the plaintiff should have been able to proceed with the case, since he had filed the complaint with the court prior to the running of the Kansas statute of limitations. Certainly Fed. R. Civ. P. 3, interpreted in this way, would be consistent with both the Constitution and

39.   446 U.S. 740 (1980).

the Rules Enabling Act. But the Court in *Walker* also had to deal with a troublesome precedent: In *Ragan v. Merchants Transfer & Warehouse Co.* (1949),[40] decided under the influence of *Guaranty Trust* and its emphasis on forum shopping and "outcome determinativeness," the Court held in a situation virtually identical to that presented by *Walker* that the state "commencement" rule, and not Fed. R. Civ. P. 3, should apply.[41] The Court in *Walker* was thus faced—or so it seemed—with a choice of (1) overruling *Ragan* or (2) repudiating or limiting the reasoning in *Hanna v. Plumer*. But the Court found a more palatable way out in *Walker*: It concluded that Fed. R. Civ. P. 3 does *not* in fact constitute a "commencement" rule for purposes of state statutes of limitations in federal court, and that since that left only the state commencement rule, that state rule must apply. With no "unavoidable conflict" between state and federal law, there was nothing to keep state law from applying.

The Court's reasoning in *Walker* is not very persuasive, but its resort to such reasoning is understandable. The Court in *Hanna v. Plumer* had itself emphasized that only an "unavoidable conflict" between the federal and state rules in that case permitted it to conclude that the Fed. R. Civ. P. 4 should govern; presumably, in situations in which there was no such "unavoidable conflict," the state law should apply if failure to do so would lead to different outcomes in state and federal court. Moreover, the Court in *Hanna* had not suggested that *Ragan* was *pro tanto* overruled by the decision in *Hanna*. The Court in *Walker*, reluctant to overrule *Ragan* yet faced with the analysis in *Hanna*, simply decided that Fed. R. Civ. P. 3 did not establish a federal commencement rule for limitations purposes after all, at least as to state statutes of limitations. Thus the federal rule was not "broad enough" to cover the situation in *Walker*, and there was no "direct collision" between federal and state law. The Court thus reaffirmed *Ragan*, albeit on a theory that *Ragan* itself had not adopted. The most obvious difficulty with the Court's reasoning in *Walker* is that both logic and precedent indicated that Fed. R. Civ. P. 3 provides a commencement rule for an applicable *federal* statute of limitations,

---

40. 337 U.S. 530 (1949).

41. Obviously, other things being equal, the federal "commencement" rule is more advantageous to a plaintiff than the state rule, at least if the end of the limitations period is rapidly approaching; the "*Erie* problem" in such a case isn't much different from the statute-of-limitations issue treated in *Guaranty Trust* itself. So it was reasonable for the

Court to conclude in *Ragan* that the difference between the state and federal commencement rules was "outcome determinative" in the sense specified by *Guaranty Trust*. Of course, *Hanna* tells us that this "outcome determinativeness" inquiry isn't really relevant where the federal rule is one that was promulgated pursuant to the Rules Enabling Act.

for purposes of federal questions cases; *Ragan* itself had said so. It is a stretch to read the unqualified language of Fed. R. Civ. P. 3 as providing a commencement rule for an applicable federal statute of limitations but not for a state statute of limitations. The Court in *Walker* avoided making this stretch in a footnote in which it stated it was leaving unresolved the question as to whether Fed. R. Civ. P. 3 does in fact provide a commencement rule for purposes of a federal statute of limitations. All right, but it's hard to see where else such a commencement rule would come from if not from Fed. R. Civ. P. 3.

Reading between the lines, *Walker* may reveal the Court struggling, not only with the problem of *stare decisis* and the *Ragan* and *Hanna* precedents, but at a more basic level with the "nub" or meaning of the doctrine established by *Erie* and subsequent cases. *Hanna v. Plumer* had indicated that avoidance of forum shopping and of "inequitable administration of the laws," while perhaps constituting "twin aims" of *Erie*, is not the sole consideration in these post-*Erie* cases; the federal interest in the conduct of litigation in the federal courts—in particular, Congressional power over federal civil procedure—also has its claims. But in *Walker* the Court indicated its desire not to stray too far from its concern with the forum shopping and "inequitable administration of the laws" that might be promoted by too easy a displacement of state law. It therefore admonished federal courts, implicitly if not explicitly, to ensure that there is an "unavoidable conflict" between a state rule and a federal rule, even one promulgated pursuant to the Rules Enabling Act, before determining à la *Hanna* that the federal rule should govern in a diversity case. *Walker* remains good law today; so, at least in diversity cases appearing to involve a conflict between a federal rule promulgated pursuant to the Rules Enabling Act and a state rule, one must always consider the possibility that the federal rule can be interpreted so as not to apply in the case, precluding any "unavoidable conflict" and therefore leading to the application of the state rule.

* * * *

By the time that *Walker* had been decided, one could intelligibly, though not effortlessly, summarize the basic principles that had emerged from the Supreme Court's decisions in *Erie* and succeeding cases. Such a summary might rely as much on a retrospective effort to provide some coherence to the line of cases as on the language in the Court's opinions itself, but it would at least have the virtue of clarity. Those basic principles might be stated as follows:

- Based on the *Erie* case itself, federal courts sitting in diversity have no constitutional authority to develop federal law, common-law-style, as to "substantive" areas of law concerning which Congress itself has no constitutional authority to legislate wholesale.[42] In the situation typified by *Erie*, there is no "conflict" between federal and state law because there is no constitutionally valid federal law at issue. State decisional law (like state statutes) must govern the case, by command of the Rules Enabling Act.

- An important part of the rationale for the *Erie* rule—the "twin aims" mentioned by the Court in *Hanna v. Plumer*—is the importance of avoiding craven forum shopping and the "inequitable administration of the laws" that would result if a party could benefit from a choice between a federal rule in federal court or a state rule in state court. In cases like *Klaxon* (choice of law) and *Guaranty Trust* (statute of limitations), where the plaintiff will often have a clear *ex ante* incentive to prefer either the state or the federal rule, this *Erie* rationale militates in favor of applying the state rule in cases where there is actually a conflict between applicable state and federal rules. It is difficult to argue that this principle is *constitutionally* required in the way that the *Erie* decision itself was; as noted, it would seem perfectly constitutional for Congress to provide the federal courts with a choice-of-law principle or a federal limitations period, so there truly is a "conflict" between the federal rule and the state rule in *Klaxon* and *Guaranty Trust* (as opposed to saying, as in *Erie* itself, that no constitutionally valid federal law is even involved). The source of law directing the application of the state rule in these cases would seem most logically to be the federal Rules of Decision Act. Alternatively, one can view *Klaxon* and *Guaranty Trust* as a natural outgrowth of the *Erie* rule by saying that both the state choice-of-law rule (in *Klaxon*) and the state statute of limitations (in *Guaranty Trust*) were so "bound up" with the underlying state-law cause of action (as to which the federal court of course could not devise its own rule) that to fail to apply the state rule would be tantamount to a failure to give true effect to the underlying state substantive law.

- However, in diversity cases where a state rule and a federal rule (each valid in itself) are competing for recognition, avoidance of forum shopping is not the only consideration at play. The integrity of the federal judiciary as an independent judicial system also has its claims. Federal courts sitting in

42. The term "wholesale" is used to hedge against the fact that the Constitution plainly permits Congress to legislate, for example, with respect to a subset of tort cases that amounts to regulation of interstate commerce, as in the Federal Employers Liability Act.

diversity are not simply mimes, seeking to do *everything* precisely as would the state court had the case been brought there. In particular, Congress has constitutional power to create rules for the conduct of litigation in the federal courts. The most conspicuous example of Congress's having done so is its enactment of the Rules Enabling Act, pursuant to which the Federal Rules of Civil Procedure (and numerous other rules governing the conduct of federal litigation as well) are promulgated. Where there is a valid federal rule (that is, one that is both constitutional and in conformity with the Rules Enabling Act) that is in "unavoidable conflict" with a state rule, the federal rule must apply.[43] Thus, in *Hanna v. Plumer*, a diversity case, Fed. R. Civ. P. 4(d)(1), concerning service of process, was held to apply rather than the process prescribed by state law for litigation in the state courts. The Court in *Hanna* did acknowledge the "twin aims" of *Erie*—"discouragement of forum-shopping and avoidance of inequitable administration of the laws"—and concluded that those dangers were not reasonably presented by the ability to obtain the federal process-service rule by suing in federal court. But even were those dangers present, the Court seemed to suggest in *Hanna* that neither *Erie*, nor its "twin aims," constitutes the proper test when a federal rule validly promulgated pursuant to the Rules Enabling Act is at issue. The validity of a federal rule under the Constitution and the Rules Enabling Act is a sufficient condition for its being applicable in a diversity case in federal court, notwithstanding a conflict with a state rule (or even the possibility that forum-shopping or disparities in result might ensue).

● The one case in the line that we have examined that is analytically most difficult to explain under these principles is *Byrd v. Blue Ridge Rural Electric Cooperative, Inc. Byrd* is notable for observing that the federal judicial system may have interests that compete with the simple aversion to forum-shopping identified in *Klaxon* and *Guaranty Trust*, but in resolving the conflict between the state rule (trial by the judge) and the federal rule (trial by the jury) in that case, *Byrd* seemed to engage in little more than a balancing test. Moreover, whereas the ultimate source of the federal rule in cases like *Hanna* is a federal statute—the Rules Enabling Act—the source of the "federal rule" favoring jury trial in *Byrd* is rather ambiguous. If we assume that that "federal

---

43. It would appear that the Supremacy Clause demands this result, but the Supreme Court has never ruled to this effect. Hence the qualifying phrase "it would appear."

rule" had been *judicially* created, by decisions of the federal courts, we are faced with the question of what to do when there is a conflict between a state rule and a federal judge-made rule. Is *Hanna*'s principle, mandating application of a *statutory* federal rule so long as it is in itself valid, appropriate for a situation in which the federal rule is *judge-made*? That seems quite dubious. As noted above, for those who would like to give at least a retrospective rationale for the result in *Byrd* that aligns it with the general analysis suggested thus far in this chapter, a possible (if not wholly compelling) explanation would be that the federal judicial practice/rule of jury trial, even as to matters for which the Seventh Amendment would not *require* jury trial, was established "under the influence of" the Seventh Amendment, and could in some sense be sufficiently connected with a Congressional "policy" favoring jury trial that the rule is somehow "legislative" in origin.[44]

- Finally, *Walker v. Armco Steel* reminds us that there can be a conflict between a state rule and a federal rule only when there actually is an applicable federal rule. While the Court's conclusion in *Walker* that Fed. R. Civ. P. 3 did not constitute a commencement rule for state statute-of-limitations purposes is not wholly persuasive, the general proposition that the state rule applies when there is no federal rule on the issue seems unassailable. Whether or not *Walker* stands as an injunction to federal courts to strain to avoid finding a conflict between a state and a federal rule whenever possible (the Court denied this), it remains clear that if there is no federal rule on the issue, the state rule must be applied.

I. The *"Erie* Doctrine" After *Walker v. Armco Steel*

Supreme Court decisions addressing the *"Erie* problem" since 1980 have been basically consistent with the line of cases prior to 1980, but they reinforce the fact that no simple formula is going to cover the myriad of issues that can arise in this area. Thus, for example, two Supreme Court cases in the late 1980s suggest that *Walker*'s seemingly simple principle—that there can be a conflict between a state and federal rule only if the federal rule actually purports to apply in the case—is more complex than meets the eye.

1. Burlington Northern Ry. v. Woods *(1987)*[45]

Burlington Northern presented a seeming "collision" between Federal Rule of Appellate Procedure 38, which permits a federal

44. Some commentators simply think that *Byrd* was incorrectly decided. *See, e.g.*, Westen & Lehman, *Is There Life for Erie?*, *supra* n.3, at 345–52.

45. 480 U.S. 1 (1987).

court of appeals to impose a penalty on an unsuccessful appellant if the court finds the appeal to have been frivolous, and an Alabama rule governing appeals in the state court system, which prescribes a 10% penalty for *all* unsuccessful appeals of money judgments. The federal court of appeals in *Burlington Northern* applied the Alabama rule when the appellant appealed unsuccessfully from the district court's judgment in a diversity case. The Supreme Court, however, ruled that Fed. R. App. P. 38 should apply. Unlike in *Walker*, the Court found that that there was in *Burlington Northern* a "direct collision" between the state and federal rules, and that, as a valid exercise of rulemaking authority pursuant to the Rules Enabling Act, Fed. R. App. P. 38 must control. This conclusion, however, did require a discriminating analysis of what amounts to a "direct collision," because the phrase implies that in certain circumstances a state rule and federal rule could both (1) apply and (2) be different from one another, while not presenting a collision sufficiently "direct" to mandate application of the federal rule. In fact, the appellee in *Burlington Northern* argued that, since Alabama has, "alongside [its] affirmance penalty statute," another appellate rule that mirrors Fed. R. App. P. 38, the state rule could be applied while not impeding the discretion accorded to federal courts by the federal rule to impose a penalty higher than 10%. (This reasoning was an attempt to suggest that there was no "unavoidable conflict" or "direct collision" between the federal and the state rule.) The Court's simple answer to this was that application of Alabama's mandatory penalty provision deprived the federal court of the discretion to impose a penalty of *less* than 10% if it chose to do so under Fed. R. App. P. 38. There was thus a "direct collision" and the federal rule must apply.

2.   Stewart Organization, Inc. v. Ricoh Corp. *(1988)*[46]

Ricoh presented a more interesting situation, pitting 28 U.S.C. § 1404(a), a federal statute governing transfer within the federal system, against Alabama case law disfavoring forum selection clauses. When the defendant was sued in federal district court in Alabama on a contract that provided that any such disputes be litigated in New York, it moved to transfer the case to the Federal District Court in New York under 28 U.S.C. § 1404(a). The federal district court in Alabama, citing Alabama case law disfavoring enforcement of forum selection clauses, denied the motion. The Supreme Court ruled that 28 U.S.C. § 1404(a), as a valid Congressional statute governing transfer within the federal judicial system, applied to the transfer problem; that it collided directly with

46.   487 U.S. 22 (1988).

Alabama law professing disapproval of forum-selection clauses; and that therefore 28 U.S.C. § 1404(a) should have been applied by the federal district court judge. Note that, because the law of Alabama and § 1404(a) were not "on all fours" with one another—the state rule concerned the enforceability of forum-selection clauses, the federal rule governed the discretion of federal courts to order transfer of cases within the federal system for a wide variety of situations—the two rules were not in "direct collision" in the sense of its being impossible to act in accordance with both. In particular, the Court held that Alabama's policy disfavoring enforcement of forum-selection clauses was one of the discretionary factors that the federal district court could legitimately take into account when applying § 1404(a) to the transfer motion. But because simple application of Alabama law to deny the transfer would have short-circuited the multi-factor discretionary analysis that § 1404(a) enjoins upon federal district courts when ruling on such motions to transfer, the collision between state and federal law was sufficiently "direct" to mandate application of § 1404(a) and not the state rule under *Hanna* and *Walker*.

Should it make any difference that *Ricoh*, unlike *Hanna* and *Walker*, involved a federal *statute* rather than a rule promulgated pursuant to the Rules Enabling Act? Probably not much. If anything, the presence of a federal statute in *Ricoh* dramatizes even more vividly the fact that the federal rule must prevail over a conflicting state rule when the two conflict or "directly collide." Congress's power to enact § 1404(a) seems obvious as part of its authority to regulate practice and procedure in the federal courts, and Alabama's law concerning the enforceability of forum-selection clauses should not be permitted to displace it in a federal diversity case.

At the same time, though, it is not clear that in *Ricoh*, the federal rule and the state rule are commensurable—that is, that they both regulate questions of "procedure." Alabama's rule does, it is true, affect venue, as § 1404(a) does, and perhaps its most common consequence is to keep parties from being able to oust Alabama courts of their rightful jurisdiction.[47] But might it not also reflect Alabama's substantive policy about the nature of contractual obligations, or the balance of bargaining power between the parties? In other words, if the Alabama rule discouraging enforcement of forum-selection clauses is not merely concerned with venue or procedure, but also speaks to questions of substance, perhaps a case like *Hanna* should not so clearly govern the question in *Ricoh*.

---

47. One might in fact inquire as to whether this rule on forum-selection clauses even has rational application where the court in which the case has initially been filed is a federal court. At the same time, we wouldn't want a defendant to be able to avoid the effect of Alabama's rule simply by removing to federal court once she has been sued in Alabama state court.

Neither *Erie* nor any of the Supreme Court's subsequent decisions give a clear answer to what should happen when application of the federal procedural rule (even assuming it derives from a federal statute or a rule promulgated pursuant to the Rules Enabling Act) would operate to displace a state substantive policy. Note that, if we choose to make *Erie*'s "twin aims" a point of departure for the analysis (which the Court in *Ricoh*, regarding the case as pretty clearly governed by *Hanna* and *Walker*, did not), it's not fanciful to think that there would be an incentive to forum-shop here. For example, after the *Ricoh* decision, a defendant sued in Alabama state court on facts identical to those in the *Ricoh* case might seek to remove to federal court, on the theory that it has a better chance of ending up litigating in New York (by means of § 1404(a) transfer) than if the case stays in Alabama state court, where the forum-selection clause is unlikely to be enforced.

The Court in *Ricoh*, however, did not wade into these waters.

3.   Gasperini: *A Return to the* Byrd *Problem?*

Gasperini v. Center for Humanities, Inc. (1996),[48] like *Ricoh*, illustrates that the state and federal rules at issue in an *"Erie* case" frequently are incommensurable; the interests they serve and the problems to which they are addressed are often so different from one another that it can be difficult to subject the conflict between them to a satisfying and persuasive analysis. In *Gasperini*, a journalist brought a diversity case in federal court, raising state-law claims against an organization for the loss of valuable slide transparencies he had lent the organization. The federal district court entered judgment for the journalist, in accordance with a jury verdict, for $450,000. Traditionally, federal appellate courts would not disturb a jury award for money damages unless it "shocked the conscience"; but New York law, beginning in 1986, provided that state appellate courts in New York "shall determine that an award is excessive or inadequate if it deviates materially from what would be reasonable compensation." Despite its neutral language ("excessive *or* inadequate"), the New York rule had plainly been adopted in an effort to curb excessive jury awards, and that rule conferred on New York appellate courts wider scope for the reversal or modification of jury awards than the "shock the conscience" test traditionally applied by federal appellate courts. The question in *Gasperini* was whether the federal court of appeals should apply the New York "deviates materially" rule or the traditional federal "shock the conscience" rule in reviewing the award made in the federal district court.

Gasperini indeed presents a strange and perplexing problem. The Court first concluded (over a vociferous dissent) that the

48.   518 U.S. 415 (1996).

Seventh Amendment does not bar federal appellate courts altogether from reviewing jury awards at the district court level for excessiveness. At the same time, federal appellate practice in that regard had consisted of reviewing, using an "abuse of discretion" standard, a denial by the federal district court of a motion for new trial on the ground that an award was excessive, and that practice had effectively amounted to reversal or modification by the court of appeals only when the jury's award "shocked the conscience." In other words, it was a high bar. Since the New York "deviates materially" rule for appellate review constitutes a different standard, the Court had to determine which standard for appellate review should apply. It did so principally by purporting to apply the analysis that had been used in *Byrd*, which, like *Gasperini* (and unlike *Hanna, Walker, Burlington Northern*, and *Ricoh*) involved a federal rule that had emerged from judicial practice rather than from a federal statute or a rule promulgated pursuant to the Rules Enabling Act.

Unlike in *Byrd*, however, the Court regarded the difference between the state and federal rules in *Gasperini* as implicating *Erie*'s "twin aims," because that difference could foreseeably affect the choice of a party to make a selection between state and federal court, and thus lead to substantially different outcomes in the two systems.[49] Therefore, even while acknowledging the substantiality of the federal interest in the allocation of decisionmaking authority between trial and appellate tribunals (similar to *Byrd*'s recognition of the importance of the federal interest in its judicial system's allocation of authority between judge and jury), not to mention the command of the Seventh Amendment, the Court in *Gasperini* regarded it as important to provide for substantial effectuation of the state rule. It attempted an accommodation of the state and federal interests through the Solomonic expedient of requiring that the federal *trial* court apply the New York "deviates materially" standard when ruling on new trial motions, without disturbing the

---

49. The idea, presumably, is that a plaintiff would prefer to litigate in federal court, because any award he might obtain in the trial court would be subject to more limited review on appeal than would be the case in the New York state courts. This reasoning rests on the conclusion, which the Supreme Court in *Gasperini* accepted, that the purpose and effect of New York's adoption of the "deviates materially" standard for appeal was to *reduce* awards overall, even though the statute provides for such review of "inadequate" awards as well. Were one to conclude that the New York standard applies equally to appellate review of awards for "excessiveness" and "inadequacy," one would appear to have a situation quite similar to that in *Byrd*: The difference in standards for appellate review, like the different modes of trial at issue in *Byrd*, would not predictably cut in favor of or against plaintiffs or defendants in any patterned way—a plaintiff awarded a large amount might find his award imperiled on appeal by application of the New York standard, but might also find his meager award subjected to freewheeling review on appeal by the same standard—and the "twin aims" of *Erie* would not seem to be so plainly implicated.

traditional standard of review (abuse of discretion or "shock the conscience") to be applied by federal appellate courts in such cases. The practical effect was to subject jury awards in the federal district court to New York's appellate standard of review (albeit at the "new trial motion" stage), while sparing the federal courts of appeals the indignity of having their traditional standard of appellate review of jury awards displaced by the state rule in diversity cases wherever the state standard might be different.

If you're looking to make sense of *Gasperini* in light of the other cases we've discussed, it is closest to *Byrd*—a decision that, as we've mentioned, can itself be a bit difficult to grasp. Both *Byrd* and *Gasperini* involve a federal rule that is "judge-made" rather than statutory or promulgated pursuant to the Rules Enabling Act; in both cases the federal rule or practice rests somehow in the shadow of the Seventh Amendment, although the precise relationship of the rule to the Seventh Amendment is elusive; and in both cases the Supreme Court engaged in something of a balancing test to determine whether (and, in *Gasperini*, how) the federal rule should be applied. The result in *Gasperini* differs from that in *Byrd* because in *Gasperini* the Court attempted to give effect to *both* the state and federal interests. The importance of providing at least some vindication of the state policy was evidently more important to the Court in *Gasperini* than in *Byrd* because in *Gasperini* it could be said, with some justice, that the availability to a party of different state and federal rules threatened to imperil the "twin aims" of *Erie*. If you agree with that, then *Gasperini* is at least intelligible in terms of the principles set out by the earlier cases.

4. *The Latest:* Semtek (2001)*

What happens if an issue arises in a federal diversity case as to which it would be constitutionally permissible to have a federal rule, but no such federal rule exists and there exists a state rule that would have applied had the case been brought in state court? This odd circumstance is what generated the Court's decision in *Semtek International Inc. v. Lockheed Martin Corp.* (2001).[50] *Semtek* is probably more of a recognition-of-judgments case than it is an *Erie* case, but the Court's discussion in *Semtek* of *Erie* merits acknowledgment in view of the themes discussed in this chapter.

Semtek brought a lawsuit based on state-claims against Lockheed in California state court; Lockheed removed to the federal district court, which subsequently dismissed the case based on California's statute of limitations. Semtek then filed the same lawsuit in a state court of Maryland, which has a longer statute of limitations that, had it been applied, would have permitted the

---

* On March 31, 2010, the Supreme Court held in *Shady Grove Orthopedic Associates v. Allstate Ins. Co.* (2010 WL 1222272) that Fed. R. Civ. P. 23 conflicts with a New York statute forbidding class actions for the recovery of statutory interest, and that the federal rule must therefore govern in that diversity case.

50. 531 U.S. 497 (2001).

action to proceed. (No removal was available since Lockheed is a citizen of Maryland.) This second action should have been barred based on *res judicata* principles, right? Not so fast. Believe it or not, under California law (as well as the law of a few other states), dismissal on statute-of-limitations grounds does not preclude the bringing of the claim in a second proceeding. (How this rule could have meaningful effect when the first case was itself outside the limitations period is anyone's guess, other than perhaps to give the plaintiff an opportunity to get a more favorable ruling on the limitations question.) Had the first case been determined by a California state court, then, full faith and credit would actually have required the Maryland court *not* to dismiss the case on *res judicata* grounds (since a California court wouldn't have). But the first case was determined by a federal court, not a California court, and neither the Full Faith and Credit Clause nor 28 U.S.C. § 1738 applies to judgments rendered by federal courts.

An 1875 decision by the Supreme Court had held that, in such a situation, the preclusion law of the state where the first case had been brought should apply with respect to the claim-preclusive effect in other states of that judgment. But the Court in *Semtek* declined to view that case as binding precedent, because the outcome in that case may have been based in part on then-existing, pre-Rules Enabling Act federal law requiring federal courts "to apply the procedural law of the forum state in nonequity cases." Having discarded the relevance of the 1875 decision, the Court also considered the possibility that Fed. R. Civ. P. 41(b) might provide an answer to the question, and this is where *Erie* comes in. Fed. R. Civ. P. 41(b) provides that any dismissal, apart from three enumerated situations that do not include dismissals based on the applicable statute of limitations, is "an adjudication upon the merits."[51] If one takes the phrase "an adjudication upon the merits" to be synonymous with "subject to claim-preclusion effect," as many people understandably do and which historically has been the case, then Fed. R. Civ. P. 41(b) could be seen as providing a federal rule for the *Semtek* situation: the statute-of-limitations dismissal in the original litigation in the federal district court is *res judicata*. But the Court was reluctant to give Fed. R. Civ. P. 41(b) this reading. For one thing, to read that provision as embodying a preclusion rule, prescribing the effect in state courts of federal court judgments (based on a state statute of limitations), when the law of the rendering state does not itself provide for such preclusive effect, might violate the Rules Enabling Act by imbuing Fed. R. Civ. P.

---

51. "Unless the dismissal order states otherwise, a dismissal under this subdivision (b) and any dismissal not under this rule—except one for lack of jurisdiction, improper venue, or failure to join a party under Rule 19—operates as an adjudication on the merits." Fed. R. Civ. P. 41(b).

41(b) with impermissible substantive content. Apart from that, however, the Court added:

> [A]s so interpreted, the Rule would in many cases violate the federalism principle of [*Erie*] ..., by engendering " 'substantial' variations [in outcomes] between state and federal litigation" which would "[l]ikely ... influence the choice of a forum." ... Out-of-state defendants sued on stale claims in California ... would systematically remove state-law suits brought against them to federal court—where, unless otherwise specified, a statute-of-limitations dismissal would bar suit everywhere.

For these reasons, the Court chose to regard Fed. R. Civ. P. 41(b) as *not* supplying any claim-preclusion rule for statute-of-limitations dismissals rendered by federal courts sitting in diversity. With no federal rule to cite on the questions, the Court held that the preclusive effect of such judgments was a question of federal common law, whose content the Court then went on to announce: The Court held that the federal rule concerning the preclusive effect of the rendering federal court's dismissal would be ... to apply the rule of the state in which that federal court sits. (That's the same result reached by the Court in its 1875 decision, but in *Semtek* it was reached largely by post-*Erie* reasoning.) This solution was likewise defended by the Court as promoting uniformity on the matter as between state and federal courts, thus obviating the incentive for "the sort of 'forum-shopping ... and ... inequitable administration of the laws' that *Erie* seeks to avoid." So, let's be clear about the holding in *Semtek*: The claim-preclusive effect in another jurisdiction of a statute-of-limitations dismissal by a federal court sitting in diversity is governed by federal common law, but the content of that federal common law is supplied by the law of the state in which that federal court sits.

The result reached by the Court in *Semtek* after all the dust had cleared seems sensible, but some of its remarks concerning the relevance to its analysis of the *Erie* line of cases are somewhat puzzling. First, the Court's suggestion that interpreting Fed R.Civ. P. 41(b) to provide a preclusion rule for statute-of-limitations dismissals founders on "the federalism principle of *Erie*" is in considerable tension with *Hanna v. Plumer*. One of the major points of *Hanna* was that, if a matter was covered by a valid Federal Rule of Civil Procedure, the importance of *Erie*'s "twin aims" receded. (One could escape this tension with *Hanna* simply by holding that that interpretation of Fed. R. Civ. P. 41(b) would in fact violate the Rules Enabling Act, but of course the Court in *Semtek* did not go so far.) Second, the Court's elaborate effort to find that Fed R.Civ. P. 41(b) does not apply to the facts of the *Semtek* case is somewhat reminiscent of the Court's effort in *Walker v. Armco Steel* to establish the inapplicability of Fed R.Civ.

P. 3, so as to avoid a "direct collision" with an applicable state rule. But in the *Burlington Northern* and *Ricoh* cases, decided after *Walker*, the Court had been less skittish about acknowledging a "direct collision" between the state and federal rules. After *Semtek*, it is unclear how industrious the lower federal courts are expected to be about interpreting federal rules in such a way as to avoid a "direct collision" with a state rule. Still and all, the conclusion that there should be uniformity between state and federal courts so far as the *res judicata* effect of dismissals based on a state statute of limitations is concerned seems a judicious one. No one is going to quarrel much with the *result* in *Semtek*.

* * *

The path that has led the Supreme Court from *Erie* to *Semtek* leaves us somewhat at large, both as to what the "real" meaning of *Erie* is, and as to which of the cases decided since *Erie* will prove to be the most important precedents when the next *"Erie* case" arrives. As *Semtek* indicates, the notion that an important component of *Erie* is the avoidance of forum shopping and "inequitable administration of the laws" remains very much at the heart of the Court's *Erie* jurisprudence. At the same time, since *Hanna v. Plumer* no federal rule promulgated pursuant to the Rules Enabling Act has been subordinated to a conflicting state rule in an *Erie* case, just as no such federal rule has ever been held by the Court to violate the Rules Enabling Act itself. *Byrd* aside, federal rules for the management of litigation that are not the product of the Rules Enabling Act or other federal statute have fared less well in cases raising an "unavoidable conflict" with a competing state rule.

J. Federal Common Law After *Erie*

As we've noted, the fact that *Erie* sounded the death knell for the concept of "general law" that is enforceable in federal courts does not mean that federal courts have no power to make law, or that there is no such thing as federal common law. In fact, on the very same day that *Erie* was decided, the Court, in an opinion written by Justice Brandeis, held in *Hinderlider v. La Plata River & Cherry Creek Ditch Co.* (1938) that "whether the water of an interstate stream must be apportioned between the two States is a question of 'federal common law' upon which neither the statutes nor the decisions of either State can be conclusive."[52] Federal jurisdiction in *Hinderlider* was not founded on diversity, so its connection to the issues raised by *Erie* is, at first glance, oblique. In fact, the case had been litigated in the state courts, and thus the Court's ruling amounted to saying that the *state courts* should have

---

52.   304 U.S. 92, 110 (1938).

applied federal (common) law in the case. Yet *Hinderlider* foreshadowed a line of post-*Erie* decisions that have made clear not only that there is such a thing as "federal common law," but that some issues in cases that fall within the diversity jurisdiction of the federal courts are to be governed by such federal common law.

Admiralty and Diversity Jurisdiction Contrasted. Identifying precisely the kinds of issues that qualify for such treatment is the more difficult part. Let us begin by recalling that Article III (as implemented by the corresponding Congressional jurisdictional statutes) vests jurisdiction in the federal courts to hear a variety of types of cases, not just diversity and federal question cases. For example, Article III declares that federal judicial power extends to "all cases of admiralty and maritime jurisdiction." The jurisdiction subsequently reposed in the federal courts by Congress pursuant to this provision is called "admiralty jurisdiction." It has long been recognized that this grant of jurisdiction to the federal courts by itself implies the authority of those courts, exclusive of state authority, to "evolve and apply a national substantive law," presumably with reference to traditional and transnational principles of maritime law. So the federal courts not only have the power to develop and apply maritime law for cases falling within their admiralty jurisdiction; they are expected to do so where Congress has not itself acted. In this instance, the Constitution's grant of *jurisdiction* to the federal judiciary has been taken to mean that the federal courts should develop *substantive law* in the area.

Notice how dramatically this state of affairs differs, as least since *Erie* was decided, from the power of the federal courts sitting in diversity. The grants of diversity and admiralty jurisdiction in Article III are parallel; but only with respect to admiralty jurisdiction are the federal courts conceded to have ample lawmaking power. The way in which this discrepancy is usually explained is that it is important to have national uniformity in maritime matters and that the drafters of Article III and of the Judiciary Act of 1789 had such uniformity in mind in creating the admiralty jurisdiction. The same can't be said of diversity jurisdiction, which evidently was created to provide a neutral forum rather than uniform substantive law (although Justice Story might have replied that it was precisely this distinction between matters requiring a uniform national law and those of merely "local" concern that animated his views on "general law" in *Swift v. Tyson*).[53] The contrast between the diversity situation and the admiralty situation

---

53. One might argue that it is the Rules of Decision Act, which applies only to "suits at common law" (which admiralty cases are not), that explains the distinction between the power of the federal courts to make substantive law for diversity cases and their power to do the same for admiralty cases. But since *Erie* did not clearly rest on an interpretation of the Rules of Decision Act, it's hard to credit that rationale.

suggests that, when determining whether a constitutional grant of jurisdiction to the federal courts implies a delegation of authority to those courts to develop rules of substantive law in that area, the key inquiry will be whether the area is one in which the federal government has a distinctively important interest. The fact that the Constitution confers jurisdiction on the federal courts to hear a certain kind of case does not, by itself, imply that it has empowered the federal courts to make substantive law for those kinds of cases.

Clearfield Trust **and** *Parnell***: The Requirement of a "Uniquely Federal Interest."** Certain other kinds of issues call for the development and application of federal common law by federal courts, not simply by virtue of the fact that Article III vests jurisdiction in the federal courts to hear the kind of case in which the issue arises, but because there is a uniquely federal interest involved that requires the application of federal rather than state law. In *Clearfield Trust Co. v. United States*,[54] one of the leading cases on post-*Erie* federal common law, a check drawn on the U.S. Treasury was issued to an individual who had performed work for the federal Works Progress Administration. Someone else, however, obtained the check "in a mysterious manner" and fraudulently endorsed it before it reached the correct individual. The check ended up in the possession of Clearfield Trust Co., which was initially unaware of the forgery. When the United States sought reimbursement from Clearfield Trust so it could issue another check to the correct individual, the federal district court held that, under *Erie*, the law of Pennsylvania—which barred the United States from recovering against Clearfield Trust because of the government's "unreasonable delay" in notifying Clearfield Trust of the forgery—applied. The Supreme Court took a different view, holding that, because of the uniquely federal interests implicated when the U.S. issues funds for services rendered to it, the matter must be governed by federal rather than state law.

> The rights and duties of the United States on commercial paper which it issues are governed by federal rather than local law. When the United States disburses its funds or pays its debts, it is exercising a constitutional function or power. This check was issued for services performed under the Federal Emergency Relief Act of 1935 ... The authority to issue the check had its origin in the Constitution and the statutes of the United States and was in no way dependent on the laws of Pennsylvania or of any other state.... The duties imposed upon the United States and the rights acquired by it as a result of the issuance find their roots in the same federal sources.... In absence of an applicable Act of Congress it is for the federal

54. 318 U.S. 363 (1943).

courts to fashion the governing rule of law according to their own standards.[55]

The interest of the United States in having a uniform legal standard with respect to rights and duties arising out of its issuance of commercial paper was of particular important to the Court. Interestingly, the Court in *Clearfield Trust* suggested that a useful source of such federal "standards" would be the "federal law merchant" that had developed in the century after *Swift v. Tyson*, even though the basic concept of the "general commercial law" on which *Swift* rested had been fundamentally undermined in *Erie*.

Federal jurisdiction in the *Clearfield Trust* case had been founded on the fact that the controversy was one to which the United States was a party, and one possibility for the Court would have been to rest the result in *Clearfield Trust* on that jurisdictional grant alone. That is, as with the admiralty jurisdiction, the very grant of jurisdiction in Article III and the implementing Congressional statute could be seen as implying federal judicial power to make and apply the substantive rules of decision to govern cases to which the United States is a party. Nevertheless, the Court did not use this reasoning in *Clearfield Trust*. It is the more prosaic fact that the rules governing the rights and duties of the United States with respect to its commercial paper implicate a distinctively federal interest that accounts for the holding in *Clearfield Trust*—not the fact that federal jurisdiction in the case was based on the U.S.'s being a party in the case. One might think that *any* case in which the United States is a party might implicate a "uniquely federal interest," and that—unlike with the diversity jurisdiction—this is the reason underlying the conferral in Article III of jurisdiction on federal courts over cases to which the U.S. is a party. But the Court in *Clearfield Trust* may have been on solid ground in declining to rest its decision on this idea. There might be cases in which, even though the U.S. is formally a party, the substance of the dispute does not implicate any important or "uniquely" federal interests.

Thirteen years after *Clearfield Trust*, the Court considered a case between private parties, which concerned federally guaranteed bonds. The jurisdiction of the federal courts, importantly, rested on diversity (unlike in *Clearfield Trust*, where jurisdiction rested on the fact that the United States was a party). The disputed issue in *Bank of America v. Parnell* (1956)[56] concerned whether plaintiff or defendant bore the burden of proof on the question of whether the defendants had acted in good faith in accepting and cashing the bonds, without notice of a previous defect in title to them. The

55. 318 U.S. at 366–67 (footnote omitted).

56. 352 U.S. 29 (1956).

Court held, notwithstanding *Clearfield Trust*, that that question should be decided by state law and not by federal common law. The fact that, unlike in *Clearfield Trust*, jurisdiction in the case was founded on diversity (since the litigants were private parties) did *not* account for the difference in result. What mattered was that the federal interest was much more attenuated in *Parnell* than in *Clearfield Trust*; in *Parnell*, the rights and duties of the United States were not at issue, and the outcome of the litigation was at best of remote importance to the federal government. For this kind of issue, there was not a strong federal interest in having a uniform legal rule. Taken together, *Clearfield Trust* and *Parnell* suggest a rather loose and subjective test for determining whether federal common law should govern in disputes involving financial instruments issued or guaranteed by the United States, in which the more clear and direct the federal interest is, the more appropriate it is to have federal law govern the issue. Of course, all these cases presuppose that jurisdiction properly rests in the federal courts. Clearly, this is true for any case that is founded on admiralty, diversity, or the fact that the United States is a party. The proper source of law for the rule of decision in the case—state law, federal common law, or something else—is a separate question from the question of jurisdiction.

It's worth noting that, although the Court concluded in *Parnell* that the issue should be governed by state and not federal common law, it explicitly left open the possibility that, in a diversity case featuring different facts, application of federal common law might be called for. This reminds us that the *Erie* decision does not mean that the application of state law is constitutionally required in diversity cases. Obviously the wide-ranging, free-floating "general law" of the pre-*Erie* federal judiciary is forbidden, but just as clearly, the "federal common law" idea as set out in *Clearfield Trust*, *Parnell*, and other cases contemplates that, in appropriate if narrowly limited circumstances, federal common law can provide the rule of decision in a diversity case. This underscores the virtue of seeing the Rules of Decision Act as the source of law dictating what law should provide the rule of decision in a diversity case. Remember that the Rules of Decision Act specifies that the laws of the states should govern "in cases where they apply." It seems more than reasonable to interpret that phrase as excluding the kinds of cases in which the Court has determined that a uniquely federal interest (whether in uniformity of legal result or for some other reason) militates in favor of applying federal common law.

Perhaps the most illuminating discussion by the Supreme Court of the problem of federal common law is in *Banco Nacional de Cuba v. Sabbatino* (1964),[57] the leading case on the "Act-of-State" Doctrine. That case is discussed in greater detail in Chapter 8, because the "act of state" doctrine is central to the question of when federal courts should apply U.S. law in cases involving the interests of foreign countries. For present purposes, we will simply note that the *Sabbatino* case emerged from the Cuban government's expropriation of property from a corporation controlled by American citizens. The ensuing litigation in the federal courts featured a lawsuit between two nominally private parties, and was based on alienage jurisdiction; in formal terms, the cause of action was for breach of contract, a claim itself not arising under federal law. The corporation defended on the ground that the act of expropriation on which the plaintiff's claim depended was unlawful under international legal norms. The Supreme Court held that the "Act-of-State" Doctrine, which states that federal courts will not rule on the legality of a foreign sovereign's acts within its own territory, barred the federal courts from ruling on this defense. The substantive merits of the doctrine and its application in the *Sabbatino* situation are discussed in Chapter 8. But, putting aside the substantive question, where does the "Act-of-State Doctrine" come from? As the Court noted, it is compelled neither by the U.S. Constitution nor by international law. The Court concluded that the doctrine is a question of federal common law.

The "federal interest" in the determination of issues relevant to the foreign relations of the U.S. is unarguable—certainly clearer than its interest in uniformity with respect to the rights and duties arising from the checks issued by the federal government. As explained by the Court in *Sabbatino*, the interest of the executive branch in determining sensitive matters of foreign policy counsels against rulings by the federal judiciary concerning the legality under international law of actions taken by a foreign sovereign. Some of the same concerns underscored the Court's conclusion that federal common law was the source of authority for this proposition. Of course, there may be a tension here in empowering the federal courts to develop a doctrine designed to limit the power of the federal judiciary, but the tension is more apparent than real. The Court in *Sabbatino* explained why the alternative—relying on a disuniform body of state law to resolve the question of whether and to what extent courts should pass on the validity of such state expropriations—was undesirable.[58]

57. 376 U.S. 398 (1964).

58. In reaching this conclusion, the Court adverted to an important article published by the legal scholar and diplomat Philip C. Jessup, *The Doctrine of Erie Railroad v. Tompkins Applied to* *International Law*, 33 AMERICAN JOURNAL OF INTERNATIONAL LAW 740 (1939). Jessup presciently noted that, while many legal issues under international law and raising questions of U.S. foreign relations might well arise in federal cases founded

Reconciling Federal Common Law With the Constitutional Framework of *Erie*. As sensible as *Sabbatino* and the other cases may seem, we should assess them in the light of our analysis of the constitutional underpinnings of *Erie*. Recall our suggestion that one might measure the constitutionality of exercises in lawmaking by the federal judiciary against the dual requirements that (1) the subject matter of such lawmaking power be within Congress's power to make law under Article I (and other constitutional grants of Congressional lawmaking power), and (2) judicial action be somehow linked to explicit or implied invitation from Congress to develop rules of law. Thus, for example, the exercise of wholesale judicial power to make substantive rules of tort law (as in *Erie* itself) clearly fails this test, but judicial power to develop procedural rules for the conduct of federal litigation can fairly be inferred from the fact of Congress's having created the lower federal courts. It would be nice if the affirmation of federal common-law-making power in cases like *Clearfield Trust* and *Sabbatino* could be easily explained using this test, but things may be more complicated than that. It is one thing to say that Congress, in conferring admiralty jurisdiction on the federal courts, has instructed those courts to make law for such cases. It is another to say that Congress has somehow, somewhere, indicated its intention that the federal courts develop substantive law concerning the government's rights and duties with respect to the checks it issues. Obviously, Congress has the power under Article I to make such law itself, but it may be a bit of a stretch to say that the relevant federal statutes in *Clearfield Trust* and *Sabbatino* contemplate that the federal courts will take over the job. We may have to fall back on the less satisfying and somewhat formalistic notion that one can infer such a Congressional invitation to the federal courts from the very fact that the issue implicates a "uniquely federal interest."

There are, of course, instances in which an invitation from Congress has been easier to discern. A canonical example is *Textile Workers v. Lincoln Mills* (1957).[59] In that case, the Supreme Court held that the federal Taft–Hartley Act, which conferred jurisdiction on the federal courts to hear disputes concerning enforcement of agreements to arbitrate under collective-bargaining agreements, should also be read as a directive to the federal courts to develop rules of law to govern such disputes. Congress quite obviously has constitutional authority to regulate in the area, and it is not unreasonable to say that the Taft–Hartley Act (as well as other federal statutes on collective bargaining) established a federal "poli-

on diversity or alienage jurisdiction, it would imprudent to conclude from *Erie* that such issues must be governed by state law.

59.   353 U.S. 448 (1957).

cy" that federal courts should implement by the development of common-law rules.[60]

Should the Federal Courts Look to State Law for the Content of Federal Common Law? A final question of interest here is that, assuming we have a situation in which federal interests call for substantive federal common law to be developed by the federal law, to what should those courts look in devising that substantive law? In *Clearfield Trust*, for instance, the Court intimated that the federal courts might take as their starting point the "federal law merchant" that had been developed prior to the *Erie* decision. An alternative, depending on the nature of the issue, might be to adopt *state* law to supply the federal common-law rule. The rule of decision would thus be federal in nature, but its content would be supplied by the law of the state in which the federal court was sitting. This was precisely what happened in the Supreme Court's decision in *Semtek* (2001), described above: When a federal court sitting in diversity renders a judgment in Case A, the preclusion law to be applied by a federal court hearing Case B is a question of federal common law, but the content of that law is to be supplied by the law of State A.[61] In the abstract at least, it might appear odd to first find that the existence a "uniquely federal interest" in a particular kind of situation calls for the development and application of federal common law by the federal courts, and then conclude that the content of that law should be supplied by the very state law that the first conclusion operates to displace. The two conclusions are easier to reconcile, however, if one remembers that the determination that an issue should be governed by federal common law is, in principle, based in part on the notion that some law or policy established by *Congress* fairly invites or authorizes

---

60. There is a different conceptual problem with *Lincoln Mills*: Whether and how the jurisdictional provision of the Taft–Hartley Act can be read to have created a federal cause of action. Without that step, and without a holding (which the Court did not announce in *Lincoln Mills*) that federal jurisdiction in such situations was valid only where diversity of citizenship exists, it is hard to see how the Court's reading of the Act could be consistent with Article III. Congress may not confer jurisdiction on the federal courts to decide cases where there is no federal cause of action and where diversity (or one of the other heads of federal jurisdiction) does not exist. It is conventional today for courts

today to read *Lincoln Mills* as having conferred a cause of action on parties aggrieved by a refusal to arbitrate—a reading that solves the "federal question" problem, but that neither the statute nor the *Lincoln Mills* decision seems to support.

61. A related situation obtains under the Federal Tort Claims Act, over which the federal courts have exclusive jurisdiction. The Act directs federal courts to apply the law (including the choice-of-law rules) of the place where the allegedly tortious conduct occurred. Of course, this a federal statutory command, not an application of federal common law.

that enterprise by federal courts. It may be artificial, but not fantastic, to posit that Congress has in a particular instance "asked" the federal courts to apply rules of federal common law founded on the law of the states in which they sit.

Chapter 8

CONFLICT OF LAWS IN THE INTERNATIONAL SPHERE

The problem of conflict of laws, of course, long predates the creation of the American republic. The *lex loci* principles that have long influenced American conflicts law were developed and debated by civil-law jurists in large part to resolve conflicts between the laws of states that today we would call sovereign—states, that is, that were under no enforceable duty to respect or apply foreign law. And while most of this book has been preoccupied with conflicts in the American (or "domestic") context, between the laws of different states of the United States, conflicts in the international sphere obviously remain an important issue—one that the process of globalization has made increasingly salient.

Most of this Chapter is concerned with international conflicts from the point of view of an American court faced with the question of deciding which law to apply in a case that has connections with more than one country. There are numerous other perspectives, of course, from which one could view the problem of "international conflicts"—investigating how courts outside the United States approach conflicts issues, the role of international tribunals, the relationship between local and international law, and so on. For our purposes, however, the focus is on American courts—and, within that focus, the emphasis will be on federal courts.

A. Some Introductory Comments

On the surface, it might appear that much of what we have said about conflicts in the domestic sphere can be applied without great difficulty in the international sphere. For example, several of the New York "guest statute" cases involved the laws of Ontario, Canada, and the New York Court of Appeals treated those conflicts problems no differently from how they would have treated conflicts between the laws of New York and, say, Connecticut. In reality, however, conflict of laws on the international stage—even as to cases brought in American courts—is a subject unto its own. There are several reasons for this.

First. Adjudication of conflicts between state or federal law in the United States and the law of another country inevitably confronts the fact that most of the rest of the world views conflicts from a different perspective—principally, a civil-law perspective—than does American law. An American court faced with an international conflict of laws might well be advised to be cautious about applying a "modern" choice-of-law method (which often embodies a preference for forum law) that much of the legal world outside the United States regards as something of a curiosity.

Second. Conflicts in the international sphere are far more likely than domestic conflicts to implicate political and diplomatic considerations. A questionable disregard of foreign law, which might be merely irritating in the domestic context, can have far greater repercussions where the laws of foreign countries or the interests of foreign nationals are concerned. Moreover, the international implications sometimes bring into play structural features of the U.S. Constitution, namely federalism and the separation of powers. If the subject of the litigation concerns a matter of interest to the political branches of the U.S. government, especially the executive, state and federal courts might be well advised to factor this into their rulings, or to decline to exercise jurisdiction altogether.

Third. The outer limits of choice of law in the international domain are not specified by the U.S. Constitution, but rather are guided by principles of international law defining the boundaries of the "legislative jurisdiction" of sovereign states. To this we might add that the Full Faith and Credit Clause, of course, does not apply to the judgments rendered by courts of foreign states. Recognition of such judgments by American courts, then, are subject to a different kind of analysis from that applied in the purely domestic context.

Fourth. Conflicts between foreign law and federal law—usually, the statutory law of the United States—raise distinct issues and tend to be analyzed somewhat differently from how conflicts between foreign law and state law are analyzed. In particular, the question of whether U.S. laws governing national economic policy such as the antitrust, intellectual property, securities, and employment discrimination laws should be given "extraterritorial" effect has been an oft-mooted one during the late twentieth and early twenty-first centuries.

Fifth. Some of the most pressing conflicts problems in the international sphere have been addressed in treaties or international conventions, which then serve as rules of decision for conflicts issues raised in the courts of the signatory nations.

Sixth. We have seen that commercial agreements that are wholly domestic to the United States frequently include choice-of-law and choice-of-forum clauses, and that increasingly these contracts incorporate an agreement to submit specified disputes to compulsory arbitration. This is even more important a consideration where international business transactions are concerned. It stands to reason that where one or both parties to a contract are reluctant to litigate in a distant forum that applies unfamiliar rules of procedure, those parties will agree in advance to submit their grievances to a tribunal and a procedure that are, at least in some sense, "neutral," and governed by procedures less cumbersome than most judicial processes (especially discovery under U.S. law). The enforceability of such compulsory arbitration provisions, and the proper interpretation to be given them, can raise judicial questions that are akin to conflicts questions. Here the subject matter of conflicts converges with that of what might be called "international civil procedure."

Seventh. Some international conflicts problems heard in U.S. courts implicate principles governing the foreign relations law of the United States. Thus, such topics as the Act-of-State Doctrine and pre-emption of state laws affecting the conduct of U.S. foreign policy must play a role in any discussion of international conflicts as seen from the U.S. point of view.

All these features of conflicts in the international arena will be touched upon in what follows. In addition, we will briefly discuss conflicts law in comparative perspective, including the emerging conflicts provisions in the European Union.

B.   Jurisdiction to Prescribe Under International Law

Throughout this book, we've assumed that there is a distinction between what we call "choice of law" and what we call "jurisdiction." Although the word "jurisdiction" has many uses in American law, it most frequently refers to the power of a court to act—whether it has legitimate authority over the defendant and over the subject matter of the case. The concept of "choice of law," however, also connotes a kind of jurisdiction, even though in contemporary American conflicts law we don't usually use the term "jurisdiction" in connection with it. When we say that application of a state's law in a particular case is legitimate, we are in effect saying that the state whose law it is had jurisdiction to provide a rule of decision for that set of circumstances. To say, for example, that Alabama could legitimately apply the Alabama Employers Liability Act to the *Carroll* case would be to say that it was within the legitimate bounds of Alabama's "legislative jurisdiction" to provide a rule of decision for that situation.[1] It is the U.S. Constitution, as we have seen in Chapter 4, that provides the (rather weak) limitations on a state's "legislative jurisdiction" in the domestic choice-of-law context.

The Five Bases for Legislative Jurisdiction Under International Legal Norms. In international law, the phrase "legislative jurisdiction" or, more often, "jurisdiction to prescribe," is much more common than it is in the United States. (You should also note that the phrase "private international law" is commonly used outside the United States to describe the legal field we know as conflict of laws.) "Legislative jurisdiction" is contrasted with the term "judicial jurisdiction" (or "jurisdiction to adjudicate"), which corresponds to our conventional use of the term "jurisdiction" in the United States. In this section, we will focus on the international law conception of "legislative jurisdiction" or "jurisdiction to prescribe." The boundaries of a state's jurisdiction to prescribe are of fundamental importance in the international sphere; to a greater extent than in domestic conflicts of law in the United States, the issue of prescriptive jurisdiction raises questions of sovereignty and diplomacy where the prerogatives of sovereign nations vis-à-vis one another are concerned. The concept applies not only to civil causes of action arising under private law, but also to the power of states to apply their criminal law.

Although at one time the law of nations defined the legitimate exercise of jurisdiction to prescribe strictly in territorial terms (where have we heard this before?), over time international law has come to identify five distinct bases for the exercise of legislative jurisdiction. (Not all, as we will see, are universally accepted.) These bases were first articulated in the context of determining limits on the exercise of "penal" jurisdiction—legislative jurisdiction with respect to punishment for *crimes*—but they have also proved useful in marking out the limits of legislative jurisdiction to create and enforce private rights of action, particular those that may be said to have a "penal" dimension in that they reinforce prohibitory or regulatory policies of the state. As stated in an influential 1935 study published under the auspices of Harvard Research in International Law, the five "general principles" are:

1. The *territorial* principle—"determining jurisdiction by reference to the place where the offence is committed";

---

1. Recall that in *Loucks v. Standard Oil*, 224 N.Y. 99, 120 N.E. 198 (1918), the leading case on the "public policy exception," Judge Cardozo noted that application of the exception (where Massachusetts law would otherwise have been the choice-of-law reference) would have resulted in dismissal of the case on grounds of jurisdiction. This use of the term "jurisdiction" reflects the "legislative jurisdiction" concept discussed in the text.

2. The *nationality* principle—"determining jurisdiction by reference to the nationality or national character of the person committing the offence";

3. The *protective* principle—"determining jurisdiction by reference to the national interest injured by the offence";

4. The *universality* principle—"determining jurisdiction by reference to the custody of the person committing the offence"; and

5. The *passive personality* principle—"determining jurisdiction by reference to the nationality or national character of the person injured by the offence."[2]

The "territorial" and "nationality" bases are the least controversial and most widely accepted of these five bases of legislative jurisdiction. Clearly, a nation can prescribe with respect to actions that take place within its territory; equally clearly, a nation has authority to prescribe when the offender is a citizen or national of that country. While the other three bases of legislative jurisdiction are more controversial, the debate over them typically concerns efforts by courts to assert penal or criminal jurisdiction and will not be discussed further here.

The *Lotus* Case and the "Effects" Doctrine. Originally, the norms of international law had suggested that territoriality was the sole basis for the assertion of legislative jurisdiction, and that the courts of a sovereign state could not legitimately apply the law of that state to persons found, or activities occurring, outside that state. By the early twentieth century, this limitation had come to appear narrow and impractical—for many of the same reasons that strict notions of territoriality were coming to seem inadequate in American domestic choice of law. International law scholars usually point to the *Lotus* case, decided in 1927 by the Permanent Court of International Justice, as the crucial event in loosening the strictures of pure "territoriality" in defining the limits of a state's legislative jurisdiction.[3] In the *Lotus* case, Turkey sought to prosecute a French officer whose negligence, it claimed, had resulted in the death of several Turkish sailors. The accident had taken place at sea, not on Turkish soil. The Permanent Court overruled France's objections to the application of Turkish criminal law, rejecting the notion that "[t]he territoriality of criminal law ... coincides with territorial sovereignty." The insight of the *Lotus* decision has had great influence on general conceptions concerning the boundaries of legislative jurisdiction, including with respect to

---

2. *Harvard Research in International Law, Jurisdiction With Respect to Crime*, 29 AMERICAN JOURNAL OF INTERNATIONAL LAW 435, 445 (Supp. 1935).

3. *S.S. Lotus (France v. Turkey)*, 1927 PCIJ, ser. A, No. 10.

non-criminal proceedings in which a court attempts to apply the forum's regulatory laws, such as the U.S. antitrust laws.

The *Lotus* decision suggested that legislative jurisdiction might legitimately be premised on a basis other than literal territoriality—a state's undoubted sovereign power to apply its law to activities occurring within its territory. Today, some might justify Turkey's assumption of legislative jurisdiction (*i.e.* its application of Turkish law to the case) on the "passive personal" basis mentioned above, since the victims were Turkish nationals, although the validity of this argument is still subject to debate in the international community. But the real import of the *Lotus* case is that the legitimacy of Turkey's jurisdiction to prescribe in the case was actually deemed to be an instance of *territorial* jurisdiction. The Permanent Court suggested that the territorial basis of jurisdiction could actually be satisfied by events taking place outside the state, but which were felt within the state. This "effects" doctrine, which formally constitutes a variant on territoriality rather than a jurisdictional basis distinct from territorialism, has achieved doctrinal importance in the United States, providing a justification for application of U.S. law to persons and events outside the boundaries of the United States.

The *Alcoa* Decision. The leading case in the U.S. is *United States v. Aluminum Co. of America* (2d Cir. 1945) (colloquially known as the "*Alcoa*" case).[4] The United States brought a civil action under the federal antitrust laws against both Alcoa and "Alcoa, Ltd.," a Canadian corporation. Alcoa, Ltd. had allegedly formed a cartel with other non-U.S. corporations, whose actions the United States argued violated the antitrust laws. The actions attributable to Alcoa, Ltd., of course, took place outside the United States. The Second Circuit, in an opinion by Judge Learned Hand, stated, "[I]t is settled law ... that any state may impose liabilities, even upon persons not within its allegiance, for conduct outside its borders that has consequences within its borders which the state reprehends." The court went on to hold that the cartel agreement violated the Sherman Act, in part because the actions taken by the cartel had anticompetitive effects in the U.S. market for aluminum.

What is important for present purposes is that the *Alcoa* case fundamentally incorporated into American law the "effects" doctrine—the notion that the effects within the United States of behavior carried on outside the United States could legitimately

---

4. 148 F.2d 416 (2d Cir. 1945). Interestingly, the *Alcoa* case had been referred to the Second Circuit by the U.S. Supreme Court, which due to a spate of recusals was unable to muster a quorum to hear the case. This circumstance has given the *Alcoa* decision a status somewhat higher than the typical Court of Appeals decision, although not co-equal with that of a decision by the Supreme Court.

establish a basis for legislative jurisdiction, *i.e.* the application of U.S. law. Although the *Alcoa* court somewhat cryptically intimated that it was not *obliged* to accept the international legal norms establishing the scope of legislative jurisdiction, it accepted as a matter of policy that it should adhere to those norms: "[W]e are not to read general words, such as those in this Act, without regard to the limitations customarily observed by nations upon the exercise of their powers." To this extent, then, *Alcoa* is a case about how "effects" within the forum can serve as a basis for the forum's jurisdiction to prescribe (that is, the application of U.S. law), as an instance of the traditional territorial basis for such jurisdiction under international law. *Alcoa* thus embodies a somewhat self-contradictory idea: In any real-world assessment of the matter, the United States was indeed applying its antitrust laws *extraterritorially*, in that those laws were reaching conduct outside the United States; but, in terms of formal doctrine, application of the "effects" doctrine made application of the antitrust laws an instance of the "territorial" basis for legislative jurisdiction. This, of course, was the very usage that the Permanent Court of International Justice had validated in 1927 in the *Lotus* case.

The "effects" doctrine is, realistically, a necessary corrective to rigid conceptions of territoriality in the modern world, but when employed too liberally it can provoke friction in the international context. If a foreign national situated in a foreign country sends a product into the United States that harms the purchaser, there can be little objection to the legitimacy of applying American law to the resulting dispute; the "effects" within the United States are obvious. But in other situations, such as application of the U.S. antitrust laws to activities conducted abroad, use of the "effects" doctrine to justify the application of U.S. law can be more controversial. Anticompetitive "effects" are not always tangible in the way that a toaster oven is; and, unlike a toaster oven, they can emerge in many different places at once. The federal antitrust laws reflect an approach to economic policy that sometimes conflicts with the priorities of other nations, including close allies of the U.S. If legal enforcement of the policy reflected by the antitrust laws were left solely to the federal government as such, the possibility of conflict might be reduced; presumably the executive branch would take considerations of international comity into account when deciding whether and when to bring a prosecution or a civil action under those laws. But the Sherman Act also confers a right of action on private individuals and corporations to sue, and provides for treble damages to boot. Its application, at the behest of private plaintiffs, to foreign nationals acting within their home country can elicit significant resentment.

The risks of an excessively liberal interpretation of "effects" have been recognized in some quarters. For example, § 402 of the Restatement (Third) of the Foreign Relations Law of the United States recognizes the legitimacy of the "effects" doctrine as an instance of the territorial basis for legislative jurisdiction, but it specifies that the "effects" must be "substantial" in order to justify the application of U.S. law; moreover, § 403 of the Restatement provides that the United States (or a state of the United States) should not exercise its legislative jurisdiction in a particular case if to do so would be "unreasonable." (Although the Third Restatement does not itself constitute U.S. "law," some of its provisions, including §§ 402 and 403, have had considerable influence in the lower federal courts.) Particularly when U.S. laws having a prohibitory or regulatory character are invoked by private plaintiffs in civil actions (as opposed to being invoked by the U.S. in a criminal action), the burden rests on the judiciary in individual cases to determine whether the extraterritorial application of U.S. law, though technically valid under the "effects" doctrine, is appropriate. Among the devices that have been developed and applied by the federal courts in support of this enterprise is the "presumption against extraterritoriality."

C.   The Presumption Against Extraterritoriality

To say that Congress *can* (consistently with international legal norms) legislate extraterritorially on the basis of the "effects" doctrine, or on some other basis, does not mean that, in any individual case, Congress *has* done so. Recall that state legislatures rarely specify the territorial reach of their regulatory statutes; the same can be said of numerous federal statutes. Therefore, even in cases where extraterritorial application of U.S. law would be legitimate under the international norms itemized above, one must interpret the statute to determine whether it, in fact, applies extraterritorially. This is a judicial inquiry that frequently implicates sensitive issues of policy and diplomacy. In the international domain, giving forum law "extraterritorial" effect—that is, to apply it to events taking place largely or wholly outside the forum—is far more likely to raise hackles than is the case within the United States. The realities of relations between sovereign nations would seem to require a greater sensitivity to the prerogatives of the locus than would be the case in a dispute wholly domestic to the United States.

The "presumption against extraterritoriality" is a canon of statutory construction that is meant to take account of these concerns. It states that courts will not apply a particular U.S. statute extraterritorially unless it appears that Congress intended that that law be given extraterritorial application: "It is a longstanding principle of American law 'that legislation of Congress, unless a contrary intent appears, is meant to apply only within the territorial jurisdiction of the United States.' '[5] According to this principle, if the evidence from the statute's text and other indicators of Congressional intent is ambiguous concerning its application extraterritorially, the statute will not be given extraterritorial effect. The Court's formulation of this canon of construction makes clear that Congress certainly has the power to exercise legislative jurisdiction extraterritorially; but, based largely on considerations of comity and diplomacy, the courts will not lightly conclude that it has exercised that power.

1. *The* Aramco *Case: Title VII*

The clearest recent statement of this doctrine was given by the U.S. Supreme Court in *EEOC v. Arabian American Oil Co.* (1991) [*"Aramco"*].[6] *Aramco* involved Title VII, the leading federal statute on employment discrimination. Boureslan, a naturalized U.S. citizen, had been employed by Aramco (a U.S. corporation) at the latter's plant in Saudi Arabia. After he had been discharged, Boureslan sued Aramco in federal court, claiming under Title VII that he had been discriminated against on the basis of his race, religion, and national origin. Citing the "presumption against extraterritoriality," the Supreme Court examined the text and legislative history of Title VII, and held that the presumption had not been overcome; the Court regarded the evidence of Congress's intention with respect to extraterritorial application of Title VII as at best ambiguous. Therefore it ruled that Title VII could not be applied in the case and that Boureslan had stated no claim for relief under the statute. Note that, while the "presumption against extraterritoriality" doctrine is itself based on *general* considerations of diplomacy and sovereignty, its specific application in *Aramco* did not feature an extended independent analysis of those considerations in the particular case. Nothing was said concerning whether U.S. relations with Saudi Arabia might be affected by application of the employment discrimination statute, or of what Saudi law and policy was with respect to employment discrimination. The Court simply examined the the text of the statute, evidence of Congress's intent with respect to extraterritorial application when passing it, the purpose of the overall statutory scheme, and interpretations of the statute that had been rendered over time by the Equal Employment Opportunity Commission, the federal agency charged with enforcing it.

---

5. *Equal Employment Opportunity Commission v. Arabian American Oil Co.*, 499 U.S. 244, 248 (1991), *quoting* *Foley Bros., Inc. v. Filardo*, 336 U.S. 281, 285 (1949).

6. 499 U.S. 244 (1991).

Questions Raised by *Aramco*. *Aramco*'s holding is clear enough. But both the specific holding in *Aramco*, and the cases decided before and since *Aramco*, raise a host of questions as to how properly to apply the presumption against extraterritoriality, and even when it should apply at all.

First, although Chief Justice Rehnquist's majority opinion in *Aramco* suggested that the presumption against extraterritoriality had been clearly established by prior precedent, in reality the Court had been far from consistent in its use of the doctrine. Prior to 1991, it had been applied to some statutes and not others; by the late 1980s it no longer appeared to be a clearly-established principle. It is not simply that the Court had applied it differently in different cases; some cases appeared not to acknowledge the doctrine at all. Moreover, as explained below, the Court has not even been able to give the presumption consistent application *since Aramco* was decided.

Second, to the extent that the doctrine does find its source in earlier Supreme Court cases, changes over the course of the last century with respect to the role of strict territoriality in choice of law have rendered the authority of those earlier statements somewhat questionable. For example, consider the following famous statement in Justice Holmes's majority opinion in *American Banana Co. v. United Fruit Co.* (1909),[7] often regarded as a primordial statement of the "presumption against extraterritoriality":

> [T]he general or almost universal rule is that the character of an act as lawful or unlawful must be determined wholly by the law of the country where the act is done ... For another jurisdiction, if it should happen to lay hold of the actor, to treat him according to its own notions rather than those of the place where he did the acts, not only would be unjust, but would be an interference with the authority of another sovereign, contrary to the comity of nations, which the other state concerned justly might resent.[8]

Justice Holmes therefore held that the U.S. antitrust laws did not apply to activities alleged to have taken place in Panama. It is clear that Holmes was heavily influenced by the territoriality paradigm that dominated conflict of laws in 1909.[9] His opinion in *American Banana* predated both the dethronement of strict territoriality in American choice of law and the acknowledgment in international

---

7. 213 U.S. 347 (1909).

8. 213 U.S. at 356.

9. Similarly, Holmes shared the "vested rights" theory justifying the *lex loci* principle that had been set forth by Joseph Beale: "The theory of the foreign suit is that, although the act complained of was subject to no law having force in the forum, it gave rise to an obligation, an *obligatio*, which like other obligations, follows the person, and may be enforced wherever the person may be found." *Slater v. Mexican National R.R.*, 194 U.S. 120, 126 (1904).

law circles that "effects" within the forum might serve as a legitimate basis for the application of the forum's law. In addition, the facts of *American Banana* did not present, in as stark a way as emerged in later cases, the specter of economic activity being carried on outside the United States having substantial and intended effects within the United States. To Holmes it seemed "startling" to suggest that the U.S. antitrust laws could be applied to events taking place in Panama. This is not to say that Holmes's comments on comity and sovereignty are wholly lacking in force today; territorialist principles have proved more durable in the international context than they have in domestic American conflicts law. It is, however, to say that it is today hardly "startling" to contemplate the possible extraterritorial application of U.S. law, and thus the presumption against extraterritoriality may require a rationale different from that underlying Holmes's opinion. Understandably, the Supreme Court did not cite *American Banana* in *Aramco*.

Third, *Aramco* involved not only a U.S. complainant, but a U.S. defendant. As the Court states, avoiding "unintended clashes between our laws and those of other nations which could result in international discord" is the basic justification for the presumption against extraterritoriality. But, under international law, "nationality" (of the defendant) is by now almost as venerable a basis for the application of forum law as is territoriality itself, and this is true even though the locus state would likewise have the right to apply its own law. Is it imperative that the "presumption against territoriality" be invoked where the defendant is a U.S. corporation? If an American company discriminates against an American citizen within the territory of Saudi Arabia, are "clashes" and "discord" as likely to result from the application of U.S. law to the company's behavior as would be the case, say, if the company had been a Saudi Arabian entity?[10]

Not only do the early Supreme Court precedents on the presumption against extraterritoriality date from the heyday of "vested rights" thinking; some of them also predate the Harvard Study's influential identification of the baseline criteria for legitimate exercise of legislative jurisdiction in 1935, as well as the *Lotus* decision of 1927. The abhorrence of extraterritoriality expressed in *American Banana* and other early cases seems now to be anachronistic. If it is today considered unremarkable under international legal norms for legislative jurisdiction to be predicated on, say, the

---

10. Also, should the *complainant*'s nationality play a role in the analysis? (The term "complainant" is used in the context of *Aramco* because, technically, the EEOC was the "plaintiff" in that case.) This would be an application of the "passive personality" basis for prescriptive jurisdiction, and thus controversial. Of course, the defendant's status as a U.S. corporation in *Aramco* eliminates the need for consideration of the complainant's nationality.

wrongdoer's nationality, should U.S. law contain a canon of statutory construction embodying a presumption against extraterritoriality regardless of the parties' nationality? In other words, would it not make sense to limit application of the presumption to cases where "effects" in the forum constituted the only clear basis under international law for the exercise of legislative jurisdiction?

Fourth, it remains unclear after *Aramco* precisely what kinds of evidence would suffice to overcome the presumption against extraterritoriality in cases where that presumption is applicable. That is, what is sufficient to demonstrate Congress's "intent" that its statute be applied extraterritorially? This, of course, is the kind of statutory construction question that courts face in many contexts. The Court's determination in *Aramco* itself that the presumption had not been overcome—that Congress had not given clear evidence of its intention that Title VII be applied extraterritorially—was at least arguable. Among other things, there were inferences that could have been drawn from the text of the statute suggesting that extraterritorial application was contemplated, at least when the plaintiff was a U.S. citizen.[11] The Court was unpersuaded by this, as well as by the EEOC's own interpretation of the statute revealed in positions taken on several previous occasions. In any event, Congress overruled the Court's decision in *Aramco* (which was, of course, a construction of a U.S. statute, not an interpretation of the Constitution) in the Civil Rights Act of 1991, which included a provision clarifying that Title VII should have extraterritorial effect in appropriate cases.[12]

11. Title VII's "alien exemption clause" provided that the state "shall not apply to an employer with respect to the employment of aliens outside any State." This would seem to suggest that the statute *was* meant to apply to the employment of U.S. citizens (such as Boureslan) outside the U.S., but the Court did not find that to be "unambiguous" evidence of Congressional intent.

12. Another problem in the wake of *Aramco* is that neither *Aramco* nor succeeding cases make clear precisely what it means for application of U.S. law to be "extraterritorial," and thus whether the presumption even comes into play, in a particular case. It thus does not resolve the seeming contradiction between saying that, for purposes of determining the legitimacy under international norms of exercising prescriptive jurisdiction, activities outside the forum could sometimes be regarded as authorizing the forum's "territorial" jurisdiction if they had substantial "effects" there and saying that those activities, because "extra-

territorial," trigger a presumption against the application of U.S. law. Of course, it couldn't have been argued in *Aramco* itself that the defendant's treatment of Boureslan in Saudi Arabia had meaningful "effects" within the United States, so the tension didn't arise in that particular case. The question does become more pressing, with respect to federal statutes regulating economic activity in a more wide-ranging way, such as the antitrust and securities fraud laws. One might argue, for example, that economic activity carried out wholly abroad that has significant anticompetitive effects within the United States should be regarded as occurring "within" U.S. territory (*a là* the "effects" doctrine); one might also argue, conversely, that actions clearly taken within the United States that *only* have effects abroad should *not* be regarded as occurring within the United States, and that application of U.S. law to such actions must be subject to the presumption against

2. Extraterritorial Application of the U.S. Antitrust Laws

Aramco is now the leading case on the presumption against extraterritoriality. But the larger debates concerning the extraterritorial application of U.S. law have focused, not on Title VII, but on federal laws that regulate economic behavior and that implicate national economic policy. The most important example, already discussed briefly, is U.S. antitrust law. U.S. antitrust law reflects distinctive American policies concerning competition, business consolidation, and private markets; to a significant degree, its provisions are enforced by private parties bringing lawsuits in federal court; and the available remedies can be harsh, including treble damages in certain cases. Some or all of these features of the U.S. antitrust laws may differ dramatically from their counterparts under the laws of other nations, yet the realities of multinational business enterprise (especially under the influence of globalization) make it clear that activities taking place abroad can have real economic impact within the United States (and vice versa, of course). Whether or not some or all of U.S. antitrust law applies extraterritorially is therefore a question of great importance. In *Hartford Fire Insurance Co. v. California* (1993),[13] the Supreme Court upheld extraterritorial application of the Sherman Act. Before analyzing the Court's somewhat perplexing decision in *Hartford Fire*, however, some brief background is necessary.

Alcoa and Extraterritorial Application of the Sherman Act. As noted above, as early as 1909 the Court considered the possible extraterritorial application of the Sherman Act in *American Banana* and dismissed the idea as inconsistent with basic legal principles. But by 1945 it was well accepted in international law circles that the kind of strict territorialism reflected in Holmes's formulation—in effect barring a state from exerting legislative jurisdiction with respect to activities occurring outside its borders— failed adequately to recognize the legitimate interests of nation-states in applying their own laws to activities causing significant effects within those states, even when the relevant "conduct" occurred elsewhere. The "effects" doctrine announced in the *Lotus* decision (1927) established as a matter of international practice the "effects" doctrine; the Harvard Study of 1935 reinforced the idea. Of course, as we've seen, to say that Congress *can* legislate extraterritorially is not to say that Congress *has* done so. But, once the strict territorialist underpinnings of Holmes's *American Banana* opinion had been discarded, it remained to be determined anew

extraterritoriality. Although the Supreme Court's decision in the *Hartford Fire* case, discussed *infra*, offers some tantalizing hints on this score so far as the antitrust laws are concerned, it remains unclear as a general matter whether palpable effects within the United States are sufficient to make the presumption inapplicable.

13. 509 U.S. 764 (1993).

whether the Sherman Act should be read as applying extraterritorially in light of the newer principles.

In *Alcoa*,[14] the case in which the Second Circuit recognized the "effects" doctrine, Judge Learned Hand held that the Sherman Act was applicable to activity occurring outside the United States that caused effects in the United States. As we've already observed, *Alcoa* amounted to recognition by American law of the "effects" doctrine. But let's distinguish between (1) the "effects" doctrine as a basis for affirming the exercise of legislative jurisdiction under principles of international law, and (2) the conclusion that the relevant federal statute should indeed be interpreted to apply extraterritorially. Although Judge Hand did not clearly distinguish question (2) from question (1), the decision in *Alcoa*, together with some later Supreme Court decisions citing it approvingly,[15] has been taken to mean that the presumption *has* been overcome with respect to the Sherman Act: "[I]t is now well established that the Sherman Act applies extraterritorially."[16] Whether that conclusion would emerge today from a *de novo* application of the *Aramco* standards for overcoming the presumption against extraterritoriality is questionable, since there is not a great deal more in the text or legislative history of the Sherman Act and its subsequent amendments than there is in the text of Title VII to suggest that extraterritorial application is contemplated by the statute. But by the time of *Hartford Fire*, the question was no longer open.

The *Hartford Fire* Case. In *Hartford Fire*, both private plaintiffs and several states sued members of the insurance industry for engaging in a conspiracy that affected the American insurance market; several of the defendants were English companies, and some of the activity alleged to be part of the conspiracy took place in England. The numerous complaints were consolidated for litigation in the U.S. District Court for the Northern District of California. Among the many issues raised was the argument by the foreign defendants that principles of international comity should result in the dismissal of the federal antitrust claims against them; as the U.S. Court of Appeals for the Ninth Circuit acknowledged, "application of [U.S.] antitrust laws to the London reinsurance market 'would lead to significant conflict with English law and policy.' "[17] The Supreme Court held in *Hartford Fire*, however, that application of the U.S. antitrust laws (the Sherman Act) to the

---

14. 148 F.2d 416 (2d Cir. 1945).

15. *Continental Ore Co. v. Union Carbide & Carbon Corp.*, 370 U.S. 690, 704 (1962); *Matsushita Elec. Industrial Co. v. Zenith Radio Corp.*, 475 U.S. 574, 582 n.6 (1986).

16. *Hartford Fire Ins. Co. v. California*, 509 U.S. 764, 814 (1983) (Scalia, J., dissenting).

17. *In re Insurance Antitrust Litigation*, 938 F.2d 919, 933 (9th Cir. 1991), *quoting In re Insurance Antitrust Litigation*, 723 F.Supp. 464, 489 (N.D.Cal. 1989).

actions of the English defendants was appropriate, even though some or all of the activity taking place in England would have been regarded as legal under English law. The Court's decision provoked a strong dissent from Justice Scalia.

The Court's decision in *Hartford Fire* would appear to be easily explained by formulaic application of the principles we've explored thus far. The *Alcoa* doctrine, long recognized as valid by the Supreme Court, seemed largely to preordain the result in *Hartford Fire*. The defendants' activities plainly had non-trivial effects within the United States; thus application of the Sherman Act posed no problems under norms of international law. Moreover, it was no longer open to question that the Sherman Act, as a matter of U.S. law, applies extraterritorially. *Ergo*, application of the Sherman Act to the activities of the English insurers was valid. The Court's opinion confused the issue somewhat, by conceiving the issue as one of subject matter jurisdiction (should the lower court have declined to exercise subject matter jurisdiction over the Sherman Act claims against the foreign defendants?). Still, the result in *Hartford Fire* seems consistent with what we have seen thus far. Why, then, was Justice Scalia's dissent so vociferous? Answering that question requires consideration of some further background to the *Hartford Fire* decision.

The *Timberlane* Case and the Third Restatement of American Foreign Relations Law. *Hartford Fire* underscores the fact that an "effects" analysis alone, wedded to a conclusion that the "presumption against extraterritoriality" has been overcome with respect to a particular U.S. statute, may pay insufficient attention to the conflicts and tensions that may be latent in the circumstances of the *particular* case. Specifically, application of U.S. antitrust law to the behavior of foreign defendants acting in England—and acting with the blessing of English law—presents questions of a different order from those involved in *Aramco*, where it is doubtful that application of Title VII would have constituted an affront to Saudi Arabian law and policy. The inadequacy of a wooden application of the *Alcoa* doctrine in particular antitrust cases has been noted by several federal courts in the past. The best-known of these decisions is *Timberlane Lumber Co. v. Bank of America* (9th Cir. 1976),[18] in which the Ninth Circuit considered an antitrust action based on actions that occurred in Honduras, in part by citizens and government officials of Honduras. The Ninth Circuit recommended a "jurisdictional rule of reason" to govern extraterritorial application of the U.S. antitrust laws:

> The effects test by itself is incomplete because it fails to consider other nations' interests. Nor does it expressly take

18. 549 F.2d 597 (9th Cir. 1976).

into account the full nature of the relationship between the actors and this country.... [Courts must consider] whether the interests of, and links to, the United States including the magnitude of the effect on American foreign commerce are sufficiently strong, vis-à-vis those of other nations, to justify an assertion of extraterritorial authority.... What we prefer is an evaluation and balancing of the relevant considerations in each case ... a "jurisdictional rule of reason."[19]

Professing to apply concepts native to the field of conflict of laws, the Ninth Circuit stated:

The elements to be weighed include the degree of conflict with foreign law and policy, the nationality or allegiance of the parties and the locations or principal places of business or corporations, the extent to which enforcement by either state can be expected to achieve compliance, the relative significance of effects on the United States as compared with those elsewhere, the extent to which there is explicit purpose to harm or affect American commerce, and the relative importance to the violations charged of conduct within the United States as compared with conduct abroad. A court evaluating these factors should identify the potential degree of conflict if American authority is asserted. A difference in law or policy is likely one sore spot, though one which may not always be present. Nationality is another; though foreign governments may have some concern for the treatment of American citizens and business residing there, they primarily care about their own nationals. Having assessed the conflict, the court should then determine whether in the face of it the contacts and interests of the United States are sufficient to support the exercise of extraterritorial jurisdiction.[20]

The analogy here with the concepts emphasized by modern choice-of-law analysis is pretty obvious. In effect, *Timberlane* appended to the "presumption-against-extraterritoriality" analysis a more discriminating analysis of the factors *in the specific case*. If one were to incorporate the *Timberlane* analysis into what we have said so far, one could conceive the problem of extraterritorial application of U.S. antitrust law as a three-stage inquiry: (1) Would application of the Sherman Act be consistent with international legal norms (yes, *per* the "effects" doctrine); (2) has Congress authorized such extraterritorial application (yes, per *Alcoa*); (3) do the facts of the particular case justify such extraterritorial application (it depends, per *Timberlane*).

Timberlane has been influential in other federal courts deciding on the extraterritorial application of the federal antitrust laws,

19. *Timberlane*, 549 F.2d at 611–12, 613 (footnote omitted).

20. *Timberlane*, 549 F.2d at 614–15 (footnotes omitted).

but the Court in *Hartford Fire* appeared to give the decision the back of its hand (without disapproving it explicitly). *Timberlane* does underscore the complex play of separation-of-powers concerns in the antitrust/extraterritoriality context. The multiple-factor test posted by the Ninth Circuit in *Timberlane*, like the "presumption against extraterritoriality" itself, seems, on the surface, to be a gesture of deference toward Congress and the Executive Branch: The federal courts should not apply U.S. antitrust law extraterritorially where, based on consideration of the various factors mentioned in *Timberlane*, there is a risk of creating or exacerbating tensions with other countries. At the same time, however, the very enterprise of applying such a multi-factor test, focused as it is on the real-world "interests" of the United States vis-à-vis those of other countries, would appear to be a rather non-judicial task (even if informed by *amicus* briefs from the relevant U.S. agencies urging application or nonapplication of U.S. law). One might say that, once it has been determined that Congress intended *generally* for the statute to apply extraterritorially, it would actually be an affront to the separation-of-powers principle for courts to apply it in some cases and not others, according to their assessment of the interests in the individual case. This is precisely why the Supreme Court majority in *Hartford Fire* cast the case, at least in part, in terms of subject matter jurisdiction: Conventional doctrine suggests that federal courts have no discretion to decline to hear cases properly within their jurisdiction. This may not have been the correct way to frame the issue—declining to apply a U.S. statute extraterritorially (even where the presumption has been generally overcome) in a particular case does not necessarily amount to refusal to "hear" the case—but it does suggest that the Court in *Hartford Fire* was expressing its disapproval of the case-by-case, balancing-of-interests approach advocated by the Ninth Circuit in *Timberlane*.

Justice Scalia's response in his *Hartford Fire* dissent was not only to deny that the case involved a question of subject matter jurisdiction, but to suggest that the prudential analysis recommended in cases like *Timberlane* (a case he cited with approval) was itself sanctioned by federal law. To this end he cited the venerable *"Charming Betsy"* doctrine. In *Murray v. The Charming Betsy* (1804), Chief Justice John Marshall had stated, "[A]n act of Congress ought never to be construed to violate the law of nations if any other possible construction remains."[21] This would mean that Acts of Congress (including the Sherman Act) presumptively incorporate, or are intended to be consistent with, the law of nations. Assuming that what Chief Justice Marshall referred to as the "law of nations" is synonymous with what today would be called "customary international law," it might nevertheless be difficult to

---

21.   6 U.S. 64, 118 (1804).

conclude that customary international law would be violated by application of the Sherman Act to the foreign defendants in *Hartford Fire*. After all, application of the Sherman Act would satisfy the "effects" test, generally regarded as a species of the "territoriality" basis for prescriptive jurisdiction. Extraterritorial application of such legislative jurisdiction can be overzealous without necessarily violating international law. But Justice Scalia professed to find a satisfactory statement of the relevant international-law principles— to be read into the Sherman Act by virtue of the *Charming Betsy* principle—in § 403 of the Restatement (Third) of the Foreign Relations Law of the United States, which we discussed above.

Section 403 does indeed proscribe "unreasonable" exercises of legislative jurisdiction, and some of the subsections in § 403(2) do specify considerations, arguably present in *Hartford Fire*, that might militate in favor of a conclusion that the exercise of such jurisdiction would be unreasonable. For example, § 403 suggests that one pertinent consideration is whether the locus state also has a regulatory policy with respect to the defendants' alleged actions, and instructs the court applying § 403 to consider "the importance of regulation to the regulating state"; plainly English law, validating the defendants' behavior, reflected an economic policy of importance to England.[22] Whether the principle of "reasonableness" and the considerations itemized in § 403 should be regarded as an embodiment of customary international law, and therefore immanent in the Sherman Act by way of the *"Charming Betsy"* doctrine, and not simply a prudential principle that should govern federal courts considering the possible extraterritorial application of U.S. law, is arguable. In any case, it is clear that the majority in *Hartford Fire* had little interest in § 403; the "reasonableness" inquiry of § 403, like the *Timberlane* doctrine, is in considerable tension with the majority's evident belief in *Hartford Fire* that application of the Sherman Act should not be a matter of judicial discretion in the individual case.[23]

---

22. Note that the considerations itemized in § 403(2) are not wholly unlike the considerations mentioned in § 6 of the Second Restatement of Conflict of Laws.

23. The Court did respond to Justice Scalia's analysis of the Third Restatement of Foreign Relations Law by quoting Comment e to § 403, stating, "No conflict [between English and U.S. law] exists, for these purposes, 'where a person subject to regulation by two states can comply with the laws of both.'" 509 U.S. at 799. The Court's reference to Comment e was confusing; in its use of the phrase "true conflict,"

to describe a situation in which the law of one country would require that which the law of the other would prohibit, it unwittingly suggested to some commentators that the Court was engaging in a choice-of-law analysis. In fact, the Court's reference to Comment e was simply intended to rebut Justice Scalia's contention that conflict between U.S. and English law was a consideration militating in favor of the conclusion that extraterritorial application of the Sherman Act in the case was "unreasonable." The Court's observation was inapt, because the quoted comment refers only to the possible application of

Many questions concerning antitrust and extraterritoriality remain unanswered after *Hartford Fire*. What about when antitrust plaintiffs (either domestic or foreign) allege harm due to violation of the U.S. antitrust laws when the harmful "effects" occur outside of the U.S.? In the Foreign Trade Antitrust Improvements Act of 1982 (mentioned in *Hartford Fire*), Congress excluded from the coverage of the Sherman Act anticompetitive conduct causing foreign harm. But Congress excepted from this exclusion situations in which the allegedly anticompetitive conduct also leads to harmful effects within the United States. In *Hoffmann–La Roche v. Empagran, S.A.* (2004),[24] domestic and foreign purchasers of vitamins brought a class action under the U.S. antitrust laws claiming an international conspiracy to raise vitamin prices. The alleged effects of the conspiracy occurred both within and outside the United States. The "exception" to the "exclusion" from Sherman Act coverage specified by the 1982 Act would seem to apply here, thus allowing the Sherman Act claims to proceed.

But the Court in *Hoffman–La Roche* considered that "the adverse foreign effect [of the defendants' allegedly anticompetitive behavior] is independent of any adverse domestic effect." It was troubled by the displacement of foreign regulatory law in cases where the anticompetitive effects were felt within the territory of such foreign country (and that harmed nationals of that country), even though the 1982 statute seemed literally to maintain Sherman Act coverage for such claims (since there was domestic harm as well). The Court therefore read the statute in light of the *Charming Betsy* principle and of the kinds of considerations itemized in § 403 of the Third Restatement. On this basis the Court determined that extraterritorial application of the Sherman Act to claims specifically alleging harmful "effects" occurring solely in a foreign country would be "unreasonable," given the paucity of any substantial U.S. interest with respect to such claims. Thus the Sherman Act, as modified by the 1982 Act, was held not to apply to such claims.

The Court's analysis in *Hoffman–La Roche*, referencing the *Charming Betsy* principle and § 403, thus seemed to adopt the general mode of analysis advocated by Justice Scalia in *Hartford Fire*, though not the result he would have favored in that case; effects within the United States (as in *Hartford Fire*) created a substantial U.S. interest that made application of the Sherman Act "reasonable." Note that, since claims of harm occurring solely outside the United States will typically (as in *Hoffman–La Roche*)

§ 403(3) (which only applies once it has already been determined that it would not be unreasonable for either of the interested states to apply its law, whereas the whole point of Justice Scalia's

analysis of § 403 was to argue that application of U.S. law would be unreasonable).

24. 542 U.S. 155 (2004).

be brought by foreign plaintiffs, Hoffman–La Roche has the *de facto*, though not *de jure*, effect of denying Sherman Act coverage solely to foreign plaintiffs. If that result is defensible on the ground that the Court is thereby leaving "room" for the application of the law and policy of the country where the effects are actually felt, that gesture of comity may at times be of cold comfort to the foreign claimants, in precisely the manner of *Neumeier v. Kuehner* (N.Y. 1972)—although this fact may be less disturbing or ironic in the international arena.

3. The Presumption Against Territoriality as Applied to Other U.S. Laws

Federal Securities Laws. The Sherman Act is, of course, not the only U.S. law that both confers a right of action on private parties and regulates an area that is of great economic importance both domestically and abroad. Another example is the securities laws, in particular the federal cause of action for securities fraud. The Supreme Court's virtually complete disregard in *Hartford Fire* of *Aramco* (which was never mentioned in the majority's opinion) and the "presumption against extraterritoriality" leaves it unclear how, if at all, the federal securities laws are to be interpreted with respect to extraterritorial application. Plainly conduct prohibited by those laws can occur within the United States and cause harm outside the U.S.; just as plainly, conduct can take place outside the U.S. that has substantial harmful effects within the U.S. Extension of the U.S. securities laws to cover such situations would undoubtedly be consistent with international norms governing legislative jurisdiction, but the question remains whether the relevant statutes, whose text sheds little light on the matter, should be interpreted to apply in such cases.

The Supreme Court has not yet decided whether the presumption against extraterritoriality applies in the securities law context, or, if it does, what result its application would yield. There is plenty of federal case law on the issue, however, much of it coming from the Second Circuit, where many lawsuits under the securities laws are brought. In general, the Second Circuit has given the securities laws a broad reading, interpreting it to apply to foreign defendants both when the "conduct" has taken place in the U.S. (which would not in any event trigger the presumption against extraterritoriality) and when even modest "effects" can be said to have been produced in the United States. It is not possible to give a more detailed account here of federal jurisprudence regarding extraterritorial application of the securities laws, but you should keep one thing in mind: As with the antitrust laws, the actions of foreign defendants acting abroad will often be regarded as legal under the law of the locus. Some of these cases, therefore, will involve not simply an interpretation of the federal securities laws, but the risk of conflict with the laws of other nations.

U.S. Intellectual Property Laws.

Over the past twenty years, no area of U.S. law and policy has generated more discussion with respect to its international implications than intellectual property law. So far as the relationship between U.S. IP law and the "presumption against extraterritoriality" is concerned, the matter is actually rather simple. For reasons that may be rooted more in the vagaries of history than in a coherent judicial policy, U.S. copyright law and patent law are treated differently from U.S. trademark law: U.S. copyright and patent law do not apply extraterritorially (*i.e.* the presumption has not been overcome with respect to these statutes), but U.S. trademark law may apply extraterritorially. As to patent and trademark law, these propositions are the consequence of Supreme Court decisions (prior to the decision in *Aramco* (1991)) that, taken as a whole, did not necessarily reflect a thorough analysis of the relationship between the "presumption against extraterritoriality" and U.S. intellectual property law and policy. Those decisions, nevertheless, remain good law.[25] As to copyright law, most courts have concluded that it has no extraterritorial application,[26] although the Supreme Court has not yet decided this issue authoritatively.

Of course, to the extent that issues of piracy and nonenforcement abroad of local intellectual property laws are a foreign policy concern for the United States, the conclusion that U.S. copyright and patent laws do not apply extraterritorially (in the absence of any clear Congressional directive to the contrary) has considerable merit. Efforts by the executive branch to address such concerns through the medium of bilateral or multilateral agreements, negotiation within international trade organizations, or political pressure on nations in which the problem of piracy and unauthorized use is greatest may be hampered by undiscriminating application of U.S. intellectual property laws to activity occurring abroad (and against foreign nationals). In fact, this concern, sounding in separation-of-powers considerations, seems far more relevant in the intellectual property area than in the employment discrimination area that was the subject of *Aramco* itself (as, perhaps, is suggested by Congress's overruling of *Aramco* with respect to Title VII). Some have argued that the same reasoning should militate in favor of concluding that

---

25. On patent law, see *Deepsouth Packing Co. v. Laitram Corp.*, 406 U.S. 518, 531 (1972) ("Our patent system makes no claim to extraterritorial effect"); on trademark, see *Steele v. Bulova Watch Co.*, 344 U.S. 280 (1952) (extraterritorial application of Lanham Trademark Act valid).

26. See, e.g., *Subafilms, Ltd., v. MGM–Pathe Communications Co.*, 24 F.3d 1088 (9th Cir. 1994).

the presumption against extraterritoriality should bar extraterritorial application of the U.S. trademark laws as well.[27]

It is worth briefly taking account of the larger legal context in which these questions are played out. There are, of course, a variety of international conventions purporting to deal with the international treatment of rights in intellectual property. The best-known of these is the Berne Convention for the Protection of Literary and Artistic Works. This venerable instrument, to which the U.S. did not become a signatory until 1989, essentially requires its signatories to treat the copyright of authors in other signatory countries in the same manner that it would treat the copyright claims of its own nationals. More recent agreements, such as the World Intellectual Property Organization Copyright Treaty, add further protections based on a more searching consideration of new media that are deserving of copyright protection. These kinds of international agreements, though, do not necessarily bear on the question of how far *U.S. law* as applied in U.S. courts may reach to cover alleged infringing actions outside the U.S. If nonenforcement or indifferent enforcement within signatory nations renders these internationally prescribed protections ineffective, resort to U.S. copyright and patent laws will not help, due to the proscription on their extraterritorial application.

What about the possibility of applying *foreign* intellectual property law in cases where the presumption against extraterritoriality forbids application of U.S. IP law? We briefly considered an analogous question in connection with *Aramco* and the Court's decision not to apply Title VII in that case, as well as *Hartford Fire* and the U.S. antitrust laws. For the most part, federal courts have been reluctant to apply foreign intellectual property law (usually, copyright law) at the instance of American plaintiffs. It is not obvious that there should be an absolute bar to applying foreign IP law in U.S. courts when the allegedly wrongful conduct occurs outside the U.S. Applying the law of a foreign country to acts that have taken place in that country would not seem to be contrary to principles of comity; quite the contrary. Application of foreign law might in some instances give the plaintiff the prospect of a judicial remedy where the proscription on extraterritorial application of U.S. copyright and patent law would otherwise deny her one. Nevertheless, regulation of intellectual property rights, which lies substantially within the domain of the federal government, may fall into that category of questions concerning "national social and economic policy" for which application of foreign law is inappropriate. The same separation-of-powers arguments for barring the extraterritorial application of, say, the federal copyright laws may also argue against the

27. Curtis A. Bradley, *Territorial Intellectual Property Rights in an Age of Globalism*, 37 Virginia Journal of International Law 505 (1997).

assumption by federal courts of authority to adjudicate claims based on foreign copyright law. However strong or weak that argument may be, one thing is clear: We are lacking a simple and coherent explanation for why it is appropriate for American courts to apply foreign law in some domains and not in others.

Note, though, that in a different kind of situation—that in which a foreign plaintiff sues in U.S. federal court alleging infringement in the United States of its foreign copyright—a choice-of-law analysis may well be both necessary and appropriate. In *Itar-Tass Russian News Agency v. Russian Kurier, Inc.* (2d Cir. 1998),[28] the plaintiff, a Russian news agency "functioning similarly to the Associated Press," sued the defendant, a Russian-language weekly newspaper published and circulated in New York, based on the fact that the defendant had copied and republished a number of articles originally published or distributed by Itar–Tass. The Second Circuit, after discussing the possible relevance of the Berne Convention and of the federal Berne Convention Implementation Act of 1988, concluded that there was a conflict of laws with respect to each of two distinct issues: (1) ownership of rights in the content and arrangement of the original articles, and (2) infringement. The court concluded that Russian law governed as to questions of ownership, and that U.S. copyright law governed as to questions of infringement.

4. Why Aren't Aramco and the Other "Extraterritoriality" Cases Treated as Choice-of-Law Cases?

In *Aramco*, no attention was given to the possibility of applying Saudi Arabian law to Boureslan's claim of employment discrimination. This seems very different from how the question might have been treated had it arisen in a wholly domestic context—for example, had Boureslan and Aramco been citizens of California, had Boureslan been employed at Aramco's plant in Nevada, and had the laws of California and Nevada differed with respect to employment discrimination. Depending on the forum and on the choice-of-law methodology employed, one can easily imagine a court deciding that California law should not apply to the dispute—but the natural corollary to that conclusion would be that Nevada law *should* apply. Once the Court determined that Title VII should not apply in *Aramco*, why did it not go on to consider the possible application of Saudi Arabian law?

Certainly we have seen conflicts between the law of a state and the law of another country treated as an ordinary problem of choice of law. We know, for example, from the New York line of "guest statute" cases, that at least in some instances the fact that one of

28.   153 F.3d 82 (2d Cir. 1998).

the laws competing for recognition is the law of a foreign country makes no difference to the analysis. The conflict between the law of New York and the law of Ontario, Canada in those cases was treated in the same manner as was the conflict in *Tooker v. Lopez*, which involved a conflict between the law of New York and the law of Colorado. On occasion (see *Neumeier v. Kuehner*) this has even resulted in the application by an American court of Canadian law. Whether it is because the basic premises of the Canadian legal system are considered close to those underlying American law, or because this matter of cross-border torts is not thought to trigger fundamental questions of sovereignty and foreign relations, American courts conceive these situations as raising a problem of *choice* of law, just as in a purely domestic situation: To hold that forum law should not apply is to hold that foreign law should, and vice versa.[29]

Nor has this situation been limited to cases involving the law of a state or those involving traditional common-law claims. In two 1950s maritime cases, the Supreme Court considered conflicts of laws between U.S. statutory law and the law of foreign country, and—far from dismissing the claim upon a conclusion that the U.S. statute should not extend to extraterritorial matters—applied the foreign law. In *Lauritzen v. Larsen* (1953),[30] a Danish seaman who joined the crew of a ship flying under the Danish flag while the ship was docked in New York sued under the federal Jones Act for injuries he suffered while the ship was docked in Cuba. The seaman argued that either *lex loci contracti* (he had agreed to join the crew while the ship was in New York) or *lex fori* should result in application of the Jones Act, whose remedy was more generous than that supplied by Danish (or Cuban) law. The federal Jones Act, like so many of the state statutes we have discussed in the context of domestic conflicts, did not specify its territorial reach. After noting this, the Court treated the problem essentially as one of choice of law. It examined several possible solutions to the problem of selecting the correct law—including the law of the flag, the law of the place of contract, and the law of the place of injury— and concluded that Danish law, not the Jones Act, should apply. Similarly, in *Romero v. International Terminal Operating Co.* (1959),[31] the Court applied the law of Spain—which was the nationality of the seaman and the flag of the ship—rather than the Jones

---

29. A different conception prevailed in the heyday of the "territorial" approach to conflicts: The applicable *lex loci* rule specified the single state whose law could legitimately be applied, and if for some reason, such as application of the "public policy exception," the court chose not to apply that law, the result was dismissal for lack of subject matter jurisdiction—not application of the other state's law. *See* the discussion of *Loucks v. Standard Oil* in Chapter 1.

30. 345 U.S. 571 (1953).

31. 358 U.S. 354 (1959).

Act, even though the injury was inflicted while the ship was docked in New Jersey.

Why have more recent cases like *Aramco* and *Hartford Fire* been treated differently? The reasons are not easy to identify. Here is one possible explanation: *Lauritzen* and *Romero* both involved questions of maritime law, and the Court in both cases emphasized that the problems of choice of law in this context had been confronted by municipal courts both in the United States and abroad since the founding of the republic. There was thus (in Justice Jackson's words) "a seasoned body of maritime law developed by the experience of American courts long accustomed to dealing with admiralty problems in reconciling our own with foreign interests and in accommodating the reach of our own laws to those of other maritime nations."[32] That body of law had roots in an international community of commercial actors whose customs came to be regarded as part of the law of nations, on which American courts drew freely in resolving such matters well into the nineteenth century. Those courts thus had a substantial tradition of applying the law of other countries in maritime disputes where circumstances did not point to the application of U.S. law.[33]

The situation seems somehow different where the question concerns application of Title VII to activities occurring in Saudi Arabia, or of the Sherman Act to activities taking place in England. Such statutes, which have few roots in traditional common-law principles, are avowedly *regulatory* in purpose (and even, under some circumstances, penal). They embody and articulate a national socio-economic policy that may conflict sharply with the policies pursued by other sovereign nations. They certainly have not emerged from a jurisprudence, centuries in the making, based on an enterprise engaged in by all the "trading nations," as could be said (albeit with some exaggeration) in *Lauritzen* and *Romero*. It may seem inappropriate, and perhaps lacking in the spirit of comity, for a federal court to presume to apply the regulatory law of a foreign country (such as the competition law of England); more to the point, it may also seem unfaithful to the interests of the United States in the protection of her own citizens and her own economic interests.

Finally, we simply have to acknowledge that the Court has been erratic in its recognition and deployment of the "presumption against extraterritoriality." In *Lauritzen* and *Romero*, the Court

32. *Lauritzen*, 345 U.S. at 577.

33. When speaking of the pre-Civil War United States, it is probably more accurate to say that courts had substantial experience in applying law different from municipal, state, or federal law in maritime disputes. They would probably have said in such cases that the rule of decision was supplied by the law of nations or a transnational maritime law, rather than the municipal law of another country.

thought it important to interpret the scope of the Jones Act in a way that did not conflict with international conceptions of comity, but ultimately relied more on a choice-of-law analysis than on an analysis of whether any such "presumption" had been overcome. In *Aramco*, of course, the presumption was applied with great fanfare. In *Hartford Fire*, it seemed once again to disappear into the mist (although it would have been simple enough to conclude that the presumption had been overcome with respect to the Sherman Act); the Court did not even bother to cite *Aramco* or to refer to the presumption by name. Many other examples could be given to illustrate that one cannot predict with confidence whether and to what extent the presumption against extraterritoriality will be applied by the Court in the future.

D. The Act-of-State Doctrine

As the preceding sections have made clear, conflict of laws raises a host of considerations in the international sphere that either are less pressing or don't exist at all in the domestic context. The states of the United States possess only certain attributes of sovereignty and are subject to the U.S. Constitution, which (as we have seen) imposes but modest limits with respect to conflict of laws. By contrast, in the international system, a general respect for the sovereign prerogatives of nation-states remains important in constraining the actions of forum courts. Those constraints themselves are not necessarily all derived from international law, but they do have strong roots in the political realities of state action in a world of sovereign nations. The Supreme Court has developed a number of doctrines that reflect both a recognition of the sovereignty of nations and the limits on the federal judiciary when deciding cases that touch on sensitive questions of U.S. foreign policy. The "presumption against extraterritoriality" is one such doctrine. The "Act-of-State Doctrine," the subject of this section, is another.

The substance of the Act-of-State Doctrine is more easily understood by examining the cases in which it has been applied than by attempting a concise general statement of it, but let's begin with the classic expression of the doctrine, announced by the U.S. Supreme Court in *Underhill v. Hernandez* (1897): "Every sovereign state is bound to respect the independence of every other sovereign state, and the courts of one country will not sit in judgment on the acts of the government of another, done within its own territory. Redress of grievances by reason of such acts must be obtained through the means open to be availed of by sovereign powers as between themselves."[34] What this means is that U.S. courts, when faced with a party's contention that a law or official act of a foreign

---

34. *Underhill v. Hernandez,* 168 U.S. 250, 252 (1897).

government within its own territory violates international law or, perhaps, some principle of U.S. law, should refrain from pronouncing on the matter. In *Underhill* itself, a U.S. citizen brought suit against the government of Venezuela, alleging that it had unlawfully detained him (the alleged detention took place during a period of political flux in which the Venezuelan government had seized power). The Supreme Court declined to rule on the contention.

The *Sabbatino* Case. While the Court's pronouncement in *Underhill* expresses the basic concept of the Act-of-State Doctrine, today the contours of the doctrine are more complex and require careful examination. The starting point for contemporary analysis of the Act-of-State Doctrine is *Banco Nacional de Cuba v. Sabbatino* (1964).[35] In 1960, Cuba expropriated ("nationalized") the property of U.S. citizens who were then in Cuba. A Cuban corporation owned largely by U.S. residents had previously contracted to sell Cuban sugar to a commodities broker (Farr, Whitlock), but that sugar was among the property that had been expropriated by the Cuban government. The broker thereupon contracted to buy the sugar instead from the Cuban government. The broker ended up selling the sugar, but instead of forwarding payment to the Cuban government, it made payment to the receiver for the original Cuban corporation. After the Cuban government assigned its contractual rights to Banco Nacional de Cuba, a nominally private party, Banco Nacional sued the broker and the Cuban corporation to recover the money. The defendants argued that Banco Nacional de Cuba was not entitled to the money because the Cuban government's expropriation of the sugar had been a violation of international law, and so neither the Cuban government nor Banco Nacional de Cuba had any rights to the sugar or to the proceeds thereof.

The Supreme Court ruled in *Sabbatino* that the federal courts should not pass upon the issue that the defendants had raised—the legality, under international (or any other) law, of Cuba's act of expropriation: "[T]he Judicial Branch will not examine the validity of a taking of property within its own territory by a foreign sovereign government, extant and recognized by this country at the time of suit, in the absence of a treaty or other unambiguous agreement regarding controlling legal principles, even if the complaint alleges that the taking violates customary international law."[36] Under the specific circumstances in *Sabbatino*, this meant in effect that the legality of the expropriation would be presumed—and that Banco Nacional de Cuba could recover. The Court's opinion in *Sabbatino* stressed that separation-of-powers principles—particularly the notion that the Executive possesses consider-

---

35. 376 U.S. 398 (1964).   **36.** 376 U.S. at 428.

able constitutional responsibility for the conduct of foreign affairs—constituted a primary rationale for the doctrine.

The Historical and Political Context of _Sabbatino_. Before discussing _Sabbatino_ and the Act-of-State Doctrine further, it's important to get a sense of the real-world context for _Sabbatino_ and several of the other important cases calling for application of the doctrine. In most of these cases, we are speaking of challenges to an official act of a foreign government that is (virtually by definition) regarded as legal by the law of that country. Moreover, as is indicated by the phrase "within its own territory" that is used in the quoted passages from both _Underhill_ and _Sabbatino_, the doctrine concerns cases in which application of the traditional territorial conflicts approach would ordinarily call for application of the foreign state's law; actions taken by a state within its own territory have traditionally epitomized matters that lie within the exclusive sovereignty of that state. The cases involve civil, not criminal litigation. And, most important for present purposes, they tend to arise where the disparity between the foreign legal principle and American legal principles are stark, or where political relations between the U.S. and the foreign state are unsettled or tense.

Expropriation by the foreign state of property owned by aliens fits these criteria well, and it is no coincidence that _Sabbatino_ involved such expropriation. Nor is it a coincidence that _Sabbatino_ and several important subsequent decisions on the Act-of-State Doctrine concerned actions by Cuba. (Nor, for that matter, is it a coincidence that some important mid-twentieth-century cases on the Act-of-State doctrine involved acts of expropriation by the Soviet Union and Nazi Germany.)[37] While relations between Cuba and the United States since the late 1950s have never been warm, the situation was particularly tense in 1960 and for several years thereafter, with U.S.–Soviet rivalry providing the essential background. (Cuba was an important issue in the U.S. presidential election in 1960.) Both the actions taken by the Cuban government and the very strong protests they evoked (reflected in the _Sabbatino_ litigation and subsequent commentary on the Supreme Court's decision) are best understood in the context of contemporary international politics. The expropriation at issue in _Sabbatino_ was an act that simultaneously (1) struck many Americans as the epitome of lawlessness and a violation of international law and (2) reflected the stirrings of an "alternate legality" that was gaining some traction in a post-World War II, Cold War world, as many smaller nations (often under Soviet sponsorship) strove for greater self-

---

37. See, e.g., _United States v. Pink_, 315 U.S. 203 (1942); _United States v. Belmont_, 301 U.S. 324 (1937); _Bernstein v. Van Heyghen Freres, S.A._, 163 F.2d 246 (2d Cir. 1947); _Bernstein v. N.V. Nederlandsche–Amerikaansche, Stoomvaart–Maatschappij_, 210 F.2d 375 (2d Cir. 1954).

determination, experimented with command economies, and sought to resist U.S. influence. As the Supreme Court put the matter with striking tact in *Sabbatino,* "There are few if any issues in international law today on which opinion seems to be so divided as the limitations on a state's power to expropriate the property of aliens."[38]

With this political and historical context in mind, let's return to *Sabbatino.* Consider it as a conflicts problem. Then-conventional principles of choice of law indicated that Cuban law should apply, which would validate the expropriation and subsequent transactions based on it. The Act-of-State Doctrine as explained in such earlier cases as *Underhill,* however, indicated that law of the locus in such cases ought not to be *validated* as such; rather, the American court should disclaim any effort to "pronounce judgment" upon it all. But is this a *legal* principle or a *political* one? By the time of *Sabbatino,* many academics and corporate lawyers, dismayed by expropriations and other actions alien to Western legal culture that seemingly could be licensed *de facto* by the *Underhill* principle, had reconceived the Act-of-State Doctrine as a *lex loci* rule in its own right. According to this argument, the doctrine simply stated that the situation called for the application of conflict-of-laws principles, and that the law of the expropriating state in the *Sabbatino* situation should presumptively apply. As such, however, this "*lex loci*" rule was subject to exceptions, such as the familiar "public policy" exception and the principle that a law of the locus violating international law could not legitimately be given effect. Application of one or both of those exceptions thus could result in the American court's refusing to give effect to the expropriation.

The thrust of this argument should not be missed; it suggested that a judicial decision refusing to give effect to Cuba's act of expropriation was a *legal* conclusion that could be reached from within the conflict-of-laws system itself, albeit by means of the "public policy exception." Paradoxically—considering that the ultimate aim of this argument was to deny recognition to Cuba's act of expropriation—it admitted in theory the propriety of according legal validity to that action as a way-station to denying it effect pursuant to the public policy or international law exceptions; whereas the *Underhill* principle would have disclaimed the authority to pass judgment, yea or nay, on the Cuban act altogether.[39]

---

38. *Sabbatino,* 376 U.S. at 428 (footnote omitted).

39. The paradox extends even farther in the specific circumstances of *Sabbatino,* where refusal to pass judgment on the Cuban law effectively (though not formally) resulted in its actual enforcement. Thus, in *Sabbatino,* a theory of the Act-of-State Doctrine that would formally have acknowledged the intelligibility of judicial recognition and validation of the act of expropriation would have resulted in refusal to give it effect, while a theory of the doctrine that formally disclaimed judicial authority to validate the act actually resulted in its *de facto* enforcement.

It is fair to say that the Court's opinion in *Sabbatino* rejected this conceptualization of the Act-of-State Doctrine. The Court reaffirmed the concept in *Underhill* that the doctrine, where it applies, constitutes a refusal to consider the legality of the action of the foreign state at all—not a decision that that action violates international law or that some other law should be applied. Equally important, the Court in *Sabbatino* clarified both the rationale underlying the doctrine and its legal basis. The Act-of-State Doctrine must come from some *source* of law, and previous discussions had been vague and discordant on this question. The Court held that the doctrine emerged, not from international law, as had sometimes been argued, nor from the U.S. Constitution, but from the federal courts' power to make federal common law.[40] And, while the Constitution as such did not compel recognition of the doctrine, the Court held that the doctrine had "constitutional underpinnings": Its substance was shaped by considerations of separation of powers, and the inadvisability of the judiciary's wading into foreign policy waters better navigated by the Executive:

> Following an expropriation of any significance, the Executive engages in diplomacy aimed to assure that United States citizens who are harmed are compensated fairly. Representing all claimants of this country, it will often be able, either by bilateral or multilateral talks, by submission to the United Nations, or by the employment of economic and political sanctions, to achieve some degree of general redress. Judicial determinations of invalidity of title can, on the other hand, have only an occasional impact, since they depend on the fortuitous circumstance of the property in question being brought into this country. Such decisions would, if the acts involved were declared invalid, often be likely to give offense to the expropriating country; since the concept of territorial sovereignty is so deep seated, any state may resent the refusal of the courts of another sovereign to accord validity to acts within its territorial borders. Piecemeal dispositions of this sort involving the probability of affront to another state could seriously interfere with negotiations being carried on by the Executive Branch and might prevent or render less favorable the terms of an agreement that could otherwise be reached. Relations with third countries which have engaged in similar expropriations would not be immune from effect.

Sabbatino therefore locates the Act-of-State Doctrine squarely in the context of foreign policy concerns, as to which the Executive must have room to operate without being "embarrassed" by judicial rulings that touch upon sensitive matters. The Court in *Sabba-*

40. *See* the discussion of *Sabbatino* in Chapter 7.

tino clearly conceived the doctrine as resting on structural, even political considerations—somewhat analogous to those involved in the "political question" doctrine in constitutional law—rather than as a choice-of-law principle.

The reasoning in *Sabbatino* reflects a sensible view of statecraft in the international arena, but in one sense it can seem counterintuitive, even paradoxical. One sees this particularly clearly when one compares the doctrine with the "public policy exception," which, as we have seen, functions as a kind of "exception" to the *lex loci* rules of the traditional approach to domestic choice of law. Under the public policy exception, the forum is apt to decline to give effect to an otherwise applicable foreign rule of law if it seems especially abhorrent or alien to the policy of the forum. The more "abhorrent" or "alien" the foreign rule, the more likely the public policy doctrine will function to preclude its application by the forum. The Act-of-State Doctrine, however, seems to rest on something like the opposite premise: One might say it is precisely those foreign rules of law that are *most* abhorrent or alien to the American forum—those that reflect a wide chasm between American political and legal culture and that of the foreign state—that most readily trigger *Sabbatino*'s concern that the judiciary not act in such a way as to interfere with the Executive's capacity to handle those differences politically. The sense of counterintuitiveness is (as is discussed further below) heightened by the procedural setting of *Sabbatino*, in which application of the Act-of-State Doctrine resulted in the ability of Banco Nacional de Cuba to maintain its contract claim. Perhaps "counterintuitive" is too mild a word: The decision in *Sabbatino* met with a firestorm of protest, and Congress enacted a statute partly overruling it.

As suggested in an influential article by Professor Anne–Marie Burley (now Slaughter), however, the Court's instincts in *Sabbatino* were sound, and one can construct from that decision a more refined "Act-of-State Doctrine" that distinguishes between what Burley calls "liberal" and "non-liberal" political and legal regimes.[41] According to Burley, the very feasibility and coherence of using a choice-of-law approach (possibly involving the application of foreign law) in the international domain rest on the notion that the nations involved share fundamental legal premises, particularly where the very validity of a government's actions is questioned. Where the actions of "liberal" states—those that recognize the rights of private property, have democratic political institutions, and protect "liberal" values such as equality—are involved, an American court can safely resolve conflicts using one or another choice-of-law approach, because the interested nations are operat-

41. Anne–Marie Burley, *Law Among Liberal States: Liberal Interna-* *tionalism and the Act of State Doctrine,* 92 Columbia Law Review 1907 (1992).

ing within a "zone of law" due to the shared premises underlying their respective political and legal systems. It may not be necessary for the judiciary to abstain and allow the "political" branches to resolve the problem. A case like *Sabbatino*, however, is different, according to Burley. It no longer makes sense in such a case to assume that basic premises underlying the respective legal and political regimes are shared ones, and therefore the predicate does not exist for allowing challenges to the actions of a state within its territory to be adjudicated according to the formal judicial process. We have entered a "zone of politics," in which conflicts of the sort represented by *Sabbatino* should be resolved by a political process.

Thus, what might first appear counterintuitive or paradoxical is really a recognition that not all relationships between nations resting on differing legal and political regimes have the requisite consensus on fundamentals to justify resolving their legal conflicts in a juridical manner, using the law of choice of law. On Burley's account, it is as if only states that share common legal premises are granted the respect that entitles them to have their laws rejected by the forum (through choice-of-law analysis). One might think that an attitude of deference to foreign law would be the norm where courts purport to be dealing with the laws of states that are friendly to the United States (which of course does not necessarily mean that they are "liberal" states); but the Act-of-State Doctrine as applied in *Sabbatino* turns that calculus on its head. In Burley's account, *Sabbatino* can be read in symbolic terms, representing a declaration by the Supreme Court that Cuba lay outside the community of nations (those she characterizes as "liberal") whose shared values justify the use of conflicts law by courts to resolve legal conflicts. While the Supreme Court has not itself adopted Burley's distinction between liberal and non-liberal regimes, she argued in her 1992 article that decisions by the lower federal courts purporting to apply the Act-of-State Doctrine have substantially reflected that distinction.

While we're on the subject of comparing the public policy exception and the Act-of-State Doctrine, let's observe that the distinctive procedural setting in *Sabbatino* was not necessarily typical for cases raising the Act-of-State Doctrine. An equally common scenario might be one in which a plaintiff sues a foreign government's assignee,[42] claiming that that government's expropriation and subsequent assignment of the plaintiff's property violated his rights and was invalid under international law. Application of the Act-of-State Doctrine, which we would expect the government's assignee to raise as a defense, would seem to result, at least under

---

42. We hypothesize a case involving a foreign government's assignee, rather than the government itself, because principles of sovereign immunity would likely govern cases in which the foreign government were sued.

the reasoning in *Sabbatino*, in dismissal of the case for lack of jurisdiction: The court would decline to rule on the alleged invalidity of the expropriation and assignment.

But in *Sabbatino*, the alleged invalidity under international law of the Cuban government's expropriation of alien property was raised by the *defendant* as a defense. In response, the *plaintiffs* raised the Act-of-State Doctrine. The consequence, then, of applying the doctrine in *Sabbatino* was not dismissal of the action on jurisdictional grounds, but adjudication of the plaintiff's contract claim. The refusal to consider the legal validity of the Cuban government's act of expropriation was really, in practical terms, to assume its validity, even though at a formal level the Court was purporting not to address the issue at all. This is part of what bothered some people about the *Sabbatino* decision, and explains why it here appears to be almost the complete reverse of the public policy doctrine: The Court upheld a cause of action that even *it* considered (judging from its rhetorical condemnations of the Cuban government in *Sabbatino*) to be based on an abhorrent act of expropriation. There does appear to be something more disturbing about applying the doctrine to permit vindication of a claim that might appear to be invalid in the absence of the doctrine, than applying it simply to dismiss the case on jurisdictional grounds. As Justice Brandeis said in connection with a similar problem in connection with the public policy exception, the Court's action in *Sabbatino* subjected the defendant in that case to "irremediable liability."[43] But this fact did not sway the Court in *Sabbatino*.

The Act-of-State Doctrine Since *Sabbatino*. Two facts should be kept in mind in assessing the current status of the Act-of-State Doctrine in the federal courts: (1) The Court in *Sabbatino* limited its holding rather carefully; and (2) the decision in *Sabbatino* has always had its critics, and both the Supreme Court and lower federal courts have shown a disposition to limit *Sabbatino* in a variety of ways.

First, the Court in *Sabbatino* did not reaffirm the wide-ranging holding in *Underhill*, which seemed to suggest that the federal judiciary should abstain from passing judgment on *any* action taken by a foreign state within its own territory; instead, the Court in *Sabbatino* confined its holding to expropriations.[44] Although expropriation has been the type of action by foreign governments that

---

43. *Bradford Elec. Light Co. v. Clapper*, 286 U.S. 145, 160 (1932).

44. "[W]e decide only that the Judicial Branch will not examine the validity of a taking of property within its own territory by a foreign sovereign government, extant and recognized by this country at the time of suit, in the absence of a treaty or other unambiguous agreement regarding controlling legal principles, even if the complaint alleges that the taking violates customary international law." *Sabbatino*, 376 U.S. at 428.

has most often invited litigation in U.S. courts, this limitation in *Sabbatino* has enabled courts in some cases to subject some other kinds of official foreign acts to judicial scrutiny. Second, the Court in *Sabbatino* confirmed that judicial abstention was required only in cases where the foreign state's act occurred within its own territorial boundaries. Lower federal courts uneasy about immunizing what they consider to be wrongful behavior by foreign states via the Act-of-State Doctrine have taken advantage of this proviso in *Sabbatino* and found the doctrine to be inapplicable even in expropriation cases, particularly where incorporeal property was involved and an argument could be made that such property lay outside the territorial boundaries of the expropriating state.

Third, the Court in *W.S. Kirkpatrick v. Environmental Tectonics Corp.* (1990)[45] arguably narrowed the Act-of-State Doctrine somewhat by holding that it applied only to cases involving "the asserted invalidity of an official act of a foreign sovereign," not to acts of foreign officials said to have been carried out with unlawful motivations. In *W.S. Kirkpatrick*, a U.S. corporation (W.S. Kirkpatrick) obtained a contract with the government of Nigeria by paying a bribe to an agent of that government. An unsuccessful bidder for the contract later sued W.S. Kirkpatrick and the Nigerian government's agent, among others, for damages under RICO and other state and federal laws. The Supreme Court ruled that the Act-of-State Doctrine did not bar adjudication of these claims, because "[n]othing in the present suit requires the court to declare invalid, and thus ineffective as 'a rule of decision for the courts of this country,' ... the official act of a foreign sovereign."[46] Since the key allegations in the lawsuit concerned the offer and acceptance of a bribe, not the legal validity of the contract ultimately awarded by the Nigerian government to W.S. Kirkpatrick, the Act-of-State Doctrine did not apply.

At first glance the Court's distinction between the situation in *W.S. Kirkpatrick* and the situation in *Sabbatino* may appear a bit artificial, signaling a desire to cabin in the Act-of-State Doctrine. Some have suggested, however, that it is legitimate to distinguish between the foreign government in its role as sovereign maker of law and policy for the locus, and the foreign government in its role as entrepreneur and party to commercial transactions. On this view, *W.S. Kirkpatrick* was rightly decided, not simply because the case technically involved no need to judge of the legal validity of "the official act of a foreign sovereign," but because a foreign government's participation in commercial transactions is not the kind of governmental act that requires a hands-off attitude by U.S.

---

45. 493 U.S. 400 (1990).

46. *W.S. Kirkpatrick*, 493 U.S. at 405, *quoting Ricaud v. American Metal Co.*, 246 U.S. 304, 310 (1918).

courts, lest sensitive political issues concerning the fundamentals of state sovereignty be affected. However persuasive this reasoning might be as a rationale for *W.S. Kirkpatrick*, it has not yet been explicitly adopted by the Court.

Can the Executive Branch Direct the Judicial Branch Not to Abstain in a Particular Case? The most interesting loose end left by *Sabbatino* concerns whether, even in a case clearly falling within the Act-of-State Doctrine, the Executive Branch can "waive" any objections to the court's adjudicating the validity of an official act by a foreign government by notifying the court in a brief or letter that it has no such objections. One can imagine several possible answers to this question. One possibility, rather unrealistic and not to be found in the reported cases, is that the court should give such a declaration no weight whatever. Another possibility is that such a declaration is pretty much binding on the court, meaning that the court must proceed to decide the matter. An important line of lower federal court decisions decided prior to *Sabbatino*, most famously *Bernstein v. N.V. Nederlandsche–Amerikaansche Stoomvaart–Maatschappij* (2d Cir. 1954), took this position. In *Bernstein*, a Jewish businessman sued to recover property that had been converted by a Dutch corporation in collaboration with Nazi officials in the 1940s. The State Department submitted a letter to the court, indicating that the Department did not object to the court's adjudication of the validity of the defense that the conversion had been undertaken based on official Nazi policy. The Second Circuit ruled summarily that the letter removed any bar to judicial consideration of the issue under the Act-of-State Doctrine. Such a letter subsequently became known colloquially as a *"Bernstein* letter," which parties arguing against the validity of official acts of foreign governments would frequently seek from the State Department in an effort to avoid the operation of the Act-of-State Doctrine.

The Supreme Court came rather close to accepting this position in *First National City Bank v. Banco Nacional de Cuba* (1972),[47] but ultimately rejected it. What has made this case a bit difficult to interpret is that a majority of the Court ruled that the Act-of-State Doctrine should not bar adjudication in that case, but only a plurality affirmed that the reasoning behind the *"Bernstein* letter" idea compelled such a result. That plurality stated, "We conclude that where the Executive Branch, charged as it is with primary responsibility for the conduct of foreign affairs, expressly represents to the Court that application of the act of state doctrine would not advance the interests of American foreign policy, that doctrine

---

47. 406 U.S. 759 (1972).

should not be applied by the courts."[48] The four dissenters from the Court's holding, as well as one of the Justices concurring in the result, rejected the notion that a *"Bernstein* letter" compelled adjudication of the issue. In particular, Justice Powell stated, "I would be uncomfortable with a doctrine which would require the judiciary to receive the Executive's permission before invoking its jurisdiction. Such a notion, in the name of the doctrine of separation of powers, seems to me to conflict with that very doctrine."[49]

The solution that seems to have been adopted by most of the lower federal courts is to regard the submission of a *"Bernstein* letter" as a relevant factor in determining whether the otherwise applicable Act-of-State Doctrine should govern—entitled to substantial weight, but not necessarily dispositive of the question. This seems a sensible resolution. As is suggested by Justice Powell's observation in *First National City Bank*, it is difficult to square the notion that a "Bernstein letter" from the Executive should bind the federal judiciary in a particular case with the doctrine of separation of powers, which after all is, after *Sabbatino*, the basic foundation for the Act-of-State Doctrine. Were the views of the plurality in *First National City Bank* to prevail, one can easily imagine situations in which the Executive would seek, on a selective basis, to recruit the judiciary in the embarrassment of a foreign sovereign when that might suit the Executive Branch's political goals. There is nothing wrong with this from a purely political perspective, but it would seem to be an inappropriate subordination of judicial independence.

E. The Constitution and the Flag: Extraterritorial Reach of the U.S. Constitution

Thus far, we've focused on the degree to which U.S. statutory law applies extraterritorially. But to what degree does the U.S. Constitution—in particular, the Bill of Rights—itself apply extraterritorially?

Much of the power of Congress to act pursuant to Article I (and the handful of other provisions in the Constitution that confer legislative power on Congress) plainly extends to matters outside the boundaries of the U.S. Extraterritorial application of the kinds of federal laws we have been discussing up to now—Title VII, antitrust, securities regulation, intellectual property—are clearly within Congress's power to regulate both interstate and foreign commerce. One might speculate that both the reach of such federal power and the reach of the Bill of Rights coincide; wherever the government is empowered to act by the Constitution, it is re-

---

48. 406 U.S. at 768 (plurality opinion).

49. 406 U.S. at 773 (Powell, J., concurring in the judgment).

strained by the Bill of Rights. But this is far from the case. The protections of the Bill of Rights only partially extend to extraterritorial assertions of power by the federal government.

A Related Issue: The Constitutional Rights of Aliens. The question of the extraterritorial effect of the Bill of Rights is enmeshed in another constitutional question: Whether and to what extent federal constitutional rights are held not only by American citizens, but by immigrants and other noncitizens. In considering the presumption against extraterritoriality, we were concerned only with the locations of the behavior that the federal government was trying to regulate, but the relevant Supreme Court precedents on extraterritorial reach of the Bill of Rights itself also require consideration of the citizenship status of the person claiming constitutional protection. Using these two axes—territoriality and nationality— we can plot a matrix setting forth four permutations:

1 U.S. Citizen Within U.S.	2 Noncitizen Within U.S.
3 U.S. Citizen Outside U.S.	4 Noncitizen Outside U.S.

The scenarios in Box #1 and Box #2 each assume that the contested government actions took place within the territory of the United States. Obviously the Bill of Rights applies fully when a U.S. citizen challenges an action taken by the federal government (as well as state governments) within the territory of the United States. Moreover, aliens residing in the United States are entitled to many of the constitutional protections to which citizens are entitled.

The Insular Cases. Of course, what it means to be "within the U.S." may require further elaboration. Ever since the Supreme Court's decision in *Dred Scott v. Sandford* (1857)[50] if not earlier, the status of the Constitution with respect to territories that are

---

50. 60 U.S. 393 (1857). Of course, the *Dred Scott* decision is better known for its notorious rulings on Black citizenship and the unconstitutionality of the Missouri Compromise, but its discussion of the rights of those inhabiting the territories of the United States has had considerable influence.

under the sovereign authority of the United States has been an important issue. Acquisition in the late nineteenth and early twentieth centuries by the United States of noncontiguous territories populated by non-white and non-English-speaking peoples eventually forced the Supreme Court to determine whether "the Constitution follows the flag" and, if so, to what extent. In a series of decisions known collectively as the *Insular Cases*,[51] the Court marked out a line of doctrine in which the people of "incorporated territories" clearly destined for statehood (in this instance, Hawai'i) were entitled to the full protection of the Constitution, while a more *ad hoc* analysis was required for residents of "unincorporated territories"—those over which the United States intended to continue to exercise sovereign authority but that were not destined for full statehood. As to these unincorporated territories, the scope of applicable constitutional guarantees depended on an examination of the situation specific to that particular territory.

The rhetoric and holdings in the *Insular Cases* have not worn especially well. They clearly reflect what today would be called "colonialist" views and are strikingly direct in their suggestions concerning the cultural incapacity of some of the non-white and non-English-speaking peoples to adapt to constitutional democracy. A plurality of the Supreme Court in 1957 recommended that the *Insular Cases* not be extended beyond their own facts. Today they are apt to be regarded as something of a curiosity, explained only by a distinctive historical moment not likely to be repeated. The fact remains, however, that the *Insular Cases* have never been overruled. The notion that there might be a "sliding scale" of constitutional entitlements under the Bill of Rights, depending on specific circumstances, seems to have survived, and, as noted below, has reappeared in opinions of the some of the individual Justices.

***Reid v. Covert* (1957).** Box #3 and Box #4 in the table above, both of which involve the assertion of U.S. governmental authority outside the United States, are the scenarios that are of most direct relevance here, since they truly concern "extraterritoriality." What about U.S. citizens who are subjected to the authority of the United States while they are abroad? The leading case is *Reid v. Covert* (1957),[52] in which the wives of U.S. servicemen stationed abroad were court-martialed and prosecuted for the murders of their husbands. Courts martial do not provide for all the protections that

---

51. A full list of the cases regarded as being among the *"Insular Cases"* would be unnecessarily long. In addition, scholars have disagreed among themselves concerning which are the "true" *Insular Cases*. Perhaps the leading case is *Downes v. Bidwell*, 182 U.S. 244 (1901), in which Justice White's concurring opinion set forth the analysis that ultimately guided the Court in most of the succeeding cases. Other important decisions include *Dorr v. United States*, 195 U.S. 138 (1904), and cases as late as *Balzac v. Porto Rico*, 258 U.S. 298 (1922).

52. 354 U.S. 1 (1957).

would be constitutionally guaranteed in conventional criminal prosecutions within the U.S., such as trial by jury. The U.S. Supreme Court held in *Reid* that trial by jury, as well as indictment by grand jury, was required in the prosecutions even though they were being held in a foreign country. While the Court in *Reid* did not hold that every constitutional right a U.S. citizen might have while in the United States necessarily applied extraterritorially in every conceivable circumstance, the *Reid* decision has generally been read broadly. The *Reid* decision explains why the federal government has not attempted to detain U.S. citizens at the federal installation in Guantanamo Bay.

***U.S. v. Verdugo–Urquidez* (1990).** This leaves our fourth box—in which the U.S. government has acted extraterritorially with respect to a noncitizen. This question arose vividly in *United States v. Verdugo–Urquidez* (1990).[53] Verdugo–Urquidez, suspected of being a kingpin in the smuggling of illegal drugs into the U.S., was arrested by U.S. agents for violation of federal narcotics laws. The U.S. Drug Enforcement Agency ["DEA"] thereupon sought, and received, permission from a high-ranking Mexican police official to search Verdugo–Urquidez's Mexican residences for evidence. Obviously, no warrant was issued by a federal magistrate in connection with the search. The DEA agents found incriminating documents, which the defendant sought to suppress in a pre-trial motion because the search allegedly was in violation of the Fourth Amendment. The lower federal courts held that Verdugo–Urquidez was entitled to rely on the Fourth Amendment, that the warrantless search did not comport with constitutional requirements, and that the evidence must be excluded. The Supreme Court, however, reversed.

As the Court pointed out, neither *Reid v. Covert* nor the various cases holding that aliens situated within the United States are entitled to certain constitutional rights necessarily supported Verdugo–Urquidez's argument. Unlike the cases relied on by the defendant, *Verdugo-Urquidez* involved both an alien defendant and extraterritorial actions by the government. The Court in *Verdugo-Urquidez* did not hold that no part of the Bill of Rights could ever extend to such a situation; it relied instead on the particular nature and phrasing of the Fourth Amendment.[54] The Court noted that, when the Fourth Amendment is violated, the violation takes place at the time and place of the search or seizure, not at the time when

---

53. 494 U.S. 259 (1990).

54. The Fourth Amendment reads: "The right of the people to be secure in their persons, houses, papers, and effects, against unreasonable searches and seizures, shall not be violated, and no Warrants shall issue, but upon probable cause, supported by Oath or affirmation, and particularly describing the place to be searched, and the persons or things to be searched."

the evidence thus obtained is introduced at trial, reinforcing that this truly was a case concerning the "extraterritorial" application of the Bill of Rights. (The Court distinguished this situation from one in which an alien apprehended abroad seeks at trial to raise a Fifth Amendment right not to incriminate himself; here the alleged violation, if any, would have occurred at trial, when (say) the government sought to introduce an involuntary confession obtained at the time of arrest.) But the real linchpin of the Court's opinion was its emphasis on the fact that the Fourth Amendment uses the phrase "the people" in defining the intended beneficiaries of the Amendment's protections. The Court believed that this phrase "refers to a class of persons who are part of a national community or who have otherwise developed sufficient connection with this country to be considered part of that community."[55] Aliens like *Verdugo-Urquidez*, whose only connection with the U.S. consisted of his arrest (and whatever role he had in smuggling illegal drugs into the U.S.), are not members of this "community." Thus the Fourth Amendment did not apply to the situation in *Verdugo-Urquidez*.

The Court's emphasis on a "national community" referenced by the phrase "the people" in the Fourth Amendment was unconvincing. It is doubtful that the use of the phrase in some but not all of the first eight amendments reflected a considered judgment by the Framers that only those Amendments without the phrase were meant to apply to aliens situated outside the country. As many have pointed out, it is more likely that the drafters (and ratifiers) of the Bill of Rights gave little or no consideration to these questions of extraterritoriality, at a time when assertion of American power to carry out police investigations in foreign countries was scarcely foreseeable. It is also hard to see how emphasis on a putative "national community" can answer questions about the territorial scope of the U.S. Constitution (as opposed to the nationality of those to whom it applies). After all, the Fourth Amendment does restrict the power of the federal government to engage in certain unreasonable searches and seizures within the United States. But the weak points in the Court's reasoning doesn't necessarily mean that the result in *Verdugo-Urquidez* is wrong.

Justice Brennan's dissent criticized the result in *Verdugo-Urquidez* as resting on an impermissible "antilogy": allowing Verdugo–Urquidez to be prosecuted under U.S. law, while denying him the benefit of a constitutional provision that operates to protect criminal defendants in U.S. courts. As Brennan stated: "[T]he Fourth Amendment is an unavoidable correlative of the Government's power to enforce the criminal law."[56] While there is logical

---

55. *Verdugo-Urquidez*, 494 U.S. at 265.

56. 494 U.S. at 282 (Brennan, J., dissenting).

appeal to the notion that constitutional protections must apply whenever and wherever the U.S. exercises sovereign governmental authority, the *Insular Cases* cast serious doubt on that contention. To some extent, Brennan's dissent relies on resolution of a somewhat abstract debating point: Are the provisions of the Bill of Rights better regarded as a limitation on what the government may do, or as rights held by individuals? If they are limitations on government, there is some force to Brennan's argument; the limitations should operate wherever the power does. If they are rights held by individuals, then their scope and force can be analyzed independently of the government's power to prosecute crime, and the result in *Verdugo-Urquidez* is better supported. But surely resolution of the *Verdugo-Urquidez* problem shouldn't rely on so academic an argument.

Justice Kennedy, concurring in *Verdugo-Urquidez*, may have had the most persuasive position. Relying on the *Insular Cases*, Kennedy observed that determination of whether a particular provision of the Constitution "applies" extraterritorially should depend on the specific right asserted and the circumstances of the particular case. In particular, he thought application of the Fourth Amendment's requirements in the circumstances of *Verdugo-Urquidez* would be "impractical and anomalous:"

> If the search had occurred in a residence within the United States, I have little doubt that the full protections of the Fourth Amendment would apply. But that is not this case. The absence of local judges or magistrates available to issue warrants, the differing and perhaps unascertainable conceptions of reasonableness and privacy that prevail abroad, and the need to cooperate with foreign officials all indicate that the Fourth Amendment's warrant requirement should not apply in Mexico as it does in this country.[57]

An important fact highlighted by Justice Kennedy's concurrence is that constitutional provisions like the Fourth Amendment, particularly as interpreted in the domestic context by the Supreme Court over 200 years, do not operate in a vacuum; they contemplate and rely on the existence of certain institutions in order to function properly. For example, the Fourth Amendment's requirement of a warrant in certain situations depends in part on the existence of a tribunal that is able to issue such a warrant in a manner that is sufficiently timely to make its use worthwhile. This may not have been true of Mexico, whose criminal justice processes may differ in important ways from ours, under the circumstances presented in *Verdugo-Urquidez*.

What About Choice of Law? Like several other cases discussed in this chapter, *Verdugo-Urquidez* considers the possible

57. 494 U.S. at 278 (Kennedy, J., concurring).

extraterritorial application of U.S. law (in this case, the Fourth Amendment) without treating the problem as one of choice of law. If the Fourth Amendment does not apply, however, would it not be worth asking whether *Mexican* law authorized the search and seizure that took place in *Verdugo-Urquidez*? Often, as in most domestic choice-of-law problems, a correlative of the conclusion that forum law does not apply is that the law of some other jurisdiction does. Granted, the ordinary rule is that courts do not apply the penal laws of another jurisdiction. And in this case there is no indication that Mexico would *want* its law to be applied. Yet there is something unsettling about the notion that the U.S. can apply its criminal laws and investigations extraterritorially while avoiding the limitations prescribed by *either* U.S. law *or* that of the locus. Note that this is precisely the circumstance that commended to the Bush Administration the use of the installation at Guantanamo Bay as a detention center for noncitizens alleged to be "enemy combatants" after the terrorist attacks on September 11, 2001 and the subsequent fighting in Afghanistan. Formally speaking, Guantanamo Bay remains within the sovereign domain of Cuba (meaning that constitutional protections applicable when the government acts within the United States do not necessarily apply), yet the 1903 treaty between Cuba and the United States leasing the area to the United States (as well as military and political realities) has operated to keep Cuba from asserting sovereign authority there.

Guantanamo and *Boumediene v. Bush* (2008). In *Boumediene v. Bush* (2008),[58] the Court rejected the argument that the kind of strategic arrangements underlying use of the Guantanamo Bay facility should determine the scope of constitutional rights that might be asserted there by noncitizens:

> [T]he Government's view is that the Constitution had no effect [at Guantanamo Bay], at least as to noncitizens, because the United States disclaimed sovereignty in the formal sense of the term. The necessary implication of the argument is that by surrendering formal sovereignty over any unincorporated territory to a third party, while at the same time entering into a lease that grants total control over the territory back to the United States, it would be possible for the political branches to govern without legal constraint.

> Our basic charter cannot be contracted away like this.[59]

Boumediene concerned the availability to presumed noncitizen "enemy combatants" of the writ of habeas corpus, a question going beyond what we can consider here. And since the Court discerned the U.S. lacked sovereignty over Guantanamo Bay only in a con-

---

58. 553 U.S. 723, 128 S.Ct. 2229 (2008).

59. 128 S.Ct. at 2258–59.

trived sense, the case is readily distinguishable from *Verdugo-Urquidez*, where the crucial acts took place in Mexico, a sovereign fully capable of asserting its own prerogatives with respect to criminal investigation within its borders. It must be remembered that Mexican officials did, after all, approve the search in *Verdugo-Urquidez*. If the U.S. Constitution placed no Fourth Amendment constraints on the U.S. in *Verdugo-Urquidez*, it is nevertheless possible that political and diplomatic considerations can check the degree to which the U.S. pursues criminal investigations abroad that wink at the constitutional limits recognized by both the U.S. and the locus.

F. The Status of International Law in American Courts

The very concept of "choice of law" rests in part on the principle that foreign law—that is, law other than the municipal law of the forum—will sometimes be applied by the forum. International law constitutes a body of law that most nations regard as having some kind of force. To what extent are the rules and principles of international law the "law of the United States" and thus constitute rules of decisions that U.S. courts must apply in appropriate cases? Does it matter which one of the several sources of international law—treaties and conventions, custom, decisions by international tribunals, and so on—is the basis for the rule of international law at issue in the particular case? Although these questions are not always given much attention in American casebooks on conflict of laws, in certain respects they certainly qualify as "conflicts" problems. At times, American courts may be faced with the question whether a rule of international law supersedes otherwise applicable state or federal law. This is not a book about international law, and we will not attempt here to define with precision the different sources of international law or explain the different issues they can raise.[60] Identification of some basic principles may, however, be helpful.

Although scholars continue to debate the matter, international law often does provide a rule of decision to be applied in American courts—but always as U.S. law. That is, international law does not apply of its own force in American courts; it applies only to the extent that U.S. law has adopted its principles.[61] However it may

---

60. A useful brief summary can be found in RALPH G. STEINHARDT, INTERNATIONAL CIVIL LITIGATION: CASES AND MATERIALS ON THE RISE OF INTERMESTIC LAW (2002), 5–21 ("A Survival Guide to International Law").

61. Thus Congress is under no constitutional obligation to act consistently

with international law when enacting a statute. This principle is, however, moderated somewhat by a venerable judicial doctrine known as the "*Charming Betsy*" principle: A Congressional statute "ought never to be construed to violate the law of nations if any other possible construction remains." *Murray v.*

have been viewed historically, this state of affairs is consistent with one of the lessons of the *Erie* case, discussed in Chapter 7: The law applied in American courts is the law of some sovereign state or nation, not a body of transnational or "transcendental" law belonging to no particular sovereign. As a general matter, under the U.S. Constitution, Congress has the authority to legislate in derogation of international law. That is, international law is not binding in U.S. courts when Congress has clearly indicated its intention that it should not apply. At the same time, it is uncontroversial that certain bodies of law that are usually regarded as part of "international law" are also part of the law of the United States. For example, bilateral and multilateral treaties to which the U.S. is a signatory have legal status roughly equivalent to that of federal statutes under the Constitution, although there are elaborate legal doctrines governing the conditions under which such treaties will be regarded as having become part of the law of the United States. For example, federal law distinguishes between "self-executing" and "non-self-executing" treaties (the latter requiring specific implementation *via* Congressional statute).

The Law of Nations and Customary International Law. The hottest debates concerning the status of international law in American courts have to do with the status of "customary international law," which is universally regarded as an important component of international law. As its name suggests, customary international law can be distinguished from other portions of international law that emerge directly from codified sources like treaties or the decisions of international tribunals. The phrase "customary international law" connotes something similar to what prior to the twentieth century was known as the "law of nations." Several venerable Supreme Court decisions have held that this body of law is "part of our law"—that is, it is incorporated in America law. Chief Justice Marshall, for example, stated in 1815 that "the Court is bound by the law of nations which is a part of the law of the land."[62] Somewhat more recently, but still a long time ago, the Court stated in a passage that continues to provoke widespread debate:

> International law is part of our law, and must be ascertained and administered by the courts of justice of appropriate jurisdiction, as often as questions of right depending upon it are duly presented for their determination. For this purpose, where there is no treaty, and no controlling executive or legislative act or judicial decision, resort must be had to the customs and

Schooner Charming Betsy, 2 Cranch 64, 118 (1804).

62. *The Nereide*, 13 U.S. 388, 423 (1815).

usages of civilized nations; and as evidence of these, to the works of jurists and commentators, who by years of labor, research and experience, have made themselves peculiarly well acquainted with the subjects of which they treat. Such works are resorted to by judicial tribunals, not for the speculations of their authors concerning what the law ought to be, but for trustworthy evidence of what the law really is.[63]

This passage dates from 1900, and its quaint confidence in "the works of jurists and commentators," while undoubtedly gratifying to scholars everywhere, seems to be of another time. As has been suggested by a number of more recent scholars (!), there is reason to be cautious about assimilating what is today called "customary international law" to the "law of nations" that the Court in these two quotations clearly had in mind. Especially since World War II, the content of international legal norms has shifted importantly in the direction of international human rights and the restraints that should operate on tyrannical or aggressor nations in a world of multilateral legal and political institutions. Whether American courts should (pursuant to the law of nations) exempt fishing vessels from capture as prize (the issue in *The Paquete Habana*) might, perhaps, be appropriately determined by referring to treatises written by scholars sequestered in their studies, attempting to record the view that nations have in the past taken on the question. But the question of what qualifies as a basic human right, and should thus be regarded as part of modern-day customary international law, has a different quality. These questions frequently are hotly contested ones, and can rarely be answered definitively by detached examination of the "customs and usages of civilized nations." This is, at least, one reason why some judges and commentators contest the notion that Supreme Court observations like those in *The Paquete Habana* and *The Nereide* should be regarded as conclusive on the question of whether and to what extent customary international law should *today* be regarded as automatically embodied in the law of the United States. Another contention is, as suggested above, that the Court's decision in *Erie* stands in the way of any effort to apply rules of decision that derive from non-positive sources such as customary international law.

The Alien Tort Statute. An important staging area for these debates in recent years has been the interpretation of one of the most cryptic laws in U.S. history—the Alien Tort Statute ["ATS"]. This law, originally enacted as part of the Judiciary Act of 1789, provides that the federal courts have jurisdiction over "any civil action by an alien for a tort only, committed in violation of the law

63. *The Paquete Habana*, 175 U.S. 677, 700 (1900).

of nations or a treaty of the United States." The statute is obviously a grant of jurisdiction. But how are federal courts exercising that jurisdiction supposed to determine the substantive law that applies to cases brought under the ATS? That question might have appeared to be a fairly simple one in the late eighteenth and early nineteenth centuries. Presumably the kinds of acts by individuals (states as such were entitled to sovereign immunity) that violated the law of nations constituted a small list known to all educated jurists. Among these, for example, were offenses relating to piracy, which all civilized nations condemned. Since, in Chief Justice Marshall's words, the law of nations is part of the law of the United States, it would make sense to say that an alien could sue in federal court under the ATS alleging harm due to an act of piracy.

Today, though, the content of what we call "customary international law"—the conceptual successor to the "law of nations"—is a dynamic and contested thing. Especially since World War II and the development of a robust conception of international human rights, most would say that the list of acts by individuals that could violate customary international law includes more than acts of piracy and the handful of other wrongs that were condemned by the law of nations in 1789. The question is whether federal courts presented with an ATS case today may legitimately incorporate, as part of federal common law, substantive legal principles derived from customary international law. In its influential decision in *Filartiga v. Pena–Irala* (2d. Cir. 1980),[64] the Second Circuit held that the federal courts properly had jurisdiction over a claim under the ATS based on torture: "[T]he torturer has become—like the pirate and slave trader before him—*hostis humani generis*, an enemy of all mankind."[65] In other words, while jurists in 1789 might not have considered torture to violate the law of nations, federal courts are entitled to recognize under the ATS that customary international law today condemns torture, according to the Second Circuit.

The Second Circuit's decision in *Filartiga* has been controversial (although it probably has more defenders than detractors), and not because its critics deny that torture is a violation of basic human rights (they don't). The bone of contention is whether, in the post-*Erie* age, the federal courts may appropriately draw on customary international law to make rules of federal common law. As discussed toward the end of Chapter 7, the mainstream view is that exercises in the making and application of federal common law by the federal courts are legitimate insofar as they can be linked to an explicit or implicit indication from Congress that it wishes the federal courts to engage in such lawmaking. Some scholars believe

64. 630 F.2d 876 (2d Cir. 1980). **65.** *Filartiga*, 630 F.2d at 890.

that that ingredient is missing in the context of the ATS and customary international law. While one might argue that the ATS itself supplies that ingredient—why would Congress have enacted it in the first place?—it remains the case that the ATS operates to confer jurisdiction on federal courts, not to create a new federal cause of action or to state federal substantive policy on questions of international law. (Not to mention that the ATS was enacted almost 150 years before *Erie* and the subsequent development of guidelines for the making of federal common law.) Critics of *Filartiga* and cases following it argue, among other things, that it is inconsistent with *Erie* for federal courts, under the ATS, to adopt as part of federal common law principles of customary international law that derive from no Congressional policy and whose content is to be found in sources (such as United Nations resolutions) that are not politically accountable to the American electorate.

In 2004, the Supreme Court resolved some (but far from all) of these questions in its decision in *Sosa v. Alvarez–Machain*.[66] In *Sosa*, the Court surveyed the history of the ATS's enactment and concluded that its drafters most likely assumed that the statute would not serve solely as a grant of jurisdiction to hear claims based on substantive principles that Congress might adopt in the future, but that it was written against a background of widely accepted principles concerning the law of nations that could be enforced by federal courts hearing cases brought under the statute. In other words, the "piracy" claims and a few others (such as offenses against foreign ambassadors and causes of action arising out of prize captures) were part of what the Court called the "ambient law of the era," which Congress expected to be applied in cases brought under the ATS. As to whether it is legitimate for federal courts to recognize causes of action under the ATS for violation of international law norms that are of more recent vintage, the Court concluded (over a very strong dissent by Justice Scalia) that such "judicial power should be exercised on the understanding that the door is still ajar subject to vigilant doorkeeping, and thus open to a narrow class of international norms today."

The Court illustrated that "vigilant doorkeeping" in *Sosa* itself by holding that Alvarez–Machain's claim to be free from arbitrary detention was not an international norm sufficiently "definite" and "specific" to constitute a cause of action under the ATS. Interestingly, though, the Court's several, apparently approving, references to *Filartiga* in its *Sosa* opinion suggests that it found the *Filartiga*'s painstaking demonstration, using a variety of international law sources, of the universal repugnance for torture to be persuasive. The Court also noted that Congress's adoption of the Torture

66.   542 U.S. 692 (2004).

Victims Protection Act in 1991 supplied the kind of Congressional guidance, at least with respect to ATS claims based on torture, that should allay concerns about untethered judicial lawmaking under the ATS.

Sosa v. Alvarez–Machain may have resolved some of the debate over the ATS, but it is hardly the last word on more general questions concerning the status of customary international law in the federal courts. The following passage from Justice Scalia's dissent in *Sosa*, while a bit hyperbolic, aptly conveys what is at stake: "The notion that a law of nations, redefined to mean the consensus of states on *any* subject, can be used by a private citizen to control a sovereign's treatment of *its own citizens* within *its own territory* is a 20th-century invention of internationalist law professors and human rights advocates."[67] How that "invention" will fare in the federal courts in the next generation is very much up for grabs.

G. Comparative Choice of Law: Conflicts Law Outside the United States

The virtually exclusive emphasis in this book has been on the law to be applied, or the judgments to be recognized, in courts in the United States. To the extent that international law or legal norms are involved in a case, they have been relevant to our discussion only insofar as they influence how a case heard in an American court should be decided. Comparative law, which is the study of how different legal systems handle particular legal questions, would seem to have limited relevance to these issues, since courts typically apply the choice-of-law rules of the forum.

But—apart from the fact that, in an age of globalization, educated lawyers should know something about how other legal systems work—comparative conflicts law can be quite relevant to conflicts decisions made by U.S. courts. For example, knowledge of how other parts of the world handle conflicts—in particular, the circumstances under which courts elsewhere regard it as appropriate to apply the substantive or "internal" law of the forum—can assist a U.S. court in determining whether a particular extraterritorial application of U.S. law would be regarded elsewhere as exorbitant. As noted in our discussion of the *Hartford Fire* decision, the Restatement (Third) of the Foreign Relations Law of the United States advises that U.S. courts should not apply U.S. law extraterritorially if such application would be "unreasonable." The "reasonableness" of an assertion of legislative jurisdiction depends in part

---

67. *Sosa v. Alvarez–Machain*, 542 U.S. at 749–50 (Scalia, J., concurring in the judgment) (emphasis in the original).

on how other states with a plausible interest in the matter view conflicts issues and whether their own conflicts principles would be hospitable to the application of U.S. law.

One sees this idea at work, for example, in the Supreme Court's decision in *Lauritzen v. Larsen* (1953),[68] the seaman's case in federal court involving the possible application of the Jones Act that was discussed earlier in this Chapter. Having determined that the United States, Denmark, and Cuba all had an interest in the case, the Court did not simply apply a choice-of-law rule, such as *lex loci delicti*, that was familiar to American courts. Rather, it considered that a variety of choice-of-law rules had been used in such circumstances over the years by the tribunals of different nations involved in the maritime trade. After a discriminating examination of the different approaches, the Court held that application of Danish law would best accord with the understanding of all nations involved, like the U.S., in that trade. A similar approach was taken in *Romero v. International Terminal Operating Co.* (1959).[69] In neither *Lauritzen* nor *Romero* did the Court opt to apply the law of the place where the injury was suffered, even though in 1953 that remained the predominant approach to tort conflicts in the United States.

How, then, do the choice-of-law principles used in American courts compare with those that prevail elsewhere in the world? It was once thought appropriate simply to consider most of the rest of the Western industrialized world as governed by some variant of civil law, and then simply to speak of a general "civil law" approach to conflicts that contrasted with the common-law approach. This simplistic conception is no longer satisfactory, if in fact it ever was. After all, well into the twentieth century conflict of laws in the United States remained a subject whose fundamental moorings were themselves based on the law and scholarship of civil-law jurists. What *can* be said, however, is that the tendency in "modern" American choice-of-law methodologies, such as interest analysis and the Second Restatement, to reduce the analysis to an *ad hoc* assessment of various contacts and state interests, has never caught on outside the United States. While the differences in today's world between civil-law and common-law approaches to legal questions are narrower than is sometimes assumed, and continue to narrow, it remains the case that, under the civil law, *codified* law is the norm. Codifications of the law of choice of law, whether in individual countries, the European Union, or in international conventions, usually specify *lex loci* rules for particular kinds of disputes. Moreover, scholars of conflicts (or, as it is more commonly called, private international law) in civil-law countries

---

68.   345 U.S. 571 (1953).   **69.**   358 U.S. 354 (1959).

have, taken as a whole, never warmed to the insights of Currie or other American critics of the *lex loci* approach.

The European Union. The development of principles of jurisdiction, procedure, and choice of law to govern large areas of private civil litigation is one of the most significant developments in the law of the European Union since its establishment in 1993.[70] The provisions on civil procedure are particularly important in light of the many civil disputes that arise having "interstate" dimensions. With respect to choice of law, the European Parliament in 2008 enacted a set of choice-of-rules for contract issues, based largely on the "Rome Convention" that had been adopted in 1980. In 2007, the Parliament had adopted a similar Regulation to govern conflicts with respect to torts and other non-contractual obligations. Each of these Regulations is highly articulated and leaves comparatively little to the discretion of the court. For example, the choice-of-law rules for contract matters specifies rules for contracts for the sale of goods (law of the country where the seller has his habitual residence), contracts for services (law of the country where the service provider has his habitual residence), contracts for the sale of goods by auction (law of the country where the auction takes place), and so on. In addition, though, a prefatory Article specifies a number of general principles animating the system as a whole, which are to govern where the particular "type" of contract issue is not treated in the specific rules. In this respect it is not wholly unlike the Second Restatement, but it is important to note that the specific rules are not regarded merely as "presumptive."

The Regulation on choice of law for non-contractual obligations, including torts, operates similarly. Interestingly, the general rule for torts (covering those torts not specifically treated elsewhere in the Regulation) is that the law of the place of injury should apply—but an exception is made for situations in which the plaintiff and defendant are residents of the same country, in which case the law of that country should apply. Recall that some critics of interest analysis in the U.S. have suggested that interest analysis improves on *lex loci* rules only with respect to common-domicile cases. The EU Regulation follows this reasoning, while maintaining a rule-based approach with no explicit reference to "interests."

An additional proposed Regulation, not yet adopted, would provide choice-of-law rules for matrimonial matters.

Member and Non–Member Nations. Even for member nations, EU Regulations currently establish choice-of-law rules only

---

70. An excellent source of information on the subject of comparative conflicts is PETER HAY, RUSSELL J. WEINTRAUB & PATRICK J. BORCHERS, COMPARATIVE CONFLICT OF LAWS: CONVENTIONS, REGULATIONS, AND CODES (2009), upon which much of the discussion in this section is based.

for certain subject areas, such as contracts and torts, discussed above. Member nations thus have their own codes governing choice of law, which in the non-common-law world is called "private international law." Germany's codification, for example, provides that conflicts concerning succession after death are to be governed by the law of the state of the decedent's citizenship at death. Lithuania's, by contrast, provides that such conflicts are to be governed by the law of the state of domicile of the testator at the time of death. Non-member nations, of course, have their own codes of private international law as to all legal subjects. A number of nations that are deeply enmeshed in the international economy have legal systems that derive originally from neither civil-law nor common-law traditions. The choice-of-law codes of, for example, Japan and the People's Republic of China make for especially interesting comparisons with those of European and South American nations.

There is nothing in any of these codifications of choice of law that would be unrecognizable to students and practitioners of American conflicts law. What is most apparent is that, outside the U.S., most industrialized nations adhere to a rule-based approach to conflicts rather than the looser methodologies often applied in American conflicts law—and this may reflect rather faithfully the more general difference between civil-law precepts and those of the common law.

H.   Recognition of Foreign Judgments

In Chapter 5, we considered the problem of recognition of judgments. In particular, we explored the role of the Full Faith and Credit Clause of the U.S. Constitution, and of the federal full-faith-and-credit statute, 28 U.S.C. § 1738, in requiring state courts in the United States to recognize and give effect to sister-state judgments. Judgments rendered by tribunals outside the United States, however, are not constitutionally entitled to full faith and credit. What principles govern the recognition and enforcement of such judgments in state and federal courts?

1.   A Leading Case of Doubtful Modern Authority: Hilton v. Guyot *(1895)*

The leading Supreme Court decision on this question is *Hilton v. Guyot* (1895),[71] although, in light of the many changes in both U.S. and international legal principles since then, *Hilton* is only the starting point in discussing the subject. In *Hilton*, a French court entered a judgment against two U.S. citizens, in favor of a French company serving as liquidators for another French firm with which

---

71.   159 U.S. 113 (1895).

the U.S. citizens had had an account. The successful French plaintiff sought to enforce the judgment in the federal courts. The U.S. Supreme Court in *Hilton* set out the basic principles that should guide state and federal courts in the recognition of foreign-country judgments, before holding that the particular French judgment before the Court should not be given recognition. According to the Court, recognition of foreign-country judgments rests on the concept of comity:

> [W]here there has been opportunity for a full and fair trial abroad before a court of competent jurisdiction, conducting the trial upon regular proceedings, after due citation or voluntary appearance of the defendant, and under a system of jurisprudence likely to secure an impartial administration of justice between the citizens of its own country and those of other countries, and there is nothing to show either prejudice in the court, or in the system of laws under which it was sitting, or fraud in procuring the judgment, or any other special reason why the comity of this nation should not allow it full effect, the merits of the case should not, in an action brought in this country upon the judgment, be tried afresh, as on a new trial or an appeal, upon the mere assertion of the party that the judgment was erroneous in law or in fact.

This presumption of recognition sounds not all that different from the policy established by the Full Faith and Credit Clause itself; foreign-country judgments should be recognized and enforced so long as fraud or some lack of due process did not taint the judgment. But the Court added a proviso that turned out to be decisive in the case: In order for the U.S. court to recognize the foreign-country judgment, the foreign country in question must itself have a policy of recognizing and enforcing the judgments of American courts in circumstances analogous to those present in the case before the court. That is, reciprocity must exist if American courts are to recognize foreign judgments. Since there was evidence in *Hilton* that French courts did not simply recognize and enforce judgments rendered by other countries, but rather tried those disputes *de novo*, the Court in *Hilton* ruled that the French judgment should be treated at most as *evidence* of the claim asserted, and not simply recognized and enforced.

The *Hilton* decision thus contains elements both of hospitality to recognition of foreign-country judgments and of a serious limitation upon that hospitality. As an example of the former, the Court suggested that the fact that one of the plaintiffs had been permitted to testify while not under oath and was not subjected to cross-examination, was not itself reason to deny recognition. This holding, together with the general statement of principles quoted above, suggests a certain cosmopolitanism in the treatment of foreign-country judgments—so long, that is, as a reciprocal policy prevails in the country from which the judgment comes. That requirement of reciprocity, however, strikes something of a sour note in the domain of private international law, and has long been criticized by American courts and scholars. Consider, for example, that courts don't usually take reciprocity concerns into account when making rulings on choice of law.[72] Moreover, particularly in the realm of private litigation, the underlying policy of *res judicata*, whether in the domestic or the international sphere, is to establish principles of finality for litigation, not to create incentives for the courts of another country to alter their own rules of recognition of foreign-country judgments. The reciprocity idea seems to insert a policy of international tit-for-tat where adjustment of the rights of private parties should be the principal issue.

"Reciprocity" No Longer the Basic Criterion for Recognition. Whatever the merits of the "reciprocity" requirement, it is no longer an important part of American law with respect to recognition of foreign-country judgments. Most courts and commentaries reject it, as does the Restatement (Third) of Foreign Relations Law of the United States. Section 98 of the Second Restatement (of Conflict of Laws) gives a fairly mainstream statement of the modern view on recognition of foreign-country judgments: "A valid judgment rendered in a foreign nation after a fair trial in a contested proceeding will be recognized in the United States so far as the immediate parties and the underlying cause of action are concerned." This formulation essentially incorporates the principles expressed by the *Hilton* court quoted above, minus the "reciprocity" idea. Of course, § 98 begs a number of questions, such as what constitutes a "fair trial," but it is in this respect no different from the exceptions to claim and issue preclusion in the domestic context that are itemized in the Restatement (Second) of Judgments (see Chapter 5). Obviously, the rendering tribunal must have had proper jurisdiction over the parties for purposes of recognition under § 98, and the proceeding must not have been procured by fraud. But precisely what sorts of procedures are required to make the proceeding a "fair" one may not be obvious to everyone. One clear prerequisite to enforcement in the United States of a foreign-country judgment against the defendant is that fair notice have been given to the defendant in the first proceeding. Thus, for example, a Bolivian judgment was denied enforcement by a U.S. District Court because service of process in the Bolivian proceeding

---

72. The single most historically notorious exception is *Scott v. Emerson*, 15 Mo. 576 (1852), the initial "Dred Scott" case, in which the Missouri Supreme Court refused to apply the law of the free-soil state where Dred Scott had for years resided, which would have emancipated him, because the courts of some free-soil states had begun refusing to apply slave-state law to slaves who had sojourned only temporarily from such a "slave" state.

was made on a person who had been the defendant's agent three years before, but not at the time of service. It appeared that the defendant itself had not received effective notice, and the District Court held that the method of service "fail[ed] to comport with American fundamental notions of due process."[73]

Is the Doctrine Governing Recognition of Foreign–Country Judgments State or Federal Law? Wherever these basic recognition principles are stated—the Second Restatement or somewhere else—their authoritative source must be some body of law, and the natural question to ask is whether the law governing recognition of foreign-country judgments should be state or federal law. In *Hilton v. Guyot*, the Supreme Court did not consider this to be a question of overriding importance, since it could (and did) regard the recognition problem as one of "general law" under *Swift v. Tyson*. After the decision in *Erie R.R. v. Tompkins* (1938), however, that is no longer a satisfactory answer. Since *Erie*, the question of recognition of foreign-country judgments has generally been one of state law. The United States is not currently a signatory to any treaties or international conventions governing the recognition and enforcement of foreign-country judgments, and Congress has passed no law generally regulating such questions.

Despite the fact that "reciprocity" is no longer widely considered to be a basic condition of recognition, the comity dimensions of the problem would seem to militate in favor of federal rather than state law being the authoritative arbiter of recognition. After all, traces of *Hilton*'s "reciprocity" idea do still turn up in some state and federal court rulings on recognition. Regardless of whether "reciprocity" *per se* is a criterion for recognition, considerations of diplomacy and foreign policy are likely to come to the fore in at least some cases concerning recognition of foreign-country judgments, suggesting that the matter really is one for federal law or federal courts or both. Certainly it is peculiar to think that the courts of two states in the United States might come to different answers concerning recognition and enforcement of a particular foreign-country judgment. Efforts to pass a federal statute to deal with the problem, however, have thus far been unavailing. Alternatively, one could imagine these questions triggering a "uniquely federal interest" justifying the application of a "federal common law," applied by federal courts, to the issues. But the development of such a federal common law doctrine has not been forthcoming, either.

73. *De la Mata v. American Life Ins. Co.*, 771 F.Supp. 1375, 1388 (D. Del. 1991).

Well over half the states have adopted some form of either the Uniform Foreign Money–Judgments Recognition Act (promulgated in 1962, currently in effect in 27 states and the Virgin Islands) or the Uniform Foreign–Country Money Judgments Recognition Act (promulgated in 2005, currently in effect in five states). Under each of these Uniform Acts, foreign-country money judgments are enforceable in the forum, with exceptions for lack of impartiality in the rendering court, procedures that fall short of what due process requires, lack of personal or subject matter jurisdiction in the rendering court, lack of sufficient notice to the defendant, and fraud in the procurement of the original judgment. Beyond that, however, each of the uniform acts provides that a foreign-country money judgment need not be enforced if enforcement would be "repugnant to the public policy of this state." Here, then, "public policy" considerations can influence the question of recognition in a way that would be impermissible were the question one of full faith and credit to a sister-state judgment. The question becomes what kinds of "public policy" considerations American courts may legitimately take into account in deciding whether to recognize and enforce a foreign-country judgment, when excessively parochial answers to that question may provoke friction with the country from which the judgment comes.

2. *Libel Tourism: A Case Study in the Recognition and Enforcement of Foreign–Country Judgments*

The problem of recognition of foreign-country judgments can arise in many contexts, but one issue that has recently drawn considerable attention is the phenomenon of "libel tourism." The phrase refers to the fact that the law of libel in some countries, notably England, is more favorable to plaintiffs than is libel law in the United States. "Libel tourism" is thus a species of forum shopping that can subject American (and, of course, other) authors and publishers to large damage judgments that would be unavailable under American law. If the successful plaintiff then attempts to enforce the judgment in the United States, where the defendant has assets, an American court will be faced with the task of determining whether enforcement is appropriate.

American Libel Law and the "Single Publication Rule." The law of libel has always raised interesting problems for jurisdiction, choice of law, judgments, and limitations periods. A libelous statement, for example in a book or periodical, can circulate in many different places, and in theory cause a harm to the plaintiff's reputation in any or all of those places. It could even be argued that a new harm is created every time someone reads the allegedly libelous statement. But the "single publication rule," which prevails throughout the United States, limits the plaintiff to a single lawsuit against the defendant for an allegedly libelous utterance, and provides that but a single cause of action arises from the statement's initial publication. The applicable limitations period thus dates from the time of that original publication; each successive "reading" of the statement by an additional person does not give rise to a new cause of action. In that single lawsuit, however, the plaintiff can recover for *all* the harm to reputation that she has suffered, whether within or outside the forum. Principles of claim preclusion will thereafter bar any further lawsuits with respect to that cause of action. The U.S. Supreme Court has upheld, as satisfying the "minimum contacts" standard, the assertion of personal jurisdiction over a defendant in a libel suit even in a state where circulation of the allegedly defamatory publication has been minimal relative to other states. The principal consequence of this ruling is that plaintiffs can sometimes shop for a favorable statute of limitations. Otherwise, though, the differences among the states with respect to the law of libel are not great, and forum shopping *within* the United States by libel plaintiffs is therefore not a significant problem.

English Law's Greater Hospitality to Plaintiffs in Libel Cases. The situation, however, is more complex when we turn to the international stage. The substance of American libel law differs in important ways from that in some other countries, notably Great Britain. In the United States, the First Amendment places strict limitations on a plaintiff's ability to win a libel judgment when the plaintiff is a "public figure" or when the case concerns a statement involving a matter of "public concern"; English law, by contrast, does not recognize such limitations. In American libel law, the plaintiff ordinarily bears the burden of proving the falsity of the allegedly defamatory statements, while in England the falsity of a defamatory statement is presumed, and truth is an affirmative defense, for the proof of which the defendant is responsible. Moreover, English libel law does not recognize the "single publication rule"; while English courts in libel cases do award damages for all harm wherever suffered, they also consider that a new cause of action arises each time a new "reader" encounters the allegedly defamatory material. English courts are apt to assert jurisdiction in libel cases even when circulation in England of the allegedly defamatory statements is small relative to that elsewhere. To assert "jurisdiction" in such cases typically means to apply English law. For these and other reasons, libel litigation in English courts can be substantially more favorable for plaintiffs than anywhere in the United States.

The fact that English law provides, in some libel cases with multijurisdictional connections, relief for plaintiffs that would not have been available under American libel law obviously does not mean that every libel suit in England, or even every attempt to enforce in an American court a libel judgment obtained in an English court, is an example of "libel tourism." Substantive law on many matters can differ from country to country—that is the whole point of the subject of Conflict of Laws—and the courts of those countries are presumptively entitled to assert both judicial and legislative jurisdiction with respect to disputes that have a plausible connection with the forum. The specific phenomenon, though, that has raised concerns among publishers, media organizations, authors, courts, and policymakers in the United States is that of the public figure or celebrity who sues an author or publisher in an English court, hoping to gain the advantages of England's plaintiff-friendly libel law, when the circulation in England of the book or article is very limited relative to its circulation elsewhere.[74] The assertion of jurisdiction in some of these cases may technically satisfy international norms, but since damages are not limited to those incurred within the forum, there is a "tail-wagging-the-dog" quality to the judgment that can seem quite prejudicial to defendants whose home country (e.g., the United States), which is usually the location where most of the circulation occurs, would not provide for liability.[75] Regardless of the domicile or nationality of the parties, libel litigation in English courts is an example of "libel tourism" if it is an obvious attempt at forum shopping and if the connections with England are modest.

The Problem of Recognition and Enforcement. When, though, does such "libel tourism" become a matter of concern for courts in the United States? Of course, the very fact that an American author or publisher has been exposed to significant liability for defamation in an English court based on limited connections with England, when the First Amendment or other parts of American libel law would bar the plaintiff from recovering, is a source of concern. Wholly apart from the monetary consequences, the mere risk of such liability can have a chilling effect on speech. But, practically speaking, it is only the attempt by the judgment creditor to enforce the judgment in the U.S.—that is, where a court in the United States serves as "Court B"—that provides American

---

74. The most notorious recent example is the default judgment obtained in the English courts by Saudi billionaire Khalid bin Mahfouz against American author Rachel Ehrenfeld after publication of her book *Funding Evil: How Terrorism Is Financed—and How to Stop It* (2003), in which she stated that Mahfouz had helped to finance the operations of Al Qaeda. Mahfouz was awarded several hundred thousand dollars after Ehrenfeld refused to appear in the English action, where the court asserted jurisdiction based on the fact that twenty-three copies of the book had appeared in England.

75. Such cases, by the way, feature American as well as foreign plaintiffs; for example, American celebrities, stymied by American libel law in their efforts to sue gossip magazines like the *National Enquirer* in American courts, have at times resorted to English courts.

courts an opportunity to offer some legal protections to defendants in "libel tourism" cases, namely by declining to enforce the judgment. If the plaintiff is serious about obtaining monetary relief, and the defendant author or publisher maintains her assets in the United States, much will depend on how judgments obtained in English "libel tourism" cases will be treated in American courts. Should such judgments be enforced?

Now that considerations of "reciprocity" no longer loom large in the jurisprudence of recognition of foreign-country judgments in American courts, more generic considerations of "public policy" have entered the picture. Recall that full-faith-and-credit principles, which govern questions of interjurisdictional recognition within the United States, admit of no "public policy" exception. But under both the above-mentioned 1962 and 2005 Uniform Acts concerning recognition of foreign-country money judgments, repugnance to the forum's public policy is a permissible basis for refusing recognition to a foreign-country judgment. (The 2005 Uniform Act also provides that repugnance to the public policy of the *United States* is a permissible basis for refusal.) In addition, the absence of personal and subject matter jurisdiction in the rendering court *requires* that the judgment be denied recognition. Even in those states that have not adopted either of the Uniform Acts, these arguments for denial of recognition are likely to be available.

Lack of Jurisdiction in Rendering Court. Application of these principles may require a discriminating assessment of the different circumstances in each case. Consider, for example, the question of jurisdiction in the rendering court. Even in cases where sales or circulation of the book or magazine in England are slight in comparison with circulation elsewhere, assertion of jurisdiction by an English court would not necessarily violate norms of international law. Even if the defendant is not an English citizen, "territorial" principles of legislative jurisdiction (based on the "effects" idea) might well support that assertion of jurisdiction. At the same time, one might posit a standard of *reasonableness* in the exercise of jurisdiction that could serve to guide American courts in determining whether the judgment should be enforced. In the distinctive situation raised by libel law, where the effects of allegedly defamatory statements can be felt in many places at once, it may be *unreasonable* for the courts of a country where the effects are minimal to assert jurisdiction even though doing so would not violate international law. American courts, however, have not thus far employed this reasoning in the few cases dealing with recognition of foreign-country libel judgments.

Public Policy. Though "reciprocity" in the *Hilton v. Guyot* sense is no longer the main consideration, American courts cannot be indifferent to diplomatic concerns when determining whether "public policy" militates against recognition and enforcement of foreign judgments. It may be tempting to regard the First Amendment as a reason for refusing enforcement to *any* foreign libel judgment that would be impermissible (and perhaps even unconstitutional) under American law. But principles of comity suggest that an American court should consider the relative *interests* of the rendering and recognition fora in the underlying dispute when determining whether to enforce the judgment—lest the United States serve merely as a haven for libel judgment debtors to sequester their assets and make legitimate foreign-country libel judgments effectively unenforceable. The United States (and any state of the United States) undoubtedly has a substantial interest in protecting American authors and publishers from ruinous money judgments based on publications that would be protected under American law and whose circulation is small in the country where a libel judgment was rendered. But what if the defendant is not a U.S. resident, or if circulation of the offending publication was in fact substantial in the country where the judgment was rendered? And should the residence or citizenship of the *plaintiff* matter? One can imagine many situations in which the "interest" of England (or another country where a libel judgment has been rendered) could be said to predominate over that of the United States. Refusal to recognize the foreign-country judgment under these circumstances might well be regarded abroad as offensive to the principles of comity. Moreover, the concept of a legitimate "interest," which (as with interest analysis in choice of law) is likely to be informed in the United States by considerations of domicile, may not accord with the prevailing conception of the term in other countries. There is currently little guidance for American courts in giving content to the phrase "public policy" where recognition of foreign-country judgments is concerned.

Declaratory Judgment Actions. It is not necessary that a foreign-country libel judgment creditor actually seek to enforce the judgment in the United States in order for speech to be chilled, or (perhaps more to the point) for defendant authors and publishers to be placed in an anxious and vulnerable position; the mere threat may be enough. For that reason, some foreign-country libel judgment debtors have taken the initiative by seeking a declaratory judgment in an American court that the judgment will be unenforceable in the United States. Where the foreign-country judgment creditor is not a U.S. citizen and has limited connections with the United States, however, it may be impossible to establish personal jurisdiction over him in such a declaratory judgment action.[76] A

---

76. *See Ehrenfeld v. Mahfouz*, 9 N.Y.3d 501, 851 N.Y.S.2d 381, 881 N.E.2d 830 (2007) (no jurisdiction over libel judgment creditor under New York long-arm statute). *See also Ehrenfeld v. Mahfouz*, 518 F.3d 102 (2d Cir. 2008).

2008 Congressional bill proposed to create, for "libel tourism" situations, a declaratory judgment remedy in federal courts for any foreign-country judgment creditor who is a "United States person"; but that got nowhere.

***Telnikoff* and *Bachchan*.** Two leading cases in the U.S. on enforcement of foreign-country libel judgments illustrate some of these issues. In *Telnikoff v. Matusevitch* (Md. 1997),[77] the defendant, a U.S. citizen living in England, published a letter in the London *Daily Telegraph* accusing the plaintiff (an English citizen) of advocating "racialism" and a "blood test" in an earlier editorial published by the plaintiff in the *Daily Telegraph* concerning the ethnic status of those hired by the BBC's Russian-language division. The plaintiff obtained a libel judgment against the defendant in the English courts. The defendant thereafter returned to the United States, where he had assets in Maryland. The plaintiff sued in federal district court to enforce the judgment, and the federal Court of Appeals for the D.C. Circuit certified the following question to the Court of Appeals of Maryland: "Would recognition of [the plaintiff's] foreign judgment be repugnant to the public policy of Maryland?" The Court of Appeals of Maryland answered the question in the affirmative, and the plaintiff's action to enforce the judgment was dismissed. (Maryland had adopted, in pertinent part, the Uniform Foreign Money–Judgments Recognition Act, including its "public policy" provision.)

In *Bachchan v. India Abroad Publications, Inc.* (N.Y. Sup. 1992),[78] the defendant operator of a New York-based news service (India Abroad) published an article accusing the plaintiff, a figure of political and cultural notoriety in India, of holding a bank account containing sums deposited by a Swedish arms company that had been charged earlier with obtaining a government contract through the payment of kickbacks. The plaintiff obtained a libel judgment in the English courts. In *Bachchan*, the Supreme Court of New York declined to enforce the judgment against the defendant

The result in *Ehrenfeld v. Mahfouz* was overturned by the New York legislature when it enacted the Libel Terrorism Protection Act, which amended New York's long-arm statute to provide jurisdiction over foreign-country judgment creditors for purposes of a declaratory judgment action when the publication was published in New York and the judgment debtor is a resident of New York or is subject to personal jurisdiction in New York. (Of course, constitutional standards for personal jurisdiction must still be met, and it is doubtful that the mere fact that the libel defendant-debtor resides in New York will alone be sufficient to establish "minimum contacts.") In an interesting spin on "reciprocity" ideas, the Act also explicitly relieves New York courts of the obligation to enforce foreign-country judgments in libel cases if the libel law of the country from which the judgment comes offers fewer protections to defendants in libel cases than are available under the U.S. and New York Constitutions.

77. 347 Md. 561, 702 A.2d 230 (1997).

78. 154 Misc.2d 228, 585 N.Y.S.2d 661 (N.Y. Sup. 1992).

India Abroad. (New York, like Maryland, had adopted the relevant provisions of the 1962 Uniform Act.) The court did not make entirely clear whether its refusal to enforce the judgment was based on New York's "public policy" or on defective "procedures" in the English proceeding (to wit, English law's requirement that the defendant has the burden of proving the truth of the statement), but the case has generally been treated as a "public policy" decision, based on First Amendment considerations.

It is interesting to explore both the common features and the differences between the two cases. In both cases, the alleged defamatory matter would probably have been constitutionally protected under American law. The defendant's letter to the *Daily Telegraph* in *Telnikoff* was part of a public debate over a matter of public interest and probably fell more into the category of "opinion" than into the category of "fact." *Bachchan* clearly involved both a "public figure" and a matter of public concern, and the defendant had relied for its story on a reputable news agency, which under American libel law constitutes a defense. But, for our purposes, there are also important differences between the two cases. *Telnikoff* was in no sense an example of "libel tourism." The allegedly defamatory statements were published in an English paper, most of whose circulation was in England; the plaintiff was an English citizen; the defendant resided in England at the time his letter appeared in the *Daily Telegraph*. The assertion of jurisdiction by the English courts was amply justified. By contrast, in *Bachchan* the choice of an English tribunal by the plaintiff was more obviously strategic, since only 2% of the copies of the offending issue published by the defendant were distributed in England, whereas 91.2% appeared in the United States. The "libel tourism" label seems more appropriate in this situation.

Thus the argument for refusing enforcement in *Bachchan*, on the ground that enforcement would violate the public policy of New York, is relatively strong. The defendant was the New York operator of a publication distributed principally in the United States. The connections, and corresponding interests, predominantly pertained to New York and the United States. The offending statements would have been absolutely protected under the U.S. Constitution had the original libel proceeding been brought in an American court. For the plaintiff to obtain a judgment in the courts of, and under the laws of, a country where but 2% of the copies of the publication were distributed, and then to enforce the judgment in an American court, seems a fairly obvious end run around American constitutional principles. *Telnikoff*, though, may present a different picture. It is true that the defendant was a U.S. citizen and had, by the time of the enforcement action, returned to the United States and lived in Maryland. One might thus say that the

United States (and, in particular, Maryland) had in the interim acquired an interest in protecting its citizen and domiciliary. But, at its heart, the case really concerned events local to England, and the right to recovery was being asserted by a citizen of England. The allegedly defamatory statements, however protected they might have been under American law, were made in England by a person who was then a resident of England. The arguments in favor of non-enforcement, on "public policy" grounds, of the judgment are thus much weaker in *Telnikoff*.

Where a bona fide case of "libel tourism" is at hand, deference to the tribunal where the original judgment was obtained is not imperatively called for because the interests of that country are, almost by definition, weak. But the situation is different in a case like *Telnikoff*. As Judge Cardozo said in the context of the "public policy" exception in choice of law, "We are not so provincial as to say that every solution of a problem is wrong because we deal with it otherwise at home." That principle would seem to call for enforcement by an American court of libel judgments like those in *Telnikoff*, where England had the most significant connections with the case. Although *Telnikoff* itself reached a different result, it will be interesting to see whether the outcome in that case leads to similar results in the future.

Is a Federal Recognition Statute Needed? *Telnikoff* and *Bachchan* both highlight the oddity that enforcement of foreign-country judgments in the United States is governed principally by state law and is often raised in state courts. Calculations respecting comity in the international domain would appear to be best governed by federal law. The libel cases underscore this point even more vividly because, even though the law of defamation in the United States is mostly state law, the shadow of the First Amendment—a part of the *federal* Constitution—hangs over all efforts to distinguish the substance of American from that of English libel law. While efforts to establish a federal statute governing recognition and enforcement of foreign-country judgments in *all* kinds of cases have not yet borne fruit, Congress has considered more seriously various proposals to enact a law governing recognition specifically in the context of foreign-country libel judgments. None of these has as yet been enacted, although a few states, notably New York—where much of the publishing industry continues to be located—have enacted laws purporting to protect authors and publishers from enforcement there of certain foreign-country libel judgments.

Libel and the Internet. *Telnikoff*, *Bachchan*, and *Ehrenfeld* all involved traditional media, as to which one could make intelligible assertions concerning the circulation of the book or story in different countries as a basis for questioning jurisdiction in the rendering court or assessing the impact of recognition on the recognition forum's public policy. Rachel Ehrenfeld, for example, could claim that only 23 copies of her book had been published in England at the time libel litigation against her was commenced there. The kind of analysis appropriate to those cases, however, may already be obsolete in light of the increasing dominance of Internet publication. In principle, it is possible for both publishers and governments themselves to regulate access to a particular author's or publisher's website in a particular country. Nevertheless, since the "virtual world" of cyberspace often confounds traditional notions of territoriality, it may be increasingly unreal to make concrete assessments of "circulation" within particular countries. The author or publisher of a hard-back book can control initial sales of the book, but that kind of control may not rest so securely with the authors and publishers of Internet content, or even with those who host the websites on which such material appears. If this is true, then it may be more difficult than ever to determine whether "circulation" of the content in a particular country is sufficient to support a "reasonable" exercise of jurisdiction there, or would militate on grounds of "public policy" against enforcement in the United States of a judgment reached in the courts of that country.

Table of Cases

A

B

Index

References are to Pages

†